VENICE

A Maritime Republic

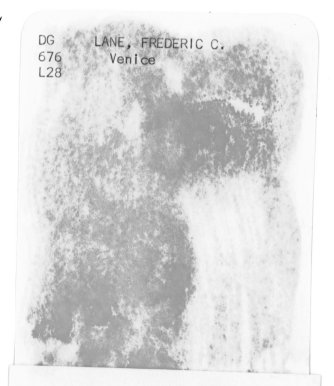

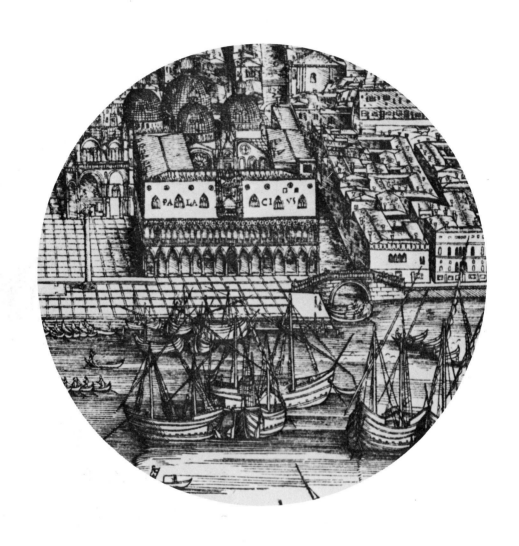

THE JOHNS HOPKINS UNIVERSITY PRESS · BALTIMORE AND LONDON

Frederic C. Lane

VENICE

A Maritime Republic

The Johns Hopkins University Press, Baltimore, Maryland 21218
The Johns Hopkins University Press Ltd., London

Library of Congress Catalog Card Number 72-12342
ISBN 0-8018-1445-6
ISBN 0-8018-1460-X (pbk.)

Library of Congress Cataloging in Publication data
will be found on the last printed page of this book.

TO

Harriet Mirick Lane
Our Children
AND
Their Children

Preface

This history aims to give an understanding of the formation and fate of that community of people who constituted the Venetian Republic. More than any previous general history of Venice, it gives space to maritime matters, to finance and manufacturing, and to economic activities generally. I have tried to treat at appropriate length other aspects of Venetian life — artistic production, political events, influential personalities, environmental and demographic conditions — but a one-volume history is necessarily selective. Any author can hope to be pardoned for writing most about what he knows best. I have put nautical affairs in the center of my story not only for that reason but also because I believe they were important in determining Venetian social structure and the city's fortunes.

Myths cluster around Venice to delight both poets and politicians. Some are personal and picturesque; others are social in their content and attribute to Venice perfect freedom, wisdom, and virtue or, at other periods, consummate tyranny, perfidy, and vice. I have not tried to deal explicitly with all the myths of Venice; they are too numerous. I find I have ignored even the legendary founding of the city by refugees from Attila's Huns! Neither have I tried to disengage my history entirely from the myths. Historical research cannot destroy them utterly except by a kind of suicide. Such is the power of imagination, that history is largely animated by the construction of myths and their unmasking.

For some readers a fuller recounting of traditional myths would serve the good purpose of making the Venetians more interesting. Other readers might be attracted by additional details on religious movements, military campaigns, and diplomatic maneuvers. I have not neglected such subjects entirely, but I hope the attention I have given to the industrial arts and crafts by which Venetians earned their livelihoods, to their commercial and financial dexterity, and to the more humdrum side of politics will serve at least as well in inducing readers to identify with the citizens and subjects of the Republic.

If some of my interpretations are sufficiently new and firmly rooted in original sources so as to interest devotees of Venetian history, I ask that they pardon passages that seem to them to belabor the obvious. In writing, I have had in mind compatriots whom I hoped would come to share a concern, not untouched by admiration, for the city of the lagoons. For them also I planned the maps, heeding the saying of George Lincoln Burr of Cornell University, my first master in historical studies, that events must be located to be understood: history has two eyes, chronology and geography. If my treatment of economic history achieves a balanced concern with techniques, statistical perspective, and human relations, it is thanks to Abbott Payson Usher, who was my teacher at both Cornell and Harvard. The pictures have been selected to illustrate and arouse curiosity, and for readers wishing to probe deeper I have added bibliographical notes as guides to my sources and to recent scholarly publications.

During many years I have been helped in Venice by the staffs of the depositories and museums which I mention, often too abbreviatedly, in the captions and bibliographical notes. I wish to make fuller acknowledgement here and to express my gratitude for their courtesies, namely: the Archivio di Stato di Venezia, the Civico Museo Correr, the Biblioteca Nazionale Marciana, the Biblioteca Querini Stampalia, the Gallerie dell' Accademia and other museums under the Sopraintendenza ai Monumenti, and the institutes at the Centro di Cultura of the Fondazione Giorgio Cini at the Isola San Giorgio Maggiore.

For assistance in research and in shaping and completing this book I wish also to thank personally many individuals who have been generous in giving of their time and skills and in sharing their knowledge, especially Richard Altobelli, G. Benzoni, W. J. Bouwsma, Fernand Braudel, A. Carile, Stanley Chojnacki, Gaetano Cozzi, Eugenio and Gilian Cucchini, James Davis, G. E. Ferrari, Lina Frizziero, Enno Gallo, Jean Georgelin, A. Giordani-Soika, P. F. Grendler, Hermann Kellenbenz, Ben Kohl, Luigi and Bianca Lanfranchi, Lilly and Angela Lavarello, Francois-Xavier Leduc, Robert Lopez, R. Morozzo della Rocca, Reinhold and Laura Mueller, T. Pignatti, G. Pillinini, Brian Pullan, Richard Rapp, Louise Buenger Robbert, Ruggiero Romano, G. B. Rubin de Cervin, Dana and Harriet Rouillard, G. Ruggiero, P. Selmi, G. Tamba, Alberto Tenenti, Maria Francesca Tiepolo, Ugo Tucci. I am gratefully indebted to Linda Vlasak and Victoria Dudley Hirsch at the Johns Hopkins University Press for the skill and imagination they used in putting the book together, and to Heberton and Elinor Evans for their gracious and sustaining hospitality at a crucial time in its production.

Frederic C. Lane

Westminster, Massachusetts
March, 1973

Contents

Illustrations

MAPS

Maps were designed by Norman Carpenter and executed by Nancy Fischman and David Spinney of the Clark University Cartographic Laboratory.

TABLES

Chronology

VENICE

A Maritime Republic

INTRODUCTORY · I

The Beginnings

CHAPTER ONE

Among the many cities men have made, Venice stands out as a symbol of beauty, of wise government, and of communally controlled capitalism. The distinctiveness of the environment in which the Venetians built gave an obviously unique quality to their city's charm. Its watery setting contributed also to an aristocratic tradition of liberty. Venice was the freest of Italy's many free cities, boasted one of her medieval chroniclers. It had no city walls but the lagoon, no palace guard except workers from its chief shipyard, no parade ground for military drill and display except the sea. The advantages of its site fostered also an economy which combined liberty and regulation in ways as unique as Venice's urban arteries and architecture.

The institutions which make Venice memorable evolved during many hundred years of effort. From the sixth century A.D. to the end of the eighteenth, the Venetians were a separate people. Looked at from the point of view of their means of livelihood, those twelve centuries divide into three periods which overlap considerably and are each of about four hundred years in length. Until about 1000 A.D., the Venetians were primarily boatmen or barge men operating small craft across their lagoons and up and down the rivers and canals leading into the mainland of northern Italy. After 1000 A.D., they became a seagoing nation, sailing, trading, and fighting in many parts of the Mediterranean and from the rivers of southern Russia to the English Channel. Finally, Venice became a city of craftsmen, functionaries, and a few aristocrats, a city renowned for its skills in handiwork, finance, and government.

The life of the Venetians before 1000 A.D. is and was relatively obscure, but a series of naval victories began in that year and came to a climax in 1204 with Venice's part in the conquest of Constantinople by Western crusaders. The conquest made Venice an imperial power, and from that date on, its history is entwined with all the shifts of power within the Mediterranean. During the following centuries the Venetians as seamen maintained the wealth and reputation of the Republic in the face of revolutions in nautical, military, and commercial technologies and in trade routes. While neighboring empires rose and fell, they elaborated a republican government in a form which aroused the envy of other Italian city-states.

At the beginning of modern times most medieval communities the size of Venice were overwhelmed by the rise of large, strongly organized monarchies. Oceanic trade routes undermined traditional sources of prosperity. Venice, however, perfected her distinctive republican institutions as a city-state, preserved her independence by diplomatic skill, and prolonged her prosperity by adjusting her trade and especially her manufacturing to new opportunities offered by an expanding Europe. By 1600, when Venice was less a nation of seamen than of craftsmen, she reached a high peak of influence as a center of artistic creation.

A remarkable degree of continuity in social and political institutions persisted throughout those many centuries, a continuity expressing the strength of the Venetians' attachment to the distinctive customs which made them a separate people.

THE FIRST VENETIANS   They became a separate people only gradually. Within the Roman Empire, the lands at the north end of the Adriatic Sea were called Venetia. When that empire was dissolving and most of Italy like the rest of Rome's western provinces was coming under the rule of Germanic tribes, the coast of Venetia remained under Roman officials appointed from Constantinople. The local center of imperial power, which still called itself "Roman" long after it had become so largely Greek that we call it Byzantine, was the city of Ravenna, some miles south of the mouth of the Po. Lagoons more extensive than those now around Venice stretched at that time from Ravenna northward. They did not reach as far around the head of the Adriatic as the major modern port on its eastern side, Trieste, but they extended as far as the city which was then the port at the terminus of the road across the Alps from Germany, Aquileia (see Map 1). In Roman times, a string of sand bars called *lidi* protected these lagoons from the storms of the Adriatic. Lido has now become the name of a particular section of these sand bars and a symbol of summer resorts. In Roman times also the lidi and the islands in the protected lagoons behind them were used as summer resorts by well-to-do inhabitants of the nearby Roman cities on the mainland, such as Padua and Aquileia. The lagoons and lidi had also their "natives," as New Yorkers would say speaking of the year-round inhabitants of some Maine harbor. These "natives" were skilled in navigating the lagoons, some parts of which were being turned into land by silt from the rivers, while a general rise of the sea level, caused in many centuries since Roman times by the melting of the earth's polar ice caps, made sailing over other parts easier. These boatmen claim our at-

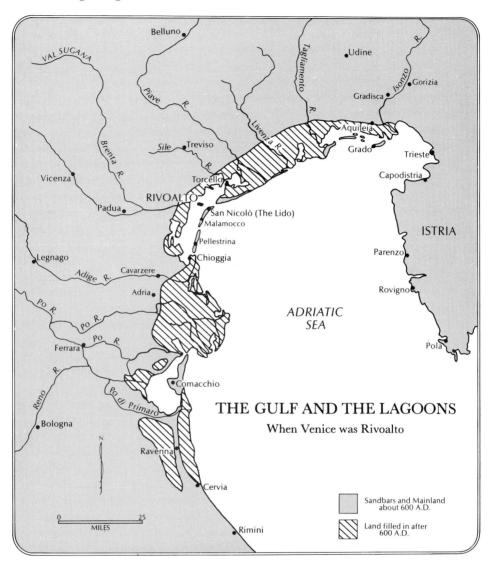

Belluno

VAL SUGANA

Tagliamento R.

Udine

Isonzo R.

Gorizia

Gradisca

Piave R.

Livenza R.

Aquileia

Grado

Trieste

Brenta R.

Sile

Treviso

Capodistria

Vicenza

Torcello

RIVOALTO

San Nicolò (The Lido)

Padua

Malamocco

ISTRIA

Pellestrina

Legnago

Chioggia

Parenzo

Adige R.

Cavarzere

Adria

Rovigno

Po R.

Po R.

Po R.

ADRIATIC
SEA

Ferrara

Pola

Reno R.

Po di Primaro

Comacchio

Bologna

THE GULF AND THE LAGOONS

When Venice was Rivoalto

N

Ravenna

Cervia

Sandbars and Mainland
about 600 A.D.

0   25

MILES

Land filled in after
600 A.D.

Rimini

MAP 1

tention as the first Venetians, the first who found a way of making a living in the mixture of mud, water, and sand peculiar to the lagoons.

Their way of life in the sixth century, before they were much affected by the Germanic invasions, was described by a high Roman official, Cassiodorus. In writing them orders to bring supplies to the fortress of Ravenna, he idealized their simple life much in the spirit in which a high-powered executive in New York, looking down on its slums from a Rockefeller tower, might slip into a letter he was dictating some glowing phrases about the one-time virtues of villagers in rural New England. Cassiodorus praised the seamanship of the Venetians, their houses, "like aquatic birds, now on sea, now on land," with their ships "hitched like animals to the walls." "You have abundance only of fish," he wrote, "rich and poor live together in equality. The same food and similar houses are shared by all; wherefore they cannot envy each other's hearths, and so they are free from the vices that rule the world. All your emulation centers on the salt works; instead of ploughs and scythes you work rollers [to pack the base of salt pans] whence comes all your gain. Upon your industry all other products depend, for although there may be somebody who does not seek gold, there never yet lived the man who desires not salt, which makes every food more savory."

Although Cassiodorus presumably exaggerated their generous egalitarian spirit, there is no reason to think he exaggerated their preoccupation with salt, fish, and boats. Deposits of silt had not yet built up the deltas of the Po and the Adige which now separate the Venetian lagoon from that of Comacchio to the south. In that area in Roman times were open bodies of water to which Pliny gave the name "the seven seas." The expression "to sail the seven seas" was a classical flourish signifying nautical skill. It was applied to the Venetians long before they sailed the oceans.

The Lombard invasion of Italy in 568 A.D. started a migration of refugees from the mainland cities and altered the social structure of the Venetians. Men of wealth moved their residence to the lagoons taking with them their dependents and as much as they could of their property. Later chroniclers and genealogists exaggerated the nobility of these immigrants and traced the ancestry of successful Venetians back to distinguished families in the plundered Roman cities as vigorously as any American ever traced his ancestry back to the passengers on the *Mayflower* or the *Ark* and the *Dove.* Actually many of these immigrants to the lagoons did possess properties on the mainland; and the few deeds, wills, and other documents that survive from before A.D. 1000 show that within the lagoons there were rich landlords with dependent tenants owing payment in kind such as eggs and chickens. Some property owners had sizable herds of cattle, horses, or pigs, as well as vineyards, gardens, and orchards. Salt pans and choice fishing spots were in private hands. Archeologists have found remains of early glass factories and expensive stone buildings. Gone is Cassiodorus's picture of primitive equality.

The refugees were widely dispersed over the lagoons. From Padua they settled mainly at Chioggia and Cavarzere, which became the southern end of the Venetian lagoon as the Po and the Adige filled with their deltas an area that had been part of "the seven seas" (see Map 1). Another important center was Malamocco, near the center of the sand bars, the lidi. The place we call Venice was then mostly open water with a cluster of small islands the chief of which was called Rivoalto (high bank), the future Rialto. The main commercial center was at first further north at Torcello. Yet further to the northeast, refugees from Aquileia made Grado important. Among them was the patriarch who had been the head of an ecclesiastical province embracing all northeastern Italy. The patriarch at Grado tried to continue to exercise these functions. Rivals supported by the Lombards appeared within Aquileia itself, which revived; but the patriarch of Grado remained the metropolitan for the lagoons.

All the area from Cavarzere to Grado remained outside the Lombard kingdom and considered itself an unconquered part of the Roman Empire. The highest Roman-Byzantine officials were at Ravenna or across the head of the Adriatic in Istria at Pola. The subordinate military officials who were their representatives in the Venetian lagoons were called tribunes, and only about A.D. 697 were the lagoons made a separate military command under a *dux (doge)*. This first doge may in fact have been selected by the inhabitants of the lagoons, as later Venetian chroniclers said, maintaining that Venice had been free and independent from its beginnings, but the doge received orders and honors from the Byzantine emperor and Venice was unquestionably considered part of the Byzantine Empire even after the Lombards had captured Ravenna in 751. A long and close association with Byzantium was reflected in the art and in the institutions developed by the Venetian Republic.

Attachment to Byzantium and independence from the mainland were reaffirmed when the Lombard kingdom was absorbed by the Frankish Empire and when Charlemagne sent his son Pepin to conquer Venice in 810 A.D. Pepin stormed and sacked Malamocco, which was then the capital, but he did not push on to capture the doge when the latter retreated to Rivoalto. The Franks withdrew from the lagoons, and the Byzantine emperor sent a fleet to reaffirm his authority. When shortly thereafter a general treaty of peace was concluded between Charlemagne and the Byzantine emperor, it explicitly declared the Venetian dukedom, the territory later called the *dogado*, to be part of the Byzantine Empire.

It soon became in fact independent. The suzerainty of the Byzantine emperor gradually faded away, and the Venetians refused pointedly to acknowledge subordination to any of the Germanic tribal kings who in the West used the title of Holy Roman Emperor to sanctify and extend their power.

TRADE AND NAVIGATION ON THE RIVERS While the Venetians were a community of boatmen living from their lagoon and the traffic of the nearby waterways, there was no conflict between their interests and those of the Byzantine emperor. The emporium of Torcello fitted into the Byzantine commercial system as a source of supplies and an outlet for Byzantine wares. A rival commercial system stretching east and west across the Mediterranean and centering in North Africa was built by Moslems after the Arab conquest of Syria, North Africa, and Spain. The rivalry of the Byzantine and Arab traders added to the importance of Venice as a Byzantine outlet to western Europe, especially after the Saracens in the ninth century conquered Sicily and the heel and toe of Italy. More than ever, Venice was Europe's portal opening on the Levant.

Being on the edge of two worlds — the Byzantine and Moslem East and the Latin-Germanic West — Venetians looked sometimes eastward, at other times westward for profits and power and for artistic inspiration. During their many centuries of independence they became very active intermediaries between East and West, but before A.D. 1000, their role was relatively passive. Some Venetians were seamen expert enough to cross the Mediterranean, but Greeks, Syrians, and other easterners carried most of the trade between Venice and the Levant. The specialty of the Venetians was transporting up the rivers of northern Italy merchandise received from the East or produced in their own lagoons.

Venice's leadership as the chief port of the Adriatic and the chief link in northern Italy between East and West was not gained without a struggle. In Cassiodorus's day the main ports in the northern Adriatic had been Ravenna and Aquileia. When they lost their position during the Lombard wars, their place was taken by cities of the lagoons which lay between them. The city of Comacchio was nearer Ravenna than Venice and equally near the shifting mouths of the Po. It threatened to become Ravenna's chief commercial heir. Unlike Venice, Comacchio formed part of the Lombard and Carolingian domains and was favored by their rulers. But in 886 the Venetians stormed and sacked the city. Thereafter the Venetians controlled the mouths of the rivers leading into northern Italy. Had Comacchio defeated the Venetians and established its control over the mouths of the Adige and the Po, it instead of Venice might have become the Queen of the Adriatic, and Venice might now be an inconspicuous village in a stagnant lagoon, as dead as the lagoon of Comacchio, famous only for its eels.

Within the Po valley, Venetian bargemen carried their search for grain as far as Pavia, which before Milan was the capital of Lombardy. There they sold eastern luxuries to the courts of Lombard and Carolingian Kings. Monasteries with large landownings scattered over central Lombardy maintained at Pavia branch offices through which to buy supplies and sell surpluses. Pavia was also the place where the route from east to west crossed the route from north to south, from across the Alps to Rome. Among the merchants who gathered at this crossroads, the Venetians were distinguished by being best supplied with the products of the east — incense, silks, and spices. They even offered the famous purple cloth which the Byzantine emperor pretended to monopolize for imperial gifts. They were known also as a queer people who sowed not, neither did they reap, but had to buy all their grain from others. In exchange they offered not only eastern wares but salt and fish. In their more immediate neighborhood — in Istria and up the valleys of the Adige, the Brenta, the Piave, and the Tagliamento — they had a near monopoly of these staples.

The dangers, vexations, and advantages which the Venetians encountered as they worked their way up these rivers are suggested by the treaties which the doges made for their protection. The supreme authority on the mainland was held by the successors of Charlemagne as Holy Roman Emperor, first his Frankish descendants, then the Saxon Ottos, and then other emperors elected by the German princes. These western rulers granted the Venetians the right to trade, subject to stipulated, moderate tolls, and promised them redress in case they were robbed. Particularly important for Venetians navigating the rivers was exemption from the medieval custom that any shipwrecked merchandise was treasure trove belonging to the lord of the region or to whoever got there first to seize it. The shifting banks and often turbulent flood waters in the rivers must have made many barges run aground more or less violently and firmly, so that some legal protection in cases of this kind of shipwreck was much to be desired. But a good legal right was probably less important than force on the spot, for the imperial power was being dissipated among local feudal nobles and emerging communes. For protection, river boats traveled in large convoys; we hear of such large fleets on the rivers in later times, when a chronicler has occasion to record how they were caught by a storm in which many perished. In the ninth, tenth, and eleventh centuries, travel in convoys on the rivers was even more necessary for safety's sake, and bargemen had as much need as seamen to be equipped for fighting.

All Venetian ships, even river barges, were subject to government regulation. When passing from the lagoon into the rivers leading inland, barges had to call at specified control points where boatmen carrying forbidden wares could be caught and fined. They would also be fined if it was found that they were overloading. Each barge was marked with a spike called "the key" which served as load line. Its location varied with the width of the barge's floor. If "the key" was submerged, the boatman was fined, the amount of the fine varying with the number of inches of overload.

Thus regulated, small individual enterprise was the rule on these waterways. Each barge was under a boatman who contracted for cargo and operated his vessel himself. He was required to transport wares on the craft specified, not on any other; to go personally, not to send a substitute; and to have his barge properly equipped with an auxiliary boat. Although we need not infer that a one-man crew was the general rule, clearly the law held one man responsible and called him the sailor (*nauta*), not captain, mate, or owner. Probably he was all four at once. Among his passengers there may have been some small traders little richer than he, traveling with wares to sell, but he carried also cargoes for wealthy men who combined large landowning with extensive commercial ventures, as did some of the early doges.

THE TURN SEAWARD   As political conditions became more stabilized in the Po valley, as its population grew and cities multiplied creating more demand for the luxury products of the East and also more wares for export, the Venetians turned increasingly from the rivers to the sea. In earlier centuries, convoys going as far as Pavia, Piacenza, Cremona, and Verona were manned by Venetians; in later centuries, they were manned mostly by men from such inland cities who had taken over the trade of their own regions, organized themselves into communes, and carried their products to Venice. The Venetians welcomed them and made treaties with the new communal governments, providing for reasonable tolls and redress in case of robbery. In return, Lombards were admitted to trade and residence in Venice, but not to Venetian overseas trade. One of the earliest Venetian customs offices was the Masters of the Lombards (*Visdomini Lombardorum*), who supervised the protection, residence, and tax-paying of Italians from the mainland.

As the Venetians pushed out to sea in their commercial enterprises, they found particularly profitable opportunities in the slave trade and the export of lumber.

Neither slaves nor serfs ever formed a substantial part of the Venetian population, but in the ninth century slaves ranked almost with salt and fish as a mainstay of Venetian commerce. Christianity had not abolished slavery, and Church leaders approved the enslavement of pagans and "infidels." They did so on the ground that the enslavement of their bodies might lead to the salvation of their souls. Among the "infidels" were counted not only the Moslems but those Christians were considered heretics. During some centuries, the Orthodoxy of the Greeks was considered heresy by Catholics, who adhered to Rome as did the Venetians. Slave raiders and merchants showed little respect for these distinctions and moral arguments; they were merely continuing a form of money-making which both antedated and survived the introduction of Christianity. To be sure, their sources of supply changed as the frontiers of Christendom spread. In the sixth century, pagan Angles and Saxons had reached the Italian slave market, as is evident from the story of the famous pun (not Angles but Angels) with which a pope expressed his resolve to Christianize them. In the ninth and tenth centuries, the yet-to-be-converted Slavic people to the east were the main source of supply. Italy was a market, and the Moslems of Africa an even better market. The Adriatic was a natural conduit between supply and demand, and Venice became the center of this trade at the same time that it became the Queen of the Adriatic. For a while Venice specialized in supplying eunuchs for Eastern courts and harems, and the Saracens bought Slavic slaves also as recruits for their armies. The sale of slaves to the Infidel was condemned by popes and emperors on both religious and military grounds, and some Venetian doges issued severe decrees against it in the tenth century. They were not obeyed, but the export of slaves from central Europe and the Balkans declined after 1000 A.D., as the Slavs were Christianized and became organized into stronger states.

Apart from slaves, the main cargo with which Venetians filled their ships as they turned from the rivers to the sea was lumber. The Mediterranean as a whole was then already feeling the effects of centuries of deforestation. The Venetians at the head of the Adriatic tapped one of the few remaining areas in which timber of many kinds was plentiful. Oak groves dotted the plains nearby, there was ash and beech further up the rivers, and in the mountains an indefinite supply of larch, pine, and fir. Since wood was a strategic war material of which the Saracens were in dire need, its sale to Moslems, like that of slaves, was repeatedly forbidden by pope and emperor. But the Venetians put business ahead of obedience to either ecclesiastical or imperial commands. Wood, like slaves, was the essential means of getting "foreign exchange," namely gold or silver, from the Moslems, with which to buy from Constantinople the luxury wares so much in demand in the West.

Their ready access to supplies of timber stimulated Venetian shipbuilding. Iron and hemp were also to be had relatively cheaply, so that the Venetians built ships both for themselves and for sale to others. Then, having their own ships and having acquired, through the sale of slaves to the Moslems, precious metal to use as capital, the Venetians took into their own hands more and more of the trade between their lagoons and the imperial capital, Constantinople.

Thus the natural resources in the immediate environment were of primary importance at the beginning of Venetian economic development. Salt and fish provided something to sell in exchange for the food they brought back from their trade along the inland rivers. When they turned from the rivers to the sea, their supplies of timber gave them not only material for their ships but also an article of export. Other parts of the Mediterranean were richer in agricultural and mineral products. It was Venice's superior supplies of timber which initially formed the basis for a division of labor between the people of the lagoons and distant Mediterranean shores more productive of wine, oil, and wheat.

Soon after 1000 A.D., political successes first in the Adriatic and then in connection with the Crusades expanded the opportunities for Venetian traders, and they used their good supplies of timber to become the leading ship operators throughout the eastern Mediterranean.

INTRODUCTORY · II

The Port-City and Its Population

CHAPTER TWO

Where Venice sate in state, throned on her hundred isles. . . .
BYRON, *CHILDE HAROLD*, IV.1

Before considering the naval actions which ushered in a sensational extension of the overseas trade of the Venetians, let us look at the special kind of port-city they built and some of the population problems which were a persistent feature of its history.

AN INTEGRATION OF COMMUNITIES The city we call Venice was formed by the coalescence of many smaller communities originating as separate units. Between A.D. 900 and 1100, as the Venetians were turning from the rivers to the open sea, they founded a cluster of new parishes around the market place of Rialto and the nearby fortress-palace of the doge who ruled the whole lagoon. Typically each parish was on a separate island. A central square had its church on one side, on another a wharf or some boatyards and workshops. On the other two sides, towering above humbler dwellings, rose the big houses or palaces of the one or two leading families who had endowed the church. The homes of the rich and the poor were never segregated in Venice as they are in modern cities in which some parts are slums and others the garden suburbs of the well-to-do. In Venice, many palaces of great nobles had basement rooms and apartments tucked in be- tween floors which provided the equivalent of slum housing, so that rich and poor lived cheek by jowl. Each parish was a diversified but integrated community. By 1200, they numbered about sixty, each with its own saint, festivals, bell tower, market center, local customs, and first citizens.

Parishes were tied together not only by ferries (*traghetti*) across intervening waters which were gradually narrowed into canals, but also by footpaths which lead from one parish to another and crossed canals on wooden bridges. By 1300, the area we think of as Venice, although more honeycombed by canals than at present, was pretty well built up, forming a dense center of population. It was one of the three or four biggest cities of western Europe, yet the local neighborhoods remained emotionally alive.

The integration within these parishes was a foundation stone of Venice's social stability. The preservation of neighborhood spirit after Venice grew more populous is one reason for considering Venice a model of city planning, even as recently as in the dreams of Lewis Mumford. Urban planning should, as he puts it, provide for each community "the reproduction on a smaller scale of the essential organs of the bigger all-embracing city, with the maximum possibilities of meeting and association on every human level." An extreme example of how Venice's parishes met this need was the parish of San Nicolò dei Mendicoli, appropriately so called, since it was inhabited mainly by fishermen and Saint Nicholas was the patron saint of all who went to sea. An assembly of its inhabitants in the parish church elected their own doge, who was then attired in scarlet to go and to be given an embrace by the real doge in the ducal palace. The strong neighborhood feeling of these parishes was reflected in the factions into which the city divided for purpose of having a festival which was a kind of annual organized riot, a free-for-all with fists and bamboo canes. Since the parish of San Nicolò dei Mendicoli was at the extreme west end of the city, the leaders of one side were called the Nicoletti; their opponents were the Castellani, from the name of Castello, the quarter at the opposite, east end of the city, inhabited mainly by sailors and workers in the nearby shipyards (see Figure 2).

Notoriously, modern cities are more successful as places in which to make a living than as places to live. Venice was successful in both ways. The parish communities were supplemented by zones with specialized functions which gave a unified life to the city as a whole. These specialized zones and the parish communities were all bound together by main arteries, such as the Grand Canal, which took heavy traffic around the edges of the differentiated zones and the separate communities, each of which had its own undisturbed center of circulation. The beauty which the Venetians created from their very special environment is justly celebrated; an equally remarkable feature of their urban layout was its efficiency.

The most important integrating center grew up near the Ducal Palace. More and more nobles built residences there in order to be near the center of government and the most important of the city's churches. This church was not the cathedral of a bishop but the private chapel of the doge. In the ninth century, two Venetians reported to their doge that they had brought back from Alexandria the body of St. Mark the Evangelist. As a home for this most precious relic, the doge built next to his palace the church we know as San Marco. In later centuries, both palace and church were rebuilt on a larger scale. The bell tower adjacent to them, the Campanile, was raised higher and higher. By 1150, it was sixty meters tall. The Campanile served not only to mark the time of day and night by its bells but also as a beacon for ships. It could be lit by a fire at night

FIGURE 1   *A Community Center. Campo Sant' Angelo, by Canaletto (courtesy of Mr. and Mrs. Charles Wrightsman Collection, New York).*

From earliest times, the daily life of a Venetian parish centered in a small campo. *The bells of its* campanile *told the time of day, its wells supplied neighbors with water. As the population grew, the* campi *were solidly ringed with shops and with palaces in various architectural styles. Venice had only one* Piazza *(Figure 16), but many* campi.

and made visible from afar by day by the gilding of its spire. The space in front of San Marco was cleared to make a paved courtyard, the Piazza, and the moat or fishing pool next to it alongside the Ducal Palace was filled and paved to form the Piazzetta. On great occasions, the Piazza and the Piazzetta were the centers of festivities; on ordinary days, the Piazza was lined with the booths of craftsmen and of officials granting permits and collecting fees.

At the other end of the Piazzetta was the busiest center of Venice's inner harbor, the Bacino San Marco. From the paved dock in front of the Ducal Palace, called the Molo, this basin extended to the island monastery of San Giorgio Maggiore and to what is now Customs House Point (La Punta della Dogana). Today, big ships go through this basin on their way to berths on the landward side of Venice near the railroad. In the days of sail, big ships moored at the Molo or where the Riva degli Schiavoni is now, or they cast anchor opposite the Ducal Palace and unloaded their cargoes onto lighters. For centuries, there was no central customs house; before unloading, a shipmaster had to have a ticket of permission from the appropriate officials. Then such wares as salt went to a governmental warehouse and much merchandise went directly to the store-rooms in the merchants' palaces. At one time, ships used this Bacino San Marco also for repairs and for taking on and off ballast, but this was forbidden in 1303, to reserve the Bacino for the movement of traffic.

The main artery leading from the water front through the city was the Grand Canal. Boatyards and stoneyards lay on its banks until the fourteenth century, and the accumulations of chipped stone and shavings threatened to fill up the canal and interfere with the ever increasing flow of traffic between San Marco and the Rialto. In 1333, boat builders and stone masons were ordered to move elsewhere. Industries concentrated in other sections, leaving the Grand Canal a thoroughfare big enough for a 200-ton ship. Its banks became a prime residential district lined with the palaces which still give it distinction. The traffic in the Grand Canal was thickest around the wooden bridge at the Rialto where barges from the mainland met barks from the sea. The open space at the foot of the bridge had originally been the local marketplace where Venetians bought their food. It became the meeting place of wholesale mer-chants of many nations — Venetians with spices and silks from the east, Lombards and Florentines offering metal work or cloth, Germans for whose exclusive use a combined hotel and warehouse (the Fondaco dei Tedeschi) was built next to the bridge, and many others from across the Alps and from other parts of Italy. To settle their deals, they had the help of money-changers (later, bankers), who set up their tables under the portico of the little church of San Gia-como at the western foot of the bridge. A little downstream on that same side of the Grand Canal was the main grain warehouse, operated by the government to keep the city supplied. During the thirteenth century the fish market, the butcher shops, and other retail facilities were pushed aside so that a space could be set apart for high finance and for negotiations concerning cargoes to and from distant ports.

As Venice became a world market, as nearly as any European city, traders crowded craftsmen also away from the Rialto. Clothmaking centered near the western end of the Grand Canal. The biggest of Venice's medieval industries, shipbuilding and ship repair, had always been more at the other end of town, between the Bacino San Marco and the Lido. Until well into the fourteenth century, some of the most important yards for the construction of ships gave on the Bacino itself, being where the Giardinetto Reale now is. Later, industrial activity was pushed out of that area, and a new grain warehouse was built where the shipways had been. The shipyards of the city became concentrated at the city's eastern end, towards the Lido. There the government built its walled "Arsenal" as early as 1104. Venice's Arsenal was more a shipyard than a center for the manufacture of arms, although it was both. Originally used mainly for storage of ships and arms kept in readiness, its extent was more than doubled between 1303 and 1325 to provide shipways and sheds for the building and outfitting of many galleys.

Next to the Arsenal was the government-owned Tana, which was both a storehouse for hemp and a rope factory. When rebuilt on the same site in 1579–80, it included a hall 316 meters long that served as a throwing yard for twisting together cables. Private shipyards, where the largest merchantmen were built, were thick along the waterfront between the Ducal Palace and the Arsenal.

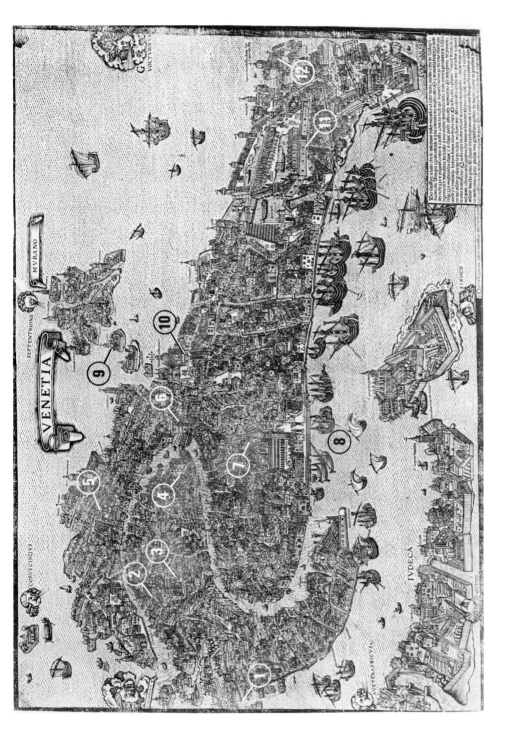

FIGURE 2 *Venice about 1500. Woodcut by Vavassore (courtesy of Museo Correr, Venice).*

(1) *San Nicolò dei Mendicoli; (2) Rio Marin, center of cloth industry; (3) Santa Maria dei Frari, Franciscan; (4) The Rialto;*
(5) *Ghetto-Foundry, became Jewish quarter; (6) German warehouse (Fondaco dei Tedeschi); (7) Mercerie, shop-lined street*
connecting Rialto and San Marco; (8) Bacino San Marco; (9) San Michele, the cemetary; (10) San Zanipolo, Dominican;
(11) *The Tana, with the Arsenal behind; (12) San Pietro di Castello, church of the bishop and, after 1451, of the patriarch.*

Other large shipyards were located on islands some distance away in the lagoons. The nearby islands in the lagoons offered opportunities to create industrial suburbs with specialized functions. The prize example was Murano, to which glassmaking was ordered transferred in 1292, so that the danger of fire in Venice itself would be lessened. Another was Chioggia which specialized in salt-making. Transport by barges, many times cheaper than by wagons, eased the movement of materials such as salt, fuel, and building materials between these suburbs and the central city.

The canals and the open lagoon eased problems of circulation and sanitation as long as the lagoon was kept alive, that is, as long as there was a tidal flow of salt water. Venice's tides were and are of two kinds. A rise and fall of about three feet is the small lunar tide, such as is found in much of the Mediterranean. An additional rise or fall of about three feet occurs frequently but irregularly as a result of the action of winds and currents, rivers and rains in the north Adriatic. When the Venetians established their capital at Rivoalto, the islands there rose more safely above high tide than they did later, for by slow geological action over centuries all the land in that part of the earth has been sinking and the sea rising. (Sinking has much accelerated recently, as will be discussed in our last chapter.) Nevertheless, in the Middle Ages as now, there were parts of the lagoon where mud flats were visible at low tide. In between were deep pools in which fish could be netted and channels usable even at low tide by vessels of considerable draft.

The principles of urban planning which Lewis Mumford finds exemplified in Venice would have been equally valid if Venice had been built on land, but it was because they were building a city on the water that the Venetians realized from an early date a need for city planning of some kind. As shown by the regulations concerning ballast and stoneyards, the waterways would have been plugged up, had individual convenience not been subordinated to some general rules. The fusion of many individual parishes into one urban mass raised many problems of the kind we associate with zoning. Dumping ballast or brush, tying up rafts of firewood, or leaving abandoned boats to rot away would cause silt to accumulate. The mud banks formed by such actions or by natural causes could be turned into "building land" by driving piles. Who then owned such land or water? Naturally, the government asserted its authority. The doge and his highest councils made the basic decisions designed to keep the canals and the channels clear and, as early as 1224, there was a magistracy in charge of channels. There developed what we might call a zoning board (*Magistrato del Piovego*) which was charged not only with claiming communal property but with giving and refusing permits to build on mud flats. Later, a *Magistrato all'Acqua* was created (1501) to handle all hydraulic problems.

More perplexing to the Republic than policing the use of the city's canals was the regulation of the many rivers which emptied into the lagoons. They brought silt and fresh water, so much fresh water into the northeastern end of the lagoon that its salt pans were abandoned. The Venetians believed the mixture of fresh with salt water was also the direct cause of bad air and its disease, malaria. In fact, the water and silt brought by the rivers nourished canebrakes in which malaria-carrying mosquitoes bred. The disease became so bad around Torcello (see Map 1) that after having been in the twelfth century the most important commercial center, Torcello declined into insignificance. To prevent the settlements around Rialto from meeting a similar fate, the government tried to divert rivers from the lagoon and build dikes and canals with locks so as to separate the fresh water from the salt water, but such an ambitious program was full of both technical and political difficulties and was not substantially accomplished until long after Venice had conquered the nearby mainland.

A SAFE HARBOR   While taking measures to protect the lagoon from the advance of fresh water, silt, and canebrakes on the landward side, the Venetians had to be alert to dangers on the seaward side which threatened its functioning as a port. Once a ship was within the sand bars (lidi) which separated the lagoon from the Adriatic, it was protected from stormy seas, but to enter within the sand bars involved special hazards. In the lidi, there were three main breaks called "mouths" or "ports": the port of Chioggia to the south, the port of Malamocco in the center, and the port of San Nicolò (now Porto di Lido) which, being closest to San Marco, was sometimes known simply as the port of Venice (see Map 1). Keeping open these passages through the lidi, as well as cleaning out the city's canals, depended mainly on the action of the tides, especially of extremely high and low tides, when the large mass of moving water carried away much debris and sediment. When the lagoons were more extensive than at present, the larger mass of water did more scouring of the channels, but also carried more silt. In the Adriatic, the waters slowed and deposited the silt so as to form shoals which were moved about by storms.

Flooding rivers, extreme tides, and the action of winds and waves on the beaches threatened to build up the submerged banks of sand and silt and move them right across the breaks in the lidi so as to close one or another of the "ports" completely, or at least make them impassible for large vessels. The channel leading from the Bacino San Marco out to sea through the port of San Nicolò began silting up dangerously as early as the thirteenth century. In 1305, the owners of two large three-deckers found their vessels too big for the port of Venice and were given permission to sell them. Big ships could not be loaded to their maximum draft inside the harbor, certainly not at low water. Although most merchantmen were inspected and cleared by port officials in the Bacino San Marco, large vessels were permitted to complete their cargo and undergo inspection after they had passed the bar at San Nicolò. The "mouths" of Malamocco and Chioggia were then relatively unimportant, and measures were taken to protect the "mouth" of San Nicolò: a breakwater was built, the loading of sand from the lidi for ballast was restricted to specified areas, and the cutting or burning of the pines there was forbidden so that the trees might anchor the soil more firmly. The "mouth" of San Nicolò remained the main port of Venice until the sixteenth century.

For the enforcement of these provisions to protect the port, "Guardians of the Lidi" were appointed and, in the thirteenth century, charged with the repair of the breakwater and the maintenance of the lighthouses. There were two lighthouses, one at San Nicolò (the northeastern end of what is now called "the Lido") and the other at Santa Elena. In 1407 port services were consolidated under an Admiral of the Port. To help ships in difficulty, instead of the tugs so conspicuous in modern Venice, a long boat rowed by twenty-eight men was kept ready, at least in winter, with a supply of hawsers and anchors. The Admiral resided in the "castle" or lighthouse of San Nicolò at the Lido and displayed above his castle a kind of ensign called "the basket," hoisting it to masthead to show when there was high water, or at half mast or lower if vessels needed to be warned of a low tide. He set out markers to show the channel; it was a great scandal in 1526 when a merchant galley returning from Alexandria was almost wrecked because its pilot presumed to ignore the channel markings of the Admiral of the Port. This official also checked on all ships entering and leaving, to make sure they had paid appropriate dues. A similar "admiral" was later in charge of the port of Malamocco.

The constantly shifting channel and sand bar made the service of pilots essential. They were tightly organized in a privileged guild. With the exception of the men who manned the long boats, all the admiral's staff — lighthouse keepers and inspectors — were retired pilots. To be available for bringing ships in during the difficult winter season, active pilots were required September 1 to March 31 to cross to the Istrian city of Parenzo (see Map 1) and wait there for ships to call and pick them up. Those called "big pilots" (*pedotti grandi*), an aristocracy of only thirteen in 1458, had the pick of the jobs on all large ships; there were "little pilots" for smaller vessels. Although they were based in Istria for half the year, these pilots were all Venetian; no Istrian was allowed to join their guild or to collect their fees.

While only experts could guide the big ships past the sand bars off the Lido, all Venetians were more or less at home on the water. Other Italians kidded the Venetian nobles on their horsemanship, saying that they handled the bridle like a tiller and blamed the horse's "pitching" on the direction of the wind. More in the Middle Ages than now, Venetians moved about their city and to the outlying islands with sailboats, gondolas, and smaller craft much like the modern sandolas. Thus they remained in a sense a nation of boatmen, even after their economy came to depend on the wholesale traders who congregated around the Rialto, on the power concentrated in the government at San Marco, and on the big ships bringing cargoes from distant lands.

Another service of the port, one which impressed sixteenth-century visitors as a notably progressive feature, was the Lazzaretto, an island which in 1423 was made a lodging place for the ill. In 1485, the Venetians began the institution called quarantine, which then meant a forty-day detention required of all vessels suspected of being infected with the plague, the dreaded Black Death.

POPULATION FIGURES AND THE PLAGUE   The Black Death dominated several centuries of Venetian demographic history. Early totals of population have to be estimated, mainly from military enrollments. They indicate that Venetians numbered at least 80,000 in 1200 and about 160,000 a century later in the lagoon area as a whole, with nearly 120,000 in the city. In western Europe in the Middle Ages, any place with over 20,000 people or even 10,000 was considered a big city, so Venice was one of the very largest. The chroniclers who report the military census may have upped the totals slightly in rounding them off, but administrative records leave no doubt that a house-to-house count of male adults was made in 1338.

The large figures for the total population at that time are the more credible because they come at the end of a long period of urban growth in Europe. Because of this general growth, Milan, Florence, Naples, and Palermo were probably about the same size as Venice in 1330. West of Italy, only Paris approached 100,000. In 1348, shortly after Venice and the other largest cities of medieval Europe topped 100,000, they were cut back by the Black Death.

The plague had two forms, not recognized as distinct until much later. One was the pulmonary disease characterized by the symptoms of extreme pneumonia and transmitted directly from person to person; the other was the bubonic form characterized by the swellings, called buboes, which turned black and gave it the name Black Death. Since the distinction was not clear to the Venetians, they did not realize that quarantine and similar attempts to isolate infected individuals, while it prevented the pneumonic form from spreading directly, was quite unavailing against the bubonic form, which is not contagious from man to man, but is transmitted by the bites of fleas that carry the disease from black rats to humans. The two forms commonly occur together, but the first infectious case of the pneumonic form almost always originates from a bubonic case, so that the spread of the plague depended on infected fleas which were carried from city to city, sometimes by merchandise, but more often by a ship's rats.

The bubonic plague came to Italy from the East. It was decimating a Tatar army that was besieging Kaffa, a trading post in the Crimea used by Genoese and Venetians. In an early instance of biological warfare, the Tatars catapulted corpses into the city, so that pestilence would weaken the defenders. But rats were more effective in spreading the disease. A Venetian galley returning from Kaffa in the fall of 1347 is signalized as bringing the rats and the plague into Italy.

Something like three-fifths of the inhabitants of Venice died within the next eighteen months. All medieval statistics are questionable, to be sure, but the Venetian government was the first to take statistics seriously, and although the earliest surviving fragments from their census records are of 1509, figures regarding the later severe epidemics of 1575–77 and 1630–31 were carefully recorded by the Board of Health and make quite credible the staggering totals for 1347–49.

Three plague-ridden centuries followed 1348, each new outbreak of pestilence producing sharp drops in population, followed by rapid but sometimes short-lived recoveries. In 1500, the population was about the same size it had been two hundred years earlier, about 120,000. During the following seventy relatively healthy years, the population within the city grew to nearly 190,000, a figure never exceeded for the same area. Then in 1575–77 and 1630–31, two severe epidemics, each killing about one-third of the population, were followed by quick but only partial recoveries. Thereafter, Venice escaped, and the bubonic plague gradually disappeared from Europe, possibly because the spread of the brown rat deprived the black rat of its food supplies. It long threatened the seaports, however, where the black rat, the carrier of the infecting fleas, being a better climber, survived on board ships. The last great outbreak of bubonic plague in western Europe was at Marseilles in 1720–21, but it persisted in the Balkans and the Levant. The Venetian Republic was on the frontier, fighting off the threat by vigilance.

The sharp up-and-down swings in population were accentuated by emigration and immigration. When it was noised abroad that plague had broken out in a city, those who could do so fled. When the plague abated, there was a flow back, not only of those who had fled, but of people seeking refuge from pestilent outbreaks elsewhere. The government encouraged the immigration in order to revive business and raise taxes to their former level.

Waves of migration from country to city were necessary to maintain the city's population. Without this in-migration, the city would have declined, for it did not reproduce itself; no city of those centuries did. The death rates in the city, especially the infant mortality, were extremely high and exceeded birth rates. In the countryside near Venice, in contrast, births almost constantly exceeded deaths. In Venice, only about one third of the population was under twenty, in the countryside about one half were under twenty, a reservoir from which Venice replenished its ranks.

The in-migrants came mainly from the Italian mainland. Of course some were attracted from the lidi or islands of the lagoons, but their population was only about 50,000, too small to replenish a city of over 100,000. Many seamen from Greece and Dalmatia moved to Venice when times were good there and the city was reported free of plague, and some became thoroughly Venetian. But in the long run, the immigrants from the mainland dominated. Skilled workers were offered special inducements and readily received rights of citizenship. While they became loyal Venetians, they and their descendants did not generally find a life on shipboard as attractive as that in a craftsman's shop, a merchant's counting house, or a government bureau. Thus the in-migration, accentuated by the plagues, contributed to changing Venice from a nation of seamen to a nation of craftsmen. There were other reasons, as will be explained, why the popular maritime tradition that was strong in Venice in the thirteenth century evaporated, but one may wonder whether the particular traditions of the poorer classes of any city could survive the demographic situation after the appearance of the Black Death.

One class at Venice, the nobility, did reproduce itself throughout the plague-ridden centuries and preserved its traditions. Even before 1000 A.D., some of the outstanding families were tracing their genealogies back to noble families in the Roman cities that had been abandoned for the safety of the lagoons. Later, stress was placed on descent from one of the tribunes who had ruled the Venetians before the creation of a doge. Families which could claim such an ancestor were called the "long" (*longhi*) or "old families"; others were the "short" or "new families" (*curti*). Actually, social mobility was rapid in the eleventh and twelfth centuries, and even in the thirteenth century some of the richest and most powerful families had only recently attained that position. Soon after 1300, however, by a process which fills important chapters of Venetian history, noble families became clearly differentiated. At that time, the nobility numbered about 1,200 men in about 150 families. At least 50 of these families had died out by the sixteenth century and only about 40 had been added, but the number of individuals in the noble class had increased. It peaked at about 2,500 in the mid-sixteenth century, when members of noble families formed about 6 percent of the total population. Thereafter, the nobility declined in numbers, both absolutely and as a proportion of the total.

Looking back over Venice's demographic history as a whole, one is struck equally by the severity of the short swings, especially by the drops during the plagues of 1347–49, 1575–77, and 1630–31, and by the stability of the long-run trend after 1300. The fluctuations of the seventeenth and eighteenth centuries were between 100,000 and 160,000 in the city; and in 1969, residents in the same area numbered about 120,000.

From the twelfth through the eighteenth century, Venice was essentially a city-state or a city-nation (as were ancient Athens and medieval Florence), with a size of population appropriate to that special and extraordinarily creative form of social entity. As a city-state it acquired great naval power in the medieval age of sprawling, loosely jointed empires, and developed a cohesive social and political structure and efficient, distinctive economic institutions. Then, well into the modern age of centralized nations, it tenaciously maintained a share of power which, though shrinking, was enough to preserve its special forms of social organization and to complete the architectural crown of its urban planning.

THE CONQUEST OF SEA POWER·I

Police and Piracy in the Adriatic

CHAPTER THREE

Wealth may be gained from seamanship in two ways, by commerce and by piracy. Well-established maritime powers such as nineteenth-century Britain have generally depended on and defended peaceful commerce, but in the early history of most maritime peoples piracy is prominent. It appears not only glorious but even respectable when viewed with the perspectives with which Victorians looked back at the founding of British sea power by such men as Sir Francis Drake. Even in Drake's day, to be sure, while English voyages across the Atlantic or into the Mediterranean were mainly for purposes of plunder, English voyages in the North Sea sought earnings from transport services rendered strictly according to law. Thus a nation could use its vessels in one area to raid foreign shores and capture ships and cargoes, while in another area it used them only for peaceful trade and its protection. On the whole, new sea powers have been inclined to piracy or privateering and have become more concerned with maintaining transportation services and the benefits of peaceful exchange later in their development.

The contrast between Venice of the twelfth and thirteenth centuries on the one hand and Venice of the sixteenth and seventeenth centuries on the other hand is in accord with this general rule, but during its earliest history Venice was in an ambivalent position. It was a subordinate part of an old, very old sea power, the East Roman or Byzantine Empire. Its earliest notable naval exploits were in defense of the peaceful exchange of commodities, of the trade which had developed under Byzantine protection. At the same time, the Venetians unhesitatingly resorted to violence to maintain and enlarge their own part in that trade, collecting in the process considerable booty.

The relative importance of the two elements varied from one stretch of water to another. Policing was first and last dominant in the Adriatic. There Venice extended in successive steps its control first over the upper Adriatic, then over Dalmatia and the middle section, and finally — less firmly — over the lower Adriatic, acting in all three areas either as a part of the Byzantine empire or as its independent ally.

The upper Adriatic and the waters always most vital to Venice may be demarcated by a line connecting Pola at the southern tip of Istria with Ravenna (see Map 2). Within this Gulf of Venice there was no room for more than one naval power. With the weakening of the Byzantine navy which had used Ravenna as its chief base, the Venetians became the representatives of Byzantium there and were responsible for protecting the flow of commerce through the head of the Adriatic. Affirming control of the Gulf of Venice was the main achievement of the doges of the Candiano family who ruled Venice during most of the tenth century. Pietro II Candiano (932–39) reduced Comacchio to ashes when, recovering from the sack of the previous century, the Comacchians began preying on Venetian commerce. He also conquered Capodistria on the other side of the Gulf, and when other Istrian cities under a local prince launched a general campaign of piracy against Venetian shipping, the doge brought them to their knees by forbidding any trade with those cities and thus cutting off their supply of salt and other necessities. His son, Pietro III Candiano (942–59), employed economic boycott successfully also in a dispute with Aquileia. The use of economic boycott as well as of military action shows that the Venetians were already the dominant merchants and carriers within this area. Not all the lands around the Gulf of Venice were under the political control of Venice, but after the decline of Ravenna, no city within the gulf produced a navy or merchant marine able to challenge Venice's fleet.

In the middle Adriatic, Venice undertook policing against pirates, for Venetian trade needed protection there which the Byzantine Empire was increasingly unable to provide. The middle Adriatic may be bounded on the north by a line connecting Ravenna and Pola and on the south by a line connecting the Bocche di Cattaro (Kotor), at the southern end of Dalmatia, with the promontory of Gargano, the spur on the heel of Italy. On its western side, there was only one important port, Ancona; but on the opposing Dalmatian coast, the maze of islands and inlets had been a center of maritime activity even before Roman times. The Slavic peoples who overran the Balkans in the seventh and eighth centuries pushed into the Dalmatian coast, sacking some of the Roman cities and accepting alliance with others who joined them in piratical raids as the Byzantine power lessened. In the ninth century, the main center of the Slavic pirates was at the mouth of the Narenta (Neretva) River. There they had a safe retreat, impregnable to attack from the sea, about 15 kilometers upstream near the site of the Roman city of Narona. Other bases were in the nearby islands such as Curzola and Lagosta. The more northerly Dalmatian cities, such as Zara, sometimes joined Slavic pirates and sometimes welcomed Venetian help and leadership. The first Candiano doge was killed in a naval battle off Zara against the Narentans. His grandson, Pietro III Candiano, led two expeditions against them, but without any decisive success. Then, for half a century, the Venetians seem to have

THE ADRIATIC
AND IONIAN SEAS

0   100
MILES

Milan

LOMBARDY   FRIULI

Verona

Venice   Capodistria

Po R.

Ferrara   Parenzo

Bologna

Ravenna   Pola

Segna

ROMAGNA   THE   Rimini

Florence

TUSCANY   Ancona   Zara

BOSNIA   45°

Recanati

Fermo

MARCHES

Tiber R.

ADRIATIC

DALMATIA

Spalato

Narenta R.

Lesina   SERBIA

Rome   Curzola

Lagosta

ABRUZZI   Ragusa

SEA   Cattaro

Mt. Gargano   Scutari

Dulcigno

Naples   APULIA   Bari

Amalfi   Durazzo

Brindisi

ALBANIA

SASENO   Valona

Otranto

40°

Palermo   CORFU   EPIRUS

Trapani

Messina   Prevesa

SICILY   SANTA MAURA

Syracuse   IONIAN SEA   CEPHALONIA

ZANTE   MOREA

MALTA

Modon

Cape Matapan

15°   35°   20°

10°

MAP 2

made gifts to the Narentans while trading along the Dalmatian coast and maintaining commercial settlements in Dalmatian cities. Export of slaves from the interior was then at its peak, and the Narentans were slave traders as well as pirates. The Venetians were their best customers, when not themselves collecting slaves in warlike raids. Increasingly, the Dalmatians found trade of some kind more profitable than piracy.

Before A.D. 1000, these Dalmatians seem to have been able to send out fleets as large as those of the Venetians. The danger that they would form a state able to continue in competition with Venice as a naval power within the Adriatic, increasing their wealth and power with the economic growth of the region, was averted by an exceptionally able doge, Pietro II Orseolo (991–1009). The fleet which sailed down the Dalmatian coast under his personal command in the year 1000 enhanced gloriously the military reputation of Venice, but its exploits were less decisive than the doge's preparatory diplomacy which defined the expedition's political meaning. Pietro II showed an extraordinarily broad and farsighted grasp of the political and economic forces at work in the European and Mediterranean worlds.

The central problem was to maintain the friendship of both the Byzantine and Germanic emperors, each of whom claimed to be the heir of the universal power of Rome, while not yielding to either any effective authority over Venice. Pietro II Orseolo was so successful in this delicate balancing act between East and West that in the end he married one son to a niece of the Byzantine emperor and another son to a sister-in-law of the Germanic Holy Roman Emperor. He secured favorable commercial treaties with both empires and supplemented them by other commercial treaties with the Moslem states of North Africa. After these arrangements had stimulated a quickening of the international trade flowing through the Adriatic, he mobilized forces to suppress the Slavic raiders who were molesting that trade from Dalmatian bases. In asserting Venetian naval power in the middle Adriatic, he thus appeared as the friend of both emperors and the protector of peaceful commerce. He came also at the invitation of the more northerly and more thoroughly Italian Dalmatian cities such as Zara to protect them against the Narentan fleets and the Slavic princes of their hinterland.

A well-managed negotiation pitted the Slavic rulers one against the other. Doge Pietro II Orseolo never penetrated up the Narenta River itself, but he soon captured forty Narentan merchant nobles returning with merchandise from Apulia and used them to make the Narentan prince come to terms. Having thus isolated the buccaneers who lived in Curzola and Lagosta (the islands opposite the mouth of the Narenta), the doge concentrated his forces against their strongholds or starved them into submission. Returning in triumph, he reminded new and old allies of Venetian might by calling at the leading cities.

They were to need frequent reminders during the next centuries. No machinery of Venetian control was established by Orseolo's expedition. Although he henceforth took the title of Duke of Dalmatia as well as of Venice, the Dalmatian cities recognized only a vague Venetian overlordship. That lordship was threatened after the princes of the hinterland accepted Christianity. The Hungarian king, Stephen, when he conquered Croatia, was in a position to give Zara and its neighbors an alternative overlord, a protector to whom they could turn for help against Venice. In one respect, the Dalmatian cruise of Pietro II Orseolo did prove decisive, however. Never thereafter did the Narentan pirates or any other fleets recruited in the middle Adriatic challenge the supremacy of the Venetian war fleet. During the following centuries, Venice was to fight many wars to maintain or regain control of Dalmatia. Mostly they were contests of Venetian sea power against cities forced to depend on help from land powers such as Hungary. In the relatively few cases when the control of these waters was in doubt, the threat came from a naval power based outside the Adriatic, such as the Genoese Republic or the Ottoman Empire.

Pietro II Orseolo successfully exerted Venetian naval power also in the lower Adriatic, the sea between Apulia and Albania. In 1002, he led a fleet that saved Bari, the Apulian capital, from Moslem conquest. Earlier Venetian expeditions into the lower Adriatic had also been directed against the Saracens, usually as an auxiliary of the Byzantine navy in its contests with the Arabs off Sicily, Calabria, and Apulia, but without notable success. The Saracens, for their part, had pushed counterattacks up the Adriatic, even into the Gulf of Venice. The first mention of large ships built by Venetians expressly for military use is in the ninth century when they constructed heavy vessels called *chelandie* to guard the entrances of the lagoons against Saracens.

Really decisive Venetian intervention in the lower Adriatic came in the 1080's. Then again, the Venetians came to the defense of the Byzantine Empire, defending at the same time their trade to Constantinople, but against a new enemy, a Norman prince ruling southern Italy. The Normans there constituted but a thin upper class, just as they did in the kingdom which they conquered in England in the same period, but Norman rulers showed extraordinary skill in organizing for military purposes the resources of their subjects. Robert, called "Guiscard" (the Crafty), the son of a minor Norman baron, rose to leadership over a handful of Norman mercenaries employed in south Italian wars. He sent home for his brothers and other Normans ready for adventure, and began waging wars of conquest on his own. While one brother mastered Sicily, Robert captured Bari and Amalfi in 1071, and Salerno in 1076. Robert, as remarkable for his boldness as for his craftiness, planned to extend his power by conquering Greece and perhaps the Byzantine imperial crown.

At about the same time that the Normans were taking over the cities which had been the Greek emperor's chief maritime centers in the west, the Asiatic maritime provinces of the Byzantine Empire were overrun or disorganized by attacks of the Seljuk Turks. These almost simultaneous blows from west and east undermined the position which the Byzantine Empire had held for centuries as the leading Mediterranean sea power. To meet the crisis, Emperor Alexius I appealed to the Venetians for naval support.

There are no surviving private diaries, confidential memoranda, or even public proclamations from which to draw statements of what the Venetians had in mind in responding to his appeal. But their acts through several centuries imply a notably consistent policy. The Venetians sought sea power, not territorial possessions from which to draw tribute. Their wars were fought to effect political arrangements which would be disadvantageous to rival sea powers, which would make Venice's established trades more secure in Levantine waters, and which would gain them trading privileges permitting commerical expansion into new areas.

During the eleventh century the number and wealth of the Venetians was growing, nourished by economic growth generally in their north Italian hinterland. Turning increasingly from the rivers to the sea, they had both the power and the will to challenge the Norman attempts to expand across the lower Adriatic. When Alexius appealed to Venice, not as a ruler commanding a subject's obedience, but as a prince seeking an ally, the Venetians responded vigorously. Their own vital interests were at stake. They already enjoyed rights to trade within the Byzantine Empire and hoped (not in vain) for reductions in tariffs. Moreover, if Robert obtained firm possession of the island of Corfu, and of Durazzo and Valona on the eastern shore, as well as Bari, Brindisi, and Otranto on the western shore, he could capture passing Venetian ships so easily that her trade with Constantinople would be at his mercy; he could bottle her up in the Adriatic. Robert obviously considered Dalmatia a part of the empire of which he meant to be the master, and he enrolled many Dalmatian ships in his fleets. Venice's future would have been very different if she had ignored these developments, if the Norman hero had been able to consolidate under his command western resources which had once supported Byzantine naval power, if he had gone on to become the heir of the Byzantine Empire or its continuator as founder of a Norman dynasty. In opposing these vaulting but not incredible ambitions of Robert the Crafty, the Venetians played a major role in a contest involving the world's great powers, the first of many times that Venice was to play such a role.

In 1081, Robert and his son Bohemond were in Albania attacking Durazzo, the city which stood at the head of an old Roman road running straight through the Balkans to Constantinople. A Venetian fleet under the personal command of the doge arrived in the harbor. The ensuing engagement is the first Venetian naval battle of which we have a detailed description. The account, written by Anna Comnena, the talented daughter of Emperor Alexius, is worth quoting at length — even if, as some critics claim, she did mix up two different engagements — because it introduces tactical problems which changed little over many centuries:

> When night fell, as they [the Venetians] were not able to approach the shore [and thus prevent being outflanked?], and there was a calm, they tied the larger vessels together with ropes and constructed a so-called "sea-harbor" and built wooden towers at their mastheads and hauled up on to them by ropes the small boats which were usually towed together at their sterns. In these they placed armed men and cut up heavy beams into pieces about a foot and a half long and studded them with sharp iron nails and then awaited the approach [of the enemy] . . . . At day-break Bohemond . . . himself led the attack against the largest of their ships and soon the rest of the fleet joined in. A fierce battle commenced and as Bohemond was fighting very savagely against them, they threw down one of the bludgeons mentioned above and knocked a hole into the ship on which Bohemond was. As the water was sucking down the vessel and they were in danger of sinking, some of the men actually jumped into the water and were drowned whilst the rest still continued fighting with the Venetians and were killed. And Bohemond being in imminent danger leapt on to one of his own boats and was saved. Then the Venetians took fresh courage and carried on the battle with greater energy until at last they routed the enemy and pursued them to Robert's camp. Directly they touched land they jumped on to it and started another battle. . . .

Two basic persistent problems for the commander of a medieval Mediterranean war fleet were how to prevent his fleet from being dispersed and defeated in fragments and how to get the maximum use in a battle from two different kinds of vessels. Most fleets contained some low and fast long ships which were rowed and had prows for ramming; and some high, wide, sailing ships with bulging bows but lofty forecastles and sterncastles. These sail-propelled round ships were hard to maneuver in an attack, but if large, well manned and well armed, especially with missile-weapons, they could defend themselves effectively. The long ships formed the main body of every war fleet, for only rowed vessels could bring the enemy to action or be depended on to act together; but if the enemy could be maneuvered into attacking the relatively slow vessels and be exposed to their missiles, he could be weakened and disorganized before the main fleet of rowed vessels was engaged.

Success in this basic tactic brought the Venetians many victories in the five hundred years between the battles of Durazzo and Lepanto. In spite of changes in rig, structure, and armament, there were always some relatively fast vessels and some other relatively slow but defensible and made dangerous by their missiles. The fastest in both the eleventh and the sixteenth centuries were the light galleys, with twenty to thirty benches to a side and more than one rower on each bench. In the twelfth century, two heavier types of rowed warships developed by Byzantine ship constructors were still in use: the *dromons*, which had two banks of oars, one above the other; and the *chelandie*, a name then applied to various types of vessels, some with oars, some without. Since the name suggests resemblances to a tortoise, it is probable that the chelandie had a second deck, or some kind of protective structure built above deck.

Although a battle's final outcome depended on hand to hand combat, sea-fights usually opened with a great deal of heaving of stones and insults, of bags of lime to get in the enemy's eyes and of soft soap to upset his footing, as well as the shooting of arrows and the catapulting of such "bludgeons" as those described by Anna Comnena. Elsewhere she describes the use of Greek fire also, but such flame-throwing endangered the ships of both sides unless done with unusual skill. Catapults were the most used big missile weapon and they could be mounted with special effectiveness on larger vessels. Anna Comnena does not distinguish between long ships and round ships, but she emphasizes the use of the "larger" ships in the sea harbor, which was probably shaped like a half moon, with the round ships at the points protecting the flanks of the rowed vessels. These heavier vessels, having been equipped for the occasion with special missile-throwing machines, withstood Bohemond's attack. When that faltered, the pursuit must have been undertaken by the lighter vessels which had been gathered in the center of the half moon.

The Venetian naval victory did not prevent Robert from taking Durazzo, for he defeated the army with which Alexius came to relieve it. The Venetian navy had served merely to delay Robert's conquests. Delay was also the chief injury inflicted by new fleets sent off Corfu in 1083, 1084, and 1085, for Robert won the main engagement. However, these and other delays occasioned by the appeals of Pope Gregory VII for protection against the Germanic emperor sufficed, since Robert died at seventy years of age in 1085. The Byzantine emperor Alexius expressed full satisfaction with the performance of the Venetians. He rewarded them by issuing the Golden Bull of 1082, a charter granting them trading privileges and exemption from tolls. In the mixture of defeats and victories, the Venetians had impressively demonstrated naval resources, skill, and resolution. Although Greek ships fought alongside the Venetians in the engagements of 1081–85, the battles of those years showed that the naval defense of the Byzantine Empire depended on the Venetian fleet.

THE CONQUEST OF SEA POWER·II

*Victories Beyond-the-Sea
and in Romania*

CHAPTER FOUR

At the end of the eleventh century, Venetian naval power began a double transformation. Hitherto Venetians had used their fleet to defend the Byzantine Empire and to protect trade in the Adriatic. After 1100, Venetian fleets sailed beyond the Adriatic and Ionian Seas and made their power felt all over the eastern Mediterranean. At the same time they supplemented trade with plunder. Both these changes were quickened by the Crusades.

THE FIRST CRUSADES Few of those who responded to the pope's appeal in 1095 for a crusade were sufficiently moved by religion to give up all worldly ambitions for the sake of the recovery of the Holy Land from the Infidel. The French and Italian nobles who pushed overland all the way to Jerusalem on the First Crusade wanted the benefits in the hereafter that could be gained by such a pilgrimage; they also wished to carve out for themselves principalities over which they could rule. This worldly ambition was particularly apparent in the case of the Norman chief Bohemond, the son of Robert the Crafty. He was quite as willing to seize lands from the Byzantine emperor as from the Moslems. As soon as he obtained possession of the great Syrian commercial center of Antioch, he let others go on to conquer Jerusalem and devoted himself to defending and enlarging his new state by attacking nearby cities held by the Greeks. Genoese fleets appeared to help Bohemond and the other crusaders, first against Antioch and then against the other coastal cities. Both Genoa and Pisa had been waging crusades of their own in the western Mediterranean for some decades and had gained much wealth by the plunder of Saracen bases in North Africa. Now they extended similar operations into the eastern Mediterranean where they obtained not only plunder but commercial privileges in the crusaders' states. There were probably some Venetians among the many Italian ship captains who turned up at crucial moments in the Syrian and Palestinian ports, heading private ventures to sell supplies to the crusading army. Without such providential or entrepreneurial reenforcement, the crusaders would never have obtained the poles and timbers they needed for scaling ladders, towers, catapults, and other indispensable siege machinery. But official Venetian participation on a considerable scale came late. Venice was more concerned with its traditional role as possessive protector of the Byzantine Empire than with conquests in Palestine.

In 1098, a large "crusading" fleet left Pisa for the east. It occupied Corfu, which was then Byzantine territory, and wintered there. In 1099, a large "crusading" fleet sailed from Venice but stopped at Rhodes to pass the winter, either because the season was late and they were still following the ancient habit of avoiding winter storms, or because their main concern was the Aegean and they did not wish to leave it to the Pisans. Rhodes is the taking-off point from the Aegean to "Beyond-the-Sea," as Europeans then called the region in which the crusaders were founding states in Syria and Palestine. In due course the Pisans arrived, at least some of their fleet did; part of it was defeated by a reanimated Byzantine navy. When the Pisans sought to winter at Rhodes also there was fighting in which the Venetians were victorious. They freed their Pisan prisoners only after requiring of them an oath that they would not try to trade in any of the ports of Romania, that is, the domains of the Greek (Byzantine) emperor. (They called these lands "Romania" because his was considered a continuation of the Roman Empire. See Map 3, insert.) The Pisans then proceeded to join the forces of Bohemond in their attack on a Byzantine-held city in northern Syria.

The Venetians showed no hurry about leaving Romania even after the Pisans had gone to "Beyond-the-Sea"; they delayed in order to seize relics of Saint Nicholas, the patron saint of seamen to whom the church at the Lido had recently been dedicated. Having by force of arms obtained his body and also relics of other saints, they finally sailed for Palestine and arrived off Jaffa at a crucial moment. No Genoese or Pisan fleets were in Palestinian waters. Some of the leading crusaders were almost literally at swords' points; their titular head, Godfrey de Bouillon, commanded but a few knights and held only the one port, Jaffa (modern Tel Aviv). He was devoting his main efforts to enlarging his control of the coasts, and in order to secure the assistance of the Venetians, he made them sweeping promises of commercial concessions throughout his domains. The Venetians then joined him in a successful attack on Haifa (see Map 3). Returning home laden with booty, the fleet arrived appropriately on Saint Nicholas Day, December 6, 1100, after being out fully a year and a half.

Venetian traders at once began using the rights granted them in Jaffa, Haifa, and elsewhere; but during the next twenty years, the Venetians were preoccupied by trying vainly to prevent the King of Hungary from establishing his authority over Dalmatian cities and by fighting again with the Normans in the lower Adriatic. The naval support for the crusaders came mainly from others: from the Genoese, for example, who sent many expeditions both public

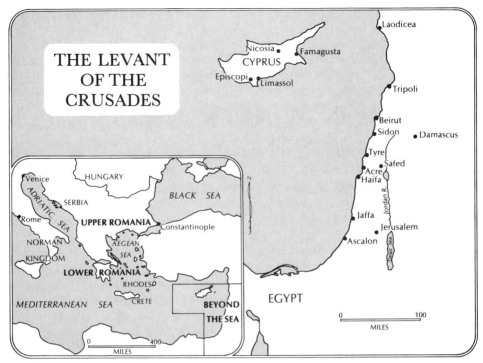

MAP 3

and private and helped in the conquest of many coastal cities in Syria and Palestine; or from the Norwegians who gave the main naval support when Sidon was taken, although a Venetian fleet helped there. The Saracen fleets were not entirely driven from the seas and the Saracens held strongly to two important Palestinian ports: Ascalon, the main base of the Egyptians in southern Palestine; and Tyre, near the border between Palestine and Syria.

In the summer of 1123, an especially well-equipped Venetian fleet under the command of Doge Domenico Michiel arrived off Jaffa, which had been attacked by the Egyptians by both land and sea. When the Venetian fleet arrived, the siege of Jaffa had just been lifted, but the Venetians went after the Egyptian fleet. In order to lure it into an engagement, the doge made a separate advanced squadron of his heaviest vessels, four large merchantmen carrying supplies, and some galleys of a large kind which were called "cats" because they carried special equipment resembling the siege machinery of that name. Being composed of higher, heavier vessels, this squadron could be and was mistaken by the Moslems for a fleet carrying merchandise and pilgrims. Seeing it approach Ascalon from the west at dawn, the Moslems hastily made sail to attack, and as the sun rose and the mist cleared, they discovered the main Venetian fleet of forty galleys coming up fast behind. Doge Michiel's galley rammed and overturned the vessel bearing the Egyptian admiral — at least that is how the chronicler of the crusades, William of Tyre, thought it should be in a naval victory. He reported that the slaughter turned the sea red for two miles around. The victorious Venetian fleet then cruised south towards Egypt and had the good luck to capture some merchant vessels on their way to

Ascalon, laden with gold, silver, and pepper, cinnamon, and all manner of other spices.

In spite of the rich spoils they had thus already acquired, the Venetians agreed to join the knights of the Kingdom of Jerusalem in their siege of Tyre and stayed until that city fell in July, 1124. The fall of Tyre left the Moslems with no naval base north of Ascalon. The Venetians had won for the crusaders undisputed control of the sea for a generation. The ports of the Kingdom of Jerusalem became secure means of receiving reinforcements from the West and the centers of exchange between Europe and Asia.

The battle of Ascalon opened a period of Venetian naval dominance in the eastern Mediterranean, but it was dominance of a kind which could be displayed in plundering others more effectively than in defending peaceful trade, and the Venetians used it primarily in plundering the Byzantine empire which they had hitherto protected. They did not turn from protection to plunder until the Byzantine emperor who succeeded Alexius I tried to take away the privileged commercial position which Alexius had given them as payment for their aid against the Normans. Alexius himself had begun to show favor to the Pisans, and when his successor in 1118 refused to renew Alexius's grant to the Venetians, they suspected that he wished to place them on an equal footing with the Pisans and play one Italian naval power off against the other. But the Pisans were too deeply committed in a quarrel with Genoa over Corsica to dispute successfully with Venice control of the Ionian and Aegean Seas. The Venetian fleet that won the celebrated victory at Ascalon for the crusaders sacked Greek islands on both its outward and return voyage, and penetrated deep into the Aegean in order to collect the body of Saint Isidore. Doge Domenico Michiel's fleet brought home some booty from Palestine but more from Romania. The Byzantine emperor was persuaded by such raids to renew the exclusive privileges of the Venetians.

Pillaging the Byzantine Empire was always a second best for the Venetians, at least from the point of view of their government. The foundation of Venetian policy was exploitation of Romania through special commercial privileges. Therefore they were ready to fight the Normans and others to keep the Byzantine Empire intact while equally ready to fight the Greeks themselves, not only for the sake of booty, but also to force the Greeks to renew Venetian privileges. Throughout the twelfth century, the Venetian navy was used first for the one purpose, then for the other, and occasionally for both at once, and the hatred felt by the Greeks and the contempt showed by the Venetians were intensified. In 1148, when the Venetians were again allied with the Greeks against the Normans and when their joint fleet was attempting to retake Corfu, Greek and Venetian seamen came to blows. The Venetians insulted Emperor Manuel Comnenus personally by dressing up a slave in imperial robes on the poop of a captured galley and parading him in mockery before the Greek fleet while they burlesqued ceremonies of the imperial court which the Greeks regarded as sacred rituals.

In spite of this insult, Manuel continued for years to ally with the Venetians because he needed their help against the Normans. But he worked to undermine their position in the Adriatic. In 1171 he felt ready for a drastic move. After special professions of firm friendship, he suddenly arrested all the Venetians in his empire and seized their property. The Venetians tried immediately to repeat the tactic that had worked so well a half century before and sent a fleet into the Aegean to sack cities until the emperor should submit. Its commander was another member of the Michiel family, Doge Vitale II Michiel. No Greek fleet challenged him, but Doge Vitale II moderated his attacks in order to negotiate about the thousands of Venetians whom Manuel was holding as hostages. Meanwhile an epidemic broke out in the fleet. When it returned in 1172, bringing pest instead of plunder, the doge faced a tumult and was murdered.

His successor, Sebastiano Ziani, the richest man in Venice, left the pillaging of Romania to private enterprise and concentrated governmental naval efforts on affirming Venetian power within the Adriatic. At the same time, this first of the Ziani doges managed Venice's foreign relations with such skill that Manuel's successors renewed Venetian privileges. But they also gave privileges to competing Italians, the various Italian colonies in Constantinople frequently came to blows, and they all were exposed to popular outbursts expressing the hate the Greeks felt for the privileged Italians.

The periodic street fights in Constantinople reflected the situation at sea. By the end of the twelfth century, piracy had become general. The Ionian and Aegean seas especially were furrowed by Genoese, Sicilians, Pisans, Anconitans, Saracens, and Greeks as well as Venetians looking for ships that could be easily captured and raiding coasts to seize treasure or enslave captives. Most wars were merely similar operations on a larger scale by the same captains and crews, who always preferred a profitable raid to an unprofitable combat with another war fleet.

The burgeoning of piracy in the Aegean gradually changed the Mediterranean slave trade. Not only captures at sea but sudden landings on unprotected coasts enslaved many Greeks, especially women and children.

Perhaps it is misleading to refer to all these slave raiders and freebooters as pirates. Unlike downright pirates, they limited to a certain extent their looting according to their political hates and loyalties, as did Sir Francis Drake later. Unlike privateers, they were not formally licensed by governments that were at war. Nor was it necessarily a hostile act against some other country to seize one of its citizens and hang him as a pirate. But none of the governments took any severe action against pirates who were their own subjects, for each felt that its nationals had suffered wrongs for which they had a right to take vengeance. Any valiant captain who had deeds of prowess to his credit received much admiration and sympathy.

The most significant naval actions in the last decades of the twelfth century took place off the coast of Palestine. The Kingdom of Jerusalem was almost completely destroyed by Saladin's victory at the Horns of Hattin (1187). Only a few coastal cities were left in Christian hands, and they could be held only through control of the sea, which was for a time lost to Saladin's Egyptian navy. It was regained by the fleets that brought out Philip Augustus of France and Richard the Lion-Hearted. Their royal expeditions, called the Third Crusade, preserved the Christians' hold on a fragment of Palestine around Acre. Transporting crusaders who came to support it boomed the business of Italian ship captains, including the Venetians, but there was no major Venetian expedition to that corner of the Mediterranean during the Third Crusade because the Venetians needed their strength nearer home. They were preoccupied with the commercial rivalry of a Pisan-Anconitan combine, the greed of the Sicilian-Normans, the ambitions of the Hohenstaufens, and the wiles of the Greeks.

THE FOURTH CRUSADE   Venice's successes depended on combining consistency in goals with flexibility in the means. Her aim was the strengthening of her sea power as a base for commercial expansion. Since the Venetians numbered less than 100,000 people all told, they could not act like a great power able to follow a planned program and to put behind it such force that others had to submit. Moreover, under the conditions of the time, military political situations changed rapidly in ways quite outside Venice's control. Success depended on adaptability. Venetian suppleness in adjusting to circumstances was never more successfully displayed than in the Fourth Crusade, a turning point in Venetian history.

At a tournament in Champagne, the heartland of French chivalry, the Count of Champagne and many other foremost nobles of France took the cross. Then they sent envoys to Venice, with Geoffrey de Villehardouin as their leading spokesman, to negotiate for transportation to the Holy Land. Ship captains of Venice, Genoa, and other cities were accustomed to making contracts for a few ships to transport crusading knights, since the sea route was now generally preferred to the long overland march used in the First Crusade, but the enthusiastic envoys from Champagne proposed a contract larger than any previously arranged. They expected a force of 33,500 to gather at Venice in 1202. In return for a promise of 85,000 marks of silver, the Venetians agreed to provide the necessary transports and food for a year for this huge number, namely, for 4,500 knights and their horses, 9,000 squires, and 20,000 foot soldiers. The operation was to require about 200 ships. So large an enterprise involved tying up nearly all of Venice's resources and it was negotiated for the Venetians as a whole by their doge. At the same time, the doge made a more clearly political deal. In return for an equal share in all booty and conquests on land or sea, the Venetians undertook to supply 50 fully armed galleys to serve also for a year. Manning 50 galleys required about 6,000 men. Even though many sailors and oarsmen could be recruited in Istria and Dalmatia, these treaties committed at least half of all the Venetians fit for fighting to service for a year with the crusaders, either on the galleys or manning the transports.

The Venetians built the ships and had them ready for departure in the summer of 1202. Constructed especially for the occasion were many horse transports of a special type which had large hatches in the bows so that horses could be led in and out. Villehardouin was enthusiastic about the way in which the Venetians fulfilled their part of the contract: "And the fleet they had got ready was so goodly and fine that never did Christian man see a goodlier or finer; as well galleys as transports, and sufficient for at least three times as many men as there were in the host." The excellence of the Venetian preparations made Villehardouin feel all the more embarrassed by the inability of the crusaders for whom he acted to fulfill their part of the bargain by completing the payment of 85,000 marks of silver. The Count of Champagne had died, some of those who had promised to rendezvous in Venice had stayed home, some others had made their own arrangements to go through other ports. Instead of 33,500 there were no more than 10,000 crusaders at most assembled on the Lido awaiting transportation. When they had paid all they could and when the richer nobles had even turned over their gold and silver plate, they still owed the Venetians some 34,000 marks.

The excessive optimism and zeal of Villehardouin and his fellow envoys, their lack of realism in handling large figures, is evident from a few comparisons. The King of France, Philip Augustus, had mustered only 650 knights and 1,300 squires to accompany him on the Third Crusade, and the force he assembled in France for the defense of his realm in his greatest battle, Bouvines, is estimated at between 7,000 and 12,000. Yet Villehardouin contracted for passage for over 30,000 men! The sum of 85,000 marks was similarly unrealistic; it was enough silver (about 20,000 kg) to coin over £60,000 sterling, about twice the annual income of either the King of England or of the King of France.

The doge who had negotiated this huge and risky shipping contract and supervised the preparation of the fleet was Enrico Dandolo, a man well over eighty and blind, but still a persuasive leader, a shrewd negotiator, and even in council with the highest feudal lords a dominating personality. Perhaps he had foreseen that Villehardouin and the other envoys were overestimating their resources and that they would start with a debt to the Venetians to be worked off. Certainly he had no trouble finding a way in which the knights could pay their debt, or at least delay payment. Zara was engaged in one of its innumerable efforts to assert its independence of Venice and to become, with Hungarian aid and overlordship, a rival power within the Adriatic. It may be doubted whether the Venetian leaders had ever really intended to engage their whole naval power in operations overseas until they had in some way used the crusading hosts to assure their control of the Adriatic. Doge Dandolo now proposed that the payment of the crusaders' debt be deferred until it could be paid out of the booty collected by the expedition, and that they begin by helping him subdue Zara. There was much objection to this diversion of the crusade to attack a Christian city, but the leading crusaders felt obligated, did not know how otherwise to get going to the East, and persuaded the majority. Thousands of Venetians and the doge himself took the cross, and "then the Venetians began to deliver the ships, the galleys and the transports to the barons, for departure. . . . Ah, God! what fine war horses were put therein," wrote Villehardouin in glowing recollection of the scene. "And when the ships were filled full with arms and provisions, and knights and sergeants, the shields were ranged round the bulwarks and the castles of the ships, and the banners were displayed, many and fair."

With equal joy in the paraphernalia of war, he described the landing at Zara: "Then might you have seen many a knight and many a sergeant swarming out of the ships, and taking from the transports many a good war horse, and many a rich tent and pavillion." Zara soon surrendered, but it was then mid-November, 1202, and it was decided to postpone further voyaging until spring.

While the Venetian fleet and the crusading host were wintering at Zara in 1202-3, a second diversion of the crusade from its presumed goal was agreed to, a detour also clearly in accord with Venetian interest and much more far-reaching in its consequences than the siege of Zara. It was decided to proceed to Constantinople and place on the Byzantine throne a claimant called "the young Alexius." To win the support of the Western knights, young Alexius offered to bring the Byzantine Empire back into submission to the papacy, to pay 200,000 marks of silver and also the cost of operating the fleet for an additional year, and join the crusade to the Holy Land himself the following year or at least contribute an army of 10,000 Greeks.

Why were the crusaders thus diverted from the Holy Land to Constantinople? The Greek emperors were suspected of having been in secret alliance with Saladin, as indeed they had been. There was some strategic justification for securing the northeast corner of the Mediterranean before proceeding to an all-out assault upon the southeast corner. But personal and dynastic ambitions were more influential. After the death of the Count of Champagne, the crusaders had chosen as their commander Boniface of Montferrat. Boniface's brothers had been active in the Byzantine Empire and through them he felt he had a claim to a part of it, the region around Salonica. Boniface was a friend of the Holy Roman Emperor, Philip of Swabia, his feudal overlord, who had close connections by marriage with the young Alexius. It seems probable that before young Alexius made his proposal to the crusading army he had come to an understanding during the previous year with Boniface and Philip, whose interests were certainly served by the diversion.

If there was such a "plot," as opponents called it, it was probably not unknown to the doge, and certainly not unwelcome. The Byzantine emperor had renewed the treaty granting extensive privileges to the Venetians just three years before, but he was extending similar privileges to the Pisans and Genoese and taxing Venetians in spite of the treaty. Ever since Manuel's seizure of all Venetians and their wares in 1171 and a popular massacre of Latins a few years later, the Venetians had felt insecure at Constantinople. Doge Enrico Dandolo had personal experience of the degenerating relations between Greeks and Latins during the recent decades. Although the report of the chronicler who attributed his blindness to a trick with a burning glass perpetrated by the Greeks was false, Dandolo had certainly been involved in many bitter negotiations at Constantinople, and the story that he was thus blinded is itself evidence of the growing hatred and distrust between Greeks and Venetians.

When the diversion to Constantinople was known among the Franks in the Kingdom of Jerusalem, who had been eagerly expecting the crusading host to bring them much needed help, it was rumored that the Venetians had from the beginning been bribed by the Soldan of Egypt to divert the crusade away from his domains. One chronicler in Palestine reports this, but there is no other evidence of such a Venetian agreement with Egypt. Venice's policies over the previous hundred years might well make one wonder, however, whether Venice had ever really intended to direct its whole naval power away from Romania and commit its whole fighting population to the conquest of Egypt or the reconquest of Palestine. For fully a century, Venice had subordinated everything to upholding its special position in the Byzantine Empire. In the precarious conditions of 1202, was it prepared to abandon Romania for new fields to conquer "Beyond-the-Sea"? Doge Dandolo signed the treaty with Villehardouin and the other envoys before Boniface had been chosen commander and before Alexius had arrived with his promises. The exact theater of operations was not specified in the treaty and Dandolo may have hoped and expected that something would happen enabling the Venetian fleet to combine action in the southeastern corner of the Mediterranean with effective furtherance of Venetian interests in Romania, as had been done in the Venetian crusading expeditions of 1099–1100

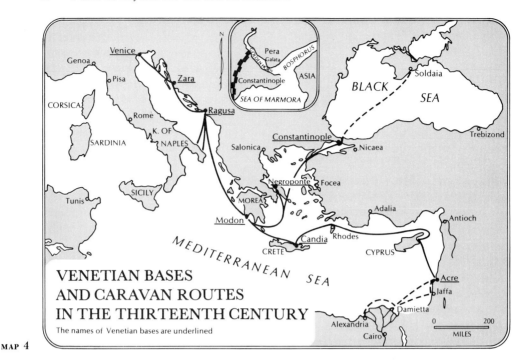

VENETIAN BASES
AND CARAVAN ROUTES
IN THE THIRTEENTH CENTURY

The names of Venetian bases are underlined

MAP 4

and 1122–24. With courage and resolution, as well as flexibility, he turned very much to Venice's advantage the circumstances which did turn up.

Many crusaders were disgusted with the decision to proceed by way of Constantinople and set off directly for Palestine, but enough remained to make the armada which sailed out of the Adriatic in the spring of 1203 and reached Constantinople in June a very formidable fighting force. Such a force was needed, for the Greeks promptly showed that they would not accept young Alexius as their emperor unless compelled to do so. Never since its foundation had Constantinople been successfully assaulted by a foreign army. It was protected on the west by a double set of walls and on the other three sides by walls along the water. Of the Byzantine navy, however, which had defended the city during many dangerous centuries, there remained but twenty rotten and worm-eaten vessels, nothing with which to challenge Venetian command of the sea. To have a base for their assault, the crusaders seized the suburb just north of Constantinople, Galata, which was separated from it by the mouth of a small river. This estuary formed Constantinople's inner harbor and was known as the Golden Horn because of its shape and the richness of the cargoes collected there (see Map 4, insert). The Greeks had sealed this inner harbor by a large chain, but it was broken when the knights stormed the castle at Galata. Venetian galleys mastered the inner harbor while the knights advanced along its northern shore.

With Galata thus secured as a base, the crusaders faced the problem of carrying the assault of the city either across the Golden Horn or around it to the west. In fact, they were to face that problem twice, once in July of 1203 and again in April of 1204, for after the first assault intimidated the Greeks sufficiently so that they accepted the young Alexius, the latter found it impossible to carry out his promises. The crusaders had either to go away humiliated and in depleted condition to carry the crusade to the Holy Land or to conquer the city for themselves.

In the first assault, that of July, 1203, which forced the Greeks to accept the young Alexius, the French knights insisted on circling the Golden Horn so that they could attack by land and fight on horseback, a style of fighting befitting their rank and one in which they had reason to consider themselves invincible. Enrico Dandolo urged instead an assault from ships across the Golden Horn, for the Venetians were experts at turning their vessels into siege machinery. The doge's judgment was confirmed when the knights attacking by land from the northwest were beaten off by Byzantium's famed Varangian guards composed of Anglo-Saxon and Danish mercenaries, while the Venetians attacking from the sea captured several towers. The chronicler from Champagne was greatly impressed by the skill and courage of the Venetians and especially of Enrico Dandolo. The doge, in spite of his age and blindness, "was standing all armed at the bow of his galley and had before him the banner of St. Mark. He called out to his sailors to put him ashore quickly, or he would do justice to their bodies; so his galley was run ashore immediately and the crew landed with his standard. All the Venetians followed his lead: those from the horse-transports sallied out, and those in the great ships got into the boats and landed as best they could." The air was full of stones and arrows. Other Venetians were crossing on boarding ramps from the mastheads of their ships to the top of the wall. When twenty-five towers had been taken by the Venetians and the Greeks were mounting a counterattack, Dandolo began to burn the adjoining houses and the north wind created a wall of fire protecting him from a counterattack. He then sent aid to the beleaguered French knights, including ironically a few captured Greek horses.

In the second assault, in April, 1204, when all the Greeks were united and opposed the crusaders more persistently, the Venetians displayed to the full their skill in siege operations. Their naval expeditions had normally included assailing fortified cities, for example, Curzola in 1000 or Tyre in 1124; in fact, such assaults were a more common part of fleet operations than were battles at sea with other fleets.

In the hand-to-hand combat of an assault the knights expected to take the lead, but the construction of siege machinery depended more on the carpenters who formed a part of every ship's crew; and sailors must have been at least as adept as knights at maintaining precarious footing atop a scaling ladder. For the capture of Constantinople, the Venetians built not only ordinary scaling ladders, battering rams, and stone-throwing slings and catapults, but fighting platforms high on the mastheads of their ships. They had rope ladders so that they could come down from above at enemies on the walls and with their spars they made structures called "flying bridges" to swing out from the high forecastles or the fighting tops to the opposing turrets. As protection against the famed "Greek fire" they covered the wooden ships with watersoaked cloths and hides.

Although the defenders were in fact not well-equipped with Greek fire, there was much other use of fire during these sieges. Conflagrations such as those Dandolo had set during the assault in July, 1203, burned over a good part of the city, and the Greeks made several efforts to burn the Venetian fleet.

One night they set afire some old chelandies filled with pitch, tow, and other combustibles. Wind and currents carried them down towards the sleeping Venetian fleet. Once alerted, the Venetians rose to the occasion, grappling the fireships with boat hooks and towing them where the current would take them harmlessly away, and cutting threatened ships loose from their moorings to avoid the danger or isolate the few that were ignited. Twice attempts to burn the fleet were foiled without serious loss. On the other hand, the fires ashore burned half the city.

For the second assault in April, 1204, the crusaders followed the advice of the doge and concentrated all their forces in an attack from the water across the Golden Horn. The Greeks had been making special preparations also, building wooden towers and platforms above the walls so that they would not be overtopped by the ships. Many of the attacking vessels did not succeed in maneuvering in close enough to the walls; the fighting men aboard had to wade ashore and depend on scaling ladders. After several hours of fierce fighting the crusaders broke off and withdrew to Galata. Some of the crusaders then proposed to attack on the east side, where the walls were not so high, but the Venetians pointed out that the current flowing south from the Bosphorus was there so strong that the ships could not be held in position. Instead, the crusaders spent two days in resting, repairing or improving their siege machinery, and planning a better ordered attack. The largest transports were lashed together in pairs so that they would support each other in attacks on the towers. The attack went on indecisively until about mid-day when, as the north wind strengthened, the pitching of one of the ships carried its masthead or forecastle so far forward that two men, first a Venetian and then a French knight, were able to leap from a "flying bridge" onto the top of one of the towers, plant their banners, and lash a rope around the crenellation so that others could come to their aid from above, while knights mounted scaling ladders below to complete the capture of that tower. Once one tower was taken, many others fell, the gates were opened, squires led horses out of the transports through the especially designed hatches and the knights mounted and rode through the streets overwhelming all opposition.

There followed three days of murder, rapine, rape, and sacrilege. Churches and houses were thoroughly plundered. When Boniface of Montferrat ordered all the booty collected for division, it was valued (apart from what may have been secretly held back) at 400,000 marks and 10,000 suits of armor. There was no trouble then in paying the overdue debt to the Venetians, besides giving them their half of the booty. The four bronze horses which had once stood on top of a triumphal arch in Rome, then over the racing stadium in Constantinople, and now stand in front of San Marco are witness to how well the Venetians picked in selecting their share.

They took also a portion of the sacred relics. Belief in the saving virtue of such relics was a powerful part of crusading enthusiasm and a part which the Venetians fully shared. On their very first crusading expedition, they made acquiring the body of Saint Nicholas almost the first order of business (second only to disposing of Pisan commercial rivals). From the capture of Tyre they brought back the block of stone from which, according to tradition, the Lord had preached. After 1204, the host of relics which the Greek emperors had collected in Constantinople during centuries of rule was distributed among its conquerors, and many added to the glory of the church of San Marco at Venice, including a fragment of the True Cross and part of the head of Saint John the Baptist.

AN EMPIRE OF   *Once did she hold the gorgeous East in fee*
NAVAL BASES   *And was the safeguard of the West . . .*
    WORDSWORTH, SONNET III.1-2

An overthrow of the Greek Empire had been no part of the plan with which the crusading barons and the Venetians came to Constantinople, but when they found that the young Alexius would not and could not fulfill his promises and that they either had to go away empty-handed or conquer the Byzantine Empire, they did not hesitate to draw up a contract providing for the second alternative — not a shipping contract this time, but a constitution for a new imperial government. It provided that a new Eastern Emperor should be elected by a committee of six Venetians and six of the barons. Boniface counted on being chosen, but since he was an old ally of the Genoese, the Venetians all voted for Baldwin, Count of Flanders, who was elected. For himself, the emperor was to receive only one quarter of the Empire, the rest was to be divided equally between the Venetians and the barons. Thus Venice was allotted three-eighths, or as it was phrased in the doge's title, he became the "Lord of One Quarter and One Half [of a quarter] of the Empire of Romania."

All the land thus allotted, including the emperor's share, was then to be subdivided into fiefs and given out in return for military service. All fief-holders were obligated to swear allegiance to the emperor, although the Doge of Venice was excepted from such an oath. Since the emperor was chosen from among the barons, the Venetians were allowed to choose a new patriarch as head for the church of Latin rite that was now established in the Empire. And in the authoritative emperor's council, alongside the great fief-holders, the leaders of the Venetian colony at Constantinople were heavily represented. The Latin Empire of Constantinople was so constituted that it had not the strength for a long life, but as long as it lasted, it assured the Venetians that the government there would be favorable to their interests.

All the privileges and possessions granted to the Venetians by previous Byzantine emperors were reaffirmed, and this time the Venetians could feel sure the promises would be kept. In addition, it was provided that no citizen of a state which was at war with Venice was to be received within the territory of the Empire. One could well say that "the Venetians had 'constitutionally' excluded their enemies from competition" (Wolff).

In the distribution of territories, the Venetian government concentrated on obtaining the essentials for naval control. An elaborately made division between emperor, crusading barons, and Venetians was largely illusory, for after the sack of Constantinople in 1204, the old Byzantine Empire was in fact "up for grabs." Large pieces were being acquired by rival Greek emperors or despots, notably Trebizond, Nicaea, and Epirus. Boniface of Montferrat insisted successfully on having Salonica and a large territory thereabouts. A nephew of Villehardouin found allies with whom to conquer the Peloponnesus, then called Morea. A nephew of Enrico Dandolo, namely, Marco Sanuto, seized the islands in the center of the Aegean and organized the Duchy of Naxos which was a fief, not of Venice, but of the Empire. One wonders what Enrico Dandolo, had he not died in 1205, would have conquered for himself, or his son, or Venice. Dandolo's successor Pietro Ziani concentrated on establishing the power of the Venetian Republic over those parts of the Empire which were of greatest strategic importance as naval bases. Consistent with the policy which Venice had previously followed and was to follow for centuries, he showed less interest in tribute-paying territories than in control of the seas used by Venetian commerce.

The most important base was of course Constantinople itself, where the Venetians had been awarded three-eighths of the city, including the area of the arsenal and the docks. The Venetian colony, having absorbed some of the polyglot native population, was counted in the tens of thousands. This colony regularly maintained a war fleet, and on several occasions the Venetian squadron of ten to twenty-five galleys defended the city against fleets fitted out by the Greek emperor of the rival empire at Nicaea.

Almost equally important strategically was the island of Crete, bordering both the southwestern and the southeastern entrances to the Aegean, and lying on the direct route from the Ionian Sea to Egypt or Syria. To obtain clear title to Crete, the Venetians paid cash and ceded claims to a large area elsewhere but to obtain possession they had to fight for it against a Genoese pirate known as Henry the Fisherman, Count of Malta, who for a time received considerable but fitful support from the city of Genoa and from the Greeks. Tolerating usurpations in many sections of the empire which had been assigned to them as part of their three-eighths, the Venetians concentrated on Crete. To push its conquest they divided it into knights' fees and sergeancies which were given in fief to Venetians, hundreds of whom emigrated to become soldiers and landlords, while others settled as merchants in the Cretan capital, Candia (now Iraklion).

Further north in the Aegean, Venice established itself firmly at Negroponte, the "Black Bridge" between classical Euboea and the mainland, and gradually extended Venetian influence over the island, making Negroponte their main base in the Aegean between Crete and Constantinople (see Map 4). In the Ionian Sea, the Venetians obtained Modon and nearby Coron at the southern tip of the Morea, and fortified them. They became the "two eyes of the Republic"; all vessels returning from the Levant were ordered to stop there to have news and give news of pirates and convoys. At the northern end of the Ionian Sea, the Venetians took Corfu in 1206, but gave it up soon after. During most of the thirteenth century, they had to depend on Ragusa, a loyal dependency in that period, as the base for their fleets operating at the end of the Adriatic.

Although there were weak links in the chain of naval bases, the colonial empire which the Venetians obtained from the Fourth Crusade, combined with their privileged position in the trade and government of the Latin Empire of Constantinople, and the firm hold on Dalmatia which Enrico Dandolo had obtained by the submission of Zara, gave the Venetians undisputed maritime preeminence in the eastern Mediterranean.

THE ORGANIZATION OF SEA POWER·I

Ships, Crews, and the Ship's Company

The lordship which Venice exercised over the eastern Mediterranean after Doge Enrico Dandolo's cagey and magnificent utilization of the Fourth Crusade was solidly based on Venetian efficiency in shipbuilding and in the operation of both warships and merchantmen. It was the high development of these industries that made it possible for Doge Enrico Dandolo to undertake the ambitious contract with the French knights and then to fulfill his share of the bargain so well as to turn the venture to Venice's great advantage. Ships were so clearly recognized by the Venetians as the basis of their power that the government forbade any Venetian to sell his ship to a foreigner unless it was old or inferior. Venetians were of course expected to build at Venice, but they did not have to be required to do so, for they had there an abundance of the materials needed and of skilled labor.

The operation as well as the building of their ships depended on free labor. It must be emphasized that references to "medieval galley slaves" are thoroughly misleading. The galley fleets of the medieval republics of Venice, Genoa, and Pisa were not rowed by slaves. Rowing and fighting were combined assignments of citizens obligated to military service because of their citizenship or of men freely hired for wages. Medieval pirates used captives as galley slaves on occasion, to be sure, but the harrowing accounts of oarsmen chained and flogged come mainly from the seventeenth century. The kind of discipline they eloquently describe had no relation to medieval conditions. This will be made clear by an examination of the kinds of ships used and by the way they were manned and loaded, topics which bring us close to problems Venetians thought about in the ordinary business of making a living.

SHIPS AND   The typical merchant ship of the twelfth or thirteenth century used no oars.
NAVIGATION   It was a "round ship," its length overall being about three times its width
or beam. It had two masts, each carrying a triangular sail. To be worthy of
the name "ship" (*navis* or *buzus* or *banzonus*), these two-masted lateeners had to
have at least two decks, a stern castle, a forecastle, and a fighting top. To meet the
growing demand of crusaders, pilgrims, and merchants, some ships of this type
were built very large, veritable castles on the sea, as the chroniclers called them.
One of the biggest was the Venetian ship appropriately named *Roccaforte* (*Fortress*) of about 500 deadweight tons. That seems tiny today, when an ordinary
freighter can carry 10,000 tons and a big tanker at least 100,000 tons but 500 tons
meant a very big ship any time before the nineteenth century. British East Indiamen of the eighteenth century were only a little larger. Americans may recall
that the *Mayflower* was rated 180 tons and Columbus's *Santa Maria* is estimated
at 100 tons. In the Middle Ages, only a few of the busiest ports such as Venice
and Genoa had ships as big as 200 tons. There were probably not a half dozen
as big as the *Roccaforte* in all the Mediterranean at any one time. The Venetians had two such giants in the 1260's and Genoa about the same number, but
the ordinary "ship" (*navis*), the standard, large two-decked cargo carrier, was
of about 200 tons.

These ships, even the biggest, were steered by side-rudders, operated on
the same principle as the paddle in a canoe and manipulated by a tiller coming
into a steerage gallery. Each vessel carried many anchors, ten to twenty, with
appropriate hawsers. Some big merchantmen had three masts, some two, all
raked forward, and lateen rigged with yards almost as long as the ship (Figure 3).
There were several sails for each mast, but they were not hoisted one above
the other; they were used alternately. A large, triangular, light cotton sail called
the *artimon* was used on the forward mast in a light breeze. If a gale threatened,
the yard was lowered, the artimon removed, and a small tough canvas sail, also
triangular, was lashed to the yard and hoisted in its place.

The lateen sails permitted sailing closer to the wind than had been possible
with the square sails common in antiquity, but the ship's course could be set no
closer than 6 points to the wind and the course made good would at best hardly
be within 7 points. Large round ships like the *Roccaforte* would fall away from
the wind more because of the wind pressure against its high sides and castles. Better
able to beat to windward were lower, longer, narrower one-deck vessels called
tarettes, generally of about 100 tons. Although better sailers and much used as
supply ships because easier to handle together with galleys in a convoy, the
tarettes were less protected from high seas and were not so useful in battle as
the two-decked *navis* or *buzo-navis*. Somewhat similar to the tarettes but heavier
in construction were the horse transports which had specialized hatches designed
so that the horses of the knights could walk on and walk off.

The type which contrasted most sharply with such fortress ships as the
Roccaforte were the galleys. They were the extreme type of "long ship," their
length being about eight times their beam. In the thirteenth century, most galleys
were biremes, that is, they had two men side by side on each bench, each pulling
a separate oar. To give the men proper leverage, the oars passed over an outrigger projecting from the sides of the long narrow hull. The virtues of the galleys
were speed and maneuverability. Against any opponent except other galleys they
could accept or decline battle at will. They could carry little cargo, having only

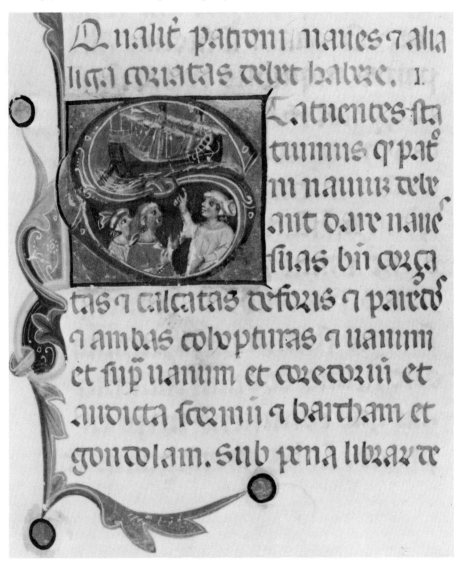

FIGURE 3   *Illuminated Initial from the Maritime Code of 1255 (courtesy of the Querini Stampalia, Venice).*

The laws codified by Doge Ranieri Zeno specified the equipment of lateen-rigged merchantmen like that pictured.

one deck and that about two yards above the keel, but when victorious, they filled their holds with shackled prisoners. If they loaded merchandise, they were a relatively safe but highly expensive form of transport.

To take advantage of favorable winds when cruising, galleys carried one or two triangular sails.

A very specialized kind of rowed vessel was the *bucentoro* (ship of gold), a broad galley with decorative superstructures which was employed only on ceremonial occasions.

Even those ships that could beat to windward, namely the light galleys and tarettes, found it such slow work that, on commercial voyages at least, they preferred staying in harbor and waiting for a favorable wind. The waters the Venetians sailed did not have dependable prevailing winds like the monsoons and the trade winds, but neither did they call for many days of sailing between ports. With a favorable wind, even at four knots (a likely speed, and frequently exceeded), a ship could cross the 90 miles from Venice to Parenzo in Istria in a day and night. Setting out from Parenzo or Pola on the outward voyage, a vessel aided by a good north wind could site Gargano more than half way down the Adriatic in three days. A fast ship might make the run all the way to Corfu in less than nine days. The winds in the Adriatic, Ionian, and Aegean Seas — the waters most sailed by the Venetians — were and are extremely variable, but a skilled pilot, able to interpret the weather signs, could hope to pick a time of departure when winds were likely to be favorable for a few days at least. The Venetians did not hug the shore out of any fear of the open sea, but the nature of the routes they sailed made it possible and sensible to sight headlands frequently, and galleys had need fairly often to put into port for supplies.

The construction of both round ships and long ships, of merchantmen and war galleys, was initiated on occasion by the government, but more frequently by private enterprise. There was no persistent prejudice either for or against the government being the builder, but most of the shipwrights and caulkers worked in small shipyards of their own on small craft or were employed in shipyards rented for the occasion by merchants who organized a group of craftsmen to build a ship for them. The government felt free to regulate in any way it might wish the product of these shipyards, and sometimes went so far as to stipulate the exact dimensions. If then later it decided to buy the ships, it would have the kind it wanted. The construction of the Arsenal in 1104 provided a place under the doge's supervision for the storage of arms, oars, rigging, and other kinds of supplies. It was used to repair galleys and keep a few in readiness, but most of the construction of new vessels, even of a war fleet, was in the thirteenth century done elsewhere. The doge could command all the shipyard workers of the lagoons to come to work in the yards in which the government was building. When so conscripted, the carpenters and caulkers were paid; the government normally depended on wages, not conscription, to recruit needed laborers. Only in quite extraordinary times were most of them working for the government. Ordinarily, the shipwrights and caulkers were in private employ, either in the shipyards or serving on board a ship at sea, as many did during the sailing season.

SEAMEN AND TRAVELING MERCHANTS   The crews of the merchant marine and the navy were the same people, but the size of the crew was much larger on a vessel prepared for combat. Before the development of cannon, the crew was a vessel's principal armament, whether it was a round ship or a long ship. Indeed, Venetian regulations distinguished between "armed" and "unarmed" ships by the size of their crews. Even a vessel built like a galley was not considered an "armed ship" unless its crew numbered at least 60 men. When "armed," a galley normally carried 140-180 men. In addition to those who manned its oars, a fully armed galley carried fighting men in its forecastle and sterncastle, along the sides between the oars, on the central gangway, and in the fighting top or crow's nest. A huge

500-ton sailing ship, such as the *Roccaforte,* had a crew of a hundred on a normal commercial voyage, but if "armed" for battle, it carried several hundred.

Narratives of medieval sea fights show that ramming was of distinctly minor importance, missiles were important but secondary, and hand-to-hand combat was decisive. On merchant ships as well as in the war fleet, each seaman was required to be provided with arms and armor—with sword, dagger, javelin or lance, shield, helmet or hat, and battle jacket—while mates were required to have additional weapons and superior body armor. The knights who were their comrades in arms during the crusades were of course better equipped. Knights wore coats of mail and had constant practice in using heavy weapons while carrying the weight of armor. But the seamen were equipped and experienced in their own kind of fighting. In an age when the priests and the military were the upper classes, seamen could make a kind of claim to be part of the warrior class.

It is hard for us to believe that service as an oarsman was not less esteemed than signing on as a sailor, but there is no evidence in the twelfth and thirteenth centuries to that effect and no reason to think that the oarsmen on the galleys were then a distinct lower class. Large numbers of oarsmen were needed only when a large war fleet was armed, and on such occasions a kind of "selective service" act was invoked. The heads of Venice's sixty-odd parishes registered all men between twenty and sixty in groups of twelve. Each dozen drew lots to see whose turn to serve would come first. Prior to 1350, he whose lot it was to go received one lire a month from the others in his dozen and received five lire from the government. He could be excused if he paid six lire towards hiring a substitute. Each citizen was ordered to keep in his house the necessary arms. This system worked as long as the common people of Venice were largely accustomed to the hardships of the sea and knew how to do what was expected of them on shipboard with ropes, weapons, or oars.

Since both ships and crews were much the same in a war fleet as in a group of merchantmen, it was easy for the government to command both and sometimes to treat them as interchangeable. Frequently the doge and his council ordered that no ships leave port until they received further orders. Indeed it was usual to close the port during the winter so as to lessen shipwrecks. The reopening in the spring was determined partly by the weather and partly by political conditions. Sometimes, all big ships were ordered to join a military expedition such as the crusade of Enrico Dandolo. More often, the shipmasters were left free to plan their ports of call according to their estimate of the commercial possibilities and to make their contracts with shippers accordingly. But specified ports might be banned for specified periods. And as often as not, the ships going on the most heavily traveled routes were ordered to sail in convoy, under an admiral appointed by the doge. The general trend of development was towards more freedom in the choice of routes, cargoes, and times of sailing, but for centuries oversea voyages were treated as community enterprises subject to government approval.

Even when the choice of routes, cargoes, and sailing dates were left to individual enterprise, the ship operators were subject to elaborate regulation. The government specified not only the dimension of ships, but also their rigging, the arms they must carry, the number of crewmen appropriate to the size of the ship, and a host of other details. All sea-going ships were officially rated according to their carrying capacity and marked with a cross, a kind of Plimsoll line, to prevent overloading. They had to pass inspection of arms and crew in the Bacino San Marco before they were allowed to leave port, and they had to post bond that they would not attack friendly peoples and would actually go where they had promised their shippers they would go.

Some of the regulations in the early laws are probably expressive only of wishful thinking, but much of it may have reflected customs which Venetians obeyed because other Venetians expected that kind of behavior of anyone who was a good Venetian. This kind of custom may have been self-enforcing in the tenth and eleventh centuries. Although still important, it did not suffice in the thirteenth. In that century, customs were formulated in maritime codes, new rules added, and in order to make all the ship's company feel bound to obey them, appropriate oaths were required. Such oaths obligated all on board, seamen as well as owners and merchants, to report each other's violations to appropriate fine-collecting officials of the government.

Under these general provisions for community control, the organization on shipboard was surprisingly democratic, at least in law, and especially on a trading voyage. Nowadays it is often said that in a ship at sea the authority of the ship's master must be unquestionable, but medieval customs provided no such concentration of power in one man. Even in a battle fleet, the admirals, called *capitani*, and the galley commanders, called *comiti* or *sopracomiti*, had limited power; they could condemn to heavy fines for disobedience, but enforcement depended on their being backed up by the councils in Venice. The law provided that anyone refusing to attack an enemy ship when ordered should have his head cut off, and the oath administered to commanders of galleys included a clause specifying that they consented and willed that this should be done to them, but it seldom happened, and no one on a Venetian merchantman had power to inflict such a penalty.

The chief officials on a twelfth-century merchant vessel were the sailing master (*nauclerus*) and the ship's scribe (*scribanus*). The former was in general command, the latter kept the record of wages and freights. Ownership of the ship was divided into shares distributed among several persons. The sailing master and the scribe were not responsible exclusively to the owners, nor were they always chosen by the owners; their position was rather that of public officials who were responsible to the whole ship's company and to the Venetian government. As late as the thirteenth century, the ship's company as a whole had the right to decide whether the vessel should change its destination, whether it should winter overseas, whether an individual seaman should be allowed to go ashore, and many other matters. Decisions about ballasting were made by a committee consisting of the sailing master, one of the owners, and two of the merchants on board, selected by the other merchants.

One reason for this relative democracy was the fact that every member of the crew was expected to be a good fighting man equipped with his own weapons. Another reason was the presence on board of a large number of merchants. In twelfth-century Europe, it was usual for a merchant to travel with his wares or to entrust them to another merchant who went with the goods and came back on the same ship to report and share the profits. Whoever shipped a fair amount of merchandise had a right to passage with appropriate personal effects. Like members of the crew, he was required to be properly armed. Some of these traveling merchants were young men of very distinguished families, looking after wares entrusted to them by older and richer friends and relatives; some were of more humble social status but of long and varied experience. Their presence meant that the ship's master was accompanied by many men equal to him in prestige, influence, and knowledge; and in this condition it is not surprising that many important decisions, such as whether to take on additional cargo or whether to go to the aid of a stricken ship, was left to the majority of the ship's company.

Among those on board there were certainly some persons of low degree, servants of the more prosperous. Some of the servants may have been slaves, since buying slaves was a commonly used method of obtaining servants in medieval Italian cities. Servants could not be counted as part of the crew, however, and sailors as well as merchants and officers were specifically forbidden by the maritime code from using servants to stand watch in their stead. There was little class differentiation between merchant passengers and sailors. The latter were expected to be traders also, at least in a small way. Each sailor had the right to load a specified amount of merchandise without paying freight. He had the same right as a merchant to his own sea chest, his own mattress, and a supply of wood, wine, or water, and flour or biscuits for the voyage. Some owners enrolled also as sailors, although the number that could do so legally was limited by law in order to make sure that the ships were adequately manned.

Loose discipline and a cooperative, egalitarian spirit is characteristic of medieval maritime law generally in western Europe in the Middle Ages. It is not at all a peculiarity of Venice. But it is all the more striking in the Mediterranean because it contrasts sharply with the tradition which Byzantium inherited from Rome. The Roman law of private property was applied at sea so as to place control of the ship entirely with the owner or his agent. He rented space or chartered the vessel to shippers and he commanded a crew composed either of slaves or of men hired for regular wages. Medieval maritime customs in contrast gave legal expression to the practical interdependence of all the ship's company and made them to some extent partners. This conception developed in the Mediterranean when the Roman-Byzantine monopoly of naval power weakened and the dangers and uncertainties at sea increased. A compilation of maritime customs made at Rhodes about A.D. 900 put more "on the general average," that is, more expenses and losses were shared among all on board. At the same time, wage payments varying with the earnings of the ship became more general. There were also local customs of this or that coast, the oldest preserved being those of Amalfi, which went much further than the earlier Rhodian compilation or the Venetian laws, which are of later date, in making owners, shippers, and operators all partners in a common fund. Compared to such three-sided profit-sharing partnerships, Venetian commercial institutions were more individualistic and capitalistic.

The financing of the Venetian voyages involved a network of partnerships and loans. A partnership between the owners financed the building of the ship, but ships were of relatively small value compared to their cargo or to the costs of manning and outfitting. Brothers belonging to rich patrician families acted together in family partnerships to load merchandise on vessels which they owned, wholly or in part, and also invested funds with many traveling merchants so as to send on many different voyages at once and enjoy the advantages of diversification. A typical cargo probably represented the stakes of something like a hundred investors who had confided sums of various amounts to more than a dozen traveling merchants, some of whom were also part of the crew.

These traveling merchants, or seamen merchants as they might also be called, had several different ways of securing funds for the ventures they managed. In the eleventh and twelfth centuries, the prohibition of usury by the Church had not yet received a legal formulation which made it practically applicable to laymen, and Venetians saw nothing wrong in borrowing money at interest. The traditional Venetian rate was 20 percent. For risky maritime voyages, money could be obtained at higher rates under the contract known in Roman law as the sea loan, in which the lender took the risk of loss through shipwreck, piracy, or enemy action.

As more and more wealth accumulated at Venice, eager investors could be induced to take more of the commercial risk. In the second half of the twelfth century, the most used form of investment was a quasi-partnership called the *colleganza* at Venice (the *commenda* elsewhere). In the colleganza, the traveling merchant did not promise any fixed percentage of return on the investment entrusted to him; instead, he promised three-fourths of the profit. If there was no profit, the stay-at-home investor or lender received no gain. At first thought, giving only one-fourth the profit to the merchant who did all the work may seem exploitative, but a seaman or traveling merchant frequently received funds in colleganza from several friends, relations, and business associates so that he made a very good thing indeed out of the voyage, even if he put up no money of his own.

Illustrative of the opportunities and methods of these traveling merchant-seamen is the career of Romano Mairano. He began in humble circumstances, to judge by the size of his wife's dowry. In 1155, he sailed to Constantinople where he sold some lumber he brought with him. With the proceeds he paid back the sea loans and a colleganza by which he had financed the purchase and shipment of the lumber. The next year he accepted employment as sailing master on a ship going to Smyrna and Alexandria. He did not own any share in that vessel but arranged through new colleganze and sea loans to ship considerable merchandise on these voyages and sell it profitably. Within ten years, he was sailing master on a ship of which he himself was the principal owner, voyaging between Venice and Constantinople, and Constantinople and Alexandria, and was part owner of another vessel. He borrowed more and more heavily — or we might say that investors entrusted larger and larger sums to his care — and he was very heavily involved when Emperor Manuel sprang his trap and arrested all the Venetians in Constantinople in 1171. Mairano's ship, a big new one, was in the harbor, and fugitive Venetians made it a center of refuge from the Greek mob incited by the emperor. The Venetians repelled the efforts of the Greeks to burn the vessel by hanging water-soaked cloths over the sides, sacrificing merchandise to save their lives. After that catastrophe, it took Romano up to twelve years to pay the debts he had contracted in 1170.

His entrepreneurial spirit was by no means crushed by this experience. Like many of his countrymen, he was in debt to Sebastiano Ziani whose wealth was so fabulous that Venetians referred to "l'haver de chà Ziani" as we would say "rich as a Rockefeller." After the debacle in Venetian-Byzantine relations in 1171–72, Sebastiano Ziani became doge and directed a striking restoration of

Venetian prosperity and prestige while his son Pietro, later to be a doge himself, took over management of the family fortune. Mairano was an experienced sailing master owning his own ship, a man worth backing. Pietro Ziani financed him for a voyage with lumber to Alexandria, and he repaid Ziani in pepper delivered to Ziani's agent in Alexandria. Encouraged, Mairano planned an entirely new kind of enterprise, a voyage along northern Africa to the west. He built a new ship for this voyage and sent it off under a shipmaster who sold it in Ceuta or Bougie. Mairano himself resumed his voyages to Syria, Palestine, and Egypt. Only after 1190, when he must have been nearly seventy, did he no longer serve as master himself of his own ships; in 1192 and 1193, his ventures to Apulia and Alexandria were handled by his son.

Members of rich old families who were themselves fully occupied in political office and military expeditions collected much of their income from diversified investment in a large number of colleganze. An example is Doge Ranieri Zeno. A summary of the inventory of his estate at his death in 1268 indicates the nature of his wealth. The high proportion invested in colleganze is evident, even if the money of account in which his assets were valued, lire a grossi, would be difficult to convert into equivalents in dollars. The items listed totaled: real estate, 10,000 lire; coin, 3,388 lire; miscellaneous, 6,025 lire; government obligations, 6,500 lire; and 132 colleganze, 22,935 lire.

A codification of Venetian maritime law promulgated in 1255 by Doge Ranieri Zeno reflected mainly the conditions favorable to sailors and merchant-seamen such as Romano Mairano, but some of its clauses reveal developments that were leading to changes in the relations within the ship's company. These clauses stipulated that one of the owners assume responsibilities that made him in effect the captain. The sailing master (*nauclerus*) became merely the mate (*nocchiero*) completely subordinate to that one of the owners whom the others selected to go with the ship to look out for their interests in negotiating with sailors and shippers. This owner was the shipmaster (*patrono*), the head of the shipping enterprise. The ship's scribe continued to be a public official subject to approval and discipline by high authorities, namely, the *Consoli dei Mercanti*, but he was selected by the shipmaster, on whose orders he acted.

On the whole, Zeno's code still showed less concern with the powers of the master than with the rights of the crew, each of whom was required to provide for himself his arms and armor. Their importance as fighting men enhanced the status of sailors and oarsmen so that they had a voice in the many decisions determined by a majority of the ship's company.

Another expression of their status was the emphasis the laws placed on their duty to report all violations of regulations by the master; in law, the seamen were as much responsible for disciplining the master as the master was for disciplining the crew. It was the shipmaster's duty to make each sailor he hired take the oath prescribed in the code, but that oath says nothing about obedience to the master; its concern was obedience to the law. The seamen's role as citizens there dominates over their role as employees.

How far the kind of democracy suggested by the laws really existed in practice must have varied from ship to ship. Much depended on whether the seamen were in fact well enough off to own their own arms, buy some merchandise with which to trade on their own, and provide adequately for their families until they came back from the voyage — all this without being burdened by debt. In some cases they could finance themselves, in other cases they had to borrow on onerous terms to be ready for a voyage. Moreover, the great families which dominated Venetian politics dominated also at sea as owners or outfitters of ships. The records refer frequently to a "galley of the Dandolo" (*la galea de Cà Dandolo*) or a "ship of the Contarini." An ordinary seaman on such a vessel knew he was serving a great family: its representative on board spoke with an authority not dependent on the letter of the law.

THE ORGANIZATION OF SEA POWER·II

The Lordship of the Gulf

CHAPTER SIX

Keep safe from stormy weather, Oh Lord, all your faithful mariners,
safe from sudden shipwreck and from evil, unsuspected tricks of cunning enemies.

This prayer was part of the ceremony at the church of San Nicolò of the Lido on the day of Ascension, the day the doges wed the sea. In the *bucentoro*, a galley especially designed and gilded for stately occasions, the doge was rowed out through the port of San Nicolò. With the leading men of the Republic and envoys of foreign states looking on, he cast a golden ring into the sea as a symbol, he said, that he was taking thereof dominion as that of a husband over his wife. A legend purporting to be history declared that the ring and with it title to the lordship of the Adriatic had been given to the doge by the pope in 1177. The legend told of a Venetian victory over an imperial fleet and of how Emperor Frederick I Barbarossa then came to Venice to kiss the pope's feet. There never was such a naval victory, nor even such a battle. And the above prayer, which is found in the oldest records, sounds like a prayer of seamen, not of politicians. One wonders whether, before the ceremony became more magnificent and political, it was not a Christianized version of some ancient pagan offering to Neptune, the sea god.

Those who elaborated a century and a half after 1177 the tale of imperial humiliation and papal gratitude embodied two truths in the legend, however. In 1177 Doge Sebastiano Ziani did play host to both pope and emperor and did preside over a peace which marked one stage in the failure of the emperors to assert control over northern Italy. Power there passed to many independent cities. By playing these cities off one against the other, Venice was able to use her sea-power so as to organize the trading area on her own terms. In this sense it is true that the peace of 1177 was a step toward Venice's assertion of the lordship of the Adriatic. A second element of truth underlying the legend and the ceremony was the fact that Venice gradually imposed formal treaties, bonds appropriately symbolized according to the customs of the time by a marriage ceremony.

While others used the crusades to acquire territory, the Venetians, as we have seen, used them to gain sea power; and as soon as they had firm control of waters important for their commerce, they applied their naval power so as to make themselves and their city richer. They regulated the flow of trade so as to increase governmental revenue and so as to create more and better business for Venetians: more employment and more favorable terms of trade.

SALT, WHEAT, In Acre or Constantinople Venetian naval power was used to check or
AND THE channel the flow of silks or spices; when used in the Adriatic, it regulated
HINTERLAND salt and cereals. These humdrum cargoes may not have contributed as
much to the quick making of mercantile fortunes as did the exotic products of the East, but the way they were controlled was equally basic to the general wealth and well-being of the city.

Much of the government's own revenue came from the sale of salt. All Venetian producers were required to place their product at the disposal of the Salt Office (*Camera del Sal*) which issued licenses to exporters with directions as to where, how much, and at what prices they could sell. The mainland cities, as far away as Milan, which bought from Venice had their own salt monopolies selling also at very profitable prices to their citizens or subjects. They needed more salt than Venice could supply. Many of its salt pans ceased production as rivers reduced the saline content of the northern and central parts of the lagoons. Venice's production concentrated around Chioggia and its output was supplemented by imports from as far away as Cyprus and the Balearic Islands. The Salt Office set special prices to attract supplies from these distant sources.

There were rival producers nearby, to be sure, at Ravenna and Cervia (see Map 1), but they were rivals of each other also, and Venice could use against them not only its naval power but its leverage as potentially their best customer. In 1238, Ravenna agreed to export grain and salt to Venice only, while being left free to import food for its own needs directly from Apulia and the Marches. In 1250, the treaties by which Venice agreed to supply Ferrara and Mantua with salt provided that these cities would not buy from any other producer. That left Venice's most dangerous competitor, Cervia, in the position of either finding almost no market for her salt or agreeing to sell to Venice. The Venetians were willing enough to buy, and contracted for all of Cervia's export except for a specified amount which Cervia was allowed to send to Bologna and to Bologna only. By thus tying up the consumers on the one hand and the producers on the other, Venice controlled a complete cartelization of salt.

Also in the grain trade Venice gained a dominant position over its neighbors. Here was no monopoly; prices were fixed by competitive bidding and by supply and demand. Venice's normal supply came partly from the territories of such nearby cities on the mainland as Padua and partly by sea from Romagna, the Marches, and other shores of the Adriatic (see Map 2). Wealthy Venetians who owned estates on the mainland brought wheat directly to their households in Venice, just as wealthy men did generally in other Italian cities, and merchants supplied themselves from the local markets when prices were low, going as far upstream as Pavia and Piacenza, which normally had a surplus. But the conditions of the harvest varied greatly from year to year; an area exporting one year might be importing the next and in a really bad year northern Italy as a whole needed to import.

Although Venice's main concern was feeding its own population, it made itself the center of wheat marketing for all northeastern Italy. When harvests in that region were bad, Venetian ships scoured the whole Mediterranean in search of places that had a surplus, importing from Sicily, Barbary, Egypt, Greece, the Balkans, and beyond. In 1268 Venetian ships brought large quantities of wheat from many ports in the Black Sea. The idea that trade over long distances was confined in the Middle Ages to expensive luxuries is not at all true of places that could be reached by water.

When a shortage seemed imminent, special inducements were offered to foreign ships to bring wheat to Venice, and Venetians were both urged and ordered to do so. Grain Commissioners posted attractive guaranteed prices, with option of free sale on the market, to anyone importing within a definite time from specified regions. Throughout Venice's extensive colonial ports in Romania, anyone loading wheat was threatened with heavy fines if he did not bring it to Venice. Within the Adriatic the Venetians insisted that all cargoes, whether on Venetian ships or not, be bound for Venice. In practice every city requisitioned any cargo it could lay hands on in time of famine; there are cases when Ragusans took to their city cargoes intended for Venice; but the superior naval power of the Venetians generally gave their needs priority.

While Venice vigorously imported grain from afar, it was equally vigorous in directing to Venice all it needed of the farm products of the immediate neighborhood. Each mainland city was of course concerned with feeding its own population, just as Venice was, but in the countryside some producers were happy to take advantage of the higher prices which could be obtained by sending to a distant market. There was a continual tug of war between different cities and between consumer and producer interests within the cities, and in these conflicts Venice generally came out on top. During a general shortage in 1270, Bologna tried to secure its supplies independently of Venice by importing through Ravenna in defiance of the Venetian order that ships bringing wheat into the North Adriatic unload at Venice. Hunger fought on the side of the Venetians. Without any decisive military action, Bologna was compelled in 1273 to conclude a treaty with Venice whereby, in return for access to the Venetian market, the Bolognese agreed not to buy at Ravenna more than a specified quantity, an amount which left them still dependent on supplies from Venice.

As in the case of salt, Venetian dominance of the grain market depended partly on the ability of Venetian ships to bring to her own market the needed supplies and partly on naval patrols coercing traffic in the northern Adriatic. In the thirteenth century, there were thirteen control points around the lagoons. At each, a half dozen men with two or three vessels inspected all passers to make sure that their cargoes were covered by permits to go where they were headed.

The coast between Grado and Istria was patrolled by a galley armed at Capodistria, which in 1180 was the main Venetian stronghold in Istria.

Not only these patrols but the size and enterprise of Venice's population made it the center of exchanges between nearby districts in many products. Venice sent onions and garlic as well as salt to Aquileia; Aquileia exported to Venice pigs as well as wheat. Istria sent Venice wood, charcoal, and stone. Trieste, which by the thirteenth century was competing with Capodistria in importance, sent skins, hides, and meat. The Marches sent their wines. In return, the metropolis met the needs of the countryside and of small towns for specialties in woodwork, leather, pottery or glass, and metal work. Once Venice had become a large city, it was the natural market for farms over a wide area and their main source of fine manufactured goods. This intra-regional trade was a mainstay of the Venetian economy throughout the centuries.

THE TRANSIT TRADE   More variable was the inter-regional trade, especially that which passed through Venice on its way from northern or western Europe to Asia, Africa, or Romania. A vital use of Venetian sea power was the channeling of this commerce through Venice to the exclusion of potential competitors, especially of nearby Ferrara, Ancona, and Zara.

This East-West transit trade expanded enormously in the twelfth and thirteenth centuries because of the economic growth of western Europe. The crusades helped by stimulating a demand in the West for eastern wares, such as sugar, spices, and silken garments, but the essential change was the production in western Europe of wares that could be sold in the East. The most important were textiles and metals. No longer were slaves and wood the chief Venetian exports overseas. The center of slave supply was shifting to the Black Sea and before 1250 wood had become a less important export than woolens.

A striking contrast between medieval economic life and that of antiquity is that in classical times we hear almost nothing of cloth production except by the women of the household, whereas in medieval times cloth was extensively produced for sale by specialized craftsmen. The result was much superior cloth and a large variety of fabrics. The woolens industry developed first and foremost in the Netherlands. Flemish cloth, made largely of English wool, became the merchandise most acceptable to Italian merchants who went northwest across the Alps to sell silks and spices. They met at the fairs of Champagne in France. These fairs, half way between Flanders and Italy, became the center of western European commerce. Venetians were one of the twelve groups of Italian merchants with recognized status at the Champagne fairs, though merchants from northwestern Italy were naturally the most prominent, especially in the early thirteenth century when the most used route over the Alps left the Po at Pavia and went northwestward over the Great Saint Bernard Pass (see Maps 8 and 9).

The traditional transshipment point for merchandise going up or down the Po was Ferrara. Located between two branches of the Po at about the point where it divided into several mouths, Ferrara had military control of the lower portion of the river. This made Ferrara a potentially dangerous rival as center of the East-West transit trade. During the eleventh and twelfth centuries, the semi-annual fairs at Ferrara were the main meeting place to which the Venetians, for example, went to find customers for the silks they imported from Constantinople. As trade quickened in western Europe and as industries developed, Ferrara received more wares from the West and more merchants from the fairs of Champagne.

The Ferrarese fairs were visited also by Germans bringing linens and metals to exchange for the products of the East. One feature of Europe's industrial development was the growth, in Constance and in towns north of present-day Switzerland, of linen makers sufficiently skilled to command an export market. By the thirteenth century, German and Italian cities were also making a softer cloth, called fustian, by weaving into a warp made of linen thread a woof composed partially or entirely of cotton, which came from the Levant.

In return for cotton, spice, incense, and other imports, the Germans offered not only linen but also silver. Important silver mines were discovered in the heart of Germany in the twelfth century, methods of mining were improved, and German miners pushed out into other regions to apply their skills. Financed by merchants in such German cities as Nuremberg and Augsburg, German miners increased their production of copper, iron, and gold as well as silver, and produced many skilled metalworkers. Metals were in demand not only in Italy; silver and copper especially were even more highly valued in the Levant.

In competing with Ferrara to attract the merchants from across the Alps, Venice had several advantages, especially for the Germans. Venice was nearer to the relatively low passes over the eastern Alps. The most important route of the Germans descended from the Brenner pass to Verona and then continued down the Adige River to its mouth in the Adriatic, only a little south of the lagoons, with which it was connected by canals (see Map 8). For the Germans as for all visiting merchants, the Venetians tried to provide attractive lodgings and warehouse facilities along with careful regulation. They began in 1228 to build for them the Fondaco dei Tedeschi next to the Rialto bridge. Germans were forbidden to ship their wares overseas from Venice, but that was not what most of them had in mind. What they wanted was to sell in Venice and obtain a wide choice of products to take back across the Alps. This Venice could offer; as its navy and merchant marine flourished, its appeal as a market for the Germans increased. Venetian ships were required to bring to Venice, not to Ferrara, wares loaded in Palestine, Greece, or other lands outside the Adriatic. The colonial empire conquered in the Fourth Crusade swelled the amount of the East-West trade that was in Venetian ships and handled by Venetian merchants. Forbidding Venetian ships to unload cargoes anywhere inside the Adriatic except at Venice was the important first step in making Venice the only center for the region's contact with other regions.

The big second step came as a by-product of the contests between the emperors and the popes, who claimed political as well as religious power in Italy. In these contests, Ferrara's commercial interests suffered. She was not even able to assert the right to have unloaded for sale within her walls all wares passing through on the Po. On the contrary, the Venetians succeeded in maintaining the right, which had been given them first in treaties with the Carolingian emperors at the time when Venice was primarily a nation of boat- or bargemen, to bring unhindered through Ferrara wheat and other wares bought further upstream. A treaty of 1230 exempted Venetian ships from tolls at Ferrara unless they chose to anchor there. The other mainland cities also opposed any staple rights for Ferrara. On the rivers, Venice was the champion of a freedom of trade which knit the region closer together.

The freedom stopped of course where the rivers entered the Gulf. There Venice claimed mastery. A chance to impose its will at the mouths of the Po came in 1240, when a ruler of Ferrara took the side of Emperor Frederick II. The pope needed the aid of the Venetians to conquer the city, which he claimed was part of the Papal States. The Venetians enthusiastically sent a fleet which displayed some of the skills in siegework which the Venetians had shown in the conquest of Constantinople, but the victory depended mainly on an uprising within the city in favor of the Este family. The Este then accepted a treaty, giving the Venetians control of Ferrara's trade with the Adriatic.

The first clause of the treaty stated explicitly that all merchandise coming from the sea to Ferrara must come from Venice. To enforce that provision, the Venetians depended for a time on a patrolling squadron off the mouths of the Po. In 1258 they reinforced this control by building a strong fort or castle near the most southerly of the mouths of the Po, then the most important for navigation, the Po di Primaro (see Map 1). They called the fort Marcamò (Sea Call) because it was near enough to the sea to hear its roar in a storm. It became the symbol of Venetian power to stop any ship and require proof that it had been cleared in Venice.

Venetian fleets also policed the Po upstream: an admiral with sixty men on six vessels protected convoys up as far as the junction of the Po with the Mincio just below Mantua. Another squadron went up the Adige as far as Legnago, where the Venetians also had a fort (see Maps 1 and 8). These river patrols protected not only the Venetians but also Ferrarese, Mantuan, and Veronese merchants on their way to or from Venice.

A STAPLE AND ITS LIMITS   Each medieval city strove to be what was called the staple. This meant that it imposed, on as large an area as feasible, staple rights which required the wares being exchanged between different parts of the region to be brought to the staple city, unloaded there to pay taxes, and offered there for sale. Merchandise from outside the region was required to be brought similarly to the staple city and not to any other place within the region. Venice's "lordship of the gulf" was unusual only in being an especially successful assertion of staple rights.

This does not mean that Venetians monopolized the trade in the sense of excluding foreigners. On the contrary, they welcomed foreign merchants and ships, and made extensive provision for housing and protecting the many foreigners who were an important feature of the Rialto. Except in time of war, they welcomed into the port of San Nicolò the vessels of their commercial rivals, even of Pisa and Genoa; indeed, they insisted that these rivals had to use the port of Venice if they came into the northern Adriatic. Neither did it mean that merchants from subject cities, such as Zara, were banned from Venice, unless in rebellion; on the contrary, they paid the same customs in Venice as did Venetians. But patrols, backed by warships whenever necessary, required that no other city than Venice be the place where they exchanged merchandise. The Venetian staple would have been completely undermined if Florentines took cloth directly to Zara to exchange for spices which Zara had received directly from the Levant. The Venetian's staple meant that all such exchanges should take place in their wholesale market, the Rialto, where Venetians would be the middlemen and would have a chance to make a profit on both cloth and spices. To make sure of this middleman position, the navigation laws required that the merchandise imported into the region come either in Venetian ships or in those of the country the wares came from.

Although Venetian staple rights are often identified with their lordship over the Adriatic, the middle and lower Adriatic were not subject to the same commercial regulations as its northern end. Direct trade between Dalmatia on the one side and Apulia and the Marches on the other was permitted. In spite of efforts, Venice never succeeded in including Ancona in the territory for which Venice was the staple. After a series of expeditions, commercial wars, and blockades, Venice forced Ancona in 1264 to recognize the Venetian system of staple in regard to its trade to the north. A treaty limited to specified quotas Ancona's direct shipments of wine and oil to Ferrara and Bologna but left relatively free its trade with Dalmatia and Apulia. Ancona promised, as had Ravenna thirty years earlier, not to compete with Venice in the very profitable tourist trade to Palestine, but to take to Venice pilgrims who embarked at Ancona. To further limit Ancona's direct trade with the Levant, Anconitans were forbidden to transport around the Adriatic one of the chief Levantine products, cotton. They were ordered to pay a 20 percent import duty on imports from outside the Adriatic, but that tariff was practically unenforceable. Ancona as well as Recanati, Fermo, and other cities of the Marches were given very favorable customs privileges in Venice itself in return for Venetian rights to export wheat, lamb skins, and wine. Since these, especially wine, were their chief exports, they were partially dependent on Venice commercially because it was their chief market. But all these cities could trade independently with Dalmatia; by keeping up its relations with the Levant, Ancona remained always a potentially dangerous rival.

The Fourth Crusade reestablished Venetian authority in Dalmatia so that it too could be subjected to Venetian navigation laws. Its most important cities, Zara and Ragusa (modern Zadar and Dubrovnik), were important sources of supplies: from Zara came food stuffs, from Ragusa hides, wax, and silver and other metals mined in its Balkan hinterland. Both had important merchant marines of their own, and Venice did not object to their ships going outside the Adriatic for cargoes, or southward across the Adriatic for grain and oil; but it did require that, if they sailed northward or westward towards the Po Valley, they load and unload in Venice. There was little friction with Ragusa in the thirteenth century because Ragusa had not yet begun to compete with Venice as an alternate carrier in the trade between East and West. Ragusan exports from the nearby Balkans were exempt from customs duties in Venice. Venice gave Ragusa the protection it needed against neighboring Slavic princes and used Ragusa as the main Venetian naval base in the lower Adriatic. Zara, on the other hand, was rebellious because an active faction there preferred the overlordship of the King of Hungary, under whom Zara might hope to become a rival of Venice in receiving, for distribution to northern Italy, wares from the East brought not only by

Zaritans themselves but also by Pisans, Genoese, and others. This faction led a revolt in 1243, Zara's fifth. After its suppression, Zara was more tightly controlled.

Apulia, being a much more fertile region than the rocky Dalmatia, was of much greater economic importance. It was not only the granary for Dalmatia, but a main source of wheat and also of olive oil, cheese, salt, meat, and wool for the Venetians. In return Venice sent iron, copper, cloth, and oriental wares and also considerable quantities of gold and silver, often needed to clinch purchases of wheat. The rulers of Apulia granted Venetians wide freedom to export, hoping to gain political support from Venice; in 1257, they accepted Venice's lordship of the Adriatic to the extent of forbidding Apulians to carry the products of their country to any place north of Ancona and Zara except to Venice. Danger of competition from Bari or other Apulian cities in the East-West trade, where they had been active, was limited by a provision forbidding them to carry foreign wares into the north Adriatic. This fitted the Venetian aim that all imports to Venice come in Venetian ships or in the ships of the country of origin.

Thus the Venetian navigation laws and treaties did not directly limit the trade of the Anconitans, Dalmatians, and Apulians among themselves or overseas, but limited them indirectly by channeling through Venice their trade with their best potential market — the richest part of the Adriatic coast and the river valleys at its northwest end. At the same time, these treaties gave Venice control of much of the imports into Lombardy, a control at the source which did not depend on the strategically placed fort of Marcamò.

THE WAR OF FERRARA After this Venetian system of navigation laws had been in effect for about two generations, the hate and envy it aroused exploded in the War of Ferrara. Marcamò was located directly across the path of the trade between the food exporting centers of Romagna such as Ravenna, Cervia, and Rimini, and the sizable cities of Ferrara and Bologna which largely depended on Romagna for food supplies. Marcamò was used not only to force interregional trade to go through Venice, but also to enforce Venetian rules and treaties concerning salt and wheat. Especially the Venetian assertion of prior claims to food supplies in times of shortage aroused hatred. Lombards complained that, through Marcamò, Venice held all Lombardy in servitude.

In 1308, Venice overreached herself by trying to bring Ferrara into political as well as commercial subjection. The opportunity seemed just too good to pass up. The death of the city's ruler occasioned civil war between his natural son, Fresco, and his brothers. Fresco appealed to the Venetians and was sent troops to which he turned over the fortress, Castel Tedaldo, commanding the bridge over the Po. The pope, who was the city's lawful overlord, sent legates demanding its surrender. When the Venetians proposed negotiations about recognizing the pope's rights as overlord but refused to give up the fortress, the pope placed Venice under an interdict and issued a bull of excommunication which was extraordinarily sweeping. Besides ordering the cessation of all religious services in Venice, the pope declared all the doge's subjects released from their oaths of obedience, forbade any trade with Venetians, and declared all their property everywhere confiscated and their persons subject to enslavement. The pope was a Frenchman, resident in Avignon, and had no army of his own with which to drive the Venetians from Ferrara, but his fulminations encouraged Venice's mainland neighbors to plunder Venetian merchants and to send soldiers who stormed successfully Castel Tedaldo.

In spite of the disaster to her army at Ferrara, Venice did not knuckle readily to the pope's demands. She maintained her patrol of the mouths of the Po. When Zara revolted in 1311 (the "sixth" time), the revolt was vigorously suppressed so that Venetian control of the sea was not shaken. It enabled her to keep up her own trade, taking advantage especially of her treaties with Moslem lands, while cutting off that of Ferrara. Moreover, she had an ally in Verona, which had its own reasons for regarding the pope as an enemy, and Verona's position on the Adige opened the way to circumventing Ferrara and the pope. Venice made a treaty with Verona, providing for the construction of a canal between the Adige and Po big enough for vessels going in opposite directions to pass each other. This canal would make it possible for the traffic which used to enter Lombardy through the mouth of the Po to enter through the mouth of the Adige instead and reach the Po upstream from Ferrara. The prospect that this new competing line would ruin Ferrara was a factor in persuading the pope to lift the interdict in 1313 and annul excommunication. Another factor was Venice's readiness to supply immediately the wheat that Ferrara badly needed.

This War of Ferrara was clearly a defeat for Venice, one of its worst in centuries, for the Venetians failed to gain Ferrara, suffered large material losses, and agreed to pay the pope an indemnity of 100,000 ducats (about one-tenth of Venice's public debt). But the peace treaty in which Venice gave up the canal project reaffirmed that all merchandise coming to Ferrara from the Adriatic must come from Venice.

While Venetian lordship of the Adriatic was generally recognized as a fact by the fourteenth century, it was diversely viewed. Some commentators mixed envy with admiration, praising the astuteness of the Venetians and their readiness to sacrifice personally for the glory and power of Venice. Others added malice to their envy and accused the Venetians of utter faithlessness, greed, and ambition to rule others. The Venetians themselves, as interpreted by their chroniclers, believed that they had exercised rightful dominion over the Adriatic from time immemorial and had won it by clearing the Adriatic of pirates and making it safe to sail.

Their lordship was in fact less extensive and much more recent than they cared to recognize. The whole of the Adriatic Sea was indeed called the Gulf of Venice, and the Venetians undertook to police all of it, to exclude war fleets except by their permission, and to inspect all merchantmen within its waters to see whether their trade was in accordance with the Venetian navigation laws and treaties. However, this did not mean that Venice insisted on being the staple for the whole area. Only in regard to the lands around what we call the Gulf of Venice and the mouth of the Po was Venice able, after the middle of the thirteenth century, to channel all trade through its own market place. This strict ordering of the routes of trade north of a line running through Ancona and Zara was reinforced by the less restrictive control that Venice exercised over the whole Adriatic Sea.

THE ORGANIZATION OF SEA POWER · III

The Trade of the Levant

CHAPTER SEVEN

Outside the Adriatic, Venice faced quite different problems in the utilization of its sea power. What "command of the sea" can mean has varied from one age to another. Britain had what could be called a cut-and-dried command from the Napoleonic wars to World War I. It was enforced during the age of sail by patrols which were able to keep the sea in all seasons and could be stationed at the strategic points along trade routes determined roughly by prevailing winds. With the coming of steam, the possession of strategically located coaling stations and their denial to the enemy enabled the British navy to sweep the seas of enemy warships and merchantmen alike, once the main enemy fleets had been defeated and bottled up, and to subject neutrals to search and detention or seizure. In contrast, a kind of command of the sea, called cut-and-run, was almost obtained by the Germans through the use of submarines in World War I. Such a cut-and-run command is purely negative; it cannot protect one's own shipping; it is successful if it denies to the enemy the use of essential trade routes.

In medieval Europe, no navy exercised a cut-and-dried command over any extended body of water, but the Venetians very nearly did so in the Adriatic. Their patrols on the rivers and off the mouths of the rivers were reinforced as need be by fleets of galleys strong enough and fast enough to suppress all opposition. The boost given Venetian naval power by the conquest of Constantinople made the Venetians feel more responsible for the suppression of piracy, especially in the Adriatic. Every year, not only in time of war but as a routine measure, they outfitted a fleet of galleys devoted to making the seas safe.

Naturally it accompanied the merchant ships going to Apulia and Romania and used the Dalmatian cities, especially Ragusa, as subordinate bases. A separate squadron for the protection of commerce in the Gulf was felt necessary in 1330. Frequently thereafter it was patrolled by a Captain of the Gulf, while the main war fleet was operating in the Aegean or Beyond-the-Sea.

To organize any cut-and-dried command over the Mediterranean as a whole, i.e., to deny the use of these waters to its enemies and to make navigation safe for its own citizens and friends at all times, was quite outside the range of possibilities. Neither Venice nor any of her rivals was able to sweep the enemy from the seas. They lacked the technical means of setting up effective blockades. Trade moved, or could move, by short hops through many alternate routes. Vessels were not built and rigged so that they could patrol off a port indefinitely in variable weather to the extent that the British did at the end of the eighteenth century. War fleets had even more difficulty finding an enemy who wished to avoid battle than Lord Nelson had when he crossed the Atlantic twice in search of Napoleon's fleet. And even after an overwhelming victory, the winner was unable to blockade effectively the enemy city. He could not prevent the defeated from sending out a new fleet, even if only a very small one, for a quick raid on an exposed point or an attack on merchant shipping.

Under these conditions, the kind of "command of the sea" at which the Venetians could aim consisted essentially in being able to protect its own convoys of merchant shipping and to send support to colonies while inflicting losses on the trade of an enemy or raiding his coasts or colonies. After the conquest of Constantinople, Venice organized this kind of maritime control in the eastern Mediterranean. Since merchant shipping was the main concern, the most strategic bases were the ports in which convoys could be organized or could stop for refreshment and refuge.

CARAVANS
OVER SEA
AND LAND
The ports most important for these convoys were determined by two streams of trade: one which went to Romania, and the other to Beyond-the-Sea. Romania meant not only the Greek peninsula and the Aegean islands but all the neighboring lands which had been part of the Byzantine Empire. Beyond-the-Sea (*Oltremare*) meant the coasts east and southeast of the Aegean, or more specifically Cyprus, Syria, and Palestine (Maps 3 and 4).

The trade in Romania employed the larger number of ships and merchants. Privileges which the Venetians had gained by aiding the Byzantine emperors against the Normans gave them preferential treatment; indeed, the Golden Bull of 1082 freed them from all tariffs in most cities. The native Greeks themselves paid 10 percent, whereas the Venetians paid nothing. This competitive advantage assured the Venetians profits, since they were operating in established markets where prices were set by the costs of native merchants who were paying the tolls from which Venetians were exempt. For a while, Genoese and Pisans obtained preferential tariffs also, but not the complete exemption enjoyed by the Venetians. When the Latin Empire of Constantinople was established in 1204, the Venetian exemption was reaffirmed and extended over the whole Empire. The Genoese and Pisans obtained a confirmation of their former position only as a favor from the Venetians and subject to the express stipulation in the treaty between the Venetians and the Empire that any peoples who were at war with Venice would be expelled from all Romania. Under these conditions it is easy to understand that the Venetians interested themselves not merely in finding in Romania wares that were in demand in Venice and the West, but also in moving merchandise from one part of Romania to another. They settled at Corinth, for example, to trade in the products going from the Peloponnesus, which the Venetians called Morea, to other parts of Greece. They exported wine, oil, fruits, and nuts from the Greek islands to Egypt and brought back wheat, beans, sugar, etc. They exported to many places the silk for which Sparta and Thebes were then famous. But the biggest element in the trade within Romania was the supplying of the city of Constantinople and the marketing of its products. Even after the sack of 1204, it was still a huge city by medieval European standards, with many productive industries and a large population to feed. Its normal grain supply came partly from Thrace and Salonica but largely from Black Sea ports in areas now parts of Bulgaria, Roumania, and the U.S.S.R. Previously excluded from the Black Sea by the Byzantine emperors, the Venetians became active there after 1204. Some settled at Soldaia on the eastern coast of the Crimea, from which they exported to Constantinople grain, salt, fish, furs, and slaves.

For the protection of all this trade, the best base was of course Constantinople. Its location made it seem for a time as desirable a center for Venetian power as Venice itself. The Venetian colony there was so large during the thirteenth century that it rivaled in size the settlements around the Rialto. There is a legend, originating much later, that immediately after the conquest in 1204, Venice's governing councils held a formal debate over the possibility of a mass migration and of moving the seat of government to Constantinople. The only truths back of the legend were that for a few years the Venetians in Constantinople, headed by the podesta they elected, continued to act, as Enrico Dandolo had, without waiting to consult the authorities in Venice, and that the Venetians within the former Byzantine Empire, at Constantinople and elsewhere, may for a while have been almost as numerous and as rich as those around Rialto.

While many Venetians settled within Romania and made their fortunes by trade within it or between the Black Sea and Egypt, the exchange between the West and the Levant became increasingly more important. Western Europe was producing more and more woolens and metals, which were in demand in the Levant and which enabled western Europeans to buy more of the products of the East. From Romania to Venice came raw silk and, above all, silk fabrics and other products of Constantinople's skilled craftsmen, alum, kermes (the red dye from the Morea), wax, honey, cotton, wheat from various ports according to the harvest, furs and slaves from the Black Sea, and sweet wines from the Greek islands.

Sailings between Venice and Romania were organized by seasons and those sailing in the same season kept somewhat together to form what was called a caravan. In the thirteenth century, such a caravan consisted typically of 10 to 20 tarettes or other rather small ships (*naves*), with one or two really big round ships or a few galleys for protection. One caravan left in the spring and returned in the fall; another left in August, wintered overseas, and returned in the spring. Their timing was regulated by law: the code of 1255 provided that shipmasters must conclude contracts with their seamen two days before the end of July for the fall *muda*, a word that meant both ships in convoy and a loading period. They were to be outside the port of San Nicolò by August 15. These ships would not return until the following Easter, or even May, not because the voyage to Constantinople took that long (it could be done easily in a couple of months each way) but because winter storms were avoided and because the merchants needed a long stay at the terminus to dispose of wares and find return cargoes. They also took time to buy and sell at various way stations. The terminus of the fleet was Constantinople, where wares from the Black Sea ports were collected. The main regular stop in the Aegean was at Negroponte, where vessels which had been trading to lesser ports in Greece could join the ships returning from Constantinople. After passing Cape Malea and Cape Matapan at the southern end of Morea, the ships called at Modon or Coron to load the products of that region and be joined by local traders from the Morea before proceeding north to Ragusa and Venice (see Maps 4 and 7).

The second great stream of trade was that to the crusaders' states, Beyond-the-Sea. For this voyage also there were spring and fall caravans. The outbound routes of the ships to Romania and to Beyond-the-Sea did not diverge until after they had rounded the southernmost points of the Greek peninsula, Cape Matapan and Cape Malea, headlands that it was often difficult to pass because of contrary winds. The caravan going to Beyond-the-Sea then went to Candia, the capital of Crete, sometimes accompanied by the Romania caravan but not normally. Crete was thus even more important as the intermediate base for voyages to Beyond-the-Sea than for voyages to Constantinople. More-over, Crete was no mere naval base; it was an important producer of grain, wine, oil, and fruits. The estates held there by Venetian nobles yielded them good revenues in the course of time. Many revolts had to be suppressed before the native population became submissive to Venetian rule; but when not absorbed in suppressing revolts, the duke through whom Venice governed the island was able to send out four to ten galleys to add to the Venetian fleets.

Sailing east from Crete, a merchant fleet was likely to call at Rhodes and Cyprus, but the terminus was St. Jean d'Acre, just north of Haifa, where the modern road takes off from the coast for Safed and Damascus. Of all the ports conquered by the crusaders, Acre underwent the most vigorous commercial de-velopment, and after the loss of Jerusalem it became the capital of what re-mained of the Kingdom of Jerusalem. Some shiploads of pilgrims disembarked further south and nearer Jerusalem at Jaffa when truces favored the pilgrims, but Acre was the center of all the business of crusading, the assembly point for convoys, and the meeting place of trade routes tapping the wealth of Asia and the spice islands.

Pepper, cinnamon, cloves, nutmeg, ginger were then even more in demand for seasoning than now, especially for seasoning meats in an age with little refrigeration. Europeans in Germany, Flanders, and England could buy more spices with which to satisfy their taste for highly seasoned foods because they were producing more of the wares in demand in the East, such as silver, copper, and woolen cloth. The Italians, who were the middlemen in this exchange, profited from being in a "growth industry" of the thirteenth century.

Some products in demand in the West came from the Levant itself, others came from the Far East. Bales of eastern drugs and spices were brought by Indian merchants to the Red Sea, which provided the most nearly all-water

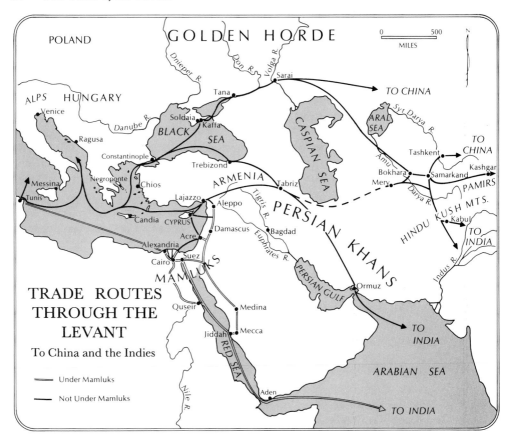

MAP 5

TRADE ROUTES
THROUGH THE
LEVANT

To China and the Indies

route between the Indian Ocean and the Mediterranean. But, for merchandise of such high value per pound, the routes were determined less by freights than by taxes, less by the costs of transport than the costs of protection, less by physical conditions than by social conditions. On all counts, there were good reasons why the spices which entered the Red Sea from India should stop at Jiddah, the port of Mecca. The merchants were all Moslems, whose religion enjoined a pilgrimage to Mecca. North of Jiddah, the navigation of the Red Sea becomes increasingly difficult, especially in certain seasons. For these reasons, the route of the spices divided at Jiddah (see Map 5). Part went from Mecca on the backs of camels. These "ships of the desert" proceeded via Medina along the old caravan route running north through desert, wadi, and grasslands east of Jordan, to Damascus. Itself a fertile oasis on the edge of the desert, Damascus was an important center of industry, famous alike for its steel and its brocades, as well as the home port of camel caravans. Three or four days sufficed to cross from Damascus to any one of several Mediterranean harbors. Acre was the most important as long as it was in Christian hands.

The other spice route reached Acre from the opposite direction, from Egypt. One way from Jiddah, that which looks easiest, was up the Red Sea to Suez and then across to the Nile at Cairo, but a route more used because of the firmer control it gave to the Egyptian soldan went ashore near Quseir, crossed to the Nile and descended the river from just below the first cataract. In either case, these Egyptian routes passed through Cairo to the ports of the delta, of which the chief was Alexandria.

Egypt had much beside spices to attract the Venetians and other Europeans. In the twelfth century, it was a main source of alum, sugar, and wheat and a major market for wood, metals, and slaves. Alexandria had been one of the busiest ports of the world almost from its foundation, but it had two disadvantages from the point of view of Italian ship captains. One was political: Alexandria was a strongly fortified harbor in which the merchants, crews, and vessels felt at the mercy of the soldan. To make sure that no ship left without his permission, the Moslem commander of the port ordered that ships turn over to him on arrival their yards and rudders. The other was technical, derived from the direction of prevailing winds. All during the summer, winds blew from the northwest. They favored a voyage to Alexandria from the west but made departure directly westward impossible for round ships and difficult for galleys except in late fall or early spring. But in these seasons storms and clouds made navigation more dangerous. Merchantmen leaving Alexandria for the west in the summer began by heading northeast or north northeast, as had the Roman grain ships. They made port in Cyprus or Syria before finding winds with which to turn west. In the existing state of seamanship, a Venetian merchantman bound from Alexandria to Venice was not really going out of its way therefore when it went to Acre to join a convoy.

At Acre the Venetians could feel quite at home. In return for their help to the crusaders after the celebrated naval victory of Ascalon, the Venetians had complete control of an entire section in Acre and also in nearby Tyre. Here was everything necessary to enable them to live as a community apart; their own church, their consulate or governmental center, their warehouse, their own special oven, bathhouse, and slaughterhouse, and perhaps also grinding mills reserved for their use. In addition, there were many Venetian palaces or private homes large enough to house not only a Venetian family and their Venetian guests who came and went with the fleets but also to house natives of Palestine or Syria from whom the Venetians collected rent. Many of these "palaces" contained workshops where the Venetians employed native workmen skilled in fancy weaving and glassmaking. Around Acre and particularly around Tyre the Venetians owned many country estates that had been awarded to Venice as part of the division of booty agreed on with the crusaders when the city was taken with the help of Doge Domenico Michiel. This was a part of the coast famous for its lemons, oranges, almonds, and figs. Syria and Palestine also produced cotton, silks, and sugar to add to the exportable merchandise brought by the caravans from Damascus.

Most of the trade by which cargoes were concentrated at Acre was in the hands of Levantines, for few Venetians went inland to Damascus. In addition to the Moslem merchants, there were many Christian Arabs and Armenians, as well as Jews and Greeks, who had been accustomed to trading back and forth over the eastern end of the Mediterranean in spite of warring armies. Crusaders added a little to the risks of being robbed but did not stop the usual caravans coming across Syria and Palestine or up from Egypt. Except when crusading armies were directly attacking Egypt, the Venetians continued to sell Egyptians even wood and metals, which scandalized newly arrived crusaders but was licensed by the kings of Jerusalem who needed revenues. Of course, selling arms to the enemy was illegal, but raw metals and plain planks were not always considered munitions of war, which was ill defined then as later.

The two caravans of ships, one through Romania to Constantinople, the other to Acre and Beyond-the-Sea (see Map 4, p. 39), brought to Venice not only the products of the eastern Mediterranean but also the most sought-after wares of the Indies. Their protection was the test of Venetian sea power. After 1250, Venice's control of these routes and her maritime supremacy generally was fiercely contested by Genoa.

GENOESE RIVALRY   Starting their expansion later than the Venetians, the Genoese found plunder and profit first in the western Mediterranean, which continued to be of basic importance in their commerce, but they exploited the opportunities opened by the crusades to Beyond-the-Sea even more vigorously than the Venetians who were held back by their concern for Romania. Although the city of Genoa never had more than half the population of Venice, it grew rapidly between 1100 and 1250 and established at least nominal control over all of Liguria. It strove to be the staple for all the coast between the Rhone River and Tuscany, just as Venice was for all the northern Adriatic.

Whereas Venice was cut off from the mainland by its lagoons, the Genoese littoral was cut off by mountains which rise sharply from the sea. Yet Genoa was not as unified a city-state as Venice, for the Ligurian coast was not thoroughly absorbed into the Genoese commune. Genoese nobles, when out of power, were often able to defy the city government from some retreat along its mountainous shore. Rivalry between different factions was more implacable at Genoa than at Venice, and control of the communal government frequently passed from one group to opponents who sent the defeated into exile. These factional fights did not interfere with commercial expansion; indeed, exiles frequently went to the Levant to make fortunes. In mid-century, the Genoese were as well entrenched as the Venetians in Acre and Tyre and were more active in Syria as a whole since their initiative in helping crusaders had won them extensive rights in the more northerly cities.

Before 1250, the rivalry between Venice and Genoa was muted by their mutual fear of the Pisans who were more dangerous to the Venetians in Romania and to the Genoese in the western Mediterranean. Pisa was overwhelmingly Ghibelline, that is, it supported the German emperors against the pope. Genoa was mainly Guelf, that is, siding with the pope, as did Venice in mid-century. After the Ghibelline party throughout Italy was weakened by the defeat and death of Frederick II in 1250, Pisa became a distinctly secondary preoccupation for the Venetians, while the Genoese became more and more energetic as commercial competitors. In the wars that followed, profits were at stake, but the wars were kept going more by hate and vainglory than by economic calculation.

The first Venetian-Genoese war was touched off by a series of incidents in Acre. A Venetian murdered a Genoese, the Genoese attacked and pillaged the Venetian quarter, and there was a fight over a monastery on the border of the two sectors. In Europe, the pope and others tried to mediate; in Acre, all the various factions lined up on one side or the other; the Knights Templar,

FIGURE 4 *The Square Pillars from Acre next to San Marco (Photo Ferruzzi).*

These trophies, richly carved by Syrian artists, were believed to have been brought home in triumph by Lorenzo Tiepolo from the Genoese stronghold.

the Pisans, and the Provencal merchants on the side of Venice, many of the local barons on the side of the Genoese. When the Venetian trading caravan left in the summer of 1257, the doge sent with it a war fleet judged sufficient to take care of the situation. In command was Lorenzo Tiepolo, the son of a doge and a warrior already renowned for his part in a reconquest of Zara in 1243. He broke through the chain by which the Genoese tried to keep him out of the harbor, burned their ships, and retook the disputed monastery. Next year, a big Genoese fleet arrived, but Tiepolo had been reinforced meanwhile, partly from Crete, mainly from Venice. When the Genoese appeared off Acre in June, 1258, he came out to give battle, and the Genoese, strangely enough, stood on the defensive so long that he was able to get to windward and form his battle line. The Genoese fleet was slightly larger, 50 galleys and 4 large round ships, against the 39 Venetian galleys, 4 large round ships, and 10 tarettes, but the Venetians had strengthened their armament by hiring from the very mixed population of Acre large numbers of men attracted by good pay and hatred of the Genoese. The Venetian victory was overwhelming; the Genoese lost half their galleys and about 1700 dead or taken prisoner. The rest fled to Tyre, and the Genoese who were still holding a strong tower in Acre fled also when they saw their fleet defeated. The Venetians carried home the columns from the Genoese great tower in Acre and set them up in triumph beside San Marco (see Figure 4).

Genoese prisoners were also carried to Venice in fetters. They were considered useful in peace negotiations but there was no thought of enslaving them. Wars against pagans, Moslems, and heretics helped supply the slave markets; indeed, wars and slave raids seemed in some cases indistinguishable. But citizens of the Italian cities did not enslave each other; captives were held for ransom or freed by the terms of a treaty. Those taken at Acre were released on the pleading of the pope, while the Venetian merchants in Acre lorded it over any surviving Genoese competitors and refused entry into the harbor to any ship showing the Genoese flag.

Three years after this victory Beyond-the-Sea, Venice suffered a severe setback in Romania. The Latin Empire, established in 1204, had always been a weak structure unable to overcome Greek rivals, several of whom set themselves up in parts of the former Byzantine Empire and claimed to be the true successors of the Roman-Byzantine emperors. Michael Paleologue, the Greek emperor whose lands lay closest to Constantinople, seized the capital in July, 1261, by treachery and a surprise attack through secret passageways, at a time when the Venetian fleet, which had always been a mainstay of its defense, was at sea. On the fleet's return, the best it could do was to rescue compatriots and the last of the Latin emperors and take them to Negroponte.

Michael Paleologue's capture of Constantinople was a big step towards his goal of restoring the Byzantine Empire as it had been before the Fourth Crusade. It threatened all Venice's colonial possessions in Romania. It might be expected therefore that the Venetians would have made a mighty effort to recover Constantinople and restore the Latin Empire, but two circumstances prevented clearcut action. One was the weakness which had always been shown by the Latin emperors at Constantinople and the fugitive emperor's lack of family resources. The other was the Genoese war which had started at Acre and was now transferred to Romania. Michael Paleologue might not have been able to hold Constantinople had not Genoa earlier that year concluded with him a treaty of alliance. By this Treaty of Ninfeo he promised to expel the Venetians and grant to the Genoese within Romania the privileged status the Venetians were enjoying. The Genoese in return promised to put their navy at his disposal, at his expense, for war against Venice and for his campaigns to restore the Byzantine Empire. As events turned out, Michael Paleologue took Constantinople himself without Genoese aid and within a few years decided that the Genoese fleets were not worth the high price they were charging. But the Treaty of Ninfeo at least brought into the Aegean Genoese fleets strong enough to rule out the possibility of a direct Venetian assault on Constantinople.

The war fleets sent by the Genoese were not, to be sure, very successful in battle. In 1262, the Genoese sought refuge in the harbor of Salonica and there the Venetians found them barricaded so strongly that they dared not attack. After challenging them to come out and fight in the open sea, which the Genoese refused to do, the Venetians sailed away. In 1263, a Genoese fleet of 38 galleys convoying supplies to Monemvasia (Malvasia), a Greek stronghold in the Morea, encountered 32 Venetian galleys on their way to Negroponte. The resulting battle of Settepozzi was clearly a Venetian victory, for of the four admirals who were commanding the Genoese, two never fully engaged, and the two that did both lost their galleys. Apparently the Genoese fleet had been outfitted in part by contractors and was partly under the command of admirals interested in returns to their investors. In 1264, the Genoese deliberately misled and evaded Venetian galleys, and also in 1265 they avoided battle. In 1266, their fleet was attacked by the Venetians off Sicily at Trapani. As the Venetians bore down rowing hard, the Genoese crews panicked and tried to swim to the nearby shore, thousands dying in the attempt. The Genoese blamed the cowardice of their admiral, or said that the crews were not real Genoese but a riffraff of all nations, hired for pay. In 1267, a Genoese fleet that was blockading Acre left without a fight when a Venetian fleet appeared. The Venetians clearly had the better of it in all the battles between main fleets: at Acre in 1258, at Settepozzi in 1263, and at Trapani in 1266.

In spite of their naval victories, the war was proving very costly to the Venetians. Their privileged commercial position in Constantinople and other parts of the Latin Empire was lost. Michael Paleologue granted the Genoese an area across the Golden Horn where, settling in large numbers, they formed a suburb all their own, known as Pera. He did not, however, grant them all the privileges the Venetians had had, and he readmitted the Venetians in 1268 while their war with Genoa was still on. Venetian merchants resumed their trade in Constantinople, but they never again held as highly privileged a position as they had before 1261.

Venice was suffering also from Genoese raids on its shipping. Even in times of peace, there was a tendency for vessels to keep company for protection from pirates. During the war, they were required to keep together, although that must have been difficult as a practical matter considering the different sailing qualities of the galleys, the tarettes, and the big lateeners of two or three decks. In order to concentrate strength, only one convoy a year was sent to Acre, and the caravan of Romania went only as far as Negroponte, where it could be reinforced from Crete without too much difficulty if threatened. Times of departure and routes were carefully stipulated, and escorts of 15–30 war galleys were provided. The system worked well enough, so that the contemporary Venetian chronicler, Martino da Canal, boasted that the Venetians sent out their caravans as usual, whereas the Genoese could cross the sea only by stealth like pirates. But that boast obscured the fact that the Genoese were really doing very well for themselves without escorted convoys. Some of their ships sailing singly or in small groups were taken by the Venetians — after Lorenzo Tiepolo's attack on the Genoese in Acre, Genoese and Venetians fought wherever their ships met — but many others got through safely. The Venetians did not have galleys available for raids on commerce since they were all tied up in escort duties. Many Genoese galleys, armed by private adventurers, were meanwhile out looking for booty. For example, three Genoese galleys and a scouting vessel, cruising together in the Aegean, pounced on a large Venetian ship which had become separated from its convoy and was keeping poor watch. They took a rich cargo and 108 prisoners, of whom 42, including Bartolomeo Zorzi, troubador poet, were Venetian nobles.

The convoy system used by the Venetians had the disadvantage not only of tying down the war galleys, but also of presenting a concentrated target. If the escorting warships could be defeated or lured away and the convoy captured, that inflicted on the enemy an even more serious material loss than the defeat of its battle squadron. The Genoese admiral Grillo achieved such a coup in 1264. The Venetian admiral to whom was assigned the protection of the caravan to Acre, wishing to clear the way for his convoy by finding and destroying the Genoese fleet, fell into a trap. Grillo called at south Italian ports, where he spread the word that he was leaving for Acre, and then sailed off — to Malta. When the Venetian galleys came seeking him, they believed the misleading reports and went east, leaving the Adriatic and Ionian seas open. Returning north from Malta, Grillo with sixteen galleys caught the unprotected Venetian convoy at sea near Durazzo and Saseno. It consisted of one very large round ship, the *Roccaforte*, a dozen tarettes, and a half-dozen other vessels. After defending their tarettes and other smaller vessels for some hours, the Venetians all withdrew with their most valuable merchandise in the *Roccaforte* and there defied the Genoese. The engagement provides a good example of the composition of thirteenth-century convoys and the military value of such a large vessel as the *Roccaforte* with its high castles. It enabled the Venetians to avoid complete disaster, but their loss was very heavy; not only were the smaller vessels and the bulk of their cargoes lost, but also a whole year's trade Beyond-the-Sea.

No other attack on a convoy was equally successful, but Grillo's success made other Venetian admirals excessively cautious about leaving the merchantmen they were escorting. After years of war, convoying was proving much less profitable than privateering. The Venetians were ready for peace, for their honor was satisfied and their commerce suffering. But the Genoese were not, for they were smarting from defeats and were making out better with their cut-and-run warfare than were the Venetians with their attempt at a kind of cut-and-dried command of the sea. Peace was made in 1270 only because King Louis IX of France insisted on having a fleet for the crusade he was planning. He threatened that, unless the Genoese stopped capturing and pillaging Venetians, he would arrest the Genoese in France and confiscate their wares. At the same time, he offered the Genoese attractive prices if they would put their

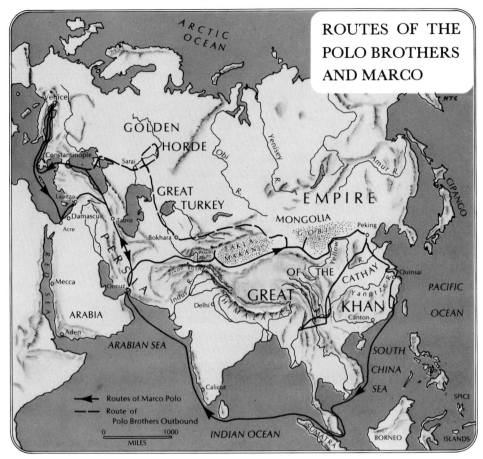

ROUTES OF THE POLO BROTHERS AND MARCO

ARCTIC OCEAN

Venice

GOLDEN HORDE

Constantinople   Sarai   Obi

Lajazzo   GREAT TURKEY

Damascus   Tabriz

Acre   Bokhara

Mecca   Ormuz   PERSIA

ARABIA

Aden

ARABIAN SEA

Calicut

INDIAN OCEAN

Yenisey

EMPIRE

MONGOLIA   GOBI   Peking

TAKLA MAKAN

HINDU KUSH   OF THE   CATHAY   Quinsai

Delhi   GREAT   Yangtze   PACIFIC

HIMALAYAS   KHAN   OCEAN

Canton

SOUTH CHINA SEA

SUMATRA   BORNEO   ISLANDS

RED SEA

Indus

CIPANGO

Amur R.

Yellow R.

SPICE

→ Routes of Marco Polo

--- Route of Polo Brothers Outbound

0   1000
MILES

MAP **6**

ships at his disposal. The resulting treaty was in effect only a truce between embittered enemies.

During the next twenty-five years, the Genoese continued their sensational economic and naval expansion. In the western Mediterranean, they decisively crushed Pisa, which never recovered from the defeat of its navy at Meloria in 1284. Genoa was then the undisputed leader in the Tyrrhenian Sea in both naval power and commercial shipping. Sailing through the straits of Gibraltar, the Genoese merchant ships carried Levantine spices and silks to Bruges and England and brought back cloth and wool. In the East they were particularly expansive in the Black Sea and Asia Minor. Although the clauses in the treaty of Ninfeo expelling the Venetians from Romania were reversed within a few years, the restoration of the Greek empire had ended the period in which the Venetians held a predominant position in all Romania. Their colonies at Negroponte, Crete, Coron, and Modon and their alliances with the Latin princes who had possessions in the southern part of the Greek peninsula gave the Venetians a superior position in the south and west of Romania, but the Genoese overtopped the Venetians in its northern and eastern parts. Their colony at Pera in the harbor of Constantinople flourished, and they built up another shipping center on the northern shore of the Black Sea. Picking Kaffa because of its excellent harbor, well protected from the north winds which prevail in that region, they made it the base for penetration into the Crimea and up the rivers of southern Russia. Other Genoese commercial centers were the island of Chios, famed for its mastic, and the very valuable alum mines at Focea near modern Smyrna (Ismir). These colonies made Genoa a far greater naval power than the size of Genoa itself would suggest.

Venice also was growing in the decades 1270–90. Her shipping profited from the opportunities open to it as a neutral when the two other main naval powers, Genoa and Pisa, were at war and from the general growth in Europe's wealth and population in those years. The textile industries of Flanders and the mines of Germany were still increasing their output and providing a means of paying for oriental wares, such as silks and spices, for which the European appetite seemed insatiable. At the same time, Venetian industrial output was growing, and Venice was just then making the most of enforcing her position as the staple of the northern Adriatic.

The Levantine trade was also changing in character. Less than formerly were Venetian ships employed in supplying other metropolises such as Constantinople and Alexandria. They concentrated more on the trade that passed through Venice itself. It was not their exclusive concern; much money was still to be made by transporting products from one part of the Levant to another, but gradually Venice was replacing Constantinople as the chief market for the raw materials from many parts of Romania, such as wine, wax, oil, honey, cotton, wool, and hides, and also as the manufacturing center from which they received supplies.

THE MONGOLS
AND NEW
TRADE ROUTES

In thys Booke I do mind to giue knowledge of strange and maruelous things
of the world, and specially of the partes of Armenia, Persia, India, Tartaria,
and of many other prouinces and Countrys, whiche shall be declared in this worke,
as they were seene by me, Marcus Paulus of the noble Citie of Venice; . . .

PROLOGUE TO ELIZABETHEAN TRANSLATION OF *THE TRAVELS OF MARCO POLO*

In seeking oriental wares to satisfy their western customers, both Venice and Genoa found especially satisfying opportunities on the shores of the Black Sea. The commercial importance of what is now the southern part of the Soviet Union increased when it was united with China under the rule of the Mongols. The conquests of these horsemen-bowmen were sensationally destructive in their first stage, which carried them to a victory over Poles and Germans in western Poland in 1241 and to the sack of Bagdad in 1258. But once their supremacy was established, the Mongol emperors organized very efficiently armies, roads, posts, tribute collection, and trade from the borders of Hungary to the Sea of Japan, the vastest empire ever created down to that time. The Great Khan, whose capital was at first in Outer Mongolia and later in China, ruled over lesser khans; furthest west was the Khanate of the Golden Horde (the Kipchak Empire), supreme over the rivers of southern Russia which were visited by Venetians, as well as Greeks, Armenians, Jews, and others, seeking supplies for the city of Constantinople. In what is now Iran and Iraq was formed the Khanate of Persia (Ilkhan Empire). Mongol expansion southward into the Arab world was stopped by the defeat inflicted on the Persian khan in 1260 by new rulers of Egypt, the Mamluks. The Mamluks remained the masters of Syria, Palestine, and the routes through the Red Sea; but the Mongol Khanate of Persia developed an overland trade between the Persian Gulf and the West. One terminus of this route was at Lajazzo, just north of Syria. A second western terminus was the city of Trebizond at the eastern end of the Black Sea. The Persian capital of Tabriz became a flourishing link in the chain of trade from Lajazzo and Trebizond to Ormuz at the head of the Persian Gulf (see Map 5).

The opportunities opened by the Mongols are illustrated by the story of Nicolò and Matteo Polo. They were among the Venetians who, after setting up business in Constantinople, extended their commerce across the Black Sea to Soldaia on the southern tip of the Crimea. In 1260 they decided to explore commercial possibilities further inland. Taking jewels and some other wares they rode from Soldaia to Sarai (near modern Saratow) on the Volga River, the capital of the Golden Horde. It proved to be a very good time indeed to be away from Constantinople and out of the Black Sea, since it was precisely in July, 1261, that the Greeks retook Constantinople and encouraged the eager Genoese to seize all the Venetians they could. Some fifty Venetians were captured trying to escape from the Black Sea and treated by the Greek emperor as pirates, being punished by blinding and having their noses cut off. How much the Polo brothers heard of this, possibly exaggerated in the telling, can only be imagined, but it seems an adequate reason why they should not try to go back by the way they had come, although it is not the reason given by Nicolò's son, Marco Polo, who wrote of their travels. Even Sarai may have seemed unsafe if the Polo brothers were sufficiently informed, for the Greek Empire became for a few years the connecting link in an alliance with the Golden Horde on the one side and the Mamluks on the other, an alliance directed partially against the Khanate of Persia and partially against Venice. It is ironic but typical of the commercial conditions of the period that the coup at Constantinople in 1261, a commercial disaster for the Venetians, should have set in motion the finding of a new route and the most celebrated of all Venetian journeys.

If Nicolo and Matteo were well-informed about commercial conditions, as seems likely, they knew about the routes through the lands of the Mongol khan of Persia. At least they must have heard about the rich city of Tabriz and of merchants that went there either through Trebizond or Lajazzo. To reach Tabriz from where they were, in Sarai, there was a route going south on the west side of the Caspian Sea, which one western traveler before them had used, but this way was closed to the Polos by the war being waged for possession of the Caucasus between the khans of Persia and of the Golden Horde. Therefore, they journeyed east from Sarai to Bokhara, in Great Turkey which was under a third Mongol khan (Chagatai Empire). From Bokhara they hoped to find a route, as yet unknown to westerners, that would lead from Bokhara to Tabriz and so back to the Mediterranean. If they had succeeded in reaching Tabriz, they would have found one Venetian already living there, Pietro Viglioni, and if they had arrived in time, they might have been called on to witness his will, which he had to have witnessed by persons not Venetian, for in Tabriz there were no other Venetians, although there were other Italians. The Polo brothers could hope to go home to Venice from Tabriz by the same route over which Viglioni had come, provided they could find "the unknown route" between Bokhara and Tabriz.

Instead, they found wars going on also between khans in Great Turkey, blocking the roads west. But they were ready to take whatever opportunity knocked, and after about three years in Bokhara, during which they learned Mongol and Persian, they met a high Mongol official traveling with a formidable caravan eastward from the Khan of Persia to the Great Khan in China. Invited to accompany him because the Great Khan had never seen Latin Christians and would be interested, so they were told, Matteo and Nicolò made the three thousand mile trip over or around the mountains called the "roof of the world" (the high Pamirs), through the populous oases of central Asia, skirting some of the earth's largest deserts until they came to the Mongol capital at Peking. Other westerners had been to the Mongol capital when it had been in Mongolia, but the new Great Khan, Kublai Khan, had moved it southward, and the Polo brothers were the first from the Mediterranean to cross the Great Wall of China.

The Great Khan knew the Moslems as difficult enemies (the defeat by the Mamluks rankled), but he knew little of Christians, and after the Polo brothers had spent some time at his court, he sent them west as his ambassadors to the pope, asking that missionaries be sent to instruct his people concerning Christianity. On this return journey, the Polo brothers finally found a route which brought them through the Khanate of Persia to the Mediterranean at Lajazzo, and so home.

When they set out again for China in 1271, they had collected only two missionaries, who fearfully turned back almost as soon as they started, but they took with them Nicolò's son, Marco, a young man of twenty-one. Marco caught the eye of the Mongol emperor, entered his service, and traveled back and forth over China for most of the next twenty years, becoming familiar with a civilization quite different and in many respects more admirable than his own, with bigger cities, a larger, highly organized state, and a different world of refined art, science, and courtly custom. When the Polos finally returned to the west, they traveled by sea from China to the Persian Gulf, and then across Persia to Trebizond (see Map 6). Back in Venice, Marco Polo recounted his travels and the wonders he had seen until he became a legendary figure. By that time, to be sure, many other western merchants had found the route to Cathay. In the 1260's, Marco's father and uncle had been pioneers in pushing east from Sarai to Bokhara. In the 1290's, other Venetians and many Genoese were taking advantage of the relatively safe roads kept open by the Mongol khans. Other Venetians who had trips of their own to talk about may have listened with less than enthusiasm to Marco Polo's tales of his travels; one legend about him is that his book was named "Marco's Millions" by those wearied with what they called his exaggerations.

Another legend is that, on his return at the age of forty to the palace in Venice which he had left as a youth, no one recognized him or his father and uncle. No one believed their story until they slit open the seams of their clothes to let piles of jewels tumble out. In fact, his uncle and father seem to have made their journeys primarily as traders in jewels and precious stones, making rich gifts to the rulers of new countries on their arrival and receiving gifts appropriate to the magnificence of the ruler on their departure, a procedure more profitable than haggling trade. Jewels were an ideal commodity for such long and arduous routes.

The most important among the routes opened by the Mongols and described by Marco Polo was that through Persia to the Indian Ocean. The

a   *b*

FIGURE 5   *Travel Posters from Marco Polo (Photo Bibliothèque Nationale, Paris).*

Marco's account shaped for centuries Europe's impressions of Asia, as shown in the miniatures adorning the narrative of his travels which was presented by the Duke of Burgundy to another member of the French royal family about 1400.

(a) Polo brothers riding to Bokhara; (b) Their reception by the Great Khan; (c) On their second trip, entering an industrial town in Armenia; (d) The merchants they met in Ormuz; (e) The pepper harvest in southern India; (f) Gathering diamonds from a riverbed in mountains guarded by poisonous serpents.

much wanted spices from India and the East Indies found there an alternative means of reaching the Mediterranean in case the routes through the Red Sea were closed. While the access to this route through Trebizond contributed to enhancing the commercial importance of the Black Sea, the branch leading through Lajazzo had many advantages. It passed through the Christian Kingdom of Lesser Armenia and enabled traders to avoid both the lands under the control of the Greeks and those under the Moslem Mamluks.

Bypassing Moslem territory became of crucial importance when the Mamluk Soldan of Egypt wiped out the last remnants of the Kingdom of Jerusalem. In 1291 Acre fell, and Tyre and Tripoli also. The pope placed a ban on any trade with lands under the rule of the soldan, even trade in wares not contraband. Cyprus might serve as an intermediary for surreptitious trade, but Lajazzo was the only port on the mainland legally open to Christians, and it immediately became the destination of the Venetian fleets to Beyond-the-Sea. Marco Polo was there on a trading voyage when war broke out between Venice and Genoa, and he was taken back to a Genoese prison, still full of tales about the days in China. In prison he found someone willing to listen, a fellow prisoner, Rustichello of Pisa, who gave Marco's narrative the literary style which was fashionable in that day and which ensured it wide circulation.

THE SECOND   The fall of Acre made Lajazzo a natural center of conflict in a new Genoese
GENOESE WAR   War. The truce of 1270 had been renewed several times, although frequent
acts of piracy as well as commercial rivalry kept mutual hatred inflamed. Both Venice and Genoa were ready to turn a casual incident into a war because each wished to expel the other from the Black Sea, more important than ever after the fall of Acre. The Venetians had been readmitted to trade in the Black

c

d

e

f

Sea after the First Genoese War, and had made their own commercial treaty with the Khan of the Golden Horde in 1291.

After an unplanned clash in which some Venetian galleys were plundered, the Venetians sent a large escort of war galleys with the caravan leaving for Cyprus and Armenia in 1294, expecting apparently to repeat what they had done at Acre in 1258. On the way the Venetians captured or destroyed Genoese possessions in Cyprus. When the news of this reached the Genoese at Pera, they armed their ships and, enlisting all those they could gather in Romania, they headed for the lands Beyond-the-Sea. By the time they caught up with the Venetians, the latter were off Lajazzo. Since the Venetians had more ships, they hardly expected to be attacked and had their sails up, which made it harder to maneuver the vessels, especially as they had not unloaded their mercantile cargoes. Many got in each other's way and ended up broadside against the enemy prows. The Genoese won a complete victory, capturing nearly all the ships and much merchandise.

Enthusiastic over this success, The Genoese conducted this second war very differently from the first one. Like the Venetians in the 1260's, they went looking for more victorious battles. In 1295, they armed the biggest fleet yet, 165 galleys with crews totaling 35,000 men! The Venetians also conscripted men and ships for a large armament but did not seek the enemy. The Genoese fleet sent a challenge to the Venetians and sailed as far as Messina. Then it sailed home again. In the letdown after that excessive effort, the Genoese began fighting among themselves and sent out no fleet in 1296. The Venetians despatched a war fleet which collected some plunder at Pera, Focea, and in Kaffa. Neither side concentrated on the protection of convoys; both used their fleets to raid the colonies of the other. As pirates, the Venetians this time did as much damage as did the Genoese, and the Venetian government showed more concern with making their armaments pay.

After several attempts, the Genoese in 1298 induced the Venetian again to risk a battle between war fleets. The Genoese commander, Lampa Doria, forced the Venetians to meet his challenge by ravaging the Dalmatian coast where the two fleets met off the island of Curzola. This was the largest battle ever fought between these two contestants, about 90 Venetian vessels against 80 Genoese, with heavily armed war galleys on both sides. Contemporary accounts differ excessively in describing the action, but agree that it was very hard fought, with heavy losses on both sides, and that the Genoese had the better of it in seamanship, maneuver, and combat. They captured most of the Venetian galleys and thousands of prisoners.

Victory in battle was of no more benefit to the Genoese in this war than battle victories had been to the Venetians in the earlier contest. Doria's losses were such that he did not feel able to push on and attack the lagoons. Venice was not blockaded and was able to outfit new fleets the following year. Indeed, Domenico Schiavo, a Venetian pirate who had commanded some ships which survived Curzola, revived the spirits of his countrymen by a surprise raid on Genoa itself and boasted of having struck coins with the insignia of St. Mark on Genoa's own breakwater. The following year, peace was made between Venice and Genoa on terms of comparative equality.

If Domenico Schiavo was really able to coin ducats on the breakwater in the harbor of Genoa, it was because he could use nearby Monaco as a base. Monaco had been taken over in 1297 by Francesco Grimaldi, who was the leader of the Guelfs in Genoa. The Doria and Spinola families, leaders of the Ghibelline faction which had gained power earlier, drove the Guelf nobles to open rebellion by confiscating and selling their property. After its defeat at Curzola, Venice allied with the Genoese Guelfs at Monaco, and it was fear of its internal enemies, the Guelfs, quite as much as respect for Venice's unbroken power that motivated the Genoese rulers in accepting the terms agreed upon in 1299.

By these terms Venice recognized Genoese primacy over all its Riviera and Genoa recognized Venetian lordship over its "Gulf" by agreeing that, if there was war of any kind in the Adriatic, no Genoese ship would enter the Adriatic except to go to Venice. Venice abandoned any support of the Guelfs of Monaco, an act which made the Grimaldi feel free to prey on Venetian commerce as well as that of Genoese Ghibellines. Neither Pisa in the west nor the Byzantine emperor in the east were included in the treaty. Venice was left free to continue its war against the Greek ruler, really a series of plundering raids which they had begun as part of the Genoese war. The question as to which was to take the lion's share of the expanding trade through the Black Sea was left quite unresolved, as was their rivalry Beyond-the-Sea. Judging from these terms one might almost say that again the side which won the battles lost the war. In 1270, the Genoese had not wanted to conclude a truce because their "honor" was unsatisfied and their purses were profiting. In 1299, victories had sated their pride and profits were suffering.

So much was left unsettled by the peace treaty that everything depended on how the rivals used the opportunities it offered. The weaknesses of Genoa's internal political organization, which had interfered with her deriving any real profit from her naval victories, appeared in more glaring form during the next century. Over the long run, the outcome of Venetian-Genoese rivalry was not to depend on superiority in seamanship or naval operations; after 1270, Venice had no such superiority. It was decided by their relative skill in arts of another order — those of social organization, in which the Genoese and the Venetians had very different talents.

ARISTOCRATIC POLITY·I

From Dukedom to Commune

The myths of Venice have enduring vitality. "Time dissipates to shining ether the solid angularity of fact," as Emerson boasted, but myths enthrall the imagination and defy trial by documentation. Some myths have even been makers of reality and moulded Venice's history.

MYTH AND REALITY IN THE DUKEDOM The oldest powerful myth proclaimed Venice's sovereign independent birth. A feeling for the integrity of the state, for its ultimate authority over all persons and groups, strikingly distinguishes Venice from such other Italian city-states as Genoa or Florence. No doubt it was derived in large part from habits of political behavior formed when Venice was part of the Byzantine Empire, for there was no sudden break with the Byzantine tradition. But, paradoxically, this feeling of state sovereignty was enhanced by a myth of original independence and self-government. Other Italian city-states of the Later Middle Ages acknowledged a theoretical sovereignty of the emperor or pope, but the Venetians looked to no such high authority to legitimatize their government. They believed it legitimate and possessed of final authority because it expressed the will of the Venetians, a people who had always been free, that is, independent of outside control. Andrea Dandolo, a doge and the authoritative fourteenth-century chronicler, ignored the fact that the first doge of Venice was a Byzantine official, created when Venice was part of the Byzantine Empire. He pictures the Venetians gathering in 697 on their own initiative from the various settlements in which they then lived scattered over the lagoons and deciding, nobles and common people together, on the creation of a single leader, the dux or doge, to replace the officials called tribunes by whom their settlements had been hitherto separately governed. (See Chronological Chart preceding Chapter 1.)

The cult of Saint Mark strengthened this feeling of sovereign independence. Italian cities generally affirmed their autonomy and power by adoring a chosen saint as their patron. For example, Genoa extolled Saint George. Venice identified with Saint Mark the Evangelist. Dandolo began his chronicle with the story of how Saint Mark was carried by a storm to the Venetian lagoons and there founded the church at Aquileia, from which was derived the Patriarchate of Venice. Legend elaborated on how he found refuge one night on the site where the church San Marco was to be built and how he dreamed of the building to be erected there in his honor. When two Venetians returning from trade in Alexandria reported to the doge that they had brought back the body of Saint Mark, their possession of the body strengthened the Venetians' conviction that the Evangelist was their special protector and patron. His cult became a symbolic expression of their loyalty to each other, of their unity.

Significantly, on its arrival in Venice, the precious relic was taken to the doge, not to the bishop or to the patriarch. Although, like other medieval Christians, the Venetians thought of themselves as a religious community, tracing their original identity, as the legends of Saint Mark showed, to the Christian community formed by the Apostle himself within the Roman Empire, they looked to the doge rather than to any ecclesiastic as the head of that community. The doge built as his private chapel the church called San Marco in which the sacred relic was placed. It was not the cathedral of the local bishop; his cathedral was the church in the Castello district called San Pietro in Olivolo. Important among early centers of settlement, Castello later became an out-of-the-way seaman's quarter, while San Marco and Rialto became the centers of Venetian life (see Figure 2). Even in ecclesiastical affairs, the bishop at Castello was secondary, overshadowed by the patriarch. As explained in Chapter 1, the seat of the patriarchate was not at Venice at all but at Grado, away at one end of the lagoon, because there it could claim rights as a continuation of the old patriarchate of Aquileia. In most cities of the Middle Ages, a bishop was the center of government before the development of communal institutions. It was not so at Venice, partly because of the strength of the Byzantine tradition of subordinating the clergy, and partly because the patriarch neither was Venice's bishop nor was San Marco his church. The doge and civic officials administered the wealth attracted by veneration for the saint's relics, and it was the power and glory of the Venetian state which was symbolized by the Lion of Saint Mark.

Another myth which, when fully formed, contributed to the solidarity of the state was a belief that Venice was free of factions, that all worked together for the glory of their city. This myth flourished in the sixteenth century, when the contrast between Venetian unity and recent civil strife elsewhere was sufficiently striking to make it believable and to outweigh the record of open violence in the first five or six centuries of Venetian political history. When doges of the Candiano family were battling for Venetian control of the northern Adriatic in the ninth and tenth centuries, they were also seeking power for their family and trying to make the Venetian lagoons an hereditary dukedom. Pietro IV Candiano put away his first wife in order to marry the sister of the richest prince in Italy, the Marquis of Tuscany. He sent Venetians as soldiers to fight in various parts of Italy for the lands that were her dowry. He brought foreign soldiers to Venice to reinforce his authority, and looked to Otto, the German emperor, for support. He was opposed by powerful families which leaned on Byzantium. His rivals roused a mob to storm the ducal palace in 976; when beaten off by Candiano's guards, they started a fire in adjoining structures. The fire spread through all that island of the city, destroying the church of San Marco as well as the ducal palace. When the doge was driven by fire and smoke to seek a way out, he was waylaid by his enemies and killed, as was his infant son, a babe in arms. This was the most savage outburst of rivalry between ducal families, but in the early centuries many of the doges were assassinated or deposed. Pietro IV Candiano was succeeded by the first of the Orseolo, who rebuilt San Marco. The second Orseolo, Pietro II, who led the brilliant expedition to Dalmatia in the year 1000, strengthened his position by marriage alliances with imperial families, but during the dogeship of his son, his dynasty also was violently overthrown.

Meanwhile, murderous feuds flourished. A member of the Caloprini family murdered one of the Morosini. For a time, the Caloprini sought and obtained a kind of protection from the German emperor, Otto II, but after his death, three Caloprini brothers were killed by the Morosini. These episodes show that, in the tenth and eleventh centuries, Venice suffered from feuds and ambitions among its great families similar to those which so conspicuously plagued other Italian city-states, both then and in later centuries. The orderly subordination of individual ambition for which Venice was later much admired was an acquired characteristic, not an inheritance of original virtues. It was not true that Venice had never known the bloody strife of factions; it was true that she found means of taming them.

Another kind of myth about Venetian government developed very much later, in the last centuries of the life of the Republic, a kind of countermyth which had historical influence not in strengthening the republic but in contributing to its downfall. It pictured Venetian government as a tyrannical oligarchy maintained by a terrifying efficiency in the use of spies, tortures, and poisons. This countermyth began among Venice's Spanish enemies during the Counter Reformation, but it matured in the eighteenth century, when there was some truth in it, and reached full flower in the propaganda by which the Jacobins and Napoleon justified their destruction of the Republic. Abandoned in its extreme form, in a mild version it still dominates many accounts. In fact, Venice did in later centuries come to be governed by less than a hundred families that closed ranks and came to believe firmly in their sole right to govern by reason of their birth. But to attribute to earlier centuries the aristocratic and democratic beliefs of the eighteenth and nineteenth centuries is a modern kind of mythmaking.

What we would call a democratic principle has been ascribed to their selection of the doge by a popular assembly and the submission of basic laws for approval by the people. But when early chronicles or legal formulas refer to "the people" (*populus*), they have in mind the whole community, or at least all the laity of the community (as in referring to the election of the bishop by *clero et populo*); they do not necessarily have in mind "people" as distinct from "nobility." There were families which were considered noble because of their wealth, military services, ecclesiastical connections, and style of living. Although they had no well-defined legal or political privileges separating them from commoners, they were the leaders of political life and were at first accepted as representing the people, that is, the community.

In the Middle Ages, there were two schemes of thought and emotion by which power was made to seem legitimate and right. One was the descending theory which held that all rightful power was handed down by God to the pope and emperor and passed on by them to those below. The other was the ascending theory which held that lawmaking and similar political powers resided in the community and could be handed over by it to those it designated. Rightful rulers were in this sense representatives of the community and were responsible to it. Of these two contrasting theories, the Venetians wholeheartedly embraced the second. They used it to justify their strong belief in their sovereign independence. While emphasizing it to defend their freedom from any emperor, they used it also to justify imposing restrictions on their doges and even deposing them.

On the other hand, they believed the Biblical teaching that all power came from God. The doge avowed in his oath of office that he attained his position through election not out of his own strength and wisdom but "by clemency of the Creator on whom all depends." He received the rod or the standard which was the symbol of his office from Saint Mark, as was clearly depicted on the Venetian coins (see Figure 12), and as was symbolized in the ceremony by which he was installed when he received the standard from the altar at San Marco. Thus elements of the descending and ascending theories were combined. Only the people, the community, could designate who was to be doge and define his powers; but the governmental authority which he exercised was thought of not as a mere human device but as a divine institution.

In the ninth, tenth, and even the eleventh centuries, the doge was a monarch of unlimited power. Later, after he had been hemmed around with advisory councils, he still remained the symbol of the unity and authority of government. He was also at the center of the practical problems of commanding the armed forces, conducting foreign affairs, dispensing justice, and supervising administrative officers. In this situation, his moral authority as representative of both the community and of Saint Mark added to the forcefulness and effectiveness of the executive branch of the government.

A beginning of the process of hemming him in with advisers appears on the occasion of the revolution which overthrew the Orseolo dynasty in 1032. Along with the new doge, two ducal councillors were elected to prevent any attempt at the kind of monarchic rule which had been practiced by the Candiani and the Orseolo. These safeguards were not immediate needs, however, for the new doge, Domenico Flabianico, was of a different stripe. He was a "new man," of a family which had not previously held high office, but he had gained great wealth as a silk merchant. He showed his shrewdness also in a peaceful term of office.

Men like Domenico Flabianico became more and more numerous in Venice during the next two centuries. Agricultural growth and general economic expansion in the Po Valley on the one side and increasing Venetian naval power and commercial privileges within the Byzantine Empire on the other side enabled many new men to rise into the ranks of the nobility. While trade, or perhaps piracy, was a main source of wealth, fortunes were also made by those who invested in real estate within the neighborhood of Rivoalto. Rich families claiming descent from the tribunes called all other nobles "new families," but really old, pretended old, and frankly new families all had much the same sources of wealth. They were all active in maritime commerce and warfare, they all bought land when they could, and they all had an interest in competing for the dogeship and for influential positions among the doge's advisers.

In accordance with the ascending theme in government, the highest authority in early Venice was in theory the General Assembly (*Concio* or *Arengo*). In this general gathering of the people occurred the selection of the doge and the approval of new laws, but it seems clear that its proceedings were dominated by the powerful families. A contemporary description of an early ducal election assumes the initiative of the leading nobles and stresses the divine inspiration which was felt to be an essential part of the process of choice. On word of the doge's death in 1071, countless boats bringing Venetians from all over the lagoons gathered between the church of the bishop at Castello and the monastery of San Nicolò at the Lido. Within church and abbey resounded fervent prayers that God give to the Venetians a capable and universally acceptable doge. Suddenly, there was a general cry through the multitude: "We wish and elect Domenico Selvo." Promptly a throng of nobles brought him forward in a bark which moved toward San Marco at the head of a procession of boats which made the water white with their oars, while the people shouted approval, the clergy chanted *Te Deum Laudamus*, and the bells of the Campanile rang triumphantly. Humbly entering the church of San Marco, the newly elected doge took from its altar his staff of office and then went to the ducal palace to receive an oath of obedience from the assembled people.

The throng of nobles around the doge when he took office were men accustomed to acting as judges and as his councillors. The growth of population and traffic made it necessary for every doge to have such a group to assist in the government. Before the councillors were organized into well-defined bodies with specified numbers and terms of office, they appeared as prominent and experienced persons whom the doge was expected to consult, sometimes a few only, but on important matters fairly large numbers. Then, in the mid-twelfth century, these men acted as the representatives of what was called the Commune. They competed with the doge for the leadership of the community, they acted particularly as spokesmen of the rapidly growing Rivoalto — the city we know as Venice — and asserted its supremacy over all the other settlements in the lagoons. Some earlier doges had tried to treat their office as a king might treat his crown, namely, as a personal or family possession; from the second half of the twelfth century on, they were called on to treat it as a public trust and to consider themselves in a position not essentially different from that of their councillors, namely, as one of the officers of the Commune, although its head.

DOGES WITHIN A COMMUNE   In becoming a commune, Venice was doing what other north Italian cities were also doing in the same period, but Venice was able to create a more solid communal allegiance. In Padua, Milan, and Florence, communes were formed as new organizations fighting to take powers away from bishops or feudal lords. The Commune of Venice was a continuation of the dukedom under a new name and with a gradually transformed structure. Long after the name of Commune was adopted and used officially, the doge continued to act as the personification of the state, giving justice and negotiating treaties. The feeling of group loyalty and the sense of state sovereignty which had been focused on him and on Saint Mark enabled the Commune to command solid loyalties.

The turning point in which this solidarity of allegiance was essentially preserved came in 1172, after Doge Vitale II Michiel brought home the fleet he had been leading against Byzantium, not rich with plunder as hoped, but decimated by a pestilence.

The ducal office or throne had then been occupied for most of a century by members of the Michiel family — for sixty-two out of the last seventy-six years, if we count in one son-in-law. Vitale II Michiel had quarreled with his councillors over his effort to advance his sons and nephews. After the disastrous outcome of his naval expedition had turned the populace against him, he faced a General Assembly without the support of his councillors, for he had not followed their advice in his dealing with the Byzantine emperor. The assembly was so hostile that he fled for refuge towards the church of San Zaccaria. He was assassinated at its doorway.

What made the events of 1172 decisive were the actions of the Ducal Council which then took charge and, more basically, the attitude of the whole group of remarkable men who exercised power for the next two generations: Sebastiano Ziani and his son Pietro, Enrico Dandolo and his son Ranieri. They accepted the principle that the doge should never act contrary to the advice of his councillors. Vitale II Michiel had tried to treat the dogeship in traditional manner as a kind of personal monarchy, though elective. His successors treated it as a republican magistracy, working together in a team even when one of them was called on to step aside and let a rival be elected to the highest office. In the transformation of the dogeship into a magistracy, the institutional changes in 1172 were less decisive than were the successes of the leading personalities of the next century and their exhibitions of restraint.

If any one constitutional reform was crucial it was the creation in 1172 of an official nominating committee to name the new doge. A body of wise men (*sapientes*) had functioned as ducal councillors at least as early as 1143 and presumably had consulted or maneuvered among themselves so that, when the people were summoned to choose a new doge, the leading men had nominations ready. But after 1172, there was just one official nominating committee and it made a single nomination, which was equivalent to election. Through this committee, the leaders of the Commune, placed in control by Michiel's debacle, made sure that the man named as doge would thereafter be one of their own members whom they thought they could trust to act as a member of the team, that is, to abide by the decisions of his councils.

The first two men chosen by this official nominating committee were two of the richest, probably the two richest, men in Venice, Sebastiano Ziani and Orio Mastropiero. A few years earlier, when the commune pledged all the revenue from the Rialto market in order to borrow a huge sum from a dozen leading citizens, Sebastiano Ziani and Orio Mastropiero had each contributed a sixth of the total. Most of the members of that consortium of creditors belonged to the old tribunician families, but Ziani and Mastropiero were relatively new names. The fabulous fortune of the Ziani had been built up by Sebastiano through many years of trade in the East and by investment in colleganze such as those handled by Romano Mairano. It was further multiplied by loans on real estate, some of them of a character that in a later period would certainly have been regarded as usurious. He can be considered the founder of the glorious Piazza di San Marco, for he bequeathed to the city a cluster of structures, which he had acquired piecemeal, that were then torn down to make an open space in front of the church. In 1172 he was already in his seventies and had served in many important embassies, while his son Pietro was busy adding to the family fortune.

In consolidating the new regime, Sebastiano Ziani proved as successful in politics as he had been in business. He vindicated the prestige of his office by executing the assassin of his predecessor, whom chroniclers wrote off as a madman, obscuring the political shift which it punctuated. And although Ziani was the first doge formally chosen by the official nominating committee, he was also the first one to add to the role of the populace in the inauguration ceremonies by being carried around the Piazza on the shoulders of workers from the Arsenal while he scattered coins among the crowd. He added to the international prestige of the Venetian doge and the Venetian Commune by conducting intricate foreign affairs in such a way as to enjoy the confidence of both pope and emperor, in spite of their being at war with each other for years. He arranged for them both to come to Venice to conclude a truce. This famous meeting of the German emperor Frederick Barbarossa and Pope Alexander III in 1177 with the doge of Venice in the role of a sovereign independent power acting as peacemaker was the climax of Sebastiano Ziani's career. He died the following spring in a monastery to which he had retired a few days before.

His successor, Orio Mastropiero, also resigned the dogeship before his death, either because of ill health or because "the Venetians wished it," as the chronicler says, although his service, while not as brilliant as that of Sebastiano Ziani, had yet been on the whole successful.

The choice of the electors fell next on a member of one of the most securely established old families, Enrico Dandolo, who as doge then led the Fourth Crusade and won for himself and his successors the title of Ruler of One Fourth and One Half of the Empire of Romania. The way in which he dominated events showed that, although the doge of Venice could not go against the views of his councils, he could be as powerful a ruler as any king, especially if he personally commanded the fleet and led it to victory. Enrico Dandolo's leadership was economic as well as military. He minted the first of the famous Venetian coins, the big silver penny or *grosso*, taking advantage of the silver bullion paid by the crusaders. He thus created a means of paying for supplies and for imports from the East. Since it was maintained at unchanged weight and fineness, the grosso added to Venice's reputation and attracted business.

The conquest of Constantinople by the crusaders in 1204 increased the wealth and power of the Venetian nobility enormously. With the Byzantine Empire "up for grabs," they were in a good position to seize lucrative lands to hold as vassals either of Venice or of the Latin emperor at Constantinople. The 200 knight's fees created in Crete were allotted to Venetian nobles and the sergeantries to commoners. Larger fiefs were gained by the Venetians who undertook the conquest of the islands of the Aegean and then held them in fee from the Latin emperor. The leader there was Marco Sanuto, son-in-law of Enrico Dandolo. A dozen other Venetian families held Aegean islands, mostly as Sanuto's vassals. Any growth in the prestige of the ducal office because of Enrico Dandolo's magnificent use of it was counterbalanced by growth in the prestige of many Venetian noble families.

Also significant at this juncture of Venetian history was the role played by Enrico Dandolo's son, Ranieri. When leaving with the crusaders and the Venetian fleet, the doge persuaded the Venetians to accept his son as vice-doge, serving in his absence. As vice-doge, Ranieri was by no means a nonentity; he was responsible for compiling an improved code of Venetian law. But, at his father's death, he stepped aside and presided over the election of Pietro Ziani. Ready to take second place under the new doge, Ranieri was given command in the fleet sent to effect the conquest of Crete. He was killed in the ensuing campaign. Overshadowed by his father, Ranieri Dandolo is not generally considered one of the heroes of Venetian history. His name is not on the list of doges, but should be on a list of those who established the tradition of behavior which gave viability to the Venetian political system. In that list, the non-doges, those who gracefully accepted second place, are as important as those who filled the highest office successfully.

Pietro Ziani had added much wealth to the fortune he had inherited from his father Sebastiano and was able to make gifts to various churches and monasteries. His generosity contributed to his popularity and, in the years between his father's death in 1178 and his own election in 1205, he had held many high magistracies. During his long term of twenty-four years as doge, he consolidated the Republic's hold on its territories in Romania: regulating to mutual satisfaction the bonds between the huge colony in Constantinople and the mother city, getting a firm foothold in Negroponte, conquering and colonizing in Crete, yielding in Corfu, but securing Coron and Modon and upholding Venetian power in Dalmatia. His many successes gained him much prestige among contemporaries, and many embassies came to seek his good offices or Venetian alliance. He had a facility for listening to many long speeches with his eyes closed and then summarizing clearly afterwards all that had been said. Like his father, he did not die in office; he retired in his last years to his family palace.

Pietro Ziani had been chosen almost unanimously, but the choice of his successor in 1229 led to a tie vote in the nominating committee, which now numbered forty. There were twenty votes for Marino Dandolo, a nephew of Enrico Dandolo who had been with his uncle at the conquest of Constantinople and then became the ruler of an Aegean island, and twenty also for Giacomo Tiepolo, who had carried on the conquest of Crete and then been the governor (*bailo*) of the colony in Constantinople. The dispute was decided in Tiepolo's favor by casting lots and Marino Dandolo accepted that result. But when the new doge went to pay his respects to old Pietro Ziani, the latter refused to see him. This episode, or the report of it handed down in family chronicles, contributed to a growing split in the Venetian nobility between a faction headed by the Tiepolo and a group composed mainly of the older families centering around the Dandolo.

Giacomo Tiepolo made his name famous by codifying Venetian law into five books of Statuti. He also issued a separate code of maritime law, that which shows most clearly the high status then enjoyed by merchant seamen.

Both Pietro Ziani and Giacomo Tiepolo used the prestige attached to being Doge of Venice to arrange marriage alliances with neighboring princes, such as the King of Sicily or the King of Rascia (part of what is now Jugoslavia). Giacomo Tiepolo's successor as doge came from the Morosini family which was allied by marriage with the Kings of Hungary. Such marriages caused alarm and were forbidden by an addition to the doge's oath of office.

It was impossible to prevent a successful doge from enhancing the status of his family through the glory which reflected on them from his notable achievements, but the Venetians attempted to restrain his use of the position for either personal or family gain by adding restrictions to the oath of office of each new incumbent. These oaths (*promissioni*) record a continual limiting of the doge's powers and freedom of action. At the death of each doge, a committee was appointed to consider additions to the oath before it was taken by the new doge to be elected. Later, another committee was appointed to examine the record in office of the dead doge and to prosecute him so that his heirs might be forced to pay compensation if he had wrongly received any gifts and to pay fines for any derelictions of the duties specified in the doge's oath.

Such inquests emphasized that the dogeship had lost all of its quasi-regal character. It became merely the most distinguished among several magistracies. Gradually, the additions to the doge's oath diluted the power of the position excessively. The series of exceptionally able men who were elected during the century after 1172 are notable for having loyally accepted the restrictions on the office as well as for the vigor and wisdom with which they exercised the very considerable power which in that century was still retained by the doge as the leader of the Venetian Commune.

THE CONSTITUTIONAL FRAMEWORK Venice had no single written document like the Constitution of the United States embodying a basic law with which all other laws had to conform. The nearest to it in early times was the doge's oath, the Promissione. Later basic laws are also to be found in the statutes sworn to by other magistrates such as the Ducal Councillors. We may speak of a Venetian constitution, however, in the same way that we refer to the British constitution, although it is embodied in no single document but is found partly in scattered statutes and partly in customs long adhered to. Custom was equally important in defining the powers and procedures of the various organs of government in Venice. Although these powers and procedures changed, they did so a little at a time during about six centuries. With a few additions and one deletion, the main lines of structure clearly discernible already in the thirteenth century were kept until 1797.

The central organs of government formed a pyramid (see Figure 6) with the General Assembly at its base and the doge at its apex. In between them were the Great Council, the Forty and the Senate, and the Ducal Council. Distrust of individual power made the Venetians depend on committees and councils. Even in their judicial system, sentences were not imposed by an individual judge but by several judges acting together. Each committee or council was checked by some other committee or council so as to assure the rule of law, even at the cost of losing some executive efficiency. While thus insisting on a division of power among the different elements in the pyramid of councils, the Venetians made no effort to separate executive, legislative, and judicial functions.

The General Assembly usually met not in boats as described for the election of Doge Domenico Selvo in 1071, but within San Marco. It was summoned only to ratify basic legislation and to acclaim a nominating committee's choice of doge.

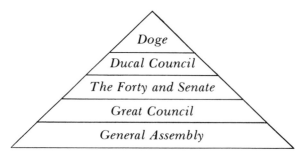

FIGURE 6   *The Constitutional Pyramid.*

Later elaborations and modifications are shown by Figure 40.

More carefully composed and regulated in its proceedings was the Great Council, which in the thirteenth century was the center of power. It elected all magistrates and the members of all the other councils and settled disputes between them. It passed laws, decreed punishments, and granted pardons. Important officials such as the Ducal Councillors were ex-officio members and together with its regular members made a total of three or four hundred. Roughly speaking one can say that the Great Council contained all the most important people who were available in Venice and a sprinkling of others named to it because someone thought they were potentially important.

So large a council was too big for frequent deliberation and debate. Those functions were performed by councils of intermediate size, of which the most important at first was the Forty (*Quarantia*). It formed the court of appeals at the top of the judicial system and at the same time was charged with preparing for approval by the Great Council legislation concerning coinage and finances. Later the Council of Forty was overshadowed by the Senate (*Consilium Rogatorum* or *Consiglio dei Pregadi*), which originated as a committee of sixty men charged with preparing decrees concerning commerce, the sending of embassies, and the movement of fleets. The Forty and the Senate acted jointly when that seemed appropriate, but in the thirteenth century the Forty was the more authoritative council and the three Heads (*Capi*) it elected to be its presiding officers rivaled in importance the Ducal Councillors.

At the top was the Ducal Council, which initiated most of the work of all the other councils while being at the same time bound to obey their decisions. After 1178, the Ducal Councillors were six in number, one for each of the *sestieri* into which the city was divided. They held office generally for a year but sometimes for six months and were not eligible for reelection until two years had elapsed since their previous term. They met under the presidency of the doge and the attendance of the three Heads of the Forty, who had a vote on many issues and could substitute in exercising councillor functions if one of the Ducal Councillors had to be absent.

These ten men — the doge, the Ducal Councillors, and the Heads of the Forty — constituted what was called the *Signoria*; in a narrow sense, they were the government. With the doge at their head, they were responsible for meeting crises as they arose, for formulating proposals and summoning the appropriate council to consider them, for seeing that various subordinate officials were duly elected and performed their duties. Justice also was their responsibility. The doge personally, accompanied by Councillors, was required by his oath of office to visit the law courts periodically and give ear to any complaints of denial of justice.

At the beginning of the thirteenth century the Signoria named the commanders of galleys and fleets, and in the Great Council made nominations for membership on councils and administrative boards. Later this latter function was assigned to special nominating committees, and fleet commanders were elected in the Great Council. As the volume of business to be done increased, many functions once performed by the Ducal Council were assigned to others, but it remained the central unifying executive authority. At the death of a doge, the six Ducal Councillors initiated proceedings for the choice of a new doge and for proposing any reforms in the process which they thought desirable. The senior Ducal Councillor was in the interim the head of the Republic and it was he who placed on the head of the newly chosen doge the final symbol of his office, the ducal beret which took the place of a crown.

One function of the Ducal Council was to force the doge to act in accordance with the decisions made by a majority of its members or by a majority of the Great Council. The oath of office of the Councillors required explicitly that, whenever they found the doge not executing a decision of the councils, they must say to him that he must do so. If a doge showed any intention of overriding his councils, they might feel that they had to oppose him constantly, lest he become too powerful. But so long as the doge avoided that kind of opposition by accepting the principle that the will of the majority should prevail in case of disagreement, the structure of the Signoria was such as to make it likely that the doge would be its most influential member. The other members came and went, some every two months, others every year, while the doge was there as long as he lived. Between 1172 and 1354, doges were in office eleven to twelve years on the average. They had the authority that went with being the presiding officer in the Signoria, the Senate, and the Great Council and during many functions and ceremonies in which they represented the Republic.

If we compare the Venetian constitution with that of other Italian communes of the Middle Ages, we find that the most prominent difference is in the nature of their chief executive. In the twelfth century, communes such as Genoa, Milan, or Florence were generally governed by a small group of "consuls" who formed a body similar in many ways to the Ducal Council at Venice. To give more unity and impartiality to the administration, nearly all the Italian communes created at the beginning of the thirteenth century a one-man executive and judicial head entitled the podesta. Like the doge in Venice, the podesta in other cities was bound by an elaborate oath and was subject to prosecution at the end of his term. But he was a very much weaker executive than the Venetian doge. The podesta held office for only a year or a few years; the doge held office for life. Moreover, the podesta was always a foreigner, never a political leader of the city in which he held that office. The other Italian communes felt it necessary to employ a foreigner in order to have a supreme judge and an executive in whom impartiality could at least be hoped for. The Venetians had more confidence in themselves and in each other. Never having been subject to the Western emperor, they had that feeling of sovereign independence that precluded bringing in any foreigner as chief executive. The doges were all men thoroughly experienced in the special Venetian way of running a government and well known to the leading men of the city, by whom they were selected and with whom they had to work. The basic difference between Venice and the other Italian city-states was the greater unity and solidity of allegiance at Venice. The doge was the expression of this unified allegiance.

Such unity, with an experienced executive officer able to appeal to it effectively, was all the more desirable because administration was very loosely organized. There was almost no bureaucracy, no especially trained officials named by superiors to perform specialized tasks. The management of the Arsenal, of the mint, of the grain warehouse, the collection of taxes, and the inspection of ships — all such functions originally the responsibility of the doge and performed by *gastaldi* and a few other subordinate officials whom he appointed — were one after another assigned to elected committees of from three to six nobles who held office for only a few years at most and were not eligible to succeed themselves. They were elected by the Great Council, at least formally; in practice, in many cases they were chosen by nominating committees. Although the doge and his Council were in a general sense responsible for seeing that these officers did their jobs — and in a crucial matter, such as the ships and weapons in the Arsenal, the doge did for a while inspect personally — the doge could not remove or directly punish the members of these administrative committees. Those charged with enforcing regulations were inspired to diligence by receipt of a portion of the fines they levied, and often two or three were given overlapping jurisdiction so that they competed in collecting penalties. If they were overzealous and unfair, their victims could appeal and ask an exemption or pardon from one of the higher councils.

The church of San Marco gave rise to a special kind of magistracy, the Procurators of San Marco. Their original function was the administration of the endowments of the church, which included much revenue from Venice's colonial possessions in the Levant, the upkeep and embellishment of the building, and the supervision of its chaplains. Their duties emphasized that San Marco belonged more to the Commune than to the bishop. In addition they acquired very extensive functions in administering wills and in the guardianship of minors and persons not of sound mind. At first they were paid a substantial salary: later they were told to expect only "divine rewards" for such pious labors. These posts brought more certain this-worldly honor, however, and gave their holders many opportunities to do favors to their friends, so that the post and title of Procurator was much sought after by aspiring politicians. Once elected Procurator of San Marco, a man held the post for life; it was the only Communal office other than the dogeship in which a noble could have life tenure. A man elected Procurator was assured of a place of honor on all ceremonial occasions for as long as he lived, and this was one reason why ambitious men desired the honor. The number of Procurators increased from one in the twelfth century to four in the thirteenth century. After they ceased to draw any salary, their number was generously raised to nine.

Local government was only slightly more bureaucratic than the central government. Venice contained 60 to 70 parishes (*contrade*), each of which had its cohesion as a small community. Each had of course its priest, who was chosen by the houseowners of the parish before being installed by the bishop, and each had also a parish chief (*Capo di Contrada*). These capi were named and supervised by the doge and his Council; to that extent, their position was bureaucratic; but the choice of the doge was limited to the inhabitants of the parish, in practice to one of the great families living there. These capi made tax assessments for forced loans and registered all the adult males of their district and supervised their selection for military-naval service. They were also charged with keeping a special eye on taverns and on foreigners.

At first, police was entirely the responsibility of these capi, who had the powers of a police magistrate in judging minor offenses. Later, special officials were created, the Lords of the Nightwatch (*Signori di Notte*) who had special responsibility for the marketplace at Rialto and for executing orders of the courts and of the Ducal Council. Although their authority extended over the city as a whole, the 100-120 men they hired as police officers were required by law to be inhabitants of the quarter (i.e., the *sestiere*) in which they served, a symptom of how much local policing was identified with the people being policed. For some centuries, the parish chiefs and the Lords of the Nightwatch competed in enforcing such regulations as those concerning taverns or the carrying of weapons.

Outside of Venice, the other settlements in the lagoons, such as Chioggia and Murano, had their own statutes and councils, but had as their chief executive a podesta chosen by the doge or Commune of Venice. Podesta or *rettori* were sent also to the chief cities of Istria, where they frequently had to fight to maintain Venetian authority. When Venice extended its power over Dalmatia, it allowed local institutions to continue but insisted that the counts, who were the chief officials, should be Venetians or men from local families distinguished as strong partisans of Venice. In all cases, the counts had to approved by the Venetian Commune and take an oath of loyalty to it.

Outside the Adriatic, Venetian colonies originated in two quite distinct ways. Some were formed by merchants enjoying grants of self-government from the local rulers, such as those gained through the crusades at Tyre and Acre. These settlements were at first informally self-governing much as was a ship's company under the maritime statutes. There was one clear difference: on land, a church and its priest provided an initial focus of organization. Later colonies of purely commercial character were under consuls elected in Venice. Quite different in origin were the colonies acquired in the partition of the Byzantine Empire. They were immediately placed under governors sent out from Venice. The most important among these had the title Duke of Crete. The Venetians who received fiefs on the island and the few Greek landlords who kept their land reported to the duke for the defense of the island. Venetian governors and feudal relations were established also in other parts of Greece, such as Coron and Modon. All these colonial governors were elected by the Great Council and had relatively short terms of office, usually two years. Each had his council which he, like the doge in Venice, was bound to consult.

Constantinople was a special case: in 1204 what had been a merchant colony became, temporarily and in conjunction with the crusading Venetian fleet, co-ruler of an empire. When the death of Enrico Dandolo in Constantinople left them leaderless, the Venetians there elected their own ruler, Marino Zeno. In Venice, Dandolo's successor, Pietro Ziani, accepted that action and confirmed Zeno in office. But Zeno's successor was sent out from Venice, as were later local governors, who had the title of bailo. The bailo had a position of great power and responsibility, for he combined the functions of a local governor, a commercial consul, and an ambassador to whatever emperor ruled in Constantinople.

All the Venetian officeholders — those within the city itself, in the lagoon settlements, and in distant colonies — were liable to prosecution for abuse of office by a distinctly Venetian group of officials, the State Attorneys (*Avvogadori di Comun*). These Attorneys had the general duty of prosecuting all cases involving the interests of the Commune, both to recover property and to inflict punishments. They were charged specifically with bringing suit against officials who failed promptly to turn over funds due to the State Treasurers (*Camerlenghi di Comun*), with prosecuting for violations of the maritime code reported to them by crewmen or shippers, and with investigating charges of bribery in the courts. They imposed on minor officials a variety of penalties for such offenses as failing to report to their offices, that is to the places assigned them, on days when they were told they should be there by the bells in the Campanile.

The most striking function of these Attorneys was the enforcement of what we would consider constitutional law. If a council or magistracy was proceeding contrary to the rules laid down for it (for example, acting on a motion made by someone who had no right to make such a motion), the State's Attorneys could intervene. They could suspend proceedings and call for a meeting of the Great Council to hear their charges. If they believed a Ducal Councillor was not doing what the statutes of his office required, they could bring a suit against him which would be judged by The Forty. They in turn could be sued for dereliction of duty by the Heads of The Forty and in last resort the case would be heard by the Great Council. Having no single document which could be pointed to as its constitution, Venice also had no institution such as our Supreme Court undertaking to enforce it. For enforcement of the basic laws distributing political power among the various magistracies and councils it depended on the fact that every official from a parish chief to the doge could be sued and fined by some other official, most notably, by the State Attorneys.

The multiplication of elected officials in councils, fleets, and administrative boards was an essential part of the transformation of Venice from a dukedom to a commune, that is, from a monarchic form of government to one which can best be called aristocratic. It gave occasion for about 500 men to be engaged in administrative posts and voting in the various councils (out of a total population of around 100,000 inhabitants). Those actively participating in the government belonged to some hundred different families, of which between 20 and 50 might be considered great families, having both commercial and landed wealth and being able to boast of ancestors who had endowed churches and had held such high positions as Ducal Councillor, Duke of Crete, Bailo at Constantinople, Captain General of the Sea, or even Doge of Venice. Although none of these positions except the dogeship could be held very long by the same man, many of the same men held first one and then another high office so that a group of leading men rotated through such posts and through important diplomatic missions abroad or special commissions at home. The doge could not oppose the will of this group effectively, but many a doge was the most influential individual within the group, formulating its will. And these leaders owed their position to their ability to command the confidence of the hundreds who formed the Great Council.

Calling the Venetian government in the mid-thirteenth century an aristocracy classifies it as one form of government by the Few, distinct from either government by the Many or government by One. For that purpose it might also be called an oligarchy. But, in referring to Venice, "oligarchy" is usually used to designate control by a smaller group within the aristocracy, generally with the implication that this small group governed oppressively. Aristocracy refers to the rule of the whole body of the nobility, conveying at the same time the favorable implication that they were the part of the population best able to rule well. The extent to which in practice they ruled in the interests of the whole community or considered only benefits to themselves is to be seen in the history of the Republic.

ARISTOCRATIC
POLITY·II

*The Growing Structure
of the Commune*

CHAPTER NINE

Elsewhere the aristocracy of the first-to-arrive defended themselves as a class and were beaten. In Venice they defended themselves as the State and fully won their fight.

G. MARANINI, *LE COSTITUZIONE DI VENEZIA*

Venetian constitutional development differed from that of the other Italian city-states of the Later Middle Ages in that it had a different starting point, namely, its Byzantine connections and its doge; but the direction of political development was the same in Venice and other northern Italian cities from 1000 to 1250. In all of them the formation of a commune placed in control an upper class of nobles or magnates.

After 1250, men hitherto excluded demanded a share in the honors and benefits of office and in shaping communal policies. This latter movement is commonly called the "rise of the people" (*il popolo*), but the lowest classes, the unskilled laborers, the slaves who served as domestics in the cities, and the tenant farmers of the countryside, did not count at all politically and did not share in the "rise of the people." Of those who did share in it, one part were those called "the little people" (*popolo minuto*), who were really a middle class of shopkeepers and artisans. The other part were "the fat people" (*popolo grasso*), merchants and landowners with economic interests very similar to those of the nobles and magnates.

Although they were somewhat more commercial, what decisively distinguished the "popolo grasso" from "the nobles" was their more recent acquisition of wealth. In most of the communes at the beginning of the thirteenth century, the old rich, the magnates, monopolized power, and the newly rich were allied with the little people to force their way to power. After a few generations, they had become old rich themselves and were fighting against a new group of newly rich and against their former allies, the little people.

All these conflicts were made more complicated and bloody by the personal and family rivalries which divided each ruling group as soon as it gained power, and by the constant warfare between the cities. Feelings of communal solidarity and pride in the freedom of the commune were so weakened by these conflicts that, by the early fourteenth century, most communes were subjected to the rule of a single individual who set himself up as the city's master, *il Signore*. At Venice, there were movements composed of the same elements which elsewhere constituted the "rise of the people" but the Venetians maintained their unifying loyalty to the Commune.

THE GUILDS AND THE LITTLE PEOPLE   The formation of guilds was a major factor in the rise of the people, or went hand in hand with it, for guilds were the organizations through which the "little people" made their influence felt. In many cities, as in Florence, guilds were also the chosen instrument of the "fat people" in establishing themselves in power in place of the magnates. Rich merchants formed their guilds initially to take care of their special interests in foreign trade and later used them in the struggles for power within the city. Venice in the twelfth century was much more purely commercial than was inland Florence. Venetian merchants engaged in international trade felt no need of any special organizations, such as guilds, to look after their commercial interests, for their Communal government made that its chief concern. No rival in that field was needed or would have been tolerated. At the same time, men who made fortunes in foreign trade were accepted as part of the ruling aristocracy even if they did not belong to the old families, as was demonstrated at the end of the twelfth century by the elections of Doges Sebastiano Ziani and Orio Mastropiero. In addition to such rich merchants, Venetian prosperity was by 1200 nourishing also many craftsmen and shopkeepers, and at Venice as elsewhere they formed guilds to satisfy their group interests.

Craftsmen were particularly numerous in industries connected with shipping — carpenters, caulkers, coopers, sailmakers, and cordage makers. Venice's connection with the East, where in the Early Middle Ages many techniques were further advanced, stimulated highly skilled crafts such as those of the glassmakers, apothecaries, jewelers, and organ makers. From the beginning, these experts probably worked for export on a small scale. Other craftsmen, such as the makers of woolen cloth, worked then only for the local market, but that was sufficient to support thousands of artisans as Venice's population approached one hundred thousand. A market of that size encouraged many shopkeepers catering to various tastes in clothing and food. Some artisans and shopkeepers who met these local demands grew wealthy, but most of them would be classified as "little people."

From early times, some distinctive crafts were organized in the sense of being subject to a particular set of rules pertinent to their kind of work or trade. These regulations were the responsibility of three Justices (*Giustizieri*) insti-

FIGURE 7   *Shipyard Workers. Caulkers and sawyers as portrayed on the central portal of San Marco, soffit of third arch (Photo Alinari).*

tuted by Sebastiano Ziani in 1173 to enforce standard weights and measures and to police markets generally, probably in imitation of officials at Constantinople with which he was familiar. Officials of another kind were the *gastaldi*, appointed by the doges; their original function was to see that the doge received the labor services which were owed him by some of the industrial workers, notably the shipwrights and ironsmiths.

The multiplication of shopkeepers and craftsmen produced not only new regulation by the government but new associations which formed themselves spontaneously. The earliest of these were not strictly along occupational lines. They were associations for religious devotion and mutual aid, open to persons of various occupations. Each such fraternity had its own special place of worship, usually a chapel or altar. It had a meeting place maintained by a contract with one of the parish churches or one of the monasteries. These religious fellowships included both rich and poor and gave aid to members who fell into misfortune. There were at least fourteen such religious fraternities, called *scuole*, before the end of the twelfth century.

By that time, some scuole were composed exclusively of men engaged in the same craft or trade. When the scuola then undertook to regulate the commercial or professional activity of its members, it became what we call a guild. As long as they appeared as associations with voluntary membership for worship and mutual assistance in misfortune, guilds were viewed as unobjectionable. Even when they began making rules about their profession and electing officers to act for them, they were still quite legal, and their guild regulations could be quite compatible with those of the Justices, for a prime concern of both was to eliminate certain varieties of what we would still call "unfair competition," namely, shoddy workmanship, excessive hours (after dark), inferior materials, etc. But some guilds felt strong enough, as did the tailors, to act as a cartel setting prices and boycotting consumers who would not meet their terms. The Justices, being charged with protecting consumer interests, forbade unilateral price-fixing and boycotts by the tailors' guild. In 1219, they revised its statutes and in so doing laid down a series of basic regulation which all in the trade were bound by oath to obey.

Significantly, the guilds for which there is the earliest evidence did not represent the most important professions or occupations. Not only was there no guild of merchants engaged in foreign trade, nothing comparable to the *Arte di Calimala* of Florence, nor any guild representing judges, lawyers, and notaries (although such a guild for the legal profession played a dominant role in nearby Padua); there was also no guild of mariners, neither of masters and mates, nor of ordinary seamen, at least not until a very late date (see Chapter 28). The seamen lacked a guild for the same reasons general merchants did; they were too numerous and the functions performed by the Commune left no sphere in which such a guild might have operated. There were, to be sure, a number of religious fraternities honoring Saint Nicholas, the patron saint of seamen, and containing mainly fishermen, or pilots, or mariners, but the oath required of seamen was prescribed by the maritime code of 1255, not by any guild statutes, and seamen had no organization of their own in the thirteenth and fourteenth centuries to advance their professional interests. The guilds first recorded and officially regulated were the tailors, the jacket makers, the goldsmiths and jewelers, the dyers, the coopers, the cordage makers, and the barber-surgeons which included the physicians. On the whole, they represented a newly rich element, or at least men who had gained moderate wealth, derived from other than maritime activities. Later in the thirteenth century, when many more guilds were approved, two types are distinguishable: those that spoke for employees — and to that extent, resembled labor unions — as did the guilds of caulkers, masons, and carpenters; and those that resembled trade associations, in that they spoke for businessmen who were employers of labor, although mostly on a quite small scale. The latter were the more numerous and more powerful and it was probably this new type of businessman, mainly shopkeepers distinct from the merchants managing maritime trade, who presented an element of ambitious unrest.

That there were movements of some kind among the guildsmen in the 1260's threatening the existing order is evident from a law passed by the Great Council and inserted thereafter in every guild statute. It strictly forbade, under threat of banishment or death, any craft to form any sworn association against the honor of the doge and his Council, or against the honor of the Commune, or against any other person — vague but sweeping language clearly showing that subversion of some kind was afoot, or at least feared. The number and activities of the Justices were increased. It was a time of political dangers. The First Genoese War was inflicting commercial losses in spite of Venetian victories. There was a tax riot in 1265 of such violence that the doge, Ranieri Zeno, a leader in the wars for the lordship of the Gulf and promulgator of the maritime code of 1255, pretended to give in to the rioters, although later he hunted out and hung the leaders. About the same time, a quarrel between two of the most prominent families reached the point of open violence when Lorenzo Tiepolo was injured in the Piazza by Giovanni Dandolo or one of his partisans. The common people began lining up on one side or the other by displaying the arms of the faction they favored, and to prevent any generalized party alignment, a law was passed forbidding commoners to display the arms of any noble house.

The dangers were dissipated through the leadership of Lorenzo Tiepolo. A national hero ever since he had broken the boom at Acre and burned the Genoese ships at the start of the war, he was elected doge in 1268. He yielded at once to the entreaty of nobles who came to reconcile him with Giovanni Dandolo. The latter, as it happened, had been one of the Ducal Councillors who presided over the electoral proceedings from which Tiepolo emerged as doge. Moreover, Lorenzo at once made clear to the guilds that the laws passed during the last years of his predecessor would not be used to destroy or cripple their organizations. Immediately after his inauguration, and as soon as he had reviewed the fleet, he ceremonially received festive delegations from guild after guild.

Within a few years, a score of important guilds had had their statutes newly revised and approved in a form which left them considerable self-government. The gastaldo who was the head of each guild was not a ducal appointee but a selection of the guildsmen, subject to the approval of the Justices. Statutes which took the form of orders by the Justices were quite often drafted by the guild's officers and voted in its general assembly. While the gastaldo's position and term of one year were standardized, the number and functions of other officials differed from one guild to another. There were usually about a dozen, chosen by a nominating committee named by outgoing officers or by lot. Some acted with the gastaldo in such technical matters as approving the promotion of apprentices; others handled the collection of dues, etc. The arrangements guilds made for religious devotions and mutual aid in illness were hardly touched at all by the Justices, except for approving the assignment of certain fees and fines to these purposes and making all practitioners of the craft or trade liable for such payments. Minor disputes in professional matters were judged by the guilds' own officials. Some guilds, such as the masons and the barber-surgeons, were even permitted to boycott an employer who failed to pay masters their due.

On the other hand, the Justices and, at a higher level, the governing councils did not hesitate to legislate on industrial questions and to cancel any measures taken by a guild but deemed contrary to public interest. Guilds were not closed monopolies; qualified immigrants could set up shop in Venice, provided they paid the dues and observed the rules. Moreover, the political subordination of the guilds was matched by an economic subordination of many guildsmen to merchants who drew their main profits from foreign trade. The shipwrights, for example, were employed by merchant owners who supplied the capital for the construction and outfitting of ships. Cordage makers were largely dependent on merchant employers who imported the hemp. In short, the suppliers of capital were in control of many branches of industry, and the chief suppliers of capital were in the governing merchant aristocracy. The policy which Venice adopted towards the guilds gave artisans and shopkeepers substantial freedom in organizing, so much so that the guilds came to number more than one hundred, but there was never any question but that the guilds were subject to the state. Guildsmen had an honorable but subordinate position in Venetian society. This combination of subordination and limited self-government was to continue for five hundred years.

If some guildsmen were dissatisfied with that status, they were probably rich members of such guilds as that of the jewelers. It has been noted that at Padua, where the guilds gained formal representation in the governing councils of the Commune in 1280, the guilds composed of modest shopkeepers and craftsmen did not furnish leaders of the republic but were content to leave that to other sections of the Paduan population, especially the lawyers. And at Florence, after its guilds became political constituencies, the small guild masters were less of a threat to the ruling class than were newly rich merchants of large affairs. The "little people" of Venice showed no discontent at being excluded from political power; one reason may well have been the outlet given them through the guilds to hold some offices of honor and have some voice in matters which concerned their daily work.

The "little people" had their part also in the festivals which were instruments of government at Venice. The chronicler who most fully records the dogeship of Lorenzo Tiepolo, namely, Martino da Canal, makes no mention of guild regulations, but he devotes many pages to describing the festival in which the doge and dogeressa received the guild masters. His choice of subject matter probably reflects what was important in the feelings of many other contemporaries. Pageantry was a vital means of communication, not so much of information, which spread like wildfire by word of mouth, so that the outcome of ducal elections was on the lips of the children in the streets before it was formally announced from the palace balcony, but as a means of communicating attitudes and feelings. In medieval cities, processions and pageants enlisted emotional participation by those being ruled more than do the television programs which are their modern equivalent. The shared experience of public ceremonies strengthened social solidarity.

Of the many festivals which occurred each year, the Wedding of the Sea on Ascension Day and the reception of the doge of the Nicoletti by the doge of the Commune have already been mentioned. Colorful parades were also marshaled for special occasions; Da Canal describes as follows part of the reception of the guilds by Doge Lorenzo Tiepolo.

The master furriers-of-new-skins had decked their bodies with sumptuous robes of ermine and squirrel and other rich furs of wild animals and had dressed their apprentices and servants richly. At their head was a fair banner, behind it they came two by two and were well marshalled with trumpets and other instruments in front. And so they came to the palace and mounted its staircase, and there where they found their new lord, Messer Lorenzo Tiepolo, they saluted him ceremoniously. And each master wished that God give him long life and victory and our lord the doge courteously returned their greeting and they all cried: "Viva, viva, nostro Signore Messer Lorenzo Tiepolo il doge," and they turned back at the command of their marshalls and went, apparelled as they were to see Madonna la Dogeressa (at the Tiepolo palace) and saluted her. . . .

The master barbers, richly decked with circlets of pearls . . . had with them two men on horseback fully armed as knights errant and with them four maidens, two on horses and two on foot, all strangely dressed. . . .

The combmakers . . . had with them a lantern full of many kinds of birds and to give delight to the doge they opened its doors and the birds inside all flew out and went flying hither and yon as they wished, and if you had been there, my readers, you could have seen everyone burst out laughing and such shouts that the birds flew every which way. . . .

Such gay festivals and guilds that were allowed autonomy without political power helped keep "the little people" acquiescent in the rule of the aristocracy. Another reason for contentment, one which the Venetians themselves emphasized and which was most important for the really poor, was an adequate supply of food. Ships and its domination of the Adriatic enabled Venice to avoid famine more effectively than did most cities and to moderate the swings in bread prices. The aristocracy boasted also of its impartial justice. Certainly the ideal of equal justice for both the great and the small was repeatedly avowed, and it was protected by elaborate safeguards, although how much it was violated in practice can only be guessed. All these factors, combined with the very topography of the city — its canals accentuating its division into some sixty to seventy small parish communities — explain why an aristocracy could govern Venice without use of force to keep down the lower classes and without any case of a genuinely popular revolt.

THE RESTRAINT OF FACTION Unity within the aristocracy was equally important in maintaining peace within the city. In communes that were shaken by uprisings of the middle or lower classes, fights between members of the ruling class gave the rioters their chance. Venice could restrain family rivalries more easily because it inherited from the Byzantine Empire a tradition of unified allegiance to a sovereign state. This unity was reinforced by many institutional arrangements some of which have already been referred to: the large number of offices and councils, the brief terms of office holders, and their ineligibility to succeed themselves. These practices made it possible to disperse powers and honors widely. No family was allowed more than one member on the Ducal Council, on any important nominating committee, or on any important administrative board. Whenever a nominee for office was being voted on, his relatives were required to withdraw.

Rivalries were reduced also by outlawing campaigns for office. Theoretically, the office sought the man, and anyone elected to office was required to serve. If he refused, he was subject to a heavy fine and made ineligible for other offices, unless excused by the Ducal Council, as he would be if he was legitimately absent from the city or about to leave on a trading voyage for which he had made contracts. Some offices were profitable and were desired on that account, so there were restrictions on the extent to which members of the nominating committees could name each other for such posts. Others, such as some of the ambassadorial missions, entailed heavy expense, and even rich men would have avoided them if possible — unless they had political ambition to match their wealth and desired the honor. But a man was not supposed to choose offices he wished to stand for; he was obligated to accept the posts for which he was picked. The requirement that a man must serve when selected expressed the Commune's claim to unqualified allegiance and accustomed members of the ruling class to subordinating their individual interests to those of the state.

We regard political parties as an essential part of any government reflecting

the will of the community, but George Washington and other founders of our
nation shared the view which was that of the Venetians and indeed all earlier
republicans, namely, that party rivalry was vicious, the destroyer of freedom.
Like the Venetians, our Founding Fathers tried to avoid it by various devices,
such as the Electoral College — unsuccessfully, as events proved.

Among the devices which they did not adopt but which the Venetians applied quite effectively, in addition to obligatory office-holding, was nomination
by lot. It was quite common in the Italian city-states of the Later Middle Ages
to place the names of qualified citizens in a bag or urn and to draw them out
blindly. Such practices, used in various ways, introduced an element of chance
and of rotation into the selection of officeholders. Drawing lots prevented a few
men, those best known on account of achievements or family, from being the only
ones to obtain the honor and power that went with office-holding. It also prevented election campaigns which would intensify rivalries, hatreds, and the
organization of factions. Its disadvantage of course was that it gave out offices
without distinguishing between men of more and less zeal and capacity.

The Venetians found a compromise which lessened the disadvantages while
keeping the one main advantage, the moderation of factionalism. Selection of
men for councils and magistracies at Venice consisted of two parts: nomination
(which they called *electio*) and approval (which we would call election). At first
the nominations seem to have all been made by the doge and his Council, but
before the end of the thirteenth century, important nominations were made by
committees whose members were chosen by lot. It was provided after 1272 that
at least two nominating committees, each chosen by lot, be required to meet
immediately and report a candidate or a slate of candidates to be voted on immediately, the same day if possible. The selection of the nominating committee
by lot and the immediacy of the nominating and the voting were expressly designed to prevent candidates from campaigning for office by appeals that would
inflame factions. On the other hand, the need of obtaining the approval of the
Great Council was a protection against the choice of incompetents.

In spite of the laws, men did seek particular offices, sometimes for personal
advantage, as is illustrated by one of the very few tales of practical personal
politics in late thirteenth-century Venice. Nicolò Querini, a member of one of
the richest and most powerful families, sought to be chosen governor of Negroponte, hoping to use the post to advance an inherited personal claim to a nearby
Aegean island. After he had failed in spite of great efforts ("gran practica," a
contemporary called it), his son Matteo Querini was named as one of the two
nominees for that post chosen by the nominating committees. When this was reported to the doge at noon as he was dining, he exclaimed: "Then the son will be
where the father could not get to be!" But the Great Council approved the
other nominee instead of Matteo Querini.

The most sought-after office, that on which party rivalries were sure to
focus if there were parties, was the dogeship. The closely contested election of
1229, when Giacomo Tiepolo and Marino Dandolo received equal votes in the
nominating committee and Tiepolo obtained the honor by lot, showed the danger.
While the dogeship gave many advantages in providing a strong executive, it
had the disadvantage of focusing family ambitions and rivalries. To obfuscate
these rivalries as much as possible and to remove their poison, the Venetians

elaborated a series of nominations of nominating committees by nominating committees and by lot. In its completed form in 1268, the process was as follows:

From the Great Council there was chosen by lot 30;
the 30 were reduced by lot to 9;
the 9 named 40;
the 40 were reduced by lot to 12;
the 12 named 25;
the 25 were reduced by lot to 9;
the 9 named 45;
the 45 were reduced by lot to 11;
the 11 named 41;
the 41 nominated the doge,
for approval by the Assembly

This seems like the *reductio ad absurdum* in indirect election of a chief executive, but it worked. The result was not absurd, its aim was achieved; the interjections of selection by lot blurred factional alignments.

In spite of all the efforts to moderate their influence, factions persisted. The denunciations and safeguards are in themselves evidence of the concern with family rivalries. In overcoming them the crowning measure was a reform in the composition of the Great Council.

ENLARGEMENT OF THE GREAT COUNCIL Although the Great Council elected all magistrates and had the final word in settling issues, the methods of selecting its own members were rather casual, easily changed, and somewhat haphazard until nearly the end of the thirteenth century. A majority of its members were in the Great Council because of some office they held or had held, such as a judgeship or a post in the Forty or Senate. Each year a nominating committee chosen partially by lot or by a system of rotation, and frequently as small as four, named one hundred additional members for the following year, members who would not be distracted from attendance by having other functions. Since only one slate of nominees was prepared, nomination was practically equivalent to election. To give to just four men chosen almost at random the power to name each year members of the supreme legislative body would have been extremely unsettling if the committee had not been bound, as were the censors in ancient Rome in their naming of the Senate, by some well-established customs about who should be chosen. Indeed membership lists show that all sections of the city and a few score families were always represented.

But there was a margin of uncertainty which widened in the latter part of the century. The majority were nobles, but some commoners also were members of the Great Council. And among the nobles there might be some question as to who was really Venetian, a question which could arise especially in regard to men whose families had been living for some time in the East, and in regard to some of the Dalmatian counts. Two dangers created a desire for change. On the one hand, a member of the nominating committee might name someone he personally admired or to whom he was personally beholden but who did not belong to a family traditionally represented in the Great Council, being instead from a family of recent immigrants and recent wealth and without any distinguished record of public service. On the other hand, as the population multiplied, which it did markedly during the thirteenth century, the nominating committee might not find room among its hundred nominees for all those who had been members and felt that their family and their public services gave them a right to continue to belong.

Proposals were made in 1286 and 1296 for changing the procedures in the yearly selection of members for the Great Council and were voted down. They were designed to deal with the first of the above mentioned difficulties, the selection of undesirables. All of them would have made the men named by the nominating committees subject one by one to a vote of approval in whole or in part, by the Ducal Council, the Forty, or the Great Council, or some combination of these councils. The resolution of 1286, that about which there is the fullest record, would have excepted from such a vote those whose paternal ancestors had been a member of one of the governing Venetian councils. It was opposed by the doge then in office, Giovanni Dandolo, who favored continuing the existing system. He was a member of one of the most solidly entrenched old families, and the majority which voted down that proposal and two others consisted overwhelmingly of nobles from relatively old families. Probably they had less objection to the emphasis on ancestors than to the provisions which would in effect have reduced the importance of the electors chosen by lot and would have given any faction which gained control of the approving bodies a chance to eliminate opposing factions from the Great Council and thus from all participation in Venetian public life.

This objection did not apply to the reform which was adopted in 1297. It contained provisions dealing simultaneously with both dangers — the danger of undesirable additions and that of excluding men who were accustomed to being included. It took care of the second of these difficulties by removing all limitations on the size of the Council and providing that all those who were already members of the Great Council or had been members during the last four years were to be members thereafter if approved by as many as twelve votes in the Council of Forty. No wonder that this proposal, giving practical assurance that those already in would continue to be members, gained a sufficient number of the members' votes! At the same time, the new law provided that other persons might be proposed for membership by a nominating committee of three when this was proposed by the doge and by his Council. These other nominees were subject to approval also in the Council of Forty, where at first they also needed a mere twelve votes out of forty to be approved. Under this procedure and the doge's sponsorship, a number of commoners of old Venetian families were made permanent members of the Council. Also a dozen or so families from Beyond-the-Sea, refugees after the fall of Acre in 1291, were admitted to the Great Council. Its membership more than doubled, rising to over 1100.

This enlargement of the Great Council was put through by a relatively young man, Pietro Gradenigo, who succeeded Giovanni Dandolo as doge. The change he directed in the composition of the Great Council was probably designed deliberately to increase its authority and enable it to eclipse the General Assembly. At the death of Giovanni Dandolo, the populace was clamoring for the election of Giacomo Tiepolo, son of the former doge Lorenzo and himself also a victorious admiral. Since Giacomo's father and grandfather had both been doges, his election might seem to recognize an hereditary right and be a return to the dynastic politics of which Vitale II Michiel had been the last, ill-fated practitioner. The popular demand for Giacomo Tiepolo made the other nobles all the less willing to name him. They did not wish to return to the selection by unruly popular assemblies such as were vaguely recalled to have functioned before 1172; they meant to keep the choice of the doge in the hands of their elaborately selected nominating committee. In view of the Dandolo-Tiepolo rivalry, there might have been civil war in Venice in 1289 if Giacomo Tiepolo had tried to use his popularity to gain the dogeship. On the contrary, he withdrew from the city in order to avoid a conflict, yet another man who made a major contribution to the solidity of Venetian institutions by his readiness to step aside. After the usual interlude of twenty days and after going through the sequence of selection procedures established in 1268, the nominating committee of forty-one named Pietro Gradenigo, a member of one of the oldest established families who, at thirty-eight, had already held many offices and was serving as the podesta of Capodistria. The choice was not popular, and Doge Gradenigo is said to have cherished a resentment against the common people who had shouted for the selection of Tiepolo. This is one explanation of his leadership in reforming the Great Council. Certainly one effect of the reforms was that the General Assembly became less important than ever.

Other effects were that the line between nobles and commoners was redrawn and the admission of new families into the governing class was made more difficult in the future. True, Gradenigo's reform had involved the acceptance, in about 1300, of many new families as noble. It is a mistake to consider it a move directed against commoners as a class and resented by them for that reason. To be sure, some commoners who thought they ought to have been made members of the Great Council and who were not among those admitted hated Gradenigo and conspired to kill him. For such a plot, a certain Marino Boccono was hanged between the two columns in 1300. On the other hand, there was no general movement of rebellion among commoners. The reform was put through in the middle of the Second Genoese War; it became effective just after the most costly of Venetian defeats, that in 1298 at Curzola, where the fleet was under the command of a Dandolo, a son of the former doge Giovanni. In contrast, the naval hero of the war, who even after the defeat made a daring raid into Genoa's own harbor, had the suggestively humble name of Domenico Schiavo. The giving of high naval commands to commoners in the last years of that war argues against any general antagonism between nobles and commoners. While some commoners had reasons to feel aggrieved, others had reasons to be pleased with the way the doge had widened the ruling class.

Liberality in accepting new men was short-lived. Within a few years, curbs were imposed on their admission to the Great Council. First they were required to have not merely twelve approving votes in the Council of Forty but a majority, then 25 approving votes, then 30. Additional restrictions were climaxed by a clear declaration in 1323 that, in order to be a member of the Great Council, a man must show that he had an ancestor who had held high posts in the Commune. By that date, membership in the Great Council had become permanent and hereditary and a prerequisite for election to any other council or magistracy.

Thereafter, the old line between nobles and commoners disappeared. Membership in the Great Council became the basis for that distinction. All members of the Great Council were considered nobles, and nobility was viewed not as a matter of personal life style, but as hereditary.

In thus enlarging and giving hereditary status to Venice's ruling class, Gradenigo cushioned the impacts of factional rivalries. In cities such as Florence, in which such rivalries led to abrupt shifts of power from one faction to another, the usual instrument for effecting the shift was a general assembly of the populace, for that could be relatively easily packed or swung one way or the other by changes in mood or by intimidation. Venice's Great Council, which completely replaced the General Assembly as the supreme body, could not be so manipulated. Hereditary life membership in that Council gave assurance to all members of the ruling class that they would not suddenly find themselves excluded. They were "locked" into an assured place in Venice's political life; for this reason, the reform of 1297 may with good reason be called the *"Serrata,"* as is customary. But the main moderating effect of the reform came simply from having so many different families, nearly two hundred, sharing power. The bitter animosity between some of them was submerged by the concern of other families with other issues. It became less difficult to find nobles who would act with impartiality.

In short, Gradenigo strengthened the hold of the aristocracy by enlarging its membership. A nearly contemporary lawyer and political thinker, Bartolus, who praised Venice as a successful aristocracy, regarded this as the essential. Venice, he said, was the kind of government classified as a Rule by the Few, but, he went on, "although they are few compared to the whole population of the city, they are many compared to those ruling in other cities, and because they are many, the people are not resentful of being governed by them. Also because they are many, they are not easily divided among themselves; moreover, many of them are men of moderate wealth, who are always a stabilizing force in a city."

CONSPIRACY AND THE COUNCIL OF TEN   In spite of all the measures devised to restrain factionalism, it led to one violent explosion under Doge Pietro Gradenigo. Like the crises which in most cities destroyed republican government and established tyranny, this crisis at Venice also came after a failure in foreign policy. It exploded in 1310, during the war with the pope over Ferrara, already referred to in describing Venice's assertion of her lordship of the gulf. Doge Gradenigo was the leader in the aggressive policy; he sought to take advantage of the situation within Ferrara to bring it definitely under Venetian rule, in spite of the opposition of the city's overlord, the pope. Even when smitten by the papal excommunication and interdict, by the defeat of the Venetian army in Ferrara, and by the heavy material losses suffered abroad by Venetian merchants whose wares and persons were subject to seizure under the terms of the pope's interdict, the doge refused to yield.

Gradenigo's readiness to defy the pope had been opposed all along by some rival leaders, notably by a branch of the Querini family. Personal quarrels embittered the relations between them and the doge's leading supporters, the Giustiniani and the Morosini. A member of the Morosini family who was serving as a Lord of the Nightwatch tried at the Rialto to search a Querini to see if he was violating the law against concealed weapons. The zealous official was tripped up and humiliated, and the offending Querini fined, so both were resentful.

Other Querini of the branch called the Querini of the Big House (de cà Mazor) wished revenge on a Dandolo who, when serving as State's Attorney, had been zealous in prosecuting them for an outrage committed against a Jew in Negroponte. Bitterest of all was Marco Querini, son of the Nicolò mentioned earlier, because he felt he had been inadequately supported when in command at Ferrara and unjustly blamed for the defeat. A conspiracy to kill the doge and seize power was initiated by Marco Querini who brought in his son-in-law, Bajamonte Tiepolo, to lead the revolt. Bajamonte was a son of the Giacomo Tiepolo who had stepped aside at the time of Gradenigo's election. In contrast to his father, Bajamonte was the kind of a man who justified the artistocracy's fear of giving too much prestige to any one family. When castellan at Modon, he had entertained in princely fashion and boasted of it, claiming it justified his appropriation of funds while in that office, an offense for which he was condemned to a heavy fine. Feeling that his honor was affronted, he withdrew from the city until called by Marco Querini to lead a revolt, which, if it had succeeded, might have made him the city's Signore. In other Italian cities, partisans of the pope in quarrels with the emperor were called Guelfs, and the Tiepolo-Querini faction were regarded as Venetian Guelfs since they were plotting against a government at war with the pope. But the conspiracy was motivated less by attachment to the pope and respect for his claims than by personal ambitions and hatreds.

The palaces of the Querini and Tiepolo were located across the bridge and behind the markets and shops of the Rialto. Their plan was to assemble their supporters there at night and next morning to cross the Grand Canal and proceed in two streams to the Piazza San Marco, one down the Mercerie to the eastern end of the Piazza, the other through the Calle dei Fabbri to its western end. Then they would unite in storming the ducal palace and be joined therein by a contingent which was to be brought across the lagoons by Badoero Badoer, a noble who was related to the Guelfs of Padua and who had large possessions on the mainland. But the doge received a warning, for in seeking supporters the conspirators approached at least one commoner who had second thoughts and turned informer. Gradenigo then acted with the decisiveness which characterized all his career. That same night he called to the Ducal Palace his Councillors and the chiefs of the great families on whose support he could count, and who brought supporters; he alerted the Arsenal; and he instructed the Podesta of Chioggia to intercept Badoer's band. The conspirators failed to synchronize their attacks. Tiepolo's column was delayed while his supporters plundered the public treasury at the Rialto, and Badoer did not get started on time because of a violent thunderstorm. Querini's column arrived first at the Piazza San Marco. It was at once engaged, and Querini was killed in the fighting. Tiepolo's column found itself under attack in the narrow confines of the Mercerie before it ever arrived at the Piazza. At the peak of the tumult, a woman looking out from an upstairs window let fall a heavy pot or mortar which struck Tiepolo's standard bearer so that the flag fell to the ground. Lacking a rallying point, his men retreated. The doge was thus victorious: Marco Querini was dead; Badoero Badoer was captured in armed rebellion and immediately executed; Bajamonte Tiepolo and the other nobles who had retreated safely to their palaces accepted terms which required them to go into exile.

Because the Tiepolo family enjoyed such a large popularity through many generations, some historians of later centuries pictured Bajamonte Tiepolo as a champion of the common people against a jealous oligarchy and the revolt of 1310 as an expression of popular discontent with the way in which Doge Gradenigo had reformed the Great Council. That is part of the Jacobin myth about Venice. Jacobins proposed to erect a monument to Bajamonte Tiepolo as a champion of democracy! In fact, he seems to have been simply a disgruntled noble who would have put his clique of nobles in power and might have proceeded to become the Signore of Venice, creating the kind of one-man rule that was at about that time being created in Milan by the Visconti, in Padua by the Carrara, in Verona by the Scaligers, and so on. Certainly, he had considerable support among the common people, attracted by his family name, unsympathetic towards Gradenigo, and resentful of the suffering imposed by the war. Also, many of the parish priests participated in his conspiracy. But there was no general uprising; the "little people" were divided. Nor is there any sign of a link between the Querini-Tiepolo conspirators and the guilds; the only guild mentioned in connection with the revolt was that of the painters who completed the rout of Querini's column by valiant fighting around their headquarters at San Luca. They were rewarded by the right to hoist their banner on a flag pole set up in the square where they had fought. The woman whose falling mortar had struck down Tiepolo's standard bearer received the reward she requested: permission to fly the banner of San Marco from her window on holidays, and assurance that the rent on her apartment would never be raised by the Procurators of San Marco, her landlords. (The Procurators did raise it in 1436, when her great grandson was serving in the fleet, but he successfully petitioned in 1468 for restoration of the old rate.) The palaces of the Querini and Tiepolo were destroyed, and a marker set up instead, to assure that Bajamonte would go down in history as the vilest of traitors ("il pessissimo traditore").

The difficult problem faced by the government immediately was the punishment of those implicated, and especially of those who had been permitted to go into exile. In other Italian cities, factional fights led to the formation of large bands of exiles (*fuorusciti*) who continued sometimes for generations to plot a revolution which would permit their return. The Genoese Ghibellines were able just about this time to create a government-in-exile which waged war on its own account and controlled several of the Genoese colonies. The many exiled Florentines who hoped for an overthrow permitting them to return to their native city are well known, because one of them was Dante. It seemed in 1310 that Venice's rulers might similarly be threatened by fuorusciti plotting their return. The terms under which Bajamonte Tiepolo and his band were permitted to leave Venice limited the places where they might go, but the leaders at once violated these limits and began seeking support among the Guelfs in nearby Padua and Treviso and among friends and relatives in Dalmatia and the Balkans. To counter such moves and to suppress any new plots, a special commission of ten men was created in 1310. It proved so useful that this Council of Ten became a permanent and prominent part of the Venetian system of interlocking Councils.

The Ten had chairmen of their own, three *Capi*, each of whom held his post for just one month before it passed to a colleague. Membership in the council was for only one year, and no two members could be of the same family. At first, its business consisted in overseeing the sentences against the exiles. It alleviated the penalties for those who showed themselves submissive, but tracked the others from place to place and set a price on their heads. Ten to twenty years later, it was making payments to successful killers. Partly by leniency but mainly by efficiency they eliminated Venetian fuorusciti.

After the danger from Bajamonte Tiepolo and his followers was elim- inated, the Council of Ten almost lapsed, but gradually it built a permanent place for itself in a dual role. Firstly, it was small enough so that the doge and his Council could take to it for action matters whose urgency and secrecy made seem undesirable consultation with any larger council. Secondly, it took the initiative in internal police. It was on the look-out to suppress not only any possibility of armed insurrection, but also any noble acting as if above the law, and any attempt to organize a faction or party even if merely by soliciting and swapping votes. They permitted no organized opposition. Indeed, any beginning of organized parties, even if initiated by those in power, would have been judged a corruption of public spirit.

The enlargement of the Great Council and the addition of the Council of Ten rounded out the aristocratic structure of governing bodies. They provided steadiness, fast action in emergencies, and involvement of the whole aristocracy in the deliberations leading to important decisions. Compared to the conditions in most cities, there was a general feeling of solidarity and loyalty among the Venetian nobility, and even in the relations between the ruling class and the rest of the people. But this cohesion was only relative and it was severely tested later in the fourteenth century.

A REORGANIZATION OF SEA POWER · I

The Response to the Nautical Revolution of the Middle Ages

While the Venetian aristocracy was consolidating its position domestically, reaffirming Venice's lordship of the gulf, and recovering from the defeat received in the Second Genoese War, it had to adjust its maritime and commercial institutions to profound changes in both the nautical arts and in business methods. If one may apply the term revolution to changes which went on over a period of a hundred years, one may properly call the changes about 1300 in the methods of navigation and in the construction, rigging, and armament of ships the Nautical Revolution of the Middle Ages. It was a necessary preliminary to that more celebrated nautical revolution of the Renaissance which accompanied the oceanic discoveries about two hundred years later.

THE NEW TECHNIQUES   In the medieval nautical revolution, new methods of navigation are symbolized by the mariner's compass. The compass was one element in a new haven-finding art conceived about the middle of the thirteenth century, an art known as dead reckoning. It was a triumph of mathematical thinking. Elementary arithmetic and geometry had been used for centuries by navigators in estimating distances and directions from one port to another. As information of this kind became more and more accurate and more and more in demand, it began to be compiled in "port books," which listed port by port the distances from one landmark to the next. Such a port book for the whole Mediterranean was compiled about 1250.

Then someone conceived a new method of pulling together all the information about distances and directions: he constructed the first marine chart. He did it by marking out on a full-sized parchment (a skin about 3 feet across) a grid of lines enabling him to plot the directions stated in the port books. Then he selected a scale appropriate to the size of the skin and he drew coast lines locating them according to the distance and direction from one landmark to the next. He may have had freehand sketches of small sections of the coast to work with, but he put them together by strictly mathematical methods to produce the first marine chart. It was the first map drawn to scale, indeed, the first extensive map ever made with accurate picturing of landforms. Since it was derived from the port book, it has been called a "portolano" or "portolan chart."

The earliest known portolan chart, dated about 1270, is called the *carta Pisana* because it probably came from Pisa, which may also have been the home of the first port book. Although no other examples from that century survive, portolan charts were in wide use before the end of the thirteenth century. Among the best chart makers of the fourteenth century were two Venetian mariners, Marco and Francesco Pizzigani.

About the same time that the portolan chart was created, a way was found of attaching a magnetized needle to a compass card so that it swung freely on a pivot in a box fastened in line with the keel of the ship. It indicated always what course the ship was on. By using such a compass, direction could be determined within about 5 degrees, that is, sixty-four points of the compass were distinguished. Navigators were also supplied with a traverse table, the *tavola di marteloio*. It enabled them to reduce a zigzag of courses to a straight line and thus know how next to set the helm in order to proceed on a desired route. Traverse table, compass, and sea chart provided the essentials of dead reckoning, a method of navigation still adequate for the Mediterranean and the method used by Columbus. It is notable that the basic conception of dead reckoning developed at about the same time and apparently at about the same place as another masterpiece of practical mathematical thinking, double-entry bookkeeping.

The chief practical effect of the new methods of navigation in the Mediterranean was the opening of the seas in winter. In antiquity, ships were pulled ashore or tied up at the dock from October until April. At the beginning of the thirteenth century, the seas were still closed in winter, ships being kept in harbor by fear, not so much of winter winds, as of rain, fog, or any kind of overcast in which a navigator unable to see the sun or stars might lose all sense of direction. The compass changed that; dead reckoning with a good compass enabled the navigator to plot his position in cloudy weather as well as in clear. The effects were noticeable at Venice at the end of the century, particularly in the 1290's. Instead of declaring the port open towards the end of March, as had been usual, the Great Council declared it open in February or even January. Extending navigation into the winter months changed the rhythm of voyages to Romania and Beyond-the-Sea. A spring convoy could leave late in the winter and return in May or early summer. A second, fall convoy could then leave in mid-summer and return the same fall or early winter, instead of wintering overseas as had been the rule earlier. Thus the use of winter months made possible two round trips a year.

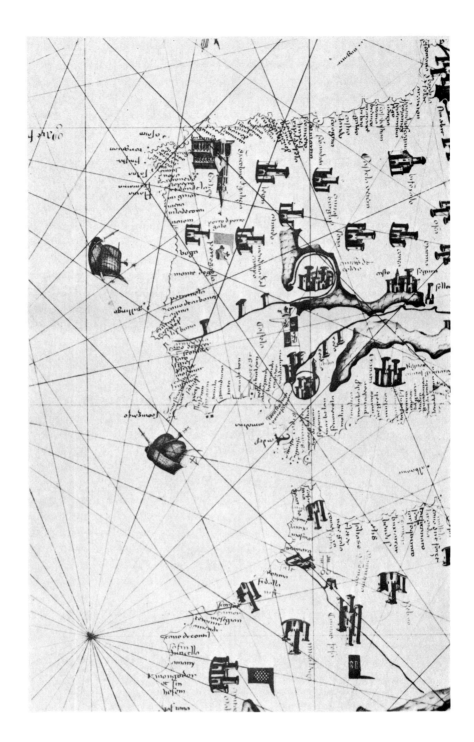

FIGURE 8 *The Pizzigani Nautical Chart of 1367. Reproduced from Prince Youssouf Kamal, Monumenta Cartographica Africae et Aegypti.*

This small section shows the 32 compass bearings for plotting courses and some of the many pictures of two-masted cogs. At the northwest corner of Spain is the church of St. James of Compostella, a famous center of pilgrimage.

The speeding up of voyages is not to be attributed to the compass alone. Essential also was the economic growth which created a demand for more voyages and markets sufficiently well organized so that ships could find cargo awaiting them and could make a quick "turn-around." Also important was the introduction, at about the same time, of new types of ships.

The change which preoccupied the Venetian government most in the 1290's and 1300's was the increased use of galleys for commercial cargoes. Triremes were then replacing biremes (see Figure 9). The larger dimensions which gave the triremes room for a third rower on each bench also provided a larger hold in which to stow cargo. The first triremes carried only approximately 50 tons; but about 1320 a more capacious galley specifically designed for trade was developed, a type called the great galley or merchant galley. It could carry about 150 tons in its hold. Even when 50 tons is added to allow for the weight of seamen's chests on deck, the total carrying capacity was small compared to the size of the crew, which numbered nearly 200. There was approximately one crewman for each ton.

The large crew, although mostly oarsmen, were not hired in order to increase the speed of the vessel. A heavily loaded merchant galley waited in port for favorable winds as did any sailing vessel and if it was a faster sailer than most, this was due mainly to its long sleek lines. The oars served as an auxiliary motor serves on a sailing ship; with oars, the vessel could maneuver better when entering or leaving harbor, could make some headway even in a calm and, when beating to windward, was not entirely dependent on tacking. The function of the oars was auxiliary but it enabled galleys to move much more on schedule than could round ships. Finally, the large crews were justified by their utility as a protection against enemies.

The change in round ships was more basic and permitted a notable saving in manpower. Innovations that had developed in northern Europe in a type called the cog were introduced into the Mediterranean after 1300. The cog was a relatively high-sided vessel with two features that wrought a revolution in Mediterranean ships: a rudder attached to the sternpost, and a square sail together with reef points and bowline (see Figure 10). The essential superiority of the single stern rudder over the two big side paddles used earlier has been contested. After the Venetian galleys adopted the stern rudder, they also carried side rudders for supplementary use. But these galleys had curved sternposts: on the straight sternposts of the cog, the stern rudder was easier to use. It entirely displaced the side rudder on large round ships.

The square rig of the cog was its main labor-saving feature. The single large square sail of the cog could turn either edge to windward, while a bowline prevented the windward edge from curling away from the wind. It had reef points to permit shortening sail and a bonnet to enlarge the sail area. In contrast, a lateen sail was cut so that the same point or corner had to be kept to windward. Shifting from one tack to another with a lateen rig, it was necessary to swing the yard around the mast, a laborious and dangerous operation with a long yard. Laborious also was the changing of the sails on a lateener as the wind freshened or lightened. For these operations, the big two-masted lateeners required more hands than were needed for the square rig of the cog. The saving in labor was sufficient to account for the adoption of the square rig in the Mediterranean.

FIGURE 9   *A Great Galley, Early Fifteenth Century.*

Because it was a trireme, the oars projected in groups of three. The rowers were seated three on a bench, each pulling a separate oar. (See also Figure 35.)

Triremes called "light galleys" which were designed for patrol and battle had one lateen sail. When the great galley was developed for commercial use, it had two or three lateen sails with the largest forward as shown here. The picture on Fra Mauro's chart of slightly later date (Figure 27) seems to be a clumsy attempt to depict a similar rig. For the sails of great galleys at the end of the fifteenth century, see Figures 21, 33.

The change from two-masted lateeners to one-masted cogs took decades, however. The first mention of a cog at Venice is in 1315, and not until after the middle of the century did *"cocha"* become the common designation for a large round ship. Nor is it by any means sure that all vessels called "coche" were one-masted. The ships sketched for decoration on the Pizzigani chart show a square sail on the mainmast, but also a second mast aft with a lateen sail (see Figure 8). There is no reason to doubt that lateen sails continued to be used on fishing boats and other small craft, as they certainly were on galleys. It is to be presumed, therefore, that the Venetians and other Mediterranean seafarers very soon experimented with adding some lateen-rigged sail to the square-rigged cog. The size of their ships suggested more than one mast. At the end of the fourteenth century, the Genoese were building many round ships as big as 1,000 tons. The Venetians were restrained by the shallowness of their harbor, but they also built vessels bigger than even such thirteenth-century giants as the *Roccaforte.* A cog built by the government for military use in 1422–25 and then hailed as the biggest ever, at least for Venice, was 92 feet long in the keel and was rated as 720 tons (1,200 *botti*). It seems likely that a vessel of that size had more than one mast.

The crews even on vessels without oars were extremely large compared to the size of the ship, at least by modern standards, but were diminishing relatively. Approximately 1 man for each 5 tons was required in the thirteenth century; the law specified 50 seamen for a 240-ton lateener of that date. No person under eighteen and no soldier or pilgrim could be counted as part of this crew. Approximately 1 sailor for each 10 tons was legally required on the cogs which came into use during the fourteenth century; regulations called for 20 adult sailors and 8 apprentices on a cog of 240 tons. To be sure, these cogs were ordered to carry for their defense additional crew classified as bowmen, numbering 4 to 8, according to the danger of the voyage. For comparison, it may be noted that when English ships first competed for cargo in the Mediterranean

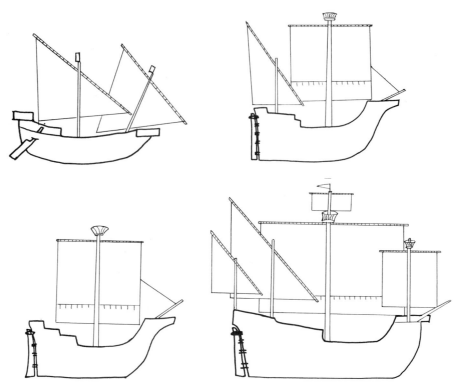

FIGURE 10   *Sail-Plans of Round Ships.*

(a) Two-masted lateener (compare Figure 3); (b) One-masted cog (compare Figure 27); (c) Two-masted cog (compare Figure 8); (d) Four-masted carack (compare Figures 2, 17, and 37).

in the seventeenth century they, like the old lateeners, carried 1 crewman for each 4½ to 5 tons. Seventeenth-century English ships did not need that large a crew to work the sails; they had large crews in order to fight off pirates or indulge in a little piracy themselves. After the introduction of the cog with its labor-saving features, the size of crews on big merchantmen was determined by how much provision was made for combat.

CONVOYS AND THEIR PROTECTION   The share of particular cities in inventing the new techniques of navigation and shipbuilding can not be determined in any detail. The different uses made of them are more clearly distinguishable, for they varied according to the political and economic situations. At Venice, a respected government focused on providing regular and secure transportation on well-defined routes. For some types of ships, the government selected the ports of call. Year by year it revised a voyage plan in the way it thought would contribute most to Venice's position as a staple city and a golden link in the chain of trade between East and West.

In this regulatory plan, great galleys and cogs were treated differently. While cogs and other round ships which formed the bulk of the Venetian mer-

chant marine were given freedom in timing their voyages for grain, salt, and
other such commodities, great galleys were operated on regularly scheduled
freight lines and carried the most precious cargoes. In the first few decades
of the fourteenth century, the Senate worked out the pattern of voyages and the
methods of administration which continued with some interruptions and exten-
sions for about two hundred years.

The crucial factor in the success of these voyages was the protection they
offered against various forms of organized violence, or, to put it differently,
the advantage they gave to Venetian shippers by providing them with better
protection at less cost than was available to their competitors. Improvements
in nautical techniques were of course productive in the long run through
lowering the costs in men and materials that were involved in overcoming the
hazards of wind and wave and other natural obstacles to maritime transportation. That was their main importance for economic growth as a cumulative
process and for the very long run. But the immediate effects on costs of such
"inventions" as the mariners' chart probably entered into the calculations of
merchants and shipmasters far less than the changing tariffs, the risks of spolia-
tion by a foreign prince or by ships of a rival city, or the price of adding soldiers
to the crew in order to prevent such loss. These costs of protection were among
the most important factors in business success.

To some extent, they were variable costs from the point of view of the individual businessman. They varied according to his choice of the kind of vessel
on which he paid freight. They varied according to the vessel's armament and
the ports to which it went. Generally, the lowering of protection costs or
gaining an advantage over a competitor's cost of protection required some form
of cooperative action, such as that undertaken later in oceanic commerce by the
chartered joint-stock companies of commerce and colonization, for example, by
the East India companies. The Venetian Commune was so completely dominated by merchants engaged in international trade that they needed no separate
organization for such purposes. The government organized convoys and took
all other necessary measures for the protection of Venetian merchants abroad.
Significantly, the planning body for overseas shipping became the council in
charge of foreign affairs, the Senate. Its frankly avowed purpose was to help
Venetian merchants make profits. It did so chiefly by organizing fleets and
commercial privileges so as to lower the protection costs of Venetian merchants.
The resulting flow of trade through Venice raised most gratifyingly the tax
receipts of the Commune.

In organizing protection for Venice's international trade, the Senate took
advantage of the new types of ships and new techniques of navigation. The
amount spent on protection had to be appropriately related to the value of the
commodities being protected. This meant that the most valuable merchandise
was most appropriately carried by great galleys or very large cogs. The Venetian
Senate decided that great galleys should be used. One reason for that decision
was probably that the navigating qualities of the great galley were better
adapted to Venetian voyages than were those of the great cogs, which were
more used by Genoa. The relatively shallow draft of the galleys and the mobility
provided by their oars were an advantage in the channels of the lagoons and of
the Dalmatian coast, whereas the need of putting into port frequently for supplies was no problem on most of the Venetian routes. When it came to fighting,

the galleys had even more advantages. Most important was the large fighting force provided by the oarsmen. In addition, their oars enabled a fleet of galleys to act together as a fighting unit; if one was attacked, the others could come to its aid. To take advantage of this potential, galleys going to the same ports in the same season were under orders always to go in convoy; round ships were only exceptionally ordered to keep together, and then did so less successfully. Galley fleets were regularly provided with a *capitanio* with command over the whole convoy. If necessary, the great galleys could be given an escort of light galleys. Great and light galleys could operate together much more effectively than could light galleys and cogs. For all these reasons, the great galley was the type of merchantman offering the maximum security, and the Venetian Senate encouraged or required its use for precious cargoes and in a regular, repeated pattern of yearly voyages.

The pattern was so fixed as to give Venetian merchants the advantages of relatively rapid turnover. Although galleys depended basically on favorable winds for long runs, they could keep to a schedule much better than could cogs. The Senate stipulated a timetable they should strive to follow and, in timing the voyages, considered not only political dangers but also the coordination of the movements of several fleets. It aimed with some success at concentrating exchanges in foreseeable periods in which wares could be quickly sold and capital readily invested in new cargo. For this purpose it provided that specified wares could be loaded only on galleys and only during specified periods.

The most striking of the voyages of the merchant galleys was that from the Mediterranean out into the Atlantic and through the English channel to the North Sea. Even before the Nautical Revolution of the Middle Ages, fleets had occasionally sailed around western Europe, as did Sigurd the Norseman, who helped the crusaders take Sidon in 1110; but merchants had preferred overland routes through France and the fairs of Champagne. The essential of Venice's trade westward was access to the markets and woolen goods of Flanders; and as the fairs of Champagne were hurt by actions of French kings, more and more use was made of the all-water route to Bruges, which was a point of juncture of many of the trade routes of northwestern Europe. At Bruges, the Venetians could find a market for their spices and other oriental wares and a supply of Flemish cloth, produced partly in Bruges, partly in nearby towns, as well as other products from the northwest, such as English wool and tin.

Shipment all the way by sea from the Mediterranean to Bruges was begun by the Genoese in the 1270's, and early in the next century Venetians also were making the voyage. Ships called at Lisbon and then sailed north-northeast by the compass from Land's End in Galicia, Spain, to Land's End in Brittany, or until soundings brought up gray sand followed by ooze, which told them they had gone far enough north to turn east-northeast into the English channel. Some stopped at Southampton for part of their cargo, but their best markets were beyond the Straits of Dover. If politics made Bruges impractical, they went on to Antwerp, but Flemish products and the Flemish trade center so dominated initially that they were called the "galleys of Flanders" even if no Flemish port was visited.

Both cogs and great galleys were used, but the Venetian government contracted to have great galleys built for the voyage when it decided in 1314 that private initiative in the field was not adequate. Operators of galleys wanted them large so that they could collect more freight; the government wished them not too large lest they be less maneuverable and so less secure, and less fitted for operation in convoys with other galleys on the Mediterranean voyages. Dardi Bembo, the leader of the operators, built galleys bigger than the government had specified and then obtained from the Senate a pardon for the offense. He made the voyage to Bruges between spring and fall with three galleys in 1317 and five in 1318. A fleet of five galleys meant a fighting force of about 1,000 men, an armament sufficient to give some assurance of safety to merchants and their cargoes, even in unfamiliar situations where local force was decisive. Dardi Bembo's voyages were not altogether peaceful; in Majorca he "liberated" some Greeks who had been enslaved by the Catalans (stole their slaves, the Catalans said) and in Southampton his crews were involved in a fight which had the effect of interrupting trade between Venice and England for several years. But at Bruges and Antwerp, relations were more friendly; the Venetians obtained trading rights and established consulates.

After about twenty years, the officially regulated voyages of the Flanders galleys were suspended for a couple of decades. One reason was the beginning of the Hundred Years War between France and England. Another was the war in the Mediterranean between the Genoese Guelfs and the King of Naples on one side and the Genoese Ghibellines and the King of Sicily on the other. In 1336, two Venetian galleys were separated by a storm from the rest of the fleet returning from Flanders and put into a Sicilian port. There they were seized by a Grimaldi, the Guelf whom contemporaries always referred to as "the monk" because he had used a monk's cowl as disguise in seizing the castle at Monaco which became and remains his family's stronghold. In fact, neither Genoese war fleet, Guelf or Ghibelline, could be trusted to refrain from pillaging Venetians, especially if the prize was attractive. A merchant galley fleet was a rich prize indeed, and although these fleets of 5 to 10 vessels formed a formidable fighting force when they kept together, they were no match for a war fleet that might number 15 to 30 war galleys. Moreover, the Venetians had no secure base in the western Mediterranean in which to regroup and refit in case of need. On the other hand, the routes over the Alps through Germany were being improved, and Venice's access to them became more secure after she overthrew the Scaliger rulers of Verona and in 1339 secured Treviso. For forty years thereafter Venetian trade to the northwest went mainly through Germany and Switzerland.

In the East, politics were even more decisive in determining trade routes; and in Romania, where Venice had once ruled as co-conqueror of the Byzantine Empire, she was not ready to give up galley voyages merely because they might face hostile fleets. After the Greeks re-established the Byzantine Empire, Venice never recovered the kind of monopoly she had had when there were Latin Emperors of Constantinople, but for decades she clung to the hope of doing so by restoring the Latin Empire. Claims to the imperial throne of Constantinople had been inherited by French nobles who were kings of Naples. They sometimes seemed strong enough to make serious efforts at rewinning Constantinople, and in that hope the Doge of Venice kept his title of "Lord of One Fourth and One Half of All the Empire of Romania." By the peace of 1299 which ended the Second Genoese War, the Genoese had abandoned the Greek emperor who had been their ally. The Venetians were left free to pillage his subjects, and did so profitably, but could not then trade advantageously at Constantinople.

Venetian raids finally induced the emperor to conclude a truce and pay reparations for damages Venetians claimed to have suffered, but the Genoese had gained a dominant position at Constantinople and the Black Sea while the Venetians were settling their war with the emperor. The self-governing Genoese colony at Pera, just across the Golden Horn from Constantinople, grew larger and larger and made its own rules on trade and tariffs. They routed so much of the commerce of the Black Sea through Pera that it was soon handling more commerce than Constantinople itself. They fortified their colony at Kaffa in the Crimea and surrounded it with outposts. With these strongholds and that in the Aegean at Chios, they dominated Upper Romania, its northern part, while the Venetians continued to dominate economically as well as politically Lower Romania through their possession of Crete and their outposts in the Morea and Negroponte.

While the Byzantine Empire was being thus weakened within, Turkish armies, firmly planted just east of the Bosphorus, threatened it from without. To repel the Turks, the Greek emperor called in a company of Catalan mercenaries, but they revolted and lived by plundering until they systematized plunder into a local government of their own. On both land and sea there was a lack of dependable protection.

Under these conditions, Venice generally organized as war fleets the great galleys she sent to Romania to carry merchandise. Not only the commander of the whole flotilla, the capitanio, but also each master (*patrono*) in command of an individual galley was a salaried official appointed by the Commune. The master was operating a state-owned ship for the profit of the Commune and was personally bound by oath to make sure that all cargo paid freight, to be present whenever wares were loaded, to search in the straw in the hold to make sure there was no hidden cargo, and to keep the hatches bolted down when he and the ship's scribe were not present. He was also responsible, of course, for fighting the ship. All departures and ports of call were determined by the capitanio according to the instructions from the doge and various Councils.

Fleets so organized could easily be dispersed for trade or concentrated for offensive or defensive military operations, or reinforced by a fleet of light galleys. In addition, there was much private shipping in the Aegean including some galleys and smaller long ships as well as cogs and smaller round ships. These vessels not only carried humbler cargoes, such as grain or salt, they concentrated higher-priced wares at the great galleys' main ports of call — Constantinople, Negroponte, Coron, and Modon. Smaller ships acted as feeders for the main line, provided by the Communally owned great galleys.

The economic decline of Upper Romania made Constantinople less important in itself than it had once been, but it remained crucial as a way station to the ports of the Black Sea. The Venetians increased their activities there after the Byzantine emperors began favoring Venetians in order to check the Genoese. Black Sea ports were active not only in supplying Constantinople itself but also as outlets for trade from the East and in slaves. Trebizond under its independent Greek emperor had a common frontier with Persia and, although Persia's Mongol Khans turned Moslem, disappointing the efforts of Christian missionaries, they remained enemies of the Mamluks who ruled in

Egypt and Syria. They kept open, as a rival to the Red Sea route, the route from Trebizond to the Persian capital of Tabriz and then across the Iran plateau to Ormuz (the route Marco Polo had taken on his return — see Map 6). Moreover, Persia itself yielded many products in demand in the West: silk, drugs, pearls, indigo, and brocades. The immediate hinterland of Trebizond was rich in minerals. In 1319, Venice, concluded a commercial treaty with its emperor and ordered the galleys of Romania to extend their voyage to Trebizond. Apparently, they found coasting northern Asia Minor a relatively dangerous operation. If any ran aground, and two or three did, they were plundered and the crews enslaved by the Turkish rulers of the region around Sinope. But the Venetians built themselves a large fortified quarter in Trebizond, as the Genoese had already done, and in the 1320's and 1330's were sending nearly every year eight to ten great galleys into the Black Sea.

In 1322, the admiral of the Romania fleet was ordered to detach two galleys which would go from Constantinople to Tana, while he went with the rest of the fleet to Trebizond. Tana was located at the mouth of the Don river and to reach it required navigating nearly the whole length of the Sea of Azov. When the elder Polos went from Soldaia in the Crimea to the Don and Volga they went overland, as did other western travelers in the thirteenth century. In 1320 the main base of operations for Venetian merchants on the northern shores of the Black Sea was still at Soldaia (compare Maps 5 and 6). The Genoese base at Kaffa was closer to the Sea of Azov, and probably the Genoese were the first Italians who learned how to navigate the Sea of Azov with large vessels. At least its coasts and ports first appear on portolan charts which were made by Genoese. They were already in Tana in 1322. But if the Genoese were the pioneers in the Azov voyage, as in the Atlantic voyages, the Venetians did not propose to let the Genoese have a monopoly, nor even to take second place there. Tana had distinct advantages over Soldaia and even over the Genoese stronghold of Kaffa. It was five hundred miles nearer to a route that ran from the Don to the Volga and then along the Caspian to the chief silk-producing region of Persia. It became also the main point of departure in the fourteenth century for a number of Italian merchants who went all the way to China. Tana also offered the largest and most varied supply of slaves, who were in demand for domestic service in Venice and Florence, as plantation labor in Crete and Cyprus, or as soldiers in Egypt.

As the Romania-Black Sea voyages became less military and more commercial, the Senate voted to turn the operation over to private enterprise. But it decided to keep control of the galleys, for if the political situation worsened, the Senate might wish to place them again under Communal operation. The Communal Arsenal was being enormously enlarged and it seemed wise to give it employment in time of peace. In 1329 the Senate established the practice of auctioning government-owned galleys so as to charter them to the highest bidder. He undertook to operate them for one voyage on a specified route under designated conditions. The successful bidder became the master (patrono) of the galley which he, or the syndicate which he headed, had won at the auction, provided he was subsequently approved by the Senate as an appropriate person of suitable age. He then hired the crew and arranged for cargo. But the capitanio of the fleet was still a salaried government official elected in the Great Council. Wages, freight rates on the main categories of cargo, times of sailing, and ports of call were all determined by the Senate and were taken into account by the galley master when he made his bid.

The system of auctioning Communally owned galleys for private operation proved so successful on the Romania run that it was soon applied to the third main trade route, that to Egypt and Beyond-the-Sea. Trade with Egypt had resumed soon after the fall of Acre, in spite of the papal ban against it. In 1302, Venice concluded a treaty with the Mamluk Moslem ruler, the soldan, which restored her trading rights. During the next decade, a few fleets operated directly by the Commune made voyages which combined calls at Alexandria and at Cyprus or Syria. In years when those seas were judged safe, the trade was left to private shipowners. But the pope persisted in forbidding all trade with Egypt — not only trade in contraband, but all commerce. In 1322, a papal envoy came to Venice and excommunicated many leading citizens, including the Procurators of San Marco, in an effort to collect the penalties claimed by the pope from the many persons who had violated his ban. The Signoria protested the excommunications vigorously, but yielded to the extent of forbidding the trade, so that for the next twenty-three years no Venetian ships went to Egypt.

A substitute for direct trade with Egypt and Syria was provided by the little Christian kingdom of Armenia and its port of Lajazzo. As explained in connection with Marco Polo's travels, Lajazzo was a Mediterranean outlet for trade coming from India through the Persian Gulf. It was also an export center for silk and other products from Persia and from Armenia itself. Its Christian rulers, being surrounded by Moslem Turks, Mongols, and Mamluks, were very friendly towards the Christians of the West and readily renewed treaties granting favorable commercial terms to the Venetians. In the early decades of the fourteenth century, Lajazzo was the main terminus of the Venetian fleets that went to Beyond-the-Sea.

In spite of the pope's ban on trade with Egypt, much of the merchandise that the Venetians loaded at Lajazzo came from Mamluk lands to the south — cotton and other products from Mamluk-ruled Syria and drugs and spices brought through Syria from far-off Asian sources by way of the Red Sea. The Mamluk soldan permitted this trade to Lajazzo, for he received directly or indirectly most of the tolls that these wares paid as they crossed the frontier. The kings of Armenia turned it over as tribute to avoid Egyptian conquest.

Another big gap in the imagined blockade of Egypt was Tunis. Venetians were very active there in the early fourteenth century. The government negotiated with the ruler of Tunis treaties for their protection but left shipping in those waters entirely to private enterprise, not even organizing protective convoys.

Cyprus, a third intermediary in Egyptian trade, was sometimes a terminus of regulated galley fleets. More often it was a way station for convoys going to Armenia. Its kings had inherited a shadowy title to the extinct kingdom of Jerusalem and also its colonies of foreign merchants. In Cyprus these colonies continued an obstreperous autonomy such as they had practiced in Palestine, with similar obligations to join in the defense of the realm, and the same rivalry among themselves.

The ships which the Venetians sent to Cyprus and Lajazzo in the 1320's were privately owned and privately operated. In most seasons, the Commune did not even determine how many might go nor offer any special inducements.

Owners of a private galley could decide, each partnership for itself, whether to send the vessel on that trip or on some other. If they did send it to Beyond-the-Sea, they had to register it in advance, place it under the command of a government-appointed admiral, obey his orders about navigation, and obey a number of regulations concerning the commodities freighted. In that sense, they were "regulated voyages," but their operation was basically a matter of private initiative.

In the 1330's, these privately owned vessels were replaced by state-owned galleys auctioned for private operation. Thereafter, the number of galleys and their routes were determined not by decisions of private partnerships but by a vote in the Senate. Freight rates and general rules about the handling of cargo and the treatment of crews were continued as they had been. In determining the number of galleys and the ports of call the Senate was guided, as the private companies of shipowners had been, by their judgments on the political situation and the demands of merchants with wares to ship.

Striking changes in the eastern trade routes occurred in the 1340's. Direct commerce with Egypt was resumed as crusading energies turned away from the Holy Land and focused on the Turkish threat in the Aegean. These Turks appeared increasingly dangerous, and it was recognized that control of the Aegean was a prerequisite for any new attack on Egypt. In accord with these conceptions, the crusading order of Knights Hospitalers of St. John was established on the strategically placed island of Rhodes, and a league of crusaders conquered Smyrna in 1344. Christian control of Smyrna somewhat checked Turkish piracy, and the Venetians gained at least that benefit from the 5 to 10 galleys they contributed to that crusading fleet. Moreover, Venetian cooperation with the pope in organizing crusades in the Aegean, together with large payments for papal licenses, moved the pope towards granting Venice permission in 1344 to send again ships to Alexandria.

The opening of Alexandria was all the more vital in the 1340's because the Persian khanate dissolved in civil war so that its routes were unsafe. Lesser Armenia, having lost its vital role as an intermediary, succumbed to Mamluk attack. In the same decade, a riot at Tana, touched off when a Venetian killed a native, roused the Khan of the Golden Horde to an attack which closed that port for some years after 1343 and placed Kaffa in danger. Political events in the 1340's thus heightened the natural advantages of the Red Sea route as the main thoroughfare to India and the Far East.

Adjusting to these kaleidoscopic political changes in Asia and to the occasional waves of crusading fever, the Venetian Senators rapidly negotiated new treaties whenever necessary and directed the fleets of auctioned government galleys, now to one port, now to another, wherever they judged the costs of a safely protected trade would be least. Lajazzo in Lesser Armenia was of course abandoned. One fleet went almost every year to Cyprus and sometimes continued on to Palestinian ports or to Syrian ports, such as Beirut (see Map 9). Another fleet went regularly to Alexandria, except for such interruptions as those occasioned by the next two Genoese wars. And after these conflicts, the voyages to Flanders were resumed, so that at the end of the fourteenth century there was established, in spite of variations and interruptions, an enduring pattern of four main routes for merchant galleys: (1) to Romania, (2) to Cyprus or Syria, (3) to Alexandria, and (4) to Flanders.

FREE These galley fleets were only a small part of the total Venetian merchant
VOYAGING marine. Most merchantmen did not sail in convoys. Even merchant galleys,
which were privately owned to a considerable extent in the fourteenth
century, made many voyages in isolation, since the laws required that they
convoy each other only in case they were going to the same port. Many sailed
unarmed, that is, with a crew of less than sixty, and in that case they were
more than ever dependent on their sails. Small craft, those of less than 100 tons,
were hardly ever in convoys, and although the big round ships — the cogs which
ranged from 200 to 500 tons and which very often carried cargoes of high value —
were frequently ordered to convoy each other, they did not do so as a general
rule.

Because the routes and times of sailing of these "unarmed ships" were
determined by contracts between operators and shippers, their activity may be
called "free voyaging" (*navigazione libera*) to contrast with the closely controlled voyages of the state's merchant galleys. On many routes, free voyaging
supplemented or for long periods took the place of officially scheduled voyages.
Trade to Tunis, already mentioned, is one example. Another example in the
western Mediterranean was the salt trade at Iviza. This smallest of the Balearic
Islands attracted ships of many nationalities because its salt was so useful in
completing cargoes. The Cocco family of Venice for some generations operated
both round ships and galleys between the Balearic Islands, ports in the western
Mediterranean, and the English Channel. Wine was another important item in
the cargoes of many cogs going beyond the Straits of Gibraltar. In freighting
such commodities as wool, these ships had to compete with wagons or pack animals going over the Alps, but wine casks could not stand the joggling of such
travel by land. The growing taste of northerners for the sweet wines of Greece
could be satisfied only by water transport and of course cogs which loaded tuns
of wine carried other merchandise as well.

Cogs became also the chief grain carriers all over the Mediterranean. Most
of Venice's food supplies came by sea from Adriatic or Ionian ports, but ever
since the 1260's more and more had come from further away, particularly from
Upper Romania and the Black Sea. Constantinople in its prime had absorbed
the grain surpluses produced around the Black Sea, but as it declined both economically and politically, those surpluses were more and more used by Venetians and Genoese to meet Italian demands. Much wheat and salt fish also came
to Venice from as far away as Tana.

Tana was likewise the main source of supply for a flourishing slave trade.
Slavery in the medieval Mediterranean differed markedly from the slavery
known through American history. It was not associated with any particular race
or color. Characteristics of the yellow race were prominent among those offered
for sale in Tana because many of them were Tatars from Central Asia, but many
others were Russians or blond types from the Caucasus. Neither was slavery
always associated with menial labor. In the Turkish and Mamluk states, the
crack army regiments were composed of men who had the legal status of slaves
of the ruler and who kept that status even when they rose to high commands. In
the Aegean, raiders carried off rich and poor, educated and uneducated alike,
and sold them as slaves while their families or friends made efforts to buy them
back. But the biggest markets were for slaves to serve in inferior positions: in

Crete and Cyprus for plantation workers, in Egypt for additions to the lower ranks of the soldiery (which were all recruited by purchase), and in Venice, Florence, and other Italian cities for domestic servants.

The slaves were exported from the Black Sea mainly in cogs; carrying them on Venetian galleys was against a law to which there were many exceptions, and of which there were even more violations, as the Senate complained in 1412 when reinforcing the prohibition. On round ships, the number allowed was limited, probably not altogether because of fear of revolts, since most of the slaves were young women and children. In 1381, the number allowed was raised from three to four for each member of the crew, so that a 400 ton ship with a crew of 50 could carry 200 slaves. The cogs of that size at Tana loaded mainly grain or slaves.

Venice was gradually ceasing to be the emporium of slave traders which it had been when a plentiful supply came from central Europe and the Balkans. At the beginning of the fourteenth century, most of the slaves bought or sold by Venetians were Greeks. The number of Greek slaves was increased by the raids of the Catalan Company, but later in the century, a feeling against enslaving Greek Christians developed in the West, and the Black Sea became the main source of supply of human merchandise. Although the slave trade in Crete boomed because it became a center for reshipment to markets in Africa and western Europe, in Venice itself slave auctions at the Rialto were forbidden in 1366. For about a century thereafter, many slaves were imported to Venice from the Black Sea, especially Tatars and Russians, but sales were by private contracts. Export to other Italian cities required permits. The high proportion of boys and young women in recorded sales accords with other indications that slaves were used mostly as domestics or concubines.

In Lower Romania and Beyond-the-Sea, cogs loaded not only heavy cargo such as grain, salt, hides, alum, and soda or potash but also much cotton and other merchandise classified as "light goods." In regard to such "light goods" the government tried to impose a rough timetable of loading periods, called *mude*, somewhat as it did more rigorously on the merchant galleys. It set dates within which cogs must load "light goods" in the Levantine ports if they were to clear the Venetian customs in the same season. The loading periods varied by regions and were adjusted to changing circumstances. The following was the general plan laid down in 1328 for ships from Romania:

> From Constantinople and Upper Romania:
> March 15 — April 15 and September 15 — October 31
> From Lower Romania (including Crete and Negroponte):
> April 15 — 30 and September 15 — October 31

One purpose served by these loading periods was to make the cogs move sufficiently on the same schedule so that they could be organized into convoys if the political situation justified it. Another result was to define predictable periods of arrival and departure in the eastern ports so that merchandise would be concentrated there at those seasons and ships would not have to wait long to secure return cargoes. At Venice, arrivals and departures were concentrated so as to intensify trade and turnover in two seasons, roughly at Christmas and in July. The rhythm of Venetian voyages in both galleys and cogs was thus adjusted to take advantage of the new nautical techniques and to meet the demands of the Venetian market, especially the desire of Venetian merchants for a rapid turnover of their capital.

A couple of centuries earlier, the Venetian ships had carried out a swarm of traveling merchants who stayed two or three months in the Levant, selling the wares they had brought with them and finding new merchandise in which to invest. At that time, Venetians had been using their military power, political privileges, and cheap shipping to cut into a system of commercial exchanges which had been organized around the capitals of the Byzantine and Moslem worlds. In the fourteenth and later centuries, the trade of the Venetians centered in Venice, and their profits were based on a system of voyages appropriately timed and protected.

A REORGANIZATION OF SEA POWER · II

The Commercial Revolution of the Resident Merchants

Compared to commercial changes in later centuries when trade vaulted from one side of an ocean or continent to another, the shifts occurring about 1300 may seem minor, but they have been characterized as a "Commercial Revolution." Especially striking geographically were the changes in western Europe, when the new routes to Bruges replaced those that had tied northern and southern Europe together through the fairs of Champagne. But the most significant aspect of the commercial revolution of about 1300 lay not in the geographic shifts but in changes in commercial practices. The ways of doing business which became current in the fourteenth century persisted until long after Europe had expanded into America.

BUSINESS ORGANIZATION Resident or sedentary merchants took the place of traveling merchants in much of western Europe and in the Mediterranean. When voyages became more regular and colonies were established in distant centers, traders no longer had to travel with their wares. With trade concentrated at familiar ports, it was no longer necessary to send special agents who would wander around looking for buyers and sources of supply. There were many Venetians at the eastern termini, at Tana, Trebizond, or Cyprus, who resided there for years on end, receiving wares consigned to them and sending shipments in return. In the west, there were groups of Venetians residing in Bruges, the western terminus of the galley voyages. Not only Venice but other leading European commercial cities developed such colonies abroad. As long as each shipment meant a separate journey, fairs moving from one town to another as did those of Champagne were practical; but such movable fairs declined when merchants began shipping without going with their merchandise. They found it more practical to ship again and again to the same city.

A major problem of the resident merchant was to know people in the distant market places whom he could trust. One solution was a family partnership in which one brother lived in Venice and other brothers overseas. Partnerships of this kind were so common in Venice, especially among the rich families, that at a father's death his sons became automatically members of such a partnership, unless they took specific legal steps to separate their inheritances. An example is the partnership of Venice's richest man at mid-century, Federico Corner, with his two brothers. One brother in Cyprus shipped spices, cotton, and other Levantine wares to Venice; another marketed them there and sent back cash for further purchases, or sent such manufactured articles as a 1,600 pound copper kettle for use on the sugar plantation the Corner acquired in Cyprus. In such a partnership, each brother was fully liable for his brother's debts.

Full partnerships between persons not of the same family were also common enough at Venice by 1300. Although less enduring than family partnerships, these "terminal partnerships" lasted for a term of years specified in the contract, usually about three or five. But Venetians did not contract together to form huge partnerships embracing many persons of various families for long periods as did the famous Florentine firms of the period, such as the Bardi and Peruzzi. A Venetian family which felt it needed more capital or more personnel for its ventures was likely to employ agents on salaries or on commissions, or to form a temporary, limited kind of partnership which is best called a joint venture.

Among the most ordinary kind of joint ventures were those of the tax farmers; for example, several men contributed to a fund used to pay in advance for the right to collect the tax on wine sales. Frequent also was the pooling of funds to make a large purchase, as of pepper from the soldan of Egypt. In that case, what was jointly owned could and often was distributed physically among the participants in the venture. A jointly owned ship could not of course be thus distributed; it bound the joint owners together to share liabilities and profits during the life of the ship.

A kind of joint venture peculiar to Venice developed when the government began auctioning galleys for a particular voyage. Companies called galley companies were formed to pay the expenses and receive the freights of a galley for that voyage. Sometimes all the share owners of all the galleys in a convoy formed a single pool, what the Venetians called a *maona*, in order to make purchases that would assure them enough cargo, or the right kind of cargo, or some extra profits from buying and selling as a unit. The rapid changes in international trade and shipping gave the Venetians reason to prefer temporary and limited joint ventures of this character.

Another kind of temporary partnership was the colleganza, already described in connection with twelfth-century shipping. These contracts, by which one party contributed capital and the other labor, continued to be used in the fourteenth century for those branches of trade in which conditions still resembled those that had faced earlier traveling merchants. A striking example of a colleganza combined with a joint venture is provided by the tragic affairs of a Giovanni Loredan, who sailed with five other nobles on the galleys of Romania to Tana in 1338 to start a trip to Delhi. After the Polos, a number of Venetians had gone across Central Asia to China, but striking out east from Tana and then turning south around the edge of the Pamirs to cross the Hindu Kush mountains to India was trying something new (see Map 5). Giovanni Loredan had just come back from a trip to China. His wife and one of his brothers tried to dissuade him from the new venture, but he believed there was a fortune to be made by a visit to an Indian prince who had a wide reputation for cruelty but also for generosity to foreign merchants. Five other Venetian nobles joined in the venture: they pooled funds in order to take with them gifts they hoped would please the Indian prince, mechanical wonders: a clock and a fountain. Each also took some wares on his own account, Giovanni taking Florentine cloth, of which he sold some along the way to pay expenses. In order to raise his share of the pooled funds, Giovanni Loredan accepted money in colleganza from his father-in-law. The Indian prince must have been pleased by the gifts, for he gave the Venetians a rich present. They invested it in a joint purchase of pearls. The expedition turned out badly, however, for Giovanni Loredan and two of the other Venetians died in the course of the journey. On the way home, the pearls were divided among the partners, but Giovanni was not there to make the most of the opportunities he had dreamed of. His father-in-law sued the guardians of Giovanni's young sons to recover not only his investment in the colleganza but also the usual three-fourths of profits, asking in this case three-fourths of all the profits on Giovanni's share of the joint venture in pearls. The one-fourth left to his heirs proved small compensation for the risks of such a voyage.

For voyages in relatively unknown territory, the colleganza was still the best arrangement from the investor's point of view because it assured the stay-at-home of his claim but put the traveling merchant in charge of the enterprise, negotiating in his own name, and it made his rewards depend on the profits realized. On the relatively safe trips, however, to well-known market places such as Constantinople or Lajazzo, there was so much money seeking investment that already in the thirteenth century a sharp operator could take advantage of the less wary investors. He could accept funds from several parties, partly friends and relatives and partly small investors, then pad his expense account, charge an undue proportion of his expenses to one investor instead of another, hand over to other merchants wares he had agreed to handle himself, and perhaps even delay making a report and settlement promptly on his return to Venice. Late in the thirteenth century, a whole series of laws were passed to prevent such practices, either because the financial markets were really in such condition that the unwary investor needed protection (as he was to need it later, in the days of stock markets and the Securities and Exchange Commission), or simply because stay-at-home investors had more influence in the councils than the traveling merchants.

During the fourteenth century, the merchants who stayed at home in Venice turned increasingly from the colleganze as a means of investing in overseas trade to the use of commission agents. Instead of receiving a share of profits, a commission agent received a percentage of the turnover that he handled. His reward was the same regardless of whether the man for whom he bought and sold was making a profit. In fact, he did not need to know whether the principal was making a profit or not. He bought and sold on the account of men who sent him wares to sell and orders to buy, and he was bound to act according to the instructions sent him.

Obviously, a Giovanni Loredan could not make a trip like that through inner Asia to India as a commission agent because it would have been quite impossible for his father-in-law who was financing him to give him instructions about the opportunities or difficulties he would face. But between Constantinople and Venice or Cyprus and Venice, there was a constant stream of letters in the fourteenth century, and a merchant in Venice was sufficiently well informed about prices so that he could send instructions to his agent and could check up afterwards to see how advantageously his agent had traded for him. Because a commission agent's earnings depended on the volume of his business, he strove to satisfy his customers and gain such a reputation that many would send him more consignments and orders. In the colleganza, the agent was paid by receiving a percentage of the profits (one-fourth); in a commission agency, he was paid by receiving a percentage of the turnover he handled (3 to 5 percent). If actually the average rate of profit was 12 to 20 percent per venture, his rewards were about the same; but as a commission agent, he had less freedom of action.

The colleganze and various kinds of joint ventures continued in use but a transition to commission agents was hastened by measures restricting the colleganze, especially by a law designed primarily to exclude foreign capital. After the enlargement of the Great Council about 1300, the rulers of Venice tightened the regulations concerning admission to citizenship, as well as those concerning admission to the Great Council. They passed much legislation designed to reserve to native born or legally naturalized Venetians the profits of trade between Venice and the Levant. Venetians were forbidden to act as stand-ins for foreigners or in any way to loan their names to foreigners so that the latter could avoid taxes or participate in business reserved for Venetians. But while the colleganze was being widely used to raise money with which to buy in the East and import to Venice, how could one be sure that the importer was not really working for foreign capitalists who had given them money in colleganze? To stop that, a party among the Venetian nobles who may be called "protectionists" put through a law forbidding anyone to import from the Levant merchandise of more value than the amount of personal worth for which he was assessed for fiscal purposes. Special officials forming an *Officium de Navigantibus* were created to enforce this law, but it was in force only a few years at a time. The Officium de Navigantibus apparently received general support only when the vicissitudes of the trade routes resulted in a glut of Levantine wares in Venice. Even then it did not affect men content to act as commission agents, for they shipped not on their own accounts but in the names of those for whom they acted. But it must have galled many ambitious merchants on the make, even if they depended more on collecting colleganze from fellow Venetians than from foreigners.

The use of resident agents instead of traveling merchants was facilitated by a number of improvements in commercial technique. One was the system of double-entry bookkeeping. This way of grouping and checking the records of every transaction made it easier for a resident merchant to keep tract accurately of what his partners or agents were doing. Tradition has assigned its invention to Venice: but the evidence is against that. Earlier examples have been found in

Genoa and Tuscany. The Venetians seem to have been responsible for a number of features of arrangement and of style, however, which were later widely adopted, for example, the placing of all debits on the left, credits on the right in parallel columns. Bookkeeping and arithmetic, using Arabic instead of Roman numerals, were taught in Venice by pedagogues called "masters of the abacus." They disseminated rules for beginning each entry the same way and for making cross references from Journal to Ledger and from one Ledger account to another (see Figure 11). More closely connected with business management was the organizing of entries under various "Ventures," and the closing of venture and merchandise accounts into a "Profit and Loss Account." This kind of bookkeeping enabled a merchant operating simultaneously on many market places to know the extent of his liabilities and the extent and nature of his assets.

An essential for the resident merchant was assurance that wares entrusted to a ship could be recognized and claimed by the agent to whom he was sending them. The foundation for such assurance was laid in the provisions of the thirteenth-century Venetian maritime codes regarding the ship's scribe, who was required to keep a careful record of all the cargo, a sort of ship's manifest, and to give official copies of extracts from it on demand. From this practice developed the bill of lading, which the merchant sending the wares received from the ship's scribe and could send to his agent overseas who would use it to claim the wares consigned him.

Another important commercial technique which became common during the fourteenth century was marine insurance. In return for a premium payable in advance, the insurer promised to compensate for loss due to shipwreck or piracy. Many merchants thought insuring wares on the galleys was a waste — these vessels were so secure — but they used insurance to cover cargoes on round ships and the ships themselves.

Of yet more importance was the bill of exchange, which enabled a resident merchant to send funds to his agent, or to receive quickly the proceeds of a sale without having to run the risks either of making a new investment in merchandise or of shipping bullion. In addition to giving more flexibility to importers and exporters, the bill of exchange facilitated all kinds of political payments in distant parts, such as the expenses of a fleet or an embassy.

These techniques enabled a variety of different kinds of business organizations to exist side by side. At one extreme were the men of great wealth, heading powerful partnerships. They usually mixed politics and business, as did the Federico Corner already referred to. He affords an example of how Venetians could make money in territories which might be called colonial even if they were not politically subject to Venice. Cyprus was ruled by French nobles who had inherited also the title of King of Jerusalem — an empty title, except that it inspired them to continue the crusades in some form. When the King of Cyprus made a trip through the West in 1361, seeking allies against the Moslems, he lodged in the massive palace of Federico Corner on the Grand Canal at San Luca, and he received from Federico thousands of ducats in loans that were spent on wars. The most solid recompense that the Corner received in return was the grant of the village of Episcopi and surrounding plantations. They were watered by one of the few Cypriot rivers flowing the year round. The river was so thoroughly used by the Corner for both power and irrigation that neighbors suffered, especially the

FIGURE 11 *Mercantile Records. A Cargo List and Double Entry (courtesy of [a] the Archivio di Stato and [b] Museo Correr, Venice).*

(a) Distinctive marks were used to identify each merchant's shipment, as is shown in this portion of a cargo list of the galleys reaching Alexandria in 1418. Then came the names of the consignees, the commodity—for example, cloth (pani), quicksilver (arzento vivo), honey (mieli), copper wire (fil di rame), lead (piombo)—and then the quantities.

(b) Venetian styling of double entry is illustrated by the double crossing-out of each entry in the Journal, as in this page from the Journal for 1505–35 of Lorenzo Priuli, father of the diarist and banker Girolamo Priuli. The same style is more fully illustrated, although in more difficult handwriting, by the Journals and Ledgers of Andrea Barbarigo a century earlier. Described in the treatise on mathematics published in 1494 by Luca Pacioli, who had taught accounting at Venice, it was widely followed for centuries.

Every transaction was analyzed into a debit and a credit and entered day by day in a Journal with <u>Per</u> *(p) before the name to be debited and, after two strikes / /, an A before the name to be credited. For example: in the very simple second entry for July, 1510 (p. 143), the debit is to the account of "Hier°," that is, Girolamo Priuli, his bank; the credit is to the account of an Alvise de Franco, who made payment for a purchase of wool (lane) by a transfer from his account at the bank to Lorenzo's account.*

After each transaction was thus analyzed and recorded chronologically, each debit and credit was recorded also in a larger book, the Ledger (Quaderno), in order to group together for analysis transactions concerning the same person or the same venture. When the debit was thus posted in the Ledger, the first of the two strokes was made across the Journal entry and the number of the page in the Ledger on which the debit was recorded was written in the left-hand margin. The second stroke showed that the credit had been similarly posted and the cross-reference to the appropriate page entered also in the left-hand margin.

Although the cross-references are in Arabic numerals, as are sums in ducats within an entry, sums paid and received are recorded at the right in the more traditional Roman numerals in lire di grossi, each worth 10 ducats.

Knights of St. John, whose nearby castle and sugar mill at Kolossi can still be visited by tourists (about 10 kilometers from Limossol). The lush plantations nearby still testify to the choiceness of the Corner grant. Its produce, mostly refined on the spot, made Federico Corner a fourteenth-century sugar king.

Federico Corner, with his huge plantation and huge loans to the King of Cyprus, and Giovanni Loredan, journeying with borrowed funds to little known lands, were less typical of the kind of business organization favored by the new techniques than a merchant of later date, Andrea Barbarigo, the first from whom we have account books complete with Journal and Ledger. The moderate fortune which he left at his death in 1449 was accumulated by using the institutions favorable to resident merchants that had developed during the previous century. He bought standard commodities, such as cotton, wool, spices, copper, or cloth, shipped mainly on the regulated galley fleets, and employed a score of different commission agents, some relatives and some not. He kept his books carefully in double entry and invested up to the hilt, buying or selling bills of exchange to make the best use of his money. He had been abroad in his youth, but for decades he never went further than the Rialto. He had to go there to make and receive payments and, above all, in order to collect the news. Whether or not he made profits depended largely on what instructions he wrote to his many agents. With no newspapers giving quotations, a resident merchant relied on receiving letters from the merchants to whom he gave business and on what his ears could pick up. Without access to the Rialto, he was cut off from the flow of the information on which to base his decisions. A court sentence forbidding a merchant to go to the Rialto was the equivalent of putting him out of business.

CARTELS AND COMMON CARRIERS Venetian government was frankly and efficiently capitalistic in the fourteenth and fifteenth centuries in the sense that its decisions were aimed at enabling Venetians to make profits by commercial investments. At the same time, the contrasting kinds of merchants within the mercantile community created conflicts of interest. Rich, well-established merchants were sometimes able to use antagonism towards foreign competition so as to restrict the activities of up-and-coming Venetians, especially of those ready to use foreign capital in expanding their activities. On the other hand, some of the policies adopted seem designed to favor middling or minor merchants, so long as they were Venetian born, or achieved naturalization by twenty-five years of tax-paying residence in the city.

One expression of these policies was in the attitude of the government towards monopolistic cartels. It tried to distinguish between combines which were open to all Venetians and those that excluded some Venetians for the benefit of others. Venetians were encouraged or even compelled to join cartels in purchasing Levantine wares. In 1283, all wishing to buy cotton at Acre were required to pool their funds in such a cartel if 80 percent of the merchants voted in favor. And all Venetians in Acre were given a right to contribute to the pool and receive a share of the cotton purchased if a cartel was decided on. A cartel was usually formed also for large spice purchases in Egypt from the Mamluk soldan, who used his customs officials to organize a selling monopoly on the other side.

In contrast to these inclusive, all-Venetian cartels which were favored were those formed by a few Venetians in order to sell some commodity to other Venetians at high prices. When two producers succeeded in controlling the production of cement, tiles, and similar building materials, the government acted with a thoroughness which might arouse the admiration of the Antitrust Division. It sequestered all the kilns and then auctioned them off for operation by bidders, but no more than one furnace to a bidder. Each operator had to post bond to assure his obedience to rules that forbade having an interest in more than one kiln and that specified the prices at which he was required to sell to all comers.

Some combines were not so easily classified. For example, a group of Venetians headed by Federico Corner formed a consortium which gained a strangle hold on the export from Cyprus to Venice of sugar, salt, and cotton. A Senatorial commission of three was appointed in 1358 to inquire and formulate remedies. It did not even consider disturbing the contracts or concessions which Corner's combine had obtained from the King of Cyprus in regard to salt and sugar, but the commissioners recommended curbing the cartel's limitation on the cotton exports from Cyprus. Apparently, Corner's combine was forcing ships to accept its allocation of cotton quotas by denying any salt or sugar cargoes to those who would not obey its rules. But a proposal to simply abolish the cotton cartel was defeated. The most the anti-monopolists could gain was a general injunction that Corner's combine must furnish cargoes of salt and sugar to anyone who asked for them, and that the cartel must not be used to raise prices in Venice. Obviously, in so far as the cartel permitted cheaper purchases in Cyprus, it was considered unobjectionable, probably indeed highly desirable.

Merchants maneuvering for profits could hardly fail to appreciate the advantages of being the only buyer or the only seller, or having a representative in that position. One way to achieve it was to control all the shipping between the place where a commodity was in supply and the place it was in demand. Apparently, the Corner combine was at least close to that position in 1358 in regard to Cypriot cotton. Because his concessions from the King of Cyprus gave him control of the salt which was essential to ship captains wishing to balance their cargoes, he sought to dictate how much cotton they could load. This cartelization threatened to raise the price of cotton in Venice. And when in 1358 Federico Corner bid in three of the galleys auctioned to go to Cyprus, he may have hoped to use control of the galleys to form a similar cartel in sugar. In some years, control of the Flemish galleys was the basis for efforts to control the commodity of which these galleys had a transport monopoly for a season — English wool. The possibility may have occurred to Marino Cappello who, as head of a combine, registered as many as 7 of the 8 galleys destined for Flanders in 1333–34. They were privately owned galleys; the system of auctioning government-owned galleys was not applied to that voyage until later. Organizing a cartel, if he had such ideas, must have been made easier for Marino Cappello by the government having elected him to the post of capitanio of the whole fleet.

At first glance, it may seem that the way the Senate organized the merchant galley fleets increased the chances for monopolies. Since the Senate's decisions limited the number of ships that could make a specified voyage during a stipulated period, it restricted the number of competitors. Indeed, there must have been many occasions in the fourteenth century when monopolists took advantage of these restrictions but there would probably have been more monopolization of transport facilities if shipping had been left entirely to private enterprise. In that case, the family partnerships which were rich enough would have owned their own fleets of galleys and operated them year after year. While some might have gone bankrupt now and then trying to monopolize too much or miscalculating the mercantile opportunities or the political dangers of a voyage, they would, on other occasions, have been in a good position to make big profits by shipping their own wares only, or the wares of their business allies.

In fact, the regulations under which the government auctioned galleys included many provisions hampering efforts at monopoly. They reflect the force of broad egalitarian tendencies within the Venetian nobility. Their professed aim was to provide secure transport to all Venetian citizens equally. The regular scheduling of these voyages supplied predicable service which an individual merchant, such as Andrea Barbarigo, could use without having to take any initiative or to make any commitments of his personal capital in organizing it. The terms of the auction obligated the galley master to act fairly as a common carrier. Specified commodities had preference over others, spices generally having the highest priority. The galley master was ordered to load these in the order presented. The collection of freights on return to Venice was in the hands of customs officials, although of course for the account of the operators. Freights collected overseas, in Bruges for example, were paid to the capitanio appointed by the Commune to manage the whole fleet. This was supposed to assure that all would be charged equally.

In practice, the rules did not prevent galley masters from either giving rebates in some form or from arranging the loading of wares in ways more advantageous to some shippers than to others. If more merchandise with priority was offered than could be lawfully loaded, the capitanio was supposed to see to it that all shippers had a fair proportion loaded on the merchant galleys and that provision was made for the rest (the left-over shares, called *rata*) to be loaded on some other vessel, usually a round ship which might or might not be able to sail in convoy with the galleys. Whether the capitanio were able to enforce these and other rules on the galley masters, especially when the galley master might be as rich and powerful as Federico Corner, is doubtful. Some certainly tried. They could levy heavy fines, 1,000 ducats or so, on disobedient galley masters. The latter could then appeal, and might or might not get absolved by the State's Attorneys, the Forty, or the Great Council. Clearly, the laws were evaded many times, but their existence shows an effort by the Venetian Commune to assure to all its merchants a fair chance to ship on the main routes of trade. It acted in the same spirit as did many guilds in making rules designed to give every guild master an equal chance.

USURY AND   In the twelfth century, the Venetians showed no concern about usury; they
FINANCE   collected 20 percent on well-secured loans and called it "old Venetian cus-
            tom." Later, as the Church made its prohibition of usury more specifically applicable to laymen as well as clerics, the Venetians partially fell in line and passed laws against it. At the same time, they developed their own standard of what was legitimate gain and what was usury. Their own standard was notably different from the official doctrine of the Church. Theirs might be called a businessman's standard, not very different from that generally accepted today. It approved as non-usurious the payment on commercial investments of a rate of return determined by market conditions.

In accord with this spirit the Venetians developed a kind of loan contract, not found in the same form elsewhere, and called the "local colleganza." After the colleganza became rare in overseas trade, a contract similar in form was used to invest in local shops, industries, and banks. These contracts no longer specified that the investor was taking the risks of shipwreck and pirates. Neither did they specify what proportion of profits he should receive. Often it was stated only that the rate would be that which would be paid by some well-known shop or bank. According to the stricter church lawyers, these contracts were usurious, but the Venetian courts enforced collection so long as the rate of interest was moderate, 5 to 8 percent. Because the rate of return was uncertain, there was room to argue about whether they were a form of participation in equity or a straight-out loan, and only in the latter case usurious. Whatever the quibble over that legal question, the Venetians did not regard the loan as really usurious unless the borrower was charged an unusually high, predetermined rate of interest or was required to put up security which was sold to his great loss and the gain of the lender.

Another way of borrowing, more free from any taint of usury, was by selling a bill of exchange. Essentially, the bill of exchange was an order to pay in one place in one kind of money because of a payment received in a different place in a different kind of money. There was always a time lag between receipt and payment (for example, sixty days on bills between Venice and Bruges), so that one of the parties was extending credit to the other in the meantime. If a merchant in Venice had sufficiently good standing with an agent in Bruges (if, for example, they were together in a family partnership) and if he was hard up for cash, the Venetian partner might draw a bill on his partner in Bruges. He would sell that bill for cash to someone in Venice who would send it to Bruges for collection. When the bill arrived in Bruges, the partner there, in order to get the money to pay it, might sell in Bruges a new bill drawn on Venice. When that new bill arrived in Venice, the Venetian partner had to pay considerably more than he had received by selling the first bill, but he had the use of the money for 120 days in the meantime.

The bill of exchange was used in all western Europe to borrow money in this fashion, and each big commercial center such as Genoa and Florence developed other credit devices also, different in form but very similar in effect to Venice's local colleganze. For example, the famous bankers of Florence accepted funds on deposit and gave the depositors "gifts."

In Venice, banking developed a distinctive style which we associate with the name giro-bank. The main function of a Venetian banker was not making loans but making payments on behalf of his clients. Even if a merchant had plenty of coins in his treasure chest, it was a bothersome and dangerous business to get them out and count them every time he made a purchase, making sure each coin was genuine and in good condition. Nor did he want to go through a similar process every time he made a sale. He was happy to receive payment by being given credit on the books of a well-known banker. He could use that credit to pay for his next purchase. These credits were not transferred by writing checks, as is done today, but depended on the person who was making a payment appearing in person before the banker, who sat behind a bench under the portico of a church at Rialto, with his big journal spread out in front of him. The payor orally instructed the banker to make a transfer to the account of the person being paid. The banker wrote as directed in his book, which was an official notarial record, so that there was no need of receipts. There were normally four or five such bankers with booths on the campo next to the Rialto bridge. Everyone of any consequence in business had an account so that he could make and receive payments through the banks. They were called *banche di scritta* or *del giro* because their main function was to write transfers and thus to rotate (*girare*) credits from one account to another at the command of the merchants.

As a general legal principle, bankers could not permit anyone to overdraw his account, not even a friend or a partner, but the temptation was irresistible. Many who had deposited coins in the bank were content to leave them in the banker's hands year after year, while the size of their account grew or declined according to the payments received or made for merchandise. There was nothing to prevent the banker from using that cash in the meantime to make payment of some kind that required coins, for example, the paying off of a galley crew on behalf of the government. That would in effect be a loan to the government and many such loans were made by bankers. There were other loans that the banker could make by simply crediting the borrower with a deposit which he had not really made. Ordinarily, the borrower would not withdraw cash. The credit given him on the banker's books could be transferred to some other merchant to pay for purchases. So long as all the transactions were within the relatively small group of wholesale merchants who gathered at the Rialto, the banker could create deposits in bank credit. To be sure, if he made too many loans in this way, he would find himself over-extended when some untoward event shook confidence and caused depositors to wish to withdraw cash. And, of course, he could over-extend himself in other ways, as by buying bills of exchange and paying for them in credits on his bank.

GROSSO AND   One set of circumstances which occasioned many bank crises but on other
DUCAT   occasions meant profits for bankers was the frequent change in the coinage
or in the values of gold and silver. The large silver penny or groat minted
extensively by Enrico Dandolo in financing the Fourth Crusade was kept at its
original weight (2.18 grams) and the same fineness (.965 pure silver). Government obligations and international transactions were recorded in a "money of
account" based on the grosso. A *lira di grossi* meant 240 of those big silver coins.
Because it was kept at uniform weight and fineness, the Venetian grosso gained
wide currency throughout the eastern Mediterranean. Venetians paid for eastern
imports by sending out bags of grossi and silver bars refined to the same degree
of fineness and so stamped by the mint.

For retail transactions within the city smaller pennies (*piccoli*) were minted,
containing less silver (see Figure 12). A second money of account was formed by
calling 240 small pennies a *lira di piccoli* and 12 small pennies a *soldo di piccoli*.
Since successive issues of small pennies contained less and less silver, the grosso,
originally worth only 26 piccoli, came to be worth 32 piccoli.

Gold as well as silver came to Venice from German, Hungarian, and Balkan
mines, and the crusades yielded much golden booty, but gold flowed into western
Europe mainly from the North African trade which passed through Genoa, Pisa,
and Florence. Genoa and Florence were the first western cities to coin gold, and
the florin issued in 1252 achieved wide acceptance as the standard gold coin
before Venice in 1284 minted its ducat with the same weight and fineness as the
florin. Until then, Byzantine mints had provided the gold coins used in Venetian
trade. While Byzantine issues deteriorated, varying in weight and fineness, the
Venetian ducat or *zecchino* was kept at 3.5 grams of almost pure gold (.997 fine)
from its first issue in 1284 until after the fall of the Republic in 1797. Gradually,
it became more widely known and trusted than any other coin, but during the
first decades of the fourteenth century, many Venetian conservatives distrusted
gold. Ducats were merely an alternative or supplementary means of making payments. Wholesale prices, all the obligations of the state, and the credits on the
books of the bankers were stated in a money of account based on the grosso.[1]

Banking had developed in connection with money changing, and one of the
functions of the bankers was to have large quantities of coins available for such
operations as hiring galley crews. Although they did not have strongboxes at
their banks, they kept cash in the strong rooms of the State Treasurer's palace
which was beside the Rialto bridge right next to bankers' booths. A sudden
change in the relative value of gold and silver might catch them with too many of
the wrong kind of coin, but more often they managed to profit amid shifting
values. So long as the value of gold compared to silver was rising (it went from
below 1 to 10 in 1252 to almost 1 to 14 in 1305 or 1310), bankers profited from accepting deposits in gold ducats and making payments in silver grossi, as they had
a right to do. Sometimes they could make payment in the smaller silver and copper coins which were widely used in retail trade and in paying wages.

A sudden drop in the value of gold began in Venice about 1326. Gold fell
until it again was worth only about 1 to 10. For about twenty years (1305–25),

---

[1]In addition to the lira di grossi, there was a second money of account based on the grosso, namely,
the lira a grossi: 1 lira di grossi = 26 lira a grossi.

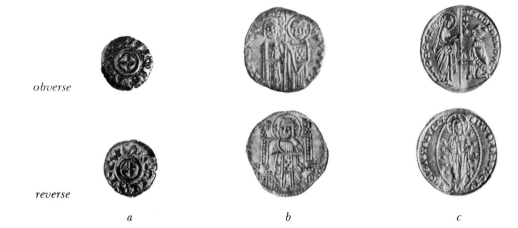

obverse

reverse

a   b   c

FIGURE 12   *Venetian Coins (courtesy of the Smithsonian Institution, Washington).*

(a) Actual size of a small Venetian penny (piccolo), issued under Doge Enrico Dandolo. Its design was similar to the penny of Charlemagne from which it took its Latin name (denarius), but it was much smaller, weighed only .362 grams (about 1/100 of an ounce), and was only 25 percent silver. Later piccoli contained much less silver.

(b) This well-worn specimen of the groat (grosso) was minted under Doge Bartolommeo Gradenigo, 1338–42. It was among the last minted with the same weight (2.18 grams), size (as pictured), fineness (96 percent pure silver), and design as those issued by Enrico Dandolo about 1200. The design echoed that of Byzantine coins, which had been used earlier at Venice for large payments, in that there were two figures in the principal design on the obverse, and one figure on the reverse. On the obverse, instead of an emperor and an archangel, the Venetians pictured the doge receiving the symbol of his office from Saint Mark. On the reverse is Christ enthroned.

When a groat of inferior weight and fineness was coined in 1379, it was distinguished by a star on the reverse to the left of the enthroned Christ.

(c) The ducat, later called the zecchino, always contained 3.55 grams of pure gold. It was the same size as the grosso and imaged the same themes more skillfully. Its obverse showed the doge kneeling to receive the standard from Saint Mark. Behind the doge was his name, in this specimen Andrea Dandolo. Behind the saint one reads S. M(arcus) Veneti. On the reverse is Christ the Redeemer, erect, holding the Gospels, and giving benediction.

one gold ducat had been worth 24 silver grossi on the market place and had been given and received by bankers on that basis. Suddenly, gold seemed plentiful and silver relatively scarce, so that a merchant offering ducats might receive only 20 or 22 grossi. Since debts were recorded in grossi, the decline of the ducat and the scarcity of the grossi made it harder for debtors to pay their creditors, banks to pay their depositors, and the government to pay its bondholders. Not surprisingly, the government stepped in and declared gold ducats to be legal tender for 24 grossi. All debts recorded in grossi could thereafter be paid in ducats at that rate. Grossi promptly went to a premium and soon ceased to be minted, at least in the old form. Thus the Venetian Commune shifted from a silver standard to a gold standard in the middle of the fourteenth century.

THE PUBLIC   A funded debt had been established in Venice in 1262 and was thereafter **DEBT**   a vital factor in Communal finances. Like other governments of the time, Venice financed wars by borrowing and depended on indirect taxes to cover peace-time expenditures and interest on loans. Income taxes and direct taxes on property were not tolerated, unless the Commune made a pretense of intending to repay. One important indirect tax was collected at the Rialto and at the Fondaco dei Tedeschi on every wholesale transaction. Although it was less than 1 percent, the flow of goods through Venice made its yield large. Even more important were the taxes on wine, salt, meat, oil, etc. Since these taxes on consumption were most burdensome to the poor, the rich did very well indeed under such a system, especially if their loans to finance wars paid 12 or 20 percent, as was common for short-term loans.

Extensive borrowing at 20 percent, or higher rates such as were paid by many medieval cities, not only enriched the wealthy, it weakened the Commune. Venice strengthened the state by its consolidation in 1262 of all outstanding loans into what was later called the *Monte Vecchio*, on which it paid only 5 percent. But it paid that 5 percent without a break for more than one hundred years, as we shall see. All Venetians having a minimal amount of property were required to subscribe proportionally whenever more was borrowed. Repayments were similarly made proportionally whenever taxes on transit and consumption yielded a surplus. Short-term loans were made from time to time through the banks and such government bureaus as the Mint, the Grain Office, and the Salt Office; but these were later liquidated by receipts from taxes or by new forced loans added to the Monte Vecchio. Venice was the first European state to fund its debt so that interest was regularly paid from one fund to all bondholders equally.

Until the Second Genoese War, the debt was small or relatively quickly repaid, but at the end of that war, the Monte Vecchio totaled over 500,000 ducats, and at the end of the War of Ferrara in 1313, it was well over 1,000,000 ducats and obviously would not be repaid for decades — if at all. But its payment of 2-½ percent every half year made it an attractive investment, and holdings could readily be bought and sold. Investments in Monte Vecchio added an element of stability to the income of resident merchants and provided a desirable means of providing for a widow or endowing a charity. The pennies collected by the sawyers guild from its members in order to make payments to those out of work because of accidents were kept in a chest with multiple locks; but the larger funds accumulated by the carpenter's guild so as to provide dowries to daughters were invested in the government bonds. Bankers were allowed and even encouraged to buy them. Venetian bonds were bought also by rulers of neighboring cities who wished to put money aside where they might enjoy it in the not too unlikely event of being chased from power, but most of the Monte Vecchio belonged to Venice's upper class and the charities they endowed.

WEALTH AND   By the end of the fourteenth century, Venetian society was much more clear-
STATUS   ly and elaborately stratified than it had been a couple of centuries earlier.

The reforms in the composition of the Great Council, the changes in ships and seamanship, and the dominance of resident merchants all tended to diminish the ease with which men could move up the social scale, especially when in the mid-fourteenth century there was a contraction of the economy, accentuated by the Black Death.

At the very top were some twenty or thirty great families that enjoyed a combination of traditional prestige, political power, and outstanding wealth. They were largely the same families which had been prominent for centuries. Another hundred families also ranked as noble because their members were accepted as members of the Great Council. They had a monopoly of membership in all the other governing councils, of magistracies, judgeships, and top naval commands, and of all the highest posts in the administration. Some spent nearly all their adult lives in legal and political activities, but most nobles were merchants and ship captains familiar with distant market places and they became office holders, if at all, only after they had passed middle age and had made an economic contribution to the family fortune.

Not all nobles were rich, nor were all rich Venetians noble. Our best information on the distribution of wealth is from the assessments made to control the levying of the forced loans. The list of assessments survives for one year, 1379. Only the relatively well-to-do were listed as obliged to make loans, namely those assessed at about 120 ducats or more, which meant, in view of the system of assessments used, those with known property worth more than 300 ducats. The value of 300 ducats at that time may be roughly indicated by comparison with the earnings of a really skilled craftsman. It was unusual for a foreman shipwright to earn as much as 100 ducats a year. Yet 2,128 persons were considered rich enough to be assessed. Since this was during the plague-stricken decades, the total population was certainly below 100,000, probably little more than 60,000, so that the assessed were about one-eighth of all heads of households. Out of this total, that is, out of 2,128, 1,211 were nobles and 917 were commoners. Outstandingly rich were 91 nobles and 26 commoners, with assessments indicating that their real wealth ranged from 10,000 to 150,000 ducats, the latter figure reflecting the assessment of the richest of all, Federico Corner. Obviously, "wealthy" and "noble" were distinct categories, although they overlapped considerably. Of the moderately rich with between 300 and 3,000 ducats, 817 were nobles and 755 non-nobles. These figures show that many nobles, indeed a majority of them, were not really wealthy. In addition, there were some nobles too poor to be assessed at all, and some rich nobles who were not assessed because they had no home in Venice but lived overseas.

Among the non-noble Venetians who were comfortably well-off, additional distinctions developed during the fourteenth century. A middle class distinguished itself from the general populace and acquired the rank of "citizens" (*cittadini*). They held themselves above manual employments considered merely "mechanical." Within this middle class, the highest status, although not necessarily the largest fortunes, belonged to those called "native-born citizens" (*cittadini originari*). From their ranks were recruited the clerks of the Ducal Chancery, notaries, and many practitioners in the law courts. Although there was no lawyers' guild at Venice as there was in Padua, Florence, and many other cities, native-born lawyers below the rank of noble acquired status as a select group within the cittadini.

Others of the native-born citizens engaged in international trade with the same rights as the nobility or directed a local business, such as a glass furnace. An equally rich although less esteemed section of the cittadini were immigrants. If they made their homes in Venice, as by marrying a Venetian, and if they did not engage in "mechanical" labor, they received after ten years a grant of half-citizenship (*de intus*), permitting them equal rights with Venetians in trading within the city. Twenty-five years of residence were required for full rights of citizenship (*de extra*), enabling them to rank as Venetians in shipping merchandise and paying customs in international trade.

The common people below the rank of the citizen enjoyed economic rights according to the guild to which they belonged and their rank in it. One aspect of these guilds (or scuole) was their provision of religious fellowship and some degree of social security. Those cittadini who did not belong to guilds, and some who did, found similar aid in misfortune and an outlet for their religious yearnings and desire for fellowship through the many fraternities which had no occupational or professional requirements for membership.

One group of these non-professional fraternities stood out in social importance. They were the four, later six, *Scuole Grandi*, so called because they were officially entitled to admit between 500 to 600 members. They were also called *Scuole dei Battuti*, for at their origin the members scourged themselves on ceremonial occasions. Self-flagellation, widespread in the thirteenth century, was soon replaced by other expressions of religious enthusiasm; in the processions for which these Scuole were celebrated in later centuries, they carried not whips for their backs but jeweled incasements containing sacred relics. To devotional exercises, they added very extensive dispensation of charity and built themselves magnificent meeting halls. Their membership included both nobles and commoners; some members were givers, other receivers of charity. They were managed entirely by laymen and were not subordinated either to the bishop or to the magistrates who governed the craft guilds. They were regulated directly by the Council of Ten, which ruled that no new fraternity could be formed without its permission. Although nobles were admitted to membership, they were not allowed to hold office in the Scuole Grandi. These posts of honor were reserved for the cittadini. Their rights to office in the Scuole Grandi and in the Ducal Chancery were privileges which made "citizenship-by-birth" appear a supplementary kind of nobility.

The major concerns of the nobles and citizens — politics, administration, finance, and the distant routes of international trade — will fill many chapters; but let us look first at everyday concerns of humbler folk. Among them also, class lines were becoming more elaborate and more pronounced in consequence of the Nautical and Commercial Revolutions.

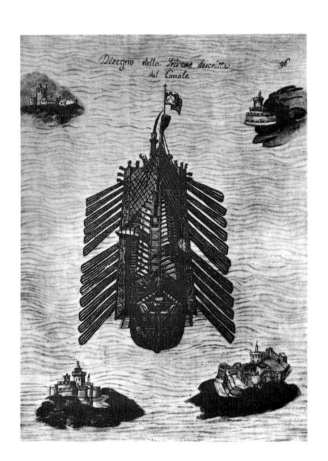

A REORGANIZATION OF SEA POWER · III

Craftsmen and Seamen

CHAPTER TWELVE

After its seapower made Venice a major trade center, its trade stimulated further industrial development. Craftsmen found many customers who were ready to buy not only for their own needs but for export. While ships thus enlarged the craftsmen's markets, they also brought them needed supplies. When production expanded to serve not only local demand but distant markets, there was a restructuring of industrial organization comparable to the change in commercial organization by which resident merchants replaced the traveling merchants.

INDUSTRIAL ORGANIZATION The greater division of labor that went hand in hand with increased production enabled the owners of the capital to concentrate on managerial functions and leave merely "mechanical" physical work to others whose labor they co-ordinated. This usually led not only to differences in functions but to contrasts in power and status, in short, to class divisions. The way in which this occurred at Venice was a contrast to the development in many other cities because of the nature of the city's early industries.

Almost every kind of manufacturing was carried on at first within the home of a craftsman, or by a farmer's family as supplement to agricultural work, or within the great house of some lord. Working at home or in an adjoining shop had so many advantages that it endured for a long time. It enabled a man to work at his own speed, to employ his whole family, to enlarge it by engaging young apprentices or journeymen whom he governed not merely as their employer but as the head of the household, and to combine for himself and his family various kinds of part-time occupations, such as housekeeping and gardening, with spinning, weaving, or some other craft. The loss of labor involved in pulling workers away from their homes was so great that manufacturing was carried on mainly by family units even when there was a separation of investor-managers from manual laborers.

In the most important of medieval industries, the textile industry, this separation took the form of the putting-out system. In that system the investor-manager was a merchant-employer. He owned the material being worked on during the whole process of its manufacture and he "put it out" to one worker after another, to spinners, weavers, dyers, and so on. Because these craftsmen could work at home, this arrangement has also been called the "domestic system," emphasizing the contrast with the later factory system which massed workers together away from their homes. In the putting-out system, craftsmen were dependent on merchants who had the knowledge, capital, and connections needed to import the material, to judge what kind of cloth could be marketed, to find workers and pay them, and to sell the product later, perhaps much later, in a distant market. Some cloth was made from local materials for local sale, to be sure, but when either the supplies or the markets were distant, the craftsman was more or less dependent on a merchant-employer. In the many cities where the merchant-employers controlled both the town government and the textile guilds, the craftsmen-employees were regulated one-sidedly.

In Venice, there was a tendency towards a similar situation, but other factors had a countervailing effect. Venice's richest merchants did not turn into merchant-employers because their talents and their capital were occupied in the complexities of Venice's very extensive foreign trade and in connected shipping or colonial ventures. Moreover, other industries were for centuries more important than textiles in Venice. In the industries which were Venice's first specialties, the technical processes were unfavorable to putting-out. They required managers who were more experts in the craft than in merchandising and who employed relatively expensive equipment and the help of a considerable amount of quite unskilled labor. Including their families and a few apprentices and journeymen, the teams they directed might number a dozen or so. These masters were men who knew how to work with their hands, but they are better called managers than laborers if "laborer" evokes the memory of tired muscles. Although they were employers, they are best characterized not as merchant-employers but as craftsmen-managers.

When craftsmen-managers and merchant-employers both existed in the same industry, as was often the case — for example, in the silk industry — conflicts between them were likely. The merchant nobles of Venice, devoted to international trade and to running the government, were just as likely to side with the craftsmen in such conflicts as with the merchant-employers.

CHEMICALS,   More important than the textile industry in early Venice and more influen-
TEXTILES, AND   tial in setting the style of industrial organization were what may be grouped
CONSTRUCTION   as the chemical industries. Makers of glass, soap, dyes, tiles or bricks, salt-
                petre, and many metal products were experts at "converting one kind of
chemical individual into another." The masters of these many crafts had a considerable store of practical knowledge of industrial chemistry, even before any of

them learned to write or to read books. Of course, the craftsmen concerned did not think of the materials they used in our chemical terms. The first writer to describe specifically the Venetian glass industry said of the product, "It is made from fusible stones and from solidified juices." He then goes on to describe the appearance of the sources of these "fusible stones" and "solidified juices." The results of mixing and heating them in various ways was well known to a medieval craftsman from experience, although he knew no chemical formulas. After giving such formulas, a modern authority goes on to say, "...the composition of the batch still standard for modern bottle and window glass is practically identical with that used by the Venetians for their glass in the Middle Ages, having remained unchanged throughout the centuries." "Scientific research," he writes, "has revealed the basis for the ancient empirical formula but has not been able to improve upon the proportions which long experience and trial-and-error proved to be the best for the purpose."

The chemical industries had a number of important characteristics in common. They required special structures, such as furnaces or leaching pits or boiling vats, which prevented their being carried on within the home to the same extent as weaving or spinning (see Figures 30 and 31). The craft "mysteries" involved manual dexterity to only a limited degree; they consisted largely in knowledge of formulas for mixtures and heating, and of skill in judging by looks, taste, smell, and feel the condition of materials. Since much of the hard manual labor consisted in tending fires and moving materials about, it could be relegated to unskilled labor more easily than could the physical labor of stone-cutting or weaving. On the other hand, horizontal specialization, that is, breaking a process down into clearly distinguishable stages, such as spinning and weaving which then became separate crafts carried on in different places, was less advantageous. Even when the workmen specialized in different tasks, employing them in the same establishment was more efficient. For these reasons, the putting-out system did not develop in the chemical industries as it did in the textile industries. Craftsmen-managers rather than merchant-employers were the chief organizers of production.

In glassmaking, for example, as many as three different kinds of furnaces were needed, although they might be combined into one structure. One was for the heating of materials at low temperature, the "fritting" which drove out some of the impurities as gases which would otherwise form bubbles in the glass and make it less transparent. Then there was the main furnace, a domed structure in which the temperature could be raised sufficiently to fuse the silicon, limestone, and soda. It had openings around the side through which pots of molten glass could be taken out in order that the glass be blown, pressed, or cast into desired shapes (see Figure 30). The art of using tubes to blow molten glass into various forms had been handed down from Roman times. These furnaces had three or four openings called mouths (*bocche*). Each mouth was tended by a team called a *"piazza"* consisting of a chief glass blower and three to five assistants of lesser skills. The third furnace was a rectangular structure for cooling the glass gradually. This third furnace was usually attached to the main furnace, so as to make further use of heat from the same fire. The very high temperatures required to fuse materials in the main furnace created such a fire hazard that glassmakers were required in 1291 to move out of the city. An exception was made the following year for small furnaces, provided that they were five paces in all direc-

a   b

FIGURE 13   *Some Crafts Shown on the Central Portal of San Marco (Photo Böhm).*

(a) Barbers served as dentists; (b) Coopers needed little capital; (c) Smiths required more expensive equipment; (d) Masons had to go out to work, as did caulkers and shipwrights, but most craftsmen worked at home.

tions distant from any house, but the exceptions were not important, since the glassmakers were content to settle at Murano, just a short boat ride from Rialto, and to make Murano famous.

Some of the owners of the furnaces were themselves glassmakers; some merely rented their furnaces to master glassmakers. Both owners and masters belonged to a glassmakers' guild which laid down rules about the contracts between owners and masters and among masters. Owners paid the highest dues to the guild, but were debarred from some of its offices. Guild rules limited the duration of contracts, the amount of advance payment which masters or laborers might receive, and the extent to which masters could bid workers away from each other. These regulations reflect a desire to assure the authority of masters over their workers but to preserve the independence of masters in dealing with the owners of furnaces.

c

d

The leaders of the industry owned the furnaces they used, employed a few other masters, and together with these masters employed something like a dozen other persons, partly apprentices and partly unskilled laborers. The capital needed to build a furnace was no more essential for these leaders than their special knowledge. This is illustrated by the story of an ambitious glassmaker named Giorgio, who began as a poor immigrant from Spalato. He was nicknamed Ballarin, the dancer, apparently because he was lame. He was employed by a long-established family of glassmakers, the Barovier. One day when they were all temporarily away, he broke into the place where they kept their secret formulas, stole them, and gave them to a rival glassmaker, whose daughter he then married, so that he was able to have a furnace of his own. Giorgio Ballarin's success story belongs to the fifteenth century, but it illustrates two factors equally essential to success a century or two earlier, namely, trade secrets and capital.

Among the skills for which the workers at Murano were most admired in the fourteenth century were their abilities to imitate pearls and other precious stones and to combine colored glass with fine enameling. Admired compositions of painters were enameled onto vases, bowls, or cups. Sometimes the decoration was a personal portrait or a design made especially for a particular occasion, such as a wedding or a state visit.

A less decorative but more useful Venetian specialty was the manufacture of lenses for eyeglasses. Spectacles may have been invented by a Venetian; certainly, the earliest evidence about the process of their production is in the regulations of Venice's glassmakers' guild. The first eyeglasses were made by using quartz crystal, and crystal workers formed a separate guild. According to the general principle of preventing fraud through imitations, they were at first forbidden to make lenses out of glass. But the glassmakers did so well in producing glass as clear as crystal that in 1302 the crystal workers were permitted to use "glass for eyes for reading." Their skill in shaping and polishing then became part of the mysteries of the glassmakers' guild.

Another Venetian specialty was making large, clear window panes. Small circular panes of crown glass with bulls eyes were widely manufactured, but the Venetians were able, by using a quite different technique, to prepare large rectangular sheets of glass, such, for example, as those supplied to Ancona in 1285 and 1305 for a lighthouse.

In addition to such expensive products as enameled bowls and eyeglasses, Murano produced large quantities of ordinary bowls, cups, and bottles. Its fancy products are, of course, the most talked about, but the glass turned out for everyday use was also of superior quality to that produced in other cities because better materials were used. Basic in the glassmaker's art was skill in picking and mixing good materials. The Venetians had the advantage of several good sources of supply. Some sands within the lagoons may have served, but the best material containing the needed silicon was found in the rivers which washed from the Alps pebbles or sand of the right consistency. The best for clear glass was found in the Adige near Verona. Excellent clay from which to build furnaces came from near Vicenza. Wood for fuel was plentiful in Friuli and Istria. Most important for the superiority of Venetian glass over that produced in the north was the use of a soda ash (sodium carbonate) whereas northern glassmakers used a potash (potassium carbonate) obtained by burning hard woods. Their product was called "forest glass," while the more translucent Venetian product was called "maritime glass." Venice imported the soda ash in large quantities from Syria where it was made by burning seaweed. Being relatively heavy, soda ash helped provide a balanced cargo for round ships loaded mainly with cotton. The vigor of the Venetian glass industry over many centuries was due mainly to craftsmen passing on special skills from father to son; but it owed much also to the accessibility of the needed materials — not that they were immediately at hand, but that Venice had the transport facilities for making them available relatively cheaply.

A good supply of raw materials was even more important to the prosperity of Venetian soapmakers. For a time in the fourteenth century, they took from Spain leadership in producing the kind of product that has made "Castillian soap" famous. Being white and hard and with a pleasant smell, it could be sold as a luxury, almost a medicinal product, in such northern countries as England, where the domestic supply of soap was soft, dark, and evil-smelling because it was made with animal fats. Instead of tallow, the Venetians used olive oil which their ships brought in large quantities from Apulia. Instead of the potash used in the north for alkali, the Venetians used ashes imported from Syria, not the sea-ash of the glassmakers, but ashes of a particular kind of scrub which contained a good percentage of soda and which therefore made a solid soap. It could be scented to suit customers' tastes.

The metallurgical industries were also well supplied with materials, and the law required that copper, silver, and gold, which flowed through Venice on its way east to pay for imports of spices, be refined before being exported. Many smiths operated middle-sized establishments in which they filled orders given them by merchant nobles. In 1304, for example, a contract to supply the Commune with 20,000 steel bolts for crossbows was awarded to three men who then sub-contracted the manufacture to master ironsmiths employing six to seventeen workers each. Coppersmiths were experts in the manufacture of large caldrons, such as were used in soapmaking and sugar refining. Silversmiths and goldsmiths staffed the Mint and supplied table services for the rich who, then much more than now, used jewelry and flat silver as a form of investment, available for melting into coin in emergencies.

In the thirteenth century, before the Arsenal was enlarged, the mint presented the largest peacetime concentration of workers under a single direction and within a single enclosure. Whereas manager-craftsmen in their enlarged family workshops directed up to a dozen or a score of men, the number employed in the mint must have risen above a hundred. If the distinction between a large workshop and a factory was merely one of numbers, the Venetian mint might be considered a factory. But it differed from a factory not only because it used no power-driven machinery, but also because craftsmen within the mint worked very much as they would have in their own homes. The purpose of pulling them together in one central workshop was not to change the process of manufacture but to safeguard the materials used and to standardize the product, the coins. And the mint was operated not by private initiative for private profit but by officials according to the rules laid down by the governing councils.

Although clearly different from the factories of the Industrial Revolution, the mint and other communal central workshops of medieval Venice presented some similar problems. The directors of the mint had to coordinate a series of operations: the assaying of all gold and silver received, the refining to specified standards, the casting and cutting of blanks which were then stamped into coins. Distinct departments, each with its own auxiliary workers and inspectors, injected an element of bureaucracy. One group of masters operated only on fine silver, another group on the alloy used for coins of smaller denominations. In the spring of 1279, the latter group included eight moneyers (men of strong biceps, who struck the coins with the dies) and an equal number of master silversmiths, preparing blanks to be struck by the moneyers. Each department had its own weighers and inspectors. Other specialized employees were the ironsmiths who made the dies and the accountants who kept the books.

In the textile industries, merchant-employers dominated some branches through the putting-out system, but not others. The wool guild and the fustian guild were both controlled by men who bought the wool or cotton and put it out to be spun in homes by women living in various parts of the lagoons, and then to weavers, and so on. The wool guild barred from membership anyone who worked for wages. The fustian or cotton-cloth guild made no such prohibition; it did not draw a sharp line between merchant-employers and craftsmen who sometimes worked for others and sometimes themselves produced for sale. Quite different were arrangements in the silk industry, which became important when experts from Lucca, refugees from political conflicts in their native city, were welcomed at Venice during the first decades of the fourteenth century. At Venice, the silk weavers owned their own looms, and formed a guild of their own from which they excluded the merchants. They required that the merchant-employers give out work to guild masters only and not engage directly the services of the apprentices and other laborers who were employees of the master weavers.

Another group of craftsmen-managers who owned their own equipment were the dyers. They worked partly for local merchant-employers and partly for general merchant-adventurers who imported undyed cloth from England or Flanders and had it dyed according to the tastes of the Levantine city to which they were shipping it.

The working of hemp fibres led to another variant from the usual putting-out system. The masters of the hemp spinners' guild, who bought hemp and had it hackled or combed, then spun, and then twisted into cordage, were employers of labor, but their early statutes specifically forbade them from having work done elsewhere than in their own homes or workshops. The technical problems of their craft apparently required that they pay such close attention to the quality of the spinning and twisting and to the different grades of hemp fibre suitable for different kinds of products that they could not put out work. Or probably it is more accurate to say that the concern of the government for the excellence of the cordage on Venetian ships forced the hemp spinners to concentrate on the processes of production. Each master was required to mark the products of his establishment by a distinctively colored thread. In the thirteenth century, the government appointed three supervisors who were to inspect the shops. No twisting of heavy hawsers was to be done without giving these inspectors notice so that they could be present to inspect at the start of the operation. If they judged one of the strands inadequately prepared, it had to be replaced.

Concentration of the master hemp spinners on the industrial process prevented them from solving problems arising in connection with their supplies. Sometimes the government stepped in; officials were elected with orders to buy the needed amounts of hemp, and also of pitch. In 1282, they alone were authorized to make purchases and they were told to resell to the masters what they needed at a price that would give the government a moderate profit. During the Second Genoese War, these officials were given special borrowing power in order to acquire large supplies. At the end of the war, this monopolistic buying was suspended amid complaints of high prices. Anyone could import, provided he paid the prescribed duty, which included a fee for keeping his wares in a government warehouse designated as the only place where hemp could be unloaded. At first that warehouse was in Canareggio, but when the Arsenal was enlarged at the other end of the city where most of the shipbuilding was concentrated, a hemp warehouse and throwing yard known as the Tana was built adjoining it.

The Tana became a central workshop which even more than the mint resembled a machineless factory. After 1328, all the hackling of hemp plants and the sorting and grading of the hemp fibres was done at the Tana, and the best grades were kept there to be made into cordage for the ships. The inferior grades were withdrawn to be made into twine for packaging or to be used in caulking. The importing of the raw material was returned to private enterprise. As a result, the importers became merchant-employers who continued to own the material while it was being worked on in the Tana or in the private shops which produced lower-grade products. They formed monopolistic combines the more easily because, at the end of the century, all the high-grade hemp came from Bologna. At one time, the government complained that one Florentine importer held all Venetians at his mercy. The government intervened, but its effort to supply master hemp spinners who wanted to own their own materials was half-hearted. Its main concern was meeting the needs of shipowners for good cordage. So long as there were no combines raising prices, the authorities were content to have the hemp spinners work on fibres put out to them either by merchant-importers or by shipbuilders who purchased material from the importing merchants after it had been hackled and graded in the Tana. For their best hawsers, shipowners "put out" hemp to spinners who worked within the Tana itself. This organization of the cordage industry at Venice should certainly not be called a domestic system, for craftsmen did not work at home. It might be called a special kind of "putting-out system" because the craftsmen did not own the material on which they worked. Its most distinctive feature, however, was the Tana, a communal central workshop.

Adjoining the Tana but under separate management was Venice's largest industrial establishment, the Arsenal, famous because of the place given it by Dante in hell. As Virgil guided him deeper down the pit, he found hell more and more crowded, and to convey this feeling Dante made comparisons with the densest throngs he had ever witnessed on earth — the pilgrims in a procession at Rome in the jubilee year 1300, the ranks of an army in which he had maneuvered, and workers massed within the Arsenal at Venice. Probably the Arsenal presented the biggest and busiest spectacle of industrial activity that Dante ever saw, or could have seen, the biggest of the time. He compared it to the crowded darkness of hell's depths in the famous lines 7–15 of Canto 21 (Longfellow's translation).

> As in the Arsenal of the Venetians
>   Boils in the winter the tenacious pitch
>   To smear their unsound vessels ov'er again,
> For sail they cannot; and instead thereof
>   One makes his vessel new, and one recaulks
>   The ribs of that which many a voyage has made;
> One hammers at the prow, one at the stern,
>   This one makes oars and that one cordage twists
>   Another mends the mainsail and the mizzen.

The Old Arsenal, where workers were most concentrated, contained docks for about a dozen galleys and storerooms for armor, spars, benches, and many other fixings, as well as the shops for sail mending, oar making, and those in which Dante saw the boiling pitch he evoked to symbolize the blackening punishment for graft.

During Dante's lifetime, the New Arsenal was added, quadrupling the area enclosed within the Arsenal walls. Previously the main function of the Arsenal had been storage and repair; great galleys as well as large round ships had been built elsewhere. Enlarged, the Arsenal was big enough so that all the merchant galleys could be constructed within its walls, although large cogs, even those built for the Commune, were made in private shipyards, which were located on the waterfront near the Arsenal and on islands elsewhere in the lagoon.

In the fourteenth-century Arsenal, as in all the large communal workshops of Venice, the central direction did not alter the process of production as it had been developed by the crafts and embodied in their craft traditions. Indeed, there was less bureaucratic provision in the Arsenal for strict enforcements of standards than in the Mint or the Tana. The government prescribed a standardization of crossbows to be sure so that bowstrings and arrows would fit all bows. In regard to galleys, it laid down a few basic dimensions to govern their size and proportions, but their sailing qualities and even to some extent the size of the galleys depended on decisions made in the process of construction by the foremen shipwrights in charge.

Foremen shipwrights were judged primarily by their skill in design, a skill which resided so much in the eye of the shipwright that it could only partially be reduced to plans that others could execute. The foreman caulker, and the less important foremen of the oarmakers, the ironsmiths, and so on, had as their chief function enforcement of the guild's technical standards. On one occasion, when merchant galleys almost sank because of imperfect caulking, the Senate held the gastaldo of the guild and the foreman caulker of the Arsenal both responsible and removed both from their posts. Half a dozen great galleys for commerce could be finished every other year by keeping employed twelve shipwrights, six sawyers, and fifteen caulkers with their apprentices and a few carriers to move lumber. Somewhat fewer men were needed to construct a similar number of light galleys at the same careful speed. A group of masters totaling about thirty, with a separate foreman shipwright for each type, was considered not too big to be supervised by craft foremen in much the same way they supervised construction in private shipyards.

The professional official in the Arsenal who came nearest to being a general manager had the title of Admiral (*armiraio*). His main concern was outfitting and the last-minute preparation of vessels about to be turned over to their commanding officers. He was concerned less with the production of hulls than with the assemblage of components at the moment when the vessel left the Arsenal. Like the central direction in the Mint and the Tana, that of the Arsenal concentrated on keeping track of materials and testing the quality of the end product.

Shipbuilding outside the Arsenal fell into two branches. In one branch were the operators of small boatyards building gondolas or sandolas and small barges; in the other were the shipwrights and caulkers who built and repaired large vessels. The latter group was in much the same situation as other craftsmen in the building trades. Craftsmen in that industry never had been able to enjoy the advantages of working at home. They went to various building sites provided by their customers who also supplied the materials. Their operations were directed by a foreman who hired other masters and who, like them, was paid weekly wages by shipowners or house owners for whom they were working. Even today, the construction industry is less bureaucratized than most and more governed by craft rules.

The chemical, textile, and construction industries, while important in themselves because of the fame of their products, do not illustrate the kind of industrial organization typical of other industries. Much manufacturing took the form of independent retail handicraft in which a craftsman bought his supplies in an open market, worked it up himself in his own home shop, and sold it to the ultimate consumer. Operators of boatyards fitted into that conventional picture of a medieval craftsman, as did those among the house carpenters who specialized in making furniture. Many similar independent craftsmen worked for general merchants as much as for ultimate consumers. Furriers, for example, dressed sable, ermine, fox, and squirrel skins imported by Andrea Barbarigo from Tana or Bruges or mountainous regions less distant. The presence of skilled masters at Venice attracted such imports. Some of these independent artisans were rich men; others were very humble folk. Most numerous were shoemakers, tailors, bakers, barbers, and others of middling status. They worked very largely on materials supplied by their customers, since clothes and household furnishings were made to order then much more than they are now.

**GUILD
FUNCTIONS** The glaring differences in the nature of their membership made the economic functions of Venice's guilds highly varied. In the building trades, they acted much as modern trade unions do, but in most industries and in the many specialized kinds of retailing, they were more like trade associations to which a government had entrusted regulatory powers. In trades where protection for unwary consumers seemed necessary, the guild statutes contained elaborate technical rules. Some were made on the initiative of the guildsmen themselves, to prevent "unfair competition" or to maintain a high reputation in the export markets; others were made by the noble magistrates elected to supervise manufacturing and retailing, the Justices (Giustizieri). In some cases, these officials fixed wages, prices, or the permitted mark-up; in other trades, there was free bargaining.

In general, guilds regulated the taking of apprentices and limited their age and number; in doing so, they made exceptions to ease the path for sons of masters. On the other hand they were prevented by the Justices, backed by the Senate, from making the admission of new men too difficult or expensive. Skilled foreigners were encouraged to settle in Venice and set up business. The most a guild could demand of them was a display of competence, obedience to guild statutes, a probationary period before they were eligible for guild offices, and the payment of dues. When the ravages of the plague made immigrants especially desired, the guilds could not even demand initiation fees.

The income of a guild came partly from fines levied by its officials, partly from initiation fees, and partly from dues which originated as levies for social and especially for religious purposes. Keeping candles lighted at a chosen altar was the original purpose of the fee called the *luminaria*, and the ship carpenters secured an early application of "the check-off" when they required that every employer must deduct the luminaria from the wages he paid. Each guild had an agreement with some parish church or monastery for the maintenance of a chapel, or at least an altar, and the richer and larger guilds put on impressive shows or floats in holiday processions. In guilds composed of masters who were on the edge of poverty, such as the sawyers, provision of some kinds of accident or health insurance was important. Nearly all guilds contributed to the decent burial of their members by requiring attendance by all masters at the funeral of every member. The ship carpenters and caulkers provided an especially desirable form of old-age benefits by requiring the hiring of one "veteran," a master over 55, in every working gang of six or more.

How much its members shared democratically in running the affairs of a guild varied. Only masters could participate, to be sure; apprentices and un-skilled laborers had no voice. The workers thus excluded must have been numer-ous in some industries, such as glassmaking; among the caulkers and ship car-penters, on the other hand, practically every adult was a master. In some cases, the officers may have run everything and restricted the business of the full membership's two meetings a year to the reading of the statute, which was their prescribed purpose. But in other cases, these assemblies voted quite demo-cratically on conflicting proposals about apprentices or about the religious serv-ices of the guild. All the decisions of a guild assembly were subject to approval by the Justices or some high council, and the Justices took the initiative in restrict-ing expenditure on sumptuous banquets. They or one of Venice's governing coun-cils had the last word on economic policies, but the guilds gave the masters a chance to be heard. They also provided opportunities for craftsmen and shop-keepers to hold positions of honor among their fellows and, above all, gave them the feeling of having a place in the social life of the city, a sense of belonging.

A PROLETARIAT   In Venice's biggest industry, shipping, there was no guild organization.
AMONG SEAMEN   Seamen were too numerous and too varied in status. When not "signed
             on" for a voyage, they were caulkers or fishermen or coopers or engaged in some other occupation. At sea, they were traders as well as sailors or oarsmen, so that it must have been difficult in the twelfth and even in the thirteenth century to draw the line between traveling merchant and merchant-seaman. During the Commercial and Nautical Revolutions of the Middle Ages they became more specialized, but in a way that degraded many.

A gap between seamen and merchants opened when traveling merchants were transformed into resident merchants. Even the most sedentary Venetian merchant could hardly be called a landlubber, to be sure, in the same class with the many pilgrims who made the voyage to the Holy Land once in a lifetime and felt merit in all their sufferings in the strange world aboard a heaving ship. But instead of going back and forth with each fleet as did the traveling merchants of the twelfth century, the overseas agents of a couple of centuries later made a sea voyage only every three or four years or much less frequently. Early maritime regulations had relied on the common mutual interests of the crew and the travel-ing merchants. Their common interest in their own safety and that of their mer-chandise had been used to prevent the owners of ships from undermanning, over-loading, using defective rigging, or cutting expenses in other dangerous ways. In the fourteenth century, the situation became quite different. Merchants and ship-owners were linked by common experiences and similar investments, sometimes by long-term partnerships. Maritime law gave more authority to the ship's mas-ter. Merchant passengers, in case there were enough on board, had some powers in settling disputes and in providing for both the welfare and the discipline of the crew, but they stood beside the master and above the seamen.

Ordinary seamen were losing status also because of a change in arms and armor. The age in which the traveling merchant was turning into a resident merchant was also that in which the supremacy of the knight was being shattered by crossbowmen and archers. There is a tendency to depreciate the crossbow as an inferior weapon by comparing it with the longbow. At Crécy and Agincourt, the longbow proved its superiority when in the hands of expert archers. But the expert archers needed for the longbow were found only in Britain and there only for a few generations. On shipboard, moreover, the longbow lost many of the advantages it enjoyed on land. Ability to place the archers in a row close together was less important on a ship. The slower fire of the crossbowmen was not so serious a disadvantage when they did not have to face charging horsemen, and the weight of the crossbow could be rested on the ship's parapet. Moreover, the crossbowman could discharge his weapon while crouching and peering over the side, whereas the archer, in order to draw his bow, had to expose himself by standing erect. All these characteristics made crossbowmen a particularly valuable kind of soldiers to have on board ship.

Defense against the bows required armor heavier than the leather jackets and helmets previously used; there was need for iron hats and steel breastplates. To be as important in battle as he had been, a seaman had to become a bowman or supply himself with the heavier armor. A highly paid mate was expected to do both. In the later thirteenth century, the efforts of the government to improve the armament of Venetian ships took the form of stipulating that the better paid members of the crew must supply themselves with additional weapons and heavier armor. This was not successful. Some of the higher ranks may have equipped themselves, but it was soon found necessary to shift the main responsibility for arms to the shipowners. They were required to hire a number of specialized bowmen and to carry weapons and armor for many of the rest of the crew.

The new types of ships coming into use in the Mediterranean also contributed to downgrading one sector of maritime labor. The introduction of the cog and the great galley reduced the number of men required per ton for each type, but the changes did not mean a decline in total demand for crewmen. During the first decades at least of the fourteenth century, the effect of the technical changes was an increase in the number of jobs on shipboard, for the change from two-masted lateeners to cogs took place very slowly and was more than counter-balanced by an increasing use of great galleys for trade, either in connection with piratical side-ventures or on purely peaceful commercial voyages. Crucial, however, was the change in the kind of labor wanted. During the first half of the fourteenth century, the demand for men skilled in handling sails and tiller decreased and the demand for oarsmen increased relatively. Many seamen who were accustomed to employment on big lateeners found that these ships were being laid up or rebuilt, that the cogs which were taking their place were sailing with smaller crews, and that the only openings were for oarsmen on the great galleys. Rowing had not been considered demeaning when it was incidental to other aspects of seamanship, to trading, and to fighting. But now the growing division of labor was separating from the oarsmen the merchants, the bowmen, the expert navigators, and even the sailors adept at handling ropes, sails, and tillers. To be an oarsman, a *galeotto*, as a regular means of livelihood became a sign of inferiority, but it was this low kind of labor that was most in demand. When the state was chartering merchant galleys for voyages to Flanders, the Black Sea, and Cyprus-Armenia, a half-dozen or more for each voyage, these ships required nearly

3,000 oarsmen and an equal number were needed for a war fleet of any size. With the industrial opportunities within the city expanding, the rewards and working conditions on the galley bench were not such as to attract that many Venetians. It became a regular practice for Venetian galley masters to recruit a third of their oarsmen in Dalmatia, and even so they complained of a scarce labor supply.

The difficulties in enrolling crews were matched by difficulties in getting them to report once they had "signed on." In order to enroll a crew, the galley master, or a government paymaster in the case of a war galley, set up a table on the Molo in front of the Ducal Palace or under its arcade on the side towards the water front and offered advances to applicants he selected. A handshake was legally sufficient, but the general rule was that the seaman received three or four months pay in advance. Competition between shipmasters was sufficiently severe so that some employers sought out seamen in their homes to make bargains. To prevent that, the government ruled that advances could not be recovered if paid elsewhere than at regular hiring places. When the vessel was to leave, a crier shouted the announcement for three days at the Rialto and at San Marco. As soon as they reported, the men received food on board, and if they did not report at the third announcement they were sought out by the policemen of the Nightwatch and either brought forceably on board or put in prison, at least if the government was the employer. Venice never depended on press gangs as much as did the British when Britannia ruled the waves, but in an emergency in 1322, the police were offered 2 grossi for each galeotto they could round up.

Like all other members of a crew, from the master on down, an oarsman had to furnish security when he received the advance in his pay. Frequently, a relative or friend went bond for him, as is evident from the records of these guarantors applying for a relief in the many cases when the seaman's failure to report was due to some misfortune on a previous voyage, such as a fall from the rigging or capture by the Genoese. There is a hint also that the bondsman was sometimes a kind of labor boss who delivered oarsmen and collected their wages. But in spite of guarantors and appeals to the Nightwatch, there were many difficulties in getting the crews on board.

One reason for the difficulties was that the men on the galleys were not paid by the voyage, as had earlier been the case on the round ships, but were paid by the day from the time of departure to that of return. And sometimes, after the vessel had been loaded and inspected in the basin of San Marco and then taken down opposite San Nicolò on the Lido, it waited there some days for the right wind and tide. Galley masters were known to delay their own coming aboard until that very last moment. A more serious cause of discontent among crews might be an unexpected change in the nature of the voyage. The daily wage was only a part of what a seaman expected to gain from a voyage. On commercial voyages, all had rights to carry freight-free some merchandise with which to trade. On military expeditions, their readiness to sign on might be stimulated by hopes of booty, especially if the commanders had the right kind of reputation. If then the mission of the fleet was changed by order of the Senate without any change in the terms previously agreed on, a failure to report is easily explained.

Whether because of such grievances, or just because men were so scarce that the galeotti thought they could get away with malingering, there was much jumping ship and failure to report for duty after accepting an advance of wages. Protests of the shipmasters were met by a modification of the maritime code. The thirteenth-century laws had provided that whoever took wages and did not report must pay the double as penalty. Such a fine could be effective against persons who had property, but not against men who owned next to nothing, not even their own weapons. Judges were empowered to inflict added penalties, but apparently did not until a law was passed in 1329 specifically requiring that those jumping ship should always be sent to jail until they paid. When the law was enforced, the jails were filled with men who had no money with which to pay what they owed. Nor could they earn while in jail. Extolling the virtues of mercy, the Great Council voted to release them from the prisons in the custody of the galley masters to whom they were indebted, so that they might work off what they owed. It even remitted some of the fines and forced the Lords of the Nightwatch to give up half of the fees that they usually collected from the debtor for the service of locking him up.

Of course, seamen were not the only persons imprisoned for debt. In those days, it was the usual way of forcing collection, and service on the galleys had for some time been one way of getting out of debtors' prison. In fact, so many people avoided paying debts by taking service on a galley and thus acquiring an immunity from arrest that, in 1312, this privilege was limited to those whose debts did not exceed 20 lire (about what a seaman earned in a month or two). But the number who were imprisoned in the 1330's and then put to work as debt slaves showed that many of Venice's seamen were in dire poverty. Such a situation was not peculiar to Venice. There were revolts by seamen in many Mediterranean maritime centers in the fourteenth century: at Genoa in 1339, at Salonica in 1345, and in Barcelona in 1391. Behind all these outbursts lay the impoverishment and loss of status of a part of the seafaring population, a degradation rooted in the widespread changes in business organization, in the art of war, and in nautical technology.

Not all the seamen had reason to be discontented, to be sure; many of them were much better off than the oarsmen. The law of 1329 requiring imprisonment for jumping ship was not applied to sailors on round ships, and an effort later to extend it to include these sailors was defeated in the Senate, though by a narrow margin. On the galleys, there were not only oarsmen and bowmen, but about a dozen real sailors, experts on working the rigging and handling the tiller. In addition to the petty officers whose duties were primarily disciplinary, there was on each galley an officer in charge of navigation (commonly called the *armiraio* or *omo di conseio*). Similar experts in the haven-finding art were of course needed on the round ships. For these experts in dead-reckoning and using and making marine charts, the claim has been made that "sailors were the first professional group to use mathematics in their everyday work" (Taylor). They were paid three times as much as a galeotto, had more extended cargo privileges, and were far from being proletarians.

The shortage of maritime labor was accentuated when the galleys of Romania returning in 1347 from the besieged city of Kaffa brought with them the beginning of the Black Death, which killed during 1348 about half of Venice's population and made similar ravages elsewhere. More efforts of a kind that had been tried even earlier were then made to remedy the shortage of oarsmen. Fugitives from justice were invited back if their crimes were not too heinous. If they would work on the galleys, they were offered reductions of the fines they had fled to escape. To ease the general dearth of seamen, the number of men required per ton on round ships was reduced, and the enlistment of boys as apprentice seamen was encouraged. But service on the galleys was not encouraged by improving working conditions. The food given crews had deteriorated since the beginning of the century, when the usual rations included not only ship biscuits and wine, but cheese and vegetable soup with salt pork in the bean soup every other day. The salt pork had disappeared. As a war with Genoa became more and more imminent, the noble who was to be the leading admiral in that war, Nicolò Pisani, sponsored a motion requiring galley masters to provide meat three days a week and cheese and sardines on other days, but the motion was voted down in the Senate. Venice entered its third great struggle with Genoa with its seamen depleted and discontented.

The Black Death was responsible for a lack of labor in all fields, but the difficulty of finding crews in Venice immediately after 1348 was an accentuation of a situation which had developed earlier and from which recovery was partial at best. Immigrants to replenish Venice's population were attracted by such inducements as exemption from the initiation fees of the guilds. The immigrants came mainly from inland Italy; they were craftsmen and shopkeepers lured by the Venetian market, not by the call of the sea.

Never again was Venice so largely a maritime nation as it had been in the thirteenth century. At that time, the lagoons had exuded seamen. In describing a nest of pirates in the Aegean about 1300, Marino Sanuto Torsello, a crusading enthusiast, wrote that it contained men from all countries and that the chiefs were mostly Genoese but the crews (*zurme e marinari*) were Venetians from the lagoons. The patriotic aspect of the popular maritime tradition of Venice had found expression in the First Genoese War at the battle of Trapani. The Genoese appeared at a time when nobles had left the Venetian fleet in order to attend to their business affairs. Consequently, the Venetian commanders hesitated to join battle. The crews, however, "le menu gent," as the chronicler Martino da Canal called them, clamored to attack and gained the victory. The Third and Fourth Genoese Wars were to reveal quite a different spirit among "the little people" of the fleet. Venice could still compete as a naval power second to none, but increasingly its strength lay in the wealth of its craftsmen and merchants rather than in its large reserve of ships and native seamen.

TRIUMPH BY COHESION·I

Symptoms of Disintegration

CHAPTER THIRTEEN

In Europe generally, the middle and later years of the fourteenth century were a period of disruption: of social revolution and the overthrow of established institutions. In England, there were peasant revolts and the throne was seized from the lawful king by the Duke of Lancaster, who thus planted the seed of the War of the Roses. In France, the king several times lost control of his kingdom. Mercenary armies subject to no government lived off the countryside. In the Church, there were two sets of popes and then three, each of whom had powerful and devout adherents. Florence suffered from bloody coups and countercoups and the revolt of the proletarian *Ciompi*. In most Italian cities the Commune was overthrown or undermined by a Signore, a kind of municipal monarch. Would the Venetian republic also be converted into a tyranny? Or racked by civil war?

Difficulties of the kind that led elsewhere to these results fermented also in Venice. After one dramatic explosion early in the century in the Tiepolo-Querini conspiracy of 1310, they sputtered to the surface confusedly but persistently. An economic depression which affected all Europe by mid-century intensified discontent. Then in 1347–49, the Black Death reduced Venice's population by about a half, as we have seen, and returned again and again to prevent full recovery. In Venice as elsewhere, the psychological effects of the plague intensified a hectic atmosphere. Men sought quick gains and quick revenges. In both business and politics they rode recklessly the wheel of fortune for high stakes and immediate satisfactions.

In this atmosphere, the solidity of the Commune of Venice was strained by new Genoese wars. Genoa as well as Venice grew in wealth and population during the Nautical and Commercial Revolutions at the end of the thirteenth and the beginning of the fourteenth centuries. The bustle and business opportunities of a great port attracted to Genoa many merchants and craftsmen from north-western Italy in spite of the city's frequent revolutions. Overseas, Genoese colonists enjoyed privileges which attracted not only more settlers from the West but adherence of many Levantines. By a liberal policy in granting citizenship, as well as by natural increase, Genoese multiplied mightily in Liguria and Romania. Genoese admirals commanded fleets for foreign princes — for the King of Sicily, the King of Naples, and the King of France. They did so for the sake of the pay and the fiefs they received from these foreign rulers, but their exploits spread the fame of Genoese seamanship and enabled Genoese admirals to maintain their own personal war fleets, composed mainly of Genoese seamen and available on appropriate occasions to serve the Genoese Commune. Throughout the fourteenth century, Genoa was Venice's most dangerous rival, and the enmity led to open war in 1350–55 and 1378–81.

In these Third and Fourth Genoese Wars, the failure of either side to obtain a cut-and-dried command of the sea was as striking as it had been in the First and Second Genoese Wars. The Nautical Revolution of the Middle Ages had made it more practical for the fleets to fight in winter as well as summer, but it left a cut-and-run strategy just as successful as ever in naval warfare. Again and again, an admiral with inferior forces was able to elude the opposing fleet while raiding the enemy's commerce and colonies. When main fleets did meet, there were heart-rending defeats, first for one side and then for the other, but the victor was never able to prevent the defeated city from putting another armada to sea within a year or two. Neither Venice nor Genoa had the means of really crushing its rival as thoroughly as Venice crushed Comacchio, or as Genoa with the aid of Tuscan allies crushed Pisa. Although each city thought at the time it could achieve "victory" in this sense, events proved otherwise.

These wars form crucial chapters of Venetian history not because of the heroic battle actions but because of the effects which victories and defeats had on the Venetian social structure and political system. The degradation from which many seamen were suffering was making its consequences felt. The hardening of class lines which had set in immediately after the enlargementt of the Great Council was engendering a bitterness made more acute by economic difficulties. The nobility was being fractured by conflicting financial interests as well as by family rivalries. The naval, diplomatic, and financial problems fired opposing ideas about the appropriate powers of the doge, the Great Council, and the smaller councils, such as the Forty or the Senate. These tensions within Venetian society were released by the fortunes of war.

THE THIRD GENOESE WAR Venetian-Genoese rivalry focused on the Aegean, the Black Sea, and the straits between. The Genoese had gained a lead there at the end of the Second Genoese War through their commercial settlement at Pera, their fortress at Kaffa, and their control of Chios and the nearby alum mines (See Chapter 10 and Maps 5 and 7). This dominant position of the Genoese was challenged more and more seriously by the Venetians after 1324 when Venice abandoned hope of restoring a Latin empire in Constantinople and sought the friendship of Byzantine emperors. Venice offered the emperors support against the pressure of the Genoese for more and more privileges and against the ever more dangerous attacks of the Turks. The role of protector of the Byzantine Empire enabled the Venetian Republic gradually to exert control over the Venetians who had made themselves independent fief-holders immediately after 1204, as had the Sanuto family on Naxos. As the Turks grew stronger, Venetian protection appeared as the only alternative to Turkish conquest. The Genoese meanwhile were hampered by their incapacity for sustained unified action. Their civil wars were extended to Romania. For example, when Guelfs gained power in Genoa in 1318, Pera and Kaffa clung to the Ghibelline side and repelled a fleet sent against them by the Genoese Guelfs. Within the Ghibellines, there were factional divisions also. Each faction disclaimed all responsibility, of course, for the raids of other Genoese factions on Venetian commerce. The Genoese made no countermove when in 1328 Venice sent a really formidable fleet, reported as forty galleys, into the Black Sea. It interrupted temporarily trade between Kaffa and Pera and exacted from the Genoese an indemnity for damage which one of the Ghibelline factions had done to Venetians at Lajazzo.

At Tana, the most northeastern outpost of Italian traders, Venetians and Genoese sometimes acted together for defense against the local ruler. When the Khan of the Golden Horde drove all Western merchants from Tana in 1343, following the Venetian-provoked riot, the Genoese invited the Venetians to trade through Kaffa. The Venetians accepted, but felt at a disadvantage there, and after a few years started to sail again directly to Tana. Considering these voyages a violation of an agreement to boycott Tana, the Genoese began seizing Venetian ships and war followed.

Events of the first year of the war, 1350, were notable chiefly in showing how much Venice had changed since the previous Genoese Wars. A fleet of about 35 galleys was armed under Marco Ruzzini as Captain General of the Sea. That title gave him supreme authority, subject always to the decisions of the councils in Venice, over the Captain of the Gulf and over commanders of other particular fleets and even over Venetian colonial officials in matters concerning fleets and their supply. Manning Ruzzini's galleys proved difficult. An effort was made to apply the same kind of conscription that had been used previously, namely, grouping all men between twenty and sixty into dozens and drafting by lot three out of every dozen. In 1294, 60 to 70 galleys had been manned in a few months by assigning the arming of the galleys to leading families and then letting the men conscripted choose on which galley they would serve. But in 1350, just after the Black Death, conscription did not produce a citizen navy. With only about 80,000 left in the population of the dogado, three-twelfths of the adult males would be only about 5,000 men, enough for about 25 galleys armed for war. It is not surprising, therefore, that crews of at least 10 of the 35 galleys came from Dalmatia or Venice's Greek colonies. But the most serious difficulty was that most of the men drafted in Venice preferred to hire substitutes. With the population halved, the average Venetian had twice as many coins in his money-chest and was less willing to fight or submit to the hardships of life at the oar. One of those who refused to serve claimed that the commanders ate good bread while the crews were given indigestible millet flour. The draft was obviously unpopular, and a proposal to forbid the hiring of substitutes was defeated.

The results showed when Ruzzini's fleet caught 14 Genoese galleys laden with merchandise in the harbor of Castro near Negroponte. He captured 10, but the engagement was considered a disgrace because 4 of the Genoese vessels got away and they would not have escaped but for the lack of discipline in the Venetian fleet. Instead of obeying orders to attack those Genoese galleys which had not yet been subdued, the crews concentrated on plundering the galleys already seized, even jumping into the water and swimming to the surrendered vessels in order to break open the hatches and get at the cargo below. This was what might be expected of mercenaries. The Venetian rules about the distribution of booty were not at that time clearly formulated in advance and a man felt he could keep what he could lay his hands on. Most significant was the irresolution of the Senate in dealing with this breach of discipline. Inquest by a commission was ordered, then delayed, then instructed to try to find out what had happened to the booty but to make no efforts as yet to recover it because, as the Senate avowed, the crews were men of many nationalities. They had been attracted by extra pay and hope of booty and if they heard rumors that their booty was to be taken from them they might rebel.

Prosecution of commanding officers was pushed more vigorously, especially after the Genoese galleys which had escaped from Castro harbor joined at Chios with a few just out from Genoa and returned across the Aegean to burn and plunder the port, although not the citadel, of Negroponte. In Venice some blamed the castellan, Tommaso Viadro, for not being on the alert and putting up a good fight; others blamed the Captain General, Ruzzini, saying that he had left inadequate forces at Negroponte, taking too many soldiers with him for a fruitless attack on Pera. One of the subordinate commanders was condemned because of the inaction of his galleys at Castro and was punished by being made ineligible for any future command, but there was no question of applying the severe punishment specified by thirteenth century laws, namely, the loss of his head. Viadro was acquitted, perhaps out of mercy, since he had just recently lost four sons to the Black Death. But neither Ruzzini nor Viadro were again chosen for a fighting command.

Realizing that they could not man a fleet large enough to crush the Genoese with their own Venetian citizens or subjects, the Venetian government looked for allies who could be hired to fight for them. In the western Mediterranean, the Catalans had for a century been coming to the forefront as a maritime people. United with other parts of northeastern Spain in the Kingdom of Aragon, they had their own reasons to fight the Genoese, notably the efforts of both Genoa and the King of Aragon to rule Sardinia. The King of Aragon agreed to furnish at least 12 galleys for which the Venetians would pay 1,000 ducats a month per galley, in addition to 18 which he agreed to arm himself. In the eastern Mediterranean, a Byzantine emperor was trying to rebuild the Greek fleet, and the Venetians promised him the same price for 8 galleys to be manned by Greeks at Venice's expense, while he at his own expense armed 12. Adding all these to the 40 for which Venice itself would somehow find the necessary sailors, oarsmen, and soldiers — either in the lagoons, in other Italian cities, in Dalmatia, or in the Venetian parts of Romania — Venice's rulers hoped to muster an armada of about 80 to 90 galleys. With a force of that size they planned to conquer the Genoese possessions in the East, turn Pera and Chios back to the Byzantine emperor, and then destroy the Genoese fleets off their own Riviera and blockade Genoa into submission.

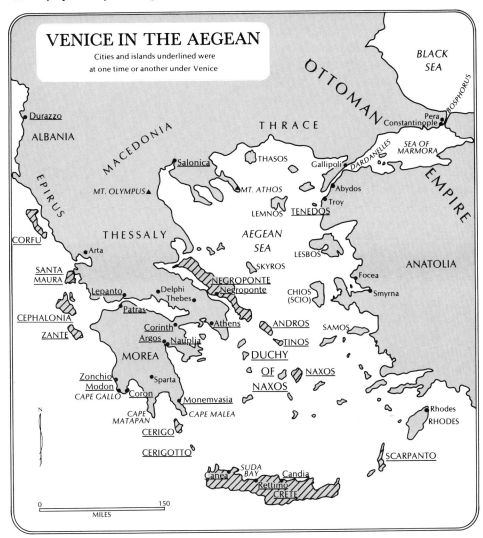

VENICE IN THE AEGEAN

Cities and islands underlined were
at one time or another under Venice

MAP **7**

But what a reversal since the twelfth century when Venice supplied the men to defend the Byzantine Empire against the Normans! Now Venice was acting as paymaster and was depending heavily on Greeks and Catalans to fight Venice's battles!

The Venetians' confidence in their wealth is no less notable than their lack of confidence in their own manpower. By their system of forced loans, they could raise the money to hire fleets without straining the resources of the rich. Earlier, the Monte Vecchio had been cut from over 1,000,000 ducats in 1313 to about 423,000 in 1343. Now, over 1,000,000 ducats were added to it between 1345 and 1363. The market price of these bonds fell, to be sure, from their par of 100, but hardly below 60 and only briefly below 80, so that in the absence of anything like an income tax the rich were not overburdened.

Coalitions are notoriously difficult to coordinate. The plan was that a Venetian fleet would join the Catalans off Sicily and either prevent the Genoese fleet from going to the east or, if it got by, follow it and join forces with the Venetian squadron in the Aegean and with the Byzantine fleet at Constantinople. Actually, the Genoese sent off a fleet of 64 galleys under Paganino Doria before either the Catalans or the Venetians were ready. A small Venetian squadron, about 20 galleys, under a new Captain General, Nicolò Pisani, was already in the Aegean taking prizes and preparing with the Byzantine fleet for an assault on Pera. When he heard that Paganino Doria's fleet was coming, Pisani fled to Negroponte, with Doria in pursuit. Pisani sank his ships to prevent their capture and used his men to successfully defend the city. When the Catalan fleet and a new Venetian fleet finally entered the Aegean, Doria retired to Pera. Pisani then refloated his vessels, joined the allied fleet and set out on the main goal of the campaign, juncture with the Greek fleet and destruction of the Genoese at Pera. By then it was November. Heavy storms and north winds delayed the allies so much that they turned back to Crete for supplies. In February, 1352, they started for the straits again. This time a south wind hampered the Genoese, who were unable to prevent the Catalan-Venetian fleet from sweeping into the Golden Horn and making juncture with the Greeks. The Genoese reformed within the Bosphorus and there fought the allies to a draw. The battle of the Bosphorus impressed contemporaries as particularly deadly and nasty because it was fought during a storm in the dead of winter and continued into the night, the maniacal slaughter being unchecked by the difficulties of telling friend from foe. The Catalan admiral and many other high officers were killed. Losses were heavy on both sides, prisoners relatively few. Some of the Franciscan friars who made it their concern to arrange for the exchange of prisoners came to the Venetians to see how many Genoese they had taken, expecting to find many because so many of the Genoese were missing. They found the number surviving as prisoners so small that they decided not to return to report to the Genoese lest the latter, enflamed by finding that so many of their companions were dead, should slaughter the Venetians they were holding.

Both sides claimed to have won the battle, but strategically the victory certainly lay with the Genoese, for the Catalans and Venetians withdrew. They had lost too much to try further assault on Pera, especially since the Genoese were receiving not only supplies but soldiers from the Sultan of the Ottoman Turks, Orkhan I, who ruled all the eastern side of the Bosphorus and the Sea of Marmora. Orkhan was looking towards expansion into Europe also. He did not want to see either the Byzantine empire or the Venetian naval power strengthened. After the allied fleet left, the Byzantine Emperor felt he had no alternative but to make peace with the Genoese and allow them to fortify Pera and the hill of Galata as they wished. Thereafter, the naval action in the Aegean consisted of much capturing of individual Genoese ships by Venetians, and vice versa.

The King of Aragon's main interest was in conquering Sardinia, and Nicolò Pisani joined him there. In 1353, Pisani won a resounding victory over the Genoese at Alghero off Sardinia, but a new Genoese fleet under Paganino Doria slipped by him and did much damage in the Adriatic. Then it eluded him again in order to plunder in the Aegean and take refuge in Chios. When Pisani found them there, he challenged the Genoese to come out and fight. Since they declined, he devoted himself to seizing Genoese shipping and then retired from the

Aegean to the Venetian bases at Modon and Coron. There he received orders from Venice telling him to avoid battle, for the Genoese now had more ships at sea than he commanded and peace was about to be negotiated. Accordingly, Pisani decided to winter in a small harbor near Modon called Porto Longo. He assigned 14 galleys under Nicola Querini to guard the entrance, and lashed together near shore his small vessels and 21 other galleys. When Paganino Doria arrived and defied Pisani to come out and fight, he declined according to his instructions, although Doria's fleet was about the same size as his. But the Genoese did not go away. A galley commanded by Paganino's nephew succeeded in slipping by Querini's squadron. One report has it that he was allowed to pass so that he could be easily captured. But a dozen other galleys slipped in after him, avoiding the protective squadron. They fell on the vessels which were tied up near shore, quite unready for action. The Venetian ships were all taken, Pisani himself and most of his men were made prisoners. Paganino Doria had been refused any triumphal honors after the battle of the Bosphorus; too many Genoese had died there. On his return to Genoa after Porto Longo in 1354, he was given a resounding triumph.

The terms of peace, however, were not those that a victor might impose. Many times in its long history, Venice was able to recover from a defeat or make good use of a victory because of skillful diplomacy based on a wide knowledge of the weaknesses and ambitions of other powers. After the defeat at Porto Longo, she had good opportunities for diplomatic maneuver because Genoa was being governed by the Visconti rulers of Milan. The defeat which Nicolò Pisani had inflicted on the Genoese at Alghero the year before had not prevented the Genoese from arming the new fleet which gained victory at Porto Longo, but that defeat had plunged Genoa into domestic strife — one faction wishing to punish the defeated admiral, a Grimaldi, the other defending him. In desperation, the Genoese accepted the Visconti as a ruler who would help them against Venice. They could always have another revolution, they may have thought, as indeed they did a few years later. But in 1355 peace negotiations were in Visconti hands, and the Visconti wanted peace. Their ambitions in northern Italy were being frustrated by allies Venice had recruited, allies which included not only North-Italian states, but the Holy Roman Emperor Charles IV, King of Bohemia. The terms agreed to left all issues open. Each republic was to stop attacks on the other and neither would send fleets to Tana for the next three years.

Revolutions so often follow defeats that there is no need to turn aside to explain why Genoa's defeat at Alghero had such consequences. It is more relevant to ask why the Venetian defeat at Porto Longo, following the failures at Castro and in the Bosphorus, did not lead to revolution in Venice. That Venice would call in a foreign prince, as the Genoese did, was in view of Venice's tradition of sovereign independence unthinkable. But the violent overthrow of nobles who could be held responsible for defeat and a reshaping of policies and even of institutions was not unthinkable. It colored the career of many doges.

ANDREA DANDOLO   Shortly before the end of the Third Genoese War, the doge died who had been at the head of the state during the most disasterous decade Venetians had ever known, 1343-54, a decade ravaged by the plague as well as by war. Andrea Dandolo's career illustrates the ambiguities which shroud Venetian internal politics of the fourteenth century. Andrea Dandolo had not made his reputation by military leadership as had so many earlier doges. Andrea was a prodigy of legal learning, so esteemed as a lawyer that he had been elected a Procurator of San Marco at twenty-two, which was phenomenally young for such a post even for a member of so distinguished a family. While Procurator, he made a compilation of pertinent acts of the Great Council. The mutual jealousies of the more experienced political leaders and Andrea's apparently "safe" preoccupation with legal detail probably explain his election as doge when only thirty-six.

As doge he applied himself to putting all the state's activity in good order from a lawyer's point of view. The terms under which Treviso and Zara were subject to Venice were spelled out in "acts of dedication," i.e., submission. Changes made in the civil law during the century since Giacomo Tiepolo's codification were collected in an additional book of the Statuti. Treaties and charters defining Venice's rights towards the popes, emperors, and other states were assembled in orderly fashion.

Andrea wrote history in the same lawyerlike spirit. His chronicle contained a mass of documents selected to prove that Venice was always right. It was organized into chapters, sections, and paragraphs so it could be cited easily and serve as a handy work of reference for Venetian statesmen.

In the writing, research, and compiling which he did as doge, Andrea Dandolo was aided by the clerks of the Ducal Chancery who were notaries by training. As the top layer in the class of citizens-by-birth, they were developing a class pride under the leadership of the head of the Chancery, the Grand Chancellor, who held a position of distinction in both the machinery and ceremony of government. Under Andrea Dandolo's dogeship, the Grand Chancellor was Benintendi dei Ravignani, twelve years younger than Andrea and his devoted collaborator. Andrea showed his appreciation and recognition of the importance of the Grand Chancellor by having the chancellor depicted with him in the mosaics of the Baptistry which he added to San Marco.

Benintendi dei Ravignani collaborated with the doge not only in legal studies but also in cultivating by correspondence the friendship of Petrarch, the outstanding poet and humanist of that day. The doge wished to raise his own prestige and that of his chancery by adding to their legal learning an ability to write elegant Latin. When Petrarch made an appeal for peace between Venice and Genoa, calling on both to recognize that they were parts of a larger whole, Italy — that they were Italy's two eyes neither of which should be put out — neither city was any more moved by the appeal than England and Germany would have been in 1915 by an appeal in the name of European nationality. But Andrea Dandolo replied with a letter in as fine Latin as he could muster, good propaganda in a medium of the time.

Although the Dandolo occupied a central position among the aristocratic old families, Andrea's history did not exalt the virtues of aristocracy. Instead, he emphasized on the one hand that the common people had taken part with the nobles in the crucial steps of Venice's early history, as in the creation of the first doge. On the other hand, he also emphasized the powers of the famous doges of the thirteenth century. In his account, the republic's decisions and victories seem like decisions and victories of the doges. Was this because he paid excessive attention to legal forms? Or was it because he thought that, in his own day too, the greatness of Venice required that doges should be powerful leaders? Did he dream of restoring the doge to a position of command such as had been held in fact by his ancestor Enrico Dandolo, the conqueror of Constantinople? Did he even entertain the idea that he might find support for such a restoration of ducal power among the citizens-by-birth rather than among the nobles? Probably he dreamed only of restoring to his Venetians the unifying spirit of patriotism which he attributed to them in their past. During his lifetime, the trend went the other way. Arrogance among the nobility and resentment at their arrogance increased and resulted in his being hated at his death. But in the long run, his learning won him a place of high honor in Venetian traditions, and his chronicles, accepted at Venice as authoritative, added to the pride of Venetians in themselves. Venetian patriotism and firmness later in the face of defeat owed much to their belief in the rightfulness of their claims and to their strong sense of having suffered and achieved together in the past.

MARINO FALIER *Those who are for a time doges I would warn to study the image this sets before their eyes, that they may see as in a mirror that they are leaders not lords, nay not even leaders, but honored servants of the State.*

PETRARCH, IN A LETTER OF MAY, 1355

Dandolo's successor did more than dream of a strong dogeship. Andrea died just before the defeat at Porto Longo. To succeed him, the electors chose on their very first ballot by 35 votes out of 41 a man whose record made him appear the perfect war leader, Marino Falier. He had been several times a commander of fleets and armies, had distinguished himself by boldness in suppressing Zara's last rebellion, had served often in the Council of Ten, and most recently, in his seventies, had conducted difficult negotiations skillfully. He was at Avignon, negotiating at the papal court, when elected. Barely a month after his return came the news of the disgraceful defeat at Porto Longo, so that in the first months of his dogeship he was occupied in the vigorous measures for full mobilization which Venice took after that defeat and while the peace was being negotiated. One exceptional step was the arming of four galleys under commanders who were commoners. Although not nobles, they were experienced ship captains, and they harried Genoese commerce quite successfully. Within Venice there were many who blamed defeats on the cowardice of the nobles. There were also many who resented the arrogance of the nobles, and one incident illustrating this also shows how Falier undertook to use this discontent. In the naval office, which was on the ground floor of the Ducal Palace next to the Bacino, one of the paymasters or naval secretaries, Giovanni Dandolo, struck in rage a galley officer, a commoner named Bertuccio Isarello, when the latter refused to accept into his crew a man the noble Dandolo wished to assign him. Isarello went to the water front and, being popular with sailors, had no trouble collecting on the edge of the Piazzetta a gang which kept walking back and forth with him threateningly waiting for Giovanni Dandolo to emerge. Feeling in danger, Giovanni went to the doge who summoned Isarello into the palace and admonished him severely. But later that night the doge called Isarello again to the palace and enlisted him in a plot to overthrow the ruling nobles and establish Marino Falier as Lord and Master, Master with the Rod (*Signore a bacheta*) as the expression went, according to the symbolism of the investiture of earlier doges. Another leader in the plot enlisted by the doge was Filippo Calendario, sometimes given more than his due as the builder of the Ducal Palace, then under construction. He was in fact a stone mason and building contractor who was also a shipowner. While many of the participants in the Falier conspiracy were connected in some way with maritime industries, the men to whom the doge made his appeal were from its upper or middle class, men with a popularity among the rank and file of seamen, and with a resentment against nobles whom they blamed for Venice's defeat.

Isarello and Calendario undertook to find twenty chiefs, each of whom would be able to call out forty men, and they were to assemble at the Ducal Palace on the night of April 15. But that evening it was clear that something had gone wrong. Too many of those approached refused to join and reported to friends among the nobility that something was afoot. Very few, even among the conspirators, knew that the doge himself was the center of the plot, but it was rumored that Filippo Calendario was about to rally all the seamen of the section around the Arsenal and from there take over the whole city (*correre la città*). First one and then another noble came to the Ducal Palace to report such rumors to the doge, who tried to make light of them, although he felt that he could not avoid calling his Councillors when that was demanded. The Councillors then pushed inquiries, discovered that the trail led to the doge himself, and sent word throughout the city to other nobles to arm men they could trust, each in his own parish, and send guards to the Piazza San Marco. The chief conspirators were all quickly seized without any fighting.

There was no lynching, no slaughter in the streets by enraged partisans. All punishments were inflicted according to due process of law as then understood. The Ducal Councillors summoned the Council of Ten the next morning, April 16. They voted to associate with their action twenty men whom they chose from among the most respected in the city. That made a body of 36, hearing evidence and sitting in judgment (the addition, called the *zonta*, of 20; the 6 Ducal Councillors; 1 of the State Attorneys, the other being disqualified; and 9 of the Council of Ten, one being debarred because he was a Falier). But they acted fast. Before nightfall, Filippo Calendario and Bertuccio Isarello had been sentenced. They were hung from an upper story of the Ducal Palace with bits in their mouths to prevent their crying out to the crowd. During the ensuing days, other condemned conspirators were hung along the loggia, until there was a line of eleven gibbeted bodies overlooking the Piazzetta. Meanwhile, the case against the doge had been heard and sentence voted. He was beheaded on April 17, 1355, on the stairway within the courtyard of the Ducal Palace, on the same spot where he had a few months before sworn to uphold the constitution of the Venetian Republic. When his head had been severed, a Chief of the Ten bearing the bloody sword strode out on a balcony to show it to the crowd and cry, "Note well, justice has been done to the traitor."

The respect of the Venetians for their republican constitution was deepened by the combination of legality, efficiency, and severity displayed at such a dangerous moment, when the head of the republic, its chief magistrate, in time of war, plotted its overthrow. To the discontented, it appeared more awesome and unassailable. By the nobles who benefited most from it and by the mass of commoners who prized the opportunity to go about their business in peace and security it was more and more revered as a work of exceptional wisdom.

What could have induced a man as universally admired as Marino Falier and so often tested in so many honored and difficult posts to attempt such a plot — a man already over seventy, with no children to whom to leave a lordship even if he could establish one? The question baffled Petrarch and is still baffling. Some later chroniclers created a romantic story to explain the mystery. They built on the undoubted facts that, soon after his election, some words insulting to the doge were written on a wall in the Ducal Palace and that Falier felt the young men perpetrating the scandal had been inadequately punished. The story grew in retelling until it was said that the words were an insult to his wife's honor, a beautiful young second wife (she was a second wife to be sure, but about fifty), by a particular young man, the Michele Steno who was later to become doge himself. This romantic legend carries no conviction because it appears only long after the event.

A more convincing explanation is to be found in the situation in Italy generally and Venice in particular in April, 1355. Nearly everywhere, government by councils was giving way to government by Signori. It was, as John Addington Symonds called it, the Age of the Despots. Venice had just been defeated in war with Genoa, and despots seemed generally more successful in war than republics. There may well have been among both nobles and commoners at Venice some who thought that more powerful doges would enable Venice to win. Falier may have been acting not from a personal ambition to be Signore but as leader of the die-hards of a war party, who were unreconciled to peace with Genoa and plotted a violent coup to impose their will. Reverence for the aristocratic constitution was not yet as firmly rooted as it was to be in the next century.

If there was such a monarchic party among the nobles, its existence was obscured as much as possible by the ruling majority. That such monarchic ideas were smoldering is suggested not only by Dandolo's emphasis on the leadership of earlier doges and by Falier's conspiracy but also by the extreme measures taken to make sure that there would be no effort to reverse the judgment on Falier. Permission to carry arms was given to all those immediately active in his condemnation or in the seizure of the conspirators, as if there was fear of vengeance from unknown sympathizers with his plot. Significant also was the curious posthumous acquittal of a later doge, Lorenzo Celsi. After his death, Celsi was officially declared innocent of unspecified charges. The likeliest explanation is in the story that Lorenzo Celsi, who was a naval commander when elected, a man who liked display and a large court and who liked to go riding with his courtiers, had one of these courtiers ride in front of him bearing a rod or staff, a *bacheta,* a symbol of power, until one day one of his Councillors had seized the staff and broken it. But it was officially decided to hush up any suspicions about his ambitions, and there was no recognition, either by official acts or in the contemporary chronicles, of any group among either the nobility or the commoners who thought that Venice needed to be ruled by a Signore and that its system of government by a complicated gearing of councils was outmoded.

TWO DECADES OF DOUBT   Enough kept going wrong, to be sure, in the interval between the Third and the Fourth Genoese Wars to give grounds for discontent. Even before the peace with Genoa in 1355, King Louis of Hungary appeared ready to join in the fight in order to make good his claims to Dalmatia. The following year he attacked, aided by several of Venice's lesser neighbors to the north and west of the lagoons. War weary and discouraged by several minor defeats, Venice ceded Dalmatia. For the first time since Doge Orseolo's famous Dalmatian cruise of the year 1000, the Venetian doge gave up the title of Duke of Dalmatia, and called himself simply, "Dei gratia dux Veneciarum et cetera"! Another humiliation for Venetians occured some years later in Cyprus, where a quarrel between the Venetian and Genoese consuls over who could take precedence in holding the king's stirrup or being on his right hand at the coronation ceremony led to a riot and then to a large Genoese expedition against the King of Cyprus, who had blamed and punished the Genoese. Venice did nothing to help the king, who had taken their side, and when the Genoese forced him to pay them a huge indemnity and to cede to them the leading port, Famagusta, Venice's only reaction was to withdraw its merchants. Meanwhile, Venice had been forced to spend heavily in suppressing a revolt in Crete, a revolt led not by the conquered Greeks of the island, as several earlier revolts had been, but by Venetian settlers joined by some of the Greek nobles who had succeeded in keeping their land. The revolt was caused by the burden of taxation imposed from Venice and by the scornful rejection of the proposal of the Cretan nobles to send representatives to Venice to discuss the matter. It was a lost opportunity to inject the representative principle into the Venetian government. The leaders of the revolt bore such thoroughly Venetian names as Gradenigo and Venier, and the rulers of Venice looked on them all as vile traitors, especially when they appealed to the Genoese for help, which was not given. An army of mercenaries sent out from Venice suppressed the rebellion but at the cost of another big increase in the public debt.

As the size of the Monte Vecchio grew, fiscal policy occasioned increasingly bitter controversies within the nobility. Its reduction between 1313 and 1343, keeping the price high, had favored bondholders, while the taxes and economies which made that reduction possible hurt the general mass of consumers and some merchants. Those who were seeking fortunes in the Levant wanted a more aggressive, even if more expensive, policy. They were less concerned with maintaining the Monte Vecchio at a high market price. Wavering policies left both interests half satisfied and the state weakened. Taxes were raised enough to hurt but not enough to prevent deficits. The debt kept rising, from the low of 423,000 ducats in 1343 to about 1,500,000 in 1363 and over 3,000,000 in 1379. Instead of making any repayment of old issues, the government provided for a sinking fund to buy in bonds when prices were low. More questionable measures were taken to sustain the market. The Procurators of San Marco, who administered many trust funds, were ordered to invest in the Monte Vecchio the endowments of hospitals and other philanthropic institutions, some of which had been in real estate.

The net result was not unfavorable to the rich old families which bore the heaviest assessments and had the biggest holdings of the Monte Vecchio, at least not according to our conceptions of taxation. Although they were forced to subscribe 24 percent of their assessment during the ten years 1363-72, that was only 8 percent of their known wealth, property being assessed at about one third of real value. Some probably had additional investments overseas that escaped the assessors. Since the price in those years hardly ever fell below 80 and frequently rose above 90 (the market price was 92½ in 1375), if they chose to sell what they were forced to buy, they recovered 80 to 90 percent of that 8 percent. In short, without any other kind of direct taxes, they paid about 1 percent of their real wealth over a ten-year period.

The instability of the coinage also gave reasons for complaint. The bondholders who had been repaid in the 1330's could have complained, if they were die-hard believers in the silver standard, that they had paid into the government silver grossi and were repaid in gold ducats at a time when it would have cost the government about one-third more to have repaid them in the silver coin at its old weight and fineness. Later in the century, bondholders benefitted from a change in the bimetallic ratio. Gold began rising, debasement of the silver coinage continued, and yet interest payments continued to be made in gold.

Waves of discontent were reflected in a fluctuating commercial policy. Relative liberalism alternated with the kind of protectionism represented by the Officium de Navigantibus with its wide powers for driving foreign capital out of the Levant trade. Opportunities for big profits by temporary monopolies in key products, such as those Federico Corner worked at in Cyprus, probably arose more in this period than in any other. Temporary monopolies based on control of merchant galleys were easier, partly because the number of galleys auctioned for the various voyages was much reduced after the plague and the general economic decline of the fourteenth century, and partly because interruptions of their voyages for political reasons were more numerous. It was an age of contracting turnover in which the merchants depended on high prices for profits.

Politically also the fourteenth century was an age of contraction. The trend toward more and more participation in government which had been notable in the previous centuries was reversed in Europe generally and in the Italian cities particularly. At Venice, the enlargement of the Great Council at the very beginning of the century was followed by erection of barriers against accepting any new families. By the middle of the century, there were signs of a concentration of power in the hands of a small group within the nobility. Important issues were increasingly decided not in the Great Council but in the Senate. The Forty acted on political and financial matters only when meeting with the Senate. During wars and other emergencies, the Great Council elected special committees of twenty or thirty, with extraordinary plenary powers, which displaced the Senate, but only temporarily. As a result, a group of about 100 men representing some thirty families decided such crucial questions as negotiating peace with Hungary or sending an army to subdue Crete.

Government by a closely knit class, a small oligarchy, had some advantages. It gave Venetian policy a consistency which contrasted with the unsteadiness of action of many of Venice's neighbors. Monarchies such as the Hungarian Kingdom, the Carrara Signory in Padua, or the Visconti Signory in Milan were subject to severe upsets when a ruler died. Venice's Senatorial oligarchy persistently strove for the same objectives decade after decade, even for century after century, and succeeded in essentials even in the dark decades between the Third and Fourth Genoese Wars. Despite the loss of Dalmatia, Venetian fleets still ruled the Adriatic and did not permit the King of Hungary or anyone else to arm a rival fleet there. They patrolled against pirates and required merchandise going to northern Italy to pass through Venice, which kept its position as the staple city of the northern Adriatic. Although the routes of trade through the Levant were frequently cut here or there, alternatives were quickly found and exploited. Westward and northward, access to the key market of Bruges was obtained by several routes. The most used route went through Germany over the Brenner Pass. Alternate overland routes went through Switzerland and Basel to the Rhine, or through Savoy to France. Negotiating security for Venetian goods along these routes was made easier by keeping open the possibility or threat of going by sea. For a couple of years after the conclusion of the Third Genoese War, government galleys were auctioned for the voyage to Flanders. Then the Anglo-French wars and other circumstances made it seem wiser to leave that voyage to private enterprise for many years, but official galley voyages to Bruges were resumed in 1374.

In that same year, galleys were offered at auction to go directly to Beirut and Alexandria. Until then, Famagusta on the east coast of Cyprus had been the assembly point of Syrian wares and the terminus of one merchant galley fleet, while another had gone directly to Alexandria, except in years when the crusading of the King of Cyprus interfered. When the Genoese seized Famagusta in 1374, they thought they were getting the treasure house of trade for all the lands Beyond-the-Sea. But the Corner continued to export sugar and salt from their concessions on the south side of the island. Moreover, Venetian galleys and the regulated cogs carrying cotton by-passed Cyprus, going directly to Beirut and other ports in Syria and Palestine, as well as to Alexandria. The Genoese were left holding a half-empty bag, while the Venetians gained a leading position nearer main sources of supply. They established themselves in Egypt and Syria as the leading customers for the spices of India, which came increasingly through the Red Sea as the routes through the Persian Gulf and Persia were more and more disrupted.

These successes of Venice's commercial diplomacy enabled her to keep pace with rival Genoa, which continued to change its government frequently. Their domestic strife did not prevent Genoese shipping and trade from competing vigorously all over the Levant. Whenever its whirl of revolutions put the government for a time in strong hands, Genoa pushed aggressively for privileges that would assure it commercial superiority in Romania.

The competition of the two republics was bitterest in the Black Sea. The trade of Trebizond suffered from disorders in Persia, but Tana regained its former importance, especially for the slave trade. At Constantinople, Venice and Genoa sought favors from rival Greek emperors who depended on one or the other of the two ambitious republics. Venice and Genoa both sought the island of Tenedos just south of the Dardanelles, for if properly fortified, it could be used to control access to the straits and keep rivals out of the Black Sea altogether. The Genoese had made themselves so hateful to the Greeks through their lordship of Pera and Galata that their efforts to seize Tenedos were resisted and its Greek governor obeyed a Venetian-backed emperor when in 1376 he let in the Venetians. The Venetian occupation and fortification of Tenedos was the signal for a Genoese attack and open war.

Venice entered the new war without having resolved the problems which had been festering ever since the previous contest. Although her institutions had proved strong enough to absorb many shocks without violent revolution, the discontent among seamen was still troublesome, the public debt was mounting to unprecedented heights, an oligarchy was asserting domination within the nobility, and even the viability and the legitimacy of the aristocratic constitution was in question.

TRIUMPH BY COHESION·II

The Climax of the Struggle with Genoa

CHAPTER FOURTEEN

This Fourth Genoese War proved to be the most severe test of the cohesion of Venetian society and of the strength of its republican institutions. Partly this was because the plague and the technical and economic changes already described had decimated and demoralized Venetian seamen. At the same time, the concentration of power in smaller councils such as the Senate had bred a jealous arrogance within these councils, suspicious of any threat to their authority, and on the other hand a resentment against that arrogance. Partly it was because a coalition was formed against Venice more formidable than any she had faced previously. She had waged war separately against Genoa and against Hungary. Now they, together with Francesco Carrara, Lord of Padua, and a number of lesser mainland neighbors, were allied against her. In earlier wars, Venice had drawn strength from its possession of Dalmatia. This time, Dalmatia was in the hands of her enemies.

THE WAR OF CHIOGGIA The war arose from competing efforts to control the trade of the Black Sea by possession of the tiny island of Tenedos, as has been explained. Its crises revolved around two outstanding personalities. The most picturesque was Carlo Zeno, a descendant of Doge Ranieri Zeno. Carlo Zeno was one of ten children left impoverished, at least comparatively impoverished, when his father was killed while commanding the crusading force that took Smyrna from the Turks early in the century. His family planned to provide for Carlo through a career in the church and sent him to Padua to study. There he fell into riotous living and gambling, lost his money, had to sell his books, and for a livelihood enlisted in a mercenary band as a soldier. When he came home to Venice some four or five years later, his family had almost given him up as dead, but they had kept for him an ecclesiastical post assigned him in his youth in a church in Patras, Greece. Carlo's leadership in fighting the Turks in that neighborhood was welcome, but when he challenged to a duel a Christian knight who had insulted him, his conduct was considered unseemly for a cleric. He resigned his post, married, and went to Constantinople to make his living as a merchant. Family tradition recorded that he there became involved in an intrigue to rescue an imprisoned emperor and obtain from him the cession of Tenedos to the Venetians. The tale is hardly more credible than the highly romantic nineteenth-century novel based on it (*Arethusa*, by F. Marion Crawford). Much that is recorded about Carlo's early life may be half fiction, but he certainly turned up at Tenedos at the right moment and was a leader in driving off the Genoese who attempted to occupy it at just the time that the Venetians moved in.

Whereas Carlo Zeno was as much soldier as admiral, Vettor Pisani, the other Venetian hero of the war, was first and last a seaman. He was the nephew of the Nicolò Pisani who had won a brilliant victory off Sardinia in the Third Genoese War and then suffered humiliating defeat at Porto Longo. The treatment of his uncle helps somewhat to explain how Vettor was treated. Following Nicolò's defeat and release from a Genoese prison, he had been prosecuted by the State's Attorneys, condemned by the Great Council to a heavy fine, and declared ineligible for further high commands. Nicolò was not accused of cowardice or inaction at Porto Longo, but of picking a bad anchorage and of having disobeyed his orders earlier in the campaign by failing to bring Doria to battle in the Aegean and by fighting against a city in Sardinia for the King of Aragon. In fact, that king had rewarded Nicolò by granting him a fief in Aragon. Some other commanders at Porto Longo received more severe sentences, and among those accused was the nephew, Vettor; but Vettor was acquitted by a vote of three to one.

In the interval between the Third and Fourth Genoese Wars, Vettor Pisani was active in outfitting and commanding merchant galleys. After he had served as the capitanio of the merchant galleys going to Tana, an episode occurred which illustrates the kinds of quarrels among the Venetian nobility that often arose from such service and reveals a side of Vettor's character which proved important during the later war. One of the galley masters had been fined for bringing back from Tana some dried salt sturgeon loaded in the arms room of the galley. The condemned galley master claimed he had been given a right to that much extra cargo and he appealed to the Ducal Council. Vettor Pisani was present at its hearing of the case. It was asserted by the ship's scribe that the galley master had loaded the dried sturgeon without the required *bolletta*, namely, the written authorization to load which he was by law required to have from the capitanio of the fleet for all wares loaded, one of the devices used to prevent overloading and to prevent the masters from playing favorites among the shippers. Vettor Pisani then spoke up and said that he knew the master had had the bolletta because he had given it to him. Vettor asked that his word be believed. One of the accusing officials, Pietro Corner, son of the rich Federico, the sugar king, replied sarcastically, "Yes indeed, but the scribe says otherwise."

Stung by being given the lie indirect, Vettor stopped Pietro Corner later in the day and asked him if he was armed, telling him he better be next time they met. Dagger in hand he waylaid Corner that evening near his palace. Corner escaped only by ducking into the nearest house. For this attempted assault Vettor Pisani was fined 200 ducats and deprived of an office in Crete to which he had been elected. But he was promptly chosen for another office in Crete and won distinction in fighting against the rebellion there in 1363. The episode shows Vettor Pisani as quick to anger, impulsive when his honor was questioned, but ready to pull in harness as part of a team when he had cooled off. Moreover, he was extremely popular with the men of his fleets because he had none of the haughty manner by which many members of the old nobility of Venice made themselves obnoxious.

When full-scale hostilities opened in 1378, Vettor Pisani was chosen Captain General of the Sea and sent west with 14 galleys to attack the Genoese in their own waters. The relatively small size of the battle fleets in this war showed how much the plagues and the general depression of the mid-fourteenth century had weakened both cities. Venice, moreover, felt acutely the severe shrinkage of her naval power as a result of the loss of Dalmatia. In this war Dalmatia, being under the King of Hungary, provided bases for the Genoese and contributed galleys to the Genoese fleets when they carried the war into the Adriatic. Venice recruited some Greek seamen (especially by sending galleys out from Venice to Crete with skeleton crews of only one man to a bench). But the enemy's possession of Dalmatia threatened Venice's connection with this source of manpower, as well as threatening the city's food supplies. Pisani won a brilliant victory in the West and brought back many noble Genoese prisoners. That did not prevent the Genoese sending out that same year another fleet which reached the Adriatic. After a voyage to the Aegean where he picked up the galleys armed there, Pisani came back to the Adriatic and became fully occupied trying to control the waters which the Venetians regarded as their own gulf.

At the end of 1378, Pisani asked permission to return to Venice to replenish his crews and refit, but the Senate ordered him to winter at Pola in Istria because from Pola he could more quickly move to protect convoys. They sent him supplies and some men to fill out his depleted crews. After a spring voyage escorting a convoy of grain ships from Apulia, he was reorganizing, and had some of his ships ashore being careened and cleaned when a Genoese fleet appeared flying flags with insignia inviting battle (a sword pointing upward). Pisani ordered the trumpets sounded to collect crews. He had about 24 galleys, including some great galleys laden with supplies. The Genoese numbered about 22, but only some 16 were visible, for the others, which had recently arrived from Genoa, were keeping out of sight behind a headland in order to later take the Venetians from the rear by surprise. Despite his apparent superiority in numbers, Pisani was against accepting the challenge because of the condition of his fleet, but when in the council of war his fellow commanders implied that failure to fight was cowardice, he ordered as many ships as possible prepared speedily for battle. He reinforced his crews with some mercenary soldiers from the garrison of Pola, probably Slavs of the neighborhood, and with his own galley led the attack. The Genoese admiral was killed and his galley overwhelmed. The Venetians seemed victorious until struck by the Genoese reserve waiting in ambush. Thereafter, the fight went against the Venetians. Despairing of victory, Pisani led the escape of five or six Venetian vessels. Hundreds of Venetians were killed and many more taken prisoner, including twenty-four nobles. They were held to be exchanged, but the Genoese commander reported to his ally in Padua that he had beheaded the eight hundred mercenaries after a council of war so advised and had thrown the butchered bodies overboard.

Considering Pisani's force adequate to protect the Adriatic, the Senate had sent Carlo Zeno off just a month earlier, in command of five well-equipped galleys, to prey on Genoese commerce. Even after the defeat, they sent six more galleys to join him. They hoped that a strong attack near Genoa on Genoese commerce would draw the Genoese fleet home from the Adriatic to the protection of their own Riviera. Neither Zeno nor the Senate realized how desperately he and his galleys would be needed at home before the end of 1379.

In that year, the city of Venice came nearer to being taken by assault than at any other time in the history of the Republic. The troops of the King of Hungary closed in on the routes northward, the Carrara lord of Padua blocked those to the west, and the Genoese fleet, instead of going home, received reinforcements. It seized ships within sight of Venice, and burned exposed towns along the Lido. Blockaded on all sides, Venice began to run out of food and supplies. The city itself seemed about to be invaded when the Genoese and Paduans joined forces within the lagoons and on August 16, 1379, took Chioggia by storm, a stunning blow. Venice asked for negotiations, but their enemies replied that they would not negotiate until after they had bridled the horses of San Marco, the four famous bronze horses which had been brought from Constantinople in 1204 and stood then as they do now above the entrance to the church of San Marco.

Among the Venetian nobility, there was no lack of will to resist. The San Nicoló entrance at the Lido was barricaded with large cogs chained together. Forts and palisades were built at key points. Large sums were raised by forced loans, and mercenaries were hired to man the forts and to break through the blockade of routes inland. The traditional system of taking men by lot out of every dozen was turned into almost universal conscription for service either in the home guard or in the army or fleet. But the common people, especially the seamen, were disgusted by the treatment of Vettor Pisani. When draftees were ordered to man 16 galleys by signing on for the galleys of their choice, only enough for 6 galleys reported. The rest refused to go to the Naval Office to enroll, refused to report for induction, we would say. They swore not to serve under the new Captain General, Taddeo Giustinian, a personification of the haughtiness of the old families. They wanted Vettor Pisani back in command. Instead, he was in prison.

He had been arrested as soon as he returned from his defeat at Pola. The formal charges presented against him by the State's Attorneys were (1) that he had led the fleet into battle in disorderly fashion, not allowing commanders time to prepare, and (2) that he had quit the fight while the battle was still going on. In fact, it seems he was guilty on both charges, as was indeed voted, 70 to 48 with 14 abstentions, by the special court of Councillors, Senators, and members of the Forty which tried him. Deceived as to the number of the enemy, as well as stung by charges of cowardice, he hurried into a trap. That was a mistake of judgment. Leaving before the battle was over was probably a wise effort on the other hand to retrieve what could be saved, but it was a clear violation of a law passed years before, which provided death for any galley commander and for any fleet commander if he withdrew from the battle before it was over. It was a law made to discourage cowards, but Vettor Pisani had not shown cowardice in the fighting, quite the contrary. The State's Attorneys asked for the death penalty prescribed by law, the doge suggested that his only punishment be a fine and ineligibility for future offices and commands. The majority voted a compromise, ineligibility and six months in the lower dungeons.

Whatever the case against Pisani technically, the people did not blame him for the defeat. They blamed galley commanders who had not supported him and cursed the Senate for having refused his request to return to Venice and having forced him and the crews to winter and refit at Pola. They attributed his condemnation to the jealousy aroused among the nobility by his extreme popularity among seafarers. He was loved, says a chronicler in the city at the time, Daniele di Chinazzo, as the "chief and father of all the seamen of Venice" ("cavo e padre de tuti i marinari de Veniexia").

After the fall of Chioggia, the nobility realized that they had to have popular support to defend the city. They made sweeping promises of political changes and of rewards to be given once the war was over, and they released Vettor Pisani from prison. Pisani went first to church to hear mass and receive communion and then to the doge, to whom he gave assurance that he would put aside all resentment and serve "el stado e honor del Chomun de Veniexia." In the Piazza, he was cheered by a mob of seamen and other supporters, indeed half of all Venice, says the chronicler on the scene. They followed him home shouting "Viva Messer Vettor," to which he replied, "Enough of that, my sons, shout *viva San Marco!*" ("Taxè, fiuoli. Dixè: viva el bon evangelista miser San Marcho!")

The Senators yielded grudgingly. At first, they gave him a minor command and did not make him capitanio as the people wanted. Four hundred men from Torcello and other towns of the lagoon arrived with banners before the Ducal Palace, announcing they had come to serve under Pisani. When they were told to report to Taddeo Giustinian, they threw down their banners and went home uttering words the chronicler thought too indecent to record. Then Vettor was commissioned to command six galleys to protect the southwesterly approaches to the city. When at last he was sitting at the bench on the Molo to enlist crews, the clerks could not write fast enough to enroll all the experienced bowmen, oarsmen, and sailors who crowded around to sign on.

The doge himself, Andrea Contarini, who had been in that office ten years and was well over seventy, gradually emerged as the central figure in a unification of commands and of sentiment. Means were found to arm 34 galleys. Every day the doge went on board and presided over the rowing of the galleys from the Giudecca to the Lido and back. This exercise was necessary, for the crews were mostly craftsmen with other skills, and needed training at the oars. When the Venetians felt that they must launch a counterattack against Chioggia or be starved within their lagoon, Doge Contarini himself was named the Captain General of the Sea and Vettor Pisani was his chief of staff or executive officer.

Pisani's plan for counterattacking aimed at cutting the enemies' lines of communication by sinking stone-laden ships or barges in the channels connecting Chioggia with the mainland and with the open sea. Most of the lagoons were shallow waters in which only small craft could operate. Galleys or barges loaded with supplies had to use deeper channels, such as those that are now most likely to be seen on a trip to Torcello or to the airport. In small craft, the Venetians were clearly superior. By plugging up the deeper channels and the openings leading out from the lagoon, Pisani aimed to separate Chioggia from both the mainland and the Genoese fleet.

Stone-laden barges and cogs, with galleys and long boats to defend and place them, left Venice for Chioggia on the longest night of the year, December 22, with the aged doge in command. At dawn, a substantial force landed just south of Chioggia. It was beaten back, but served to divert attention while plugging operations were carried out. Then the barriers that had been erected had to be defended from the Genoese efforts to remove them. That required constant patrolling and fighting from ships, from small craft, and at strategically placed strong points on the sand bars separating the lagoons from the sea. Shopkeepers and craftsmen unaccustomed to exposure and wounds began talking of giving up and going home. Doge Contarini said he would stay there until he died or the Genoese in Chioggia surrendered, but it was doubtful who could hold out longest. The Venetians pinned their hopes on the return of Carlo Zeno, who had been gone eight months and whose whereabouts was unknown.

Zeno returned triumphant on January 1, 1380, with 14 galleys, all in topnotch shape after the most successful conceivable raiding of Genoese commerce all over the Mediterranean. The Genoese had concentrated so heavily at the heart of their enemy's power that Zeno had been able to sail back and forth between Genoa and Sicily a couple of times burning Genoese ships and taking Genoese cargoes off neutral vessels. He then went east to Tenedos and Constantinople, seizing more booty along the way and reinforcing Tenedos's blockade of the straits. Picking up galleys that had been armed in Crete and others stationed off Tenedos, he continued his depredations as far as Beirut. He was on his way back to Crete for supplies and refitting when he received the command to return to Venice. He had already collected so much booty that he and galley masters under him had been sending cargoes of loot to Crete for sale. The proceeds safely accumulated there would later be distributed so that each member of Zeno's crews would receive his due share in accordance with the rules made after the disorder at Castro had shown the need of firm regulations. Even after he was told that he was needed in Venice, Carlo Zeno could not resist, any more than Sir Francis Drake would have in comparable circumstances, a special opportunity discovered by his advance guard when they put into the harbor of Rhodes. There was the biggest and richest of all Genoese cogs, the *Richignona*, with a cargo worth a half million ducats and a crew of three hundred, including one hundred and sixty merchants, distinguished men who would pay good ransoms. The cog got away from the three galleys, but when Zeno came up with ten to a dozen more, commandeered a cog in Rhodes harbor to give high battlements for his attackers, and succeeded in setting the *Richignona*'s sails on fire, it surrendered. The booty from this ship alone was worth 20 ducats for each oarsman and 40 ducats for each bowman. After this feat, Zeno stopped in Crete for a month to careen and clean his galleys and reorganize so that, when he arrived at Venice, he would be ready for battle. He could not foresee what Genoese fleet he might meet in the Adriatic.

Once home, Zeno was promptly sent to the point of greatest danger and suffered another of his innumerable wounds in defeating a desperate Genoese effort to open a passage from the lagoon to the sea. By forts, barriers, and sunken barges, the Venetians kept them blockaded. Even after Zeno's return, the Venetians refused to go out into the Adriatic and give battle to a Genoese fleet which came to relieve Chioggia. They kept their stations which held the enemy forces separated. Zeno fully supported Pisani and the doge in imposing this strategy upon impatient compatriots who were suffering from shortages and wanted quick decisive action. Bit by bit, the Venetians were gaining more and more control of their lagoon and the routes leading to it, so that the Genoese in Chioggia were more and more tightly trapped. Presently, they began to run out of food and powder.

Gunpowder was important in this Fourth Genoese War, commonly called also the War of Chioggia. Although there had been sporadic use earlier of various incendiary mixtures such as the Greek fire so expertly employed in earlier centuries by the Byzantine navy, and although cannon had been used in the West since very early in the fourteenth century, the War of Chioggia was the first in which cannon were used on Venetian ships. Cannon were mounted on the forecastles of the galleys and they were placed also on the smaller long boats much used in the fighting around Chioggia. Of course, they were also useful against attacking ships; as soon as the Venetians occupied Tenedos, they posted cannon to strengthen its defenses. Whether firing from land or sea, early cannon were so inaccurate that the stone cannon balls were much less to be feared than the steel bolts of the crossbows, by which both Pisani and Zeno were wounded more than once. Cannon were chiefly useful in battering walls. The Genoese commander at Chioggia, Piero Doria, was killed when cannon fire toppled a tower which fell on him.

Much of the fighting on the sand bars close to Chioggia was being done by several thousand of the professional mercenaries who had become in that century the core and curse of every army. Carlo Zeno was invaluable in maintaining authority over them through his understanding of such men and the prestige of his personal prowess and courage. He stopped a fight between the English and Italian mercenaries and foiled a last-minute Genoese attempt, when food and powder were exhausted, to buy over the mercenary captains. After that failed, in June, 1380, the Genoese in Chioggia surrendered.

After Venice had parried this thrust at its heart and, in doing so, inflicted a severe wound on the enemy, it still had to fight vigorously to regain control of the Adriatic. Vettor Pisani died in that fighting while serving as Captain General of the Sea, the title of supreme command to which he was finally elected. Carlo Zeno succeeded him and gradually cleared the Adriatic. On land, Venice remained on the defensive. While Chioggia was under siege, Pietro Corner, the same who had quarreled with Pisani years before, was working effectively as ambassador in Milan to obtain help from its able Visconti ruler. Visconti's advances alarmed his neighbor on the west, the Count of Savoy, who called a peace conference at Turin. Because of her victory at Chioggia, Venice demanded the right to propose terms, but the terms she proposed showed how exhausted she was, how satisfied to have survived. By the Treaty of Turin of 1381, Venice gave up the fortification of Tenedos, agreed that neither Venetians nor Genoese would trade at Tana for the next two years, acknowledged the special rights of the Genoese in Cyprus, gave Treviso to the Duke of Austria to prevent it from going to the Carrara, and for recognition of her staple rights in the northern Adriatic paid a yearly indemnity to the King of Hungary, who of course kept Dalmatia. Judged by the Treaty of Turin, the Fourth Genoese War was a defeat for Venice and was as inconclusive as the three earlier Genoese wars. But events were to prove that Venice, merely by surviving with its spirit, its institutions, and its key colonies intact, had in fact won the long duel with Genoa.

REGAINING LOST GROUND The rebuilding on the home front began immediately along the lines laid down by promises made when the danger was most acute. In September, 1381, a month after the conclusion of peace, thirty new families were added to those having hereditary membership in the Great Council. The persons selected were among those who had made the biggest contributions to the war effort but the previous status of the individuals and their families was also influential. Raffaino Caresini, for example, was elected because of previous service as Grand Chancellor. The addition of these thirty families was important because they increased the number and wealth, and therefore the power, of the nobility, and also because it indicated a possible willingness on the part of the families already noble to share their honor and power.

A shift in the distribution of power within the nobility itself occurred at the same time. Hitherto the doges had been members of the "old families," those called the *longhi*, which were believed to be descended from the tribunes who had governed in the lagoons before the election of the first doge. The familiar names Dandolo, Michiel, Morosini, Contarini, Giustiniani, Zeno, Corner, Gradenigo, and Falier had reappeared again and again in top commands and embassies as well as in the dogeship. After 1382, they continue to reappear in positions of prominence but not in the dogeship. A different group — the "new families," long prominent but called the *curti* — succeeded in preventing any member of the longhi from attaining the highest honor during the next two hundred and fifty years. Beginning with the election of Antonio Venier in 1382, the curti were able to elect a member of their own group as doge.

The reasons for this shift are obscure. Probably the thirty new families added at the end of the War of Chioggia shared a jealousy of the "old families" and felt they had already been sufficiently honored. Perhaps the wealth of the longhi as a whole was depleted by the way the war was financed. The system of forced loans which had worked well in the past turned into a disaster for those families with large holdings of government bonds. In a couple of years, the Monte Vecchio burgeoned from about 3 million to about 5 million ducats. The forced levies were 107 percent of assessments, which meant one quarter to one third percent of known wealth. Family accumulations of government bonds and even real estate were dumped on the market in order to have the cash to pay these levies. For the first time, there was a catastrophic drop in the market price. From 92½ in 1375, it fell to 18 in 1381, when interest was suspended. Real estate prices also fell drastically, as the government condemned the property of defaulters. Commercial capital, especially if invested overseas, was less fully counted in making assessments and harder to get at. No doubt, some of the "old families" maneuvered through the crisis successfully, but as a whole they were probably relatively hard hit because of holding more bonds and real estate than liquid capital.

At the conclusion of peace, the Senate succeeded by many dodges and devices and by stringent economy in reestablishing the bonds as a worthwhile investment and a useful instrument for the financing of future wars. The government still avoided any general system of direct taxes, preferring taxes on consumption and on goods in transit. Interest payments were resumed in 1382, but at 4 percent. The size of the debt was gradually reduced by the sinking fund, so that it was down to about 3,500,000 ducats in 1402, and the price was up to 66. But there had occurred in the meantime a big turnover in the ownerships of bonds and of real estate.

The parsimoniousness which made possible this financial recovery kept Venetian naval power at a very low level for several decades. The main concern was to set in motion the currents of trade which were the support of both private fortunes and the tax revenue of the state. As usual, special attention was paid to the transport of the precious merchandise yielding high profits and customs duties, and for this purpose merchant galleys were again sent to Romania, to Beirut, to Alexandria, and to Flanders. The fleets were notably smaller than those of the 1330's, only 2 to 4 galleys instead of 6 to 10; for the wars, the repeated attacks of the plague (an outbreak in 1382 is said to have killed 19,000), and the general economic contraction had lowered the whole level of activity. Indeed, providing full crews for 15 merchant galleys, which required 2.500 to 3,000 men, was a severe strain on Venice's supply of maritime labor. The city's laborers and tradespeople who had been mobilized in the fleet which Doge Contarini led against Chioggia went back to their shops when the war was over. New immigrants from the Italian mainland increased Venice's industrial production and quickened the return of prosperity but did not make up the wartime losses in seamen. The recruiting grounds of Dalmatia were closed, being under the King of Hungary. Greeks from the Venetian portion of Romania were a major reservoir of seamen, however. In the decades just after 1381, more than half of the war galleys armed to patrol against pirates or to keep the Turks in check were manned in Crete or Negroponte. For a decade or two, Venetian oarsmen were so fully employed on the merchant galleys that from Venice itself not more than two to four war galleys were armed annually to serve on patrol under the Captain of the Gulf.

Fortunately for Venice, she faced no serious challenge in those years from any rival naval power, and her diplomacy did much to compensate for lack of military force. The Venetian Senate kept well informed about political changes affecting her interests from the passes of the Alps to the most distant shores of the Mediterranean. Many states were experiencing civil war or revolution. With a good sense of timing and with concern — as always — for naval power and trade, not territory, Venice used the opportunities opened for her by the mere fact that she had survived with her integrating spirit intact. She was therefore in a position to profit from the break-up of neighbors and rivals. The Genoese were either exhausted, demoralized by civil wars, or turning their attentions westward. In the Adriatic, there was a dynastic union of the Kingdom of Hungary and the Kingdom of Naples which would have been extremely dangerous for Venice had not both these kingdoms been distracted by the rivalry of various claimants to their thrones. Neither kingdom had any navy in the Adriatic. Venice maintained her lordship of the gulf, required shipping in the northern Adriatic to load and unload at Venice, and treated as pirates any warships which were in the Adriatic without having obtained her permission to be there.

To compensate for the lack of Dalmatian bases, Venice acquired Corfu. When Venice had first occupied Corfu, just after 1204, she could not have held on to it without incurring the enmity during the next two centuries of the kings of Naples who were then powerful and were then often needed by Venice as allies. Prudently, Venice had been satisfied to use Ragusa as the way station visited by her fleets between Pola and Modon. In the late fourteenth century, Ragusa ceased to be available, and the kings of Naples were easier to handle. Venice purchased from one Neapolitan claimant a new title to Corfu, after occupying it in 1386 by agreement with the leading Corfiotes. The island was thoroughly fortified and held by Venice thereafter as long as the Republic lasted.

Venetian control of the lower Adriatic was strengthened also, curiously enough, by the advance of what was to prove in the long run her most exhausting foe, the Ottoman Empire. As the Ottoman Turks expanded over more and more of the Balkans, restricting the Byzantine Empire to small territories around Constantinople and Salonica and subduing the Bulgarians and the Serbs, it looked as if all the port cities and islands of the Aegean would ultimately come under Moslem Turkish rule. There was hope in only one alternative, namely, Venetian protection. The war fleets which Venice maintained in Greek waters were small, but they were as large as those of any other power, and behind them stood the Venetian bases at Negroponte, Crete, Modon, and Corfu.

Although the Ottoman Turks had yet to develop a navy, their army seemed invincible. In 1396, it completely overwhelmed at Nicopolis a large crusading army which included the flower of French chivalry as well as Hungary's forces. Venice was very careful to avoid a direct challenge to the Ottoman Empire, both because it could not hope to match the power of the Ottoman army and because it had merchants scattered through Turkish domains. But when it could buy up some seaport offered for sale by a local Greek prince or by the heir of one of the French crusaders, and could buy it at a bargain price because the seller knew that he could not himself defend it from the Turks, Venice bought, fortified, and then made some temporizing agreement with the Ottoman emperor. Operating on these principles, Venice acquired Durazzo and Scutari in Albania; Lepanto; Patras, Argos, and Nauplia in Morea; and Athens, as well as more land around Negroponte and more islands in the Aegean (see Map 7).

One motive in the acquisition of many of these places in Romania was to prevent them from falling into the hands of the Genoese. Even when the Genoese Commune was paralyzed by revolutions, there was always some danger that a group of Genoese would form a company to act on its own in taking over some place in the Levant, as a Genoese maona had taken over Chios and much of Cyprus. Since the Byzantine Empire was bankrupt, it was an open question how much the Turks would take over by conquest, and how much would be acquired by the Empire's Christian protectors, and by which of its protectors. The big prize was of course Constantinople. There the Genoese were still powerful in their fortified settlement at Pera and Galata on the northern side of the Golden Horn, while the Venetians were established along the southern shore. Venice and Genoa each maintained galleys to help defend the city at the time of the crusading disaster of Nicopolis and immediately afterwards. But they were not mainly responsible for saving the city from the sultan's victorious army. That army might very well have extinguished the Byzantine Empire within a few years but for the campaigns launched by a new conqueror erupting with tremendous force from Central Asia, Timur (or Tamerlane, as he was known in the Western tradition). He crushed the Ottoman army so completely in 1402 that he may be said to have given the Byzantine Empire a new lease on life. Although Tamerlane's plundering of Tana and destruction of cities in its hinterland made the Black Sea ports less valuable, his defeat of the Ottomans delayed the Turkish conquest of Constantinople for half a century and thus enabled the Venetians and Genoese to continue to trade around the Black Sea and to bring back to Italy cargoes of fish, grain, hides, furs, and slaves.

Beyond-the-Sea, there was only one survivor among the crusaders' states, the Kingdom of Cyprus. It was left by the Treaty of Turin at the mercy of the Genoese who demanded ever larger payments from its kings and tried to center all trade at Famagusta, which they ruled directly. The Venetians felt no vital interest in fighting for the King of Cyprus, since Venetian traders seeking the spices of the Indies were by-passing Famagusta and shipping directly to and from Tripoli, Beirut, and Alexandria. Ever since crusading efforts had been largely directed against the Ottoman Turks in Romania and papal approval had been obtained for Venice's official galley voyages to the lands ruled by the Mamluks, Venice had tightened its commercial ties with Egypt and Syria. Venetians penetrated so far into Syria, Lebanon, and Palestine in search of such crops as cotton that their chief consulate was placed in the interior at Damascus.

Although not vitally concerned about Cyprus itself, Venice became alarmed when a large fleet left Genoa, headed for Cyprus under the command of a French noble famous for his feats of arms and for his adventuresome, imperious spirit, the Maréchal Boucicault. After changing their doges ten times in five years, the Genoese had conferred the rule of their city on the King of France who had sent Boucicault as governor. The size of the fleet and the reputation of Boucicault made the Venetians fear that it had some other goals in addition to its announced purpose of enforcing demands on the King of Cyprus. In fact, having settled affairs in Cyprus, Boucicault indulged in what he regarded as crusading, namely, pillaging the Moslem seaports. He raided Alexandria, Beirut, and Tripoli — precisely those ports used by the Venetians as they by-passed Famagusta. In Beirut, Boucicault plundered not only Moslems but also the warehouses containing the merchandise of the Venetians. Consequently, the Venetians were not sure whether his intentions were hostile or friendly and felt that in any case they had a grievance to avenge. Under Carlo Zeno they had meanwhile mobilized what seemed to them then a large fleet, 14 galleys of which 5 were manned at Venice. While Boucicault was on his way home in the fall of 1403, he anchored off an island opposite the Venetian base of Modon where Zeno was stationed. Next day the fleets engaged, and Zeno sent Boucicault on his way with the loss of three galleys. Boucicault claimed he had been treacherously assaulted, but neither the King of France nor the Genoese took up his quarrel so that a peace was quickly arranged which left the Venetians enjoying an indemnity and the prestige of their victory. They had captured some celebrated French knights and proved that Venice could muster men of unexcelled valor and prowess even if its fleets were small compared to those of earlier days.

Besides the lack of men and of money, another reason for the small size of the Venetian war fleets during the first decades after the War of Chioggia was preoccupation with events on the mainland a few miles from the lagoons. During the War of Chioggia, Francesco Carrara, Lord of Padua, had clearly revealed his ambition to humble Venice, although Venice had earlier helped him and his family to power with the hope that Padua would serve Venice as a buffer against more powerful mainland states. The aggressive policy of Francesco Carrara turned his state from a buffer into a menace. He bought Treviso from the Duke of Austria and interfered in disputes in Friuli. By extending his domains all the way from Padua to Udine, he was threatening to cut Venice off from the Alpine passes leading to Germany. The Senate checked him for a while by supporting his opponents in Friuli and finally took the extreme step of allying with the ruler of Milan, the dangerous Gian Galeazzo Visconti. Together they overthrew the Carrara and divided his lands. Acute danger to Venice from the mainland was removed for some time by reacquiring Treviso and then by the death in 1402 of Gian Galeazzo, the too-powerful neighbor with whose help they had gained Treviso.

Gradually, as trade revived, as revenues increased, as the Turkish danger was eclipsed through one set of circumstances and the Carrara danger through another set, and as Genoa became less and less able to conduct a foreign policy of her own, Venice felt restored in power and prosperity. The climax of the recovery came with the restoration of Venice's rule over Dalmatia. The competition of various princes for the thrones of Hungary and Naples had subjected the Dalmatian cities to so much misrule that many of them, including Zara but not Ragusa, were ready to offer themselves to Venice. Content that her fleets patrolled the Adriatic and guided its commerce, Venice held off until she was able to buy out one of the princely contenders at a bargain price in 1409. When she then began asserting full authority over Dalmatia, she was strong enough to win the resulting war with a King of Hungary, who received no aid from Genoa. By this time Venice's trade and wealth had fully recovered, if not to the levels preceding the Black Death, at least to a range and volume above what they had been before the War of Chioggia.

Throughout the troubled fourteenth century, in spite of periods of weakness, Venice had maintained the essential of her economic position, namely, being a go-between in the commercial relations of East and West. Within the Adriatic, she held onto her monopoly in that role. In the Mediterranean as a whole, she had no monopoly; Genoese and other Italians and Catalans and French offered competition, but only Genoa came abreast, and none surpassed Venice as an intermediary in exchanging the wares of western Europe for those of the eastern Mediterranean. Taxes on the transit trade replenished the Republic's treasury, and Venetian merchants calculated profits on it twice, once on their imports and again when they exported or sold to such visiting merchants as the Germans. Interruptions of trade were frequent but temporary, making prices jumpy. Whether prices were high or low, the Venetians, being like brokers the men in the middle, took their commissions or found other ways to profit.

The internal social repercussions of the strains of war had not altered but reinforced Venice's basic class structure and political institutions. The framework developed earlier to adjust to the "rise of the people" and to restrain factionalism endured. The ruling class of merchant nobles had again strengthened their dominance by admitting some additional families to their ranks, just as they had done when the Great Council was enlarged at the beginning of the century. The criterion of nobility then established, namely, membership in the Great Council, was maintained; and only nobles could serve on Venice's governing councils and administrative boards. Guilds gave craftsmen-managers and merchant-employers opportunities to decide many economic issues of immediate concern to their business, but they could have influence on such issues as tariffs and commercial treaties only by appearing as petitioners before the governing nobles. Among commoners, only the emerging class of citizens-by-birth was directly involved in the formulation or execution of state policy. They were restricted to secretarial posts but confirmed in their monopoly of staffing the Ducal Chancery and felt honored as a class by the honors given their head, the Grand Chancellor. Among the general mass of craftsmen and merchants were many immigrants. Welcomed for their skills and attracted by the city's reputation for relatively plentiful food and equal justice, immigrants replenished its population after each visitation of war and plague.

The structure of the governing councils underwent only one basic change during the fourteenth century, a concentration of power in the Senate. With the need for more complicated international diplomacy, its authority increased. By absorbing the Forty, it absorbed also the latter's initiatives in regulating money and finance. In the bitter contests over fiscal policies, the Senate in the end prevailed. To be sure, the Senate was frequently replaced or supplemented during the fourteenth century by special commissions that were granted full powers by the Great Council for handling a war or other emergency. Early in the fifteenth century, the naming of such special commissions ceased; the Senate directed the conduct of wars, as well as ordinary diplomacy, finances, commercial policy, and maritime regulation.

In spite of the defeats its fleets had suffered in major battles, Venice at the beginning of the fifteenth century was still basically a maritime republic looking seaward and eastward. Its colonial empire seemed secure. A supply of maritime labor was gradually being rebuilt, partly by immigrants from Greece and Dalmatia. The Venetian nobility supplied commanding officers for both war galleys and merchantmen. A combination of seafaring and trade continued to be the normal way of life for Venetian nobles until in their middle years they retired from the sea to devote themselves to their families, their investments, and the political careers which were the monopoly of their class.

THE TURN
WESTWARD · I

Arts, Sciences, and Literature

CHAPTER FIFTEEN

During the early fifteenth century Venice turned westward, although the ties to the East were too strong to be broken completely or sharply. The change permeated political life and even penetrated maritime activity but was evident first in the arts and sciences.

BYZANTINE AND GOTHIC For centuries the Venetians looked eastward for models of beauty. The city's most famous building, San Marco, impresses on every visitor the Eastern origin of Venice's early art. During the thousand years since it was first built, it has been embellished by additions in many styles, but its basic similarity to churches of the Byzantine East is unmistakable. Like the most famous of these, Santa Sophia in Constantinople, San Marco has walls of brick, even of rubble, covered with more precious material. In contrast to the towering cathedrals of the West, it is roofed by low domes and lighted by small windows. Many of its five hundred columns are single stones cut from eastern quarries and topped by capitals carved into intricately braided or flowering patterns. The interior glowing with the golden background of its ubiquitous mosaics suggests the magic and mystery of the East.

The Adriatic, however, had its own artistic tradition. Modern Venetian historians stress the continuance in the lagoons of the methods of building and mosaic making which flourished in late Roman times at Ravenna, as the buildings still surviving there brilliantly testify. After Ravenna was conquered by the Lombards, Venice fell heir to its artistic tradition, one may well believe, just as it fell heir to the policing of the Adriatic for the Byzantine Empire. Examples of this post-Ravenna art are notable at Torcello, the early commercial emporium of the lagoons, and at Parenzo, mentioned above as the Istrian port of Venetian pilots. But the style which succeeded the Roman and made its influence felt from Syria to Sicily and from Venice to Moscow found its main center in Constantinople and is therefore called Byzantine.

The Byzantine emperors collected apostolic relics at Constantinople in a church which was also the burial place of famous emperors and became a shrine and symbol of their imperial power. When the Venetians acquired their own apostolic protector through possessing the body of Saint Mark, they took the Church of the Holy Apostles as their model in building a resting place for the relics. They built it as a chapel of the doge, as already explained, not the church of any bishop, and it symbolized the power and independence asserted first by Venice's doges and later by the Commune.

Like the Church of the Holy Apostles, San Marco had the form of a Greek cross which the Venetians modified slightly so as to make the building more suited for public participation in ceremonies. They added an apse at one end and a vestibule at the other and accentuated in the vaulting the east-west axis. The structure, begun in the 1060's, was quite plain inside and out. In shining contrast to the brick walls not yet covered with marbles and mosaics there stood by the high altar the Golden Screen (*Pala d'Oro*). This altarpiece was all of gold, studded with hundreds of gems and covered with religious scenes and images in cloisonné enamel. More precious stones and enameled plaques were added over the centuries, some made in Constantinople, others masterpieces of Venetian goldsmiths. It seems fitting that the earliest masterpieces of art cherished by a maritime people for whom travel was a way of life should have been portable treasures of patient, painstaking craftsmanship.

Gradually, San Marco's walls, arches, and domes were covered with mosaics programmed in accord with religious symbolism. At the highest level were presented the divine mysteries: Immanuel, Ascension, Pentecost; at a lower level more human events, first those of the life of Christ, then those of the saints, with particular attention, naturally, to the life, relics, and miracles of Saint Mark. The narthex or vestibule was judged appropriate for scenes from Genesis and Exodus, since the Old Testament was regarded as an introduction, a preparation. Executing the program of mosaics took centuries, and as it progressed, desire to have more space on which to display mosaics led to walling up some windows. Wide differences in style reflect the tastes and capacities of various master mosaic-makers from the eleventh century to the fourteenth, and show their diverse responses to new art forms developed by Romanesque artists in mainland Italy or new waves of influence from Greece. An example is the contrast between the relatively naturalistic narrative style of the Old Testament scenes in the narthex and the more stylized symbolic figures of the central cupolas.

Byzantine architecture was overwhelmingly concerned with the interior of a place of worship. It cared little about the building's external appearance. Until the thirteenth century, San Marco's exterior was plain brickwork relieved on the façade by only a few niches containing colored stone or mosaics. Attached to the brickwork to the right of the main entrance, as revealed during recent reparations, was a lateen yardarm, a trophy of some naval victory.

FIGURE 14 *The Mosaic on the West Wall of the Cathedral at Torcello (Photo Böhm).*

The church of the Bishop of Torcello was older than the doge's chapel, San Marco, and some of the mosaics of his cathedral were copied from mosaics at Ravenna; but the Apotheosis of Christ and Last Judgment *on the wall over the main door is a distinctive composition executed in the same epoch as many famous mosaics of San Marco, namely, the twelfth and thirteenth centuries.*

During the thirteenth century, naval commanders sent home more sumptuous trophies. Most famous are the four horses, part of the loot brought back from Constantinople after its sack in 1204. They were supplemented during the following decades by shipments of other pieces of ancient statuary, by choice marbles, revered relics, and jeweled reliquaries. The doorposts from the Genoese stronghold at Acre taken by Lorenzo Tiepolo were used to flank an entrance, now closed, on the side towards the Piazzetta and the water front (see Figure 4).

While the Venetians were building San Marco and decorating its interior in the Byzantine style, the Romanesque and Gothic styles developed in the West. Both these styles gave much attention to the outward appearance of a church and especially to its doorways. Under Romanesque and Gothic influence, the Venetians added adornments to the entrances of San Marco. An open square in front of the church had been created by Sebastiano Ziani, the doge who gave such a decisive turn to both external and internal politics when he took charge in 1172. He used some of his fabulous wealth to buy up properties in front of the church and then in his will left the land to the Commune for use as a piazza. The portals leading from this square into the vestibule of the church were ornamented with groups of columns and with arches covered with sculpture. In the interior, stonecutters had carved Byzantine capitals and moldings with designs and symbolic figures in low relief. The many arches now built for the western portals were covered with figures in high relief. They show the naturalistic style which came to Venice with workmen from Lombardy and Emilia. One of the finest of the many medieval representations of craftsmen at work is on the third arch of the central portal of San Marco. It begins with fishermen, includes ironsmiths and barbers, and features especially workers in wood: carpenters, coopers, and caulkers (see Figures 7 and 13).

Palaces as well as churches were at first built in Byzantine style. These featured round arches and arcades after the manner of the Roman palaces at Spalato and Ravenna. Although showing Byzantine features, their distinctive character reflected Venice's domestic tranquility and security against attack. Palaces were also fortresses in most cities, but not in Venice. Open arcades were a feature not only of upper stories but of the ground floor or, as we may call it, the sea floor. Later it was more closed in. A typical plan came to include a facade ornamented by a central loggia and balconies overlooking a canal. The most elaborate were on the main floor, what we call the second floor. On both sea floor and second floor, a long central room ran through to an enclosed courtyard (see Figure 15). Up one side of the courtyard ran a staircase. The sea floor was used for the storage of boats, wood, and other supplies and of merchandise. The big room on the main floor, lighted through the central loggia, was designed for ceremonial occasions. Ordinary living concentrated in the smaller rooms placed on the sides which were heated by fireplaces in cold weather. Quarters for slaves, servants, and other dependents were among the storerooms on the sea floor or in an attic, or in low-ceilinged mezzanines tucked in corners between the main floors. The courtyard was the source of water supply, since it was graded so as to catch water from the roofs and filter it through sand into a cistern tapped by a well. The palace of a great family was a relatively self-sufficient and imposing unit, with its own supply of water, fuel, food, boats, servants or slaves, and several generations of brothers and cousins.

a

b

c

FIGURE 15   *Homes of Nobles in Byzantine and Gothic Styles (Photo Ferruzzi).*

(a) The two lower floors of the Palazzo Dandolo-Farsetti, now the city hall, show Venice's Byzantine style of palace architecture; (b) The fully developed Gothic palace had three or four stories with the main loggia on the second or third floor as in the Palazzo Bernardo; (c) Behind the loggia, a ceremonial hall extended to an interior courtyard like that of the Cà d'Oro.—The many fireplaces in the medieval palaces were evident from the forest of chimney tops (see Figure 17).

The round arches of the early palaces were gradually replaced by pointed arches — at first, arches pointed only at the top, an ornamental touch suggestive of contemporary Moorish or Arab styles, then by true pointed arches like those basic to the Gothic style developed in France. Gothic style was formed for church architecture and was used by the Friars beginning about 1330 when they built their churches in Venice; the Dominicans built, in Gothic, San Giovanni e Paolo (San Zanipolo to Venetians), the Franciscans built Santa Maria Gloriosa, commonly called dei Frari. Like other Italian Gothic churches, they do not accentuate the vertical lines as much as do the cathedrals of northern France, but they use Gothic vaulting to create interior spaciousness and graceful windows. Gothic contributed also to the gaiety of the façade of San Marco as we know it. Gothic touches such as the pinnacles between the arches were added after a fire in 1419 necessitated some rebuilding.

The masterpiece of Venetian Gothic is the Ducal Palace. The arcades extending across the whole front, one above the other, were features retained from earlier Venetian palace architecture. It was not unusual to place above them a wide wall pierced by few windows. In the Ducal Palace, the wall is forty feet high and yet does not make the building appear top-heavy! The expanse of wall is lightened by the diamond-shaped pattern of colored stones woven into it, by the rope-like stone stitching at the corners, by the framing and the placing of its few windows, and by the fanciful parapet which crowns it. The transition from the colonnade at the sea floor with its wide arches on heavy columns is eased by the more closely spaced arches of the loggia above and the quadrifoil tracery above them (as in the corner shown in Figure 16).

The harmony of the façade of the Ducal Palace makes us wish to know more of the architect who conceived it, but the records are conclusive only in regard to the nature of his problem. When Pietro Gradenigo enlarged the Great Council, he also began construction of a larger hall for its meetings. At that time, about 1300, the main structure of the Ducal Palace was along the Rio di Palazzo where is now its east wing. One end of it came down to the embankment on the harbor front, the Molo, where there were also smaller buildings housing government offices. Within these structures Gradenigo enlarged a hall which served while the size of the Great Council grew from 400 to 1,000, but by 1340 it numbered 1,200 members. With this record of past growth, a bigger room was planned for the future. To accommodate conveniently at the same time the other expanding organs of government, including naval administrators, it was voted in 1340 to build a wing parallel to the water front and to devote its top floor to a bigger hall for the Great Council. Soon after construction was begun, the Black Death stopped the city's growth. Membership in the Great Council shrank and did not expand again so as to make use of the new hall necessary until about 1420, although work on it continued according to the original intentions. In 1365, the great hall was so far built that a painter from Padua was called in to start decorating its walls, and in 1400–1404 Pietro Paolo delle Masegne designed and executed the central balcony overlooking the harbor. In 1424, a third wing was begun in the same style, the west wing facing the Piazzetta.

Regrettable as is the loss of the name of the architect who conceived the general design of the Ducal Palace, his anonymity emphasizes that the building we now admire was created over centuries by many craftsmen-artists each of whom, like Pietro Paolo delle Masegne, shaped his particular assignment with a feeling for how it fitted into the scheme of the whole. The sculptures woven into the arcades, for example, give variety and special meaning to many corners and columns. The capitals of the columns of the portico or lower arcade depict, one set, the seasons; another set, the races of men; a third set, famous emperors; yet others, the cardinal virtues and vices; and so on.

Early in the fifteenth century, Gothic tracery of the kind used in the loggia of the Ducal Palace became the dominant style for private palaces. While no private building was as impressive as the Ducal Palace, many were more pretentiously ornamented. The Cà d'Oro, although relatively small, outshone rivals by its many-colored stones and the complexity of its stone tracery as well as by the gilding from which it took its name.

Architects and sculptors all had the social status of craftsmen and were members of the stonecutters' guild (*tagiapiera*). Hundreds of masters were manual laborers who shaped blocks according to instructions or copies as exactly as they could traditional designs as, for example, in making the well-curbs that ornamented the courtyards of palaces and centered the small squares (campi) where the common folk drew their water. Such stonecutters used "Byzantine" designs for well-curbs or capitals long after the Gothic had become fashionable. A few master stonecutters, in contrast, proved themselves first-class artists. They fused influences from East and West and Venice's own past according to their personal genius. Their best sculpture was in relief, however, not in the round. Venice did not develop, as did Renaissance Florence, a distinctive school of sculpture radiating influence afar.

THE PAINTERS Such a Venetian school did develop in painting. Its roots lay in the shops of the mosaic makers, from whom the painters inherited concern with luminosity and color. A sensitivity to color and its function in composition was heightened in Venice because it has streets of water. Reflected light, which changed with every wind and tide, gave a special strength to variations in color where, as Lionello Venturi wrote, "every stone takes on the luster of enamel."

At first, painters were employed mainly to decorate altarpieces which served as aids to devotion in churches and private chapels. They worked in tempera on wood, depicting in strong colors saintly figures set in contrasting backgrounds, often richly gilded. Their style was still partly Byzantine, like the many beautiful mosaics added in San Marco in the fourteenth century. Some of the painted altarpieces were quite small, others large and almost as imposing as the Pala d'Oro at San Marco, although nowhere near as costly.

In the middle of the fifteenth century, Venetian painting was transformed by two influences from the West. From the Flemings came a new technique, the use of oil paints. More fruitful and far-reaching than any such change in technique was the new spirit which came at about the same time from Florence. Building on an earlier Florentine emphasis on line, form, and tactile values, Brunelleschi, Donatello, Masaccio, and Leon Battista Alberti between 1420 and 1440 wrought the revolution which in the history of Western art is called "the Renaissance." They combined a mastery of perspective, a mathematical conception of composition, a close, admiring study of classical antiquity, and a striving for the kind of ideal form which they saw in Greek and Roman art. Their achievements were accompanied by the blossoming of the movement in literature and learning called "humanism," which glorified Greek and Latin literature as the guides to a full and worthy life. Humanism came to Venice in many ways, as we shall see; the corresponding movement in painting came through Padua.

After the Venetian conquest, Padua and Venice became artistically and intellectually so united that the French have sometimes called Padua Venice's "Left Bank." In 1440–60, three outstanding firms of painters operated in both cities. One was headed by Antonio Vivarini. A son of a glass-blower, he set up his *bottega*, first in Murano. There he contracted for altarpieces fully carved and colored. Then he moved to Venice and continued such production in partnership with an immigrant from Cologne, Giovanni d'Alemagna. They trained Antonio's gifted younger brother Bartolomeo, and his son Alvise. When there was a big job to be done in the church of the Eremitani at Padua, they were among the painters engaged to decorate one of its chapel walls.

The biggest of the three firms was headed by a Paduan, son of a notary, more a contractor than a craftsman, Francesco Squarcione, who was said to have had one hundred and thirty-seven apprentices. Squarcione was a collector of ancient art and open to all kinds of influences, but his "apprentices," whose work he exploited or organized, seem to have learned more from others than from him.

The most important of the three botteghe was headed by Jacopo Bellini, the son of a tinsmith whose family belonged to the Nicoletti of Venice's fisherman's quarter. He became an admirer and perhaps an apprentice of the Florentine, Gentile da Fabriano, who was hired in 1408 to paint the hall of the Great Council in the Ducal Palace. Jacopo probably followed Gentile back to Florence, for in Florentine records there is mention of a "Jacopo of Venice" who took ship in 1423 or 1424 for Flanders. In Flanders, Jacopo could have seen the brilliant color produced in the new oil technique being used by the Van Eycks at Bruges. The artistic conceptions which the Florentines were developing in those years certainly influenced Jacopo Bellini strongly. A sketchbook which he compiled and passed on to his sons includes studies in perspective, in foreshortening of figures in various positions, of architectural backgrounds and landscapes — studies preparatory to presenting men not as isolated figures but as located in space with reference to each other. So little of Jacopo's painting survives that he is best known for his sketchbook and the work of his sons, Gentile and Giovanni.

A youngster who learned from Jacopo even quicker than his own sons was Andrea Mantegna, an apprentice of Squarcione whom Squarcione is said to have adopted in an effort to retain his services. But Jacopo Bellini had more to teach and had a daughter. Mantegna married Jacopo's daughter and became associated with his bottega. There Mantegna not only learned but exerted strong influence, for he had a powerful style of his own and imbibed the new spirit directly from the Florentines. In the 1440's, when Mantegna was in his teens, Florentine influence was directly felt in Padua through the presence there of Donatello and of the leading patron of Florentine humanists, Palla Strozzi, exiled by his rival, Cosimo de' Medici. Donatello, a very positive personality, was much admired in Padua; after ten years, he returned home saying that only in Florence could he receive the stimulus of constant criticism. As one proof of his powers Donatello left in Padua a statue of the Venetian condottiere, Gattamelata, the first equestrian statue worthy of comparison with those of

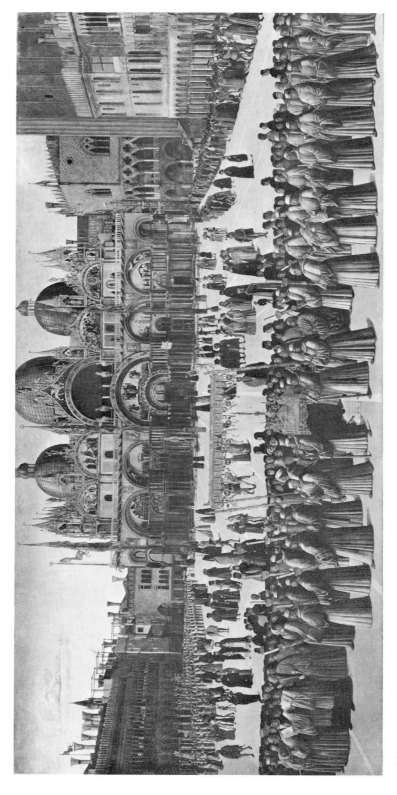

FIGURE 16 *The Piazza San Marco as painted by Gentile Bellini (Photo Alinari).*

In painting The Procession of the Cross for the Scuola Grande di San Giovanni Evangelista, Gentile Bellini depicted meticulously the façade of San Marco with the mosaics then in place, the corner of the Ducal Palace, and the Campanile abutting the hospital which at that time fronted on the south side of the Piazza. In the center foreground are the members of the Scuola carrying the reliquary containing the fragment of the True Cross.

antiquity and recalling indeed the statue of Marcus Aurelius in Rome. The same feeling for antiquity that enthused Strozzi and Donatello inspired Andrea Mantegna to depict soldiers in Roman armor against backgrounds of Roman architecture. He won fame in 1450, when only nineteen, by his paintings in the church of the Eremitani (paintings destroyed by bombing in World War II). By their power they quite outshone those of the competing Vivarini. Having established himself as the foremost painter in northern Italy, Mantegna went off to work for the Duke of Mantua. The Bellini returned to Venice where they and the Vivarini found a good market for their treatments of religious themes.

In the 1470's, the new technique of painting with oils on large canvases was thoroughly assimilated in Venice, partly under the influence of an outsider, Antonello da Messina. The new techniques immediately enlarged the market for paintings since frescoes, watercolors on plaster, did not last long in Venice's humid atmosphere. The frescoes which Gentile da Fabriano and others had painted in the Ducal Palace were fading. A commission to cover them with huge canvases depicting the same famous scenes from Venetian history or legend was given to Gentile and Giovanni Bellini, who were thus recognized as the leaders among Venetian painters.

Although the big murals which the Bellini brothers painted in the Ducal Palace were later destroyed by fire, Gentile Bellini's ability with large scenes is manifest in other canvases which have been preserved, for example, in his meticulously accurate depicting of the Piazza during a festival procession. He was the first of the long series of notable artists who have delighted to depict Venice itself (see Figure 16). He also showed great skill in portraiture (see Figure 19). The portrait he did for the German emperor was rewarded with a knighthood, and when Sultan Mohammed, the Conqueror of Constantinople, asked Venice in 1479 to send her foremost painter to do his, she sent Gentile Bellini.

Giovanni Bellini collaborated with his brother at the Ducal Palace, but he maintained a separate bottega and developed a quite individual style. Much influenced at first by Mantegna, he departed from the hard, sometimes harsh though compelling qualities found in many of Mantegna's conceptions and attained a delicacy and a depth of religious feeling peculiarly his own. He expressed it in many highly treasured Madonnas and in original compositions of mystic meaning. Millard Meiss describes Bellini's *St. Francis Receiving the Stigmata*, at the Frick Gallery, New York: "An unseen power symbolised by light regenerates the saint and, so it seems, the whole visible world too — the wild flowers and vine sprouting from the rocks, the dry branches bursting into leaf and the quiet lonely donkey, who is mysteriously touched with life like Adam at the creation." A more obscure symbolism enriches his imaginatively designed *Sacred Allegory*, sometimes called *Souls in Paradise*, at the Uffizi, Florence.

Between Gentile's death in 1507 and his own in 1516 at near eighty, Giovanni Bellini was ranked by Venetians as the finest of all painters. Classical themes and details were not a central concern to him but they enter into some of his compositions, for during his long life he responded to many influences, including those of his own apprentices, Giorgione and Titian.

Giorgione is sometimes called the first modern painter because he did not draw a design before putting on paint; he designed by applying colors. Unlike previous painters, he worked less on altarpieces or monumental decorations for large halls than on small canvases which nobles could enjoy in the privacy of their own rooms, lyrical combinations of color and form free from religious specifications. Since he was an apprentice and collaborator in the Bellini bottega and a teacher and co-worker of Titian, who continued his style with greater fame, the pictures attributed by all experts entirely to Giorgione are few. Among those few are *The Three Philosophers* and *The Tempest*, sometimes called *The Soldier and the Gypsy*. But all agree that, before he died in 1510, not yet thirty-five, Giorgione had revolutionized the way of painting and the market for paintings.

The Bellini, Giorgione, and Titian gave Venetian painting such a reputation that, when Florence and Rome faltered in their leadership, Venice for a time became, as we will see in our last chapter, the foremost art center of the West.

Meanwhile a contemporary, Vettor Carpaccio, perfected a distinctive style, most expressive of the beauties of the city and the feelings of its people. Carpaccio was born on one of the small islands in the lagoon. He mastered his craft without being apprenticed in any of the leading botteghe, but he learned much from the works of such older masters as the Bellini brothers. Like Gentile Bellini he enjoyed painting Venice itself. In his *Healing of the Demoniac*, that miracle is to one side, so as to leave room to depict the old wooden bridge of the Rialto and the glittering of gondoliers beneath (see Figure 17).

Carpaccio worked mainly for less distinguished customers than did Giorgione or Titian. He had assignments in many churches to be sure, and for a time in the Ducal Palace, and his *Lion of San Marco*, with the harbor as its background, was painted for the State Treasurers; but his highest commissions were from the fraternities, the scuole. In addition to the guilds of craftsmen and the large, rich Scuole Grandi managed by Venetian-born cittadini, there were also fraternities formed by foreign colonists resident in Venice, notably those of the Greeks (San Giorgio dei Greci) and of the Slavs (San Giorgio degli Schiavoni). Many lesser ones, called *scuole piccole*, also honored a particular saint or a particular relic. They vied in decorating their meeting halls with the newly demonstrated beauties of oil paintings on large canvases. The best known views of Venice by Gentile Bellini and Carpaccio were part of a series painted for one of the largest of these fraternities, the Scuola Grande di San Giovanni Evangelista, depicting the miracles performed by the fragment of the True Cross of which it was the proud possessor.

The legends of the patron saints of the scuole provided themes in which Carpaccio was at his best. His *Legend of St. Ursula* is a tale of arrivals and departures in strange lands, as well as of chastity and martyrdom, of much journeying by sea, and of messages received and sent, and Carpaccio depicted the story by canvases in which innumerable small designs were woven together within a larger framework, like the episodes of a rambling romance. The harbor scenes, with their somewhat fantastic imaginary castles but meticulous realistic ships, have a luminosity which suggests that of Venice itself. In no other painter do ships have so important a part. Adding to the depth and mood of a picture by a selected background of hills and dales had become commonplace. Jacopo Bellini's notebook contained many such studies of landscape, but ships appear only in one, an abandoned wreck contributing to a picturing of desolation surrounding St. Jerome. Carpaccio showed ships under full sail in the open sea. It seems appropriate that this most Venetian of artists should have been not only a giver of life to legends but also the first great marine painter (see Figures 35 and 37).

FIGURE 17   *The Wooden Bridge at Rialto, as painted by Carpaccio (Photo Böhm).*

When the Rialto was at the peak of its importance as a financial center, it was reached not by the present impressive stone structure, but by a wooden drawbridge. In a painting commissioned by the Scuola Grande di San Giovanni Evangelista to commemorate a cure performed by their sacred relic, Carpaccio used the carrying of the fragment of the True Cross over the bridge as an excuse to depict the Grand Canal.

SCIENTISTS   Mundane interests did not seriously compete with religion in painting until
AND   the end of the fifteenth century. In science and literature the change began
HUMANISTS   earlier and in two opposing currents.

At first, popular science was embraced within religious art; the creation
was depicted in the vestibule of San Marco and the four elements — earth, air,
fire, and water — in a corner of the Last Judgment at Torcello. Anyone wishing
to enquire more deeply turned to the treatments of natural history by theologians
or to the writing of the ancient Greeks and Romans. For guidance in theology the
Venetians looked less to Constantinople than to the interpretations accepted in
Latin Christendom. Although their handling of the relations of Church and state
showed Byzantine influence, in regard to ritual and to doctrines on such matters
as the nature of the Trinity, Venice accepted the authority of the Roman popes,
and its clergy studied the writing of the leading churchmen of the West. While
correcting the pagan "errors" of Greek philosophers, these churchmen bowed to
the Greeks, and to Aristotle in particular, as the authority in logic and in natural
science.

As wealth, learning, and curiosity grew in the West, there was a demand for
direct knowledge of more of what Aristotle himself had written. Manuscripts of
his works and understanding of the language in which they were written were
best preserved at Constantinople, and Venice's close contacts with the Levant
made it one of the centers through which, during the twelfth and thirteenth
centuries, the West came to know more fully Aristotle's many treatises. A leader
in this transmission was called James of Venice. He went to Constantinople in
1135–36, found Aristotle being vigorously taught in the schools there, and
during the next decade or so translated from Greek to Latin many of Aristotle's
works on logic, metaphysics, physics, and psychology.

These subjects were intensely studied in the medieval universities, where they
competed with law and medicine, which had a more strictly professional utility.
The University of Padua, which became Venice's own, had been formed centuries
earlier by a secession from the University of Bologna. As at Bologna, lawyers
formed the most important faculty at Padua; not only was it the biggest, it
contained many men of political prestige and wide influence. Law was also the
faculty most attended by Venetian nobles looking forward to government positions in which knowledge of the law would be useful. Once Padua was under
Venice, the Venetian government forbade its nobles to go anywhere else for
their studies. While ensuring the university of customers by such laws, Venice
also provided funds to lure distinguished professors, and they in turn attracted
many students from outside Venetian domains, especially from Germany. To
select professors for all the faculties and to regulate their privileges and those
of the students, who had their own organization, the Great Council elected a
board of *Riformatori dello Studio di Padova*, generally choosing Senators who
had themselves taken doctorates there.

All professors not in the Faculty of Law were grouped in what was called
the Faculty of Arts but which taught mainly science, especially medicine. For
centuries before it took over Padua, Venice had had a highly respected corps of
physicians and surgeons. Their guild passed on the qualifications of practitioners,
required its members to steer clear of financial involvement with pharmacists,
and ordered them to meet, surgeons and physicians together, once a month to

discuss interesting cases. Many of the physician-surgeons of Venice were practically health officers salaried by the government. One of the most highly esteemed, a Master Gualtieri, petitioned in 1318 to found a home for aged or ailing seamen. He stipulated that no cleric should have a hand in running it, perhaps for unknown personal reasons, perhaps because just about that time the leading professor of medicine at Padua was posthumously convicted of heresy and his bones dug up and burned. Master Gualtieri served as chief physician or Head Surgeon for several fleets of merchant galleys, and his unstinting services to battle victims in the War of Ferrara was cited by the government in voting him privileges. While building the seamen's hospital, he went deeply in debt. The Great Council continued to favor him but, when voting him loans, appointed guardians to administer his money because he was believed to be too open-handed. Such acts show the respect in which Venetians held their own medical profession while at the same time foreigners of high reputation were welcomed and richly paid. Padua's medical faculty became as distinguished as its law faculty, and no competing medical schools within the Venetian domains were permitted to grant degrees. Even for the preliminary arts degree other schools could only prepare students for the examination conducted by the Paduan faculty. Its degree also became necessary, in the course of time, for full status in the Venetian medical guild.

Union of all sciences and philosophy in the same faculty with medicine was not as unreasonable as it may now seem. The study of medicine led to the probing of all the mysteries of nature. It led into astrology and astronomy, since the movement of the stars was believed to affect various organs of the body. Guided by Aristotle, a first-class biologist in his time, it led to consideration of what was the basic nature of matter and the proper methods of scientific inquiry. Important distinctions which prepared the way for the kind of scientific method that Galileo was to clarify two centuries later, also at Padua, were being thrashed out in Western universities. One professor, known as Paul of Venice, made a three-year trip to Oxford where interest in scientific method was strong. He returned to teach the new methodology at Padua until his death in 1429. Meanwhile, interest in natural science and philosophy was strengthened in Venice by a private endowment of public lectures at the Rialto. They became so popular under a vigorous and ambitious pupil of Paul of Venice that the Council of Ten threatened him with severe punishment if he did not stop trying to organize his students so as to rival the University of Padua. Thereafter, the Senate took care to elect to that lectureship distinguished members of the nobility who could be trusted not to become academic empire builders and who would inculcate doctrine deemed good for young fellow nobles.

About that time, a Venetian who was not of the nobility but the son of a notary and who was a merchant by occupation although a physician by education, Simone Valentini, drew up his will with specific provisions for the education of his children. First, he wished them to receive the training in reading, writing, and arithmetic which was basic alike for governmental positions, merchandising, and even some crafts and which was provided by scores of private tutors and schoolmasters. He could count on those who were called "masters of the abacus" to teach his sons bookkeeping as well as basic mathematics. When one of these tutors of mathematics, Luca Pacioli, exceptional in his intellect, arranged to publish a comprehensive treatise, *Summa de Arithmetica, Geometria, Proportioni e Proportionalità* (Venice, 1494), he included full instructions for double-entry accounting (see Figure 11). But Simone Valentini wanted his children to learn more than "the three R's" and business skills. He asked his executors to arrange, if possible, that the children should also study authors, logic, and philosophy. But not, he specified, to make them doctors or lawyers; they should be merchants ("sed non fiant medici nec iuriste, sed solum mercatores").

There were no public schools at Venice for elementary or secondary education. Just as craftsmen learned by apprenticeship to their fathers or some other master, young nobles, after private tutoring, learned by accompanying their fathers or uncles on business trips or political or naval missions. But as Valentini's will illustrates, there was a growing desire for more educational opportunities in addition to the professional training offered at the University. The endowed lectures on philosophy at the Rialto offered one response. In the long run, the desire was more largely met by another kind of study, that of Latin literature, in the mood set by Francesco Petrarch. Having gained wide fame as a poet by his sonnets and as a scholar by the graceful and eloquent Latin in which he conducted a Europe-wide correspondence, Petrarch came to Venice to reside. In return for a promise to leave to Venice his celebrated collection of manuscripts as the foundation of a public library, the Signoria provided him with a house on the Riva degli Schiavoni, where he enjoyed the busy life of the harbor. He had professed admiration for the learned Doge Andrea Dandolo and encouraged him to write Latin in a more classical style. Petrarch made many friends at Venice but before he died he went off to enjoy at Padua the hospitality of Francesco Carrara, who became Venice's enemy, and to relax in a country villa nearby in the Euganean hills. When he died there in 1374, his library was scattered.

Petrarch's humanist tastes did not find immediate general acceptance at Venice. Just as he was leaving, he learned that four of his "friends" had met to talk about him. They had agreed that he was a good man, but rather ignorant. They judged him "ignorant" because he disdained to pay attention to the refined logical distinctions dear to the Aristoteleans, whereas his "four friends" shared the common view that the ideas of Aristotle, "the master of those who know," as Dante had called him, must be understood by anyone who wished to be accepted as a man of learning. Infuriated, Petrarch counter-blasted with a tract denouncing that sort of learning as a Godless kind of quibbling, unworthy of man's nature. In contrast he extolled qualities which could be developed by the study of imaginative literature, especially eloquence, by which he meant persuasive power in writing and speaking. But interest in Aristotelean science grew more vigorously for a time at Venice than did Petrarchian humanism. The public lectureship at the Rialto was endowed by one of the four "friends" who had so offended Petrarch; a public lectureship devoted to Latin literature was not established until much later.

Petrarch's firmest friends and admirers were among the officials in the chancery, particularly the Grand Chancellor, Benintendi dei Ravignani. The staff of the chancery had received hitherto the lawyer-like training of notaries; now they became enthusiastic for adding to it the acquaintance with Latin literature which would enable them to write that language elegantly. When the lectureship in Latin literature was finally established, it was at San Marco, near the chancery. It was supplemented by twelve fellowships offered each year to boys who would attend and train for the chancery positions. Some distinguished Latin scholars were called in to teach in this school at San Marco, but Venetian nobles did not become its lecturers as they did in philosophy at the Rialto. When nobles acquired distinction as humanists, they were kept busy on diplomatic missions.

For two generations after Petrarch's death, his ideas aroused enthusiasm in other cities more than in Venice. Humanism found support mainly in Florence and at the courts of the princes. Many humanists praised one-man rule and disparaged republics, especially Venice. In the latter, they claimed, men of letters were not properly appreciated, for everyone was absorbed in making money. For a time, the humanist movement found Venice a relatively unsympathetic environment because of a divergence in their ideals both of learning and of government.

About fifty years after Petrarch's death in 1374, the situation had radically changed. Venice had grown richer, more secure, more interested in the embellishment of life. On the other hand, the most learned and original humanists, those of Florence, had developed a highly self-conscious republicanism while fighting the aggressive Visconti dukes of Milan. The humanists employed by these dukes extolled the benefits of a unified, centralized monarchy that would give peace to Italy. In opposition, a group of Florentines who are called "civic humanists" celebrated the ideal of liberty which the Florentines associated with their form of government. The Florentine constitution was not integrated as well as the Venetian, and it was more subject to corruption and violent overhaul, but it gave more political opportunities to new men. Moreover, both embodied the same basic principles: the submission of all individuals to the law of the commune and the decisions of its councils; a wide diffusion of membership in councils and magistracies; short terms and rapid rotation in office; and the calling of office holders to account when their terms of office were over. Rich men of distinguished families dominated the government in both Venice and Florence but they did so by commanding the confidence of a free following of men equal in rights. This kind of responsible public service was possible only in a republic, so declared the civic humanists, and it developed the highest type of human character, the type represented in their minds by Cicero, whom they praised not only for his eloquence but for his public spirit. This emphasis on republicanism heightened humanism's appeal to Venetian nobles.

Another change from Petrarch's day was the humanists' fuller knowledge of Greek. Although Petrarch believed the Greek language was a key to beauty and wisdom because the Romans had praised Greek writers, he could not read Greek; and the sounds made by Greek seamen under his windows on the Venetian water front were not the language of Socrates and Plutarch. Two generations later, humanists were able to read in the Greek original the works of Greek philosophers, orators, and historians. They drew directly from Plato and Demosthenes in building their conceptions of human personality and civic virtue. Florence had led in importing a Greek professor and supplying students for him, but once the movement was under way, Venice served as the gateway to Greece for scholars as well as merchants, and Greeks coming to the West felt most at home among their many commercial compatriots in Venice. A second lectureship in the humanities was established at San Marco, and lecturers were appointed who were experts in Greek as well as Latin literature. The Riformatori established at the University of Padua a chair for Greek, Padua having become a center of humanistic as well as scientific studies. The crown on Venetian leadership in the field was set in 1468, when the most distinguished of all Greek refugees, Cardinal Bessarion, donated his library to Venice. By sending most of it from Rome to Venice before he died, he made a reality of Petrarch's dream of a fine public library open to scholars. It is now part of the Biblioteca Nazionale Marciana.

An industrial development, printing with movable types, also enhanced Venice's importance for the humanists. During the last quarter of the fifteenth century, Venice became the busiest producer of printed books in all Europe, as will be described in Chapter 22. Humanists turned to Venice to publish their own works and to obtain the best editions of the classics, especially those produced by Venice's Aldine Press.

Among the first of the Italians to go to Constantinople to learn Greek thoroughly was Guarino Guarini. When he returned, he began teaching in Venice and formulated the program for what is deservedly called a "liberal education." His aim was to teach young men how to handle themselves. He taught Greek and Latin not for their own sake but to inspire boys to speak up and express themselves, winning a friend or overawing an adversary in conversation or debate. That was a skill they would need in order to be effective in princely courts or city councils. Sensitivity to language and literature would thus become part of their lives as well-rounded individuals. Knowledge of the great literature of Greece and Rome served to supplement, not to replace, the training young nobles received in trade, in war, and in politics by the coaching of their fathers or uncles, or in law at a university.

Guarino, like many other humanist educators, did not stay long in Venice; apparently, they found the shifting patronage of Venetian nobles too insecure a means of livelihood, and the Signoria less munificent than upstart princes. But one aspect of their educational ideal, the aspect allied to civic humanism, took deeper roots in Venice than elsewhere in Italy. To Venetians, the perfection of manhood through classical studies was not an end in itself but a preparation for service of the Republic. At princely courts, the ideal of public service derived from Cicero and Plutarch could flourish only by being adulterated into the picture of the perfect courtier. At Florence, its realization was made difficult by the vindictive strife of factions. In Venice, humanism ministered less to intellectual originality or personal achievements than to the disciplining of character according to a social ideal. As later in nineteenth-century England, where the classics also colored an aristocracy's ideals of public service, they were accepted in Venice as the best preparation for public life.

This ideal was personified at an early date by Francesco Barbaro, a pupil of Guarino. As a young man, Francesco showed his mastery of Greek by translating two of Plutarch's lives, those of Aristides and Cato, two ancient models of civic virtue. He wrote a treatise defending marriage because it was through a family that a man could perpetuate his nation. Its elegant Latin won praise from even Florentine humanists. All his life he collected manuscripts of ancient authors and corresponded with leading men of letters, but after being chosen Senator at the exceptionally early age of twenty-nine, he was kept busy in political office. He was ambassador to Rome, Ferrara, and Florence, and podesta in Treviso,

Vicenza, Bergamo, and Brescia, and became a national hero by his resolute defense of Brescia against Milan. Francesco Barbaro did not claim literary glory as a humanist, but was proud of his services to his republic.

Bernardo Giustiniani, a son of one of Francesco Barbaro's good friends, grew up equally devoted to both Latin literature and political service. His distinguished father spent much energy seeking good tutors for Bernardo and gave his son political experience by taking him with him as he moved from one position to another. From this upbringing, Bernardo acquired fame as a man of letters skillful in negotiations. At about seventy years of age, after decades of diplomatic service, Bernardo Giustiniani applied himself to the writing of history. Orations and history were the forms of literature that appealed most to Venetian humanists. From antiquity, they had learned a view of historical writing different from that of the lawyer-minded Andrea Dandolo. On the one hand they learned to stress a search for the truth of what happened. On the other hand, they regarded history as a branch of literature, to be written in flowing emotion-stirring rhetoric, while also giving a rational explanation of events. Bernardo Giustiniani applied these views to the early history of Venice, comparing chronicles and documents one with the other, and — more surprisingly — comparing them with archaeological findings and with geographical study to decide which of the traditions seemed most probably true. Along the way he went into long digressions, somewhat after the fashion of Herodotus, to accentuate his conception of Venice's place in history and her mission. He upset none of the myths to which the Venetians were most attached, such as belief in the city's freedom ever since its foundation, but he pruned out some of the least credible tales. Compared to Dandolo's chronicle, his history provided a more rational and more moving historical basis for belief in Venice's great destiny.

To the politically minded majority of Venetian Senators, Giustiniani's history seemed less useful than that written by a second-rate professional humanist called Sabellico, who carried the story down to the mid-fifteenth century. Sabellico also wrote Latin in humanist style and he took pains less in finding the truth than in leaving out disagreeable truths. He was rewarded with pay and the lectureship at the school at San Marco, so that his history came to be regarded as Venice's "offical history." Having an official history then seemed to Venice's rulers such a good idea that, after Sabellico's death, they made provision for its continuation, but sought a Venetian noble for the task. After delays, in 1530 they assigned the position to Pietro Bembo, who indeed was then the highest ranking Venetian man of letters (see Figure 19).

Pietro Bembo was different from the kind of person idealized by the civic humanists a century earlier, quite different from Francesco Barbaro or Bernardo Giustiniani. He illustrates the wide diversity of personalities in Venice as elsewhere in Italy during the period called the High Renaissance (roughly 1492–1550). To be sure, he also was trained for public service by a distinguished father whom he accompanied on embassies to foreign capitals. But Pietro preferred love-making and poetry to negotiations and administration. Until his father died at eighty-five, loaded with honors, Pietro lived away from Venice, thus avoiding both the wearisome minor offices with which a noble was expected to begin his political career and his father's reproaches for neglect of his calling as a member of the nobility. Not that Pietro Bembo was an idler. His learning, his correspondence with important people, and his literary production prove the

FIGURE 18 *The Courtyard of the Ducal Palace as painted by Guardi (courtesy of the Louvre, Paris). Although painted much later, Francesco Guardi's* Crowning of a Doge *shows the lavish use, about 1500, of classical decorative detail on the courtyard side of the east wing of the Ducal Palace.*

contrary. Leaving to his father and brothers the handling of the small family fortune, he sought and received from princely courts, especially from Rome, favors that provided a good income. In the end, he thus repaired the family fortune. After his father's death, when the family's problems really required his attention, he returned to Venice, married the mother of his three children, and settled down in a villa near Padua.

To earn the stipend and the honor assigned him as offical historian, Bembo at sixty took up vigorously the continuation of Sabellico's story. He was distracted from his writing when the pope rewarded him for past services to the papacy and for literary eminence by making him a cardinal, but before he died in 1547 at the age of seventy-six, he had narrated in a favorable light Venice's policies during the difficult years 1487–1513, exciting years as will be explained in the next chapters. Where eloquence was called for, he quite outclassed Sabellico, but Venice's rulers did not find Bembo's history entirely satisfactory. Before publishing it, they had it revised to remove passages in which Bembo used his literary skill to express his opinion of some popes and cardinals he had known personally and of some other individuals, particularly in a Venetian family, the Grimani, who seemed to him to have profited unduly amid their country's difficulties.

In the history of Italian literature, Pietro Bembo is important for his championing of the vernacular. He wrote his history in Latin but himself supervised a translation into Italian. He published a tract devoted to defending the language of Dante and Boccaccio and attacking humanists who said that all enduring literature had to be in Latin. His own popular composition, reprinted in many editions, was *Gli Asolani*, a dialogue on love which contained many echoes of Plato's dialogue on the same subject but which pictured in Italian a very courtly, very Italian gathering at the villa of Caterina Corner, the exiled Queen of Cyprus, at Asolo. In his middle age, Bembo acquired a reputation as an authority on Platonic love, but in this dialogue, begun in his twenties when he was still throbbing from affairs with his first three mistresses, he is equally eloquent about the agonies, joys, and benefits of the physical attraction between men and women.

Italian gradually prevailed over both Latin and the Venetian dialect as Venice's literary language, although the Venetian dialect was the medium for many official papers, for personal diaries and letters, and for much popular poetry.

EARLY Admiring imitation of the ancient Romans was only one of many elements
RENAISSANCE in Venetian civilization in the sixteenth century. Even when Venice, com-
ARCHITECTURE bined with Padua, had become one of the half-dozen cultural centers leading
the Western world in the creation of its arts and sciences, she still showed in many respects her Eastern connections. The oriental strain was evident in the pomp of her ceremonies and also in her first uses of the Renaissance's new style in architecture. Florence, where the new style took form, demanded order and proportion in planning a building as a whole. Venice adopted details of the new style, such as classic columns, round arches, and pediments, but without much concern for orderly harmonious structure. Venetians were more interested in color and picturesque variety.

Prosperity crowded Venice's palaces together, especially near the Grand Canal. They jostled each other on all sides but one, and all architectural design was concentrated on that one façade, usually overlooking a canal. Only an occasional doorway, or a balcony on an angle where it could catch the sun, or some feature of the interior courtyard, might also be carefully decorated. In this respect, the Late Gothic palaces and those of the Early Renaissance were the same. And they were the same also in heaping-on decoration, often in disregard of the lines of structure.

In going back to rounded arches, many Venetian stonecutters went back also to other features of earlier Byzantine palaces, such as the extensive use of colored marble, serpentine, and porphyry. They handled Roman arches and pilasters with a light touch which makes their Early Renaissance façades as gay and fanciful as those of the flamboyant Gothic. The profuse decoration of these Venetian palaces and of most of the churches of the same period expresses a taste very different from that of the rather austere early Florentine Renaissance. John Ruskin, the eloquent English art critic of a century ago, called the Venetian style "Byzantine Renaissance" (*Stones of Venice*, Vol. II, chap. 1, par. xxiii).

Even in this rather unclassical variation, the "Renaissance" in architecture affected Venice only many decades after it was conceived in Florence. The formal entrance to the Ducal Palace joining its west wing with San Marco was built in mid-century in a most flamboyant Gothic. The first thorough expression of the new style was the gateway to the Arsenal, built in 1460 (see Figure 32). It flowered in the Ducal Palace only when its old east wing was destroyed by fire in 1483 and was then rebuilt on lines laid down by Antonio Rizzo in the new style (see Figure 18).

Most of the stonecutters who built these profusely decorated Venetian palaces were like Rizzo from Lombardy. Their own Lombard traditions as well as those of Venice explain their distaste for the relatively severe Florentine style. But the best architect of the group, Mauro Coducci, drew inspiration from the most articulate of the Florentine artists, Leon Battista Alberti. Coducci was from Bergamo and must have been taken in his youth by his father, also a stonemason, to Rimini, where he may have worked on Alberti's Tempio Malatestiana. Many of Alberti's conceptions were incorporated in San Michele in Isola, the church which Coducci built on Venice's cemetery island. He set the style also for many important buildings which were begun or finished by other stonecutters: for example, the Clock Tower, the Procuratie Vecchie, San Zaccaria, and the Scuola Grande di San Marco (see Figure 20).

The style which Coducci perfected did not last long. Within a generation after his death in 1504, Venetian architecture became more thoroughly dominated by Roman examples, those of both Ancient Rome and the Rome of the High Renaissance. When we return in our last chapter to sketch the completion of the building of Venice, we will find her foremost architect, Palladio, setting standards for all the West.

THE TURN WESTWARD · II

Contests for Power: The Fifteenth Century

CHAPTER SIXTEEN

Political as well as cultural developments in fifteenth-century Italy invited Venice to devote more energy to Italian affairs. She became deeply involved in controlling the nearby mainland and parts of Lombardy, and these contests broadened out until the dominance of Italy was at stake. Then, when Spain and France became united kingdoms, the Italian balance of power was submerged into the European state system. Against foreign armies, Venice made efforts to pose as the champion of Italian freedom but failed. At the same time, she was facing new rivals for sea power, first the Turkish and then the Spanish fleets. The problems of power within Italy became interlocked with control of the Mediterranean Sea.

EXPANSION ON THE MAINLAND Among Venice's several basic interests in the Italian mainland, the most important was her need to draw on it for supplies: for food and wood, for example, and even for water on the occasions when an extra high, wind-driven tide overflowed the courtyards and campi and salted all the wells so that bargemen sold fresh water by the quart. Some of Venice's early wars and treaties with mainland rulers have been mentioned in describing how Venice established staple rights in the North Adriatic, her lordship of the gulf (see Chapter 6). These treaties not only assured that trade would flow through Venice but also assured her of food supplies from the immediate hinterland. As the city grew as a manufacturing center, her demand for raw materials became more intense and more varied: hemp from marshy lands near the Po, iron and copper from the foothills of the Alps, masts and spars from as far away as the Dolomites.

A second vital interest was in the overland routes to the western outlets for spices and to the textiles and metals offered in exchange. There were four or five feasible routes through the Austrian Alps to southern Germany and two or three through Lombardy to France or the Rhineland so that the blocking of a few could be countered by the more intensive use of others, but Venice had a vital interest in preventing any one power from surrounding the lagoons and closing all the routes to the north and west. So long as Venice had as neighbors many cities competing one with the other, and so long as the claimants to wider powers, such as popes and emperors, had no means of effective local control, it did not much matter to Venice which of the neighboring potentates was gaining and which was losing. But the instruments of state-building — administrative and judicial bureaucracies backed by armies and taxation — were in the fourteenth and fifteenth centuries creating larger and more centralized units. The consolidation of all northern Italy became a distant possibility.

Should the Venetians stay out of Italian politics until such a strong North Italian state actually interfered with its supplies and trade routes? Or should it intervene to prevent any such consolidation? Venice's concern with preserving a scattering or balance of power was logically subordinate to its interest in supplies and trade routes; psychologically, concern with a balance of power became dominant and led to impatient ambition. There developed in Italy a state system the members of which were of rapidly changing weight or force. Any equilibrium was precarious. Fighting for a balance of power led to considering a different solution. Some thought the best way to make sure no one else upset the balance to Venice's disadvantage was to upset it in her favor.

A number of material benefits which imperialism brought to some members of the Venetian nobility reinforced this will for power as an end in itself. The subjection of more territory meant more jobs. The cities which came under Venice kept their own laws and magistracies, to be sure, and only a few high officials were sent out from Venice; a podesta or rettore, a military commander, and perhaps a treasurer; but as dozens of cities were acquired, these posts became important as sources of livelihood and dignity to some members of the Venetian nobility. Wealthier Venetians bought land and welcomed opportunities to acquire more farms when, after a conquest or reconquest, the estates of "rebels" were put up to auction. Although larger material interests supported Venice's maritime imperialism, a self-interested support was building up for an expansionist policy also in Italy.

The first threat of a centralized state on Venice's western frontier came from the Scaliger family which ruled Verona, Padua, and many other cities, some as far away as Tuscany. A Florentine alliance and a short war won Treviso for Venice in 1339 and drove the Scaligers from Padua. Then the Carrara family in Padua became a threat, although the Venetians had earlier helped the Carrara take power in Padua. At first, Francesco Carrara il Vecchio seemed dangerous only because of his alliances with the Genoese and the King of Hungary during the wars culminating at Chioggia in 1379 (see Chapter 14). But even after Venice had bested those two enemies, Francesco il Vecchio persisted in trying to extend his power all around Venice's western frontiers, from Ferrara, whose duke was his ally, to Friuli, where he sent men and money to win sup-

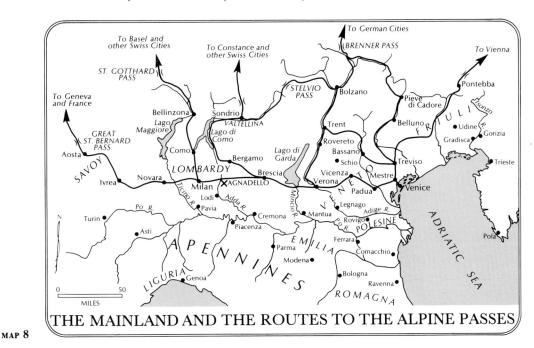

THE MAINLAND AND THE ROUTES TO THE ALPINE PASSES

MAP 8

porters in a district still loosely organized in feudal fashion. In order to dispose of the danger of a great Carrara state based on Padua, Venice allied with the ruler of Milan, Gian Galeazzo Visconti. The Carrara were exterminated and, after Gian Galeazzo's death. Venice added to its dominion in 1404–6 Vicenza, Verona, and Padua.

A notable feature of Venice's triumph over the Carrara was the thorough, implacable fashion in which Venice killed off the family and obliterated as far as possible all memorials of it at Padua. At Verona, in contrast, Venice preserved the monuments of the Scaligers as if seeking legitimacy as their successors. Lords of some cities that submitted to Venice were handsomely pensioned off to retirement in Dalmatia or Greece. But all three captured members of the Carrara family were strangled by order of the Council of Ten. A rumor that they had died of pneumonia may have been given out, but such subterfuge was unnecessary. The Carrara were hated by the Venetian populace because they had again and again turned on Venice and were accused of trying to poison the city's wells. Killing captured enemies who were still dangerous was not unusual in that age. The soldier cardinal who was reducing Rome to order at about this time beheaded many a captured noble. Gian Galeazzo owed his control of Milan to capturing by trickery an uncle whom he then poisoned. Venetians approved the execution of the Carrara, muttering "dead men wage no wars" ("uomo morto non fa guerra").

The Council of Ten was moved by these same feelings and, in addition, by evidence that the Carrara, who had been honored by admission to the Venetian nobility when they had been allies of Venice, had been boring from within the aristocracy and might even have had some success in building up a pro-Carrara faction. In accord with the general Venetian principle that its nobles should not form attachments with foreign princes, as did so many Genoese nobles, the receipt of gifts or pensions from the Signore of Carrara had been explicitly forbidden. When the secret accounts of the Carrara were captured, they showed payments to a number of nobles, including Venice's foremost war hero, Carlo Zeno. He was condemned to loss of all offices and a year in prison. The vote was far from unanimous in the Council of Ten, but Zeno submitted. He was proved technically guilty, although there was not much doubt of his basic loyalty. In the operations leading to the capture of Padua, he had again played a heroic role, personally testing the passability of a ford by wading through its waters himself up to his neck. It was a tribute to the moral power of the Venetian constitution that even the most valiant and most lauded Venetian obeyed the will of his fellow aristocrats. When he died in 1418 at the age of 84, he was accorded at his funeral the highest honors.

In killing the Carrara, Venice showed that its republican machinery was quite as capable of decisive ruthless action as any of the contemporary self-made princes, the signori typified in the "New Prince" later idealized by Machiavelli. In destroying the Carrara, Venice was protecting its interests in supplies and trade routes, but in strengthening Milan it ignored a need for a balance of power in Italy as a whole. When Venice allied with Gian Galeazzo Visconti, he was already in control of all Lombardy and parts of Tuscany and the Romagna. At the very time that the overthrow of the Carrara brought Gian Galeazzo deep into the Veneto, the civic humanists of Florence were shouting to the skies that the diabolical Visconti tyrant was about to conquer all Italy and stamp out its liberty. However, the Black Death hit Milan in 1402, and by carrying off Gian Galeazzo proved to the satisfaction of the witty Florentines that even the plague was good for something. His sons were minors, his state dissolved in civil war. Before a new "Visconti tyrant" became strong enough to threaten again, in Florentine eyes, the liberty of Italy, Florence had ended by conquest the liberty of Pisa, consolidating its control in Tuscany. In that interim also Venice finished off the Carrara and strengthened its dominion over Friuli and Dalmatia.

In 1423, there were three main states in northern Italy: Milan, Florence, and Venice. The Papal States in the center of the peninsula and the Kingdom of Naples in the south were moving toward consolidations that would soon enable them to play effective roles in a five-power Italian state system.

A threat to upset the balance of power among them again came from Milan in 1423, when Filippo Maria Visconti, having rebuilt the Visconti control of Lombardy, reached out into Romagna. Again the Florentines felt threatened, and they appealed to Venice to join them in a defense of Italian liberties. Nobles influenced by the civic humanists favored the Florentine alliance, but the leading advocate of such an alliance was a man known primarily as an aggressive politician, Francesco Foscari.

The resulting debates among Venetian rulers are the first of which some verbatim reports have survived. Opposing Francesco Foscari, who had pushed himself into the high position of Procurator of San Marco at the relatively early age of 43, was the 80-year-old doge, Tommaso Mocenigo, who counseled caution. Mocenigo had gained reputation years earlier as Captain General of the Sea, and as doge had presided over substantial territorial acquisitions in Dalmatia and Friuli. Mocenigo directed his arguments especially against those who thought that they and other Venetians could gain wealth from wars in Lombardy. He extolled the high prosperity brought by peace, the satisfactory state of the merchant marine and navy, and the reduction of the public debt. After being raised to almost 10 million ducats by the wars at the beginning of the century, it had been reduced during his dogeship to 6 million ducats. He described with statistical detail the flow through Venice each year of goods worth 10 million ducats and compared Lombardy to a fertile garden from which the Venetians, through commerce, gathered the fruits but to which war would bring devastation. In a speech which we may call his "Farewell Address," made just before his death in 1423 when Francesco Foscari seemed likely to be elected as his successor, Mocenigo praised other men as candidates but said of Foscari: "Why some say that they wish to elect Messer Francesco Foscari I do not know, for said Ser Francesco Foscari spreads lies and other statements without foundation and swoops and soars more than a hawk or falcon. And if you make him doge, which God forbid, you will shortly be at war; and whoever has 10,000 ducats, you will find yourself with only 1,000, and who has ten houses will have only one, and who has ten suits, coats or shirts, will have difficulty finding one. . . ." But Foscari was elected, and the acceptance of the Florentine alliance against Milan proved to be the beginning of thirty years of almost constant warfare in Lombardy, becoming every year more costly.

The issue setting Francesco Foscari against Tommaso Mocenigo was not the relative priority of Italian politics compared to the Turkish menace in the Aegean, although it came to appear that way later. Foscari was for an adventuresome assertive policy in both directions. Immediately after Foscari became doge, Salonica, the largest city left in the Byzantine Empire outside of Constantinople, offered itself to Venice, hoping for enough support to be able to resist a Turkish attack. Venice accepted and in 1424 sent a fleet under Pietro Loredan, who had decisively defeated the Turks in an encounter at Gallipoli some years earlier and had been Foscari's chief rival for the dogeship. Venetian superiority at sea was not yet in question. It was used less to keep Salonica well supplied than to harry Turkish coasts with hopes of booty and of inducing the sultan to make a compromise peace. Within a few years, Venice was sending a bigger navy up the Po River, however, than to the Aegean Sea, and Salonica was lost. Once deeply engaged in wars in the Po valley, Venice devoted fewer men and less money to the defense of her colonial empire. A century after Mocenigo's death, when the Ottoman Turks had become a great naval power and Italian wars were still absorbing Venetian resources, Venetians who believed that Venice's greatness depended on the sea looked back on Mocenigo's "Farewell Address" as a warning against seeking dominion on the continent, a warning that should have been heeded.

Aggressive action in Italy and in the Levant seemed all the more in harmony at the beginning of Foscari's dogeship because Genoa was subject again, for a time, to the Duke of Milan. War with Milan gave opportunities to strike blows at Genoa, the traditional enemy who still seemed more dangerous as a maritime rival than the Turk. In 1431, after the main Venetian fleet under Pietro Loredano won a brilliant victory at Portofino near Genoa, another fleet composed mainly of converted merchantmen unsuccessfully attacked Chios, the main base of the Genoese in the Aegean. This might be called Venice's

FIGURE 19   *Venetian Faces.*

(a) The ambitious politician Francesco Foscari, leader of the Venetian "hawks" and doge for thirty-four years. Portrait by Lazzaro Bastiani (courtesy of the Museo Correr, Venice).

(b) The saintly patriarch Lorenzo Giustinian, under whom the patriarchate was moved in 1451 from Grado to within Venice at San Pietro di Castello. Uncle of the diplomat-historian Bernardo Giustinian. Portrait by Gentile Bellini (courtesy of the Accademia, Venice, Photo Böhm).

(c) The elegant humanist Pietro Bembo, poet, courtier, and finally historian and cardinal. Portrait by Titian (courtesy of the National Gallery of Art, Washington).

a

Fifth Genoese War, except that it was so subordinate to the struggle with Milan that it ended as soon as one of Genoa's innumerable revolutions drove out the Milanese governor.

Meanwhile Venice had acquired Brescia and Bergamo, stretching her domain deep into Lombardy, but these acquisitions did not bring peace. Without crippling Milan, they gave Filippo Maria a grievance which he fought to redress. He made an ally of Alfonso, King of Aragon, who became also King of Naples after one of Naples' innumerable civil wars. The adherence of the Papal States to the Florentine-Venetian block then served to keep a balance of power. Smaller princes such as the dukes of Mantua and Ferrara were now on one side, now on the other. All Italy was thus deeply involved, but the center of Venice's military efforts was Lombardy.

These Lombard wars were in part naval wars. Control of the Po and Adige rivers was strategically important, and the Venetian Arsenal built and equipped a type of vessel especially designed for river warfare, the first type that the Venetians called "galleons." They were rowed and they carried artillery. During a period when Brescia was under siege, shipwrights and seamen were sent from Venice to arm a fleet on the Lago di Garda because the Milanese forces were so strongly entrenched to the south of that lake that the only way to send supplies to the beleaguered city was across the lake (see Map 8). Six galleys and 25 smaller long ships were taken from Verona up the Adige nearly as far as Rovereto and then with 120 oxen to a galley, pulled the fifteen miles over hills to the northern end of the Lago di Garda. It took 15 days and a total of 2,000 oxen, with innumerable heavy hawsers controlling the vessels as they descended to the lake. Once there, they suffered a defeat, to be sure, by vessels

b   *c*

which the forewarned Milanese mobilized against them, but the success in carrying ships over mountains aroused great admiration in an age when humanists celebrated such feats of human ingenuity. When later reinforced, the Venetian vessels finally won on the Lago di Garda a victory which contributed to lifting the siege of Brescia.

Five centuries earlier, mainland rivers had attracted the energies of the Venetians as traders. Then they had turned to the sea and the East. Now in the fifteenth century, they were returning to the mainland, not as bargemen peddling salt and Eastern fabrics, but as rulers directing fleets and armies.

CONDOTTIERI AND THE BALANCE OF POWER IN ITALY Venetian river fleets were commanded by Venetians just as were seagoing armadas. Venetian nobles sometimes provided able military leadership also in the defense of the cities of which they were the governors. The magnificent 3-year defense of Brescia was inspired and guided by Francesco Barbaro, the humanist statesman, and fought through by the men of that city. In the Scaliger war, Venetians had commanded field armies also; indeed, armies had then been largely composed of conscripts from Venice just as were the war fleets. But before the end of the fourteenth century, land war had passed almost completely into the hands of highly equipped and skilled mercenary specialists. Victories in the Lombard campaigns were often won by bloodless maneuvers which cut an enemy's lines of supplies or caught his troops in disarray. For warfare of that kind, Venice did what all the other Italian states were doing; it hired mercenary captains. They were called *condottieri* because they operated according to a contract, a *condotta*, which stated the amount they received for their services and for specified numbers of soldiers whom they recruited. One or two Venetian nobles called Commissioners (*Provveditori*) were elected to advise the commander in determining his plan of campaign and to report on him. Some Commissioners also commanded troops in battle, but that was particularly the function of the professional condottiere.

Although the expertise of the condottieri was indisputable, their loyalty was often in question. For them to terminate their employment by one government and seek a contract with one of its rivals was not considered disloyal. No one felt they had any obligation beyond the time and circumstances specified in their contracts. But if a condottiere began secret negotiations with a potential new employer whose army he was at the same time facing in the field, and especially if he refrained while negotiating from seizing military opportunities, he was suspected of breach of contract and deemed deserving of punishment as a traitor. It was also considered a breach of good faith when he sold to one government a city he had captured when in the service of a rival. Florence was more than once thus tricked by her condottieri; Machiavelli's wounded patriotism added vitriol to his denunciation of these mercenaries.

On the whole, Venice was one of the most successful employers of condottieri, but she had difficulties. The most dramatic case occurred early in the Lombard wars. At their start, she obtained the services of the very ablest condottiere, Carmagnola, who, while in the service of the Duke of Milan, had proved himself at the top of his profession by beating the famous Swiss infantry. During his first years in Venetian service, he justified his reputation, but after he had won Brescia and Bergamo for Venice, he failed to follow up victories and became suspiciously inactive. The Council of Ten learned that he was treacherously negotiating with Filippo Maria Visconti. Without revealing their suspicions, they invited Carmagnola to Venice in March 1432, to explain more fully his ideas about the feasability of various operations in the coming campaign. Although a decisive step towards his condemnation had already been taken in the Senate, no word of it leaked out. Carmagnola was received with the utmost cordiality and high honors until he had conferred with the Ten in the rooms high in the Ducal Palace. Then, as he turned to descend by the way he had come, he found attendants blocking that door and pointing instead to the door which led to the prisons. A month later, after a formal hearing of evidence he was beheaded in a public ceremony between the two columns of the Piazzetta.

Earlier, when Filippo Maria Visconti learned that Carmagnola was leaving his service to be employed by Venice, he had plotted to have him poisoned. Handling a somewhat similar situation with more legality and efficiency added much to Venice's prestige.

Removing Carmagnola proved easier than replacing him with as brilliant a general. Among the condottieri Venice employed later, two are especially memorable, less for their victories, to be sure, than for their statues. Gattamelata, for whom the equestrian statue at Padua was made by Donatello, commanded Venice's efforts to relieve Brescia, and some historians give him credit for the hauling of ships over the mountains to the Lago di Garda. He served without brilliant successes but with constant loyalty. Bartolomeo Colleoni became Venice's leading general a little later, and after many times

FIGURE 20   *The Condottiere in Front of San Marco (Photo Böhm).*

The statue of Bartolomeo Colleoni by Verrocchio, erected on a finely designed pedestal by the Venetian caster Alessandro Leopardi, looms in front of the Scuola San Marco, an example of the Early Renaissance style of Mauro Coducci. On the right, in contrast, is the rather sedate Gothic of San Giovanni e Paolo, the Dominican church.

changing sides. As a businessman, he was one of the most successful of the condottieri, piling up treasure and landed estates as he shifted among competing employers. At his death, he left in cash 231,983 ducats, an amount comparable to the riches of the leading banker of the age, Cosimo de' Medici. Colleoni was a Venetian subject, being born near Bergamo where he also had his principal estate, and he realized that the Venetian government was likely to seize much of his wealth, as indeed it did, as soon as he was dead and his army and skill was no longer to be feared. Hoping to soften the blow, he added a codicil to his will in 1475, leaving 100,000 ducats to Venice, "for the war against the Turk and the defense of the Christian religion," and expressing the wish that a bronze statue of him be erected in the Piazza San Marco. After sequestering all his estate and doling out portions to the heirs he had designated, the government commissioned the statue by Verrocchio and erected it, not in the Piazza San Marco, but in front of the hospital or Scuola di San Marco and the Church of San Giovanni e Paolo (see Figure 20). The latter church contained many monuments to famous Venetians, but such glorification of any individual person was not permitted at the center of government, at San Marco. In spite of all his shifting about, Colleoni had never treacherously broken a contract with the Venetian Republic; and in accepting the legacy from his estate, the Republic cannot justly be accused of breaking faith with him either, for it erected in his honor so excellent an equestrian statue that it, and it alone, has made his name truly memorable.

The most successful of all the Italian condottieri was Francesco Sforza, who blocked Venice's ambitions by making himself Duke of Milan. While being employed at one time or another by Venice, Florence, and the Papacy, he used these contracts to accumulate army, income, and lands so as to become himself a member of the state system. Then he accepted Milan's bid for his services and married Filippo Maria Visconti's daughter. When in 1447 Filippo Maria Visconti died leaving no male heir, Milan's leading citizens proclaimed a republic. Champions of civic humanism, such as Francesco Barbaro, hailed this triumph of republicanism and urged a warm alliance of the republics of Venice, Florence, Milan, and Genoa. But Florence was now ruled in effect by Cosimo de' Medici, who resolved to support Sforza in order to check Venice. Francesco Foscari and the other leaders of Venetian policy made their alliance with the Milanese Republic conditional on Milan's cession of some cities, Lodi and Piacenza, where an anti-Visconti party had proclaimed freedom and let in the Venetian forces. That enraged many Milanese. Francesco Sforza was able by astute diplomatic and military maneuvering to make himself the Duke of Milan. He then fought the Venetian-paid armies to a standstill, until mutual exhaustion, the Turkish conquest of Constantinople, and papal mediation induced the combatants to accept a general peace in 1454. In this Peace of Lodi, the unity of an Italian state system was expressed by providing for an alliance of its five leading members — Naples, the Papal State, Florence, Milan, and Venice — for the professed purpose of defending Italy from the Turk.

When Venice began her wars against Milan in 1425, she was joining the Florentines in protecting the "liberties of Italy" by maintaining a balance of power against Milanese expansion. At the death of the last of the Visconti, Venice itself loomed as the threat to the balance of power. Even after Sforza's victory, in the state system formalized in the Peace of Lodi, Venice stood out as the most powerful member.

There is a report of a conversation among several condottieri about their business interests. One leader urged that they all avoid winning victories for Venice because, if she became any stronger, she would be able to impose peace on Italy and put them all out of work.

THE OTTOMAN TURKS IN THE BALANCE   If Venice had had Italy only to think about, she might indeed have proved strong enough to upset completely the Italian balance of power and gradually force the other Italian states to follow its leadership, its will.

But in fact Venice had to think not only of Italy but of the Balkans and the Aegean, where the Ottoman Empire was increasing its power. The Turks were the weight which kept Venice from bringing the balance of power down definitely in her favor in Italy.

In fighting the Turk, Venice was, to be sure, not alone. Her wars with the Ottoman Empire were within the framework of a political system distinguishable in the fifteenth century from that of Italy, one that might be called Balkan-Anatolian, but one which impinged on that of Italy not only through Venice but also through the papacy. Anti-Turkish diplomacy carried a crusading mantle. Again and again, popes renewed appeals for a crusade against the Ottoman

Turks. The popes backed their rhetoric by helping to levy special taxes to support crusaders. Most of the money thus collected was used by rulers for other purposes — except in countries that were directly threatened, as were Albania, Hungary, Poland, Transylvania, and Roumania, as well as Venice.

In spite of popular feeling against the "Infidels," every Italian state including Venice tried at one time or another to come to an understanding with the Turk against its Italian rivals. Even if it did not, it was believed to be doing so. Venice was most vociferously accused of this by other Italians because they were jealous of Venice's greater power and because Venice, being the most exposed to Turkish aggression, appealed loudly for crusading aid when at war and yet was ready to make peace with the Infidel whenever it suited her interests. All Western states made promises in terms of romantic chivalry and Christian piety and then made excuses in terms of political necessities. Venice counted among her political necessities not only the preservation of her colonies but the continuation of her commerce.

Basically the policy of Venice was to maintain control of the sea, to defend cities that could be protected from the sea, to pick up more when that was easy, and to retaliate for Turkish acts of aggression by seaborne raids. A shattering of the Ottoman Empire by the destruction of its army was more than once attempted by such large military states as Hungary and Poland, with support from French or German crusaders. Their efforts ended in defeats which confirmed Venice's belief in the wisdom of avoiding any offense to the Ottoman sultan that might require her to confront on land the full power of the Turkish army.

To accord with its policy of defending key outposts that were well fortified and could be supported from the sea, Venice should have made a major effort to keep Constantinople out of the hands of the Turk, even if the privileges of the large Genoese colony there and the hatred of the Greek population towards the Roman Church made the city a constant problem. But reports of preparations by Mohammed the Conqueror were not taken as seriously as they should have been. The struggle with Francesco Sforza was at its peak; reports of danger to Constantinople had been coming in for decades, and the threats of a very young sultan who had just come to the throne were generally discounted. A man of nineteen was considered too young to be taken seriously even in that century. The last Greek emperor appealed again and again for help, but that sent from the West was all too little or too late or both. When the city fell in 1453, some Venetian merchants and seamen in the city played a prominent role in its defense as did a number of other Westerners in residence. Many were killed in battle or decapitated by the vengeful sultan. Cutting its losses and playing for time, Venice merely negotiated a new treaty in which Mohammed promised protection to its commerce and colonies.

Ten years after the fall of Constantinople, Venice felt ready to strike back, for Italy had been relatively peaceful in the meantime. There was a better than usual prospect of a crusading coalition because of the efforts of Aeneas Sylvius Piccolomini, the humanist pope who took the name of Pius II. He devoted his renowned eloquence and his last ounce of physical strength to the cause. He announced he was leading the crusade himself, and set a dramatic example of personal sacrifice by going to Ancona to embark, although he had to be carried there ill in a litter, and died just as his ships were joined by the fleet from Venice commanded by the doge in person. The collapse of the crusade left

Venice facing a long war against the Turk with only wavering support from the papacy and more hostility than aid from other Western states, especially those of Italy.

The hostility was naturally most evident when the fortunes of war favored Venice, and abated only a little when Turkish victories threatened even Italian soil. At first Venetian arms were successful and conquered most of the Morea. Milan, Florence, and Naples formed an anti-Venetian alliance. They had the more reason to make their alliance anti-Venetian because Venice refused to join them in curbing Venice's old condottiere, Bartolomeo Colleoni, who was no longer in Venetian pay but acting, Venice protested, on his own and with help from Florentine exiles, enemies of the Medici. He tried to carve out a principality for himself in the Romagna. The hostile Italian coalition dissolved only after the 75-year-old Colleoni had been bought off and after Venice began to suffer reverses.

Venice's staunchest ally against the Turks, Scanderbeg, the Albanian "Athlete of Christendom," died in 1468. In his mountains he had held his own against the fury of the Ottoman army even when it was led by the sultan in person. He bequeathed his country and his cause to Venice as "the most faithful and valiant of his allies," but Venice was able to defend only a few Albanian cities while Turkish armies occupied others, hardly more than fifty miles by sea from Italy.

In 1470 Mohammed, for the first time, took the field personally against the Venetians. His army and a huge newly constructed fleet attacked Venice's main base in the North Aegean, Negroponte. In a campaign which was a kind of turning point in Venetian maritime history, as will be explained in a later chapter on the life of the fleets, Mohammed took Negroponte. Never thereafter did Venice hold "the gorgeous East in fee" in the way she had done sine 1204. But she did not give up the fight. She found new allies by embassies to Persia and other eastern neighbors of the Ottomans. After the taking of Negroponte, the Turkish fleet retired within the Dardanelles and left the Aegean unprotected from Venetian raids. In some years, Neapolitan and Papal squadrons joined in these raids. The Florentines remained implacably hostile, taking advantage of the war to increase their trade in Constantinople, acting as spies, and sabotaging peace negotiations. Turkish cavalry raided Dalmatia and Friuli, penetrating so far into northern Italy that the smoke from the villages they burned could be seen from the top of Venice's Campanile. Admitting defeat, Venice ended by a treaty in January 25, 1479, this 16-year war. She renounced Negroponte and some other Aegean Islands and agreed to pay 10,000 ducats a year for trading privileges. She also surrendered the Albanian fortress of Scutari, which had bravely held out for years.

Venetian naval supremacy during the later years of the war brought one territorial gain. The Venetian fleet turned aside from ravaging Turkish territory long enough to assure that a Venetian, Caterina Corner, was enthroned as Queen of Cyprus and would in time make that island a Venetian possession. This gain intensified the envious hostility with which Venice was regarded by other Italian states.

As soon as Sultan Mohammed made peace with Venice, he signalized the opening he had won on the Adriatic by seizing Otranto, the city on the heel of Italy closest to Albania. This Turkish invasion of Italy shocked the Italian princes enough so that they stopped fighting each other for a year or two. But they were at it again in 1482, when Mohammed died and Otranto was evacuated. The pope sought Venice's alliance against the King of Naples and promised Venice as reward Ferrara, where Venetians were not getting all the favored treatment to which they felt their treaties entitled them. Venice yielded to the temptation. Just three years after the conclusion of the Turkish war, she felt rich enough to start a new war that she knew would be expensive. At first, the condottieri whom Venice hired were very successful, but then the principle of the balance of power came into play. Milan and Florence supported Ferrara. The pope, alarmed by the extent of Venetian victories, changed sides, ordered Venice to stop its attack on Ferrara, and placed Venice under an interdict when she refused. Venice withdrew, but not without some return on her military investment; by the peace treaty made in 1484, Venice kept land she had conquered in the mouths of the Po, the Polesine.

THE MOST TRIUMPHANT CITY   When a worldly-wise French ambassador visited Venice at the end of the fifteenth century he wrote of it: "It is the most triumphant city I have ever seen, does most honor to all ambassadors and strangers, and governs itself with the greatest wisdom. . . ." (Philippe de Commines, *Memoirs*, 1495). Venice was then the outstanding naval power of the Mediterranean and the strongest state in the Italian peninsula.

How much the Republic had changed since the fourteenth century is emphasized by an analysis of its budget about 1500, roughly tabulated as follows:

BUDGET OF VENICE ABOUT 1500, IN ROUND FIGURES
*(Omitting Cyprus and recently acquired Polesine,
Cervia, Cremona, and cities in Apulia)*

Receipts	*Ducats*	*Expenses*	*Ducats*
Sales taxes in Venice (on consumption and goods in transit)	230,000	Ordinary Misc. and Salt Office Salaries	59,000 26,000
Direct taxes	160,000	Interest on government	
Salt sales	100,000	bonds	155,000
Miscellaneous	130,000	Expenses of mainland	
Mainland cities	330,000	cities	90,000
Overseas domains	200,000	Expenses overseas	200,000
		Total	530,000
Total	1,150,000	Available for extraordinary expenses (wars)	620,000
		Total	1,150,000

Two of the largest items of receipts had been absent a century or two earlier: the payments from the mainland cities and the direct taxes collected in Venice. Perhaps income from domains overseas had at some time been larger; but if the costs of the navy and the fortresses for the defense of those domains were charged against the income, the costs would probably have exceeded the income at most any period. After the acquisition of the mainland domains, revenues from that source helped support the cost of overseas empire.

Direct taxes had been resisted as long as possible. The system of forced loans, which had with difficulty survived the War of Chioggia and had been restored to health under Doge Tommaso Mocenigo, was again relied on for the wars in Lombardy, but these wars proved so costly that interest payments were reduced and postponed. In 1423, bonds of the Monte Vecchio had paid 4 percent and sold at 66 (so as to yield 6 percent); by 1474, they were paying only 1 percent irregularly and selling at 13. This cut in the interest payments on the Monte Vecchio crippled many of Venice's old philanthropic foundations, such as those supporting hospitals, for a century earlier they had been compelled by law to shift investments from real estate into government bonds (see Chapter 13).

Long before the Monte Vecchio fell to 13, it was evident that the traditional system of financing wars would no longer work. As the price of the bonds fell, the levies of forced loans became practically equivalent to direct property taxes. Those taxed refused to pay. It was necessary to condemn them as tax delinquents and seize and sell their property. This was a painful, slow process, and it was inequitable because the assessments on which the levies were allotted were very imperfect reflections of capacity to pay. The Senate was already gradually shifting to direct taxes when the Turkish conquest of Constantinople in 1453, in the midst of the Sforza war, created an atmosphere in which it could vote sweeping, drastic direct levies on income. These levies were then moderated and regularized and, in 1463, assessments were made more equitable. A cadaster was drawn up, listing all of the city's real estate, building by building, and its value. In theory, income from freights, merchandise, farms on the mainland, and bonds was also taxed. When loans were again levied in 1482 during the War of Ferrara, these income taxes were drawn on to pay the interest on the new series of bonds, called the *Monte Nuovo*. The assurance of its regularly paying 5 percent in perpetuity seemed so good that the Monte Nuovo were bought voluntarily by both Venetian and foreign investors. Their purchases expressed faith in Venice's bright future.

In the closing years of the fifteenth century, Venice's expansion on the mainland seemed to have been a huge success. The extent of her domains, the financial strength of the government, and the general air of opulence in the city fostered self-confidence. Weaknesses such as her dependence on condottieri and their mercenaries did not seem serious. Neither was there much concern about the lack of a political program and structure that could inspire an Italian army and win the cooperation of the leading citizens of other cities.

The nearest approach to such a program was that of the civic humanists. Of their ideals, it has been said that for that period: "Such a dream constituted in truth the most authentic and positively constructive force in Italian political history. . . ." Instead, princely particularism triumphed with Francesco Sforza and Cosimo de' Medici and led to foreign domination in the next century. Even the program of the civic humanists was not altogether "authentic." Francesco Barbaro's advocacy of an alliance of free republics was as inflated with wishful thinking as was Machiavelli's dream of the union of Italy by a "new prince." The republican liberty which civic humanists glorified contained the seeds of its own destruction. Big cities, such as Florence and Milan, whether republics or not, asserted their liberty by suppressing the liberties of smaller cities, such as Pisa or Cremona, and at the same time refused to take second place behind any other republic, even one that was also Italian and admired for its republican institutions, as was Venice. Nor did Venice show any disposition, as its Italian domains grew, to modify its institutions with the aim of winning the loyalty of other Italians. Venice was triumphant only within the limitations set by its structure as a city-state and by the diplomatic, financial, and military standards of the Italian state system.

THE TURN
WESTWARD · III

Contests for Power:
The Sixteenth Century

CHAPTER SEVENTEEN

Although the wealth and self-confidence of the Venetian Republic was never more blatant than in the last decades of the fifteenth century, far from the lagoons and quite outside her control much larger states — units of power with which a city-state such as Venice could not in the long run compete — were being solidified by Renaissance monarchs. While the Italians were rationalizing government and refining the art of politics on a small scale in their Italian state system, units approaching national states were being woven out of feudal monarchies in England, France, and Spain. Germany was as hopelessly divided as Italy, but the princes of the Hapsburg family who held the title of Holy Roman Emperor also ruled enough territory as family possessions to make them a fourth major power. Such rivals in the west and the Ottoman Empire to the east were to prove more dangerous than the Venetians yet realized.

THE TURNING POINT A new period of power politics on a larger scale opened when in 1494 a King of France invaded Italy to make good his claim to the Kingdom of Naples. His army so easily swept all before it that Venice organized a league against him to restore the balance of power. This League of Venice was not purely Italian; its signatories included the German emperor and the King of Spain. The Italian state system was being expanded into a European state system.

To keep track of the new and larger swings of the balance of power, Venice sent resident ambassadors to all the major courts of Europe. Such a regular exchange of diplomats first became common practice in Italy between 1440 and 1460. After 1494, it gradually became Europe-wide. When preserving a balance in Italy depended, for example, on checking France, it was useful to understand the politics of the English court and whether the English would threaten to cross the Channel. Venetian ambassadors were especially notable for the sagacious, fact-filled reports in which they surveyed the strengths, weaknesses, and personalities of all countries being weighed in the balance.

In spite of the entrance into the game of so many well-heeled competitors, Venice continued to play for the highest stakes: naval supremacy in the Mediterranean and a dominant position in Italy. An important step towards both these goals was Venetian occupation of key cities in Apulia in 1495, while the League of Venice was expelling the French from the Kingdom of Naples. Not only was Apulia a wealthy province within Italy, it was also one of the keys to the Adriatic and the Ionian Seas. Cities such as Otranto and Brindisi at once began manning galleys for the Venetian fleets. At the same time, Venice supported Pisa in an effort to secure its freedom from Florence. When that turned Milan against her, Venice allied with a new King of France, Louis XII, and when he conquered Milan, Venice received the rich city of Cremona, deep within Lombardy.

At this point the Turks again threw their weight against Venice, counter-balancing her Italian successes. Without warning, the Ottoman sultan sent a huge fleet into the Ionian Sea in 1499, and when the Venetians fought poorly in "the deplorable battle of Zonchio," as will be described in Chapter 25, the Turkish army and navy combined to capture nearly all the Venetian strongholds in Greece, including Modon and Coron, which since 1204 had been considered the "two eyes of the Republic." They had been ports of call for all voyages to the Levant. Turkish troops raided Dalmatia and plundered Friuli so that again the smoke from burning villages could be seen from the top of Venice's Campanile. Groaning under the financial burden of the war and wishing to be free to face Italian complications, Venice made peace in 1503 by surrendering claims to many cities in Albania and Greece.

In any speculation about what might have been, this may be judged the turning point of Venetian history. The Venetians were worried about the extent of French dominance in northern Italy and misled by hopes of gaining additional territory there. They did not foresee in 1503 how costly would be the wars over those issues. But when their Italian wars demanded extreme sacrifices, the Venetians made extra efforts. Against the Turks, in contrast, they showed no stomach for extreme measures, even when their sea power was at stake. In 1503, they gave up keys to naval empire without making the kind of financial sacrifices which within a decade they found themselves forced to make in order to keep their mainland state. Unlike Venice's leaders of earlier centuries, the dominant statesmen of 1500 were thinking more in terms of territory than of sea power.

THE LEAGUE OF CAMBRAI   Among the many "myths of Venice," one credits the Venetian Senate with unfailing wisdom in the conduct of foreign affairs. That myth can draw inspiration from many episodes but is not supported by the Senate's decisions during the first decade of the sixteenth century. The actions of the Senate left Venice isolated; the whirl of alliances concerning control of Italy brought forth in 1509 a union of nearly all Europe against Venice. This coalition, called the

League of Cambrai, plunged Venice closer to destruction than she had ever been except in the darkest days of the War of Chioggia.

Since the French invasion in 1494, Venice had been steadily gaining territory while playing the foreigners against each other. She had made them all resentful and she relied too much on their rivalry to keep them from allying against her. France wanted Cremona and other cities that had belonged to Milan; from the Hapsburg emperor Venice had recently taken Trieste and other cities on his frontier; Spain, having conquered the Kingdom of Naples, claimed the Apulian seaports; and both Ferrara and Mantua coveted lands along their Venetian borders. When the domain which Cesare Borgia had built in Romagna in the Papal States collapsed at the death of his father in 1503, Venetians found the temptation to add territory there irresistible. This infuriated the new pope, Julius II. He became the head of a league, formed in France at Cambrai in 1509, which professed to be preparing for a crusade against the Turk by first depriving Venice of all its possessions. The pope would have all Romagna; the emperor would take Friuli and the Veneto, including even Treviso and Padua; the King of Hungary, Dalmatia; the Duke of Savoy, Cyprus; the King of France would round out Lombardy; the King of Spain, Apulia; while Mantua and Ferrara took tidbits.

Facing all these enemies at once, Venice tried to detach various members by offering them portions of what they claimed, but portions only, and meanwhile banked on an army which was the biggest and finest that had yet been collected by an Italian state. It was composed of Italian mercenary companies and militia and of some light cavalry recruited through Venetian possessions in Albania or Greece. It was posted some 20 miles from Milan, facing a French force of nearly equal size, about 20,000 men. It was commanded by two condottieri of whom the younger, Bartolomeo d'Alviano, was impressively energetic and intelligent but impetuous, and the older, Count di Pitigliano, with the supreme command, was cautious and either lethargic or bound, he felt, by orders from the Senate to delay and avoid battle. When Alviano's forces encountered the French at Agnadello in the Ghiara d'Adda, Pitigliano failed to support them, they were crushed on May 14, 1509, and the whole Venetian army scattered in rout.

The complete lack of any national feeling within Venice's mainland domain was revealed by the way this one defeat caused its immediate collapse. In city after city, from Brescia to Padua, the local nobles over whom and through whom Venice had ruled declared for the King of France or the German emperor. The general population acquiesced and joined in closing city gates against the Venetian army, fearing that if they were admitted the city would subsequently be besieged and sacked by French or German soldiers.

Being the only Italian power strong enough possibly to hold its own against the foreign monarchs, Venice tried to appeal to Italian national sentiment. Before the battle of Agnadello, the Venetian army had used the battle cry, "Italia e Libertà." It had been indeed an army composed of Italians fighting foreigners. But the nobles of the mainland cities resented being subordinate to the nobles of Venice. Once the Venetian army was defeated, Venice seemed simply a master less to be feared than the King of France or the emperor. The few Venetian officials who presided over the government of the subject cities were quite unable to rally support, except at Treviso and in Friuli. The remnants of the Venetian army fled back to salt water, to Mestre on the shores of the lagoon.

They arrived there in such demoralized condition that terrified Venetians feared the King of France would soon be assaulting the city itself. Venice prepared for a siege. Mill stones were hurriedly brought in so that the grain which ships would bring could be ground within the city. Provision was made to import enough wheat for many months. More galleys were armed. Patricians rushed barges up the rivers to rescue household furnishing from their country estates, and thousands of refugees, rich and poor, poured into the city. Each parish organized security committees headed by nobles and containing trusted men from the maritime services. Foreigners were counted and many expelled, partly to prevent their causing trouble, partly to reduce the number of mouths to feed.

The dismay and even panic within Venice is described in a diary-chronicle written by Girolamo Priuli, a banker who went bankrupt a few years later. Holding no political office, Priuli reported the news and views which he picked up on the Rialto. Although his father was elected to the most honored positions in the Venetian government during the first two decades of the sixteenth century, Girolamo interspersed his account of those years with many caustic and cynical comments on the misbehavior and miscalculation of Venice's "Senatorial Fathers." He was thoroughly patriotic withal, with a nationalism that was Venetian, not Italian. He denounced Paduans with special vigor and was most passionate in heaping abuse on the defeated army. Not even Machiavelli was more bitter in castigating those mercenaries who took your money year after year and then, when you needed them most, ran away.

But Priuli was more moralist than political analyst. He regarded the Venetian defeat at Agnadello as punishment for the sins of the Venetian nobles, on which he elaborated (but, being a banker, he said nothing about usury): arrogance, delay and denial of justice, violation of oaths, lay control of church benefices, lechery in the nunneries, sodomy, effeminate dress, and luxurious and lascivious entertainments. The feeling that God was punishing Venice was widespread. In June, the Senate strengthened the laws protecting the virtue of nuns. To appease God's wrath, the Patriarch ordered fasting on Wednesday and Saturday as well as Friday.

When Julius II heralded the League's attack by excommunicating Venice, that did not disturb the conscience of Venice's rulers. They simply forbade the publication of the papal bull and Venetian priests did not obey it. But the defection of city after city following the defeat at Agnadello shattered the self-confidence of the Venetians and threw their leaders into confusion. They at once surrendered their Apulian seaports to satisfy the King of Spain and made offers to the pope and the emperor in efforts to detach them from the League. Some Senators seriously discussed appealing to the Turks for aid!

Spirits revived in July, when reports began coming in that the common people in the lost domains were rising against the invaders. Unlike the upper class of the subject cities, the peasants and artisans had found satisfactions in Venetian rule, and the arrogance and savagery of French and German soldiers stirred them to revolt. Venetian troops were reorganized at Mestre and Treviso under the fiery Andrea Gritti, the Commissioner accompanying the army (see Figure 25). Gritti proved more resolute than the condottiere, Count Pitigliano, in rallying the defeated troops, and emergency measures decreed by the Council of Ten kept enough coin flowing from the Venetian mint to the camp so that he was able to hold the remnants of the army together. Since ordinary taxes or loans could not be collected fast enough, special bonuses were offered to those who would open their treasure chests and bring coin or turn in jewelry and tableware to be melted down into coin. At his father's behest, Girolamo Priuli took to the mint some of the family silverware. By such methods between 120,000 and 200,000 ducats in coin were made available. To supplement the professional army, a kind of miniature *levée en masse*, reminiscent of the dark days of the War of Chioggia, aroused patriotic response within Venice and its lagoon cities. Again, it was for nearby action; the goal this time was Padua. On the evening before July 17, the canals were full of barges crowded with armed men, while all exits from the lagoons were patrolled to prevent news of the preparations from reaching Padua. Next day, recruits from Venice reinforced the army which Gritti brought from Treviso and retook Padua, welcomed by partisans within the walls shouting "Marco, Marco."

Regained, Padua had to be defended against a sustained attack by the emperor, who arrived belatedly with the most formidable artillery yet used in any siege. It was successfully resisted by Venice's mercenaries and by many volunteers who went out from Venice to join in the brave defense under Andrea Gritti. Meanwhile, the pope and the King of Spain changed sides. The war turned into an effort to expel the French. When that had succeeded, Venice also reversed alliances, allying with France in order to regain Brescia and Verona. After seven years of war, in which many of its cities had been sacked and the countryside ravaged, Venice regained in 1516 the essentials of the territory it had won on the mainland almost a century earlier.

In the later Italian wars, Venice used her army cautiously to protect her own territory and, after 1529, successfully followed a policy of neutrality. By her diplomacy as much as by her arms she defended herself against the Renaissance monarchs who plundered and subjected the rest of Italy, but any fear or hope of Venetian dominance over Italy was gone.

A SECOND-CLASS SEA POWER   Meanwhile, Venice as a sea power was also losing its preeminence. The Ottoman and Spanish empires were expanding naval armaments in the Mediterranean to new dimensions.

In 1470 and 1499–1500, the Turks had used a fleet merely as a temporary adjunct to army operations, disbanding the fleet at the end of the army's campaign. Shortly thereafter, they began to patrol the Aegean fairly regularly against Christian crusaders or pirates. Another step in the spurt of Ottoman sea power was the conquest of Syria and Egypt in 1517. A third was the conquest of Rhodes in 1522, expelling the Knights Hospitalers of St. John from the Aegean. Then came the biggest leap, adding the Barbary pirates under the leadership of the Greek-born red-bearded Khaireddin who took control of Algiers in 1529. With this addition the Ottoman Empire circled the whole Mediterranean Sea from Albania to Morocco (see Map 10). Even under the best of leadership, Venice could hardly hope alone to match year after year the fleets then at the disposal of the Ottoman sultan.

Only through Spanish and Hapsburg leadership was a naval power of possibly countervailing strength developed in those same decades. "Spanish" sea power had been partially composed of Italian ships and seamen ever since Spaniards had acquired Sicily. It became more so when Spain conquered Naples in 1501-3, and in 1509 took the Apulian ports from Venice. When the Spanish throne was inherited by the Hapsburg who became in 1519 Emperor Charles V, he added Spanish power to the moral authority in Italy of a Holy Roman Emperor, his claims to Milan, and his resources from Germany and the Netherlands. He was a truly international ruler and thought of himself as the emperor of all Christian Europe. Indeed, he sought and obtained loyal service from notable men of many nationalities. To command his fleets, he won over from the service of France Andrea Doria, who brought with him Genoese maritime resources. With Spain's own naval forces supplemented by those of all Italy outside of Venice, Charles was able in 1535 to lead against Tunis the most powerful fleet yet assembled in the Mediterranean. In attacking the Moslems in North Africa, Charles had enthusiastic Spanish support, for Spaniards had followed up the conquest of Granada by carrying their crusade across into North Africa and already held several cities there. Charles took Tunis and gave it to a Moslem ruler who was ready to become his vassal. About the same time, he gave the Knights of St. John, ousted from Rhodes, a new home at Malta.

Crowded by the two giants that had grown up on either side of her, the Ottoman Empire and the Spanish Empire, Venice began to maintain, year after year, fleets larger than ever before. But she did not feel capable of waging war alone against either empire. On sea as on land, she relied on playing the balance of power. An essential in that game was France, for within Italy and in the Western Mediterranean, Charles V's power would have been overwhelming had not France, the richest and most populous kingdom of Christendom, been his determined enemy. After Charles V's armies had conquered all the Italian states except Venice, sacking even Rome in 1527, Venice feared to ally definitely with him lest he become yet more powerful. She also feared to ally definitely against him lest he crush her. The Turks openly threatened Venice's empire, Charles V and Spain implicitly threatened her independence. Venice needed France's alliance against Spain, while she also needed Spain's alliance against the Turk.

Venice performed this double balancing act for the rest of the century with sufficient skill so that she was engaged in only two major wars after 1529, both brief and both naval contests in which she was allied with Spain and the Hapsburg against the Turk. In both these wars Venice had to subordinate her own naval operations, which will be described in Chapter 25, to those of a crusading league dominated in 1537-40 by Emperor Charles V and in 1570-73 by his son and successor as King of Spain, Philip II. In the earlier of those two wars, the combined Christian fleet was commanded by Andrea Doria and suffered a humiliating reverse at the battle of Prevesa when Doria commanded its retreat at a crucial moment. He had secret orders from the emperor not to fight unless absolutely sure of victory because the emperor was negotiating with the admiral of the Turkish fleet, Khaireddin, even on the eve of the battle, hoping to win him over. Charles wished to strengthen his position in North Africa; he had no real intention of strengthening Venice's position in Greek waters. That would only make Venice more able to oppose his complete dominance in Italy. His intentions and the consequent untrustworthiness of Doria as an ally were so clear that Venice made a separate peace in 1540. The war lowered her prestige because of the retreat at Prevesa, unpunished Turkish plundering, and the extinction of the last hold of Venetian nobles on the islands of the Aegean north of Crete.

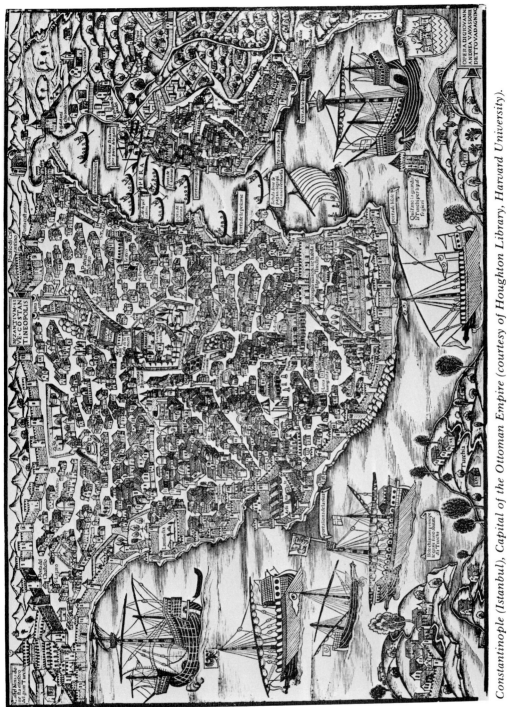

FIGURE 21 *Constantinople (Istanbul), Capital of the Ottoman Empire (courtesy of Houghton Library, Harvard University).*

This perspective view, composed early in the sixteenth century by Giovanni Andrea Vavassore, shows Santa Sophia still labeled as a Christian church, but next to it, on the heights overlooking the entrance to the Golden Horn, is the New Palace of the Turkish emperor ("El seraglio novo dove habita El Gran Turcho").

In 1571, in contrast, the Christian League under the command of the Hapsburg prince, Don John of Austria, won the sensational victory of Lepanto. It halted the advance of Ottoman sea power and saved from Turkish conquest Venice's Ionian Islands. If the Turks had won on that day, Venice would probably have lost Zante and Corfu and most of Dalmatia. But Philip's policy was much like that of his father. He and his Spanish advisers wished to use the Christian fleet to add to Spain's domains in North Africa. He wished Venice as an ally against the Turk, but he did not wish to strengthen Venice unduly. He refused to let the victorious fleet go east to serve Venice's interest. Again, Venice gained peace by concessions, yielding Cyprus which the Turks had conquered.

The defeat at Prevesa and the victory at Lepanto, both followed by humiliating peace treaties, revealed how much Venetian naval power had declined since 1424 when, at the beginning of the Milanese wars, her naval preeminence in the Mediterranean was practically unchallenged. But the fleets Venice put to sea in 1538 and 1571 were four or five times as large as those manned in the 1420's. The scale of naval warfare had been elevated by the growth, in the meantime, of two large Mediterranean empires, the Ottoman and the Spanish. Much as Venice had increased her own war fleets, she had not been able to keep up.

THE TURNING POINT RECONSIDERED Could she have built and manned yet larger fleets if she had never fought to become the leading power in Italy? Among Venice's ruling nobles, those who favored acquiring more and more territory in Lombardy and in Romagna, the landward-looking party, might argue that only by establishing a kind of hegemony over Italy could Venice command resources equal to those of the giant empires which were developing at the eastern and western extremities of the Mediterranean. The only hope to hold her own against them was to be dominant in that sea's central peninsula.

On the other side, there was a seaward-looking party which regarded the possessions in Lombardy as just a malignant tumor sucking the maritime vitality that had made Venice great. Its views were agonizingly expressed by lines that Girolamo Priuli wrote in his diary in the darkest days of the War of the League of Cambrai. He reported that some Venetians were saying that, if the mainland was lost, "the Venetian nobles, citizens and populace would devote themselves to the sea and going on voyages and, besides gaining profits would become valiant men and experts in the ways of the sea and every other undertaking, and perhaps that would be of more benefit to the Venetian Republic than the income received from the mainland." A love of luxurious country living was corrupting the nobility, said Priuli, who had spent his own youth as a merchant in London, and young nobles were growing up like ignorant peasants having seen nothing of the world. He blamed the Senate for its failure to fortify and supply adequately maritime bases such as Modon, and lamented the millions of ducats spent in fortifying Italian cities and hiring Italian mercenaries. The latter was pure loss, he said, soldiers took the money away, whereas what was paid out for the fleet came back because the recipients spent it in Venice. But Priuli knew that there was no serious question of Venice giving up voluntarily its mainland domain. It would, he said, have been too great a blow to Venice's prestige.

Whether Venice's turn westward into Italian conquests was in itself a mistake or a necessity, clearly Venice failed to make the many institutional changes that were called for in order to exercise the power to which she aspired. One weakness was her dependence on the condottieri. Machiavelli scornfully reproached Venice for not conscripting her own citizens and subjects into her armies as she had done in her navy. In fact, for crews as for soldiers, she relied primarily on volunteers, not conscripts. The navy was commanded entirely by Venetian nobles, to be sure, but the number prepared by experience for naval commands was declining. The decisions made in 1502–4, surrendering key naval bases to the Turks and seeking lands to rule in Italy, were symptomatic. Nobles were becoming more interested in land than in the sea. The top naval commands went to diplomat-politicians, not to seamen or adventurers comparable to Vettor Pisani or Carlo Zeno.

In order to compete with the Ottoman, French, and Hapsburg empires, a military organization of a new kind and on an unprecedented scale was called for on sea as well as on land. Venice's deep involvement in land warfare no doubt distracted energies and attention from making a maximum effort to maintain her position among sea powers. But her traditional superior position could not have been maintained by traditional means. She did arm and man more and larger ships for longer periods than ever before and made changes in ships, arms, and crews, in the Arsenal and in naval administration, as will be described in Chapter 25. The extent and direction of development was limited by her political system, however. She did not develop a hierarchy of real professionals supported by a naval bureaucracy. Discipline and appointments to high commands depended on the votes of fellow nobles in Venice's governing councils. In a negative sense at least, changes within the internal structure of the republic were quite as crucial as any weavings of diplomacy or any vicissitudes of battle in determining Venice's future.

THE TURN
WESTWARD · IV

The Corruption and
Perfection of the Constitution

CHAPTER EIGHTEEN

During the centuries in which the Venetians had imposed restrictions on their doge so as to make him merely a magistrate of the Commune, they had given concrete form to an ideal of political liberty. That ideal had blossomed during the Later Middle Ages in other Italian city-states also. Distrust of personal power was institutionalized by short terms of office, by limitations on re-election, and by delegating powers and responsibilities not to individuals but to committees. In the sixteenth century the conflicts with powerful monarchies called for an efficiency in armament, diplomacy, and finance which was difficult to reconcile with these institutions and the ideal they embodied. Nearly everywhere the republican principles, derived from the communes and extolled by civic humanists, were abandoned, if not completely in theory, at least in practice. Venice alone survived with independence while perpetuating republican institutions.

No sixteenth-century government was efficient by standards applied to modern states, nor did it possess comparable powers to collect taxes and enforce regulations, but those most nearly successful were, except for Venice, monarchies. Observers of that century found it amazing that Venice could hold up its head among the great powers while still a republic. Thanks to her navy and diplomatic juggling, she even preserved much of her empire. Venice aroused admiration then as now for many political and administrative achievements. Her populace was relatively well-fed and creative. It enjoyed domestic peace, many municipal services (such as the ministrations of a Board of Health), and a system of justice which had a high reputation of impartiality to all classes.

Venice was renowned also for skillful diplomacy and a navy which, though no longer supreme, was at least still a force to be reckoned with, backed by an Arsenal which was the largest industrial establishment of the age.

In the eyes of many Venetian nobles, however, none of these was Venice's finest achievement. The most precious was the vitality of their republican constitution. Not being written out in any one document, the constitution consisted of a style and tradition of political behavior based on custom as much as on particular laws. It included the checks on irresponsible personal power, developed in the age of the Communes, and also the aristocratic principle that power belonged by right to the well-born. Top leadership depended on the admiration and confidence of others in the governing group, not on catering to the greed or ambitions of those below. Considered subversive was any seeking of power either through popularity among the non-noble populace or by serving the selfish interests of the more needy, least educated, and least well-informed members of the nobility. Republicanism required virtue, as Montesquieu said later when summarizing in a word the needed spirit; in the sixteenth century, some observers explained Venice's success by praising the Venetian nobles' devotion to duty and to public welfare.

Like the modern democratic ideal, the Venetian republican ideal called for more virtue than is to be found in examining the realities of practical politics, that is, day-by-day pursuit and use of public office. At the very time that Venice's political system was being idealized, it also seemed to many Venetian nobles to be showing disquieting signs of corruption. Many distinctive Venetian practices, such as the secrecy of the ballot, for which Venice was in that age distinctive, were perfected as measures against corruption. The contrasts between unrealized but not abandoned ideals on the one hand and attention to personal and group interests on the other hand made Venetian politics quite modern in spirit although quaint in details.

NOBLE GENTLEMEN, SOVEREIGN AND EQUAL   All the changes, whether for efficiency or for combating corruption, were within the aristocratic framework established early in the fourteenth century and reaffirmed after the crises in the War of Chioggia. The doge was called "The Prince" (*Il Principe*), but he could do nothing without one of his councils. The nobles eligible to these councils came from families which formed six to seven percent of the city's population. Their sovereign power, long established in fact, received full symbolic expression when the General Assembly was abolished and, in 1423, the Great Council declared that its own decrees, even if they changed the basic law, were valid without the ceremonial of popular approval. The words "and it please you" were omitted from the presentation before the people of each new doge chosen by the committee of forty-one nobles. The changing spirit of the republic was reflected in its name. In 1462, the doge's oath was altered to remove all references to a "Commune of the Venetians." The government was commonly referred to by the adjective proudly associated with it, *La Serenissima*.

While parading their sovereignty more confidently, the nobility became more exclusive. There were no new admissions like those of 1381. A proposal made in 1403 to admit to the Great Council a new family of native-born, middle-class Venetians whenever one of the old families died out, was killed by the Ducal

Council. Nobles of the cities which became subject to Venice, such as Verona, were not given any part in the Venetian government; they were restricted to subordinate roles in their own cities. Very rarely, by a special personal privilege, one of them was made a member of the Great Council of Venice, but he was not accepted by the Venetians as one of themselves to be trusted with high office.

Although nobility itself was hereditary, there were no hereditary differences in rank within the Venetian nobility. Real differences in wealth were of course both obvious and painful. They were paraded in the jewels and luxurious costumes of the women and of young men who organized social clubs called *compagnie delle calze* because each distinguished itself by the fancy many-colored hose and tights which the young men wore. Extravagant displays of wealth increased in spite of being forbidden by sumptuary legislation. At home, both men and women wore highly varied costumes, and the women added to their finery when they went out. But mature nobles went about in plain black robes or togas, except that magistrates were required to wear the red, purple, or violet robes of their office. Thus their clothes symbolized the fact that all nobles had equal rights except when raised up temporarily by the offices they held. Legally all nobles were eligible for all offices unless disqualified by an office they were already holding, by a crime, or by failure to pay taxes or other debts to the government.

Marriage of nobles with commoners both women and men was not uncommon, and nobility depended on one's father, not one's mother. If the mother was a menial or a prostitute, the child could not be registered in the Book of Gold in which noble parents registered their sons at birth to assure their admission to the Great Council. But there was no difficulty with such registry if the mother was the legitimate daughter of a rich merchant, a master glass blower, or one of the class called "citizens by birth" (*cittadini originari*). Two of the richest doges, Antonio Grimani and Giovanni Bembo, had mothers who were commoners. It is notable also that the sumptuary legislation made no distinctions between commoners and nobles. Extravagant displays were equally forbidden to both and, in practice, upper-class commoners went about in the same plain black togas worn by ordinary nobles. Thus both dress and marriages softened the line between the nobles and upper-class commoners.

THE ORGANS OF GOVERNMENT AND THE IDEAL   The success of this government by the several thousand nobles, all of equal rights, was attributed partly to Venice's system of interlocking councils. The distribution of power among them entirely ignored the separation to which we are accustomed of legislative, judicial, and executive functions. All three were given in some measure to most every layer of the pyramid of councils depicted in Chapter 8. The Great Council, for example, not only voted on basic changes in the laws, it voted also on the guilt of some accused officials, and conferred offices and granted pardons under stipulated procedures. If any principle other than tradition governed the distribution of power among councils, it was that of mixing appropriately efficiency, deliberation, and broad participation.

All nobles except clerics were members of the Great Council by age twenty-five and many became members before twenty-five, so that this body was almost the size that we associate with political conventions. The number of nobles was about 2,500 in 1500. Frequently, over a thousand men attended the Great Council (see Figure 22). Its regular functions were to elect officials and approve the acts of smaller councils (see Figure 40).

Since the Great Council was too large for thorough discussion and wise decision about war and peace, armaments and negotiations, laws, loans, and taxes, the deliberative function passed to the Senate. Originally sixty men, nominated and elected by the Great Council, the Senate was enlarged by inclusion in it of the Council of Forty (*Quarantia Criminale*), which also functioned independently as a court of appeals in criminal cases, and by the addition of sixty more Senators called the *zonta*. These sixty were nominated by the Senators whose terms were expiring. Practically all important officials were ex-officio members of the Senate during or after their terms of office. Ambassadors and high naval commanders were admitted to the Senate from the time of their election to the end of the year after their return from their assignment. In short, everybody who was anybody politically had a place in the Senate. The number with the right to attend rose to about 300 men, of whom about 230 had a right to vote. They had so many other duties that only 70 were required for a quorum, and the usual number recorded as voting was about 180. Although a Senator's term of office was only one year, many of the same men were elected again and again in a way that fostered continuity and assured that Senatorial decisions were made by well-informed men of long experience.

Freedom of debate in the Senate stimulated eloquence. In men raised in awe of Cicero's orations to the Roman Senate, the Venetian Senate aroused admiration both as an example of republicanism and as a guarantee that important questions would be well considered. Every Senator had unlimited right to speak so long as he did not introduce irrelevant matters. Even if he did, it was up to the doge to call him to order, and the doge could not do that effectively unless backed up by his Councillors and the State Attorneys or the Chiefs of the Ten. But there were no filibustering speeches to empty benches, for once a session had begun, only the Senators over seventy could leave without formal permission from the chair. Conversations on the floor were forbidden, but long harangues produced much shufflings and clearing of throats. Sessions frequently went on late as the darkening hall was lighted by candelabras, and were ended only by a motion "to delay," i.e., to continue consideration another day.

Although sometimes lengthy, the debates in the Senate were made to focus on well-defined practical issues by rules of procedure and the preparations of steering committees. At first the doge and the six Ducal Councillors acted as the Senate's steering committee. Forming with the three Heads of the Council of Forty the body called the Signoria, they acted as a bench of officers which presided over the Senate, the Great Council, and indeed the whole government. The Signoria had so many functions, however, administrative, judicial, and ceremonial, that about 1400 the Senate created six *Savii del Consiglio* to prepare its agenda, frame resolutions, defend them, and supervise their execution. They were also called *Savii Grandi*, which might be translated as "Chief Ministers." For the conduct of the Italian wars, the Savii Grandi were supplemented about 1430 by five Ministers for War and the Mainland (*Savii di Terra Ferma*). To them were attached an older special committee of five Ministers of the Marine (*Savii ai Ordini*) concerned with commerce, navy, and overseas colonies. (The

FIGURE 22   *A Session of the Great Council (courtesy of Museo Correr, Venice).*

The Great Council met in a hall seating more than fifteen hundred. This seventeenth-century engraving shows the Doge, Signoria, and Grand Chancellor presiding beneath The Paradise *by Tintoretto. Raised benches along the sides were assigned to various magistrates, the most prominent being reserved for those who, like Chiefs of the Ten, were charged with overseeing enforcement of election proceedings. Passing between the benches, carrying "ballot boxes" or sacks, are the collectors of "yes" and "no" votes.*

"ordini" referred to were the maritime regulations.) These three groups of Savii formed, together with the Signoria, a sort of council of ministers. Meeting all together, they were called the Full College (*Pieno Collegio*). Frequently present also at this joint meeting of steering committees was one of the three State Attorneys, who had a right to attend any meeting of any council, for an important function of these Attorneys, in theory, was to prevent a council from exceeding its authority. In some cases, they forced the Collegio or Signoria to refer an issue to the Great Council instead of the Senate.

An ordinary day's business started with a morning meeting of the Full College, with the doge presiding and the Savii Grandi directing the agenda. This included reading dispatches received, giving audience to foreign envoys and to delegations from subject cities, receiving reports of officials, and deciding what should be placed before an afternoon meeting of the Senate, if a meeting seemed in order. Once the main steps to be taken were clear, the Signoria withdrew, leaving the Savii to work out details of motions, and perhaps counter-motions, to be submitted to the Senate. No proposals which had not been presented first to the Collegio could come before the Senate. Many ex-officio members of the Senate, even some without the right to vote, could make motions regarding matters pertaining to their offices, and an individual Senator could initiate a measure, but only after giving the Collegio a chance to accept or revise.

In handling crucial issues of foreign policy and of finance, the Signoria could by-pass the Senate by taking proposals to the Council of Ten. It did so increasingly in the sixteenth century, when the whirls in the balance of power made speed and secrecy more important, especially at the time of the League of Cambrai. Having proved its efficacy as a special court for the discovery and trial of traitors, as illustrated by the cases of Marino Falier and Carmagnola, the Ten asserted more and more widely its authority to handle emergencies and to defend the constitution. The Ten became the defender of aristocratic or even oligarchic practices against what it considered demagogic subversion. In such matters, the three Chiefs of the Ten took the lead, and their own secretaries kept the records and made up the agenda. The Ten intervened also in a wide variety of municipal problems, even bank failures, in order to maintain law and order. More in dispute was the extent of its authority in finances and in negotiations with foreign powers.

At a later date, the Ten came to be thought of as the stronghold of a small oligarchy within the aristocracy, in conflict with the more broadly representative Senate. Conflicts between the Ten and the Senate were rare, however, because both were generally managed by the same men and almost the same steering committee. As already explained, the Ten never acted entirely alone. Regularly it had seventeen voting members, including the doge and his Councillors. It met with one of the State's Attorneys present, who, if he thought the Council was exceeding its authority or disobeying its statutes, could appeal the case to the Great Council. For important decisions an addition (zonta) of fifteen to twenty Senators was called in. When foreign affairs were considered, the Savii Grandi were required to be present. As a result, decisions in the Ten and in the Senate were initiated by the same leadership; there was no conflict between them in that sense. But measures could be taken through the Council of Ten with the kind of speed and secrecy required for changing alliances in the middle of a war. Leaders who felt responsible for acting on issues as they arose could do what they thought necessary, provided they obtained approval in the Ten, even if that required an action generally so unpopular that its approval by the Senate would have been doubtful. For example, in order to make peace with the Turks in 1540, the Ten authorized negotiation of terms which the Senate would not have approved in advance but felt forced to accept.

These leaders, who constituted the effective government of the *Serenissima Repubblica*, consisted at any given moment of the sixteen men holding the positions of doge, Ducal Councillors, Savii Grandi, and Chiefs of the Ten. This was the inner circle. The rest of the Ten, the Savii di Terra Ferma, the three Heads of the Forty, and the three State Attorneys were on the outer edge of the inner circle. Altogether it numbered about forty counting ambassadors and commanders out of the city on important missions. Its members could not be re-elected immediately to the same office. Each Ducal Councillor, Savio Grande, or Chief of the Ten was required when his term expired to take a "vacation," usually of a year or two, before again holding that particular office. But the man who had been Ducal Councillor one year could be and often was Savio Grande before the end of the next year and then a member of the Ten, perhaps one of its Chiefs. Their terms were all short, none longer than eighteen months, and were so staggered that some member of the inner circle left it each month only to reenter it immediately a few months later in some other similarly important post. When such moving around occurs in modern Italy's equally frequent changes of cabinet, it is scornfully referred to as "musical chairs." In the Venetian Republic it occasioned no "cabinet crises"; it was planned that way, so as to avoid concentrations of power in single individuals and yet to keep the government in experienced hands.

The way the Venetians liked to think their government worked was described about 1520 by Gasparo Contarini, himself an attractive illustration of the kind of careers it fostered. Gasparo was a descendent of the doge who had presided over the victory in the War of Chioggia. This family background and the talents which made him a tactful and eloquent ambassador enabled him to advance rapidly up the Venetian *cursus honorum* once he was launched on a political career. But he started relatively late. Through his twenties, he devoted himself to a combination of literary and theological studies. He was one of a group of deeply religious nobles uprooted from their studious life at Padua by the defeat of 1509. Like many men of his and Luther's generation, Gasparo questioned how he should live in order to enjoy the blessing of eternal salvation. Two of his closest friends resolved the issue by becoming monks and urged him to do the same. Deciding that salvation depended on God's grace and did not require such a withdrawal from the world, Gasparo turned to an active life in service of his family and his commonwealth. After service, at thirty-six, in a magistracy concerned with surveying and draining some lands reclaimed from the Po, in which he himself made a big investment, he went as envoy to young Emperor Charles V at Worms in 1520 and won the emperor's esteem. On his return, he was taken into the edge of the inner circle of Venice's rulers as a Savio di Terra Ferma. Another embassy being brilliantly successful, to Rome this time, he entered the center of the inner circle and began rotating through the key positions: Savio Grande, Chief of the Ten, and Ducal Councillor. Then the pope stole him, as one old Senator growled disgustedly, depriving Venice of its finest gentleman by making him a cardinal. As a cleric, he was debarred thereafter from ever again holding any office in the Venetian Republic. The pope kept him busy in negotiations which came nearer than any others to giving a peaceful turn to the Reformation. His international reputation as a statesman and churchman won for his view of Venetian government wide acceptance by succeeding generations.

Gasparo Contarini's treatise began by considering what form of government was ideal. He had learned from Aristotle and other ancient writers the advantages of a mixed form containing some elements of monarchy, some of government by "the Few," and some of government by "the Many." Believing the Venetian Republic close to perfection, since it had already preserved its freedom longer than any ancient city, even Rome, he described Venice's system of interlocking councils as a harmonious combination of the three forms. For that purpose, the Great Council represented the Many, which he also called the popular element, or the whole body of citizens. He considered citizens only those we call nobles. He felt the need of only a few words to justify the exclusion of the working masses from citizenship, that is, from any share in supreme power, since that was then a universal practice. He used only a few more words to defend the principle, which he felt distinctively Venetian, of basing citizenship (nobility) strictly on ancestry, not wealth. Within the body of citizens thus circumscribed the Senate and the Ten represented, he said, the Few who deserved more power because of their abilities, their possessions, and their training, while the doge gave Venice the advantages of a monarchy without its disadvantages. Writing at the time when Venice had impressed contemporaries by surviving the Italian Wars with its mainland domain essentially intact, Contarini presented as an explanation of the greatness of his city this harmonious blending of constitutional forms "by the marvelous virtue and wisdom of our ancestors." Many non-Venetians also, even some Florentines, analyzed the Venetian constitutional structure admiringly.

PRACTICAL *Where all corrupt means to aspire are curbed,*
POLITICS   *And Officers for virtues worth elected. . . .*
SONNET IN PREFACE TO LONDON EDITION (1599) OF
CONTARINI'S *THE COMMONWEALTH AND GOVERNMENT OF VENICE*

In an ideal republican government men are chosen for high office because of services to the whole community, as by negotiating a peace or proposing a wise law. Corruption, as Machiavelli stressed in analyzing the way the Medici ruled Florence, put in power men who rendered particular services to the private interests of their supporters, perhaps in connection with taxes, perhaps in the distribution of government jobs. The Venetians were not immune to that kind of corruption; on the contrary, it was constantly present more or less, challenging the virtue demanded by the republican ideal.

Analysts of the realities of modern democratic politics emphasize the importance of primaries. Similarly, an examination of the seamier side of Venetian political life must consider in detail not only elections but how men were nominated. Although in theory the job should seek the man and no one could campaign for office, in practice offices were eagerly sought after and by methods which included many appeals to the selfish private interests of voters.

To a few of the most important offices, the Senate both nominated and elected by a procedure, called *scrutinio*, which was relatively simple. Each Senator named the man he preferred, all Senators then voted for or against each name on the list. Ability to vote against a candidate directly, not merely indirectly as we do by voting for someone else, was a feature of all Venetian balloting. The Venetian practice involved the possibility that for every candidate there would be more negative votes than favorable votes. In the scrutinio, after the Senators had all voted on each name, the one with the highest number of favorable votes was declared elected only if he had more votes in his favor than against him.

Savii, ambassadors, and many commissioners (*provveditori*) were chosen in this way, and special provision was made for filling disagreeable posts, such as an expensive embassy foredoomed to failure. Troublesome politicians were likely to be nominated for such posts by their rivals. If they refused, they were not only fined, but lost popularity because of their unwillingness to take responsibility. If they accepted, their opponents had hopes they would fail. At least they would be out of the city for a while, unable to compete in shaping the deliberations of the inner circle. Generally the list of nominees recorded the men who had made the nominations and who were held responsible in case of any defalcation by their nominees. For unpopular posts, however, provision was made for anonymous nominations, so that Senators would not fear to nominate an able but vindictive person.

To most offices, election took place in the Great Council which chose among several candidates nominated by a variety of processes. Some were nominated from above, that is, by the Signoria or the Senate. They represented the choices of what Contarini called "the more noble among the citizens," the Few. Others were nominated from below, that is, by committees chosen by lot from the Great Council itself. The use of lot strengthened the role of the Many. It was what Contarini called a "popular" feature (we would say "democratic" in a relative sense) because it assumed that one citizen's opinion was as good as another's. It gave ordinary members of the Great Council a chance to be important.

Since it was the core of the "popular" aspect of the Venetian constitution, the selection of nominating committees by lot received much time and attention. The Great Council normally met every Sunday and was all the better attended because each meeting was like the drawings of a lottery from which one might emerge with a rich prize for himself or for a friend. Officers to be chosen had been announced in advance by criers at the Rialto and San Marco or, later, by printed handbills. All afternoon was spent in "balloting" (see Figure 23). The ballots were, as their name implies, small round balls. Most of them were silver, but a certain number were gilded. To determine the membership of nominating committees — there were usually four — all the members of the Great Council rose one by one from the long benches on which they sat and came to the platform at the front of the hall where the doge and his Councillors presided, and where there were urns full of ballots. These urns were of such a height and shape that the member could not tell until after taking a ballot whether he had drawn a gold or silver ball. If he drew a gold ballot, he stayed on the platform to form part of a nominating committee, having shown the ballot to a Ducal Councillor who verified through recognizing a secret mark that it had indeed been drawn from the urn that day and was not a counterfeit brought with him by a noble eager to be on a nominating committee. Every stage of the election procedure at Venice contained similar evidence that cheating was expected unless provision was made to prevent it — a sign of the intensity of competition for honors.

Members lucky enough to be on a nominating committee took places on the platform facing the doge, their backs to the assembly so that no signs might be exchanged between them and men anxious to be nominated. Further drawing of lots reduced the number to thirty-six and divided them into the four committees, each of which withdrew immediately to a separate room where it again drew lots to see which member would have the first chance to nominate for the first of the offices to be filled. In most cases the first nomination made was accepted by other members of the committee who wished to have accepted the nominations they would make when their turns came. A member could nominate himself or swap turns with another member. When the four committees reported to the Great Council, its members proceeded at once to vote yes or no on each of the candidates nominated. Sometimes all candidates were voted down. Attendance at the Great Council must have been more attractive because of the ample opportunities (which we lack) for voting explicitly against.

In making nominations, there was no restriction on naming members of one's family, but no nominating committee could contain two men with the same family name, and when a nominee was voted on, he and his relatives had to leave the hall.

Secret balloting on the names proposed was assured by ballot boxes containing two compartments, a white part for favorable votes and a green part for unfavorable. They were so designed that when the voter put his hand within, no one could see into which compartment he was casting his ballot. Since leaden balls made a noise revealing where they were put, pieces of linen were substituted. Secrecy was the more necessary because there was so much voting against; secrecy made the resentments of those defeated less personal. Any open declaration during the balloting was subject to severe penalties. The nominees had to be voted on the same day they were named, so that there would be no chance to drum up votes over night.

In most elections in the Great Council there were in addition to the nominations from below, by its own nominating committees, other nominations from above. Some were made by the Signoria, and the most influential were the nominations made by the Senate through its procedure of scrutinio. For each election of a Ducal Councillor, for example, there were four nominations made by committees of the Great Council chosen by lot and one nomination made by the Senate. The man with the prestige of Senatorial backing almost always won. But not always, sometimes the winner had been reported second or third on the Senate's list.

Nominations from above were so likely to win out over those proposed by the Great Council's committees that they had to be limited if the mass of nobles were to feel that their participation was affecting the final results. To give the Great Council's nominees a better chance, the rights of Signoria and Senate to nominate were reduced. In 1500, a reform-minded Ducal Councillor, Antonio Tron, induced his colleagues in the Signoria to renounce their right to make nominations. Previously they had agreed among themselves to take turns in picking nominees. There was much naming of relatives and talk of the sale of nominations. In sponsoring the motion to abolish their own rights to nominate, the Ducal Councillors were relieving themselves of that kind of pressure. Probably their experience had anticipated that of the American president who said hundreds of years later that under the spoils system every appointment he made produced "ten enemies and one ingrate."

The same urge to escape solicitation by job seekers moved some Senators to favor limitations on the Senate's nominating power also, but the Senate's procedure of scrutinio recommended itself as the way of selecting the best men

a

b

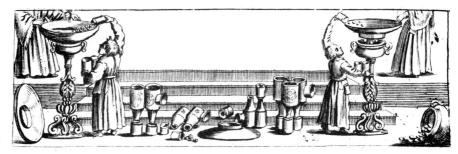

c

FIGURE 23   *Balloting in the Great Council. Woodcuts in 1578 edition of Gasparo Contarini, Della Repubblica.*

(a) Members of the Great Council advancing to the urns under the eyes of Ducal Councillors and Secretaries to draw the gilded or silvered ballots (pellets) which determined membership on nominating committees; (b) Drawing from the urns; (c) Refilling the urns.

for important posts. Even after the Great Council passed a law saying that only its own committees could nominate galley commanders (*sopracomiti*), the Senate and, in emergencies, the Council of Ten still named commanders for galleys, even if it had to give them a different title (*governatori*). And in the most important elections, as of a Ducal Councillor or Captain General of the Sea, the Senate's right to nominate was uncontested and its backing generally assured election.

Reducing the number of positions for which the Signoria and Senate could nominate tended to reverse the trend towards oligarchy. Nomination by the Great Council only would have weakened the leadership of the inner circle if there had been no corruption in the nominating and balloting. But corruptions favoring an oligarchic trend are depicted by several contemporary diarists. One was the merchant-banker, Girolamo Priuli, mentioned above, who repeatedly expressed a businessman's disdain of "politicians." He wrote with self-satisfaction that he had held no offices himself because he would not engage in the bowing, scraping, pleading, and bargaining of those who aspired to places in the government. A fuller account of the maneuvering and manipulation in elections is given by a man who took some part in it, Marino Sanuto. He did not share Priuli's scorn of politicians nor Priuli's tendency to attribute any misfortune befalling Venice to the stars or the city's sins. Sanuto was a hard-headed, highly trained student of politics. Like Gasparo Contarini, he had good family connections, received a humanist education from an early age, and made a name for himself by his studies before holding office. Finding the history written by the humanist Sabellico too sketchy and superficial, Sanuto put together a *Life of the Doges*, based on his own hunting up of old chronicles, laws, and letters. All his life, Sanuto was a glutton for facts, for detail. He collected a library famous for its maps as well as thousands of books and manuscripts.

Day by day Sanuto also kept track of everything going on in Venice. Fires, murders, lectures, weddings, concerts, bank failures, cargo lists, and market reports as well as dispatches received, state visits, council meetings, and political scandals — he recorded all these in a diary of fifty-eight large volumes. He began it in the expectation that it would serve him as notes for writing a history of his own times. His pride was grievously wounded when, after he had been collecting such notes for some twenty years, the government appointed Pietro Bembo official historian instead, because Bembo commanded a finer Latin style. Sanuto was pensioned and told to let Bembo use his notes, that is his diary, and he consented reluctantly.

Even while he was personally compiling this equivalent of a daily newspaper for thirty-eight years, Sanuto found the energy for a political career which was quite as significant in its way as Gasparo Contarini's. Sanuto began well, as a Lord of the Nightwatch, and moved up to be Savio ai Ordini, a post which Contarini twenty years later said was of great importance as long as Venice's main concern was seaward. Then it was used to try out young men before they mounted to a more responsible position, such as Savio di Terra Ferma. Sanuto never went to sea, but he was Savio ai Ordini several times in his thirties, and worked hard and effectively in mobilizing the fleet prior to the battle off Zonchio in 1499. He was given a term as Treasurer at Verona, re-elected Savio ai Ordini in his forties, and nominated a number of times for more important posts, such as State Attorney, once by himself when the luck of the draw gave him a chance and more often by relatives. Once when a close relative drew the golden ball and could have nominated Marino Sanuto but failed to do so, Marino felt wronged. He never quite made it into even the outer edge of the inner circle. He had inherited enough to live on, but not enough to advance his political career with money, as many did. He won his way into the Senate for a few years, and spoke relatively frequently there and in the Great Council. He describes his speeches as eloquent and listened to with such attention that there was "no clearing of throats" ("niun sputava"). But he did not make himself popular with the men running things. When he was nominated to go as inspector (*sindico*) on a three-year tour of Venetian colonies, a powerful, well-paying job, he considered that a foul blow by some personal enemy. He wanted to stay in Venice, write his diary, make speeches in the Senate, and compel his fellow nobles to obey the law at home.

Sanuto not only lacked the kind of eloquence that benefited Gasparo Contarini and Pietro Bembo, he also lacked political tact. He was a stickler for legality and he spoke his mind regardless, even on some occasions when, as he honestly admitted afterwards in his diary, he was wrong. "My conscience goaded me to speak," he wrote, "for God has given me a good voice, strong memory, and much knowledge from years of studying the records of the government. I felt I would be untrue to myself if I did not voice my opinion of what was under discussion." He resented the successes of richer or more pliable men and wrote bitterly of his failure to become State Attorney or to win a permanent place in the Senate, expressing the wounded vanity of an unsuccessful scholar-in-politics who felt that his learning and devotion were unappreciated.

Sanuto depicts corrupting pressures concentrating on the Great Council after the nominating powers of the Signoria and Senate were restricted. They were intensified by the fiscal strains of war in 1509–16. On the one hand, high taxes made men more eager for office and for favors from those who held office. On the other hand, all kinds of expedients were used in desperate efforts to raise cash. To men whom it approved and who put down 2,000 ducats, the Council of Ten granted the title and toga of Senator and admission to that body, though without the right to vote. Minor offices were sold. The doge made an eloquent appeal to all officeholders to make large cash loans or gifts, and the amounts they offered as loans or gifts were announced in the Great Council. Nobles began announcing their contributions just before their names were to come up for a vote. On one occasion, Sanuto put up 500 ducats, "found God knows how," in order to win election to the Senate, and he lost some desired offices when rivals put up more than he felt he could. Under these conditions, a law which required electors to take an oath that they had not been solicited was repealed, because nobles taking it were said to be endangering their souls' salvation. Not always were the men offering the largest gifts or loans elected; Sanuto considered some cases when they were rejected dangerous expressions of ingratitude which would make raising money more difficult in any future emergency. But when a clear-cut sale of positions to the highest bidder was proposed, Sanuto made a long speech against it and took warm satisfaction in his contribution to its defeat.

As soon as the essentials of the mainland domain were recovered, the bidding in the Great Council was stopped, and new laws were passed against electioneering. New officials, called the Censors, were created especially to stop it. They were immediately effective! But only temporarily, and after four years, the office was abolished. It was re-created, to be sure, in 1524, and the Council of Ten issued new decrees against soliciting votes, but these laws were then so openly violated that they served merely to obfuscate any workable distinction between legitimate and illegitimate electioneering. They forbade any form of political rally, but they did not prevent the buying of votes. Sanuto lamented bitterly in October, 1530: "Votes are being bought for money. Everyone knows it; it is evident that no one can win an office of any importance who does not have a group of impoverished gentlemen to whom he has to give money before he is nominated and after being elected. God help this poor republic lest the proverb be fulfilled: A venal city will quickly perish (urbs venalis cito peritus). Those in power do not occupy themselves with steps against it, and especially not against those who give out the money and win honors in that way. But the poor are pardonable, because poverty cannot do otherwise. May God, who guides all, provide; otherwise I foresee much evil."

Among the richest prizes to be won through politics were ecclesiastical benefices. Although no politician could hold office both in the Church and in the Republic, he could add enormously to the prestige and wealth of his family by winning a bishopric for a brother, son, or nephew. The formal appointment was made by the pope, of course, but the Senate imitated contemporary monarchs and insisted on telling popes whom to appoint. If any Venetian accepted a bishopric in Venetian territory contrary to the will of the Senate, it responded by inflicting punishment not only on him but on his family. For men with influence in the Senate, however, an important by-product of a successful embassy or governorship could be the winning of a church living for a relative. There were devices by which such a living, once gained, could be kept in the family.

Among the lesser prizes were many positions paying salaries large enough to attract noblemen of moderate means. Minor nobles seeking such posts sought the favor of the powerful who could throw votes their way. This form of corruption as well as more overt bribery increased the concentration of power in a few hands.

Wealth cast a dark shadow over the competition for honors within the Venetian nobility. Its corrupting power had no place in Contarini's ideal. On the other hand, public service also counted heavily in the selection of leaders. The impressive wealth of some families and the established reputation for public service of others, while a few enjoyed both, dominated the nominations and elections, even the nominations made by the committees chosen by lot, and nourished the oligarchic trend within the aristocracy.

Contrary trends were still strong enough, however, to give some truth to Contarini's picture of the Venetian constitution as a mixture of diverse elements. There were real differences in interests and sentiments between the general body of the nobility assembled in the Great Council and the potential oligarchy of about one hundred men, members of some twenty or thirty families, who held or had held and were likely to hold again offices in the inner circle. Both influenced policy and the style of governing.

The Great Council could make its influence felt by votes of no confidence. One way was to reject nominations for the Senate's zonta. An opportunity came each year on the last day of September, when the sixty additional Senators were all voted on at once. Ordinary Senators, like members of the Forty and the Ten, were elected a few at a time from lists of nominees proposed during the summer months by nominating committees. Then, just before the Senatorial terms expired, the outgoing Senators individually made nominations for the following year, these names were combined in a list usually totaling about 120, and the Great Council spent a day voting on that list. There was no obligatory "vacation" for Senators; usually the same men were reelected again and again. But not in years of military defeats! In 1500 and 1509, Priuli and Sanuto considered the results equivalent to the fall of a government. The foremost men of the city who had been the core of the inner circle failed of election because they were held responsible for the recent disasters. Many officers of the fleet were judged guilty of cowardice in the action off Zonchio and their relatives suffered defeat. Men whose relatives had given a good account of themselves in battle were elected in 1500 even if of little experience or personal reputation.

Such a revolt in the Great Council could weaken even a united inner circle. Usually the inner circle was not united; it contained strong-minded men of divergent views, rivals sometimes envenomed by personal grudges. Their conflicts were normally argued out and decided in the Senate, but the final arbiter was the Great Council. While Contarini did not begrudge it that role, he feared lest this "popular" element became too strong. There was indeed danger that the Venetian republic would be weakened by catering to the desire of the general mass of nobles for low taxes and plenty of well-paying jobs, including many sinecures. There was also danger that members of the inner circle, to which Contarini belonged, would be attentive only to their own interests. Against both dangers worked the faith shared by both Contarini and Sanuto that honor was to be gained by serving the welfare of the whole commonwealth.

ADMINISTRATION AND THE DOGES   All the successes and failures of Venetian administration depended on the quality of the men chosen by the system of balloting employed in the Senate and Great Council. To their credit must be put the beautifying of the city and the success, in spite of mistakes and controversies, in keeping the lagoon alive and the port open. In many fields of municipal administration, as notably in medical care and the regulations for controlling the outbreak of the plague, the Serenissima was widely looked to as a model. The governors whom Venice sent to administer justice and collect taxes in subject cities also enjoyed a good reputation compared to others of the time, not an excessively high standard. In naval administration they succeeded much better in producing the needed warships than in providing the needed crews, as will be explained in Chapter 25.

The diplomatic service of the Serenissima was of especially high quality. Earlier than any other state except Milan, Venice sent to foreign courts resident ambassadors who kept the Senate and Ten extremely well informed. On their return, they made in the Senate reports which analyzed acutely the personalities, resources, and developments of the countries in which the ambassadors had served. Sometimes the reports were too long for one session and had to be continued at the next, yet they were listened to with great attention, for many of the Senators had been ambassadors themselves, or expected to be. Moreover, the returning ambassador, if he came from a major post such as Rome, had probably already served as one of the Savii and would be kept busy the rest of his life in high office if, after hearing his report, the Senators judged him worthy.

Administration by boards of elected officials limited Venice's development of bureaucratic structures like those employed by contemporary Renaissance monarchs. Their brief terms of office, rarely as much as four years, prevented noble office holders from acquiring entrenched bureaucratic interests or highly specialized expertise. These qualities affected Venetian government for better or worse only through the officials of lower class, the secretaries, notaries, and accountants. These permanent employees tended to the details of administration, and the chief accountant at the Grain Office or the Arsenal, for example, understood many of its problems better than his noble supervisors. Indeed, some offices for nobles became mere sinecures, providing a salary and requiring little attention, although that was notably not true either of the Grain Office or of the Arsenal where the nobles in charge were often under severe pressure to meet the demands made on them by the governing councils.

The upper level of secretarial positions were reserved for the citizens-by-birth (cittadini originarii). Their class became as proud of its status as were the nobles and registered the births of its members in a "Book of Silver" just as the nobles registered theirs in the "Book of Gold." At its head was the Grand Chancellor who took precedence in ceremonial processions over nearly all other office holders, even important nobles. Like the doge and the Procurators of San Marco he held office for life. The whole class of citizens-by-birth could feel that their importance received recognition by the high honors bestowed on their representative, the Grand Chancellor. Secretaries immediately beneath him handled the papers at the meeting of the Ten, the Collegio, and the Senate. These confidential secretaries were occasionally sent on diplomatic missions requiring a combination of skill and low profile.

Such delicate posts were never for sale, but lesser positions were sold during the financial crisis in 1510. Current holders were called on to pay eight to ten times their salaries in order to acquire a life-time right to the job and the right to bequeath it to a son or close heir. If the current holder did not buy it, the post was sold to the highest bidder. Such sales were common practice in Europe in that period. They had advantages from two points of view: raising money for the government, and protecting bureaucrats from the spoils system. The purchasers probably felt no shock or much pain in paying a stated price instead of making appreciative gifts to the patrons on whose good will they would otherwise have relied.

Although the secretaries and lesser functionaries at Venice provided material for a bureaucracy, they were not under centralized bureaucratic control. They were supervised only by the shifting body of elected nobles. The powers of these nobles were so defined that for each there was some other officer charged with checking against maladministration. The banker-diarist Priuli said nobles were tolerant of each other's failings lest they make enemies who would work against them in the elections, but there is also record of many who tried to move up by demonstrating zeal against wrongdoers. There was little except common repute by which to judge efficiency, however, and the coordination of the activities of the hundreds of nobles moving from one office to another every few years depended primarily on their common spirit. The chief mechanism of routine coordination was supervision by interagency committees on which the inner circle was represented by one or two Savii or a Ducal Councillor. These Savii and Councillors, and the Chiefs of the Ten, were in effect the top administrators, under the doge, but they lacked the clear-cut powers of the chiefs of a bureaucracy. They had no ministries directly under them, just a few secretaries assigned from the ducal chancery. They had no power to remove the governors, naval commanders, or other officials to whom they transmitted the orders of the Senate. Appeals from their judgments and difference among them were decided by winning a majority in the Senate or the Ten, so that these Councils exercised directly many executive functions.

Contarini's claim that the doges gave Venice the advantages of a monarchy without its disadvantages was a bit of nostalgic wishful thinking. Correctly he emphasized that the doge was the unifying center of the administration. But even when supported by his Ducal Council, he lacked the powers to appoint and remove subordinates that would have made him an effective executive.

Although they lacked executive powers, the doges could function as political leaders, using not commands but persuasion. Within the Signoria, a doge had preeminence not only formally but for practical reasons. He alone held office for life, while other members of the inner circle were continually changing. A Ducal Councillor served in the Signoria only eight months. The doge stood at the center of the inner circle, presided over the meetings of the top councils, and in all of them could make motions on his own. Almost always the doge was a man who had been Procurator of San Marco, an honor conferred by a direct vote of a majority of the Great Council in lively electoral contests which brought out record-breaking attendance. For example, the number voting in 1510 was 1,671. He thus came to the dogeship backed not only by a majority in the committee of 41 electors who chose him, but also by popularity among the general body of the nobility. For years he had been rotating through the offices of the inner circle. When so many experienced Senators failed of re-election in 1509, Priuli expressed relief that there would be at least one man of experience left at the center of affairs, the doge. (Priuli not only criticized the politicians in power, he criticized throwing them out!) Although the doge did not have personal power anywhere near equal to the honors formally paid him, he was expected to be a real leader.

At the beginning of the fifteenth century and occasionally thereafter, that expectation was fulfilled. Certainly Francesco Foscari led in formulating and executing the policy which gained conquests in Lombardy. So long as that policy was successful, he was able to override even such rivals as the naval hero Pietro Loredan, victor over both Turks and Genoese. In doing so, he stirred up hatreds which took revenge when the expansion in Lombardy was checked by Francesco Sforza, when war taxes became a bitter burden, and when he was made vulnerable by the misbehavior of a son. After thirty-four years in office, the proud, imperious Francesco Foscari was deposed in 1457 by vote of the Ducal Councillors and the Ten, led by a Loredan.

Most of the next eight doges were in office only a few years. For example, Pietro Mocenigo reigned less than two years, 1474–76, near the end of the Turkish war in which he had been a victorious admiral (see Chapter 25). At the end of the century, the fifteen-year term of Agostino Barbarigo re-echoed faintly that of Foscari. He, too, was an imperious man of executive abilities, at his election the popular leader of a triumphant faction, at his death a discredited

FIGURE 24   *Doge Leonardo Loredan. Portrait by Giovanni Bellini (Photo Böhm).*

A smooth chairman and an effective orator, Leonardo Loredan was doge during the dark days of the War of the League of Cambrai.

FIGURE 25   *(opposite page) Doge Andrea Gritti. Portrait by Titian (courtesy of National Gallery of Art, Washington).*

A merchant for many years, then a leader of armies, in his old age Andrea Gritti was a forceful but frustrated doge.

member of a demoralized faction. A struggle between the "new" families, to which he belonged, and the "old" families, who had occupied the dogeship before 1382 but not at all since that date, preceded his election. By generous treatment of the rival candidate he did much to heal the bitter feelings then aroused, and he conducted his office with impressive dignity, assisted by a full white beard. He backed the building of the east wing of the Ducal Palace by Antonio Rizzo, a Veronese stonecutter he particularly favored, who responded by placing insignia of Barbarigo's family among the decorations of the Palace. At Barbarigo's death, Rizzo fled to avoid prosecution for profiteering. Agostino Barbarigo was intensely unpopular at his death because of both military defeats

and charges that he used his office avariciously. In addition to the Correctors, appointed at each ducal election to revise the oath to be taken by the new doge, Prosecutors were appointed to investigate the dead doge and bring suit against his heirs. They collected thousands of ducats from a son-in-law who had managed Barbarigo's personal finances. Such Prosecutors were regularly elected thereafter, and the restrictions added to the ducal oath by the Correctors made ducal action more circumspect than ever.

Next elected was the suave, smooth-shaven Leonardo Loredan (see Figure 24), popular in 1501 because a French alliance he had favored was proving successful at the moment, and because a member of his family had just died a hero's death in the Turkish war. He was famed for eloquence and good sense, but when the Venetian army was shattered at Agnadello, his popularity dropped. Marino Sanuto describes him as acting half-dead at receipt of the bad news and contrasted his despondent behavior with the way Foscari had rallied men's spirit after a defeat by appearing in the council confidently dressed in his most gorgeous golden robes. Later in 1509, Doge Loredan roused himself on some occasions to exert the leadership expected of him. When a severe measure to force payment of heavy war taxes on real estate was defeated in the Great Council, 700 noes to 650 in favor, Doge Loredan took the rostrum to plead eloquently for the needs of the emergency and swung the Great Council around so that it passed an amended version, 864 to 494 noes.

More influential than any other man in reanimating the fighting spirit of Venetians after Agnadello was Andrea Gritti (see Figure 25). He was a grain merchant at Constantinople until well along in his forties when his skill in negotiating with Turks was called on to arrange the last details of the peace treaty of 1503. On his return to Venice, he was accepted at once into the inner circle. As Commissioner with the army he led in the reconquest and defense of Padua. Captured by the French in a later engagement, he turned that to some advantage by winning the confidence of the French king. Besides his native tongue he knew Latin, Greek, French, and Turkish. After the brief dogeship of the octogenarian Antonio Grimani as Loredan's successor, Gritti, then 68, sought the honor in defiance of opponents who held against him his fiery temperament and the entanglements they feared might result from the four illegitimate sons he had sired in Constantinople, one of whom enjoyed high favor at the Turkish court as a merchant supplying its armies. Andrea Gritti was a master of the grand manner and too domineering to be popular, although he sought popularity by selling his wheat at low prices. With absolute monarchy on the rise everywhere in Europe, some Venetians feared he would act the tyrant. The granddaughter he sent home from his inaugural reception because she wore a golden dress in violation of sumptuary laws probably agreed. But Gritti's temperament was no threat to the republic; the shackles on ducal action were too strong, indeed too strong for the public good. Sanuto describes Gritti's impotent anger during the election of Senators at the end of September, 1529, when he was unable to inflict punishment for illegal soliciting of votes even though he himself had witnessed it. Before he died in 1538, he was futilely opposing the actions by which the Serenissima was drifting into war with the Turks.

Doges who were effective leaders became increasingly rare. As in many other elective monarchies in which oligarchs chose the monarch, the men chosen were rarely of such a kind as to increase the power and prestige of the office. When they were elected, most of the doges were already at what is now considered an age for retirement. Not infrequently contenders compromised on someone they thought would die soon and give them another chance to get elected themselves. No office in the Venetian political system gave the advantages of a strong executive or invited men to exert political leadership firm enough to check the seepage into the nobility of a tendency toward self-satisfied self-indulgence.

THE CONSENT OF THE GOVERNED In spite of weaknesses in the Venetian constitution, it provided better government than was generally found elsewhere, and all signs indicate that it enjoyed popular support. There was no need for troops in the city to intimidate the populace; the common people never tried to throw off the rule of the nobles. On special occasions, such as the death of a doge, when it was felt desirable to have extra protection at the Ducal Palace, an honor guard was temporarily recruited from the workers in the Arsenal. Some particular doges became hated, but the system was not attacked. The devices for the restraint of faction woven into the machinery of government were sufficiently successful so that none of the men disappointed in the intense competition for honors tried to overthrow the system, at least none after Marino Falier. The lower classes were never incited to revolt, or given the opportunity to revolt, by vengeful nobles offering to be their leaders. Personal ambitions were blunted and contained within the network of councils and magistracies.

The loyalty and obedience which garlanded the Serenissima is to be explained less by the machinery of government than by many of the features of Venetian social structure which have been mentioned in earlier chapters. The vitality of the parish communities, some sixty in number, each containing both rich and poor, palaces and workshops, cut across class lines which, on the other hand, received recognition in the occupational associations, the guilds. Both local and professional groupings gave a sense of belonging which found symbolic expression in a variety of ceremonies and festivals. The most elaborate and impressive festivals were those which the government organized in order to parade its own magnificence. The richness of the doge's robes, the gilded splendor of the huge galley, the bucentoro, in which he went to wed the sea, the glittering elegance of the ambassadors and dignitaries accompanying him on such occasions, and the sumptuous masques staged by the guilds to honor the doge or by the doge to honor visiting potentates were not mere catering to vainglory. They were part of the Serenissima's artistic mastery of government by pageantry.

As important as pageantry was food. Her fleets and her regulation of navigation kept Venice's markets relatively well supplied, and even her lower classes relatively well fed. Her acquisitions on the mainland gave added assurance that her graneries would be full. The Grain Office was one branch of administration in which the Venetian system of committees was successful.

Venice maintained also the high reputation it had gained in earlier centuries for equitable administration of justice. Nobles and commoners had equal standing in court. Late in the sixteenth century, Bodin, a French champion of monarchy, considered Venice in general an example of aristocracy, yet he said of it, in the words of a contemporary translation: "Yea moreover an iniurie done by a Venetian gentleman unto the least inhabitant of the city is right severely corrected and punished; and so a great sweetnesse and libertie of life is given unto all, which savoureth more of popular libertie than of Aristocraticall government." The rich could of course hire smarter lawyers than the poor could, as in any capitalist society, but to defend prisoners too poor to hire any lawyer one of Venice's corps of licensed lawyers was officially chosen by lot to act for the accused, and in the doge's oath of office he swore to see that equal justice

FIGURE 26 *The Fisherman and the Doge (Photo Alinari).*

When the doges wed the sea, the golden ring was a symbol of Venetian dominance in the Adriatic, but in the story behind The Presentation of the Ring *by Paris Bordone, the ring symbolized the protection of Venice from the sea by its patron saints.*

On the night of February 15, 1340, while flood waters driven by a howling scirocco seemed about to submerge and destroy the city, a poor fisherman was approached by three old men of distinguished mien who insisted, in spite of wind and wave, that he take them out towards the Lido. As they approached the open sea, they encountered a huge galley propelled by demons, "fiery fiends swinging red-hot oars that hissed everytime they dipped in the water." The three passengers, majestically upright, made the sign of the cross, the ship of devils plunged beneath the waves, and the water calmed. (At the peak of the flood of November, 1967, the suddenness with which a change of the wind flattened the waters seemed to me also a miracle.)

The three saints directed that they be taken to their dwelling places, so some chroniclers tell the story, namely, to the monasteries of San Nicolò and San Giorgio and to the church San Marco. When at the end of these arduous journeys their boatman asked for his fee, Saint Mark took a ring from his finger and told the fisherman to present it to the doge from whom he would receive his pay.

As Bordone pictured the scene, it conveys the intimate magnificence of Venice's aristocratic governance.

was done to all, great and small. How completely this ideal was lived up to is doubtful, but Venetian courts had that generally high reputation for impartiality which Shakespeare echoed.

Equal justice did not imply equality in honors or in economic opportunities and interests. The native-born citizens eligible for posts in the Ducal Chancery and at the head of the Scuole Grandi ranked as a kind of quasi nobility. Below them were the rich members of guilds, such as clothiers or grocers, who had many workmen under them. So many of these shopkeepers were recent immigrants that Philippe de Commynes, the French ambassador who wrote a laudatory analysis of Venetian institutions at the beginning of the sixteenth century, after declaring that "the people" had no part in the government, added: "Most of the people are foreigners."

The workmen had their guilds too, even if with restricted functions. Through these many subordinate organizations the Serenissima permitted the common people of various ranks to satisfy on a modest scale their desires for honors and office-holding. Shipwrights at the Arsenal enjoyed one set of privileges, stevedores at the customs house another set; bakers were governed by one set of rules, gondoliers by other rules made by a different magistracy. Each had its own special reasons to be more or less satisfied with the status the government afforded them. This diversity in rights to organize and in job opportunities divided the populace into separate interest groups in a way that impeded any coalescence among them in opposition to the ruling nobility.

Government by catering to or threatening the self-interest of separately organized groups within the society would become a form of corruption if not guided by any conception of the general welfare. In practice, the long-lived stability of the Venetian government rested on the attention its rulers gave to both special interests and the general welfare of the beloved city.

THE OCEANIC CHALLENGE·I

Participants in Oceanic Discoveries

The date 1492, conventionally used to separate medieval from modern history, serves as well as any other dividing point, for in the perspectives of world history, Columbus's voyage symbolizes the beginning of a new relationship between Western Europe and the rest of the world. The effects on Venice were less lethal than is commonly supposed, but its central position in the old system of relations between East and West made crucial for its future the success of its economy in reacting to the West's oceanic expansion.

Venice had its own part in creating the situation which thus challenged her traditional role in world commerce. Some explorers of note were Venetians, as was to be expected in view of Venice's leading position among maritime peoples. Moreover, Venice's position as a "world market" gave it a leadership in collecting and systematizing geographical information. "Discovery" involved more than seeing for the first time; it involved fitting new knowledge together with the old in evaluating what was seen. For centuries before 1492, Venetians had been pushing beyond the Mediterranean in their search for profits and for the kind of specific, accurate information which contributed to profits, and they were leaders in synthesizing this knowledge.

MAP MAKERS As a new and more accurate conception of the globe was gradually built up by travelers and seamen, this knowledge was brought together on world maps. Most of the "maps" made in medieval Europe were mere diagrams showing features of religious importance such as the Garden of Eden or Earthly

Paradise and the Holy City of Jerusalem. Very soon after Marco Polo returned from his journeying in Cathay, as he called China, and while he was still living in Venice and talking about it, a new type of world map emerged from the joint efforts of a Venetian friar, a Venetian noble, and a Genoese maker of marine charts. The two Venetians were political thinkers primarily, only secondarily concerned with maps. The friar, Fra Paolino, wrote a short treatise on government, a long chronicle, and a brief geographic work in which he argued that verbal descriptions of the world needed to be supplemented pictorially. Accordingly, he appended to his history and his geography a map of the world based mainly on traditional geographic writings and showing the three continents of Europe, Asia, and Africa, surrounded by water. But even in its earliest version, Fra Paolino's map paid some attention to new knowledge, to what travelers of his time were reporting. Cathay, unknown to the ancient Romans, was located in the northeastern portion of his map and it showed the Caspian as a closed sea, not an inlet from a northern ocean.

The Venetian noble who took up his ideas was Marino Sanuto the Elder, called Torsello, who is to be distinguished from the historian diarist of the same name who lived two centuries later. Torsello was a persistent advocate for a new crusade. When he submitted his plan for it to the pope about 1320, the pope referred it to Fra Paolino, who was then attached to the papal court. Torsello had probably met Paolino when both were in Venice a few years earlier. Certainly Torsello enthusiastically applied Paolino's doctrine that geographic material should be presented through maps. He accompanied his exposition of plans for a crusade with a set of five portolan charts covering all the Mediterranean and drawn for him in Venice by a skilled Genoese maker of nautical charts, Petrus Vesconte. To the set of sailing charts, which by this time had become quite accurate and standardized, Petrus Vesconte added for Torsello a detailed scale map of Palestine, plans of Acre and Jerusalem, and a world map. The world map was like that of Fra Paolino, except that the form of the Mediterranean was corrected to more nearly agree with the nautical charts. In some later copies which Torsello circulated to arouse interest in a crusade, improvements were made also in depicting the Caucasus Mountains and Scandinavia. Marino Sanuto Torsello's pleading and planning did not lead to the crusade he dreamed of, but through the cooperation of Fra Paolino and Petrus Vesconte, they occasioned the best compilation of geographical knowledge yet made in the West.

The finest charts surviving from the early fourteenth century were made by Genoese. A native Venetian school developed later during that century, while the Catalans were becoming the leaders. Francesco and Marco Pizzigani of Venice, like their Catalan contemporaries, added to their depicting of coasts a mapping of the interior of Europe and of other lands around the Mediterranean, applying the same principles of drawing to scale which created the marine charts. They adorned their maps also with pictures, banners, and legends (see Figure 8).

In the next century, when the Portuguese became the leaders, but either wore out their own charts or destroyed them for the sake of secrecy, Venetians made the most accurate known records of newly discovered coasts. The history of America begins cartographically in the view of many scholars with Andrea Bianco. His maps of 1436 and 1448 record first one then another report of what had been found west of the Madeira Island. The chart he made in London in 1448 indicates a large "authentic island" resembling the eastern bulge of Brazil somewhere near that location. It may reflect the report of Portuguese who had been blown to the west, just as his earlier picturing of an island of Antilla probably reflects a combination of some other landfall and legend. Andrea Bianco did not make his living entirely from maps. Between 1437 and 1451, he served as chief navigation officer on the Venetian merchant galley fleets to the Tana, to Beirut and Alexandria, to Romania, to Barbary, and most frequently — seven times — to Flanders. These posts brought him into intimate and honorable association with the "Atlantic pilots" whom the Flemish fleets took on for the crossing from Lisbon to Southampton, and the varying islands and coastlines which he pictured in the Atlantic probably reflected what he learned from them, some of it accurate and some not.

While producing nautical charts of ever greater accuracy and range, Venetians also continued to make world maps in the tradition of that of Fra Paolino. The world map which Andrea Bianco included in his 1436 atlas depicts quite accurately the coasts he knew at first hand. It uncritically follows old traditions, however, regarding regions he could know only from books. In eastern Asia, its most prominent feature is the terrestrial paradise. The world was better mapped in that century by a friar of the Camaldolite monastery in the glass-making island of Murano. There Fra Mauro maintained a workshop which combined the methods and information of the chart makers with what could be learned from scholars. The latter had recently rediscovered Ptolemy's geography, whose errors began to acquire weighty authority. Fra Mauro filled his map with inscriptions reflecting his use not only of Ptolemy but also of Marco Polo and many other travelers and he showed good judgment in weighing their accounts one against another. While Prince Henry was spurring Portuguese navigators to sail further down the African coast, his brother, Prince Peter, visited Fra Mauro in the lagoons. Since Fra Mauro's maps showed more knowledge of lands far south in the interior of Africa than any others did, Prince Peter ordered for his brother a world map which Fra Mauro made with the aid of Andrea Bianco and which he delivered to Prince Henry just before his own death in 1459. A copy of this map, the climax of Fra Mauro's labors of coordination and compilation, survives in Venice (see Figure 27).

EXPLORERS AND THEIR NARRATIVES The relations between Venice and the Portuguese princes were maintained through the calls made in Lisbon by the galleys of Flanders. In 1454, while the fleet was waiting off Cape St. Vincent for a favorable wind, envoys from Prince Henry came down to trade and visit. One of the young Venetian merchants aboard, Alvise da Mosto, was so attracted by their tales of unknown lands and chances for untold profits that he converted his merchandise into wares suitable for that purpose and set out the next spring southward, down the African coast. He found trading in the Senegal River exciting and profitable; local chiefs were ready to pay from nine to fourteen men for one horse, and there was a good market in Portugal for Negro slaves. He returned the following year to trade in the Gambia further south. On the way down the coast he was blown off to sea by a storm and thus discovered some of the Cape Verde Islands. But Alvise is more notable as an observer and as a reporter of new lands than as an explorer. It is even doubtful whether he was indeed really the first to see the Cape Verde Islands, for there is no record of his having attempted to settle them or to have them enfeoffed to him. That was done a few years later by a Genoese, although Alvise da Mosto stayed in Portugal for a decade, writing up not only his own voyages but also those of the Portuguese. Then he returned to Venice, fought in the wars against the Turks, and served as a Senator and as a commander of fleets and fortresses. Meanwhile, the vivid account of his youthful part in the oceanic discoveries of the Portuguese earned him legendary fame as a navigator. In fact, he is most praiseworthy for writing the first general description of equatorial Africa which brought into relief its characteristic features.

Far more important in oceanic discoveries, and far less firmly attached to Venice, were John and Sebastian Cabot. Caboto is a Genoese name, and Giovanni Caboto obtained Venetian citizenship after fifteen years residence about 1472. He married a Venetian and his son Sebastian was born in Venice, but he was often away on one kind of a project or another. As a merchant he visited the sacred cities of the Moslem world, even Mecca he said, and gained a first-hand knowledge of the spices coming from the East. He was in Valencia in 1493, engaged in a project for harbor improvement, when Christopher Columbus, freshly returned from his discovery, passed through that city on his way to report triumphantly to the Spanish sovereigns that he had found the best and shortest way to the Indies. Cabot, who had read Marco Polo and had talked in the Levant with merchants from India, could not believe that the natives and the trophies which Columbus brought home really came from the wealthy Eastern realms. But Columbus's voyage fired his imagination and intensified his ambition to do what Columbus claimed to have done, and Cabot was well enough informed to know Columbus had not done — to sail west to Cathay.

Cabot believed the practical way to sail to Asia was to cross the western sea in high latitudes where the earth was not so big around and then to work down the coast of Asia to Cipango (Japan), whose wealth Marco Polo had described, and on to the tropical regions whence came the spices. Cabot had the good judgment to take his project to England where he interested King Henry VII, who was alert for commercial opportunities. He also won the support of some merchants of Bristol who had had experience in crossing the western ocean. The seamen of the west of England had been trading and fishing off Iceland for more than a century and may have discovered the Grand Banks off Newfoundland. They were not eagerly spreading any news that would attract competitors to their fishing grounds, but probably Cabot had heard of their voyages and went to Bristol for that reason. Certainly he came to think of Newfoundland as a part of Asia and a confirmation of his theory that Asia could be reached relatively quickly in high latitudes.

Accordingly, John Cabot and his family settled in Bristol and then obtained from King Henry VII a grant of special rights in whatever lands previously unknown to Christians he might discover across the ocean. In 1497 in a small ship, the *Matthew*, named after his Venetian-born wife Mattea, with a crew of only eighteen including two Bristol merchants, he crossed the Atlantic in thirty-five days and made a landfall on Newfoundland or perhaps Cape Breton. There he planted not only the banners of England and of the pope, but also, as he told a Venetian friend, the standard of Saint Mark. Then he sailed 300

FIGURE 27 *The World Map of Fra Mauro (courtesy of Biblioteca Marciana, Venice).*

This small segment of Fra Mauro's big Planisphere shows how he used the skill of nautical chartmakers in delineating the shorelines of the eastern Mediterranean. It is upside down by our standards. Included are pictures of a one-masted cog and a three-masted galley, and several of Fra Mauro's learned inscriptions. That above the galley expounds the relation of the Nile flood to the sun's movement through the signs of the zodiac—Cancer, Leo, Virgo, and Libra.

leagues along the coast. Since he found lands richer and showing more signs of habitation than those first seen in Newfoundland (which is not saying much) he felt that he had proved the existence of a large land mass and had confirmed his theory. So did those to whom he reported, including the English king and the merchants of Bristol. They financed a new and larger expedition. Five ships sailed the following year, expecting to push on far enough to find the trade centers of Cathay. But John Cabot and his ship never came back.

John Cabot's achievements have been obscured by the misrepresentations of his son, Sebastian, and by the reticence of the men of Bristol who after his death returned to exploiting the Newfoundland fisheries and saying little about such voyages. John Cabot had acquired credit among them as an authority on the spice trade. He also knew how to make maps and a globe to illustrate his ideas and won acceptance with them and in the English court as a geographer and cosmographer. He seems to have enjoyed less acceptance as a practical expert in navigation. His English companions had had more experience than he in those waters and when returning from the 1497 voyage his judgment of their latitude, although correct, was overruled by his companions. He was described by the envoy from the Duke of Milan as "of kindly wit and a most expert mariner."

Sebastian Cabot made no voyage before 1508 in furtherance of the grant given his father. Then, according to his own account, which many scholars disbelieve, he went to the northwest looking for a passage to Cathay and was turned back by ice from what was later called Hudson's strait. Sebastian must have been in impressive person, and he received credit for his father's voyages as well as for his own. After settling in Spain — when the new English king, Henry VIII, showed a notable lack of interest in exploration — he became the Spanish Pilot Major. During the thirty years that he held that high post, it was Sebastian's duty to examine all the pilots guiding the Spanish fleets to and from the New World. He was in charge of their instruction in the methods of determining latitude by the sun and stars which had been developed by the Portuguese at the end of the fifteenth century and which were just coming into general use. Where Sebastian learned celestial navigation we can only guess. If he learned it from his father, then John Cabot was far ahead of most of the navigators of the time, including Columbus.

While Sebastian was in Spain, he said nothing about the northwest passage to Cathay, which he claimed he had discovered only to be blocked by ice, but he had thoughts of transferring his services back to England in order to explore that route. In this connection he recalled that he was a Venetian, as indeed he was by birth. He made proposals to the Venetian authorities about using his secret route to Cathay for the advantage of Venice. Thinking in terms of political geography, they judged that impractical. Probably it was just a ploy to try to raise some capital. In fact when he did go to sea in command of an expedition it was in the service of Spain to the River Plate. He stayed in Spanish service until 1548 when, at the age of seventy, he went back to England. There he was much honored, claimed to be an Englishman by birth, and gave the English valuable encouragement in their search for passages northeast and northwest to the Indies.

On an occasion when Sebastian Cabot was playing with the idea of coming to Venice for funds, one of the men charged with investigating what he had to offer was Giovanni Battista Ramusio, a secretary of the Council of Ten whose personal interests had already made him a correspondent of Sebastian. Ramusio was a university man and closely linked to publishers and printers. Venice contributed to Europe's understanding of the geographical discoveries through its leadership in the printing industry as well as by map making and explorations. Ramusio assembled for printing at Venice the first of the many systematic collections of travels through which Europeans were informed of the discoveries, including those which the Portuguese would have preferred to keep secret. He naturally included in his collection such famous Venetian travelers as Marco Polo and Da Mosto, but his collection was international in its sources and world-circling in its scope.

Stimulated by the lively interest in voyages of discovery, other Venetians looked into their family archives to seek records of exploits by their ancestors. The most extraordinary resulting tale of exploration concerned Nicolò Zeno, a brother of the fourteenth-century naval hero, Carlo Zeno. This Nicolò Zeno was in fact like Alvise da Mosto a noble whose career at sea was so successful that he was chosen one of the commanding admirals of the merchant galley fleets. He commanded the fleet to Flanders in 1385. He was also for a time reputed to be so wealthy as to own more Venetian government bonds than any other man. But he was indicted and condemned for extortion while governor at Coron and Modon. Then he disappeared from the official Venetian records, and if he ever made the voyage of discovery attributed to him, it must have been between that disgrace and his death which is recorded as occurring in 1400. According to the account attributed to him by his grandnephew, he went north beyond the British Isles to Engroneland (Greenland ?), a land of ice where he found a monastery of Dominican Friars which was most miraculously heated by a fountain of boiling hot water, which served them also to do all their cooking. In a nearby country which he called Frisland he and a brother, Antonio, won the confidence of a great king whom they helped extend his power further to the west to a country called Estotiland, which could be nothing if not America. The descriptions of North American Indians, of Eskimo igloos, and of kayaks is quite convincing, and one section reads like a description of the Norse settlement in Labrador which did not die until late in the fourteenth century. But the account of exploits by Nicolo and his brother Antonio in the service of a King of Frisland (Faeroe Islands ?) are in conflict with extant Venetian records about his family. One would conclude that the grandnephew, also named Nicolò, had made it all up except that the younger Nicolò Zeno was both a man of learning and a highly respected Senator. The truth may be hinted at in the younger Nicolò's statement that letters and other writings concerning these exploits came into his hands when he was a small boy and was unappreciative of their value, so that he "tore them and rent them to pieces." Probably what he read in childhood about some voyage of an ancestor in northern seas made him an enthusiastic collector of maps and travel tales of that region. Late in life, filling in details from his studies and from the exciting reports of recent explorations, he composed around the family traditions a narrative which was essentially fiction. Perhaps he deliberately perpetuated a fraud; probably he really confused fact and fiction.

Such confusions have always added much to the fascination of travel literature and the geographies based on them. Many were to be found in the ancient geographies revered as authoritative in the sixteenth century, such as those of Ptolemy and Strabo. Ramusio's absorption in collecting accounts of the discoveries was in no small part a desire to compare what had hitherto been known from ancient authors with what contemporaries were describing as seen with their own eyes. He translated the ancient Greek accounts of navigation between Africa and India, for example, and compared their information on spices and winds with that in the accounts he had of the Portuguese voyages. Ramusio took pride even in the Portuguese achievements. As in the 1960's men were proud of conquests in space through rocketry, so Ramusio took delight in the enormous progress during his life time in the science of geography. He thanked God that he had been born in an age that was not only imitating the ancients but surpassing them in the acquisition of knowledge.

THE OCEANIC CHALLENGE · II

The Spice Trade

CHAPTER TWENTY

Quite different from Ramusio's detached scientific interest in the oceanic discoveries was the emotional and materialistic concern of Girolamo Priuli, the banker-diarist already introduced as a critic of Venice's mainland expansion. In August, 1499, Girolamo Priuli picked up on the Rialto his first news of a Portuguese fleet's arrival in India. It was a garbled account contained in a letter from Egypt (the commander's name was given as Columbus), and Priuli only half believed it. When more reports came in, both from Alexandria and from Lisbon, he was quickly convinced that a new route for eastern spices had been found. In the excited buzz on the Rialto, many merchants insisted that the new-found route of the Portuguese would never amount to anything, it was too long, the Moors in India would oppose it, too many ships would be lost. Priuli went to the other extreme and prophesied that the voyages would not only continue but would enable the Portuguese to sell spices at a fraction of the cost the Venetians paid and that Venice would be utterly ruined.

Pruili's prophecy was about half right, half wrong. The Portuguese voyages did continue, but the Portuguese did not sell spices below the prices customary in Venice, and Venice was not ruined by the circumnavigation of Africa. For reasons which Priuli did not foresee, Venice was able in the mid-sixteenth century to recapture much of the spice trade; and even in the decades when that trade was largely lost, the city remained prosperous, for its wealth did not depend so exclusively on the spice trade as Girolamo Priuli's laments would lead one to believe.

EXPLOITING THE
RED SEA ROUTE

To understand the effects of the oceanic discoveries on Venetian commerce, it is necessary to examine how Venice's trade had developed during the fifteenth century, particularly in relation to Asiatic products. The routes into Asia through the Black Sea and through Armenia and Persia became blocked by wars and banditry as the Mongol states disintegrated (see Map 5). Tana, over which the Genoese and Venetians fought so bitterly, was sacked by the meteoric conqueror Tamerlane in 1395. It revived but only as a center for the trade in slaves and such local products as furs, grain, and salt fish. The routes from Tana into Central Asia and those from Trebizond to the Persian Gulf became so unsafe that products of India, China, and the Spice Islands came to the Mediterranean almost entirely through Syria and Egypt. The Mamluk soldan who ruled both these territories had an uneasy control over much of Arabia also, but not over Mesopotamia (modern Iraq), so that the trade route that went through the Persian Gulf to Basra and Bagdad, and then up the Euphrates and across the desert to Damascus or Aleppo, like the route across Persia to Trebizond, was quite inadequately policed for the protection of merchants (see Map 10). The trade from India went almost entirely into the Red Sea.

Among the attractions of the Red Sea route was the opportunity for the Moslem merchants to combine business with religious duty by making a pilgrimage to Mecca. For that reason they stopped at Jiddah, the port of Mecca. Caravans so big they took two days and nights to pass out of Mecca's gates were escorted by soldiers around the edge of the Arabian desert either to Cairo, whence the spices went on to Alexandria, or to Damascus. Syria was enormously important to the Venetians because of its own products, above all cotton and cotton fabrics, and as a market for manufactured products. It needed to import manufactures more than ever after Tamerlane carried off from Damascus all the skilled craftsmen he could gather and sent them to his capital, to Samarkand in Central Asia. And Beirut and Tripoli were important for the spice trade also because they were the ports giving access to those spices which reached Damascus from the Red Sea (see Maps 3 and 5).

Of course the safety of the Red Sea route was only relative. Even the huge camel caravans from Mecca were sometimes raided successfully by desert Arabs in spite of the escorting soldiers; and in addition to the taxes paid to the Egyptian soldan, who at least furnished some protection in return, there were exactions by rulers of Red Sea ports. The most important of these were Aden and Jiddah. The ruler of Aden was particularly rapacious in the 1420's and an Indian sea captain named Ibrahim tried to find some other port wherein wares from India could be reloaded into vessels more adapted to the Red Sea. In 1422 he tried Jiddah, and his ships were pillaged by the sharif who ruled both Jiddah and Mecca. In 1424 he tried Jiddah again and was well pleased with the treatment he received from a Mamluk governor whom the Egyptian soldan had sent with a detachment of soldiers to accompany the pilgrim caravan to Mecca the previous year. These Mamluks brought Mecca and Jiddah directly under the soldan's control. The extortionate ruler of Aden found his port deserted and even Chinese vessels went directly to Jiddah. The elimination of the high levies at Aden and Jiddah through the concentration of control in Egyptian hands reduced the costs of protection on the Red Sea route and confirmed its superiority over any other known route between Europe and the Indies.

At Alexandria, the chief western outlet from the Red Sea funnel, the Venetians held a predominant position among the Western buyers of spices. They had two large and impressive warehouse-palaces, which were among the handsomest structures in Alexandria; the Genoese had only one; the Catalans and French had much smaller establishments. Each was a complex of buildings, walled in around a central courtyard used for packing and loading, and was surrounded by pleasant gardens. Within, merchants had storerooms and shops on the ground floor, lodgings above, their own baths, their own oven, and all the other facilities they needed. In the courtyard, they had animals including a pig which they kept, so a pilgrim-tourist reported, to scandalize the Moslems. Like other Christians, the Venetians were forbidden to go outside their compound during the hours of prayer on the Moslem holy day of Friday, and they were locked in at night. But Venetians were allowed their own church for Christian worship.

A large part of the silver and copper marketed in Venice by the Germans was carried by Venice's merchant galleys to Alexandria, together with much fine cloth and other wares. The Venetians were the best cash customers of the Egyptians and that gave them advantages in bargaining for privileges. Their consul had rights which in theory protected them from arbitrary arrests and confiscations, but in fact the resident Venetian merchants, who in good times lived luxuriously in their palace compound, were now and then locked up, beaten till they bled, and threatened with death. What was surest to arouse the wrath of the soldan was to hear that some of his subjects, Moslem traveling merchants, had been seized at sea and sold into slavery. If a Venetian was guilty in such a case, the Serenissima took strong measures. For example, in 1442, word reached Venice that a certain Piero Marcello, who had business in Acre with a Syrian whom he felt was not making the payments promised, enticed him on board his ship and sailed off to Beirut. There he lured ten more Moslems on board for a conference, set sail again, and went to Rhodes where he sold them all as slaves. The Venetian government promptly sentenced Marcello to be hanged, offered 4,000 ducats reward for his capture alive, 2,000 dead, and despatched an impressive embassy to the soldan who was thus induced to release the Venetian merchants he had seized and affirm the Venetian privileges in even more favorable terms. Venice's rivals were more frequently and grievously endangered, for after the raids of Maréchal Boucicault the Genoese as well as the French and Spanish were considered by the Mamluks as in league with such crusaders as the Knights of St. John, who generally considered all Moslems fair game and were not easily distinguished from other Christian pirates who were also mostly French and Spanish.

The predominance of the Venetians owed much to the regularity and security of the voyages of their great merchant galleys, which returned to Venice at the beginning of each winter (see Chapter 24). Those from Alexandria and Beirut sometimes numbered together as many as ten. Venice's navigation laws provided that only with these fleets could spices be brought to Venice, and the control which the commanders of these fleets exercised over the Venetian merchants, in conjunction with the consul, helped the Venetians to bargain successfully with the Mamluk soldan. Barsbay, the same soldan who took direct control of the whole Red Sea route by placing Mamluks in Jiddah, tried at the same time to keep prices in Alexandria high. He meant to keep for himself all the benefits from reduction of protection costs in the Red Sea, being there the monopolist of tribute-taking and, in Alexandria and Beirut, the sole seller to Europeans. To make him be reasonable, the Senate ordered all Venetians to withdraw gradually their investments from Mamluk lands to way stations such as Crete and Modon. (There was much traffic through small ships bringing fruits and oil from the Greek isles to Egypt. Although round ships could not bring spices to Venice, they could carry them from Egypt to Greek half-way points there to be picked up later by galleys returning to Venice.) When at least most of Venetian wealth was safe from the soldan's seizure, the Senate sent merchant galleys under strict orders not to unload on arrival their cargo of coin and precious metals but to trade only from the galleys. As a result, the galleys brought back very few spices in 1430, but the next fleet returned with a full load which had been purchased without hindrance from the soldan's monopolistic ideas. Pepper prices in Venice went to a new low.

It has been believed that spice prices were rising in Europe during the fifteenth century and that increasing difficulty in obtaining the products of the Indies was the reason for the oceanic expansion of that century. But merchants' account books show that spices were not growing dearer in Europe during the decades when the Portuguese were exploring around Africa. Pepper fell about 50 percent on the Venetian wholesale market between the 1420's and the 1440's and until the very end of the century remained at 40 to 50 ducats a cargo, well below the prices common during the first decades (see Figure 28). From the Genoese point of view, it may well have seemed that the Levant trade was becoming ever more difficult. The Levant was an area of relatively stagnant economies in which the Genoese faced stiff competition from experienced and better organized competitors. The Genoese found compensation by putting capital and mercantile skills into the expanding economies of Spain and Portugal. This diversion of Genoese energies was one reason why the Venetians far outstripped all competitors as buyers of spices in Alexandria and Syria. The number of galleys the Venetians sent and the prices they paid both show that from the Venetian point of view supplies were relatively plentiful and cheap.

The opposite impression has been created in good part by outcries of mistreatment, particularly those of Emmanuele Piloti, a Venetian who lived twenty-two years in Alexandria and knew the situation there thoroughly. In the 1430's he wrote a tract designed to arouse European princes to a crusade, a purpose which gave him reason to exaggerate Barsbay's cruelty and greed. And in displaying his exact knowledge of the customs barriers and warehouses through which an invading army should fight its way into Alexandria, Piloti described how, with his own hands and those of one servant, he broke a hole in the wall between a warehouse and the customs office so that he could move goods in and out without paying tolls. To be sure, Venetian letters and chronicles repeatedly complain of the greed and savagery of the Mamluks, but that may only prove how ancient is the practice of businessmen who have to deal with government officials of complaining violently about how badly they are being squeezed, even if their profits are good, in the conviction that if they do not yell bloody murder they will be squeezed harder. No doubt the Mamluks were brutal, rapacious, and unpredictable, but that did not prevent the Venetians from making lots of money out of the Egyptian spice trade.

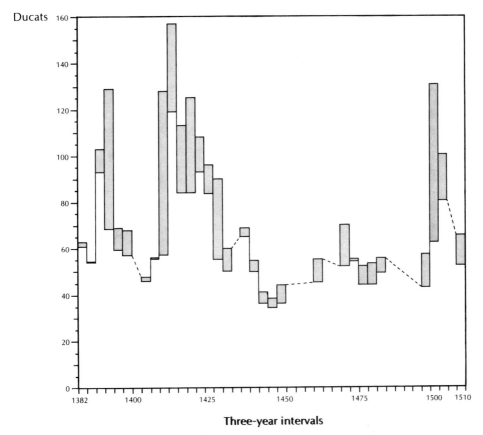

Ducats

FIGURE 28   *Pepper Prices at Venice, 1382–1510.*

Range of some recorded prices, by three-year periods, in ducats per 400 lbs. Venetian.

A particular point of conflict and compromise was the soldan's sale to the Venetians of pepper he had collected from merchants importing from India. Barsbay's efforts at monopoly were repeatedly revived, but the Venetians beat down the soldan's demands until they reached an agreement to buy just 210 loads (*sporta*) of pepper at a price well above the market but stipulated in advance. Those 210 loads amounted to only about one tenth of the total Venetian purchases of pepper, their extra cost was covered by a small levy on all Venetians trading at Alexandria, and the Venetians were then free to buy the rest of what they wanted from merchants in the bazaar.

The situation which was so profitable for Venetians ended abruptly in 1499 at the outbreak of the war between Venice and the Ottoman Turks. The galleys which had been auctioned for the trading voyages were all ordered into the war fleet commanded by Antonio Grimani; pepper prices in Venice went from 56 ducats a *cargo* (120 kg) in 1498 to 100 ducats in 1500. There was hot debate in the Venetian Senate over how long the galleys should be held up and whether additional galleys should be sent. Sanuto called it a battle between full warehouses and empty warehouses, for merchants with stocks on hand were content to delay new arrivals. The Grimani family was reputed to have made 40,000 ducats out of holding for high prices. Just about the time when the detained galleys were released there was a speculative fever. Pepper rose to 130 in February, 1501, and fell back to 62 the next month.

THE
PORTUGUESE
COMPETITION

Hard on the heels of this violent but temporary disruption of the usual rhythm came the effects of the Portuguese circumnavigation of Africa. After Da Gama's return, the Portuguese king sent a powerful fleet under Cabral, who was in India in the winter of 1500-1501 bombarding Calicut and arranging to get cargoes from the ruler of a nearby port. The effects were felt in Venice the following fall; pepper prices shot up to 95 in November, 1501, when news arrived from Egypt that the ships of the spice fleet from India had been sunk by the Portuguese. They stayed high for the next several years, at 100 ducats a cargo, while arrivals from India to the Red Sea dwindled. The rhythm of voyages was upset. The soldan demanded prices that the Venetians considered quite excessive, and in some years no galleys went to Alexandria. The French, Ragusans, and others increased their share of what trade there was.

While disputing violently over pepper prices, the Venetians and the Mamluks had a common interest in stopping the Portuguese voyages. At the first news of the Portuguese appearance in India, the Venetians urged the soldan to put pressure on the kings in India to refuse spices to the newcomers, and the soldan then appealed to Venice for aid in creating a fleet in the Red Sea to sail against them. Arab-Indian seamen made ships by lashing or sewing timbers together. They were surprisingly strong and some were fairly large, but they were no match for the heavy cannon-carrying Portuguese ships. At the same time that he asked for munitions, the soldan sent word throughout the West that he would destroy the Holy Places of the Christians in Jerusalem unless the Portuguese voyages were stopped; but the Portuguese told the pope he need not worry, it was an empty threat, for the soldan would not ruin the tourist pilgrim trade from which he derived much revenue. Later, in 1509, the propaganda against Venice at the time of the League of Cambrai, which pretended to be preparatory to a crusade, asserted that the Venetians had responded to the soldan's appeal for aid and furnished him with materials and skilled shipwrights so that he could build a fleet to fight Christians in India. No doubt, many Venetians wished him success there. Officially, the Senate refused his request, but replied sympathetically, telling him of Venice's political difficulties and advising him that he could obtain cannon and ship timbers from domains of the Ottoman Turks. Possibly they hinted that they would connive at his recruitment of crews in Greece.

Recruiting seamen and shipwrights wherever he could in the eastern Mediterranean and obtaining timber and artillery from Turkey, the Egyptian soldan prepared a fleet which sailed from the Red Sea to the coasts of India. It won its first battle with the Portuguese, but was crushed in the next fight. Materials for another fleet were intercepted by the Knights of Rhodes on their way from Turkey to Egypt. The Portuguese were left free to make raids into the Red Sea and to try to patrol its entrance, although they never succeeded in taking Aden or stopping entirely the flow of spices. When the Venetians patched up their dispute with the soldan and again became the leading Westerners trading at Alexandria, the arrivals of spices there had fallen to a fraction of what they had been.

FIGURE 29   *Negotiating with the Mamluks (courtesy of Caisse Nationale des Monuments Historiques).*

Displayed in the Louvre, Paris, as The Reception of Ambassador Domenico Trevisano at Cairo, *School of Gentile Bellini, it has been believed for nearly a century to picture the embassy sent in 1512 to arrange for resumption of trade after it had been disrupted by the high prices that resulted from Portuguese raids in the Indian Ocean. But the buildings resemble those of Damascus, not Cairo, and the scene may represent an episode that occurred before Gentile's death in 1507. In any case it depicts an oriental court as conceived either by Gentile Bellini or by that "close follower" to whom it has been attributed by the foremost American art critic, Bernhard Berenson.*

Meanwhile the Portuguese were marketing their spices at Lisbon and Antwerp and threatening to supply all France and Germany through Antwerp. Some Venetians thought that, in order to keep its German market, Venice would do well to draw its supplies from Lisbon, but when they sent their merchant galleys to Lisbon in 1521, the Venetians found the prices there too high to be attractive. Thereafter, the Senate followed the advice of those who believed that Venice's future still lay with the traditional Levantine trade. The Levant was too important to Venice to be abandoned, not only because of spices but because it was a major market for many Venetian manufactures, a source of raw materials, and the focus of Venice's colonial and naval power.

Hopes for a revival of the Levantine spice trade soon proved well founded; the Portuguese hold on the spice trade was more precarious than it seemed in the light of their first successes. They had driven Venetians out of the market in western Europe not by selling below the prices which had generally prevailed in the fifteenth century, but by cutting the supplies of the Venetians. When Girolamo Priuli prophesied Venice's ruin through the Portuguese capture of the trade, he dwelt on the cheapness with which the Portuguese could buy in India and on their freedom from the taxes of the soldan. He and other Venetian observers in the opening decade of the sixteenth century assumed that the Portuguese would organize the trade much as the Venetians organized their spice trade, namely, with fleets supplied by the government but with the purchase and sale of spices left to private traders whose search for profits would keep costs and prices relatively low. In fact, the Portuguese king imitated more nearly the practices of such Mamluk soldans as Barsbay. He decided to take a monopoly of pepper into his own hands and then to sell it at as high a price as he could get. He could keep his price high only as long as he disrupted the trade between India and Egypt across the Arabian Sea. He undertook to do that by acting as an Emperor of India and by maintaining fleets and fortresses at key points. His hold on the spice trade depended not on any economy in the circumnavigation of Africa compared to passage through the eastern Mediterranean, but on his imperial control in India. Indeed, desire for the glory of being Emperor of India may have determined his choice of policy. Having chosen to build an empire, he meant to recover its expenses from the high prices he obtained from his pepper monopoly. His success and the continued Portuguese control of the trade then depended entirely on Portuguese patrols or some other way of raising protection costs in the Arabian Sea.

The Ottoman conquest of Egypt in 1517 was a step towards revival of the Mediterranean spice trade because it brought the Portuguese in the Indian Ocean face to face with a much more formidable military and naval power. The Portuguese repelled Ottoman Turkish attacks upon their main bases in India and allied with the Shah of Persia to control the Persian Gulf, but the Ottomans controlled Aden. Portuguese efforts to patrol became less effective. In order to keep their alliance with the Persian shah, whose help they needed against the Ottomans, the Portuguese permitted spices to flow from India to Ormuz. Thence spices found their way not only into Persia but across northern Syria to Aleppo and on down to Beirut. The route through the Persian Gulf, which had been much used in the earlier Middle Ages, again became important; and the Venetians moved to Aleppo their main commercial settlement and consulate in Syria. Persian silk was even more important than spices in Aleppo, however; the largest supply of spices was again to be found in Egypt (see Map 10, p. 371).

For some years in the 1560's, the flow of spices through the Red Sea equalled that of the 1490's. The large volume of spice arriving in Egypt was not due simply to success in eluding Portuguese patrols; mostly, it was due to the sale of spices to Arab traders by Portuguese officials more interested in their own profits than those of their king, or driven to such illicit trade because their salaries were in arrears. Supplies in the Levant became so plentiful that the Venetian spice merchants reconquered their German and Italian markets, and Levantine spices also supplied most of France.

THE COMPETITORS AFTER 1570 For the Venetians, this revival of the "good old times" ceased abruptly in 1570, but during all the rest of the century there was competition between arrivals on the three routes — through the Red Sea, through the Persian Gulf, and around Africa — with violent fluctuations in their relative importance. More and more nations became involved. The French largely replaced the Venetians in the Levantine part of the trade during the War of Cyprus, 1570-73, or rather, French flags or passports did, since Genoese and many other Italians, including even some Venetians, when not adequately employed in fighting the Turks under Spanish or Venetian flags, traded in the Ottoman Empire with French passports. The Ottoman sultan gave the French special privileges in order to have the French kings as allies against the Hapsburg monarchs of Austria and Spain. Marseilles consequently began to appear as a dangerous rival to Venice.

When the King of Spain, Philip II, succeeded to the throne of Portugal in 1580, the Spanish loomed suddenly as the masters of the spices. Spain's naval and military power was then at its peak, and Philip at once showed that he meant to use it to extract more profit from the spice trade. His was the first truly worldwide empire; the sun never set on Philip's possessions in America, around Africa, and across the edge of southern Asia. The only ruler anywhere near his equal in power was the Ottoman sultan. Their forces clashed in the Arabian Sea as well as in the valley of the Danube and in the Mediterranean, and they extended opposing alliances from Ireland to Sumatra. The spice trade was one of the many battlefields they fought over in this first "world war."

One Turkish move in the contest was of a kind to change radically Venice's position, namely, the effort to build a canal at Suez. Many centuries earlier, a canal between the Nile and Suez had been dug. Although it had filled up with sand, it had not been entirely forgotten, and in 1504 the Venetians debated whether they should urge the Mamluk soldan to re-excavate it. Nothing was done until after the Ottoman conquest of Egypt. About 1530, thousands of diggers were at work, and a more serious effort was planned by the Ottoman government in 1586. All these plans envisaged the canal as a military, not a commercial advantage; the main purpose was to send the Turkish Mediterranean fleet into the Red Sea to protect Mecca from Christian raids and to carry the war to India. More pressing military expenditures elsewhere, as for the Turkish-Persian war in 1586, prevented any of the Ottoman plans being fully executed. Skeptics said a canal was impractical anyhow, so the Venetian ambassador at Constantinople reported, because of the shifting sands.

Equally abortive but also of momentous possibilities for Venice was one of the Spanish moves in the battle of the spices. In 1584, Philip offered to sell to the Venetians all the pepper imported through Lisbon. He sweetened the offer with promises of Spanish galleys to escort as far as Sicily the ships the Venetians would send for the spices, and with promises of a general lowering of customs duties. But there were several catches in the proposal. The king was offering 3,000,000 lbs. a year, and while it was doubtful whether the fleets sailing around Africa could really bring back that much, if they did, the Venetians would be obligated to buy it all at a relatively high price. It was two or three times the quantity of pepper the Venetians were accustomed to importing from the Levant. To keep up the price, they would be expected to stop imports through the Ottoman Empire, which would lead to political reprisals and the ruin of the markets there for Venetian products. They would also be expected, in order to keep up the price, to organize a Europe-wide cartel to control sales. Many such cartels, assigning districts and quotas to their members, had been organized during the sixteenth century by agreements among German, Italian, and Portuguese merchants. While apportioning out the pepper and other spices, these pools assembled enough capital so that they could contract with the Portuguese king for a huge amount at once, and supply him with the funds needed to outfit new fleets. The Venetians had joined hardly at all in these cartels. Their role hitherto had been that of the competitor outside the cartel who limited the area in which the cartel could make its monopoly effective. If the Venetians took the contract for the pepper coming through Portugal, they might have a strangle hold on both sources of supply. In that regard, their cartel would have been in a better position than any previous cartel. But it would have lacked one essential for success: ability to limit the supply in accordance with the demand. Even if King Philip and his successors kept the agreement and sold to no one else, which could be doubted, Venice could not limit what she bought from him to the amount she judged salable at the price fixed. From a strictly business point of view, therefore, the Venetians had reasons for not accepting Philip's proposal. Anyhow, Venice's leaders were not as experienced in managing international cartels of that kind as were the Augsburgers and the Genoese.

Really decisive, probably, were the political considerations. To accept the spice contract would harness Venice into a Spanish alliance. Advocates of the Spanish contract may have dreamed that Venice could take a new lease on life as a maritime republic by throwing her commercial expertise, her capital, and her shipping into the exploitation of Philip's world-wide empire. Venice had grown great by working within the Byzantine Empire. The commercial opportunities within the Spanish-Portuguese Empire of Philip were even greater. But the structures of the two empires were quite different, and Venice's own resources in men and materials, especially in men, were quite different from what they had been in the twelfth century. To be dependent on the good will of the Spanish monarch was to be avoided at all costs, so the Venetians felt in the late sixteenth century. They were committed to playing the balance between France and Spain and between Spain and Turkey in order to control their own destiny.

The growth of English and Dutch sea power in the 1590's made any Spanish-Venetian monopoly of the spice trade quite out of the question. The Dutch and English took cargoes from the Spanish-Portuguese Indiamen in the Atlantic and then found their way around Africa to India and the Spice Islands. For a time, their depredations made the Mediterranean a safer route than the Atlantic and thus contributed to the final decade of Mediterranean commercial preeminence from which Venice profited at the end of the sixteenth century. Early in the seventeenth century, however, the Dutch gained effective control of the Spice Islands. Far more effectively and permanently than the Portuguese had ever done, the Dutch cut off the flow through the Red Sea.

THE OCEANIC CHALLENGE · III

The Shifts in Other Trades

CHAPTER TWENTY-ONE

In the second half of the sixteenth century, Venice was more populous and full of riches than she had ever been. This seems paradoxical in view of the many adverse effects which the oceanic discoveries had on Venetian commerce. Some changes were to her advantage, to be sure, but the immediate shifts in many others were more damaging than the vicissitudes of the spice trade. A balanced view of the effects of oceanic discoveries requires a look at all sides of the city's economy.

COLONIAL PRODUCTS AND BULLION   The sugar trade was the first to be revolutionized by oceanic voyages. In expecting that the Portuguese would break to new lows the price of pepper and other spices, Priuli may have had in mind what had happened to sugar.

The growing of sugar cane was introduced into the Madeira Islands almost as soon as they were discovered and about 1470 Portuguese ships began taking Madeira sugar to Flanders and into the Mediterranean. Virgin soil, slaves, and plentiful supplies of wood for boiling down the cane made production cheap at the new source of supply and, by 1490, drove the price in both Venice and Antwerp down to a third of what it had been. The Genoese, who led in marketing Portuguese sugar, were by that date shipping it as far east in the Mediterranean as Chios. When Madeira no longer offered virgin soil and virgin forests, Brazil began producing yet cheaper supplies.

This shift in the center of sugar production hit the Venetians all the harder because, just at the time when the Portuguese sugar was driving down the price, they acquired control of the main Levantine source of supply, the island of Cyprus. The Genoese were driven from their favored position there in 1464 after the king they supported was ousted by a rival known as James the Bastard. Looking to Venice for support against the Genoese, the Turks, and various Italian princes who disputed his right to the throne of Cyprus, James married Caterina Corner, whose father and uncle had helped him to power with their loans. Venice gave approval and promise of support, and at the same time symbolized the intent that the glory and benefits of this royal marriage should go rather to the Republic than to the Corner family by formally adopting Caterina so that she became a daughter of the Serenissima. When subsequently James the Bastard and his infant son died, Venice supported the rule of its daughter as queen. Since Caterina's rule was shaky and it began to seem as if she might fall under the control of men who plotted to have her marry again and give birth to an heir who would take the island out of Venice's grasp, the Senate sent out her brother, Giorgio Corner, with instruction to persuade her, by threat of force only if necessary, to abdicate in favor of her adopted father, the Republic. Backed by the strong fleets that Venice kept in the neighborhood, these maneuvers brought Cyprus peacefully under direct Venetian rule in 1489. By that time, many high offices and profitable fiefs in the kingdom were held by the Corner, Contarini, Giustiniani, and other Venetians. Thus Venice definitely triumphed over Genoa in yet another field in which they had traditionally been bitter rivals. By that time, the Genoese were finding ample compensation, at least in so far as the sugar trade was concerned, handling the exports from the Portuguese islands.

On the other hand, Venetians found a kind of compensation by expanding Cypriot production of cotton. In the early fifteenth century, Venetian cotton exports from Syria and Palestine had faced the competition of Genoese exports from Cyprus and the mainland near Chios. By the end of the century, Venetians faced practically no competition, except among themselves, in supplying cotton for Europe's fustian industry. The light cotton cloths from India called "calicoes" did not flood European markets until late in the seventeenth century, and meanwhile the fustian weavers of Augsburg, Ulm, and other German cities expanded production and bought more and more in Venice. Ultimately, of course, cotton from the New World would undersell the Cypriot product just as sugar was doing, but that did not happen until later. Meanwhile, production in Cyprus expanded to more than three times what it had been before Venice took over; cotton was called in Cyprus the "plant of gold." Even after Cyprus was lost to the Turks in 1571, its cotton was still for some decades marketed through Venice.

Another branch of commerce radically changed by oceanic discoveries was the trade in dyestuffs, important because so closely linked with the main industry of the times, the manufacture of textiles. Venice was most affected by the revolution in red dyes. A main source of reds was brazilwood, called *verzino* at Venice, which had come from India but which was found so plentifully in Brazil that it gave its name to that country. Within two decades after the land of Brazil was sighted by a Portuguese fleet on its way to India, Venetian Senators were told during a debate about spices and dyes that brazilwood had been shipped from Portugal to Syria and sold for a profit in markets where it used to be bought.

Competition from the New World even more damaging to Venetian trade arose from the discovery by the Spanish that a brilliant red dye could be obtained

from insects, cochineal, found on New World cactus plants. Before that discovery, the brightest scarlet had been produced by insects found on oak trees
in Greece. The dyestuff collected from oak trees, kermes (*grana*), had been for
centuries an important part of the merchandise which the Venetians imported
from Crete and Morea and then transshipped to the north and west. After the
middle of the sixteenth century kermes was gradually replaced by the American
product.

In the bullion trade, oceanic voyages were only one of the factors affecting
Venice's position. At the same time that the Portuguese were pushing around the
western bulge of Africa to tap its gold output through the Gulf of Guinea, German
miners were improving their methods and increasing their output again, after
about a century of depression. Primarily silver and copper, but also some gold,
were sent from Germany and Hungary to Venice, and as the exports from the
German mines grew larger and larger, Venetian trade and finance profited.
Some of the silver went to Tunis and other North African ports to be exchanged
for the gold that continued to come across the Sahara even after the Portuguese
were able to import African gold by sea. Larger quantities of silver, much
copper, and some gold were exported from Venice to Egypt, whence much of
it found its way to India in exchange for spices. As long as the main supplies
of silver came from north of Venice and flowed to the south or east in exchange
for gold or for spices, Venice had a strategic position in which to profit from
coining, transporting, and exchanging the precious metals.

For some time after the discovery of America, the output of silver from
Germany and of gold from Africa continued to increase, although supplemented
by new supplies from America. After 1580, American silver reached Europe in
quantities that quite overshadowed the amount mined in Germany. None of
the new supply was marketed primarily in Venice, and even some of the German
output was diverted to Antwerp where it was used to pay for Portuguese spices.
When the flood of American silver reached its peak in 1590-1600, a part
filtered through to Venice from other trade centers, such as Seville, Lyons, and
Genoa, but Venetians complained that their trade in the Levant was suffering
because of the competition of merchants better supplied than they with silver,
especially the French, who gained much silver by selling wheat in Spain.

**LEVANTINE
MERCHANTS,
JEWS, AND THE
GHETTOS**   Political changes within the Mediterranean, as well as developments across
the oceans, adversely affected Venetian trade in a number of ways, most of
them connected more or less directly with the growth of the Ottoman
Empire. The political background of Venice's wars with the Turks has been
mentioned in Chapter 17; the naval efforts they inspired will be described
in Chapter 25. Economically, each Turkish war was a drag on the Venetian economy while it lasted; these wars gave few opportunities for plunder and privileges
such as had made Venice's wars with the Byzantine Empire so profitable, and
the lands lost suffered from the devastation attendant on Turkish conquest. But
absorption into the Ottoman Empire did not bring desolation, as many Western
Christian writers have implied. Behind their frontiers, the Ottoman rulers encouraged commerce so as to be able to tax it. In their tariffs they put the Venetians at a disadvantage, however, and the merchants native to Levantine lands
now had a powerful protector who helped them compete vigorously with West-

erners. Greeks, Armenians, and Arabs had not ceased altogether commercial activity when the Crusades gave Westerners the advantages that went with having the upper hand politically, but they had been for some centuries overshadowed by the Italians. "The victory of the Ottoman Empire symbolized, in the sphere of economics, a victory of Greeks, Turks, renegade Christians, Armenians, Ragusans, and Jews over the two-century-old commercial hegemony of Venice and Genoa," so writes a historian of the Balkans, Traian Stoianovich. The activities of merchants native to the Middle East increased not only within the Ottoman Empire, but in shipping westward. The Greek community at Venice, composed partly of mariners and refugee scholars but richly reinforced by merchants, formed their own fraternity and built their own church. Turkish merchants were interned during the War of Cyprus in a building reserved for them, where they were protected from hooting, stone-throwing mobs of small boys celebrating the Christian victory at Lepanto. After the peace, they were all housed together in a Fondaco dei Turchi, although Asiatic Turks protested against having to live with Balkan Turks, claiming that their customs were so different they were sure there would be fights.

Jews played a complex role in this revival of Levantine participation in the trade of Levant. Venetians distinguished three kinds of Jews which they called Levantine, German, and Ponentine (Western). When Venice's power had been at its peak in Romania, Jews had lived and traded side by side with Venetians in the Venetian quarter in Constantinople, and some of these Levantine Jews had been granted a kind of Venetian citizenship. Levantine Jews early gave its name to the island in Venice called the Giudecca. Those of Corfu or Crete continued to enjoy rights to trade as Venetian subjects. Many others became Turkish subjects and enjoyed the rights of resident aliens as international traders under the treaties Venice negotiated with their powerful protector, the Ottoman sultan. Although their length of residence in Venice was limited by law, in fact some settled and raised families there.

Entirely different was the treatment of those called German Jews, most of whom came from other Italian cities. They were not entitled to participate in Venice's international trade, but were allowed to act as pawnbrokers taking "usury," limited in theory to 15 percent, and to be dealers in second-hand goods, especially clothing. For some time they were restricted to Mestre, but took refuge in Venice when wars ravaged the mainland. In 1516 they were permitted to stay, but were confined to an area which had been the site of a new foundry (see Figure 2) and was therefore called the "Ghetto Nuovo" (*getto* means "casting"). There they governed themselves and had their own places of worship and their own butchers and bakers who prepared food according to Jewish rites, as well as their pawn shops and their clothing stores, some of which were very richly stocked. They were locked within the ghetto at night and on some Christian holidays. This was explained, as was the locking in of Venetians in Alexandria at night and during hours of prayer on Moslem holy days, by claiming that it was necessary to protect them from fanatics and to prevent scandal. Any of these Jews staying in Venice for more than two weeks were ordered to wear a yellow O on his back, or if that was covered by a cloak, to wear a yellow, later a scarlet, hat or turban. The rule was often evaded, but theoretically it applied even to Jewish physicians, who were highly esteemed.

The Venetian name for its Jewish quarter, ghetto, became much later a generic term for any congested district to which its residents were restricted, a symbol of segregation. But there were many examples of friendly contact between Jews and Christians in Venice, and no mob attack on Jews ever occurred there. Jews were separately taxed, however, and their right to reside in Venice was limited to a stipulated period. Every so often they had to contract for a new right of residence by payment of a sizable sum.

About the middle of the sixteenth century, a new element became of importance in Venice's relations with the Jews, namely the Marranos. In Spain during the fifteenth century, the descendants of Jews who had become Christians were first known as "Converts" or as "New Christians" and then, as they came under attack on the charge of being secretly still Jews, were called "Marranos" (meaning "pigs"). Many moved to Portugal as refugees from Spain, and being accepted as Christians became leading financiers and pepper merchants. The biggest of the business organizations of these New Christians was that of the Mendes family. Its members operated on a grandiose scale in Antwerp and Lyons as well as in Lisbon. Soon after 1536, when an inquisition modeled on that of Spain was introduced into Portugal, some of the leading Marranos came to Venice. They came as Christians, but their sincerity was suspect, and they felt that their persons and fortunes were insecure in Christian lands. The intensity of religious feeling aroused by the Reformation generated a fanatical intolerance which was likely to hit Jews and New Christians. It did so in Ancona in 1556 when Pope Paul IV ordered the New Christians arrested. Twenty-four of them were burned.

Venice was not altogether immune to religiously colored anti-Semitism and it had commercial and even political reasons to hate some New Christians. The leader of the Mendes family, christened João Miquez and better known by the Jewish name he took later, Joseph Nasi, shifted his center of operations to Constantinople. Although by being circumcized he made impossible his own return to the West, he maintained the close business connections which the Mendes family had established among New Christians in Western cities, including those with a cousin in Venice. At the same time, he developed a commercial and industrial organization among the Jews within the Ottoman Empire. His commercial operations with their ramifications, stretching from Antwerp to Palestine, were a threat to the profits of Venetian merchants. His competition hit Venice's most sensitive nerve, for it included the exchange of Levantine wares for those of Western Europe and sought to bypass Venice whenever that was practical, making use of business connections in Ragusa, Ancona, Ferrara, and other cities in which there were either Jewish or New Christian colonies.

Joseph Nasi became an enemy of Venice in politics also. He became the foremost financier and tax-farmer of the Ottoman emperor and was honored with the title of Duke of Naxos, a title which, before the Turkish conquests, had belonged to a Venetian family. He was considered a main instigator of the Turkish invasion of Cyprus in 1571.

Anti-Semitism acquired added force at Venice as a result. So long as the Jews with whom the Venetians dealt were either associates of Venetians in the Levant or pawnbrokers and second-hand dealers in Venice, the Venetians found them economically helpful. During the heyday of the Mendes firm, the Jews of the Levant were seen as the most dangerous of competitors, and a law banned Marranos from Venice. From Constantinople the Venetian envoy reported that Venetians had to sell their wares to Jews, who conspired to get a low price. In Egypt Jews bought up spices before they got to Alexandria, so that the Venetians had to buy from them. It was to meet this competition that the Venetians moved their main settlement and consulate from Alexandria to Cairo in 1555. These economic rivalries fostered a kind of anti-Semitism that was made more bitter by religious excitement and by the association of Jews and Marranos with Venice's deadly enemy, the Turks. Under these circumstances it is not surprising that, when there was a devastating explosion and fire in the Arsenal just on the eve of the War of Cyprus, Jews were accused of setting it off.

Among the cities whose competition was hurting Venice was Ragusa, which resembled the Venice of earlier centuries in many respects. When Venice regained possession of the rest of Dalmatia early in the fifteenth century, Ragusa became a practically independent republic, although nominally subject at first to the King of Hungary and then to the Ottoman sultan. In spite of their paying annual tribute to the Turk, Ragusans were treated as neutrals in time of war. Ragusan merchants took advantage of this neutral position to expand their trade by sea, all the more so because the trade inland to Bosnia and Serbia, which had previously been their main activity, was disrupted during the collapse of those states and their conquest by the Turks. Then, once Turkish rule of the Balkans was firmly established, Ragusans made the overland route from their city to Constantinople a major channel of trade. As Florence and Venice became rivals commercially as well as politically, Florentines shipped their cloth east by way of Ancona, thence by sea to Ragusa, and then overland to the centers of the Ottoman Empire. Venice's staple right as "Lord of the Gulf" did not extend far enough south to prevent this cross-Adriatic trade. Moreover, Ragusans imported from Alexandria and other Levantine centers in order to re-ship to England. This by-passing of Venice increased notably during each of Venice's wars with the Turk. Even Venetians then turned to Ragusans for help. Thus in 1537-40 Venetians were allowed to use Ragusan ships to get their possessions out of the Ottoman Empire, although at the same time the Venetians tried to prevent Ragusans from carrying cloth east to satisfy the market from which the war excluded the Venetians. At the end of each war, trade swung back from Ragusa to Venice, and the change was reflected in Ragusan custom receipts which fell from 52,000 ducats annually in 1538-41 to 19,700 in 1552-55, and fell from 106,000 ducats annually in 1570-72 to 28,000 in 1576-80. But, on both the land route and the sea route, Ragusans remained dangerous competitors.

Another port which began to lure off some of the East-West trade on which Venice traditionally relied was developed near the end of the century by the Grand Duke of Tuscany at Leghorn. He made it a free port, which meant that wares from either the Levant or the Channel could be reshipped there without payment of any duty, and he invited Jews to settle at Leghorn.

Such rival ports could never become a positively helpful factor, although the extent to which they hurt Venice could change abruptly. The commercial energies of New Christians and Jews, on the other hand, could work in Venice's favor or against her, according to circumstances.

After the death of the Duke of Naxos and of the sultan with whom he had great influence, Venice's relations with Jews improved. Many of those active in international trade chose to make Venice their base of operations and won favor with the Serenissima. Their leader was Daniele Rodriga. He initiated the development of the port of Spalato so that it rivaled Ragusa as a terminus of the overland route from Constantinople and a point of assemblage for westward shipment of hides, wax, and other products of the Balkans. He started this new development at Spalato by petitioning in 1577 for permission to rent an abandoned monastery and convert it to lodgings and a warehouse for the Jewish and Turkish merchants who brought wares from the interior, promising to bear himself all the initial expenses of repair and upkeep. He asked also low tolls that would enable Spalato to compete with other way-stations. He encouraged the sending of great galleys to protect from pirates the wares moving between Venice and Dalmatia. At first the galley masters, being interested in quick turn-around and full cargo, went to the established centers of trade, to Narenta and Ragusa, but after 1592 the government, which auctioned the galleys for the voyage, insisted that they go to Spalato. Trade from the interior then concentrated there so as to divert much of the overland trade from Ragusa and funnel it more and more in the next century through Spalato towards Venice.

Ponentine Jews such as Daniele Rodriga could not legally reside in Venice for more than a year, although some, like Daniele, were married there and their residence was winked at. Rodriga petitioned in 1579 that his kind be given rights of residence similar to those of the "German" Jews and permission to continue their trade. The petition was referred to the Board of Trade (*Cinque Savii alla Mercanzia*) which had been created to advise the Senate on commercial matters. At first, the Board recommended against it, saying that Jews would then control all the dealings of the Rialto and might provoke war with the Turk so that they alone, using the status of some relatives as Turkish subjects, would control all trade. The Board of Trade changed its advice a few years later, after second thoughts about how much the customs revenues would be increased by the trade the Jews would bring to the city. A contract was made providing for security of residence for ten years and rights to engage in international trade. It was made with a Jewish community distinct in organization from that of the German Jews but embracing the Levantine Jews and the "Western" Jews who were refugees from Spain and Portugal. They lived together in a newer part of the ghetto, called Ghetto Vecchio because of its location on the site of an old foundry. Those Marranos who wished to declare themselves Jews were permitted to come to Venice and join this community.

Under these arrangements, anti-Semitism faded and the Venetian Jewish community flourished. The provision requiring Jews to wear yellow or red hats was modified so as to permit them to substitute black hats or turbans when going on a journey. One suspects that many violations of humiliating rules were winked at, for both Jewish rabbis and Christian eulogists claimed that, after 1590, Jews were especially well treated in Venice. Christians went to concerts in the ghetto and Jews attended regattas and theatrical performances outside. They gambled together and listened to each other's sermons, those that had a taste for sermons. The number of Jews increased to at least 2,500. The highest apartment houses in Venice, some of them seven stories high, were built in order to accommodate so many in a small space. Intellectually as well as architecturally the Venetian ghetto was outstanding; before the development of Amsterdam, Venetian rabbis were recognized by other Jewish communities of the West as the most authoritative.

Economically, the advantages which Venice gained from welcoming Jews were twofold. The Jewish pawnbrokers performed under tight regulations a function which was so generally recognized as necessary that in most Italian cities institutions called *Monti di Pietà* were formed to make loans to the poor. The interest charged by the Jews was pushed down to 5 percent. It could be made that low only because the government required other Jews, rich dealers in second-hand clothing and in international trade, to help the pawnbrokers. At the same time, the rich Jewish merchants brought commerce to Venice that might otherwise have been routed through other cities.

One of the projects with which Daniele Rodriga attracted the favor of the nobles on the Venetian Board of Trade was a plan to send Venetian ships south on the Atlantic coast of Morocco to load sugar. Most of northwestern Africa became closed to Venetian enterprise, however. The extension of Spanish and Ottoman power into that region and the warfare between them had killed that branch of Venetian trade and left all Venetian shipping liable to attack from the Barbary pirates.

NEW MARKETS   But not all the effects of Ottoman expansion and of the oceanic voyages were detrimental to the Venetian economy. The power of a sultan ruling from the walls of Vienna to Arabia and to the border of Morocco turned Constantinople into a flourishing city again. Its population rose from less than 100,000 in 1453 to about 700,000 in 1580, and the wealth of the sultan's court made it a major market for Venetian merchandise. Also beneficial to Venice was the diversion to oceanic routes early in the century of Basque and Portuguese shipping which had been active in the Mediterranean. Removal of this competition was an element in the sixteenth-century revival of the Venetian merchant marine, a lopsided revival, to be sure, which will be described in later chapters. Also, before the end of the century, codfish from the Grand Banks of Newfoundland was helping to meet a demand for food that had never been met from Adriatic sources and that had called for imports from the Black Sea. Moreover, the general economic growth of western Europe, which was proceeding vigorously again in the sixteenth century when the ground lost in the fourteenth century was more than recovered, stimulated economic growth in Venice also.

The expanding volume of the cotton trade is one example of the way Venice profited from these expanding markets. Another example is the expansion of silk imports. Silk in greater quantity than ever before came from Persia through Aleppo, and in spite of some French competition, the Venetians were far and away the leading Western merchants in Aleppo. In 1549 they moved their main Syrian consulate from Damascus to Aleppo. The chief market for this Persian and Syrian silk was not in Venice itself, since Venice's own silk weavers used a lighter kind of silk grown near Bassano and Vicenza, but beyond the Alps in Nuremberg, Frankfurt-am-Main, and Cologne. The prosperous German cities looked to Venice for silk as well as for cotton, and they looked to her also for their "colonial products," even those which like sugar were increasingly obtained by Venice from the west.

Venice lost her position as the middleman drawing profit from supplying such goods to England and the Netherlands, to be sure, but she partially made up for this by finding an expanding market in northwest Europe for other Mediterranean products. The English were enjoying more and more of the sweet Malmsey wines from the isles of Greece. The cost of freighting wine from Crete to Southampton was cut in half late in the fifteenth century. Later, raisins also became a major item in Venetian shipments to England. The Venetian Ionian Islands, especially Zante, specialized in growing grapes that were dried for export to go into the famous English "plum puddings."

The development of such cities as Lisbon, Seville, Antwerp, and London made the commercial pre-eminence of Venice less outstanding than it had been, but it also provided markets for Venetian merchants and craftsmen, so that Venice was certainly more populous—reaching nearly 190,000 inhabitants—and probably wealthier in the sixteenth century than it had been in the fifteenth.

FOOD AND THE Its very prosperity magnified Venice's difficulties in obtaining food sup-
GRAIN TRADE plies. The first mention of the Venetians as a distinct people characterized
them as men who seemed strange in an almost entirely agrarian Europe because they did not sow or reap. They obtained their food in exchange for transport services and salt. In the more commercial and industrial Europe of the fifteenth and sixteenth centuries, the dwellers in the lagoons still had to buy their food abroad, and they had to do so in competition with many other urban centers. Salt, although still important and a source of substantial revenues for the government, was overshadowed as an export by many manufactured goods and by commercial and political services. Payment for food supplies was only one element in a very complex balance of payments, but it was still a most fundamental factor.

Transport by sea made food supplies a very different problem for Venice than for an inland city such as Paris which reached out gradually over an ever expanding circle of farmland. Venice, and other large Mediterranean cities, could tap any region which had a surplus and a port on the sea. Fresh vegetables and fresh meat, to be sure, came from relatively nearby, although Venetian butcheries slaughtered cattle driven from the Hungarian plains. The mainstay of Venetian diet was wheat, however, which kept relatively well and could be transported 1,000 miles by sea more cheaply than 50 miles by land. Even before Venice's population had grown to number more than 100,000, as in 1300 and again in 1400, Venetian ships were bringing wheat from as far away as the Black Sea or Egypt. Occasionally, they took on wheat in Lisbon. The normal sources of supply were chiefly Apulia and Sicily, while much came also from Albanian, Greek, Cretan, and Cypriot ports. From one year to the next, war or weather changed centers of supply into distressed importers. Sometimes the Italian mainland had a surplus, and Venice made sure it received supplies from its subject areas there when it needed them, but more generally the mainland had to supplement its own production with substantial imports of wheat from the overseas sources tapped by Venetian ships. In a record twelve months, 1511-12, ships brought 60,000 tons of wheat to Venice, enough to feed more than 300,000 people, more than twice its own population.

Keeping the city well supplied was the responsibility of a special committee which was under orders to report to the doge every morning how large a reserve there was in the city's two large grain warehouses, the one at the Rialto, the other near San Marco, next to the Mint. If supplies were low or bad harvests in prospect, the Grain Office guaranteed relatively high prices to merchants who contracted to bring grain from specified areas within a specified time. These importers were not required to sell to the government; they could sell in Venice to private parties on the open market where the price was allowed to fluctuate according to supply and demand except that there was a limit on how much the price could be raised in one day. When it went intolerably high, the officials brought it down by selling the grain they had stored, even if it meant taking a loss. All wheat entering the city was carefully registered, even that which wealthy landowners collected from their mainland estates and brought to their palaces in Venice for their own use. This amounted to about 30 percent of the total in 1595. Another 22 percent of imports was bought on the marketplace by householders who mixed their own dough and sent it to bakers (*fornai*) for baking. The rest of what merchants imported, nearly half the total imports, went to bakers who both mixed and baked (*pistori*). The Grain Office controlled these bakers very closely, allocating them supplies and fixing both their prices and the size of the loaves. The price per loaf was kept constant for long periods but, after bad harvests, the loaves were smaller.

For centuries Venice was able to shift her purchases out of high-priced areas into those where prices were lower, but cheap areas became harder and harder to find. Expanding population was pressing on food supplies in many parts of the Mediterranean. When the population of Constantinople had grown to about 700,000 in 1580, it absorbed all the surpluses from the Roumanian and Russian ports on the Black Sea which had once helped supply Italy. Moreover, when Ottoman armies were waging war on the Danube or against the Persians in Armenia, as they were during most of the late decades of the sixteenth century, the grain supplies of the Black Sea went to the armies, and Constantinople turned for supplies to various Greek ports on which Venice had come to rely. Turkish prohibitions on exports could be got around, to be sure, more or less. Licenses could be bought from high officials at court; and local lords in Albania and Greece, accustomed to supplying Venetian buyers when the price was right, continued to do so, especially if the price was even better and there were Venetian galleys in the neighborhood which would discourage Turkish patrols from enforcing orders against exports. But Venice was thrown back increasingly on the production of her own territories in northern Italy. Wheat prices kept rising even more than prices generally. At the end of the sixteenth century, they shot up so that in 1590-99 they averaged twice what they had averaged a decade earlier. In 1590-91, years of extraordinary scarcity in the Mediterranean, the price was three times what it had been in 1580.

A swing of capital investment into agriculture was a rational answer to this economic situation as well as a patriotic response to national needs. Venetians of wealth had for centuries been buying estates on the mainland, and this movement became accentuated in the last quarter of the sixteenth century. It has often been characterized negatively as a "flight from the sea," but it can equally well be characterized positively as the intelligent entrepreneurial response to the needs and opportunities of those decades. Earlier Venetians had bought land mainly to add a more solid element to a fortune made in trade, or in order to have the prestige that went with landed possessions, or the delights of a handsome villa and country life. With wheat prices soaring, many now turned to agricultural improvement as a way also of building up a fortune.

An eloquent champion of such investments was Alvise (i.e., Luigi) Corner, who is famous mainly for being able to publish proudly at 95 a fourth revised edition of a little treatise on long life which he had written at 83. He then advocated extreme sobriety but confessed that, in his youth as a law student, he had been guilty of extremes of another kind. He was not born one of the wealthy Corner nobles, in fact, he never obtained official recognition of his claim to be descended from a doge, but he inherited from an uncle some pieces of real estate. Devoting himself to agriculture, he ditched and drained until his farm lands were so productive that he could boast of having made his fortune that way and could spend generously, turning his house in Padua into a showpiece by his selection and encouragement of first-class architects. In addition to his treatise *On Old Age*, or *A Sober Life*, and one on architecture, he wrote several on the preservation of the lagoons and land reclamation.

Alvise Corner estimated that one-fourth to one-third of the Padovano, Trevisana, and Friuli was uncultivated land, of which three-fourths could be made fertile by irrigation and, above all, by proper drainage. He urged its cultivation in order to relieve Venice of dependence on foreign countries for wheat and suggested that the government itself undertake large reclamation projects. Private enterprise was hobbled, he said, by the multitude of property rights that had to be reconciled in draining a large swamp—including the rights of monasteries, local communes, trustees of various estates, and the owners of mills that backed up the waters. The broad scheme which he suggested was never carried out, but a Reclamation Commission (the *Provveditori dei Beni Inculti*) was appointed in 1556. It undertook itself a few drainage projects and was useful in encouraging and regulating private enterprise. Property owners formed consortia to distribute among themselves the expenses and benefits. Even when the Commission backed their taking of land by eminent domain, theirs was slow work—clearing out superfluous mill ponds, tapping river dikes occasionally to quicken the flow of drainage ditches, and even building canal-bridges when that was made necessary by a diked-in river that flowed above the level of the land to be drained. This, said Corner was true alchemy, turning wasteland into fertile fields. It made the Venetian domains very nearly self-sufficient in the seventeenth century and reduced the extent to which the wealth of the Serenissima depended on the sea.

THE OCEANIC
CHALLENGE · IV

The Expansion of Manufactures

The general economic growth of the sixteenth century affected Venice most strikingly by expanding the markets for her manufactures. Her traditional chemical industries such as glassmaking benefited, new industries such as printing took root, and for the first time Venice became one of the leading centers in what was then the biggest branch of Europe's industries, the making of woolen cloth.

OLD INDUSTRIES AND NEW Traditionally and still in the fifteenth century, Venice was primarily a center for the distribution rather than the making of woolens. The wars in Italy at the beginning of the sixteenth century changed the situation. Not only were other leading Italian cities sacked in the 1520's, but marches and countermarches disrupted trade and sent craftsmen looking for a peaceful refuge. Many found such a refuge in Venice, which was never entered by a foreign army and was better supplied with food than most cities thanks to its waterways and its sea power. In Florence and the cities of Lombardy, the output of woolen cloth fell. In Venice it skyrocketed from less than 2,000 in 1516, when a series of figures begins, to more than 20,000 cloths a year after 1565. Tariffs and navigation laws concerning the import of raw wool were eased in order, the laws said, that there be work for the poor people who depended on the industry for livelihood. Expanding Spanish production of wool made Spain rather than England the main source of supply.

FIGURE 30   *Glass Blowers and Their Furnace. Woodcut in Agricola, De Re Metallica, 1556.*

Glassmaking was included with mining and metallurgy in a treatise written by a German physician, Giorgius Agricola. Its products then, as centuries earlier, included not only the flasks and goblets pictured above, but also trees, ships, and animals. Agricola said he had seen all these made in glass "when some time ago I spent two whole years in Venice."

A—Blow-pipe.   B—Little window.   C—Marble.   D—Forceps.   E—Moulds by means of which the shapes are produced.

The boom in the woolen industry was the biggest factor in Venice's industrial growth during the sixteenth century, and the largest single element in the expansion of the population, but it was by no means the only element. During the same period, the silk industry at least tripled the number it employed and ranked second to woolens; at the end of the century, there were more silk weavers than shipwrights or caulkers in Venice. The various chemical industries, such as soapmaking, although not as important relatively within Venice as they had once been, were thriving more than ever. Venetian glassmakers were at the peak of their fame and multiplied their specialities (see Figure 30). Hourglasses accurately blown at Venice were sold by ship chandlers all over Europe. Mirrors gained enormously in popularity when made of crystal-clear glass, such as the Venetians had developed while imitating rock crystal in order to make spectacles. Mirror makers multiplied to such an extent that they formed a separate guild in 1564. Window glass became so common that a laudatory description of Venice boasted that every parish had its glazier. Venetian craftsmen had a widespread reputation in innumerable kinds of artistic work: in lacemaking, which made Burano almost as populous as the nearby glass center, Murano; in furniture: in leather work; in jewelry; and in many other specialities.

Among new industries, printing deserves special attention. The manufacture of standardized movable types was the key invention by which Johann Gutenberg started this new industry in the Rhineland about 1450. Within a couple of decades, two craftsmen who were experts in the crucial art of cutting the punches or dies by which to make the molds in which the type was cast — Nicolas Jensen and John of Speyer — had brought their tools and their skill to Venice. In his first publication John of Speyer took four months to print only 100 copies of Cicero's letters. Even that slow pace was strikingly faster than the hand-copying by which "book-sellers" had previously supplied their customers, and as a second edition, John turned out in the same length of time 600 copies. Venice was a good place to print books, not only because it contained a reading public but because its commercial connections made it easy to find buyers by shipping far afield, as far as to Portugal or to Poland. Although paper was not manufactured in Venice itself, it was made in excellent quality in such Italian cities as Fabriano which had been accustomed to market through Venice. Skilled laborers were available to be recruited into the new, rapidly growing industry. The government was generous in granting to printers patents or copyrights, although neither patents nor copyrights were really enforceable at Venice or anywhere else in those centuries. These advantages made Venice the leading center of the printing industry. Out of a total of 1,821 publications known to have been issued in the years 1495–97 from all presses existing, 447 were printed at Venice, whereas Paris, then next in importance, printed only 181. In the early sixteenth century, wars disrupted activity in many other Italian centers, but Venetian production continued to grow. In its second half, publishing in Rome was considered three times as expensive as publishing in Venice, and Venice's 113 printer-publishers turned out three and a half times as many books as Milan, Florence, and Rome combined.

Although the volume of output increased during the sixteenth century, Venetian printers produced their finest products at its beginning, when they were still competing for customers with the producers of beautifully handwritten and hand-illustrated codices and were selling to humanist scholars and their patrons. The most famous of these printers was a humanist himself, Aldus Manutius. While a tutor in a noble family on the mainland, he conceived in the 1480's the project of printing the Greek classics. They were then enormously admired but little known, for almost nothing had been printed in that language. He selected Venice as the location for his enterprise, not only because it was already the leading center of printing, but also because of the many Greek scholars he could recruit there to prepare copy and read proof, and because of the collection of Greek manuscripts in the library that had been bequeathed to the Serenissima by Cardinal Bessarion. Pietro Bembo, who was appointed librarian of that collection, was a friend of Aldus and encouraged him. Also, Aldus knew he could find at Venice craftsmen able to cut the punches for the Greek type which he himself designed, modeling the letters on the handwriting of a distinguished Greek scholar whom he employed to prepare manuscripts for the typesetters. As colophon, he adopted an emblem appropriate at Venice, a dolphin and an anchor, maritime symbols of speed and reliability (see picture on Chronological Chart).

Aldus made a major innovation also in the publication of books in Latin or Italian. He designed a new kind of type resembling handwriting and called *italic*. Since a big page of that kind of type was hard to read, he began to print small volumes a half or a quarter the size previously in use (called *octavos* because the paper was folded into eight printing surfaces). The octavo size and the closeness of the letters in italic type enabled Aldus to compress into a book which would fit one's pocket works that had previously been available only in large quarto or folio volumes, for example, the Virgil of 1501, his first octavo publication. This cut the cost of such a book to about one-eighth of what it had been, and opened up a large new market, especially among students. Venice issued Aldus a patent on his new kind of type, but it was immediately imitated elsewhere.

Venetian publishing covered every field and was preeminent in many fields, notably in the printing of music. Books were printed in Hebrew as well as Greek characters. They were illustrated at first by woodcuts, later by copper engravings. As books became cheaper and light literature more important, Venice as a publishing center attracted men who lived by writing what would sell. Their leader, "the first author to shake himself loose from the courts to enjoy the free life of Venice was Pietro Aretino" (Grendler), a scandalously witty blackmailer known as the "Scourge of Princes" because they feared his libels. He and imitators kept the presses supplied with snappy scurrilous plays and dialogues, while less talented hacks compiled many kinds of handbooks.

CRAFTSMEN AND CAPITALISTS   Neither in the new industries such as printing nor in the old ones such as textile manufacturing was the growth of output accompanied by any notable development of industrial capitalism. Of course, Venice had long been capitalistic in the sense of being ruled by men who accumulated wealth by investing capital and who shaped Venice's institutions and policies so that their way of making a living could succeed. But they were commercial capitalists, investing in merchandise and hiring labor for its transport and marketing. True, they readily invested in manufacturing also in the sense of loaning money or forming partnerships of some kind with makers of cloth, or soap, or glassware. Descriptions of the wealth of leading nobles often mention their possession of a soap works or a glass factory. In one case, a noble was fined because he used the wrong kind of wood in firing his kiln for making brick or tile. His only excuse was that he had been ill and left his brother in charge. But that was in the fourteenth century, and it was probably exceptional even then that a Venetian noble should be that attentive to industrial processes. Venetian ambassadors at Florence about 1500 described with amazement the extent to which the leading gentlemen of Florence supervised their own cloth-making enterprises. The Venetian nobles financed industrial enterprises, to be sure, as well as commercial enterprises, but they did not undertake a real entrepreneurial role in manufacturing as they did, for example, in shipping raisins from Zante to England, or in financing and commanding the voyages of merchant galleys.

Consequently, it is not surprising to find that while government regulations were entirely favorable to commercial capitalism, they often restricted a capitalist's freedom of operation in manufacturing enterprises. This was manifest particularly clearly in the sixteenth century in the silk industry. Ownership of a loom could not be had simply by possessing the capital necessary to buy it. Ownership of looms was forbidden, except to those who knew how to use them "with their own hands." This rule was designed to create a neat division into two groups: merchants who gave orders for silk cloth, and the craftsmen who formed the guild of silk weavers. When the silk merchants nevertheless began to get control of the industrial process by hiring loom-owning masters for yearly salaries, the guild forbade it and gained the government's approval for their rule by arguing that the practice would kill the industry, for no silk weaver would be attracted to move to Venice, they said, if the best he could look forward to was "to be a laborer in another man's house (esser lavorante in casa de altri)." It was established that all master weavers should be paid so much per yard.

Another capitalistic trend which developed within the silk weaver's craft was also suppressed. A few rich masters who operated as many as 30 looms were able to contract for large quantities while accepting deferred payments. They secured all the orders from the merchants and subcontracted at 16 to 20 soldi a yard cloth for which they were paid 30 to 32 soldi. Laws forbidding any master to operate more than 6 looms had been enacted earlier but then repealed by a vote of the Senate. A later vote of the Senate reestablished the rule. In one of the three surviving volumes of the silk guild's statutes (all three bound in silk), the parchment page devoted to recording the reestablishment of that limit of 6 is illuminated triumphantly in many colors.

How much the growth of the industry was really due to the attraction to Venice of silk weavers because of the independent status offered to them in that city and how much it was due to other conditions, such as security, cannot be demonstrated, but their number went from 500 in 1493 to 1,200 in 1554 and kept on growing. They were so numerous, they asserted in 1554, that the merchants did not keep all of them fully employed and they won the right to make cloth on their own, in advance of any order from merchants, although they could use no more than two looms for that purpose.

In the woolen industry, in contrast, the guild which made nearly all the rules, subject to governmental approval, was an employers association (the *Camera del Purgo*) which had been formed centuries earlier. The many processes involved in turning wool into cloth, processes involving a larger number of specialized crafts than the making of silks, were coordinated by merchant employers. After 1539, the men engaged by these merchant-clothiers were permitted to have guilds of their own, however, when the duty of furnishing oarsmen for wartime fleets was placed on the guilds, as will be explained below. The spinning women remained unorganized, and they were so numerous in surrounding villages that special rules were made to enable them to pass customs barriers when they came to Venice to get wool and bring back thread. But the men were in four guilds: (1) the wool combers who worked in the houses of the merchant employers, (2) the weavers who worked in their own homes, (3) the teaselers who raised a nap on cloth after it had been fulled at Treviso, and (4) the shearmen or finishers who made the nap smooth. To these might be added (5) the dyers, although they sometimes worked for other employers also.

All of these groups obtained some benefits from having their own guild. They may have felt that the benefits hardly balanced the obligation of supplying oarsmen, but they would have had that burden anyhow. It might have been administered by the employers' guild without giving workers any organization of their own. Besides religious and social benefits, a guild gave its members representatives who could petition and argue before the magistrates and governing councils on behalf of their interests. Even if the voice of their employers was more likely to be listened to, it was of some advantage for Venetian wool workers to have any voice at all, in contrast to those of Florence, called *ciompi*, who were denied any organization of their own.

The possibility that craftsmen-employees could apply economic pressure is shown by a strike of the shearmen in 1556. A couple of years earlier the shearmen (*cimadori*) had begun asking for a higher price for each piece of cloth finished, alleging as justification both a rise in the price of their tools and in the general cost of living and also that the merchants were having cloths made longer. At first they used the petitioning procedure open to all Venetian guilds, but their petitions were sent from one body to another until, tired of the "run around," the shearmen met illegally in an unusual place and took together a horrible and blasphemous oath, at least it was so described by the merchants, forcing all to swear on a crucifix erected in their midst that they would take no cloths for finishing except at new prices fixed by the guild. Thinking that such "daring and cruel action" might spark an uprising of all woolen workers, the merchant employers appealed to the Council of Ten. Its Capi admonished the shearmen. But that did not get the cloth sheared.

The strike was called at a strategic moment, as the alarmed merchants explained to the authorities. The industry was booming, on the way to producing that year a record 16,000 cloths, 3,500 more than the year before. Galleys had been auctioned to carry many cloths to market in Syria, but 3,000 were waiting to be sheared. Since that was the last stage of production, the strike was tying up many half-finished cloths which would otherwise be on their way to market overseas. The unknown leaders of the shearmen had done such a good job of organizing that orders and threats from the Council of Ten did not put men back to work. When merchant-employers called on them to come and get cloth to finish, some answered that they were waiting to see what others did, some asked for the higher prices, and some just said that they had other things to do. The clothiers petitioned the government for permission to bring in foreign workmen to finish their cloth, but when the government delayed by referring that to a commission, they yielded somewhat. Higher rates were set for the longer cloths, and a joint committee, four from the employers and four from the shearmen, was established to set down a general schedule of piece-work rates.

When such things could happen, it is not surprising that merchants objected to the organization of new guilds. The ruling nobles had divided views, however, for they were generally more interested in international trade and shipping or simply in governing. This division is shown by the reaction to a petition from candlemakers (see Figure 31) asking that they be permitted to form their own guild. The merchants who had candles manufactured for sale belonged to the grocers' guild (*spezieri*). Being composed mainly of merchants that guild did not regulate their processing of what they sold. The petition of the candlemakers was referred to the five-man Board of Trade. Two of its members favored formation of the new guild. They argued that it would help in obtaining galeotti. Moreover, they appealed to the general principle that every occupational group should have their own rules, own officials, and own saint, "their protector under whose banner particularly they can worship, as does every other guild (scuola)." But the majority opposed a new guild, siding with

a

b

c

FIGURE 31 *Artisans at Work. Water-colored sketches by Grevembroech (courtesy of Museo Correr, Venice).*

(a) Refining wax for manufacture into candles; (b) Sugar refining: much imported sugar was further refined by boiling and straining and then crystallized into sugar loaves and candies; (c) Members of the physicians' guild were forbidden to leave the city during a plague. For protection from contagious exhalations, when visiting the sick, they wore a smooth linen gown, a waxed mask over the face, a hat over the hair, spectacles over the eyes, and—to protect the nose—a beak containing drugs chosen as antidotes against both infections and the smells of death.

the merchants who argued that the industry of whitening wax and forming it into candles had grown at Venice because they were free to employ men as they wished, on day wages or piece work, and in the places they wished, and that if the workers organized, they would impose on the merchants rules that would raise costs so that the industry would go to the competing centers, Ragusa, Ancona, and Florence. Moreover, they said that those candlemakers who headed their own establishments belonged to the grocers' guild, and when oarsmen were necessary, they could come from that guild. On these grounds merchant capitalists were left free to organize the process of candle-making as they wished.

Merchants had freedom of entrepreneurial action in organizing production in a number of other industries. Printing and publishing furnishes an interesting example. The first printing shops were set up, as we have seen, by craftsmen who understood the technique which Gutenberg had introduced and had the skill to cut punches by which handsome type could be made. Nicolas Jensen had been an apprentice in the Paris mint before he went to Mainz to learn the secrets of printing. Both he and John of Speyer were admired for the handsome type which came from the punches which they cut. Those punches were the most essential element in their capital equipment. Presses were not in themselves either new or expensive. Even when supplemented with a font or two of type made from the punches, the equipment of a printer represented a capital investment hardly larger than the cost of paper for one book. But capital was needed to pay for the workmen and for paper and ink, so as to build up a large stock of books on hand or in transit to the many centers which had to be reached if a large edition was to be sold. Almost as soon as his printing was well under way, Nicolas Jensen formed partnerships which supplied capital and aided his marketing. Later, entrepreneurs did not begin as craftsmen, but as men of means who became booksellers and publishers. They decided what to publish. Then they contracted with craftsmen to cut punches, cast and set type, and operate presses. They supplied the paper and relatively prompt pay while they sought out markets.

An outstanding example of this type of businessman was the father-in-law of Aldus, who was like Aldus an immigrant from mainland Italy, Andrea Torresano. He opened a book store, acquired the type punches of Nicolas Jensen, and then showed a willingness to share entrepreneurial initiative by making Aldus his chief editor. The program of publications, which was both profitable and a real contribution to civilization, came from Aldus. For its execution, Andrea and Aldus organized a central workshop where over thirty persons were brought together under their direction. Besides the usual compositors and pressmen and their apprentices, Andrea and Aldus hired various specialists, such as the artist who cut the dies for Aldus's new italic type and to whom he gave credit on the title page of the book in which it was first used. Specialists of another kind were the copyreaders, among whom is sometimes counted the most famous European scholar of that age, Erasmus, to whom we owe a caustic description of the establishment.

Andrea was the boss, and even Aldus might be considered one of Andrea's workmen, so wrote Erasmus, who resented being called a former proofreader of the Aldine firm, which he had visited while still a young man. Later in life, he quarreled with many who had been his friends there and satirized them in an acid comic skit. He had read proof, Erasmus said, only to make author's corrections; there was a hired proofreader to correct printers' errors. But he minimized the extent to which he owed his knowledge of Greek to the Greek scholars Aldus had collected by saying that he had been kept too busy. "We hardly had time, as they say, to scratch our ears. Aldus often declared that he wondered how I could write such a quantity offhand in the midst of so much noise and bustle." Aldus's drive, putting to work everyone he could, was manifest in the inscription placed, almost like a help-wanted ad, at the doorway. It read:

> Whoever you are, Aldus earnestly begs you to state your business in the fewest possible words and begone, unless, like Hercules to weary Atlas, you would lend a helping hand. There will always be enough work for you and all who come this way.

While handling the intellectual head of the enterprise, Aldus, with relative respect, Erasmus's skit flayed its business leader, Andrea Torresano, for stinginess. It is indicative of the way the tradition of the family workshop survived even in as big an establishment as the Aldine press, with its many gradations of employees, that they were all fed by "the master," Andrea. Erasmus claimed that Andrea added to his profits by watering their wine and feeding them on next to nothing. Perhaps Erasmus was venting a finicky scholar's resentment at a businessman's efforts to keep down expenses, as well as disgust with the peculiarities and frugalities of the Venetian cuisine. He was a northerner who liked plenty of meat and had no use for "a morsel of shellfish caught in the sewer." If excessively parsimonious, Andrea Torresano was a successful businessman. After Aldus's death he kept the firm going and passed on a flourishing business to Aldus's children.

In organizing the printing of their books in one central establishment, the Aldine firm was not typical. Most publishers gave out contracts to printers who headed small shops with two or three presses. These master printers could easily turn into publishers themselves in a small way and market their product through book stores and fairs. Heading a shop with perhaps as many as ten to fifteen persons — compositors, pressmen, and proofreaders; journeymen, apprentices, and plain laborers — such master printers belonged to the class which I have called craftsmen-managers and which had always been relatively important in Venice. In the same class of course fell the silk weavers who had as many as six looms, or the glassmaker with his own furnace.

With its thirty employees and attached scholars, the Aldine printing and publishing establishment was quite possibly the largest private industrial establishment in Venice in terms of the number of men at one center under one management. The building of a palace or of a big ship might bring more workmen together at one place, but only for a short time, not long enough to develop regular bureaucratic controls. Such enterprises as a tanning yard or a sugar refinery and candy manufactory (Figure 31) may have occupied more space, but hardly more men.

Bigger in every way, of course, were the Arsenal (Figure 32 and 36) and the adjoining rope factory called the Tana, and also Venice's Mint. These were operated by the government; their managers were not spurred by the profit motive, but these communal enterprises developed controls, nevertheless, to increase their efficiency. The new Mint built in 1540 excited admiration by the orderly way in which it provided for the variety of different craftsmen employed and for a convenient, well-controlled movement of the precious material from one workman to another, from one inspector to another. Accurate accounting was of course most important at this great depository of bullion and coin, and its accountants calculated the costs and the gains to the government in minting each kind of coin. They itemized costs of each kind of labor and materials, including such small items as charcoal, but did not allow for overhead. At the Tana, more and more regulations and inspectors were imposed in the efforts to standardize the products. For example, hemp from Bologna was all spun in one room; hemp of a somewhat inferior grade, produced at a newly developed source of supply within Venice's only domains west of Padua, in another. The spinners' bobbins were marked so that inspectors could identify any spinner whose thread was not found to be of the specified weight. The best cables were marked with a white label; inferior grades had black, green, and yellow labels. At the Arsenal, where thousands were employed in Venice's biggest industrial establishment, craft standards were substantially supplemented by managerial arrangements. The Arsenal developed a kind of assembly line and some standardization of interchangeable parts, as will be explained in Chapter 25 in describing the war fleets and their administration.

THE ROLE OF   Guild regulation of techniques was scanty in many industries, and in only
THE GUILDS   a few branches of manufacturing were guilds as influential in determining
industrial organization as in the silk industry. But guilds or fraternities of some kind were important in the lives of nearly all Venetians of the middle and lower classes. In addition to the Scuole Grandi dominated by civil servants of the cittadini class, there were many other religious fraternities which were not based on occupational cohesion. Thus, before there was any printers' guild, John of Speyer and Nicolas Jensen belonged to the Scuola di San Girolamo. Its members included painters, stonecutters, glass blowers, and engravers.

Membership in a guild was made practically obligatory for all craftsmen and shopkeepers soon after 1539 when guilds were called on to furnish conscripts for the galleys. In building up the naval reserve, which will be described in Chapter 25, the government allotted to each occupational guild and to the Scuole Grandi quotas of oarsmen. The size of the quotas depended generally on the number of their able-bodied members, but the Scuole Grandi and the clothiers had quotas arranged on the basis of their wealth. When men were called for, most guilds did not in practice send their own members, but hired substitutes. In the course of time this practice became so universal that the government required the guilds to build up financial reserves for exactly that purpose and then took supervision of payments into these reserves so that the "levy of galeotti" became merely a form of taxation (see Chapters 25 and 28). To the other functions of the guilds there was thus gradually added a role in tax collecting, a role which gave Venice's governing councils added interest in increasing guild membership.

Making guild membership more universal increased the number of guilds. They came to total about one hundred, not counting the "traghetti" of the boatmen or any purely religious fraternities, such as the Scuole Grandi. About

FIGURE 32   *The Gateway of the Arsenal (Photo Ferruzzi).*

The scene suggests a factory gate at closing time, but the thousands of workers pouring from the Arsenal were not "factory hands." They differed in spirit and in discipline, for they were master craftsmen and naval reservists.

The bundles being carried contained the shavings which master carpenters could, by traditional right, take home for firewood, but they explain also the disappearance of excessive amounts of good wood, of spikes, and even of cordage.

half of the hundred were composed of various kinds of retailers, such as poultry dealers, or independent retail handicraftsmen, such as the bakers. Some, like the mercers, embraced shopkeepers who sold a large variety of merchandise, although a master who sold too large a range of wares had to join an additional guild. Some guilds tried to restrict their membership by barring foreigners, by requiring long apprenticeships, or even by admitting only the sons of masters; but the merchant-princes ruling Venice struck down any such guild rules unless they believed them helpful to the city's power. All guilds tried to collect dues from as many as possible of the city's artisans, so as to have more funds for their banquets, their accident funds or dowries, and for their payments for galeotti. Also, each guild tried to get as much work as possible for its members. For these reasons, they were constantly engaged in jurisdictional disputes. In spite of their rules, they had difficulty really enforcing membership on all who practiced their craft or trade.

The amount of democracy and of internal solidarity differed greatly from guild to guild. Of the hundred guilds, three quarters had less than 250 members, even counting members who were not masters; only two or three numbered more than a thousand. When guild organization was imposed by the government in order to have an instrument of regulation and taxation, as in the formation of the Guild of Printers and Booksellers in 1549, the membership was likely to be uninterested. There was trouble getting a quorum at the annual assembly and the government felt it necessary to impose elaborate rules to prevent financial mismanagement by guild officials. A relatively small clique ran the guild affairs and stayed in power by nominating successors to office through nominating committees which reflected on a much reduced scale the method used in choosing the doge of the Republic. In others, there was much participatory democracy. Their statute-books (*mariegole*) record large attendance and close votes in guild assemblies that made new rules. These rules were always subject to the approval of the Justices or other appropriate government officials, but the initiative regarding the guild's internal affairs usually came from the guild's officers. General participation was certainly large in the guild of the silk weavers, and far from sheeplike. In 1543, the taking of arms to the guild assembly was expressly forbidden because there had occurred tumults and scandal with the shedding of blood. Attendance at the assembly was generally two or three hundred. The peak attendance recorded was in 1561 at a meeting concerned with the guild's provision of social security or poor relief. The membership voted 578 to 42 in favor of increasing charitable payments to poor girls within the guild and of setting up at the same time more safeguards on the way in which the money was dispensed.

Economic historians of the liberal school generally picture guilds as enemies of industrial progress, preventing improvements, particularly labor-saving innovations such as machines, or holding up wages and restricting the labor supply when market conditions made lower wages and expansion of the labor force necessary. The Venetian guilds showed some tendency to act in these ways, but in the fifteenth and sixteenth centuries, they hampered economic growth less than they helped it. They did not prevent the introduction of machines and other new inventions. On the contrary, the government was liberal in granting to self-styled inventors privileges like those given the early printers. Indeed, in 1474, it decreed patents of ten-years validity available to all who registered a new device. In the sixteenth century, a kind of a gig mill was employed by clothiers to raise the nap on cloths after the fulling. When the guild of the workers affected by it, the teaselers, asked that the use of the machine be forbidden, the dispute went to the Senate which did not forbid the use of the machine but merely required that cloth be marked in some way so as to distinguish cloth teaseled by hand from that teaseled by machine. Moreover, innovations which raised the quality of the product, thereby in a sense creating a new product, were not opposed by either guild regulations or the guild spirit. As much through the attitude they fostered as through legislation, guilds channeled competition into improvement of quality rather than reduction of costs. Much of Venice's industrial growth in the sixteenth century was in producing wares of high quality, from soap to glass, from silks to books. Even in what one might call standard products, in contrast to works of high artistic merit, efficiency in manufacturing in this period generally depended not on the planning of the process of production by a capable manager, but on the skill in the hands and eyes of the workmen. To the extent that guilds attracted and nurtured craftsmen by making them feel that they were their own masters and not "laborers in another man's house," they contributed to Venice's development during the sixteenth century into "the foremost industrial city in Italy" (Braudel).

THE OCEANIC CHALLENGE · V

Finance and Income from Power

While manufacturing within the lagoon owed much of its boom to security from war's alarms, the wealth of the Venetian upper classes depended to an even greater extent and more directly on the Republic's political successes. Governing the domains of the Serenissima was for a significant number of Venetians their way of making a living.

GOVERNMENT JOBS Governmental revenue increased by more than 50 percent early in the fifteenth century with the conquest of the mainland state, as explained in Chapter 16. It was about 1,000,000 ducats a year in the late fifteenth century and then grew again to reach about 2,000,000 ducats before 1570. Much came from indirect taxes levied in Venice and from the salt of Cyprus, as well as from the subject cities of the mainland. Higher figures were recorded after 1580 but are less significant because more affected by the general change in price level following the influx of American gold and silver.

Collecting this money, keeping track of it, drawing salaries from it and "gratuities" in addition—was one of the main occupations of a growing number of those Venetians whom one might call, anachronistically, the "white-collar class." A superior status was increasingly asserted by those who did not dirty their hands actually handling things, and especially by the citizens-by-birth whose families had a monopoly of a layer of offices beneath those of the nobles. As in the Renaissance monarchies, larger revenues went mainly into armies and navies, but some went to pay the salaries of clerks, accountants, notaries, lawyers, and secretaries.

The nobility benefitted even more from the extension of Venetian dominions and the accompanying increase in government revenue. Nobles were more numerous than citizens-by-birth. When the city's population was at its peak of nearly 190,000 souls before the plague of 1575, noblemen over twenty-one numbered around 2,500–3,000. The number of citizens was about 4,000 male adults. but that probably included as many naturalized traders as "citizens-by-birth." The positions held by the nobility paid higher salaries, between 100 and 500 ducats a year to a podesta or castellan, compared to 50 to 200 ducats to a chief secretary or accountant (not counting in either case the collection of fines or gratuities).

Many of the positions for which the nobles received substantial salaries were in subject cities, but good pay was also received within Venice itself. Every member of each of the three superior courts, the Quarantie, received more than 100 ducats a year. Of course, any noble who held a position such as podesta was expected to live up to it. Some officials, like the doge who, with 4,800 ducats a year in 1582, was the highest paid, were fined if they did not spend enough of their salary. The fine of the doge was posthumous, paid by his heirs. Distinguished ambassadorships, then as now, were an occasion for more expense than could be covered by salaries or expense accounts. Men of known wealth who were elected ambassadors often went to great lengths to avoid having to serve and to spend as would be expected of them if they were not to be disgraced, especially if they thought the mission likely to be difficult and to yield little honor or influence. But for most nobles, living up to a high office meant living as they wished to live. The more than 200,000 ducats paid out in salaries annually to 700–1,000 nobles was a substantial contribution by taxpayers to the income of that class.

Church benefices supplied another kind of income that depended on political influence. For example, the bishopric of Padua about 1535 provided 5,000 ducats a year to Francesco, son of Alvise Pisani, the enterprising banker whose operations will be described shortly. A corollary of Venice's possession of a mainland dominion was the naming of Venetian nobles to many bishoprics, canonates, and other church offices which yielded lush returns.

PUBLIC FINANCE   Interest payments on the government's debt formed another substantial element in the income of the upper classes. The funded debt had originated in forced loans, as explained in Chapter 11. Although less painful for the rich than paying direct taxes on income, forced levies for the Monte Vecchio had become a kind of capital levy during the War of Chioggia and again when their price fell precipitously also near the end of the Visconti-Sforza wars (see Chapter 16). The levy of direct taxes, which was made possible by the crisis of 1453, was shortly thereafter reduced to a minimum by instituting a new series of government bonds, the *Monte Nuovo*. Returns from the income tax were assigned to pay the interest on the Monte Nuovo, which mushroomed so that by 1509 its interest payments totaled 150,000 ducats annually, a significant item in the income of many Venetians.

The defeat of the Venetian armies at Agnadello in 1509 triggered a catastrophe for Venetian bondholders comparable to the losses that had resulted from the War of Chioggia and the Visconti-Sforza wars. Interest on both Monte Nuovo and Monte Vecchio were suspended and their prices plummeted. Girolamo Priuli, whose comments on mercenaries and on the spice trade we have noted, was personally very hard hit by the crisis of 1509 because he had just opened a bank and because he had just bought Monte Nuovo at 102. When the price suddenly fell to 40 he lamented bitterly the folly of such investments. They "are based on air," he wrote in his diary, "and are mere books, namely, paper and ink."

Before these Italian wars were over in 1529, the Venetian government had issued two new series backed by new promises, the *Monte Novissimo* and the *Monte di Sussidio*. It also resorted to many financial devices for short-term borrowing, some already described in Chapter 18. At one time or another in those years, Monte Vecchio sold at 3, Monte Nuovo as low as 10, and Monte Novissimo at 25.

The losses thus suffered were not made good entirely; many nobles were left impoverished. But the handling of the debt during the rest of the century was such that it was a source of sustenance rather than a burden for the Venetian upper class. No effort was made to bring all the issues of government bonds back to par; that would have cost about half of the republic's total revenue and was never seriously considered. But as soon as Venice's political fortunes took a definite turn for the better, payments on the Monte Vecchio were resumed at the rate which had become usual, 1 percent a year. Instead of resuming interest payments of the Monte Nuovo, the government declared that no further interest would accrue but that the whole issue would be liquidated. Some were redeemed by being accepted at much above the market price in payment for lands confiscated from those who had sided with Venice's enemies during the war. The rest were paid off by annual installments which were supposed to complete the liquidation within 17 years, but which in fact dragged out over about 30 years. Meanwhile, the Monte Novissimo and the Monte di Sussidio were refunded by selling new bonds to get money with which to pay off the old, for very soon after the cession of hostilities, interest rates fell from 8 or 10 percent to 5 or 6 percent. On the resulting bonds outstanding, coupons representing 5 percent of the par value were paid regularly after 1530. (They were not really coupons, physically speaking; like the "bonds," they were credit entries on the books of the Loan Office.) Adding together all the payments the Republic was making on its long-term debts about 1550 gives a total of 300,000 ducats a year. In 1560, after the Monte Nuovo had been retired, it was about 200,000 ducats. Between 1540 and 1570, the well-to-do in Venice received more in payments on the Republic's long-term debts than they paid in direct taxes, for income taxes were still thought of as essentially war taxes and were lightly levied in peacetime. At the beginning of the sixteenth century, direct taxes on Venetians yielded about one fourth of the government's income. At the end of the century, they yielded only one tenth, for they had not increased, whereas the income from indirect taxes and from the mainland cities had about doubled the total revenue.

The general trend towards reduction in the debt was briefly interrupted by the financing of the War of Cyprus, 1570-73, but was dramatically reaffirmed soon afterwards. The war occasioned a debt of about 6,000,000 ducats, much of which was raised not by forced loans but by voluntary "deposits in the Mint." Perpetual annuities paid on the average 8 percent annually, life annuities paid

14 percent. Total interest payments, including those on the still outstanding Monti, totaled 800,000 ducats. To reduce this burden, it was voted in 1577 that the first claim on the yield of the income tax should be for 120,000 ducats a year to be devoted to liquidating these deposits, beginning first with those paying the highest interest, 14 percent, and always devoting the interest saved to paying off other deposits. The effect was quickly so impressive that the appropriation for liquidation was increased. A reorganization of accounting uncovered fraudulent claims, and the Mint was entirely "freed" of debt in 1584. Shortly thereafter, the Monte Novissimo and Monte di Sussidio were liquidated. Finally, it was the turn of the Monte Vecchio, but bondholders of that Monte were paid only what had been its average market price since 1520, namely 2½, except that holders of "virgin" bonds, which had never been sold but had been handed down from father to son ever since they had been originally subscribed to as a forced loan more than a hundred years earlier, received twice as much.

In the opening years of the seventeenth century, the Venetian Republic was entirely out of debt, except on current accounts. Charitable foundations lacked suitable securities in which to invest their funds. Their need of having such opportunities for investment was specified as the reason for reinstituting the long-term debt by accepting new deposits in the Mint at 4 percent.

While all this liquidation was going on, the rich in Venice were receiving many millions more from the government than they were paying in direct taxes. The highly solvent condition of the Venetian Republic gave them more money to spend or to invest.

The abolition of the public debt would in some circumstances have had a deflationary effect interfering with prosperity. The deflationary influence was all the greater because, when the Mint was "freed," the Council of Ten ordered that the half million ducats of interest thereby saved should be hoarded in separate coin chests in the Mint, in order that it be available for the next military emergency. And some such sum was in fact hoarded each year during the last decade or two of the sixteenth century. In 1600, Venice was reputed to have a reserve hoard in coin of 12 to 14 million ducats.

Rising prices, however, not usually associated with deflation, accompanied this hoarding, because it occurred during the decades when American silver was flooding into Europe. Whether this hoarding was a deliberate attempt to counteract the influx is doubtful.

The influx of silver facilitated the liquidation of the debt, for in mid-century Venice had abandoned the gold standard and shifted back to silver. Like the shift earlier from silver to gold, in 1300–1350, the change was gradual. As in the earlier case, it was a shift to the metal which was falling in value and it was therefore favorable to debtors (see Chapter 11). From about 1350 to 1520, the relative value of gold and silver had not changed much. It was about 11 to 1. The ducat continued to be minted with 3.5 grams of pure gold. Silver coins of many kinds to replace the old grosso had been issued with changing weights and purity and were the basis of the money of account used in all retail trade and in setting the wages of laborers, the lira di piccoli. Purchases, wages, and debts which were calculated and recorded in lire di piccoli could be paid either by using the small pennies (if the sum was not too large) or by using large silver coins which often took the name of the doge issuing them, such as *troni, mocenighi, marcelli*, or by using gold ducats. As the silver coins came to weigh less and less, partly through wear and partly through a policy of debasement, the ducat was given a higher and higher value in lire and soldi di piccoli. Its official value as legal tender was made 124 soldi in 1455 and in fact its market value stabilized at that figure for half a century.

From about 1455 to 1510 Venice had in effect one monetary scale into which both silver and gold coins fitted with fixed relations which were expressed by stating the value of coins in soldi di piccoli, both gold and silver. Government regulations called for the payment of tolls and taxes half in silver and half in gold, but it did not really matter which kind of coin was used so long as their legal values and their market values were the same. Because this situation lasted for a lifetime, Venetians became accustomed to saying "one ducat" when they meant any combination of coins equal in value to one ducat, that is, to 124 soldi.

During the difficult days of the War of the League of Cambrai, good coins of either gold or silver disappeared, and creditors who wanted prompt payment or merchants who had merchandise they were eager to sell took payment in whatever they could get, frequently accepting foreign coins at more than their legal-tender value. When good coins were to be had again, they were of silver rather than of gold, especially after mid-century, when American as well as German silver began reaching Venice. Since silver coins worth 124 soldi were legal tender for payment of one ducat, debts recorded in ducats were paid more in silver than in gold. In effect the name "ducat" ceased to refer to a coin and instead designated a unit of account. The gold coin which was still minted with 3.5 grams of gold acquired a new name, *zecchino* (from *zecca*, mint). To give the accounting unit called a ducat a material counterpart, the Mint began in 1562 issuing silver coins called "ducats" and stamped "124" to show their value in soldi di piccoli.

This change in the monetary system made paying off the public debt easier. If the older issues of government bonds had been paid in the same kind of coin which the government had, much earlier, collected, redemption would have cost approximately twice as much, for while the government was retiring the debt by paying out silver coins, the golden zecchino rose in value from 124 soldi in 1515 to 200 in 1593. The zecchino rose partly because silver was becoming less valuable compared to gold, the bimetallic ratio going from 10 to 1 to 13 to 1, and partly because the silver coins worth 124 soldi contained less silver. After the War of Cyprus, a silver ducat worth 124 soldi was minted, containing 28 grams of silver, whereas in 1515 coins worth 124 soldi had contained 36 grams.

GIRO-BANKS, PRIVATE AND PUBLIC   These changes in the coinage betokened bright opportunities and dark dangers for bankers. Basically, their opportunities arose, as explained in Chapter 11 when describing the origins of the Venetian type of bank—the transfer or giro-bank—from the convenience which merchants found in making payments by transfers on the bankers' books instead of by handling coin. This convenience was all the more appreciated the more the coinage was confusing or deteriorating. With thousands of depositors transferring credits among themselves, a banker would pay for purchases by credit on his books and thus enlarge his own commercial operations, trusting that his depositors would not ask for cash but would merely transfer credits to other depositors.

The advantages and the dangers of such a position were prominent in the career of Alvise Pisani. As early as in his twenties, he began operating in 1499 the bank founded by his father a couple of decades earlier. Suddenly the failure of the oldest of the four existing banks caused a run on all the others. Once confidence was shaken, merchants were not content to accept payments with transfers on the bankers' books; they wanted coins. If the banker had been using the cash, as Pisani had, to ship to England and to import wool or cloth, or if it was rumored that he had had much merchandise on a vessel recently lost, he was in danger of being caught short. Soon, Pisani's was the only large bank still open. There was a dense, wild crush of depositors around the booth in the little campo at Rialto where Alvise Pisani sat with his journal on the table before him, ready to write transfers and withdrawals. A contemporary described the scene: "Messer Alvise Pisani, wishing to write in the Journal as usual, there were so many wishing to draw money that the pen was snatched from his hand by those saying, 'Write for my account.' Seeing such fury, he put up the pen and said, 'Gentlemen, one and all of you will have what is yours.'" He sent word to his uncle (a member of the Council of Ten), and the Chiefs of the Ten came with a public crier to restore order and proclaim the formation of a 100,000 ducat guarantee fund. First on the list of guarantors were all the banker's relatives. "Then their friends assembled to announce themselves also as guarantors, and after their friends came, almost all the Rialto. When the foreigners saw this, to win good will (so runs Priuli's description) they all and of every country, Catalans, Spaniards, Marranos, Florentines, Pisans, Milanese, Lucchese, Sienese, Bolognese, Genoese and Romans and of every other people that is found on the Rialto made pledges. To see the gathering together of so many gentlemen who came to be the guarantors for the good and salvation of this bank, on which so largely rested the honor and reputation of Venice, this, in truth, was the finest thing seen for many a year."

In spite of Alvise Pisani's success that day in turning the psychology of the marketplace, his bank faced another run the following year. He then added further to his reputation by arriving dressed in scarlet, accompanied by a public crier who proclaimed from the steps of the Rialto bridge that all should come and take their money for he was liquidating. He did in fact then pay in full. Consequently, when he opened a new bank four years later in a period of easy money, he was able to get almost all the banking business into his hands. The wealth and high political connections of his family had saved him during the crunch of 1499, and they helped him extend his operations between 1504 and 1526. Marriages strengthened his connections among the richest and most powerful of the Venetian nobility, and one of his sons became a cardinal. Especially festive was the celebration of the marriage of his daughter to the son of Venice's richest man, Giorgio Corner, the brother of the Queen of Cyprus. Alvise became, as Marino Sanuto said, "a power in the land." During the ducal elections of 1521, he was mentioned as a possible candidate. In the contest of 1523, he was a prominent supporter of the candidate who was successful, Andrea Gritti, whose niece his son had recently married.

Alvise Pisani came in for the opprobrium frequently leveled at a banker-politician. After an especially gay party some young nobles scrawled under the portico at the Rialto insults to all the bankers who had their booths there. They were quickly rubbed off but Sanuto found out what they said. They twitted one banker about the courtesan he kept, another about being in the hands of Anselm, the rich Jew. Of Alvise Pisani they wrote: "You big traitor, under this doge you'll steal the Ducal Palace" ("Alvise Pisani rebelazzo, sotto sto doge tu vendera il palazzo"). But his good fortunes lasted until death, which overtook him in the honorific and responsible office of Commissioner, while he was serving with the Venetian-French army which was decimated by typhus while beseiging Naples in 1528.

Alvise Pisani lived before paper money had made it usual to finance wars by inflation of the currency. His significance for the history of banking is in the extent to which he enabled Venice to finance wars by inflation of bank credit. During the drainage of precious metals from Venice in the War of the League of Cambrai, Pisani's was almost the only bank. Transfers on his books became the means of payment accepted for all kinds of obligations, and he increased the volume of his deposits by making loans. Many loans were to the government in return for the assignment to him of taxes that would be collected later. Also, he paid bills of exchange which ambassadors were authorized to draw to cover their expenses. He made loans to politicians to enable them to bid for office. In all these ways and also by financing galley voyages, Alvise Pisani acquired such large liabilities to depositors that he might have had trouble meeting another crunch like that of 1499. But the condition of the coinage was such in the 1520's that he was able, as a matter of practice, to avoid demands for immediate payment in good coin. Good coins were too scarce. They were at a premium, and bank money became a separate kind of money which was quoted at a discount of 6 or 10 or even as much as 20 percent. Such a depreciation was a natural result of the expansion of bank credit, as well as a result of coinage problems.

That bank credits should be quoted below par was not to be tolerated a moment longer than necessary in the view of Venice's rulers, especially since by 1526 the inflationary situation had led to the opening of five new banks within the previous two years. Banking Commissioners were appointed who were to be supplied by the banks with a fund of good coins from which they were to pay any depositor who could not get full payment from his banker. That brought bank money back up to par and put most of the new banks out of business.

Restrictive regulation of banking was characteristic of Venice. Her laws limited a banker's dealings in credit in order that he concentrate on one approved function: namely, providing a convenient method of payment, a means of exchange. That function might have been fullfilled by a governmentally operated exchange office and giro-bank. It was proposed in 1356 and again in 1374 that the government operate such a Communal giro-bank, but the proposals were rejected, and competition was allowed to continue two centuries longer. Finally, the dramatic failure of a new Pisani bank (Pisani-Tiepolo) lead the government to create the *Banco della Piazza* in 1587 and give it a monopoly. Its operation was entrusted to a private banker who was obligated to liquidate and to apply for a new license every three years. His operations were severely restricted by the terms of his license, but he received profits or commissions from dealing in coin and exchange. The Banco della Piazza provided the desired convenience for merchants, but in 1619 a second public bank was created, the *Banco del Giro*, which had the additional function of financing government debt. The government paid for purchases by what were in effect drafts on its account in the Banco del Giro, an account which was always overdrawn. Indeed, the purpose of creating the bank in 1619 was to pay for a huge purchase of silver for the Mint. The seller of the silver received a large credit on the books of the bank. He could not use it to draw coin from the bank; indeed, the bank had no cash to speak of, only small yearly installments sent from the Mint, according to a plan for gradually extinguishing the government's debt to the bank. The only substantial security behind its deposits was the government's obligation. But Giovanni Vendramin, who had sold the silver to the government, could transfer his credits in the bank to other merchants who also had faith in the government's promise. Bank deposits did in fact circulate as a kind of money; payment through the bank was made obligatory for bills of exchange. Thus the kind of issue of bank money which Alvise Pisani had managed privately was operated publicly by the Banco del Giro.

Venice was not a leader in those practices which were to transform banking in the eighteenth and nineteenth centuries, namely, the negotiability of bills and the issuance of bank notes. Indeed, Venice was on the whole conservative ir business practices in the sixteenth century. Partnerships with limited liability were forbidden by a law requiring all partnerships to be registered and everyone who shared in the profits to share in the liabilities. Joint ventures of limited liability, such as financed the galley voyages or reclamation projects, were possible, but they were unions of capital of limited duration for limited purposes. They never developed the separate personality and long life of the chartered joint-stock companies of commerce and colonization which were appearing in England, or of the contemporary mining companies of Germany.

Nevertheless, Venice was a leader in the field of banking, if only in two respects. (1) The type of giro-bank which it developed was widely imitated in the seventeenth century, as in Amsterdam, Hamburg, and Nuremberg. In view of the monetary conditions of the time, it was useful for a commercial center to have an institution which did not make loans at interest or pay interest on deposits, but lived on fees or profits from exchange and made payment by bank entries, which was easier and safer than paying in coin. (2) Venice led also in financing wars by the issue of bank money. Alvise Pisani did it in a small way, and it may well have been done also by earlier private bankers. It was done on a larger scale during the wars of the seventeenth century by the Banco del Giro.

Giro-banks were so central in the activities of the Rialto that any bank failure had spectacular effects. It paralyzed business momentarily, but the government immediately took vigorous measures to force the bankers and their families to pay all depositors, seizing the bankers' personal property and even threatening expulsion from the nobility. Compared to other cities of the time, Venice had relatively good banking facilities and this, combined with its long-established commercial connections, made Venice one of Europe's most important financial centers, especially for the transfer of funds internationally through bills of exchange. Drafts on Venetian banks were used by Ragusa to pay its ambassador in Naples and by the popes to pay expenses of their legates at the Council of Trent. Venice was the favorite clearing house for settling accounts between northern trade centers and Italian cities.

There were opportunities for gain in the Venetian bill market, not only from the service of transferring funds, but also from the interest charges reflected in the prices of bills of exchange. Most bills were paid at a special kind of exchange fair which bloomed in the sixteenth century and with which Venice had very active dealings. Loaning money by buying bills avoided any taint of usury and, if properly managed, it gave protection against depreciation of the moneys of account. Bills on the exchange fairs were a form of investment which at the end of the century attracted money from every city where there was an accumulation of liquid funds, as there long had been and still was at Venice. Rich Venetian nobles were inclined to leave the details of drawing and re-drawing bills to Florentines and Genoese, who played an important role on the Rialto, but many Venetians directly or indirectly put money into this form of investment. Private finance as well as public finance was thus one source of Venice's sixteenth-century prosperity.

RICH AND POOR: A SUMMARY OR BALANCE SHEET All things considered, Venice had found many compensations for the economic difficulties created for it by Europe's oceanic expansion, by the growth of the Ottoman and Spanish empires, and by other changes of the fifteenth and sixteenth centuries. Just as she had adjusted to smaller revolutions in trade routes during earlier centuries, so again Venice adapted sufficiently to remain a leading commercial center. Especially during the last decade of the sixteenth century, when spices again flowed into the Mediterranean from the east, when Antwerp and many other "world markets" were suffering from political disruptions, when Jewish refugees drew to Venice trade from the Levant and Balkans, and when the boom of its textile industries reached new heights, Venice again appeared triumphant.

The renewed prosperity touched different groups unequally. A portion of the nobility became richer than ever. The paying-off of the public debt, although in depreciated coin and at less than par, added to the funds available for other kinds of investment, since it was accompanied by light direct taxes. There were still many Venetians prepared in the sixteenth century to venture to far-away lands in search of profits. For the first time, we hear of Venetian merchants in Sweden and, extensively, in Poland. Others found ways to make themselves friendly with the Portuguese and sought fortune trading in gems and fabrics in Indian cities. But no big fortunes were made in such ventures; returns were higher on investments nearer home. The growth of manufactures and of population added to the value of urban real estate. The exhaustion of wheat surpluses in areas that had been Venice's overseas sources of supply made reclamation projects on the nearby mainland highly profitable. What had been an aristocracy of merchant princes was by the end of the sixteenth century largely converted into a landed nobility.

The rich displayed their wealth in ever more grandiose fashion as Gothic style gave way to Renaissance and Baroque. The construction of sumptuous palaces was remarked on by contemporaries before 1450—witness the Cà d'Oro and Cà Foscari—and this kind of conspicuous consumption increased. In addition to great palaces in Venice, such as the Palazzo Corner della Cà Grande (see Figure 42), many Venetian nobles built magnificently on their mainland estates. Of the 1,400 mainland villas in Venetian territory that are classed today as of artistic interest, 15 were built in the fourteenth century, 84 in the fifteenth, and over 250 in the sixteenth century. The furnishings of these palaces, the clothes and jewels of Venetian women, the sumptuousness of the festivals with which the Serenissima honored visiting royalty, gave diversion to pilgrim-tourists, and dazzled the populace—all these gave Venice the reputation of being, as Fernand Braudel has said, the richest and most luxurious city in the world.

Beneath the magnificence was much misery. It was worst in years of famine; for, in spite of Venice's vigilant Grain Office, in spite of the reserves in its warehouse and its ships able to tap distant sources of supply, the city could not escape entirely the sufferings which commonly attended crop failures. The famine of 1527-29, for example, was blamed partly on war, but mainly on bad weather and floods. Careful of her own supply, Venice had swept into the city all the wheat available on mainland markets or raised on estates belonging to Venetians. Starving peasants then inundated the city. "Give alms to 200 and as many again appear," wrote a contemporary, "you cannot walk down a street or stop in a square or church without multitudes surrounding you to beg for charity: you see hunger written in their faces, their eyes like gemless rings, the wretchedness of their bodies with skins shaped only by bones. . . . Certainly all the citizens are doing their duty with charity—but it cannot suffice, for a great part of the country has come hither, so that, with death and the departure of the people, many villages in the direction of the Alps have become completely uninhabited. . . ." Any bread left in the villages was made of millet and rye, only in the next century did the cultivation of corn (maize) provide a more nourishing diet for peasants who had surrendered all their wheat to pay rents and taxes. Making up partially at least for the portion of the mainland crops which Venice had cleaned out of the countryside, she shipped some of her seaborn imports to starving areas. To assuage the flood of beggars within the city, the government built temporary shelters and, while forbidding begging, arranged to provide food in these "hospitals" until the next harvest. The crowding in the shelters bred an epidemic of typhus. Only good weather and peace in the countryside after 1530 brought real relief and made the usual methods of charity again seem adequate.

For those among Venice's own poor who fell into misfortune and faced starvation, there were more permanent institutions dispensing poor relief. The guilds were expected to look after their own impoverished members, partly from dues collected for that purpose, partly from charity. Several purely religious fraternities, including the rich Scuole Grandi, dispensed charity, as did some monasteries. Many new hospitals and other institutions to aid and reform the unfortunate were founded in the sixteenth century (see Figure 38). In each of Venice's sixty-eight parishes, the parish priest was responsible for being informed about the deserving poor too proud to beg and for collecting from his other parishioners for their support.

At the bottom level of Venice's social structure, the census of 1563 counted foundlings and beggars as about 1 percent and servants as 7 to 8 percent. Among the household servants were hundreds of slaves, although slaves were less numerous than they had been a century earlier. Import of Tatar and Russian slaves from Tana had been large before the Turkish conquest of Constantinople diverted them to other markets after 1453. The Venetian demand for domestics was then met by indentured servants brought in by ship captains from Dalmatia and Albania. In anticipation of the system of indentured servants that later supplied labor for North American colonies, the serving maids and others thus imported were required to work off the cost of their transportation by four years of labor under those to whom the ship captains "sold" them. That they were sometimes kept in bondage longer and even shipped abroad for sale as perpetual slaves is proved by regulations against such abuses.

There is evidence of black slaves among the gondoliers when near the end of the fifteenth century blacks became a larger part of the slave population; but these slave gondoliers were a tiny, if conspicuous, group compared to the one or two thousand self-employed gondoliers among whom the government organized a kind of naval reserve of oarsmen. Use of slaves in manufacturing is referred to by a few guild rules that forbade any master selling for export a slave who had learned a craft. Since the reference is to female slaves, it suggests that the industrial employment of slaves was auxiliary to domestic service. But among the thousands of unskilled workers who performed such menial tasks as stoking the fires of Venice's chemical industries or moving materials around a construction site, there must have been many who were materially worse off than slaves and who had more fear of hunger. The nearly 190,000 who crowded Venice at its peak of population about 1570 included a great many poor. There were thousands who made a precarious living by mixing fishing with other occupations, and many widows seeking more security than they could find in the countryside. A plentiful supply of cheap labor was probably one support of the boom then in manufacturing.

Venice's most famous industries depended on skilled master craftsmen, however, as we have seen. Guild masters formed a kind of lower middle class. They earned fully twice as much as unskilled laborers and at least a third more than their semi-skilled journeymen. Unskilled laborers in the Arsenal in the mid-sixteenth century were paid at a daily rate which, if they were fully employed the year round, as probably only a very few were, amounted to 15 to 20 ducats a year (8 to 10 soldi a day, 250 days a year, makes 16 to 20 ducats of 124 soldi). They were the lowest paid workers in the Arsenal, except for boy apprentices and the women sewing on sails, who received a little more than half as much per day. The base pay for oarsmen on galleys was also about 20 ducats a year, but was supplemented and discounted in ways that will be described below. A skilled craftsman, in contrast, received nearly 50 ducats. The yearly salary of a foreman ship carpenter and a ship's master was about twice as much again, namely about 100 ducats. For comparison it may be noted that writers who boasted of Venice's wealth considered nobles as well off only if they had income of 1,000 ducats a year and counted as really rich those with 10,000 a year.

Together with shopkeepers of similar economic status, Venice's lower middle class of master craftsmen numbered in the tens of thousands. In Europe generally the wages of this working class lost purchasing power during the sixteenth century, especially during its second half when prices rose rapidly. In England and many German cities, wages lagged so far behind prices that in the building trades at least, the workers received only about half as much purchasing power in 1620 as in 1520. In Venice, there was a general price rise also, in spite of the fiscal and provisioning policies, but wages in Venice did not lag as far or as permanently behind the rise in the cost of living as did wages in England. The daily wage of a master in the construction industry at Venice went from 30 soldi in 1550 to a little over 60 soldi a day by 1610. The price of wheat went up at a higher rate, but fell somewhat in the early seventeenth century, whereas wages did not fall back. Wages of the semi-skilled among masons and carpenters followed the same trends but rose less. In short, there was a comparatively moderate decline in real wages during the sixteenth century and some recovery early in the seventeenth.

Above the ordinary master craftsman in both skill and pay was a stratum which included, on the one hand, outstanding foremen and artists and, on the other hand, lawyers, accountants, and many civil servants. This upper middle class was less numerous, to be numbered in the thousands instead of the tens of thousands. It included, for example, the city's foremost marine architect, the Foreman Shipwright of the Arsenal who had a salary of 100 ducats a year in 1550, a residence, and some other prerequisites of office. It included also the Arsenal's Chief Bookkeeper who received 180 ducats a year and a residence. In the upper middle class were many, probably most, of the cittadini, both the citizens-by-birth and those naturalized, such as John Cabot. Many of its members were merchants and some ship captains. Also included, with somewhat the same range of income, were leading artists and builders of palaces: Mauro Coducci's salary as Foreman of San Marco, in charge of construction around the Piazza, was 80 ducats a year; Jacopo Tatti (Sansovino) who came from Rome with established prestige was appointed to that post at the same salary in 1529, and promptly received raises which by 1539 pushed his pay up to 200 ducats. Although the members of this upper middle class had very diverse and highly variable incomes, as a whole they shared rather fully, whether as artisans, merchants, or civil servants, in the benefits of Venice's adjustments to the new conditions of the sixteenth century.

In contrast were those among the nobles who, from the point of view of income, should probably be included somewhere in the middle classes, the impoverished nobles called "Barnabotti." Nobility being hereditary, all descendents of nobles were also nobles, no matter how impoverished their families were and regardless of whether their poverty was due to accidental misfortune or lack of capital and opportunity or lack of education and gumption. Increasingly, those impoverished found less and less chance of rebuilding a family fortune. The increasing number of Barnabotti was a sign of economic decay and a source of political corruption. Being very poor by the standards of their expectations as nobles, they yet struggled to keep up appearances. Most of the Barnabotti thus came to depend abjectly on favors received from the rich and powerful, from those who were better able or better placed to use the opportunities still open to their class in agriculture, commerce, banking, and politics.

Comparing all the signs of wealth and poverty, well-being and misery among the various classes of Venetians in 1600 with what we know of them in 1400 or 1500 gives on balance little basis for speaking of a general economic decline. Growth in some segments and decline in others had made structural changes, however. The maritime industries were less important relatively at the later date, and within the maritime industries, some segments had grown while others declined. An overall judgment of how well Venice met the challenge posed by the oceanic discoveries and the growth of the Ottoman and Spanish empires must consider the ups and downs in shipbuilding and in the operation of the navy and the merchant marine. As explained in our next chapters, it was on the seas that Venice's response was least adequate.

CHANGING FLEETS AND SHIPYARDS · I

The Peak and Passing of the Merchant Galleys

CHAPTER TWENTY-FOUR

The shifts in international trade and politics affected differently the three parts of the fleet: merchant galleys, war galleys, and merchantmen dependent entirely on sail. To be sure, the recovery of Venetian power and prosperity after the war of Chioggia was such a broad movement that all aspects of Venetian maritime life expanded until about 1430. Helped by the re-conquest of Dalmatia, the Venetian navy and merchant marine both grew. Doge Tommaso Mocenigo in his famous "Farewell Address" of 1423 estimated that Venice had 45 galleys employing 11,000 seamen, 300 sizable round ships employing 8,000 men, and 3,000 smaller vessels employing 17,000 men. The total of 36,000 seamen, when the total population of the lagoons was about 150,000, seems excessive. It is credible only if it includes many seamen from Greece and Dalmatia, and his 45 galleys must include a battle fleet of a size that was maximum for the period. Even when so interpreted, his figures show that round ships, including small types, were more important than galleys in giving employment.

EXPANSION Galleys increased in relative importance, however, later in the fifteenth century because the fleet of round ships then declined sharply while that of galleys expanded. Although their popularity did not outlast the century, merchant galleys were a highly specialized type particularly adapted to the political and commercial conditions of the fifteenth century. The size of these "great galleys" came to differentiate them sharply from the speedy warships called "light galleys."

At their largest, the Venetian merchant galleys carried 250 to 300 tons in their cargo holds and loaded more weight on deck. Their length overall was about six times their beam, whereas that of light galleys was eight times the beam. The deck of a galley was much wider than the ship's hull because all its central section was a rowing space extending to outriggers supported by brackets arching out from the beam ends. This rowing space was divided down the middle by a raised gangway on each side of which were the benches of the oarsmen (see view of galley from above on Chronological Chart). Between their benches and the parapet built on the outrigger were stations for the bowmen so that, when a galley was fully manned, about 180 men were fitted into this central deck measuring 30 feet by 115 feet.

Beneath the deck were two large cargo holds, separated by an arms room and the cabin of the ship's scribe under the main hatchway. The kitchen was aft beneath a portion of the deck where a rower's bench might be removed to make space for some fresh meat on the hoof (see Figure 33). The low peak was devoted to the carpenter's hold and sailors' gear, until at a later date it began to be used for cannon. The sterncastle rose higher and contained three tiers. The lowest had bunks and the captain's treasure chest. Above it was his main cabin, with room for the captain's table and some storage of arms. Above that was the castle proper from which the captain commanded in battle and the navigator gave directions to men in a gallery immediately behind him, handling the tiller.

Light war galleys had only one mast, but the great galleys had two or three. At mid-century, the tallest was forward and they were all lateen rigged (Figure 9). Merchant galleys depended on the wind to carry them from one port to another, but their oars gave them a maneuverability which made wrecks extremely rare and which enabled them to move more nearly on schedule.

As warships, merchant galleys were formidable enough to discourage most pirates. To be sure, piracy was on the increase, and the jagged line between piracy and war was blurred, but war fleets were seldom large. Three to five great galleys, able because of their oars to come one to the aid of the other, constituted a force of some 600 to 1,000 men. Well led and equipped, they could handle most situations. The ordinary sailors and oarsmen were armed with swords and pikes. Better equipped were the 20 to 30 "bowmen," among whom were included after 1460 cannoneers and then some arquebusiers.

Galleys were an expensive means of transport. High-priced cargo was needed to support the expense, and quick turn-around to keep it to a minimum. These conditions were most fully met on their voyages to Alexandria. Outgoing cargoes often worth 100,000 ducats per galley included much silver bullion as well as gold and silver coin. Equally valuable return cargoes were assured by the galley's prior rights to load spices. Round ships were not permitted to bring spices to Venice except when there were more than the galleys could hold. Then the extra spices were loaded on a particular cog or carack designated by the capitanio of the galley fleet to return with him carrying the spice bales which had been offered to the galleys and for which they could not find room. These rules had the effect of concentrating trade in the period when the galleys were in port. This loading period (*muda*) was fixed by the Senate; to assure a quick turn-around, it ordered the galleys to stop loading in Alexandria twenty days after their arrival or on the twentieth of November. At that season, they had a good chance of catching a wind that would enable them to cross directly to Crete and be home for the Christmas fair. On other routes also, regular yearly sailings to the same ports at approximately the same times served to concentrate cargoes so that big crews did not have to be fed during long periods of idleness.

By the 1420's, the Venetian merchant galleys were proving so successful that they had a number of imitators, most notably the galleys which the Florentines sent out from Pisa. But no other city operated so many so regularly over so long a period.

The Florentine galleys were in part a response to expanding Venetian activity in the western Mediterranean. Venice's turn westward in the opening decades of the fifteenth century, which was so pronounced in politics and in Venetian culture generally, was represented commercially by the opening of a new line serving the northwestern shores of the Mediterranean, the "galleys of Aque Morte." They stopped at many ports, such as Naples and Pisa, on their way to French harbors and usually continued on to Barcelona. This added a fifth line to the established four: Romania, Beirut, Alexandria, and Flanders (see Chapters 10 and 14). A sixth, that of the galleys of Barbary or West Africa, was added after 1436 to carry silver and textiles to Tunis and along western North Africa to Moorish Granada and then to Valencia. In the last decades of the century, a seventh fleet called *"al trafego"* serviced Northeast Africa. It went from Venice to Tunis and then to Alexandria or Beirut. Thus Venice's galley fleets facilitated dependable shipment between Venice and all the shores of the Mediterranean as well as the Straits of Dover (see Map 9).

MANAGEMENT AND REGULATION   Some of these routes had been tried out first by privately owned galleys, but after mid-century the only galleys which were not state-owned were two or three which carried pilgrims to Palestine. The other 15–20 galleys sailing each year were auctioned by the government for a specified voyage. The high bidder, if judged worthy by the Senate, received a charter to operate the galley on behalf of a group of investors forming the temporary kind of partnership we have called a joint venture (see Chapter 11). As galley master (patrono) he was at least nominally the head of the partnership and the galley's commander. To be approved by the Senate, he was supposed to be thirty years of age and to show that the group he headed was putting up security sufficient to assure the operation of the galley and the payment of full crews. The shareholders of these joint ventures were sometimes individuals, but mainly the family partnerships through which most Venetian nobles did business. Practically speaking, the galley master was often an employee of a capitalist, such as Alvise Pisani, who was financing the voyage. His duties and functions were elaborately spelled out in the terms of his charter.

One set of these regulations concerned freight rates. The rates set by the Senate for the voyages to the east were sufficiently high so that auctioning galleys for those voyages yielded the government more than enough to pay the cost of building and outfitting the galleys. For the western voyages, in contrast, subsidies often had to be offered to attract bidders. The amounts bid for the galleys of course fluctuated widely from year to year, according to the Rialto's estimates of market conditions. The amounts bid varied also because of changes in freight rates. Although most basic rates remained unchanged for long periods, some were debated each year by the Senate and were determined not by what the traffic would bear but by commercial purposes. For example, in 1423, to improve the market situation in Venice, the 4 galleys sent to Flanders and England were ordered to load all spices offered without charging any freight. On some imports from the Levant, rates were set relatively high because the galleys had a monopoly of their transport, at least at specified seasons, and merchants sending at other times on other vessels had to pay full freight or half freight to the galleys anyhow. In short, some galley freights were treated as customs duties and were not determined according to the economics of the transportation enterprise itself. Chartering a galley was in some cases a venture in tax-farming.

The close connection between freights and customs was one reason for regulating freights strictly and entrusting their collection not to the galley master but to customs officials in case they were paid in Venice or, in case they were paid at a destination overseas, to the fleet commander, the capitanio. He then took out what he needed for the maintenance of the fleet and distributed the rest among the galley masters. The scribe, whose duty it was to record all cargo loaded and all freight due, was a public official chosen by the Collegio and in many cases assigned by it to the particular galley on which he served. All freights, whether collected at Venice or overseas, were ordered put in a common pool, so that galleys would be equally and more safely loaded.

The strict regulation of freight payments was partly to prevent the galley masters from cheating the stay-at-home capitalists who were financing the voyages and mainly to assure that the auctioned galleys would really act as common carriers, giving specified kinds of wares priority over others but loading merchandise of high priority, such as spices, at equal rates for all shippers, first come, first served. According to the regulations, they had no chance to do otherwise, since nothing could be loaded without a ticket from the capitanio, and he and customs officials collected freights. But account books and law suits show that, in fact, galley masters gave rebates to business associates and made contracts specifying how illegally collected freights were to be divided.

In the fourteenth century, the capitani who commanded these trading fleets had in some cases been the leaders of combines among the galley masters, but in the fifteenth century they were strictly forbidden to own shares in any of the galley companies or to have a son or brother as one of the galley masters. They were not asked to renounce all opportunity for commercial profit, for they were allowed to invest in cargo through colleganze entrusted to agents, but they were paid salaries of from 60 to 120 ducats a month, which was more than adequate to pay for the staff they were required to hire and feed: two or three pages, two pipers, and a chaplain or notary. At some periods, they paid the keep of the chief navigator and the fleet physician. Election as capitanio was eagerly sought as a distinction and a source of revenue. On his return, the capitanio had the honor of reporting before the Senate. He described how the galley masters had conducted themselves, the vicissitudes of the particular voyage, and the general commercial situation encountered. After his report, the Senate voted approval or disgrace on each galley master. The capitanio's function was military in emergencies, but routinely it centered on policing the galley masters.

In addition to enforcing the priorities in loading and the collection of freights, the capitani were responsible for resisting efforts of galley masters to stay in a port and load for a longer period than had been specified in the auction

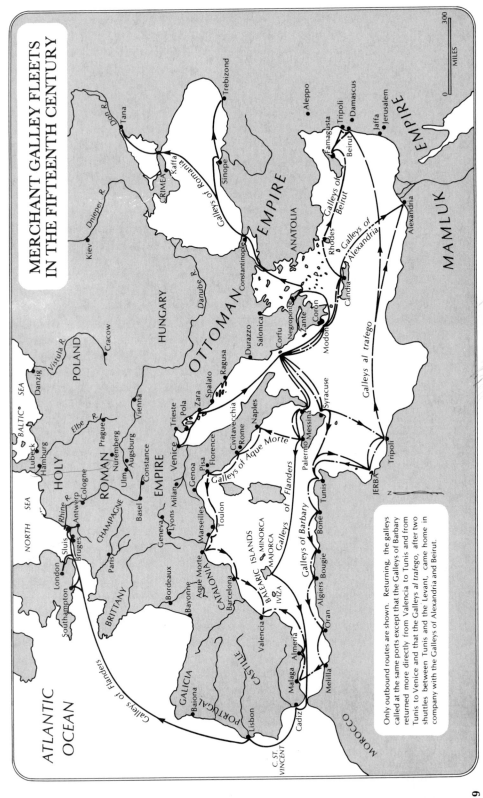

MERCHANT GALLEY FLEETS
IN THE FIFTEENTH CENTURY

Only outbound routes are shown. Returning, the galleys
called at the same ports except that the Galleys of Barbary
returned more directly from Valencia to Tunis and from
Tunis to Venice and that the Galleys al trafego, after two
shuttles between Tunis and the Levant, came home in
company with the Galleys of Alexandria and Beirut.

MAP 9

contract. Sometimes such extension was left to the discretion of a Council of Twelve, formed of merchants and galley masters, but on most Levantine voyages the loading periods were precisely set, and a capitanio who permitted later loading was heavily fined and barred from further commands.

CREWS AND The treatment of the crew formed a third area in which the capitani were
PASSENGERS charged with making the galley masters obey the rules. To make sure that
the required number were on board, the capitanio was ordered to hold a general muster as soon as the galleys had crossed from Venice to Pola. If any were missing then or at similar musters during the voyage, he was to hire substitutes. The galley masters had an obvious economic interest in cutting expenses and one way to do it was to hire a smaller crew. Another way was to skimp on the food. Part of the capitanio's function was to see that the standard 18 ounces of dried biscuits were distributed as well as appropriate amounts of wine and of bean soup. The wages of all the crew were fixed by the Senate, and to prevent galley masters from collecting kickbacks they were required, when paying the advances to the men who signed on, to "lay at the feet of the doge" money bags containing enough coin for the full amount and then disburse it in the presence of naval paymasters or one of the Ministers of the Marine.

The repetition of regulations to prevent kickbacks indicates that employment on the merchant galleys was eagerly sought. Base wages on both war galleys and merchant galleys fell markedly in Venice early in the fifteenth century, probably because of the increase in the supply of maritime labor coincident with the recovery of Dalmatia. Then a decline in the number of round ships further depressed the labor market. Merchant galleys were the one bright spot, the one segment of the merchant marine that was expanding. Although the cash wage was low, it was supplemented by fringe benefits of which the chief was the right of each crewman to his own venture, freight free. The officers had big chests piled on top of the central gangway; the oarsmen stuffed all they could under their benches and raised the benches to make more room. Among his clothes, arms, and other personal effects, each crewman found room for a variety of items which he had been able to purchase relatively cheaply in one port and hoped to sell at good profit in another. When customs officials began seizing cottons brought to Venice by seamen among their clothes, the Senate allayed protest by decreeing in 1414 that each sailor could have a customs exemption of 10 ducats. This exemption was raised in 1608 to 20 ducats. Exempt anyhow were cheeses and wine, for although basic rations of ship biscuit and soup was provided by the galley master, each oarsman was expected to carry something extra for nourishment. Sometimes the seamen did very good business selling from on board the galley. As it entered a harbor, it was surrounded by a swarm of small craft peddling a variety of foods and merchandise. On one occasion at Alexandria the soldan's customs officials and the Venetian merchants were slow in reaching an agreement under which the hatches could be opened and exchange on a large scale begun. The capitanio reported that the crews did a thriving business meanwhile with petty traders clambering over the sides.

About 1490, these fleets of merchant galleys employed about 4,000 seamen under regulations calculated to raise the condition of the galeotti appreciably above the low state to which it had been reduced in the fourteenth century. How much all the regulation for the protection of the pay, the food, and the ventures of the seamen were enforced may be doubted, but at least it can be said that, in addition to the factors of supply and demand that determined the general level of a seaman's remuneration, the merchant galleys were under regulations which were favorable to the crew and which were subject to enforcement by independent commanding officers. Behind their enforcement, there was the sentiment among Venice's rulers which was expressed by frequent references in Senatorial decrees to seamen as an important part of state power ("la marinareza di questa cittade, la quale è principal membro del nostro stato").

Even better off than the oarsmen on these galleys were the officers, the able-bodied seamen, and even the bowmen or marines. The highest paid non-noble was the chief navigator (*armiraio*), who was the capitanio's chief of staff for everything connected with navigating and fighting the galley. In the fourteenth century, the capitani picked their own chief navigators, but after 1430 the doge and other high magistrates of the republic balloted to choose a chief navigator for each fleet from among ten to twenty applicants. They were the most skilled seamen to be found in Venice, including such men as Andrea Bianco, the map maker. They compiled their expertise not only in maps but also in notebooks which reveal the range of their interests and duties. These included astronomical data, records of tides, and general mathematical problems, such as estimating the height of distant objects. Notes on the weights and measures used in various markets show their interest in trading. The chief navigators also felt some responsibility for the way the crew was worked and fed, for we find in their notebooks details about rations and work rules. One rule required that the chief navigator should, when the galley was proceeding under oar, stop the rowing at stated intervals for meals and for an hour prior to sunrise so as to enable the men to sleep and to be ready for either flight or pursuit if dawn's light revealed the sails of unknown ships. Although admitted to the captain's table at the beginning of the fifteenth century, at the end of the century the chief navigator presided over a separate table with other non-noble officers and the sailors (the oarsmen ate at their benches). He was one of the crew and they looked to him as their head.

Eating at the head table (with the capitanio on the flag ship, with the patrono on other galleys) were such merchant nobles as might have bought passage, a chaplain, and often a ship's doctor such as the Master Gualtieri already referred to (see Chapter 15). Merchants, colonial officials, and diplomatic envoys were favored as passengers, but pilgrims were allowed on merchant galleys only by special permission. The chaplain served also as notary; to judge from regulations, that was his main function. The ship's doctor was sometimes a highly educated physician, as skilled in astrology and astronomy as the chief navigator. At Venice, there was no sharp line between surgeons, who were the experts on treating wounds, and the men who were called "physicians" because they were qualified by training to prescribe physic, that is, internal medicine. In most countries these two branches of the profession were quite separate. In sixteenth-century England, for example, service in the fleets was restricted to surgeons who were forbidden to practice internal medicine, but in Venice many were skilled in both surgery and medicine and were part of the same guild. Men who were merely barbers had a distinct guild and were forbidden to engage in any surgery except pulling teeth, cutting out wens, and bleeding according to the directions of a physician. A barber who was paid the same wages as an able-bodied seaman or bowman formed a regular part of the crew of each galley, but the capitanio was expected to take with him also a physician-surgeon, who collected a grosso each payday from each crewman. Some of these were among the leading medical men of their time and became professors at Padua or Bologna.

At the chief navigator's table (*armiraio* on the flagship and *homo di conseio* on other galleys) were the two top deck officers (the *comito* commanding aft and the *paron iurato* commanding before the mast), the ship's scribe, the *penese* (an older man in charge of gear), the ship's carpenter and ship's caulker, the chief gunner (after cannon were added), and eight to twelve "mates" (*nocchieri* or *compagni*). The mates' functions were those of able-bodied seamen. They were young men on their way to becoming deck officers and chief navigators. From their ranks came the heroes of many narrow escapes. It was two of the mates who saved the galleys of Barbary from wreck in 1524 by swimming ashore carrying hawsers. They were glowingly praised by the capitanio of that fleet in his report before the Senate. Another mate saved one of the galleys of Beirut in 1526. When all the superior officers and pilots were at their wits' end in a storm, he took command and brought the galley to safety, winning such praise from the endangered galley master and merchants that he was promptly promoted by a special act of the Senate.

The deck officers were normally chosen by a committee of the Collegio, and so were the 20 to 30 bowmen. The latter, or later the arquebusiers and gunners, were selected at the shooting ranges located in various parts of the city and especially at the Lido. Again, the multitude of rules to prevent favoritism or kickbacks show how much these positions were sought. When depression in private shipyards late in the fifteenth century put many caulkers and shipwrights out of work, each galley was ordered to carry 3 shipwrights and 2 caulkers who would be counted and paid as bowmen, in addition to those who went to serve in their craft. Many caulkers also obtained jobs as mates. Although the cargo and table privileges of the mates, the master craftsmen, and the bowmen were different, their wages were about the same, 3 to 4 ducats a month, which was two and a half times as much as the 8 lire di piccoli a month of the oarsmen.

One group of bowmen were quite distinct from the others and were paid more. They were nobles who were called bowmen of the quarterdeck (*balestrieri della popa*) and ate at the captain's table. Sometimes they are referred to simply as "nobles of the galley." Going to school was a relatively unimportant part of education in the Venetian Republic, especially after the age of sixteen. The young learned by observing the adults do their work and by being included in it. While there was no formal apprenticeship among the merchant nobles, young nobles went to sea at an early age, accompanying their parents or other relatives, and the Senate created the institution of "bowman of the quarterdeck" to encourage this practice and to assist poorer members of the nobility to recoup their fortunes. Adding to their salaries what they made on their ventures, a noble bowman could gain 100 to 200 ducats on a voyage. Recipients were elected by a committee of the Collegio, later by the Quarantia. In 1400 each galley master was required to pay, feed, and provide space for 4 such young nobles. When the number was raised to 6 and then in 1483 to 8, the merchant galleys provided such help to about 150 youths each year.

One case in which it did help an impoverished young noble to get started on a prosperous mercantile career was that of Andrea Barbarigo, who was in many ways a typical fifteenth-century Venetian merchant. His father had been capitanio of galleys of Alexandria when one was wrecked coming up the Dalmatian coast in winter. Judged derelict of duty in not going to its aid, he was fined 10,000 ducats. Thus impoverished, Andrea, then about 18, began trading with only the advantages of good family connections and a couple of hundred ducats given him by his mother. He put what he earned and learned as bowman of the quarterdeck to good use in business, and before he died at fifty in 1449, he had assets of 10,000 to 15,000 ducats, no great fortune but a substantial accumulation.

The ideal example of how the institution of noble bowmen was supposed to work in breeding seamen is Alvise da Mosto, famous for his voyages to equatorial Africa. He first went to sea at 14. He was hardly 20 when Andrea Barbarigo, a cousin, entrusted him with the bartering of some cloth and beads for gold in north African ports. Writing much later, he explained why he later took service as a noble bowman of the galleys of Flanders, by saying, "Having sailed over the various parts of our Mediterranean seas, I decided to make yet another kind of voyage, to Flanders, both for the purpose of gaining profits and because my mind was set on exercising my youth, working in every way to increase my abilities, so that through a thorough knowledge of the world I might when older achieve some honorable distinction."

The bowmanship of these nobles had originally been of some importance; applicants had to prove they were 20 years old and had to present themselves with their bows at the shooting butts where the committee made its selections. In the course of time, the institution degenerated and tended to become merely a hand-out for poor nobles. The age was lowered from 20 to 18, with younger boys allowed as exceptions. Those chosen often sold their claims to wages, food, and space. Galley masters were among their best customers, for they cut expenses by such deals. The Senate found it necessary to decree again and again that those chosen should actually go or send an acceptable substitute. The institution was still fulfilling some of its educational function, however, as late as the mid-sixteenth century, as is indicated by the memorandum of good advice that a Benedetto Sanuto gave his younger brother who was going as a noble bowman on the galleys of Alexandria. Most of it concerned the merchandise he was to buy and sell, the kind of advice he should seek in business matters, and the older men on whom he should pattern himself. It opened and closed with more personal advice: show always due deference to the capitanio at whose table you will eat, don't pass the time playing cards lest you fall into a quarrel on the size of the stakes, but instead read the books you are taking with you, don't eat too much, especially not the delicious quails of Alexandria, avoid the easy women of Corfu and Crete who have *mal francese*, be sure your servant does not let any of your clothes blow overboard, keep warmly dressed.

The fullest descriptions of these galleys and the life on board is in the accounts of pilgrims who wrote up their pilgrimage as the exciting and unusual

FIGURE 33   *Great Galley Approaching Rhodes.*

The woodcuts made by Erhard Reuwich of Utrecht, who went with Bernhard von Breydenbach on his pilgrimage to Palestine in 1483–84, show the spaciousness of the hull of the great galley, the supply of fresh meat carried on deck, and the chests heaped up on its central gangway.

In contrast to the three-masted galleys pictured in the mid-fifteenth century (Figures 9 and 27), the later great galleys had only a small mast in the bow. It was smaller than the foreward masts of the caracks which Reuwich depicted above in the background and similarly it was square-rigged.

event of their lives, and sometimes as a guide for other tourists. To be sure of including what was wanted for the latter purpose, they put in tall tales told by sailors, and even copied each other for the sake of completeness. One German tourist, unable to take a camera, took along an engraver who illustrated the noble traveler's account with excellent etchings of ships, harbors, and scenes of the Holy Land. Only rarely did pilgrims travel on the state's merchant galleys, although occasionally the Arsenal was told to outfit a great galley to be operated under bareboat charter by some especially distinguished pilgrim, such as the Duke of Lancaster who became England's King Henry IV. The poorest pilgrims were stowed below on round ships, but the favorite tourist vessels in the fifteenth century were galleys very much like the merchant galleys except that they were privately owned and operated. Their noises, dirt, smells, and bustle, the groaning, sweating, and pilfering of the crews amid ships, the more decorous

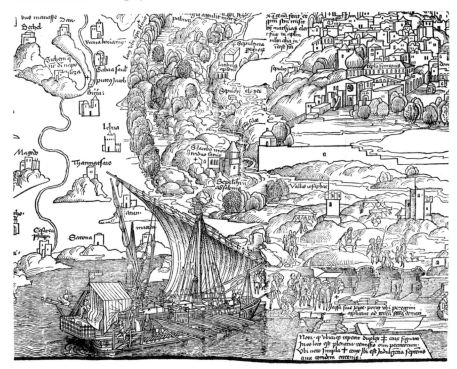

FIGURE 34　*Disembarking Pilgrims in the Holy Land. Woodcut by Reuwich of Utrecht.*

stern castle canopied to show the arms of the noble in charge, the calling back and forth during the night of the helmsman and the lookout—all these must have been much the same.

Pilgrims often referred to oarsmen as slaves. Perhaps they were merely using the term they would have applied at home to men in so menial and miserable a condition; perhaps some of the oarsmen on those privately operated galleys were, in fact, slaves of the galley master. But the pilgrims also have much to say about how eagerly the galeotti went ashore to set up booths and bargain with their ventures at every stop, or how much they overcharged pilgrims to whom they made sales. Obviously, then, most oarsmen were not slaves chained to their benches. And certainly employment of any slaves on the galleys the state auctioned for trading voyages would have been a blatant defiance of Senatorial decrees and of the commission of the capitanio.

Although left to private enterprise, dealings with tourists were elaborately regulated, for the tourist trade was then as now an important element in Venetian prosperity. Pilgrims found near San Marco special booths flying the flags of galley masters who had posted bonds with the government to guarantee their good behavior in taking pilgrims to Jerusalem. Going by galley had the advantage that you stopped at many important places. Everyone then eagerly piled ashore to get a change of diet and see the sights. As a place for sightseeing and spending money, none could of course excel Venice herself. Venice's taverns and brothels were carefully regulated to maintain the good name of the city, and pilgrims found a series of glittering church ceremonies to make less tiresome their wearisome waiting as the galley master tried to fill his passenger list and catch a favorable wind.

THEIR FINAL VOYAGES After being celebrated for two centuries as passenger liners and fast cargo ships, great galleys suddenly dropped out of commercial use almost entirely soon after 1500. Basically, their usefulness was undermined gradually by improvements in both the military and sailing qualities of round ships. Cannon were steadily being improved, and a round ship could carry more guns than a galley. Maneuverability under sail was increased by the changes in rigging which in the mid-fifteenth century transformed the ketch-rigged cog into a "full-rigged" carack or galleon. Carack and galleon were "full-rigged ships" in that they had not only the big square mainsail of the cog, they had one or two lateen sails aft and also small square sails hung on a forward mast, and above the crow's-nest on the mainmast (see Figures 10 and 37). The advantages of this rig were so well established that the Venetian merchant galleys used a somewhat similar rig in the late fifteenth century instead of rigging all three of their masts with lateen sails as they had earlier (see Figure 33).

But the suddenness with which the galleys ceased their mercantile voyages was due to changes in those political and economic conditions to which they had been particularly adjusted and which had justified their high freights. The consolidation of large states, such as the Ottoman Empire and the French and Spanish kingdoms, and the involvement of Venice in their wars exposed merchantmen to greater dangers. Even four or five galleys could not resist the war fleet of one of the new "great powers." At the same time, the precious cargoes that might have justified powerful escorts for galley convoys diminished as Venetians handled less of the inter-regional flow of spices and of bullion.

The first line to feel the effects of the changing political situation was that which had functioned longest, the fleet going to Romania and the Black Sea. For centuries it had carried out coin and cloth and brought back silk, alum, and other wares from Constantinople. In the Black Sea, it loaded furs, salt fish, and sometimes slaves from Tana, and at Sinope and Trebizond, it received the metals of Anatolia and the silks and other products of Armenia and Persia (see Map 9). Which ports they would visit in the Black Sea was often determined in Constantinople by the capitanio in conjunction with a Council of Twelve and the Venetian ambassador (*bailo*). They could be better informed than the Senate in Venice. In 1452, the galleys ignored Mohammed the Conqueror's preparations to besiege Constantinople and went on, two to Tana and one to Trebizond. On their return they anchored inside the Golden Horn and, together with the two light galleys sent to escort them, defended that harbor against the Turkish fleet. When Mohammed placed guns on the heights north of the Golden Horn and brought the galleys within range, the capitani, galley masters, and Council of Twelve decided to unload the galleys so that they could be moved to a safer spot. What happened then, as told in the account of the siege written by the physician in the fleet, reveals something about the feelings the crews had for their ships. At the first move to unload,

the crews rose up with swords in their hands around the hatches of the galley, saying "we want to see who thinks he can take the merchandise out of this galley. We know that where our wares are there is our house and home. Once the galleys are unloaded, we will be held in this city by the Greeks like slaves, whereas now we are free to go or stay. . . . We leave our fate to God's mercy. We see that all the Christians in this city are to die under Turkish swords . . . and therefore we galeotti have decided to die on this galley, which is our home, and do not wish to die ashore."

Faced with this attitude, the capitanio left the galleys loaded. Many of the crew were persuaded to go and fight on the walls, but when the Turks burst in and the city was lost, the galleys were being kedged out even before the capitanio could make his way aboard.

No merchant galleys went to Constantinople again until after peace was made between Venice and the Turk in 1479, and never thereafter did they go beyond into the Black Sea. The intermittent voyages of the galleys of Romania in later years had as their main functions carrying out Venetian manufactures and bringing back the raw silk, dyes, and wax that Venetians accumulated at the way stations in Greece such as Nauplia and Modon, or spices which had been brought to those assembly points by round ships from Egypt and Syria.

At the next Turkish war, in 1499, all great galleys were sent to the war fleet. For the first time since 1381, none went on a trading voyage. Most of the regular voyages were resumed the next year, but in 1509 the War of the League of Cambrai stopped all the western voyages. The galleys of Aque Morte never sailed again, and the efforts to reanimate the trading voyage along North Africa and that through the Straits of Gibraltar to the English Channel ran into political difficulties.

The North African voyages were all the more profitable and complicated because they carried many passengers who were both Moslems and traders in slaves. The slave trade was not nearly as important in fifteenth-century Venetian commerce as it had been earlier, but for the first time there was established a connection between slavery and blackness. Venetian slave traders had dealt at first mainly in blond slaves, Slavs, then in partially yellow "Tatars." After the Ottoman conquest of Constantinople dried up the supply of slaves from the Black Sea, Negroes from Africa were in demand.

Slave trading in North Africa was complicated by the readiness of Christian and Moslem corsairs or crusaders to sell as slaves all of the opposite religion whom they could capture. In time of war, slave raiding was hard to distinguish from skirmishing and holding captives for ransom. Crusaders like the Knights of St. John and almost all Spaniards considered themselves permanently at war with all Moslems. They claimed the right to seize Moors and their wares even if they were traveling on Venetian ships. If any Venetian ship captain surrendered Moslem passengers to the Spaniards or the Knights, the Egyptian soldan accused the captain of having himself sold them into slavery. That did indeed happen sometimes, even on the closely supervised galleys, but the highest councils of Venice's government, concerned about the safety of Venetian merchants in Alexandria, did their best to keep the Moorish passengers safe and claimed that the Venetian flag protected the goods and passengers carried. The Senate reacted vigorously when in 1464 two galleys driven off course between Tunis and Alexandria stopped at Rhodes for supplies and the Grand Master of the Knights promptly seized all the Moors and their wares in spite of the protests of the Venetian commanders. As soon as it heard of this, the Senate ordered the Captain General of the Sea, whose main assignment was supporting the war against the Ottoman Turks then beginning in the Morea, to go at once with his full war fleet to Rhodes and demand their release "before a twelve-penny candle burns out" ("in tanto tempo che dura una candela da un soldo"). He received the order in Crete and three days later was in Rhodes with 30 to 40 galleys. The Grand Master equivocated for two days, but when the Venetians began systematically ravaging the island, beginning with his own plantation, he gave in. The Moors were sent on to Alexandria, where they were received with rejoicing, especially by the Venetian merchants who were then released from prison.

Young blacks, one or two thousand a year, were in the cargoes that the Moors regularly brought to Egypt, and both black and white slaves were traded as gifts between the Moslem courts. How could one tell which of the non-Christians going on the galleys between North African ports were somebody's slaves and which were free subjects of a friendly Moorish prince? After a case in which a white Moorish merchant had been kidnapped by a galley's officers and sold as if a slave, the Senate ordered in 1490 that thereafter no slaves might be carried on those African voyages "except the blacks which the Moors take with them from place to place." In practice, this must have meant that on those ships, as a general rule, blacks were considered slaves. This is the first indication I have found in Venetian records of an association of slavery and color.

Galley voyages to Barbary grew more and more difficult as pirate fleets grew larger. In 1517, the King of Tunis engaged passage on the galleys for an embassy he was sending with rich gifts to the Ottoman sultan, including slaves for his court and harem. Especially noted were four eight-horse teams, each of a different breed or color, each team of horses attended by eight grooms also of various carefully matched colors, attired in richly jeweled costumes. The total value was rumored as 200,000 ducats. When the fleet stopped at Syracuse to get ship biscuit, pirates swarmed around like bees around a honey pot. The Tunisian embassy told the capitanio that if he did not deliver them safely to Ottoman territory they would say he had sold them. Fearing the fury of a sultan robbed of his gifts, the Senate ordered the battle fleet commander who was in Istria to go at once to rescue them. Before he could get there, the vice-admiral and other officials at Corfu had decided to unload two merchant galleys that were returning from Alexandria and with his patrolling three galleys to go at once to Syracuse. At their approach the pirates scattered; the gifts for the sultan arrived safely at the Turkish port of Valona.

Venice's system of interlocking bases, patrols, and trading convoys could cope with that kind of a pirate threat, and the gold which came across the Sahara to Tunis was so attractive that special efforts were made to get it. The banker Alvise Pisani financed a fleet that brought African gold to Venice in 1519. In 1520-22, the Barbary galleys extended their voyage westward to Lisbon in hopes of using the African gold to buy spices there at good prices, but without much success, as has been explained. The growth of Spanish and Turkish power gradually made the voyage impossible. After the red-bearded Moslem corsair of Greek birth, Khaireddin, had made himself King of Algiers and Admiral of the Ottoman Navy, his fleet and the fleet of Charles V alternated in attacking Tunis. In 1533, the last galleys on the Barbary voyage had to bring Moorish passengers to Venice because Tunis was being besieged.

The unsuitability of merchant galleys to operate as neutral carriers in the midst of war fleets was one reason also for the discontinuance of the voyages to the English Channel. The galleys of Flanders had been so named originally when their main function was moving spices to western markets centering in Bruges. As return cargoes, they brought back woolen cloth for transshipment to the Levant, and much English wool. When cargoes of wool became most important, the timing of the voyage shifted and slowed down. Instead of making a round trip between spring and fall, the galleys left in midsummer, spent three months at least in London or Southampton, and left in the spring after the sheep were clipped. They could make a fast voyage if necessary. At the outbreak of the war with the League of Cambrai, they came from Southampton to Otranto in thirty-one days without any trading stops in between. But the long months spent in English ports raised the labor costs, led to troubles between crews and natives, and tempted the English king to seize the galleys for use in his wars with France. In 1529, he did seize some of their bronze cannon. They last sailed in 1533; thereafter, the import of English wool was left to caracks and overland wagoners.

Another reason for discontinuing the "Flanders galleys" was the Venetian lack of spices. Politics would probably have interrupted their voyages in any case, but the disruption of the spice trade during the opening decades of the sixteenth century might well have seemed in itself sufficient reason to stop sending such expensive ships on that voyage.

Most affected of course by the Portuguese discoveries were the galleys of Beirut and Alexandria. During the fifteenth century, their voyages—that to Alexandria especially—typified the conditions which made the mercantile use of great galleys advantageous: precious cargoes, quick turn-around, and monopolistic bargaining. When the Portuguese began selling pepper at Lisbon and Antwerp, they attracted to those cities silver which had previously been the most precious item in outgoing cargoes to Alexandria. At the same time, their forays in the Indian Ocean not only cut in half for some decades the flow of spices to Egypt, they also made the time when the spices would arrive there less predictable and negotiations with its soldan more difficult. Infuriated by the drop in his customs receipts, the soldan tried to make up for it by demanding higher and higher prices for pepper. In 1505, it looked as if he meant to enforce his demands by seizing the galleys. They made a dash for freedom under the fire of the fort that commanded the harbor of Alexandria. A cannon ball carried away the mast of one galley, but they all escaped, and the capitanio was much praised for his courage and skill in breaking out of a harbor so strongly fortified that it was frequently referred to as a prison.

After patching up their quarrel with the soldan, the Senate decided in 1514 to let caracks bring spices from Alexandria, hoping thus to increase the amount brought to Venice. But tradition was abandoned only gradually. After galleys had returned empty in 1524 because the carack *Cornera* had just loaded, spices were again required to come by galley. Their monopoly was definitely repealed, however, in 1534, on the grounds that freedom of foreign competitors to load at any time gave them advantages. Galley voyages to Alexandria became less and less frequent, ending in 1564. By that time, pepper and other spices were again plentiful in Alexandria, but they were brought thence to Venice in caracks.

The galleys of Beirut had much the same fortunes; but there was less danger that they would be seized in Beirut or any Syrian port, they did much business at way stations such as Cyprus, and there was no lack of the main items in their outborne cargo, namely cloth and other Venetian manufactures. The conquest of both Syria and Egypt by the Ottomans in 1517 caused no immediate interruption but did of course have the consequence that in later years no galleys went when Venice and the Turk were at war, or when Turkish fleets seemed particularly threatening. Otherwise, the voyages continued until 1570. When galleys were sent, it was more in order to give some good jobs to seamen than because of any advantages that transport by galley offered to merchants.

At the very end of the sixteenth century, new demands for protection from pirates were met by a new galley line. But that was an Adriatic service, a different kind of line, with a different compliment of officers and men, and a vessel different from those that for about two centuries had flown the banner of the winged lion in all the leading harbors from the Don and the Nile to the Thames and the Scheldt, and set the bells in the Campanile ringing whenever a returning fleet was sighted off the Lido.

CHANGING FLEETS AND SHIPYARDS·II

The War Fleets

CHAPTER TWENTY·FIVE

A NEW FOE
AND NEW
WEAPONS The nature of naval warfare changed when Genoa faded out as Venice's chief opponent and was replaced by the Ottoman Empire. To be sure, the Venetians were slow in recognizing the Turks as naval rivals. Until almost the last quarter of the fifteenth century, Genoa still appeared the maritime enemy as well as a commercial competitor and often an ally of Venice's antagonists in the wars in Italy. The Turks were mighty on land but inexperienced at sea, and Venice's first naval encounters with the Turks strengthened her confidence in her own superiority. In 1416, after acts of violence on both sides had culminated in an attempt by the Turks to waylay the merchant galleys of Romania, 12 war galleys were sent under Pietro Loredan, then at the beginning of a long, distinguished career. He had orders not to engage in battle unless the Turks were attacking Venetians. He found a Turkish fleet at Gallipoli, their main base, ideally located for intercepting Venetian vessels on their way from the Dardenelles to Constantinople (see Map 7). Considering their behavior threatening, he attacked and destroyed their ships. The next encounters came about 10 years later when Venice was trying in vain to defend Salonica by retaliatory raids. This time an assault on the enemy fleet and protective palisades at Gallipoli was repulsed, but Venetians blamed this check on incompetence or cowardice and disobedience in their fleet, not on Turkish skill or valor.

A major difference in human terms between Venice's wars with Genoa and with the Turks was dramatized in the first battle of Gallipoli. No prisoners were taken. The Moslem Turks were all killed, cut to pieces ("tagliati a pezze"), as Loredano phrased it. With regard to the Christians, of whom there were many in the Turkish fleet, mostly Greeks, but some Sicilians, a distinction was made between the slaves and the mercenaries, that is, volunteers. The former were freed, the latter were all killed even after surrender. Many were hanged, as Loredan explained, in order that the Turks should lack seamen to guide their ships and so that "no bad Christians will dare to hire themselves out to these Infidels."

This pattern was repeated in later battles. It was one of the ways in which Venice tried unsuccessfully to deprive the Turks of the services of the Greeks who, as the Byzantine Empire shriveled and disappeared, became subjects either of Venice or, more largely, of the Ottoman emperor. Gradually Venetian policy toward the Greeks in her colonies became somewhat more liberal, especially toward the Greek Orthodox priests. The time came when a Venetian commander even advocated making a place on the galleys for Greek priests because the Latin (Italian) priests could not take the confessions of the largely Greek crews. In antagonism to the "Infidel," many humble inhabitants of the Greek islands and a few of the nobility and the high clergy, as illustrated by Cardinal Bessarion, directed their loyalties to Venice. Many others accepted Turkish rule as better than submission to Italians and to the Roman Catholic Church. The Turkish ships were handled mainly by Greek seamen — partly by the thousands of slaves whom the Turks carried off from the coasts of the Aegean and Ionian Seas, partly by volunteers who felt that the rewards of serving the Ottoman Turk outweighed the dangers of Venetian vengeance.

In terms of military techniques, the Turkish wars differed from the Genoese almost from the start because of the importance of cannon. Gunfire had a role in the War of Chioggia, as we have seen, but a minor role. It may have played a part also in the Turkish success in defending Gallipoli in 1429. But the first really impressive use of cannon against ships was in connection with the seige of Constantinople by Mohammed the Conqueror. As described in the previous chapter, his artillery almost forced the Venetian galleys to abandon their anchorage in the Golden Horn. At the beginning of his seige, he had demonstrated the ability of cannon to control passage through the straits by building on the European side of the Bosphorus a castle 200 feet high from which his cannon hurled stone balls weighing 400 to 600 pounds. Three Venetian cogs tried to run past without lowering sail. Two made it, the third was sunk, its crew captured and beheaded and its captain impaled. On the first naval expedition which Mohammed organized, he placed formidable guns also on some of his ships. He was ahead of the Venetians in developing artillery both on land and sea, but his effective batteries were all land-based. The effect of cannon on naval warfare was felt first not in actions between opposing fleets at sea, but in limiting the effectiveness of fleets in attacking ports. A harbor well defended by batteries could not be stormed as Lorenzo Tiepolo had stormed Acre in 1257, breaking the chain and destroying the Genoese fleet in the harbor.

In the long run, cannon were to make round ships supreme because they could carry more artillery than galleys. In addition, the improvements in their rigging increased their maneuverability, making the carack and galleon more useful as warships than the cog; but the ability of galleys for mass action without dependence on the wind made the speedy light galley the backbone of Mediterranean war fleets throughout the fifteenth and sixteenth centuries.

FIGURE 35 *Light Galley alongside a Carack (courtesy of the Accademia, Venice; Photo Ferruzzi).*

The contrast between a war galley—low, long, and narrow—and a high round ship is emphatic in this detail of background from Carpaccio's Legend of St. Ursula.

As the range and accuracy of cannon increased, many efforts were made to use them effectively on galleys. For the slaughter of opposing crews, small caliber guns were mounted on the forecastle and all around the sterncastle. One cannon or culverin big enough to pierce an enemy's hull or bring down his mast was placed in the prow. Even on light galleys there was room enough for a formidable piece at the head of the gangway which ran down the middle of the rowers' platform. The weight of these guns required special strengthening of the galley's structure. Aiming them successfully depended on skillful maneuver.

Great galleys had space and strength enough to carry more and bigger guns, and about 1460 they began to carry a few even when on commercial voyages, as we have seen. When they were disappearing as cargo carriers in the mid-sixteenth century, their armament and deck arrangements were redesigned to make them primarily warships. They then took a new lease on life as the type commonly called a galleass (*galeazza*). It had cannon not only at bow and stern heavier than those on the light galleys but also guns along the sides so that it could fire a miniature broadside.

The galleass only partially met the demand for an oared vessel serving as a gun carriage because it was not fast enough to operate effectively with light galleys. During the first half of the fifteenth century, the shipwrights of the Arsenal made many attempts to construct vessels as fast as the light galleys but bigger and heavier. Among the many solutions tried, quadriremes were most acceptable. Having four oars to a bench instead of three, they provided commanders with flagships stronger than ordinary galleys but still able to lead into battle. With speed and large crews and guns, they were good for capturing pirates.

Even more impressive for that purpose was the quinquireme built by Vettor Fausto. A humanist who gave public lectures on Greek poets, he claimed to have found in Archimedes the secret of building the kind of a quinquireme used by the ancients. There were enough humanists in the Senate impressed by this argument, or by Fausto himself, so that they assigned him men and materials in the Arsenal. At the subsequent race witnessed off the Lido by the doge and his Council, the quinquireme proved able to keep up with a standard trireme. It had the desired speed but had an overcrowded deck and was little used because of the expense of its huge crew. Light triremes remained the backbone of the war fleet and were supplemented by round ships whose use depended entirely on the wind, by some quadriremes which carried only a little more artillery than the ordinary light galleys, and by some galleasses with formidable artillery.

When Venice began her wars against the Turk, her battle fleets contained roughly these same four types of vessels although they were not as clearly differentiated as later, and did not carry as many guns. For decades the main impact of cannon was psychological, a result of their terrifying noise, their occasional devastating effect, and the very fact that their effectiveness was unknown. Psychologically at least, they were important in the first serious defeat inflicted on Venice by the Turks, the loss of Negroponte in 1470. That campaign was also the first which made Venice realize how serious for her were the consequences of the fall of Constantinople. Under Mohammed the Conqueror it was once again the capital of a powerful empire and therefore became again the central base of a great naval power, especially since the Ottoman Empire included so many Greeks skilled in shipbuilding. In 1470 there issued from the Dardanelles a fleet of 300 vessels, reported by a Venetian galley commander as "a forest on the sea, when described incredible but when seen stupefying." That fleet was an auxiliary to a campaign of the Turkish army which Mohammed was leading in person. The Venetian-Turkish war which had begun in the Morea seven years before (see Chapter 16) had moved into the Aegean. Reacting to the Venetian pillaging of its northern shores, Mohammed was striking at Venice's main base there, Negroponte.

To intercept this "forest on the sea" the Venetian Captain General, Nicolò da Canal, had 55 galleys, and one at least of his galley commanders was thankful that the wind prevented the Venetians from attacking the Turks before it was discovered how many they were and how well equipped with cannon. Nicolò da Canal retired to Crete for reinforcements. He returned with more galleys and with 18 large round ships, cogs or caracks, and entered from the north the straits between Negroponte and the mainland. Mohammed's fleet was largely dismantled and lay south of the city. Just north of the city he had built a bridge of boats across the narrowest part of the straits so as to move troops onto the island. He was pressing the siege with assaults so that the defenders were near collapse when their spirits were revived by the sight of the Venetian fleet approaching. Instead of at once attacking the bridge of boats and throwing relief into the fortress, Da Canal anchored. Seizing what looked like his last chance to overwhelm the enfeebled garrison, Mohammed launched an all-out assault. When Da Canal moved next morning to attack the bridge of boats, the brandishing of swords on the walls of the city revealed that it had fallen. His attempt to recapture it later after he had received more reinforcement was also a fiasco.

Da Canal was recalled, imprisoned on arrival, and prosecuted not only for failure to attack the Turks when he should have but also for many abuses in the fleet by which he and his galley commanders stood to profit. Condemned, he was fined and sentenced to live the rest of his life in a small village. He was a man of literary distinction, a friend of humanists, who had taken his doctorate at a university, and then for more than twenty years had served the Republic as ambassador to the leading courts of Europe. Men inured to maritime service regarded him as an example of the mistake of giving command of the fleet to one who was more a scholar than a seaman. They criticized him not only for hesitating at the crucial moment before Negroponte, but for failing to cut off and destroy a part of the gangling Turkish fleet on its voyage either to or from Negroponte.

Da Canal's failure to maintain tight discipline or to find effective use for the forces at his command contrasted sharply with the successes of his successor, Pietro Mocenigo. Although Mocenigo was not the victor in any major battle, he conducted raids all over the Aegean, collected much booty, and had his fleet at the right places at the right times so as to keep the Turkish armada bottled up at Constantinople and to enable Venice to win control of Cyprus without any fighting. After four and a half years of continual service, Pietro Mocenigo returned to a hero's welcome and in 1474 was rewarded with election as doge.

In extenuation of Nicolò da Canal's failure, it should be noted that he faced two problems which might have disconcerted a more experienced commander. His failure to attack at Negroponte at the crucial moment was attributed by one of the seamen present to his fear of the Turkish cannon. Mohammed was employing some sensationally large guns in his assault, and Da Canal might well have feared their effect on his ships. Knowing in hindsight the disposition of the Turkish forces, one can say with some confidence that Da Canal could have broken the bridge of boats and relieved the city, but it is not surprising that, before initiating a fight in which he might be engaged with the main force of the Turkish army, he should have paused to look over the situation and learn the position of their guns. More of a reflection on his ability as a naval commander was his failure to inflict any damage on the Turkish fleet during its voyages between Negroponte and the Dardenelles. Many of the Turkish ships were light vessels and they were spread over six miles of sea. The Venetians had heavier ships, caracks and great galleys, which the Turks feared. But not even the most seasoned of Venetian admirals had had much experience as yet in maneuvering with a fleet combining several types of ships carrying artillery against another similarly diverse fleet.

This same problem — the effect of gunpowder on a battle between fleets at sea — bedeviled the Venetian commander also in the next Turkish war in 1499-1503. Again, the Venetians elected a Captain General who was not primarily a seamen. He was Antonio Grimani, a financier, who had served once previously in a naval command but was esteemed above all for his business acumen and skill in negotiations. This time the Turks were carrying the war into the Ionian Sea. While their army attacked Lepanto, a Venetian base in central Greece on the gulf of the same name (see Map 7), a huge fleet carrying the artillery for the siege and other supplies rounded the Morea to assail the city from the sea. To turn back or destroy the on-coming armada, Grimani had the most powerful fleet Venice had yet assembled: about 50 light galleys, about 15 great merchant galleys, and some 20 to 30 very large caracks, some of them vessels of more than 1,000 tons carrying many soldiers and cannon. The Turkish fleet contained more light galleys but had only a couple of great galleys and two or three big caracks. Grimani tried to join battle in such a way that his big ships carrying the heavy guns would be the first engaged, and succeeded in doing so in at least one of the series of engagements fought off the west coast of Morea. But since the Venetian Captain General traditionally used a fast light galley as his flag ship (there were no quadriremes in this fleet), Grimani by these tactics lost the moral advantage of personal leadership at the point of danger. When two of his largest round ships grappled with the largest of the Turkish caracks, its powder magazine was set on fire, and all three were consumed. The spectacle threw the whole fleet into disorder. Grimani's orders were not adequate and were not obeyed and he failed to punish the disobedient. Consequently, in later encounters Venetian vessels also avoided coming to grips with the enemy fleet, so that it arrived essentially intact before Lepanto, which promptly surrendered. Again, the Captain General was made the scapegoat. A money-maker never was any good for anything except making money, said the sea dogs. Grimani was recalled, condemned, and sentenced to live on a small Dalmatian island, which he found so unbearable that he fled to Rome where, through connections at the Papal Court and through his diplomatic skill, he arranged to be welcomed back to Venice during the War of the League of Cambrai and to climax his political comeback in 1521 by election to the dogeship!

After Grimani was demoted, the Venetian fleet operated with more success when Benedetto Pesaro, a statesman and former merchant of maritime experience, was placed in command. He was criticized for keeping a mistress with him, although in his seventies, and for cutting off the heads of delinquent subordinates, including a close relative of Doge Leonardo Loredan. But he was warmly praised when he completed Venetian conquest of the Ionian Islands. He resented the restoration of some of his conquests in order to obtain peace. One may wonder how different Venice's position would have been if they had followed his urgings so rebuild their power in the lower Adriatic and Ionian Seas, where at that time they were manning some galleys from the cities they held in Apulia, instead of making peace with the Turk in order to contend with the pope over lands in Romagna and with the French over leadership in northern Italy.

The Turks considered their fleet an auxiliary to their army. Once the latter had completed its campaign against the Venetian strongholds, both in 1470 and 1500 the fleet withdrew to Constantinople. Consequently, neither Pietro Mocenigo nor Benedetto Pesaro directed a battle at sea with the Turkish fleet; neither had an opportunity to prove that he could do better than Nicolò da Canal, the man of letters, or Antonio Grimani, the financier, in combining actions by light galleys, great galleys, and round ships against a similarly heterogeneous enemy fleet.

The most celebrated Genoese admiral of the next generation, Andrea Doria, hardly did any better. He was serving Charles V, who was Venice's ally in her next war with the Turk, and commanded the allied fleet at the battle of Prevesa, 1538. His maneuvers in that battle were the result of secret instructions from Charles, who hoped to avoid battle and win over the Turkish admiral, Khaireddin, but they appeared to be efforts to do just what Grimani had planned to do, namely, use the cannon fire of his large round ships to weaken the enemy before the light galleys engaged. He was partially successful since, from the Venetian point of view, the one brilliant aspect of that otherwise disheartening battle was the defense put up by a Venetian great ship of the new type called a "galleon." It was cut off and surrounded by Turkish galleys but fought them off with gunfire. Doria's maneuvering on that day was on the whole a failure, for while his fleet was not destroyed, it retired disorganized and demoralized. For the next thirty years, the Turks felt themselves the masters at sea. Under the leadership provided by such Barbary seamen as Khaireddin, the Ottoman navy operated not as a mere auxiliary to the army but as an independent weapon.

NAVAL ADMINISTRATION AND THE ARSENAL   Complex problems were, to be sure, created by combining oared galleys and vessels dependent entirely on the wind into a single fleet at the same time that cannon were becoming increasingly effective. But it is noteworthy that in none of the major naval battles involving a combination of both types were the Venetian fleets commanded by the Serenissima's most experienced admirals. The Venetian political system operated so as to place the high naval command in crucial years in the hands of men whose capacities had been demonstrated in other than military or maritime activities. The Captain General of the Sea was elected theoretically by the Great Council, but that council merely approved the Senate's nominee. At the beginning of a war, when the hopes of victory were high, the command was sought by men esteemed already as administrators and diplomats, who hoped by adding military laurels to win election later to the dogeship. Such men were loath to enforce discipline by punishments that would make bitter enemies in important families.

The duties of the office did indeed call for the skills of a businessman and diplomat as well as those of a general and seaman. For example, the instructions issued to Vicenzo Cappello, an experienced admiral who was Captain General in 1538, were detailed on three points: (1) how he was to work with Andrea Doria and the papal admiral in determining some action, (2) the two contracts he was to negotiate for the delivery of needed tons of ship biscuit, and (3) just how he was to dispense the huge amount of coin entrusted to him, about 100,000 ducats. To judge from the contents of his instructions, the political and financial aspects of the position were those about which the Senate and Council of Ten were most concerned. There was more emphasis on orderly administration than on military tactics or fighting spirit.

Administration really was increasingly important. The size of the fleet that Mohammed the Conqueror sent out from Constantinople in 1470 shocked the

Venetians into outfitting a fleet almost twice as large as those armed earlier in the century. As Ottoman and Spanish naval power reached new dimensions during the following century (as described in Chapter 17), the number of galleys in Venetian fleets doubled again. Many disarmed each autumn, but a substantial number were kept at sea throughout the year. Fleets of such size and permanence required bases well furnished with ship biscuit, gunpowder, oars, and other supplies. The line of such bases from Venice through Corfu to Candia and on to Famagusta defined rather narrowly the waters in which Venice's fleets operated (see Map 10). Having the main base at one end of the line simplified the strategic problem of concentrating forces and protecting lines of supply, but it increased the logistic problem of keeping adequate stocks of food and munitions in the outposts.

Venice's most striking success in rising to the Turkish challenge was its expansion of the industrial output of the main base. The Arsenal became twice as large as it had been when its bustling crowds and dirt impressed Dante Alighieri. In 1473, looking ahead even in the midst of war, the Senate ordered construction of an addition called the Newest Arsenal so that, besides building and outfitting merchant galleys, the Arsenal could construct and store under cover a reserve of ships with which to match the suddenly appearing multitudinous fleets of the Turk. The reserve, traditionally 25 galleys, was raised to 50 late in the fifteenth century. Then, after fleets of more than 100 galleys had been outfitted for the war of 1537-40, the reserve was fixed at 100 light galleys, 4 (later 10) great galleys, 8 biremes, and 16 light dispatch and scouting vessels. By that time enough covered sheds or basins had been built in the Newest Arsenal so that most of the reserve galleys could be stored under cover. Twenty-five were supposed to be in basins, armed and equipped so that they could be manned and sent to sea at very short notice. The rest of the "moth-ball fleet," as we might call it, was to be kept on land, complete in hull and superstructure, ready to be launched as soon as they were caulked. As merchant galleys went out of use, the maintenance of this 100-galley reserve became the chief goal of the Arsenal's activity and remained so until the standard was lowered to 50 in 1633.

A hundred finished but unused galleys waiting in reserve constituted an ideal rarely if ever attained. The peak of the Arsenal's activity was in the 1560's, when it was trying to maintain this reserve and at the same time in many years had to put to sea 40 to 60 galleys because of the size of Turkish and Spanish fleets which, it was hoped, were directed only against each other, but of which the objectives were always in doubt. In those years the Arsenal, which then covered 60 acres, employed on an average about 2,000 men within its wall — as many as 3,000 in emergencies, and hardly ever less than 1,000. It was the biggest industrial establishment in all Christendom, perhaps the biggest in the world.

Some features of the Arsenal's organization anticipated such characteristics of modern industry as an assembly line, interchangeable parts, and vertical integration. But neither the original creation of the Arsenal nor its expansion in the sixteenth century arose from ideas for improving the process of production through the concentration of many workers in one large central workshop. The process of production were thought of as matters of craft skill, to be left to the traditions of the crafts as fostered by the guilds. The purposes for which the Arsenal was created were the safe storage of weapons and ships in such condition that they would be available in time of need. "Managing" the Arsenal meant keeping track of materials. Technical knowledge was needed by "management" only in judging the quality of the goods delivered and in assembling them on a fully outfitted vessel. Quality was judged by foremen selected from the appropriate craft. The assemblage was directed by the Arsenal's highest non-noble official, the "Admiral of the Arsenal." He was an experienced seaman of great authority, but nobles frequently had strong ideas of their own about just how the galleys they were to command should be armed.

Gradually efforts at strict accounting for materials, for men employed, and for moneys spent led to the hiring of workers with specialized duties defined by the management and not by any guild tradition. Such personnel was employed first in connection with assemblage or outfitting and slowly spread into the earlier stages of production. Under the immediate direction of the Admiral were a dozen warehouse supervisors and several gangs of stevedores and unskilled laborers who moved material to the finished galleys. He organized their work so that, as a galley neared completion, it moved down a kind of assembly line. Hulls were constructed in the New Arsenal or Newest Arsenal. They were then brought into the Old Arsenal where they moved past a series of warehouses. From these warehouses, as a visiting traveler described the scene, "they handed out to them, from one the cordage, from another the bread, from another the arms, and from another the balistas and mortars, and so from all sides everything which was required. . . ." The many different parts of the Arsenal — lumber yard, building ways, foundries, arms room, and rope walk (the separate but adjoining structure and institution called the Tana) — were located in a pattern that on the whole facilitated this assemblage. They had not been planned as a unit but over the centuries they developed by a series of adjustments into an approximate direct-line layout.

An assembly-line required some standardization so as to have interchangeable parts. Masts, spars, benches, and other deck fixings were the same for all light galleys. Standardization could be more easily applied if all equipment, for example, iron work and pulleys, were made within the Arsenal instead of being bought from craftsmen working outside. That was one good reason for bringing the production of all materials more and more within the Arsenal. The vertical integration was pushed to the point of sending masters from the Arsenal to the forests, not only to select ship-timber — foremen shipwrights were accustomed to going themselves to the woods to find the kind of logs they wanted — but also to supervise efficient cutting for oars and pikes.

Even in the framing and caulking of the hulls, craft tradition and guild discipline were gradually supplemented by supervision through specialized personnel. Such supervision was the more necessary because the management could not pick and choose its workers or fire them at will. To retain the supply of shipwrights which it needed in emergencies, the Senate gave all ship carpenters the right to work in the Arsenal whenever they could not find employment elsewhere, although at rates of pay somewhat less than they might hope for outside. Half of the caulkers selected by rotation had similar rights. These two crafts made up about two-thirds of the 2,000 men who often crowded through the Arsenal's one gate, where they were checked in and out by paymasters (see Figure 32). These same paymasters were later instructed to go around inside and cross off the payroll of the day any men they found asleep. Even when there were as many as 200 to 300 ship carpenters in the arsenal, there was no firm division into work gangs under supervisors, although there were three or four foremen shipwrights whose skills in shaping hulls made them the directors of the work of others. For occasions when galleys were needed in a hurry and a large labor force had to be made to work more efficiently, the Lords of the Arsenal devised a system of "inside contracts," much like that employed by American gun manufacturers in the nineteenth century. Using materials and equipment supplied by the management, shipwrights bid for contracts to make specified numbers of hulls. The lowest bidder received the contract and hired other shipwrights to work for him under his supervision. The Senate felt that work done by inside contracting was not of top quality. It forbade caulking to be done in that way, and permitted it for construction of hulls only in emergencies. Instead, it planned in 1569 a firm assignment of men to sub-foremen who would be responsible for quotas of production assigned them.

The masters of the arsenal could not be meticulously disciplined, for they were an elite among the artisan class and a kind of reserve corps of non-commissioned officers. Many served in battle on the galleys they had built. Fifty of them were selected to act as the honor guard of the Ducal Palace during ducal elections. They were the city's only fire department, and noble onlookers were much impressed with the prodigies they performed in fighting fires such as that which destroyed the upper story of the Ducal Palace in 1577. On the rare occasions when they were so infuriated by delays or abuses in their pay that they stormed across the bridges to the Ducal Palace, the Chiefs of the Ten or the doge needed to use cajolery as well as threats. There was no police or armed guard able to oppose and disperse them. But their loyalty was not really in question. On the eve of the War of Cyprus, the Council of Ten decreed that guards should be posted in the Piazza and in the Arsenal at night, and elected as captains three men who were not masters in the Arsenal. These men found themselves so hated that they resigned, and when the zonta of the Ten came up for reelection, none of those who had voted this unpopular measure was approved by the Great Council. New captains were chosen from among the Arsenalotti.

Although too political in structure and spirit to be a model of industrial efficiency, the Arsenal produced what was demanded of it. When the largest possible fleet was needed quickly because of the Turkish attack on Cyprus, the Arsenal turned out 100 galleys within two months in the spring of 1570 and, in the Christian battle lines at Lepanto the following year, more than half the ships were Venetian-built.

CREWS AND THEIR COMMANDERS Not lack of ships but lack of men limited Venetian sea power. Challenged at sea by two such huge empires as those of Spain and the Turk, Venice's only hope of competing lay in superior organization. Her Arsenal gave her superiority in industrial organization, but it produced more galleys than Venice could find crews for. At Lepanto, the Venetian galleys were so inadequately manned that they accepted on board detachments of Spanish soldiers as reinforcements. The Republic failed to organize effectively the manpower it needed at sea.

After other Mediterranean fleets were using galley slaves as oarsmen, Venice still relied primarily on volunteers and claimed she needed few soldiers because her galeotti were all combatants. Whereas the Spaniards, for example, put at least 100 soldiers on each galley when preparing for battle, the Venetians were satisfied with 60. They had trouble finding that many from among the militia of their subject cities, the hirelings of their condottieri, and the city's own corps of bowmen chosen at its shooting ranges at the Lido. In navy ratings these were still called bowmen (*balestrieri*) even after they were armed in 1518 with guns. Like the mates and other ratings, which were much the same as on the merchant galleys, they were no doubt more useful in close combat than the oarsmen, and Venetian cannon and cannoneers had a high reputation; but her galleys were generally shorthanded and, in spite of the free oarsmen, the crews as a whole were not first class as a fighting force.

A small select element were the gentlemen cadets (*nobili*) which each galley was required to have on board. On war galleys as well as merchant galleys these young nobles might be teen-agers serving their apprenticeship, but those who had served four years, at least, were eligible to become galley commanders (*sopracomiti*). A law was passed against fathers taking their own sons, but sopracomiti frequently took their brothers or cousins. If the commander was killed or disabled, one of the nobles took command temporarily and hoped for confirmation by the Senate. The regular second in command, the comito who gave orders to the crew, was not eligible because not a noble.

Galley commanders were the key figures in the recruitment and maintenance of the crew. Many a man elected to that honor by the Great Council, the Senate, or the Council of Ten tried to avoid serving because he knew that before he collected any salary he would have to lay out his own funds in order to man and furnish his galley in a way that would do him proud. Many another eagerly sought the honor and strove to be assigned as soon as possible one of the galleys coming from the Arsenal. When he then set up his hiring bench on the Molo in front of the Ducal Palace in order to sign on a crew, he found that if he wished good men, he had to promise them bonuses beyond the official base pay and had to give fat cash loans on the spot in addition to the advance of wages made by the naval paymasters. To recoup later, he might be tempted to skimp on the rations he gave his men, for which he received an allowance of so much per head, or to collect payment for more men than he actually had, or charge excessively for needed repairs. Having paid out considerable coin to man and arm his galley, he certainly felt that he and his family had a stake in it, so that a brother was likely to claim the command if he died, or at least a compensation from whoever was appointed. The government recognized the heavy investments which galley commanders made in their galleys by voting them lump sums as compensation.

Whether a particular galley commander grew richer or poorer depended not only on the extent and success of his padding of his accounts but also on conditions of the labor market, the fortunes of war, and his share in booty. If he took command when there was desperate unemployment among seamen, he might not have to pay any bonuses, he might even collect some kickbacks, at least from the petty officers, especially if he let them profit from such illegal practices as selling wine and cloths on credit at usurious rates to destitute galeotti. When the voyages of the merchant galleys were dwindling in the opening decades of the sixteenth century, there was unemployment whenever the political situation permitted a demobilization of the war fleet. In 1519 the Senate cut the rate of base pay for oarsmen from 12 lire a month to 8 lire, saying that galley commanders who gave their men prompt payment were able to hire at the lower rate. On merchant galleys, 8 lire had for decades been the base pay, but it had been supplemented by venture rights. The 33 percent cut in pay for service on war galleys proved excessive; the rate was raised to 10 lire in 1524. It stayed there for the rest of the century, while prices and other wages mounted. Consequently, when large war fleets were needed as in the 1530's, volunteers could not be hired without big bonuses. By keeping the base pay low and voting the galley commanders lump sums in compensation for their expenses, the Senate in effect shifted to the commanders the opportunities and difficulties of adjusting to fluctuations in the labor market. By mid-century the demand for oarsmen was so large that the shift had the advantage, from the Senate's point of view, of placing a part of the financial burden of naval warfare on the nobles who received the honors of command.

Galley commanders who were rich and public-spirited or politically ambitious probably provided well for their galeotti in order to have crews of which they could be proud but, on the whole, the first half of the sixteenth century was a second period of depression for ordinary seamen and, most markedly, for the oarsmen. After the worsening of their economic and legal status during the Nautical Revolution of the Middle Ages, Venetian galeotti had enjoyed almost a century of amelioration in their working conditions through the expansion of the voyages of the merchant galleys on which they enjoyed valuable fringe benefits and favorable work rules. When those voyages ceased, some 4,000 good jobs vanished also. The expanding war fleets were a poor substitute from the point of view of a galeotto, for the chances of loot were relatively poor against the fearsome Turks. And the food on the galleys deteriorated. To make matters worse, the government again and again failed to pay off crews promptly. Once, in hungry desperation, they sacked the bakeries and escaped unpunished because, as one high admiral who was also a chronicler commented, they were really taking only what was due them. Usually their only redress was to line in tattered garb the stairway in the courtyard of the Ducal Palace, crying out to the passing Senators and ambassadors their need for pay. Such scenes hardly accorded with the Senators' conceptions of the magnificence of the Serenissima. Many well worked-out provisions were enacted to provide prompt payment and to limit the length of time that crews were kept at sea, but they were repeatedly overruled by emergencies. Wage payments while on cruise were much delayed. One complaint of reform-minded commanders was that, when war galleys returned, the men mustered out received so much overdue pay that they never re-enlisted, for no one who had money enough to set himself up in some other occupation would return to the labors and discomforts of an oarsman.

Under these conditions, more and more use was made of conscription. In Crete and Dalmatia, conscription had been used regularly, although extensively supplemented by the hiring of volunteers who could be attracted by loans or bonuses. Conscription from the subject territories in northern Italy was begun hesitatingly in 1500. In spite of discouraging reports from fleet commanders concerning how rapidly these "Lombards" died off, not knowing how to take care of themselves at sea, enrollment of 6,000 men ready to serve partly as soldiers but mainly as oarsmen was ordered in 1522, and efforts were made to give them practice on short summer voyages. A few galleys were successfully manned by volunteers from the Lago di Garda, under the command of nobles of that area as sopracomiti. Mainland conscripts were enrolled to man half of the reserve fleet of 100 galleys presumed to be waiting in the Arsenal, although they were judged no good for the arduous year-round patrol duties requiring more seasoned crews.

To man the other half of that reserve fleet, conscription was re-introduced within Venice. Instead of returning to the organization by parishes and by "dozens" which had been used for that purpose in the fourteenth century, the Senate in the sixteenth century turned to the industrial and fraternal organizations of the artisans and shopkeepers. In 1539 each guild and each Scuola Grande was assigned a number of oarsmen proportionate to its size, or, in the case of the richest, to its wealth. Similar quotas were assigned to the traghetti into which the gondoliers and other boatmen were organized. Substitutes were hired by guildsmen whose health or status made their service at the oar unthinkable, but in the poorer guilds many of the men on whom the lot fell served in person. Substituting guilds and confraternities for parishes as the units on which to place the responsibility for finding men was in accord with the fact that these professional or religious associations had more solidarity than the traditional divisions into neighborhoods. A bargeman or gondolier who went to fill the quota assigned to his traghetto might feel that his brother guildsmen would help his family in his absence.

Aside from such moral support and incidental material aid, the guilds and confraternities paid bonuses to the men who went to fill their quotas. A normal bonus in 1537 was about half the base pay. If the quota was filled by hiring substitutes who were not members of the guild, the bonuses might be considerably larger. Although in the mid-sixteenth century some guilds filled their quota from their own members, they came to rely more and more on substitutes. The levy of galeotti then became simply a way of collecting money to be used in the hiring done by naval paymasters. Such centralization of the hiring seemed the more necessary because it was found that men who would normally be available for service at the oar refused to come to the hiring tables in a crisis, confident that they could later sell their services to some conscript from the mainland or some guildsman desperate to find a substitute. Some must have collected three kinds of advances: the regular four months of base pay, an advance bonus from a guild, and an "outfitting loan" from the galley commander. In Dalmatia also, where many of the crewmen were recruited even for the ships initially manned at Venice, men obtained high bonuses as substitutes. They obtained such high loans from officers competing with one another to fill out their crews that some galeotti, once they had collected all possible advances and had more debts than they could ever hope to pay, yielded to the temptation to jump ship and seek employment with the Spaniards or even the Turks.

This situation inspired the use of convicts, a remedy championed in both words and deeds by one of the most devoted and experienced of Venice's admirals, Cristoforo da Canal. He wrote a book on naval administration and tactics in the form of a rather flowery imaginary dialogue, such as humanists made popular. He included many references to Roman heroes, but was proud to base his own skill and judgment entirely on experience. A galley commander at 22, he had been taught at sea since boyhood by an uncle and he himself took his own four-year-old son with him, weaning him, he said, on ship biscuit. His dialogue written about 1550 evaluated the kinds of free men available. Although he spoke well of Venetians serving as officers or able-bodied seamen, or even as marines, he considered the oarsmen recruited at Venice the worst. In so prosperous a city, good men found other jobs, only penniless beggars enlisted as oarsmen. He praised highly the Dalmatians, and indeed a good part of the crews signed on in Venice must have been immigrants from Dalmatia or Greece. Da Canal considered the Greeks the very best. Although he wrote pungently of their filthy personal habits, he said they could outrow the Dalmatians and were less likely to be ill. But the number of Dalmatians and Greeks that Venice could recruit was shrinking. War with the Ottoman Empire meant Turkish raids into Dalmatia carrying off slaves and tying down other men for defense. The Turks also collected many rowers by slave raids on the Greek islands. One Venetian admiral said that if watch towers were not built along the coasts of Crete to permit warning of such raids, Crete, a major Venetian recruiting ground, would soon be as short of manpower as Dalmatia. Conscripts from mainland Italy were usable only for the brief campaigns in which all the reserve was mobilized. Some new source of oarsmen was necessary for the fleets of 30 to 60 galleys which Venice then needed on patrol even in time of peace.

Convicts were already in use in other navies but were quite subordinate to another kind of galley slave on Spanish, Genoese, or Turkish vessels, slaves who were the personal property of the galley commander — of an Andrea Doria, for example, who bought slaves collected on the Turkish frontiers. A commander such as Andrea Doria had the interest in taking good care of his crews that any property owner had in taking care of his property, and such oarsmen chained to their benches may indeed have been better fed and clothed than many of Venice's free galeotti. But why should a Venetian galley commander take good care of the convicts assigned him? Guided by his rigorous sense of duty and pervasive patriotism, Cristoforo da Canal answered that question by himself setting an example. In 1545 he was elected the commander of the first Venetian galley rowed by men chained to their benches. He operated it so successfully, keeping so many of the convicts alive, that 5 more galleys were so manned in the next two years and placed more or less directly under his supervision.

Da Canal said he preferred convicts to free oarsmen, even when the latter were available, because the men bound by chains were governed by fear and therefore more obedient. The galley as a whole could operate with better discipline, responsible to the will of its commander like a finely geared machine. He was proud of taking good care of his crews and his success was sufficiently appreciated so that he rose to the highest post in the Venetian fleets in 1555. He never attained the title of Captain General of the Sea, for the years of his command were not those of a major mobilization. His task was the hunting out and destruction of the thickening swarms of pirates, and he died in 1562 from the wounds received while destroying a pirate fleet he had waylaid between Albania and Corfu. Recognizing that he had spent his life in their service and lived and died without wealth, the Senators voted a pension to his family, dowries for his daughters, and assurance to his son of a galley command.

Cristoforo da Canal cannot be called typical of Venetian admirals of the sixteenth century; he was too much a devoted reformer. But his career shows that, while many captains may have tried to make money from their commands or have been intent only on making a show for political purposes, one at least was ascetically and dynamically devoted to the welfare of the republic. There was no higher aim for a man's life, he wrote in his dialogue, than to serve and preserve a republic in which the glory of his self-sacrificing deeds would be remembered and recounted as an inspiration to his descendants.

LEPANTO AND AFTER   All Venice's methods of manning were strained to the limit in the War of Cyprus. In the spring of 1570, conscripts from the mainland, Dalmatia, the lagoon cities, and the guilds within Venice were called up to provide crews for 60 light galleys and 12 great galleys. There were about 16 convict galleys at sea with enough "free" galleys which had been previously manned partly in Venice but mainly in Crete, Dalmatia, and the Ionian Isles to make a grand total of 140 galleys. The original crews were decimated that year by disease and many thousands were replaced by oarsmen obtained in the Greek Islands in recruiting drives that may have resembled either the raids by which the Turks often filled their benches with slaves from the same area or the possibly milder methods of press gangs. Some galleys were wrecked trying to operate in bad weather during the following winter, but reinforcements kept coming from the Arsenal. A number were abandoned simply in order to man the others more adequately.

In 1571, the fleet that sailed to the battle of Lepanto was as tabulated below. The galleys listed as manned "from Venice" included some with crews composed largely of Greeks or Dalmatians as well as those manned by convicts or by the conscripts and volunteers from Venice and the mainland. Galleys are tabulated as "from Dalmatia" or "from the Mainland" when their commanders were nobles from specified cities, for example, Spalato or Padua.

FLEET OF THE HOLY LEAGUE AT LEPANTO, 1571

Galleys under Venetian commanders

Light galleys manned from	Venice, free	38
	Venice, convict	16
	Crete	30
	Ionian Isles	7
	Dalmatia	8
	Mainland cities (Terra Ferma)	5
Great galleys from Venice, free		6
Subtotal		110

Galleys under other commanders

Light galleys manned from	Naples and Sicily	36
	Genoa	22
	Papal and Other Italian States	23
	Spain, Malta, etc.	17
Subtotal		98
Grand total		208

The victory at Lepanto was the climax of decades of effort by Venetian diplomats as well as by Venetian admirals, Arsenal, and naval administrators. The possibility of almost doubling their forces through joint action with squadrons sent by the pope and the King of Spain gave Venetian commanders reasons for not operating alone against the Turk. Failure to agree on such joint action prevented the impressive industrial effort in the spring of 1570 from yielding any military fruit. A better prospect for 1571 blossomed from the conclusion of the Holy League under the leadership of Pope Pius V. It not only specified the contingents to be furnished for a crusade by the three allies and the military objectives; it also specified that the supreme command should go to a man in whose will to fight the fleets could have confidence, Don John of Austria, born out of wedlock but raised by his father, Emperor Charles V, as a prince. In spite of the ambiguous orders that he had from his half-brother, King Philip II of Spain, Don John led the fleet into enemy waters seeking battle (see Map 10 insert). A Turkish fleet of about equal strength was taking on supplies and men at Lepanto and many of its commanders urged that it stay there, protected by batteries, until the Christian fleet withdrew, as it would almost surely have to do for lack of food and any base nearer than Corfu. But the Turkish admiral, like Don John, wished the glory of a victory and argued that destruction of this supreme crusading effort would enable the Turks easily to take Crete, the Ionian Isles, and Dalmatia, and to raid Italy at will. Turkish superiority at sea had not been shaken since their victory at Prevesa in 1538, and he did not now wish to seem to fear combat.

Seeking each other and each underestimating the other's strength, the two fleets met in the Gulf of Patras soon after dawn on October 7, 1571, and spent the morning deploying according to pre-arranged plans. All round ships had been left behind; the only heavy gun-carrying vessels involved were 6 Venetian great galleys. These galeasses were towed to the front so that their fire would disrupt and weaken the enemy before the main clash of the op-

MAP 10   INSERT—*Fleet Movements before Lepanto.*

> *At the beginning of 1571 Venetian forces were scattered. About 30 galleys were at Candia in Crete trying to run supplies into Famagusta, the one stronghold still in Venetian hands in Cyprus. At Canea in Crete were another 30 galleys. The newly elected Venetian Captain General of the Sea, Sebastian Venier, had about 50 light galleys and 6 great galleys at Corfu. About 5,000 soldiers who had been hired to serve on the ships were still in Venice. The Turkish fleet came from Negroponte to anchor in Suda Bay in Crete between Candia and Canea, and then headed west. Venier, in order to unite his forces with those of his allies, took his galleys from Corfu to Messina, where the papal, Neapolitan, Sicilian, and Genoese contingents were assemblying and awaiting the arrival of Don John from Spain. The Turkish fleet proceeded up the unguarded Adriatic, sacking the countryside of Corfu and of Dalmatia as far as Lesina but failing to take the fortified strong points. Venice felt threatened in its lagoons, blocked its harbor with a chain and a galeassa, and fortified the Lido. Before the Turks turned back to Lepanto to replenish their supplies and their crews, the Venetian contingents from Crete safely reached Messina. The united Christian fleet then sailed from Messina east in search of the enemy.*

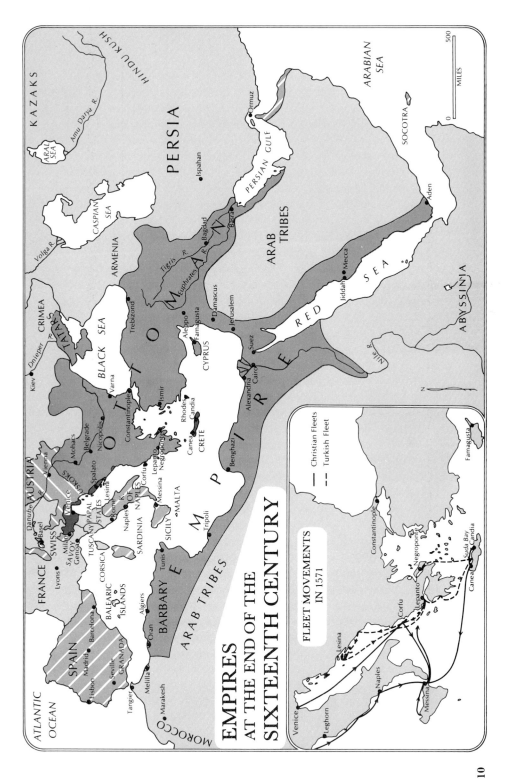

EMPIRES AT THE END OF THE SIXTEENTH CENTURY

FLEET MOVEMENTS IN 1571

Christian Fleets
Turkish Fleet

MAP 10

posing lines of light galleys, but once the Turks had rowed past, most of them were out of the action about a half-mile from the crucial fighting. Cannon were of secondary importance in this battle, although the Christians profited from superior firepower, especially in hand guns, whereas the Turks still extensively used bows. Maneuvering also had little effect on the outcome. The Turks, having more vessels, tried a flanking maneuver. Gian Andrea Doria, commanding the right wing of the Christian fleet, went so far out to sea to prevent being surrounded that he left a gap between his squadron and that in the center commanded by Don John. This hole permitted one of the Turkish pirate admirals to escape when Christian victory was evident. Meanwhile, the outcome was decided by close combat across the decks of galleys mashed together. Its crucial point was in the center where Don John, seconded by the Venetian and papal flagships, out-fought the Turkish flagship, boarded it, and killed the Turkish leaders. The Turks lost about 30,000 men, dead or captured, the Christians about 9,000. The Venetian second-in-command, Provveditore Agostino Barbarigo, was mortally wounded, and some twenty Venetian galley commanders killed. Among the spoils divided by the victors were 117 galleys and many smaller vessels.

Lepanto represented nothing new in tactics. Don John at twenty-four had proved his valor and ability fighting Moriscos in Granada, but was no expert in naval warfare. His contribution was to give the fleet unity, both through his moral leadership and the way in which he organized it. He mixed together the galleys from different ports and different commands, splitting up the Venetians, for example, so that some were assigned to one wing, some to another, although there were fewer Venetian vessels, to be sure, in the right wing commanded by Gian Andrea Doria than in the left wing under the Venetian Provveditore Agostino Barbarigo. The Venetian Captain General, Sebastian Venier, and the commander of the papal fleet, Marco Antonio Colonna, were both stationed next to Don John himself in the center of the central squadron. Finding the Venetian galleys woefully deficient in soldiers — 5,000 who had been hired in Venice were unable to reach the fleet — he persuaded Venier to accept assignment to his ships of Spanish swordsmen. The 40,000 to 50,000 men thus scrambled up together drew their unifying fighting spirit from a crusading zeal which was part of the Counter-Reformation, then at the peak of its force in Spain and Italy. The pope as head of the Holy League and the emperor's young son as commander personified this spirit. Just before the battle, Don John in shining armor went rapidly along the lines in a dispatch boat, shouting encouragement to the crews. As the fleets came within gunshot, all other flags were lowered and Don John hoisted the banner bearing the image of the Crucified Redeemer which had been blessed by the pope. A crucifix was raised aloft on every galley. Men bowed before it, confessed sins, and received absolution according to the indulgence which the pope had granted for the crusade.

Victory at Lepanto did not save Cyprus. Before the fleets met, Famagusta had fallen and the Turkish conqueror, violating the honorable terms of surrender, had flayed the Venetian commander alive and stuffed his skin with straw to be mocked by the triumphant Turks. Joint operations of the crusading fleet the next year failed to win any compensating conquest, since the spirit which had brought unity in battle did not give unity to the divergent policies of Venice and Spain. Although won under the crusaders' banner, not under that

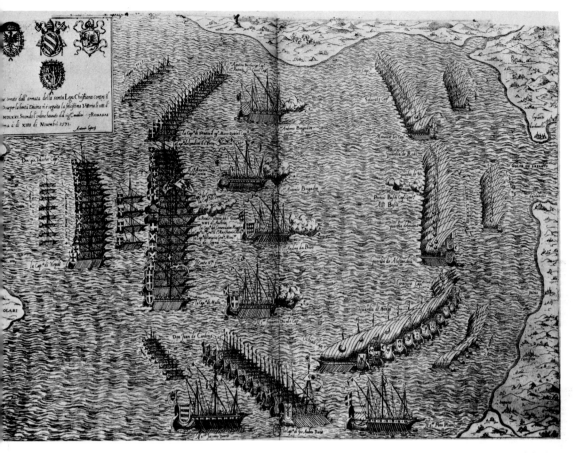

FIGURE 36   *The Opposing Fleets at the Battle of Lepanto (Photo Bibliothèque Nationale, Paris).*

of the winged lion of Saint Mark, the victory of Lepanto deserved the wild cele-bration which burst forth at Venice when a galley entered port, trailing cap-tured Turkish flags and shooting off its guns while its crew shouted: "Vittoria! Vittoria!" An Ottoman victory or an ignominious Christian withdrawal would have placed at the mercy of the Turk every Venetian who ventured to sea.

For ten years after Lepanto, there was hardly a single new galley built in the Arsenal; surviving Arsenalotti were occupied storing captured galleys and refitting. For a time, crews ceased to be a problem, because prisoners of war were used as galley slaves. Then peace brought a reduction in the war fleet. Patrolling galleys were rowed almost entirely by convicts, with only about 50 unchained men to a galley, nearly all sailors or soldiers. Only on some of the flagships were all on board free men.

The use of oarsmen chained to their benches went hand in hand with a change in the system of rowing. One large oar pulled by all the men on the same bench, instead of a separate oar for each man, became general in most navies before Lepanto and was tried out by the Venetians in 1537, but at Lepanto their galleys were still triremes, that is, they had three oars and three men to a bench (as in Figure 35). The major advantage of the single large oar was that additional slaves, no matter how unskilled, could be put on the bench to pull on it. After Lepanto, when the Venetian galleys were no longer rowed by free men, they too adopted a single oar to a bench. They had four men to an oar on the standard light galleys. On large flagships the number sometimes rose in the seventeenth century to as high as eight.

Many men to an oar and one oar to a bench also contributed to increasing the speed of the galleass and prolonging its life. These vessels became a kind of symbol of Venetian maritime skill. In many respects, Venice's reputation as a sea power was fading during the sixteenth century. Other nations were producing more skilled navigators. The humiliations at Turkish hands earlier in the century were not entirely expunged by Lepanto, but that victory did much to restore Venice's naval reputation. In that battle the performance of the Venetian galleasses had been most impressive. They stood out in front, isolated, in face of the oncoming enemy and saw the Turks break their lines in order to avoid their fire. In the campaign of the year after Lepanto, the Venetians tried to tow their galleasses to the front whenever an engagement seemed likely. They lost so much time in these maneuvers that they repeatedly failed to bring the Turkish fleet to action.

At the end of the century, some galleasses were sent to hunt pirates. To give them the speed needed for that purpose, their deck arrangements were changed after consultation with many experts, including the local professor of mathematics, Galileo Galilei. The new type of galleass had a crew of about 500, including 288 oarsmen of whom three-fourths were convicts. It was a relatively safe vessel on which to serve, for it was so powerfully armed that no rowed vessel was ever likely to attack it and, even as rearranged, it was not fast enough to force battle on an opponent unless it could catch a sailing vessel in harbor or becalmed. In these circumstances, galleasses could maneuver to use their guns while avoiding enemy fire, as they did in destroying one notorious Dutch pirate, Carstens. But on the whole, they were not effective against northern pirates who used round ships and kept the seas in winter when a galley, even a galleass, could not stay long on patrol without inordinate illness in its crew. Although built at a time when Venice's power was waning and the oarless ship-of-the-line was beginning its rule of the waves, the galleasses are among the most famous products of Venetian shipwrights. They answered the special problem of combining artillery and oars with an intricate but integrated magnificence worthy of the Baroque.

CHANGING FLEETS AND SHIPYARDS · III

Argosies with Portly Sails

CHAPTER TWENTY-SIX

The histories of the United States and of Venice are remarkably similar in one respect. In the early history of both republics, the sea was a source of wealth, contributing to the expansion of the rest of the economy. An American merchant marine advantaged by a plentiful supply of ship timber and of seamen expanded during the French Revolution and Napoleonic Wars. Soon thereafter, ships from Salem and New Bedford brought back wealth from China and polar whale fisheries. A little later, as the country as a whole was turning away from the sea, American shipwrights created their masterpieces, the clipper ships. But after the Civil War the economy grew faster in other sectors. Having lost its comparative advantage as a seafaring nation, the United States kept a merchant marine alive by subsidies and protective navigation laws, drawing on the strength of the rest of the economy for the purpose of enabling its maritime industries to withstand the competition of foreigners who had cheaper supplies and labor.

Similarly Venice, having used its ships and seamen to gain the lordship of the gulf, a colonial empire, and a leading place among centers of international trade, found later opportunities for growth in industry and finance. As its timber supplies dwindled and labor turned toward other skills, it lost its comparative advantage in building and operating ships. Against competitors who had cheaper supplies and cheaper labor, Venice used the resources provided by the vigor of other sectors of her economy. She tried, as the United States tried later, to preserve a glorified maritime tradition by protective navigation laws and by subsidies.

Of course, shipping was more important to the Venetian than to the American republic, both in youth and in maturity. After Venetians no longer enjoyed lower costs in furnishing transportation by sea, Venice remained the leading port of the Adriatic, and one of the half dozen busiest ports in all the Mediterranean. The volume of the trade moving through the city was increased by the growth of its industries, by its position as a political capital, and by the agricultural and industrial development of its hinterland. And Venice continues down to the present to be a leading port, competing with Naples for second place in modern Italy.

Galleys were in no century the major element in the movement of tonnage through the port, in spite of their importance for the value of their cargoes and the number of men they employed. If small round ships as well as large vessels are included in estimates, then round ships were the more important also in providing jobs. Moreover, the future lay with round ships, not galleys, for both war and trade. The disappearance of the Venetian merchant galleys, like the disappearance of the American clipper ships, was an inevitable result of changing technology. The future of the Venetian merchant marine depended on its adjustment to technical changes in round ships and economic conditions affecting their use and construction.

TIMBER SHORTAGE, FALLING FREIGHTS, AND SUBSIDIES A deterioration of Venice's competitive position showed first in the building and operation of the smaller and simpler types. As the forests which had once surrounded the lagoons and which had supplied timber cargoes for Romano Mairano and other twelfth-century sea captains were cleared away, shipwrights followed them back to the foothills of the Alps. Early in the fifteenth century, complaints of unemployment by Venetian shipwrights were met by banning the import of boats and barges from such cities as Treviso and Verona. Such imports were ordered burned. Then somewhat bigger vessels from Istria became a threat and were forbidden. By mid-century, a general prohibition against the buying by Venetians of foreign-built ships and against their shipping wares to Venice on foreign ships was reiterated. In earlier centuries, Venetian laws forbad foreigners to build at Venice without special license or to buy or charter Venetian vessels, assuming the plenitude of Venetian ships could be used to increase the amount of Venetian trade. In the fifteenth and sixteenth centuries, Venetian laws forbad Venetians building or buying elsewhere or shipping to Venice on foreign vessels, assuming that the volume of Venetian trade could be used to increase the number of Venetian ships.

Even after the construction of smaller craft was in decline, the number and size of big round ships increased. About 1450, there were at least 30 of 240 tons or more. Anything over 200 tons was considered big in that age. The cogs which the Venetian government armed against pirates were considered enormous, even if only a little over 600 tons. The Genoese, to be sure, used many larger vessels and did not have to worry about shallow channels in their home port, as did the Venetians. For Venice, 400 tons became a normal size for some 6 to 10 cogs carrying cotton and ashes from Syria, for 3 or 4 bringing slaves or food supplies from the Black Sea, 3 or 4 making the long voyage from Crete to England, and a dozen or so more handling grain, oil, wine, and salt on various runs. These big round ships carried a far larger tonnage than did the merchant galleys at their peak and could almost rival them from the point of view of prestige, value of cargoes, and political importance.

Suddenly in the 1460's and 1470's, a precipitous drop in freight rates plunged also this section of the industry into depression. Freights on many of the bulk cargoes, such as cotton, potash, and salt, fell by at least a quarter during the fifteenth century. Wine shipments from Crete to England, which had cost 7 or 8 ducats a cask, fell in the 1470's to as low as 3 or 4 ducats.

Since the downward movement of freights was so general, one may ask whether the drop is to be explained at least in part by the technical change which occurred at about that time, namely the displacement of ketch-rigged cogs by the full-rigged carack. That change began in the mid-fifteenth century with the addition of a small square sail on a forward mast and another above the crow's-nest on the mainmast (see Figures 10 and 37). Later, more sails were added in the same pattern; and the big, bulging mainsail which was characteristic of the early caracks as well as of cogs was divided into several smaller square sails hung on as many yards on the same mast, a change that made the canvas stand flatter and the ship better able to beat to windward (see Figure 39).

While these changes were making big round ships more secure from storms, improvements in cannon were making them more secure from pirates. They thereby became better able to compete with the merchant galleys for cargo, as has been explained. Increased security tended to decrease overall costs of operation, but the added sails tended to increase rather than decrease the crew needed. Any effect of the new rig on the freight for wine or cotton must have been very gradual.

The sudden drop in freight rates between Crete and England was the result of competition not among the Venetian shippers but from foreigners, partly from Englishmen and Spaniards who were active in the Mediterranean in those decades, and above all from Genoese. All the big caracks became more dependent on the Channel voyage when the Turks squeezed them out of the Black Sea. Moreover, for the direct voyage from the Aegean to the Channel, the Genoese had relied especially on alum which they loaded near Chios. Just when the Turks were interfering with that trade, the alum discovered in the Papal States in 1461 conquered the western markets. Thereafter, Genoese ships making their traditional voyage from the Aegean to the Channel, on which they carried also silks, spices, cotton, and other eastern products, had to replace alum with some other heavy cargo so as to balance their load. This may explain their offering such low freights on wine from Crete to England.

Nearer home, Venice's most damaging competitor was Ragusa, which was becoming in the fifteenth century what Venice had been in the twelfth. Ragusans were closer to the unexhausted oak forests of Gargano, the spur on the heel of Italy, and shipping was their chief means of livelihood. They bid cargoes away from the Venetians on all seas, even in the Adriatic.

To preserve the merchant marine against all this competition, the Venetian Senate tried a half dozen methods. It decreed that the trade between Venice and its colonies, and exchanges within the northern Adriatic which Venice's staple rights stipulated should go through Venice, must be transported by Venetian vessels only, a protective device similar to the United States' insistence that its coastwise shipping be under the American flag. Ragusan vessels were banned from Venice unless they were bringing grain. The parts of Dalmatia under Venetian rule were at one time forbidden to build any vessels larger than 30 tons and later were permitted to do so only provided they had no association with Ragusan or other foreign capitalists.

Foreign ships generally were put at a disadvantage by being made to pay higher tonnage duties in Venice and by restrictions on what they could load.

To recapture voyages to the Channel with wine from Crete, the Senate decreed a tax on each cask loaded by foreigners, so as to bring their cost up to what Venetian shipowners said they had to charge, a tax of 5 ducats per cask in 1473, 4 ducats in 1488. The King of England retaliated by levying at his end a tax on all Cretan wine brought in by foreigners, and he kept on collecting his tax even after the Venetians removed theirs in response to strong representations from Cretans who complained that these taxes forced them to sell at ruinous prices. But the government was determined to give some help in that voyage to shipowners, since it was the voyage which made profitable the biggest caracks, the kind the government wanted to have available for use in war fleets. It therefore voted a bounty of 2 ducats for each cask shipped from Crete to the Channel, a kind of differential operating subsidy for an "essential" route.

A direct construction subsidy of so much per ton for ships which were of specified size and were built within a specified period had been used as early as 1433, in an effort to get extra large vessels, and similar offers were made with increasing amounts of subsidy, as much as 4 ducats per *botte* (about 6 per ton) in 1486. These offers had so little effect in the 1480's and 1490's that the government itself built the big round ships it wanted as naval auxiliaries. Construction bounties had a good effect only when combined with an increase in freight rates. A law of 1502 setting minimum freights and providing for their prompt collection was followed by a burst of building. The legislated minimum freight rates may have been less responsible for this revival than were the diversion of Atlantic shipping to the new oceanic voyages and the conclusion of peace between Venice and the Turk. The boom was vigorous but short-lived, and after the War of the League of Cambrai a new effort was felt necessary.

One freight rate of crucial importance for the big caracks was fully under government control, namely, the amount the government paid for the delivery of salt from Iviza and Cyprus. Local sales of salt had always been a major source of revenue, and treaties with neighbors such as the Duke of Milan could open up wider markets, making an increase in supplies worthwhile. Caracks returning from carrying wine to England had plenty of room to load salt at Iviza, the smallest of the Balearic Islands, although they had to compete there with Genoese also trying to supply north Italian markets. Near the other end of the Mediterranean, salt from Cyprus served as ballast under cargoes of cotton or other light wares, and after Venice acquired Cyprus, she gave her caracks a monopoly of collecting this cargo from the great salt lake near Limassol.

The most successful program of aid to Venetian shipbuilders was begun in 1533 when the Council of Ten upped the appropriation for paying freights for overseas salt from 12,000 ducats a year to 18,000 ducats. The Senate made sure that this money would really be used to build big ships by decreeing that it be loaned to builders and collected back from them by deducting appropriate amounts from the increased freights credited to them for bringing salt. This system of loans to builders of big ships was periodically renewed. It seemed so successful that it was extended to all builders of big ships whether they loaded salt or other cargo. They were given seven years in which to repay. These loans and the salt subsidies (the nearest Venetian equivalent perhaps to the mail subsidies used more recently to aid merchant marines) accompanied a revival of activity in the private shipyards of Venice that lasted until 1570.

CARACKS ASCENDANT Whether they caused that revival may be doubted. Offers of construction subsidies and increased payments for salt made in the 1470's had not had any such effect. Probably the insatiable demand for ships created by wars, by the general economic expansion, and particularly by new oceanic voyages benefited the Venetian merchant marine. Certainly there were more big round ships in Venice in the 1560's than there had ever been before, and their carrying capacity was so much greater than the capacity of any other type that it seems probable the total tonnage of the Venetian merchant marine reached its peak in the 1560's. Such evidence as we have even indicates that more big caracks were then going in and out of the lagoons than in and out of Genoa, although at that time only the channel at Malamocco was deep enough for them. There were at least 40 of the big ships favored by the government, mostly of 600 to 700 tons. Although the Cretan wine trade had been depressed by the taxes, Venetian ships had regained most of what survived. Returning, these ships brought back the wool, cloth, tin, and lead formerly loaded on the galleys of Flanders. Big caracks also took to Constantinople and Alexandria Venetian manufactures of the kind the galleys used to freight. They trusted their size and artillery to repel pirates. They carried the heavy movement of grain and varied their ports of call with the harvests but found it hard to supply all the grain needed with the growth of population. Caracks instead of galleys received licenses to load pilgrims for Palestine.

The Ragusans, to be sure, were still annoying as competitors. Their ships were also increasing in number and size and became so well known in England that there is some ground for thinking that the term "argosies" is derived from "Ragusan." Or the word may be derived from the Argonauts of Greek myth. When Shakespeare applied it to the vessels bearing the fortune of his Merchant of Venice, he had plenty of opportunity to see in the Thames, from both Venice and Ragusa, "argosies with portly sail, like signiors and rich burgers . . . over-peer the petty traffickers."

Their cargoes would have been insured, however, as Shakespeare's Antonio's were not. During the fifteenth century, Venice had become the major center for marine insurance; the wide-flung Medici partnerships used their Venetian branch to place insurance on shipments between various ports. One of the narrow lanes leading into the Rialto was called "Insurance Street" (Calle della Sicurtà). The insurance brokers found there would give you forms (in the sixteenth century, printed forms) on which you could write your name, the ship, the wares, and the amount of insurance you wanted. The broker then took it around to men he knew who commonly acted as "underwriters." They wrote underneath, at the bottom of the form, that for a stated premium they would insure for a given amount, seldom more than 500 ducats' worth, more often 100 or 200. In this way, the risks of losing one ship and its cargo was divided among hundreds of people.

Ease in insuring cargoes favored the use of caracks instead of galleys. Even if vessels were well armed and in convoy, there was still some chance of loss through storms or piracy, a risk greater than any danger that underwriters would fail to pay. When the extra costs of a merchant galley exceeded the costs of insurance on caracks, a merchant would prefer the latter. Insurance rates naturally varied according to the ship and the circumstances. At the outbreak of the War of the League of Cambrai, rates jumped, so Priuli reports, from 2½ to 5 percent on ships from Syria, and insurance for wares on the Flemish galleys, which had been 4 percent, could not be had even for 15 percent (although in fact those galleys made it home quite safely). At the end of the sixteenth century, the rates between Venice and Alexandria or Syria were mostly 3½ or 4 percent.

As in so many other ways, caracks replaced merchant galleys also in providing an apprentice-like kind of education for young nobles. Each carack was required to carry some "poor nobles" as "bowmen of the quarterdeck." Even when the post did not serve to launch an impoverished young man on a mercantile maritime career, as originally intended, it gave useful experience in seeing the world. One young man who was particularly diligent in using it that way, Alessandro Magno, kept a full diary in order, as he said, to aid pleasures of later recollection, to while away the time, and to satisfy his curiosity. He gives the names of all the crew, their duties and pay, the courses and winds day by day, cargo lists, and much detail on his sightseeing ashore, such as how he got inside the great pyramids in Egypt. His first voyage was as a mere passenger, to be sure, providing company for a sister who was going with her husband, infant daughter, and father-in-law to a position in Cyprus. Then Alessandro purchased posts as noble bowman on voyages to Alexandria and London. He improved his education by four such voyages before he reached the age of admission to the Great Council, twenty-five, and then was promptly nominated by an older brother for a profitable office, Treasurer at Brescia.

The ships on which Alessandro Magno sailed were of 600 to 700 tons. They carried crews totaling as few as 52 for one voyage to Cyprus, and at most 73 for the voyage to England, counting everyone including the master and the deck hands. These hands (*fanti*) numbered 20 to 30 and received the same monthly pay as the oarsmen on a war galley, 10 lire, but they each had in addition a right to load a little over a half ton free of freight. There were four helmsmen and four "able-bodied seamen" (*marineri*) who had tonnage rights twice as large and one or two lire more per month. Craftsmen such as the carpenter received three times the tonnage rights and twice the salary of the "hands."

Although he mentions twenty-two ratings of specialists, including a barber who made some income from the sale of medicine and ointments, Alessandro makes no mention of a chaplain. Religious ceremonies were not lacking, however. At prescribed hours, the mate's whistle called the crew together. The mate and scribe led prayers to which the crew intoned responses of "Amen" or "And protect our ship and the ship's company."

FIGURE 37 *Caracks Setting Sail (Photo Böhm).*

In his Legend of St. Ursula, *behind the young couple taking leave of their parents, Carpaccio painted the waiting ships with the form and sails of caracks of the late fifteenth century: high forecastle and sterncastle, a very big square mainsail on the main mast, a square topsail above the crow's-nest, a square sail on a mast rising from the forecastle, and one or two lateen-rigged masts aft.*

As a noble, Alessandro of course ate at the captain's table. So also on the merchantmen did the mate, the pilot, the purser or scribe, the carpenter, the caulker, the gunners, and passengers paying 5 ducats a month. How well they ate depended on how much the ship's master wished to do himself honor, but many of the choicest mouthfulls were saved for the second table, Alessandro said, because it included, besides lesser ratings and passengers paying only 3 ducats, the steward and the cook. Even the deck hands at the third mess were much better fed than oarsmen on war galleys, for they had meat three times a week, with sardines and cheese on the other days, as well as all the bean soup (*minestre*) they wanted. At Easter, all the ship's company ate together on the best that the season and the place could afford.

On none of Alessandro's voyages was the ship's master a noble or a part owner, although he was still called the *patron*. He was a hired man like the rest of the crew, although paid by the year, "on land or sea," as were the mate, the purser, and the steward in charge of supplies (*masser*). In sixteenth-century Venice, nobles still were prominent among the shipowners (*parcenevoli*), but commanding merchantmen was a distinct occupation left increasingly to middle-class Venetians or Dalmatians. At the same time, Venice was falling behind in the art of nagivation. At the beginning of the century, Portugal was in the lead, although many individual Italians (including some Venetians, as we have seen) played a prominent role as experts; in mid-century, the Spaniards moved ahead; so did the English at the end of the century, developing new techniques which were needed for oceanic voyages. Old-fashioned methods—dead-reckoning and a knowledge of headlands, harbors, and winds— were most important to such a Mediterranean seaman as Cristoforo da Canal, but even in these traditional aspects of their art the Venetian navigators were losing their former fame.

There were many other signs that this Indian summer of Venetian shipbuilding would be followed by a bleak winter. Most obvious was the shortage of oaken ship timbers. A few good oak forests still grew around the northern Adriatic, but the Arsenal insisted on reserving them for its exclusive use; for example, the Val di Montona in Istria and the hills of Montello near Treviso, both of which were protected by ditches and by forest rangers headed by shipwrights from the Arsenal. To strengthen the Arsenal's monopoly, all shipbuilders receiving loans were required after 1559 to swear that they had cut no oak in Venetian domains.

From buying timbers abroad to buying abroad whole ships was a natural step. A step halfway was taken even before 1570; many Venetian nobles obtained licenses to export larch and fir, which were relatively plentiful in Venice, in order to build vessels in the colonies, especially at Curzola, the one Dalmatian city where the construction of big ships was encouraged. Many rebuilt foreign vessels were accorded the same rights as those built in Venice. In years of grain shortage, Venetian registry was similarly granted to some foreign-built ships as a reward for importing wheat.

THE COLLAPSE   The War of Cyprus and the Great Plague which began just two years later in 1575 disrupted both ship construction and trade. Trade revived in the 1580's, and the amount of traffic moving through the port of Venice kept on growing through the end of the century. Shipbuilding, however, did not revive. As materials became ever harder to find, the costs of construction at Venice quadrupled while seamen's wages, like prices in general, about doubled between 1550 and 1590. The benefits reserved for Venetian-built ships were not sufficient to offset these costs, plus such operating costs as carrying young nobles. More and more of the trade of Venice was carried by vessels not Venetians.

These decades of debacle for Venetian shipbuilding were the same years in which the Dutch were revolutionizing the industry by new methods of construction and by a new, cheaper type of cargo carrier. They had even less timber supplies in their own country than the Venetians, but the Dutch organized imports from Scandinavia and such Baltic ports as Danzig, stored big supplies in good order so that desired pieces could be quickly found, moved them with cranes, and sawed them with windmills. For the cheap import of the timber they developed the flyboat, a relatively low, flat-bottomed, vessel of light construction which had a very roomy hull. Square-rigged, it required a small crew. It was not readily defensible, but where pirates were scarce, it brought transport costs down to a new low.

During boom periods in shipbuilding at Venice, its business leaders were not putting their energies into cutting costs by methods such as the Dutch used. Venetian merchants who wanted a carack formed a partnership including one man who was to be the ship's master and another who would buy or cut the lumber. Either he or a third partner hired a foreman shipwright who both designed the vessel and directed the masters who helped him build it. This foreman and his workers went back and forth between receiving wages from the Arsenal and from private builders. In small shipyards, there were craftsmen-managers, to be sure, building gondolas and barges. Attempts by some of them to extend their operations to the construction of big ships had been checked in 1425 by forbidding them to take a contract for a vessel of more than 100 tons. With this limitation, there was little chance in the industry for the development of owner-managers who combined technical competence, capital, and entrepreneurial ability.

There was at least one, however, Bernardino Sebastian Rosso, and he sought government aid when depression hit the industry. A Francesco Rosso, probably his grandfather, had been the foremost builder of merchant galleys in the Arsenal at the beginning of the sixteenth century, but in the middle of the century Bernardino Rosso was turning out caracks and smaller vessels in a shipyard of his own, the limitation of 1425 having fallen into desuetude. In 1589 he said he had built twenty ships or more, but his last one had remained unsold for three years. He petitioned not only for a subsidy, but for special exemptions that would enable him to cut costs in organizing a stable labor force and in felling and transporting timbers. He was granted encouraging privileges, but his enterprise had little success. Not having earlier developed a group of entrepreneurs intent on the economics of shipyards, Venice found too few such men to face the difficulties evident at the end of the century.

Another effort in the private sector to meet the crisis is suggested by the multiplication of a type of vessel operating with reduced costs, a type called the *marciliana*. They were low, flat-bottomed, and broad, with bulging bows and square sails. They needed only a small crew and were not burdened by regulations such as those requiring caracks to carry noble bowmen. They were particularly adapted to the harbors of the Adriatic, but began to go outside, to Crete and beyond, and to grow in size. They were an easy prey for pirates, but their multiplication suggests that this could be compensated for, from a strictly business point of view, by insurance combined with lower freights. The government disapproved of the marciliane, however, and in 1602 forbad them to go beyond Zante. It wished all long voyages to be made by big caracks because they were useful naval auxiliaries, or by a type of commercial galleon developed in Crete which used high lateen sails and was favored because it trained the kind of sailors needed on the lateen-rigged war galleys.

The Senate's policy towards the merchant marine in the sixteenth century not only clung to traditional types but was guided less by economic considerations than by the concerns of naval commanders.

To induce the building of large ships, the Senate continued for a time to depend on fat construction subsidies. When that did no good, in 1590 it repealed the ban on buying foreign ships. There were then only 12 good-sized Venetian vessels, and it seemed clear that there would soon be no big merchantmen flying the flag of Saint Mark unless the demand of home shipbuilding for protection was overridden. At the same time, raises in freight rates were authorized, and in 1602 western ships were barred from carrying wares between Venice and the Levant. Thus encouraged, the Venetian merchant marine recovered enough to contain 26 vessels counted in 1605 as "large," which then meant over 360 tons. More than half of them were foreign-built. When there was a new crises in 1627, the government went so far in reversing former policy as to offer subsidies for the purchase of foreign ships.

Buying in foreign shipyards did not restore vitality to the Venetian merchant marine. The Dutch and English were proving that they could not only build cheaper, they could operate more efficiently. Merchantmen from the Atlantic had stayed out of the Mediterranean almost entirely between 1553 and 1573, but thereafter the English and others returned to bring wheat and stock fish and to load wines and raisins from the Greek isles. They obtained from the Ottoman sultan rights to trade directly with his domains. They even began handling much of the traffic in and out of Venice itself. Their vessels were smaller than the caracks favored by the Venetian government, seldom more than 250 tons. Being able to sail with less wind and to complete cargoes more quickly, they provided faster service. When Venetians bought such vessels from the English or Dutch and tried to sail them with Venetian crews so as to have the advantages of Venetian registry, they could not operate as efficiently, for the Venetian seamen did not have the skills needed on these types. Even Venetian merchants increasingly preferred loading on foreign ships because they charged lower freights or permitted lower rates of insurance.

This trend was accentuated by the burgeoning of piracy both within the Adriatic and throughout the Mediterranean. Particularly troublesome to Venice was the plundering in the northern Adriatic by the Uskoks (*Uscocchi*), who were Christian refugees from Bosnia and the parts of Dalmatia conquered by the Turks (the name Uskok comes from the Serbo-Croatian word for "escaped"). When Venice made peace after the Battle of Lepanto, the Uskoks continued their own war against the Turks. They were enrolled by the Hapsburg rulers whose territory bordered on the Ottoman Empire to defend their frontier. Their main headquarters was the city of Segna (modern Senj) just east of Istria (see

Maps 2 and 10). They seldom received the pay promised them and lived mainly by plundering passing ships or nearby towns which they accused of carrying enemy goods or trading with the enemy. The whole city of Segna lived from such robbery, the expeditions were blessed in the local church, and the monasteries of the Dominicans and Franciscans received tenths from the loot. The Uskoks operated swarms of small craft with about ten oars to a side which were very hard to catch because they were rowed with great speed by dozens of oarsmen taking turns at the oars. They were aided, Venetians believed, by their women who in caves ashore worked spells to call down from the mountains the deadly north wind, the *boro*, to destroy any fleet seeking to blockade them. They preyed equally on Ragusan and Venetian vessels, but were inclined to avoid those Dalmatian vessels which operated on shares. Crews that had an interest in safe delivery of the cargo fought back. Venetian seamen were generally on wages. On agreement that they be spared, they would stand aside and let the Uskoks carry off the goods of rich merchants, whether Turks, Jews, or Christians. The Uskoks being fellow Christians might not enslave them if they put up no fight. This aspect of the Uskoks' depredations suggests that their success was as much an expression of class war as of the crusading spirit. Both characterizations are anachronistic, in opposite ways, but they suggest how far the Uskoks were from being ordinary pirates.

While the Uskoks harried the northern Adriatic, Venetian patrols further south were kept busy by Turkish corsairs from Albanian ports. The Adriatic was more infested with pirates than it had ever been since the tenth century.

The pirate danger gave a new lease on life to merchant galleys. The Senate was willing to subsidize their use and had plenty of great galleys idle in the Arsenal. In 1588 it provided two for service to Corfu and Zante, setting a very low charter fee and giving 5,000 ducats as operating subsidy with each. Less subsidy was necessary to stimulate their use on the shorter run to Spalato when that Dalmatian city was developed into a terminus for the overland route from Constantinople and handled more and more trade as the seas became more and more unsafe. Going from Spalato to Venice this trade passed around the head-lands of the homes from which the Uskoks had "escaped." For protection from the Uskoks, Daniele Rodriga began backing proposals for galley voyages even before his improvements at Spalato bore fruit. Once docks and warehouses were ready, shipmasters from Spalato came forward to bid for galleys that would travel back and forth between that city and Venice. A new type of galley was developed for the Spalato voyage with less draft than the great merchant galleys of the past and a different kind of crew. The crew totaled only 160, and of that number 40 were soldiers. As soon as the vessel reached Venice, it was taken over by an unloading crew of 10, while the regular crew was shifted to a second galley which started back immediately for Spalato. Thus this shuttle made six voyages a year in 1614-19, eight voyages in 1636.

Outside the Adriatic also Venetian shipping was afflicted by both Christian and Moslem pirates, with the Christians doing the most damage. When Venice withdrew from the Holy League after Lepanto, it tried to maintain a neutral position between the warring Ottoman and Spanish empires. Consequently, its vessels seemed fair prey to the corsairs who formed parts of both fleets and who were released for concentration on private piratical enterprise when the two empires made peace in 1580. By that treaty, the Turkish sultan assumed no more obligation to suppress the Barbary sea captains than the King of Spain did to suppress the regular raiding of Moslem shipping by the Knights of St. John, based on Malta. What was worse, Spanish governors of Naples and Sicily aided corsairs with whom they shared the profits. Even when not so encouraged, Christians calling themselves "crusaders" claimed the right to seize from a Venetian ship any wares belonging to Moslems or Jews. Before plundering a vessel, they sometimes went to the trouble of torturing the ship's officers to make them "confess" that the cargo belonged to "Infidels." The Venetian flag was little protection unless backed by guns on board or on galleys nearby.

Most damaging of all were the pirates from England and other northern countries. When they came into the Mediterranean, they used not the one-decked lightly-manned Dutch flyboats, but a "defensible merchantman" which was more like a galleon, essentially the same type of vessel with which the English were preying on Spanish shipping. Although relatively small, they were strongly built and carried formidable batteries. The English needed guns and fighting men to protect themselves from the Spanish and the Moors, and they used them to plunder promiscuously. Venetian caracks were especially tempting victims because of the richness of their cargoes. In 1603, the Venetians figured that they had lost a dozen good-sized vessels to corsairs backed by the Spanish viceroys, and another dozen to pirates from northern waters. The English heaped injury upon insult by competing at the same time commercially, underbidding Venetian ships for cargoes of cotton, wine, and fruits.

Some Senators thought that reviving the use of great galleys for commercial voyages was the best countermove against piracy outside as well as inside the Adriatic, but the Board of Trade reported against the proposal to send them to Syria. They would lack cargoes, it said, since the trade was in the hands of a few family firms which owned their own ships and carried spices and silks cheaply because they filled up with cotton at Cyprus. Instead, convoys were instituted, composed exclusively of ships of over 360 tons which were ordered to carry plenty of guns and soldiers and were escorted through the most dangerous waters by great galleys armed at inordinate expense. Some big Venetian ships were in fact sufficiently well armed to give a good account of themselves against pirates, but the officials in charge of inspecting complained that many owners and shippers preferred spending money on insurance instead of spending it on good crews. Once they had insured, they did not care whether or not the vessel and wares were lost, so they hired green boys who hid below as soon as pirates threatened to come aboard.

Among the boys thus hiding were some pauper children. A decree of 1559 required each ship of 300 tons or more to carry three such as cabin boys on the grounds that service at sea would reform their morals by rescuing them from begging.

At the first signs in the fifteenth century that its merchant marine faced stiff competition, the Venetian government began using the general strength of the Venetian economy to support merchant shipping. At the beginning of the seventeenth century, after two centuries of subsidies and protective navigation laws, Venice was a flourishing port, but was desperately dependent on foreign shipyards and foreign seamen. The navigation act passed in 1602, which gave prior loading rights to vessels of Venetian registry and stopped Western ships from transporting wares between Venice and the Levant, pushed protection of the merchant marine to the point where it threatened to undermine the foundations of Venice's position in international commerce.

A TENACIOUS DEFENSE · I

Of Sovereignty and the Constitution

CHAPTER TWENTY-SEVEN

Esto pertetua! (Be thou perpetual!)
LAST WORDS OF PAOLO SARPI (1623)

Continental Europe in the seventeenth century is characterized generally by economic stagnation and the consolidation of absolute monarchies. As these trends became evident, the Venetians felt their republic more and more threatened. Between the two great plagues of 1575-77 and 1630-31, the cresting fervor of the Counter-Reformation worked to increase not only the power of the papacy in Italy but also that of the Hapsburg princes. During the same period, the success of Venice's response to the oceanic challenge was proved transitory, for the economic upswing at the end of the sixteenth century was followed by a devastating decline. These circumstances presented Venice with threats that were met by skillful diplomacy and a short-winded reinvigoration of Venice's republicanism.

PEACE-KEEPING DIPLOMACY Weakness forced Venice to follow a policy of neutrality after the War of Cyprus and the plague of 1575-77. She was quite unable to prevent Spanish domination of Italy during the decades when France was disrupted by its wars of religion. While France was thus crippled and while the Ottoman Empire under ineffective sultans directed its armies against Persia, the Spanish and Austrian empires, both ruled by Hapsburgs, dominated continental Europe. The Spanish Empire included Milan and the Kingdom of Naples. The Austrian

Empire included as much of Hungary and Croatia as had not been conquered by the Turks. Their territories would have been contiguous had not Venice's domains lain between them (see Map 10). To ally with them too closely or to oppose them too obstreperously would endanger Venice's independence or existence. And there was always worry lest the Turks would again turn their energies westward and attack Venice's remaining colonial empire.

In order to make its neutrality respected, Venice fortified its cities and its overseas bases according to the new principles of military engineering which developed to counter the rapid improvement in cannon. It maintained, even in time of peace, a fair number of mercenary soldiers. Italian troops having deteriorated at the beginning of the seventeenth century—"It was said of them that they were good for something only if they were outside their own country" (Ranke)—Venice depended partly on Albanians, partly on Germans, who were officered not by Venetian nobles but by foreigners. Meanwhile the Spanish, Austrian, and French monarchies were building armies many times larger. For their command, supply, and finance, these monarchies developed embryonic bureaucracies: specialized functionaries permanently employed in graded ranks under centralized direction. Venice improved its treasury records and budgetary controls, to be sure, but lacked centralized bureaucracies. It continued to rely on overlapping boards of magistrates that checked each other in the republican spirit developed in earlier centuries and that were composed of nobles elected for short terms of office. The most experienced and most powerful nobles rotated through top governing councils, changing positions about once a year. The ever-increasing number of boards and inter-council committees only made the system less efficient. Committee assignments were more productive of wise commentaries and impressive reports than of the effective large-scale action needed for military power.

A relatively passive policy of neutrality accorded with the changing structure of Venetian society. Manufacturing and agriculture were the growing segments of the economy, not overseas trade and shipping. To an increasing extent, the common people of the city were engaged in unwarlike industrial activity, and the nobility became more and more attached to their landed estates, disinclined to expose either themselves or their farms and villas to the hazards of war. Their investment in land was a result of the same profit-seeking spirit which had once prompted investments in overseas trade. It is not to be explained by a change in spirit; but the change in investments, once it had occurred, produced a change in spirit.

All these circumstances made the Venetians predisposed more toward peace than war. Their attitude was idealized and justified by Paolo Paruta, an able diplomat and man of letters who after Pietro Bembo continued Venice's official history. In an essay, *Della perfettione della vita politica*, Paruta elaborated a refutation of Machiavelli's doctrine that the highest good in political life was power, either the power of the state or of the man of *virtù*. In contrast, Paruta started from the maxim that the aim of politics was happiness and drew a corollary in praise of peace. "To enjoy the sweet fruits of peace," he wrote, "is the true purpose to which all military institutions and operations should be directed." Implicitly comparing Rome with Venice, he continued: "Therefore that prince or that republic which directs all its thoughts and attention to wars, making one give birth to another so as to enlarge the frontiers of its empire, is not on the path that can lead it to well being (*felicità*), which consists not in dominating many peoples but in ruling with justice and keeping its subjects in peace and tranquility."

Paruta was himself one of the ambassadors who kept Venice's diplomatic reputation high in spite of the Serenissima's military weakness. His finest moments came as ambassador to Rome. Venice was the first Italian state to recognize Henry of Bourbon as King of France. It did so at a time when Henry was an excommunicated heretic, and Spain and Austria were supporting a rival. Displaying both tact and persistence in presenting to the pope Venice's view that Henry IV was the only means of having a French counterweight to Spain, Paruta gave Venice a prestigeful role in the reconciliation of Henry with the papacy, a triumph of peaceful diplomacy.

EMBRYONIC PARTIES The vitality of Venetian republicanism in this period between the two great plagues created a kind of embryonic party system. There were no formal party organizations of course; the idea of party continued to be denounced, just as it was in England when men first began branding each other as Whigs and Tories. But family factions were for a time overshadowed by larger alignments determined by intellectual attitudes, constitutional issues, and foreign policy. On the one side were those called the "Young." That label had been applied for at least a century to the "outs" trying to get "in" and favoring more energetic action than the "old guard." The party labels "Young" and "Old" evolved so that they had no more literal meaning than do our labels "Left" and "Right." But something resembling a similar division is discernible in Venice between 1580 and 1630.

The Young found an intellectual atmosphere from which to draw inspiration in the parlor of the Morosini palace at San Luca, presided over by Andrea Morosini, who succeeded Paruta as the republic's official historian. This "Ridotto Morosini" is famous as an example of the new kind of social center being developed in European society, free from the ceremonial of courts and the programs of the academies. Venice had a large number of academies devoted less to literature than those of Florence and more to natural science. At the Ridotto Morosini, however, not only mathematical scientists such as Galileo Galilei and learned monks such as Paolo Sarpi, but also influential state secretaries, merchant nobles, as were many of the Morosini, and patrician statesmen such as Leonardo Donà, on the way to becoming doge, all met on the basis of equality, able to speak freely about subjects that interested them. This informality was a noteworthy circumstance in an age that rigidly stressed class distinctions. The Ridotto Morosini set the intellectual tone of "the Young." Any new ideas coming from France, England, and the Netherlands aroused interest, especially those from France. The readiness of the Young to listen to dangerous ideas was an important part of the attitude that separated them from "the Old."

The domestic constitutional issue concerned the role of the Council of Ten. The Young wished to curb what they regarded as its oligarchic activity. In 1582–83 they forced through a limitation of its interference in finances and foreign affairs. By making the Senate again the center of decision on these matters, they gave more nobles a voice in settling important issues.

Most crucial in the contrast of the two groups was their attitude towards Spain and the policy of neutrality. The Young wanted a more assertive policy; to them, the policy of balance and neutrality seemed to have become a formula for submission to Spanish dominance over Italy. They looked to France, England, and the Netherlands not only for new ideas but, above all, for allies who could help overthrow Spanish dominance. The Old might share resentment at Spanish power, but were more timid and more inclined, because of their wealth which included many church benefices, to avoid the dangers of offending Spain or the popes.

A strong cord of cohesion among the Young was their attitude toward the Church. The traditional Venetian relations between Church and state, religion and politics, were being challenged by the Counter-Reformation. Buoyed up by the revival of religious enthusiasm, the papacy was asserting its claims more vigorously and, in doing so, had in many cases the backing of Spain. Many Venetians thought of papal power as Spanish power in disguise. To some, anti-clericalism was a purely political issue. To others it was a religious issue, for they felt "a deep sense of personal responsibility in spiritual matters," and were unwilling to be guided by the pope. They objected particularly to the Jesuits because of the skill with which the Jesuits used the confessional to direct consciences in ways that had political consequences.

In the early sixteenth century, before the line between Protestant and Catholic was clearly and harshly drawn, the Veneto was important in the germination and dissemination of ideas which became influential among groups now generally lumped together as Anabaptists, but Lutheranism and Calvinism won relatively few converts. At the end of the century, as at its beginning, Venice was noted for the magnificence of its religious ceremonies and for the crowds attracted by religious relics and reports of miracles. The few Venetian nobles who went over to Protestantism were not politically important. Questions concerning the relations of Church and state, however, were inflamed by the Protestant revolts beyond the Alps and by Catholic countermeasures, and in these relations the Venetian tradition was distinctive. Although bishops served as chief ministers in most West European states, in Venice they were excluded from all political office. Until 1451 Venice's top ecclesiastic, the patriarch, had his seat at the small lagoon city of Grado (see Chapter 8 and Figure 19). His seat was then moved to Venice, but only to the church at Castello, not to San Marco, the chief church of the city, for San Marco was the chapel of the doge. The patriarch and others of the higher clergy were voted on by the Senate which sent names to the pope for confirmation. Parish priests were elected by the property holders of the parishes they administered. Church property in Venice was taxed, and clerics accused of crimes were judged in state courts. Many other resolutely Catholic countries also had special institutions enhancing the government's control over the Church. An example was royal control of the Inquisition in Spain. But in other Italian cities, papal power was not limited as much as it was in Venice, nor was the Church as firmly policed by the state.

Venetian practices regarding heretics were also distinctive. The Inquisition was permitted to function only with the addition of three lay members, the

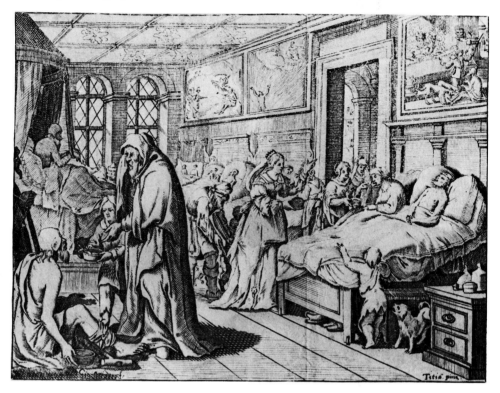

FIGURE 38   *A Hospital. Sketch by Titian (courtesy of Museo Correr, Venice).*

Institutions for the care of the sick and unfortunate were one expression of the religious fervor of the Catholic Reformation.

Savii contro l'Eresia. Another group of lay magistrates was charged with suppressing blasphemy, while the supervisors of the University of Padua handled routine censorship. Although condemned heretics were sometimes put to death, it was inflicted quietly, not in public displays for the strengthening of faith, as in Spain. No organized Protestant propaganda was permitted, and Protestantism was tolerated only marginally as an intellectual plaything of a few skeptics and as the religious custom of a few foreigners: the German merchants in their Fondaco, a flourishing colony of German bakers, and the many German students at Padua. For its Greek Orthodox colony, the government won from Rome the right for them to use their own calendar. Jews and Moslems performed their own rites in their special quarters or hostels. Venice was far from being any champion of freedom of thought in principle. When the Papal Nuncio asked that Giordano Bruno be turned over to the Roman Inquisition in view of his heretical ideas about the Trinity and his previous prosecution as a Neapolitan, the Senate asserted its authority by an inquiry and then readily complied. But men of a great variety of views succeeded one way or another in living in Venice pretty much as they pleased, and thinking as they pleased, so long as they did not attack the government. If graffiti attacking the doge appeared, as they often did, horrible penalties were decreed by the Ten against the unknown authors.

AN INTERDICT Controversies with the pope became acute in 1605, when Venice ex-
DEFIED tended to its mainland possessions practices that were traditional within
the lagoons. The Council of Ten arrested two clerics of the Veneto accused
of crimes for which the pope said they should be judged only in ecclesiastical
courts. About the same time a law was passed restricting the acquisition and
use of property by the Church. Ecclesiastically owned farm lands in the Veneto
had been greatly extended and enriched since the Mainland came under Venetian rule, partly by bequests and, to a considerable extent, by good monastic
management in drainage and irrigation. The government felt it necessary to
limit this Church holding of real estate, as had long been done within the lagoons, lest the income from an excessive amount of land come under the control
of Rome.

The pope at the time was Paul V, a distinguished legal expert on church
law. Declaring the actions of the Venetian Republic to be contrary to canon law,
he demanded the repeal of the decrees concerning Church property and the surrender to ecclesiastical authorities of the criminous clerics. Otherwise, he
threatened, he would excommunicate Venice's rulers and by an interdict forbid
any celebration of religious services in the territory of the Republic. Similar
threats had recently brought submission to papal authority from Genoa, Ferrara,
and Lucca. And had not Venice bowed the last time it had been subject to an
interdict, namely in 1509, during the War of the League of Cambrai? Confident
of his rights and of Spanish backing, Paul V expected that Venice would quickly
yield.

Just when the pope was making his threat more explicit, the Venetians
were called on to elect a new doge. They chose Leonardo Donà, a man whose
career shows that, in spite of the corruption of which Marino Sanuto had complained earlier in the century and which had become more and more notorious,
some Venetians won election to high office by respect for their hard work and
abilities. As a young man, Leonardo Donà had not commanded a galley or made
trading voyages, as his younger brothers had done, but instead he was initiated
into public affairs by acting as secretary for his father, writing letters for him
when he was a member of the Board of Trade. When his father became governor in Cyprus, he went along. Like young Alessandro Magno, Leonardo Donà
took elaborate notes during such travels; indeed, Leonardo made that trip an
occasion for research in the Cypriote archives to learn all he could about the
various parts of Cyprus and its institutions. On a later voyage to Vienna, he
took notes on the languages spoken in localities along the way and on the roads
needing repair. Government, not trade, filled Leonardo's mind and note taking.
By the age of forty, he had proved his abilities in many offices, was renowned for
his eloquence, and entered the government's inner circle as a Savio Grande.
Thirty years later, after service on many delicate missions and repeated rotation
through the highest offices in Venice, he was still at seventy the leader of the
Young and was chosen doge because of their confidence that he would preserve
against the pope the sovereign independence of the Republic.

Leonardo Donà was a devotedly religious man, governed by a stern sense of
duty, a bachelor observing throughout life the vow of chastity he had taken in
his youth. He believed strongly that a layman should be governed by his own
sense of right, not by the clergy. Secure in his own conscience, he was not the
least worried that he was personally excommunicated. He had been Venice's

negotiator at Rome in many disputes over temporal matters, always in the shadow of the threat that the pope would appeal to his spiritual powers as Julius II had done in 1509. To such men as Leonardo Donà the particular points at issue in 1606 were less vital than the general principle that the Republic must prove, when it came to a showdown, that such weapons would not force it to surrender.

Under Donà's leadership the papal interdict was resisted by decrees forbidding its publication within Venetian territory and threatening with death clergy who obeyed it. None were actually executed, although there were imprisonments and expulsions, but the legal threat of death made obedience to the Republic more pardonable from a canonical point of view. Besides using its police powers to compel obedience, the Republic challenged the pope on intellectual and religious grounds. Venice formally protested that the interdict was invalid, a perversion of papal powers so bad that to obey it was a sin. The pope's power was then at the peak of its resurgence; that it should be boldly challenged within Italy and by a public authority through the printing press attracted Europe-wide attention.

Venice's cause was argued by an exceptionally able spokesman, Paolo Sarpi. He was not a noble, but a member of the clergy recruited from Venice's middle class of citizens. An infant prodigy who made his mark first in the study of natural philosophy and who only later turned to legal and historical studies, Sarpi was one of a group from whom the Senate asked advisory opinions and legal briefs defining its position. It found his briefs so solidly thought out and documented that it came to depend on him for guidance. He was given an official salaried position of Adviser in Theology and Canon Law. In Rome he and Leonardo Donà were considered responsible for leading Venice into heresy, and Rome's leading scholars took up their pens against him. Lawyers of the university of Padua sided with Venice; those of Bologna with Rome. To cater to the wide interest aroused in Europe generally, anthologies were published containing selections from authors on both sides.

The war of pamphlets could not bring an end to the conflict. The only prospects for a conclusion lay in a compromise or in an appeal to arms with papal acceptance of vague Spanish offers to supply the needed troops. The pope had not expected such resolute resistance. Venice was maintaining religious services by the vigorous use of police powers and was subsidizing a shocking campaign of publications. The longer the papacy's ultimate weapon was successfully defied, the more its prestige suffered. On the other hand, Venice was feeling the strain. Within the city itself the interdict was ignored by nearly all the clergy except some of the religious orders, such as the Jesuits, who were expelled; but in some mainland cities, such as Brescia, the Venetian governors had to send inspectors into churches to intimidate priests who hesitated to administer the sacraments. The Serenissima's treasury was being drained by the cost of keeping a fleet and an army ready to resist any attack from Spain or from the Papal States. Venice hoped for support from monarchs interested in resisting papal claims in their own territories. Only the King of England, James I, far away and ineffectual, declared himself on her side. France equivocated. Spain offered her mediation so that she might have the prestige of seeming to impose a solution. After a year, a settlement was maneuvered by a French envoy who told each side that the other had yielded more than it really had. In an audience

before the Signoria while declaring the interdict lifted, he murmured an absolution too fast to be interrupted and made the appropriate gestures beneath his
robe so that he could report to the pope that the Venetian rulers had accepted
absolution, implying sin, which in fact they refused to confess. The offending
laws were not repealed, neither were they for the nonce enforced. The lifting
of the interdict was generally considered a victory for Venice and for the principle of state sovereignty, since Venice made no admission of guilt, refused to permit the Jesuits to return, and continued to support Sarpi in his official position
of honor.

To Sarpi and his close friends, this way of ending the interdict was a letdown, partly perhaps because it had the immediate effect of lessening his personal importance but also because he had hoped that the contest would broaden
into a religious movement of anti-papal reform. His personal popularity, however, rose to new heights six months later, when he was waylaid by three assassins on a bridge near his home. Surviving severely wounded, he expressed common belief in a famous pun, saying that in the "styletto" that had broken off
on his cheek bone he recognized the style of the Roman court. (The assassins
did indeed find sanctuary in the Papal States, but there was nothing unusual in
those days in a failure to extradite escaped criminals.)

As the attempted assassination indicated, papal supporters persisted in
efforts to silence Sarpi. The Young, equally unreconciled and alert, energetically
sought to strengthen their contacts with the English, Dutch, and French so that
they would have allies in any future confrontation. In this respect also they were
led by Sarpi who continued to enjoy the protection and patronage of the Republic until his death in 1623. In his last years, he made good his boast that he
would be more dangerous to the papacy dead than alive by writing his master-
ful and influential *History of the Council of Trent.*

THE
HAPSBURG
VISE
After the quarrel with the papacy was appeased, Venice continued to feel
threatened by the encircling Hapsburgs. Leadership in the struggle against
them passed to Nicolò Contarini. When really young, he met and admired
Leonardo Donà at the ridotto of his Morosini cousins and took Leonardo
as a model. He developed a character equally conscientious and proud, commanding respect by eloquence, intelligence, hard work, and devotion to the
Republic, but was more emotional and impetuous. He was equally anti-clerical,
but his main drive was against the passive policy of neutrality. He wanted Venice
to arm and assert its independence and defend its interests even at the risk of
a war with Spain.

The policy he favored led to two wars. In 1615, Venice's mercenaries
crossed the eastern frontier to attack the lands of the Austrian Hapsburg archduke who protected the Uskoks. Combats with these pirates had become more
savage on both sides. Venice had celebrated a victory by setting up the heads of
slaughtered Uskok pirates around the Piazza. The Uskoks waylaid a Venetian
commander and celebrated by a banquet at which he was killed and his heart
was eaten. While fleets attacked the Uskok strongholds from the sea, Venice
sent what it considered a big army against the archduke's lands along the river
Isonzo, especially against Gradisca (see Maps 1 and 10). After a favorable
beginning, the offensive bogged down, and Nicolò Contarini was sent to the

front as a Commissioner. Trained from his youth in the world of dispatches, reports, and debates, not in the command of ships or weapons, and lacking full powers of command, he was more successful in analyzing the weaknesses of the Venetian forces than in correcting them. Peace on reasonably satisfactory terms was obtained in 1617, more by diplomatic than military means. Spanish governors who commanded strong forces in Milan and Naples would gladly have backed the archduke, but the German emperor, the archduke's overlord, and the Spanish king desired peace because of involvements elsewhere. The Spanish army in Milan, the most dangerous for Venice, was engaged in a war with the Duke of Savoy. As Contarini urged, Venice subsidized Savoy heavily to keep the Spanish occupied until the War of Gradisca ended. The peace treaty left Venice's eastern frontier little changed and still poorly defined but included a promise to remove the Uskoks. In fact, a joint commission of which Nicolò Contarini was a member moved them out of Segna to the interior, and their piracies abated.

An undeclared war began meanwhile between Venice and the Duke of Ossuna, the Spanish viceroy of the Kingdom of Naples. How much backing Ossuna had from the Spanish king seemed doubtful. Ossuna mobilized a large fleet at Brindisi, enlisting Uskoks and Ragusans eager to join him in shattering Venetian lordship of the Adriatic. The fleet that Venice concentrated against him failed in half-hearted combats in 1617 to destroy Ossuna's fleet, which achieved the striking success of capturing two of the merchant galleys then operating between Venice and Spalato. The Venetian fleet was then enlarged to formidable proportions—40 galleys, 8 galleasses, and 38 sailing ships. The relations which the Young had carefully cultivated with heretic England and the Netherlands proved their worth in that they enabled Venice to hire English and Dutch ships as well as soldiers. Ossuna's fleet was withdrawn from the Adriatic, leaving the Venetian admiral free in 1618 and 1619 to make triumphal cruises up and down that sea, driving aground a Ragusan Indiaman that failed to salute respectfully, seizing a vessel carrying salt from Ravenna to Trieste, and in general enforcing Venetian navigation laws.

Ossuna's threats seemed more serious because of plotting within Venice. For the War of Gradisca, Venice had hired mercenary soldiers of many nationalities. Mutinies within the Dutch and English contingents were easily suppressed. More alarming was a plot involving many of the numerous French mercenaries who gathered within the city at the conclusion of the war. Veterans of the religious wars in France, some were convinced haters of Spanish-Catholic power, but most of them were unprincipled adventurers. In the taverns where they gathered, they talked of a scheme for seizing the Ducal Palace, killing the Senators, and joyously plundering the rich palaces of self-indulgent Venetians. These *bravi*, professional killers, had no fear of a palace guard composed of Arsenalotti. Their leader was a corsair who had served in Ossuna's fleet, from which he hoped for reinforcements. He and his friends were in touch with the Spanish ambassador resident in Venice, the Marquis of Bedmar, members of whose staff listened to and perhaps encouraged their plotting.

When the bravi recognized three corpses dangling from a gibbet in the Piazzetta one morning in May 1618, they knew their leaders had been betrayed and they fled. The taverns emptied so quickly that it was rumored that the missing could be found in the Canal Orfano where the Council of Ten usually deposited those it ordered secretly strangled. Word of the plot had indeed been revealed to the Ten by a Huguenot captain who had no wish to aid Spain. The Ten acted with its usual speed and efficacy and without public explanations. The Senate asked the King of Spain to recall Bedmar, but made no specific charges. Venice discredited her Spanish enemies more effectively by a silence which left the world free to suspect the worst, which it readily did in the decades when the English were making a national holiday of the discovery of Guy Fawkes's "gunpowder plot" to blow up the House of Parliament.

In 1620 the Young had reason to feel that they had been on the whole successful. They had curbed the powers of the Ten and elected their own leaders to the key posts in the government. The Serenissima had withstood the interdict of a wrathful pope, aided Savoy to resist the Spanish governor of Milan, gained from war with the Austrian archduke the removal of the Uskoks, reaffirmed against Ossuna its lordship of the Adriatic, and handled the "Spanish Conspiracy" so as to enjoy seeing notoriously hostile Spanish representatives removed from Italy.

The next ten years, however, revealed that Venice held too weak a hand to compete with Europe's other players in power politics. France was rising to leadership again, under Richelieu. He used an alliance with Venice in his maneuvers against the Hapsburgs, but then negotiated behind her back in ways that tarnished the prestige of the Serenissima. Most humiliating for Venice was the outcome of a crisis over Mantua. When the ruler of this small buffer state died in 1628, the Hapsburgs supported one claimant, France and Venice the other. While French troops fought the Spanish west of Milan, Venice's army tried to relieve Mantua, which was besieged by troops from Germany. After one defeat, the Venetian force disintegrated and Mantua was sacked with the horrors for which the Thirty Years War was infamous. Shuddering Venetians again thanked God for their lagoons. Only the intervention of Sweden checked Hapsburg victories and brought peace to Italy in 1631, a peace in which the Serenissima was included on terms dictated by France.

The spread of the plague made impossible the reorganization of the Venetian army after its defeat near Mantua in 1630. This last epidemic of Black Death reduced the population of Venice within 16 months from approximately 150,000 to 100,000 and was equally deadly in Verona and other mainland cities. Nicolò Contarini, who had been elected doge to lead the War of the Mantuan Succession, the bitter climax to his anti-Spanish policy, died just after the plague had lifted. A week before his death, this most staunchly anti-clerical of doges laid the cornerstone of Santa Maria della Salute, erected in gratitude for Venice's deliverance from the plague.

THE ECONOMIC DOWNTURN   Lack of the necessary military institutions was the obvious and immediate cause of Venice's loss of weight in the balance of power. Enfeebling also was an economic decline which started while Venice's political prestige was still high.

During the last decade of the sixteenth century, Venice's population, trade, and industries were all expanding. Imports from the Levant increased about threefold between 1582 and 1602. Silk imports from Aleppo and cotton from Cyprus and Smyrna were booming. Spices were coming through both the Red Sea and the Persian Gulf. This revived Mediterranean spice trade reached a new peak shortly after 1590. Much of the cotton and silk went with the spices north and west to or through Germany, but a good part was used by Venice's own weavers. Woolen manufactures, using mainly Spanish wool, reached a peak of 28,729 cloths in 1602, the output having about tripled since mid-century. Backing up this industrial growth, domestic food production was being increased by the drainage and reclamation.

There were ugly splotches on this rosy picture, to be sure, and the most depressing was in the sector which had once been Venice's strength, in the merchant marine. The superiority of the Westerners, especially the English and Dutch, in building ships, sailing them, and fighting them was so overwhelming that Venice's policy of using the strength of other sectors of the economy to support the merchant marine interfered with making adjustments to a new commercial situation. The competition of the English and the Dutch became more acute after they made peace with Spain, the English in 1604, the Dutch in 1609. Their merchantmen could then more safely pass the Straits of Gilbraltar. They negotiated commercial rights in Turkey so that they could load cotton at Smyrna. With it they shipped other Levantine wares to the North Sea to be sold through Frankfurt-am-Main to the Germans who had been Venice's best customers. The English went direct to Zante for their raisins.

Large numbers of these "Western" ships came to Venice and more would have come had they not been handicapped by Venetian tolls and navigation laws. A number of foreign merchants, with the English most prominent, showed a desire to use Venice as their main southern base. They felt they would have less to fear there from Spain and the Inquisition than in Genoa or Leghorn. They petitioned for permission to ship between Venice and the Levant in their own ships. Instead, Venice reaffirmed in 1602 its traditional policy of reserving that trade for Venetian merchants and Venetian ships, welcoming foreigners who imported wares from their country of origin, but requiring them to sell in Venice, not transship. Nicolò Contarini on the other hand recognized the need of adjusting commercial policy to foreign policy. He sought to open Venetian trade to Westerners as well as to form political alliances with England and the Netherlands. He supported the proposal of Nicolò Donà, Leonardo's brother and a merchant, to throw open to foreigners the trade between Venice and the Levant. This would encourage the settlement and naturalization at Venice of foreigners who could make up for Venice's declining number of expert seamen and enterprising traders. But the proposal was defeated. Faced with a protectionist attitude at Venice, Westerners went elsewhere, directly to the Levant or to intermediate ports such as Leghorn, Ancona, or Ragusa.

During the decade after 1602, the volume of trade moving through Venice fell forty percent to judge by the returns from customs. The inadequacy of the transport services Venetian ships were able to offer, plagued as they were by high construction costs, poor crews, and losses to pirates, was only part of the explanation. The Dutch and English found their way around the Cape of Good Hope and diverted the spice trade more thoroughly and permanently than the Portuguese and Spaniards had ever done. An economic crisis within the Ottoman Empire, which was accentuated by a debasement of the coinage, depressed that main market for Venetian manufacturers. The woolen industry was hardest hit. Its output fell after 1602 and especially after 1620, reaching a low of only 8,053 cloths in 1631. A debasement of the coinage in Turkey made it harder for Venetians to buy cotton and silk there in competition with the French, English, or Dutch because these Western merchants came supplied with gold or silver, whereas the Venetians depended on selling manufactures. Even if these fetched a relatively high price in Turkish money, the return was worth less in gold or silver. Another advantage of the Westerners was the growing popularity of the kind of woolens they had to sell, the new draperies, a lighter, cheaper kind of fabric better suited to a depressed market. Venetians still made large sales of silk and gold brocades and of glass wares and jewelry, but its manufacturing suffered from contracting markets in all the surrounding countries. The German market particularly was damaged by the Thirty Years War, 1618–48, which is conservatively estimated to have reduced the population of the Holy Roman Empire by one third. A downward trend in the quantity of silver arriving from America had a relatively depressing effect all over Europe. The conjunction of all these circumstances produced a continuing decline in Venetian economy. After the downturn about 1602, a more general depression began during the Europe-wide economic crisis about 1620.

Skillful financial management postponed the effects of war and economic decline on government finances. Normal income had risen to about 3,500,000 ducats a year. As in the past, most of this income came from taxes on consumption and trade or from the mainland cities. Rich Venetians were relatively less heavily taxed than in the past, since annual direct taxes were only about 500,000 ducats even in time of war and fell to 200,000 ducats after 1620. Some of the cost of the War of Gradisca was handled by an issue of bank money through the newly founded Banco del Giro (see Chapter 23). At its formation, the government was its creditor for 500,000 ducats. These credits, basically loans to the government, rose to about 1,000,000 ducats without weakening the bank's credit.

But the money futilely expended in the War of the Mantuan Succession raised the government's debt to the bank to nearly 3,000,000 ducats. With this overissue, bank money declined to a discount of 20 percent compared to coins. (It fell from 120 to 97; when at par, bank money was quoted at 120 in "current money" because the bank's accounts were kept in "mint lire" and "mint ducats" which had 20 percent more value than the lire or ducat of "current money.") When, about 1640, a drastic reduction of the government's debt to the bank sent bank money over par (up to 122), it was brought down to par by permitting, for the first time, depositors to acquire bank money by making deposits in cash. Previously, they could acquire deposits only by the transfer of credits against the government. As soon as it could freely accept deposits, the Banco del Giro fulfilled all the functions which had been performed by the Banco della Piazza, which was abolished in 1638. Meanwhile, the long-term debt, almost nil about 1600, had grown to over 8,000,000 ducats, and in the 1630's was taking a bite of 500,000 ducats a year out of the budget.

STAGNATION IN POLITICS   While the economy was in recession, the spirited republicanism which had drawn strength from opposing foreign enemies began to wane. The coalition of the Young which had been formed in 1582 to curb the Council of Ten splintered in 1628 in a struggle over the same issue.

The Ten had come to symbolize the concentration of power in a narrow oligarchy. Within the ranks of the nobility, the contrast between rich and poor was increasing. Members of the Ten, well-educated men able to devote all their time to public affairs and generally able to spend freely, came from a relatively few very rich families. The anti-monarchic spirit, strong in Venice in the late sixteenth century, made any concentration of power suspect, and the arrogance of the rich was resented; but the power of the Ten involved also other more complicated issues.

Some nobles hated the Ten because of the vigor with which it disciplined them when they acted as if above the law. For example, an incident which enflamed sentiment in the crisis of 1582 occurred when several nobles were on an outing on the Lido, dressed up as if foreigners and carrying arquebuses and accompanied by some bravi. When they encountered another group of pic-nickers, also with bravi, one of the nobles flung some words at a woman in the other party, at which her companions took offense. In the resulting fighting, there were casualties on both sides, although the nobles on the whole got the worst of it. The group containing no nobles promptly reported to the Ten that they had been attacked by a group of foreigners armed with arquebuses. When the nobles came the following day to complain that they had been attacked, they were harshly reprimanded by the Ten for going about dressed as foreigners and carrying guns. They responded by denouncing the "tyranny" of the Ten and trying to have their case heard instead by the Forty, where they expected to find fellow nobles, of middling rank like themselves, more sympathetic.

Another cause of resentment was the power being assumed by the non-noble secretaries of the Ten. They were the foremost members of the corps of civil servants recruited from the citizens-by-birth. Unlike noble office-holders, the secretaries did not move every year or two from one task to another; being bureaucrats with long-term assignments, they strove to increase the power of the particular bodies to which they were attached. Nobles who disliked the Ten blamed its secretaries for its encroachments on the traditional functions of the Senate in foreign affairs and finances, and on the jurisdiction of the Forty over criminal cases.

In 1582, opposition to the Ten had asserted itself in the Great Council by a refusal to elect men nominated to form the Ten's zonta, without which the Ten could not act in many cases. The Councillors and others of the inner circle tried again and again to put a slate through. They even called a meeting on a day when they knew that their most eloquent opponent, Federigo Badoer, would not be present because of the death of his sister. Resentment at such tactics caused them another defeat. Badoer argued that no zonta was needed, that the power of the Ten should be cut back, that foreign policy and finances be re-turned fully to the Senate, and the Ten be restricted to guarding the constitution from subversion, especially criminal violence, and to the spying and counter-espionage considered essential in international relations. These limitations were indeed imposed in 1582–83; the zonta was abolished, and the powers of the Senate in finances and foreign affairs reaffirmed.

The reassertion of the Senate's functions in foreign affairs gave the Council of Ten a chance to increase its role in criminal matters. To enforce on Senators the necessary secrecy, it created a special committee of three called the State

Inquisitors. At first concerned only with guarding state secrets, these Inquisitors expanded their activities until they had potential jurisdiction over all crimes committed by nobles. Both the Inquisitors and Council of Ten had strict rules of procedure to follow in passing judgment and inflicting punishment; but their proceedings were secret. The accused had no chance to face accusers, to hire lawyers, or to know fully the case against him. Judgments could not be appealed, and they were sometimes executed with unseemly speed. Some glaring cases of injustice shook confidence in the procedure. Antonio Foscarini, an ambassador accused of selling state secrets, was speedily tried and executed. A few months later it was discovered that he had been framed, his accusers had been lying. The Council of Ten publicly admitted its mistake, restoring honor but not life to the accused. In some other cases, there were shocking contrasts between the severity of sentences imposed on minor nobles and on members of the most powerful families. The feeling grew among the poorer nobles that they were being treated as inferiors by a small oligarchy which was abusing its power.

These feelings were brought to a head in 1628 by the attacks of Ranieri Zeno on Doge Giovanni Corner. This Corner was descended from the family that could boast of having brought Venice a kingdom, Cyprus. It had done favors to the papacy and to the King of France, for which they were ready to return favors. The Corner were one of the longhi, the old "tribunician" families which had held the dogeship before 1381 but from that year until 1612 had been excluded by the group called the curti (see Chapter 14). That division within the ranks of the richest, best established families was now entirely healed, and Giovanni Corner was so rich, popular, and powerful that he obtained the consent of his Councillors and the Senate for his sons to hold simultaneously Church offices and seats in the Senate in defiance of the laws of the Republic.

Ranieri Zeno, also of ancient family, denounced this ducal greed and senatorial laxity in speeches that were not only personal insults to the doge but also accusations against an oligarchy which enforced the laws drastically on others, but not on themselves. Zeno acquired a large following among the poorer nobles. He made his most biting attacks after the Great Council had elected him to the Council of Ten. The majority of the latter council opposed Zeno and voted his banishment. The Great Council repealed the decree and then showed its discontent by also refusing again and again to approve men nominated to the Ten. By this method the Great Council forced formation of a commission to reform the authority of the Ten.

Among the reforms considered was the transfer of most criminal cases involving nobles from the Council of Ten to the Forty, which was much more broadly representative of the nobility. Other proposals aimed at loosening the grip of the secretaries of the Ten, who, Zeno said, really ran that tribunal because of their expertise in its procedure and control of the paperwork.

The chairman of the reforming commission was Nicolò Contarini, then in his seventies, and supported for the post by the Young because they knew that during many years in high office he had not hesitated to offend the great in obeying his sense of duty and because he had worked with Zeno as an ally in urging policies against Spain and the pope. But Contarini turned against Zeno when the latter began bidding for clerical support in his assault on the rich. Moreover, he was alienated by Zeno's extreme language, by his setting of poor against rich, and by his implication that nobles who had been long in harness in the inner circle, as Contarini had been, were puppets in the hands of the secretaries. Nicolò Contarini was not rich himself, but his honor and pride as one of the ruling circle made him regard Zeno's proposals and methods as dangerously subversive.

Since the issue was constitutional, the report of the reform commission was debated not in the Senate but in the Great Council. During these debates it became clear that most nobles thought the criminal jurisdiction of the Council of Ten was necessary to preserve the discipline and reputation of their class. It was argued effectively that the secrecy of the proceedings of the Ten contributed to maintaining Venice's reputation of giving equal justice to all, because lawless behavior could not be curbed otherwise, since victims would fear openly to accuse evildoers belonging to powerful families. On the other hand, it was also urged that the prestige and honor of the nobility was better preserved if they were judged secretly by the Ten instead of by the equivalent of ordinary police courts. In the end, the only reforms approved left the powers of the Ten and the Inquisitors unshaken and those of the secretaries clipped only temporarily.

Neither Nicolò Contarini nor Ranieri Zeno offered a broad party program for reinvigorating the growing number of impoverished noblemen. As a movement for domestic reform, the Young fell apart. New wars with the Turks soon absorbed all Venice's political energies for almost a century. In 1657, the Jesuits were readmitted in order to assure papal support in wars still regarded as crusades. New attacks on the Ten, or on the Inquisitors who came to exercise most of their powers, were made near the end of the Republic, to be sure, particularly in 1762. They read like repeat performances of 1628 and had the same negative outcome.

From a modern point of view, the abortion of Venice's embryonic party system signified stagnation. Parties were to prove vital instruments of change in the nineteenth century's democratic development of republican institutions. In reaching out for support of conflicting programs, they provided both mechanisms and consent for new institutions. Without parties, Venetian republicanism concentrated more and more narrowly on just preserving the forms of institutions created by much idealized ancestors.

From the point of view of the seventeenth century, the lack of change in the Venetian constitution seemed the best of reasons for praising it. Revolution and civil war occurred in that century in so many countries in association with party strife that Venice was praised above all for avoiding those ills. Because its institutions had lasted for centuries and restrained violence, Venice was lauded as a model of stability.

While even monarchists praised Venice for its internal peace and its equitable administration of justice, opponents of monarchy found other reasons also to praise it. They lauded its liberty and the settling of problems by free-spoken debate and balloting. Venice was considered a model republic when such models were very rare. When, in 1647, the Neapolitans tried a short-lived rebellion unattached to princely claims, they sent envoys to Venice to find out how to form a republic. When Englishmen, having executed Charles I, engaged in vigorous debate over desirable forms of government, many pointed to Venice to show a republic's good possibilities. Their arguments were echoed a century later in the rhetoric of the revolution which created a new republic in America.

A TENACIOUS
DEFENSE · II

In a New Age of Sea Power

First and last, Venice depended on the Adriatic. Even nobles whose treasures and whose hearts were in mainland estates accepted the political principle that the foundation of Venice's independence was its control of the Adriatic. Nicolò Contarini and Paolo Sarpi may never have been to sea (no voyage is recorded), but both were champions of Venice's "lordship of the gulf." The most solid achievement in the struggle against the encircling Hapsburgs was the strengthening of Venice's naval control of the Adriatic by the removal of the Uskoks and the triumphant patrols after Ossuna's fleet had been withdrawn.

THE NEW PATTERN Ossuna's war was the last Spanish threat to Venice by sea, for in the war between Spain and the Netherlands which resumed in 1619, the Dutch destroyed Spanish fleets. Later, the Spanish were weakened by defeats at the hands of the French, by the successful revolt of Portugal, and by unsuccessful but debilitating revolts in Catalonia, Naples, and Sicily. Meanwhile, Ottoman energies were for some time diverted eastward. The pattern of sea power in the Mediterranean was basically altered. No longer did Spain and the Turk loom over the Mediterranean as world empires likely to crush Venice if she did not balance them adroitly. During most of the seventeenth century, the only navies in the Mediterranean stronger than Venice's own were the Dutch, English, and French squadrons that were occupied in fighting each other in that sea's western half.

The pattern of piracy became less disastrous for Venice than it had been in the century's first decades. Attacks on Venetian shipping by Christian corsairs diminished when notoriously hostile Spanish viceroys of Naples and Sicily were recalled and the Uskoks were moved inland. The Knights of St. John at Malta, the Papal Navy, and galleys from Tuscany made summer raids against Moslem fleets or coasts. Only occasionally did they fail to respect the Venetian flag, less tempting as Venice's trade declined. Their most coveted prizes were in the Turkish convoys between Constantinople and Alexandria. The English and Dutch gradually turned from piracy to trade, or joined the pirates in North African ports.

The Moslem raiders and Christian pirates from these Barbary states continued for centuries to damage Venetian shipping. Venice considered Algiers, Tunis, and Tripoli subject to the Ottoman emperor and tried in vain to induce him to force them to observe the treaties of peace by which he promised protection to Venetian commerce. The rulers of the Barbary states acknowledged the authority of the sultan in theory and furnished contingents for his navy, but they found excuses for not obeying his orders protecting commerce. They spared only the ships of nations that made treaties with them directly. With others, such as Venice, they considered themselves at war.

The Barbary raiders made Venetian voyages in the western Mediterranean impractical, but the Serenissima patrolled the Adriatic and the Levantine seas with some success in spite of the connivance of Turkish governors with the Moorish raiders. In 1638, the main galley fleets of Algiers and Tunis, 16 galleys in all, entered the Adriatic while the Venetian fleet of 28 galleys and 2 galleasses was off Crete. When it returned, the raiders took shelter in Albania under the Turkish guns at Valona. Tired of merely blockading and alarmed by a report of a relief fleet on the way, the Venetian commander sent his galleasses to engage the forts, while his galleys captured and towed away the pirate vessels, freeing 3,600 captives. Venice's treaties with the sultan gave her the right to destroy Moslem corsairs in the Adriatic, but the bombardment of his fortress made the sultan furious. War was avoided only because of his preoccupation with a campaign against Persia.

The Turk was still the most dangerous threat to Venice's remaining sea power. Even though the Ottoman Empire at the beginning of the seventeenth century had lost some of its efficiency and expansive drive, it was still a huge empire with great military resources. By land, it was a direct threat to Venetian control of the Adriatic, for the Venetian-ruled part of Dalmatia had been reduced in the sixteenth century to a very narrow strip, and Venice had barely a toehold in Albania. By sea, the Turkish threat was less direct as long as Venice held the Ionian Islands and Crete. But from the Turkish point of view, Crete in Christian hands threatened their communications within their empire. When the Knights of St. John cut out of the fleet returning from Alexandria to Constantinople a prize containing members of the sultan's harem who had been on a pilgrimage to Mecca, the sultan mobilized a powerful armada. He pretended it was going to attack Malta, but in fact it landed in Crete, where the Knights had stopped for supplies on their way home. Crete was easier to assault than Malta, and its possession was equally important in suppressing the Levantine raids of Christian corsairs.

By economic calculation, the defense of Crete by Venice could have been judged not worth the cost. But if it was abandoned, a direct Turkish threat to the Adriatic might be expected, and the national sentiment of honor required that Crete be defended.

THE LAST TURKISH WARS   In the ensuing war and the two others that followed, making three between 1645 and 1718, Venice fought the Turks in Dalmatia as well as in the Aegean and Ionian Seas. The Greek population of Crete showed little interest in fighting Turks for the sake of staying under Venice, but in the mountains of Dalmatia many of the peasants, especially the Morlacchi, were eager to fight their Turkish overlords. Consequently, Venice made solid gains in Dalmatia. Aided by German gunners supplied by Venice, the Morlacchi took the seemingly impregnable fortress of Clissa on the road inland from Spalato. Later, territory behind Zara and Spalato and around the Bocche di Cattaro was conquered, so that altogether the size of Venetian Dalmatia tripled. By land, Venice thus strengthened against the Turks her hold on the Adriatic.

At sea Venice won most of the battles in the war for Crete and yet could not prevent the Turks from taking it. Venetian strategists had long recognized that Crete could not be defended from Crete itself. It could be protected only by using sea power to intercept any invading army or to disrupt its lines of communications. When they realized that Crete, not Malta, was the Turkish objective, the Venetians mobilized quickly a formidable fleet which was supplemented by some galleys from Malta, the Papal States, Naples, and Tuscany. Each occasionally sent contingents of 5 or 6 galleys. All Christian crusaders or corsairs felt threatened by the Turkish attack on Crete, and the squadrons they were accustomed to outfit for cruises in the Levant operated during the war in conjunction with the Venetian war fleet; at least Papal and Maltese contingents came nearly every summer. While they added manpower, they tangled up and weakened the chain of command. In 1645, the Papal admiral successfully claimed the highest rank. Whoever was commander-in-chief, every decision was submitted to a council of war in which there were bitter divisions. The Christian force assembled in 1645 totalled 60 to 70 galleys, 4 galeasses, and about 36 galleons, a fair match for the Turkish invading fleet. But divided councils, bad luck in the weather, and irresolution in action prevented any decisive blow against the invaders that year or the following year when a Venetian was in command. The invaders received reinforcements and were soon attacking the capital, Candia.

During the twenty-four years of war that followed, the leadership and morale of the Venetian navy improved strikingly. Generally, the Venetians were on the offensive at sea, not hesitating to seek battle even when the odds were heavily against them. They won several resounding victories: in the central Aegean in 1651, and in the Dardanelles in 1655 and 1656. The Battle of the Dardanelles of 1656 is said by the historian of the Ottoman Empire, Hammer, to have been "the most severe defeat experienced by the Ottomans since Lepanto." Venice had sufficient command of the seas to collect tribute and recruits in most years from many Aegean islands. But they could not prevent the Turks from running supplies through to the army in Crete. The Turks generally avoided naval battles, except when necessary to get such supplies through. In the 1650's the Venetians concentrated on blockading the Dardanelles. They inflicted heavy damage on the Turkish fleets that tried to fight their way out, but the prevailing northerly winds and the strong current flowing out from the Black Sea prevented a constant blockade, and the Turks organized convoys of reinforcements leaving also from Chios, Rhodes, Alexandria, and Monemvasia. A major Venetian effort to capture the Turkish supply base at Canea in 1666 failed, and the arrival of strong reinforcements during the next year under the Grand Vizier sealed the fate of Candia.

The stubborn twenty-year defense of the fortress was by then exciting admiration in Europe as a romantic tale of assaults and sorties, mines and countermines, ravelins lost and rewon. "Never had a fortress, either in the Ottoman Empire or any other, been so fought over as Candia, or cost so much blood and money." (Hammer) To strike a blow for Christendom on this battle-front became the thing to do. After the long war between Spain and France ended in 1659, Christian states became more responsive to reiterated pleas of the popes that they send men and money to support Venice. Young nobles came out to show their manliness, many as individuals in Venetian pay and some in companies sent by their governments, especially French companies, which fought gallantly even if under Papal banners so as not to interfere with the French king's traditional alliance with the Turk. After a particularly gallant and wasteful sorti by a French contingent, which then at once went home, the Venetian Captain General, Francesco Morosini, in 1669 concluded terms surrendering Candia but enabling the Venetians to retire with the honors of war, to keep in Crete small bases of crucial naval importance, two Aegean islands (Tine and Cerigo — see Map 7), and the territory Venetians had won in Dalmatia.

Although much criticized at first for thus accepting the loss of Candia as inevitable, Francesco Morosini was reelected Captain General fifteen years later when Venice sought revenge. In 1683, the Austrians and Poles had turned the Turks back from the walls of Vienna. With the pope, they then called on Venice to join in shattering the common foe. A war party in Venice argued successfully that, if Venice did not respond to that appeal, she would get no support herself whenever the Turks might again strike at her. Later Russia, fighting for access to the Black Sea, joined the anti-Turkish coalition, and thirteen master ship carpenters from the Venetian Arsenal were sent to help Russia build a galley fleet.

The weakened Turks gave ground. Within four years, Francesco Morosini had conquered all and more than Venice had previously lost to the Turks in the Ionian Sea and the Morea. In September, 1687, he was assaulting Athens. One of his gunners lobbed a shell through the roof of the Parthenon and thus exploded the munitions which the Turks had stored there. Ruining the marvel of Attic art which had stood for more than two thousand years contributed little to the campaign. After a try at Negroponte and an epidemic in the fleet, Morosini decided to withdraw to the Morea. Its conquest had won him such popularity that he was elected doge. When he died, he was combining the dogeship with a new appointment as Captain General.

None of Francesco Morosini's successors added to his conquests, although many large fleets were sent into the Aegean during the next half dozen years. When Venice's allies ended the war by the Treaty of Karlowitz, 1699, Venice kept what Morosini had won for her. She was at peace then for fifteen years, while the rest of western Europe fought the bitter war of the Spanish Succession, which left Austria dominant in Italy but too exhausted, the Turks thought, to take them on again, especially since they (the Turks) felt strengthened meanwhile by a victory in the Black Sea over Russia. Thinking they would find Venice without allies, the Turks in 1714 undertook the reconquest of Morea and made short work of it. None of the Venetian commanders of her fortresses in the Morea put up much fight before surrendering, and the Venetian fleet retreated before a Turkish fleet twice its size. When the Turks moved on to assail Corfu Venetian resistence stiffened, however. Other Christian fleets, notably Portuguese and Papal contingents, came to its support, and the Austrian emperor entered the war. An Austrian victory in Hungary in 1716 helped save Corfu. The Venetians took the offensive again at sea and felt cheated when the Austrians forced them to make peace, to accept the loss of Morea, and to renounce efforts to incorporate into Venetian Dalmatia the pirate nest of Dulcigno (Ulčiny—see Map 2).

Fleet actions in these last Turkish wars seldom had decisive consequences but were far from trivial in size. In the Second Morean War, for example, while the galleys and army were attacking Dulcigno, the Venetian fleet of sailing ships was stationed off the southern tip of Greece to keep back the Turkish fleet. In accomplishing its mission, the fleet suffered heavy losses at the Battle of Cape Matapan in 1718. The fleets then engaged were much larger than those in Nelson's famous victory over the French in Aboukir Bay at the end of the century, namely:

> At Matapan — *Venetian*: 26 ships, 1,800 guns, casualties 1,824
>
> *Turkish*: 36 ships, 2,000 guns, casualties can only be guessed at but Turkish unwillingness to renew the fight suggest they suffered at least as much as the Venetians
>
> At Aboukir Bay — *English*: 14 ships, 1,212 guns, casualties 895
>
> *French*: 14 ships, 1,206 guns, casualties estimated 3,000

On the oceans, to be sure, bigger naval battles had been fought earlier: the French concentrated 75 ships to defeat the English at Beachy Head in 1690, and the English used about the same number to rewin control the next year.

SHIPS, COMMANDERS, AND CREWS   In the above comparison, all the vessels were of the type called a "ship-of-the-line." During the years of the Cretan War, naval architecture and naval tactics completed their adjustment to gunnery. While Venice was fighting its time-honored foe, the new naval powers, England and Holland, were fighting each other, and in the process they developed the tactics and specifications of the ship-of-the-line. They fought in a column, a line ahead, which enabled each vessel to deliver its broadside to the enemy. Out of the galleon developed a type depending entirely on sails, which was judged strong enough to take its place in such a line. It was stoutly timbered, with a relatively low sterncastle, almost no forecastle, heavy guns on two or three decks, and improved top sails which made it easier to handle (see Figure 39). Whereas the galleons that Venice used against Ossuna about 1620 carried only 20 to 30 cannon, many a ship-of-the-line used in the later Turkish wars had more than 70 guns.

Galleys, however, were still essential in the Mediterranean, because of their ability to move when a sailing ship could not. If a ship was entirely becalmed, a galley could avoid broadsides and inflict severe damage with the cannon mounted at its prow. Moreover, the Turks could have run supplies through to their army in Crete systematically in calms if the Venetians had not had galleys to oppose the Turkish galleys. On the other hand, galleys had to leave blockading stations fairly often to get water for their crews and to avoid bad storms.

The combined use of galleys and sailing ships was characteristic of the Cretan War and was then perfected, so far as that was possible. When a galley and a galleon teamed together, the galley depended on the guns of the galleon for protection and the galleon depended on the galley to tow it into position. Instead of fleets sailing on parallel courses and exchanging broadsides, they generally formed a line abreast as at Lepanto. Each commander tried to gain the advantages which came from getting to windward of the enemy. He then had freedom of choice in pressing the attack or breaking off the engagement. Galleys were used to tow ships into position to windward, to straighten the battle line, or to rescue a vessel whose rigging had been shot away. As gunnery improved, there was less of that clash of ships for boarding which reached its apotheosis at Lepanto. Days and nights were passed in cannonading, sometimes at deadly close quarters, more often at long range in confused formations.

With its celebrated Arsenal, Venice had been a leader in maintaining in time of peace a government-owned war fleet and, in 1499, its fleet even included three or four very large sailing ships designed for battle by shipwrights of the Arsenal. During the sixteenth century, the building of such sailing warships by the government almost completely stopped. The Arsenal built only galleys, and Venice mobilized ships like galleons by converting merchantmen that it rented or commandeered, as did other governments. Since Venice's own big ships were too few to suffice for operations against Ossuna in 1617–19, Venice arranged to hire not only foreign ships in its harbor but several that were contracted for in Holland at the same time that Dutch troops were hired. In 1617 such use of Dutch and English in the Mediterranean was an innovation, which the Spaniards and Papalists considered outrageous, being likely to spread heresy. In the later Turkish wars, it was routine for both sides to rent Dutch and English ships. Venice did not begin building its own ships-of-the-line until 1667, when an English warship was used as a model. Stimulated by the war and the demand for the new type, life in the Arsenal then quickened. Sixty-eight ships-of-the-line issued from the Arsenal in the next fifty years, about half of them "first-rates" with 70 to 75 guns.

In 1724 the Arsenal began building the smaller type of warship that was developed in the Atlantic for scouting and for raiding or convoy duty, the frigate. In Venice that name had earlier applied to rowed dispatch boats, but the frigates built in the Arsenal in the eighteenth century had sails, no oars, and 30 to 44 guns.

Galleasses saw hard service in the Cretan War and under Francesco Morosini. He valued them because they were less dependent on wind than the ships,

FIGURE 39 *A Ship-of-the-Line (courtesy of Museo Storico Navale, Venice).*

To enable big ships to move through the shallow channels of the lagoon, pontoons known as "camels" were fitted to the hull, as shown in this seventeenth-century engraving by Coronelli.

and had more fire power than other galleys. Four to eight galleasses were sent out each year, until Morosini's successors complained that they had the disadvantages of both types, slowing down the other galleys in good weather but unable to operate with the ships in really rough weather. They last took part in a fleet action in 1717 and were eliminated from the Arsenal in 1755.

Venetian conservatism was epitomized in the rule that the Captain General of the Sea must use a galley for his flagship. As late as 1695, when the Turkish admiral hoisted his flag on a ship-of-the-line, and a Venetian Captain General, Morosini's successor, suggested he do the same, he was ordered to continue to use the special type of galley built for him.

Venetian commanders were all chosen by the elective processes already described, in which the Great Council was theoretically supreme but, in practice, an inner circle acting sometimes through the Council of Ten but usually through the Senate really made the choices and fixed the terms of a commander's commission. In time of peace, commands were stepping stones in the cursus honorum through which ambitious nobles strove to reach the highest goal their life offered, the dogeship. Generally, the men in charge at the beginning of a war proved inadequate in battle. Judging military talents in peacetime was difficult in monarchies also where the highest posts often went to court favorites instead of the ablest soldiers or admirals. Viewed comparatively, Venice's choices by election, though very far from perfect, do not look so bad. The tests of combat soon revealed a number of nobles with courage and skill who could be chosen to replace those who failed. The latter were almost always prosecuted, with the Senate or Great Council passing sentences that were much affected by factional politics. Many were acquitted; those convicted of cowardice or failure to obey orders were generally only fined or temporarily exiled, but grievously injured in their honor. Victors were rewarded with triumphal receptions, pensions, and such high posts as Procurator of San Marco. If few Captains General were reappointed, that was partly because the mortality among them was high. Of the ten in command during the Cretan War, five died in service.

Although success might make a naval command profitable because of booty won and gifts from a grateful republic, it was initially a financial burden. Sizable advances had to be paid out in manning the fleet. Even on the ordinary patrolling galleys which were rowed almost altogether by convicts, some guards and free galeotti were needed and convicts were not used on the galleasses and on the flagships. Free galeotti had to be enticed by bonuses for which the commanders hoped to receive later reimbursement (as explained in Chapter 25). Such bonuses were necessary to get good men even from among the conscripts.

The system instituted in the sixteenth century of conscripting from the city's guilds, from the mainland, and from overseas colonies was relied on for emergencies. In the fleet of 70 galleys that put to sea in the crises over the papal interdict, 10 or 12 were actually manned by the Venetian guilds, and with good men according to the report of the Captain General of the Sea, while 20 were manned in Crete. A levy on the guilds was made again at the beginning of the Cretan War. Although most men supplied by the guilds were hired substitutes, not all guilds could afford that alternative. Fifteen to twenty ironsmiths served personally in the first years of the War for Crete. Recognizing that the conscripting of skilled craftsmen for service at the oar was wasteful, the government encouraged the process whereby the levy was converted into a tax, and to prevent sudden demands from bankrupting the guilds, it required in 1639 the payment of regular yearly installments into a special fund of coin kept in the Mint for emergencies. Because paid in installments and made proportionate to income, it was called hopefully the "imperceptible tax" (*tansa insensible*).

Increasingly, the crews on Venetian galleys were of mixed nationality. The thirty to forty soldier guards needed on each galley were largely Albanian refugees. Dalmatians and Greeks were numerous among the sailors of all ranks and among the free oarsmen. Convict oarsmen could not be had in sufficient number from Venetian prisons and were obtained from neighboring states, even as far away as Bavaria. As the Cretan War dragged on, Venice's oarsmen came to resemble more and more the galley slaves whom their opponents and allies obtained from raids or from the slave markets in Leghorn and various Moslem ports. Ever since Lepanto, captured Turks had been used. Gradually, more and more reliance was placed on recruiting in the Aegean Islands by methods which may have included slave raids, purchase in slave markets, impressment, and the paying of bonuses. One Captain General reported that on such occasions sopracomiti were ruined by the cost of "buying free galeotti."

Other sopracomiti not rich enough for their ambitions ruined themselves because of the amounts they spent to gild the carved woodwork of their stern-castles. Fancy ornamentation of the poops was in style. In that Baroque age, a lavish display was essential to building the kind of reputation that would advance a political career. Laws forbidding such decoration were no more effective than other sumptuary legislation.

On the galleons and ships-of-the-line, the poops were also elaborately decorated, but the conditions of the crews and commanders were different. When sailing ships were rented by the month with the services of their masters and crews, the foreign captains were naturally concerned about the destruction of their vessels and had to be given special guarantees of compensation to risk them in dangerous actions. A Venetian noble entitled "governatore" was charged with command to invigorate the fighting but he had less control of the ship than the foreign "capitano." Many vessels were commanded entirely by the foreign captains because not enough Venetians could be found who were qualified to act as governatori. A minimum requirement was to have served four years as a gentleman cadet (*nobile*) on some commander's staff. Some of the hired captains were as harshly denounced as were the foreign mercenaries blamed for Venice's defeats on land, others were highly praised for their gallant service.

On foreign ships, the crews were paid by their captains according to their national customs. On the Venetian galleons or ships-of-the-line, there were also many foreigners, especially Greeks. The decline of the merchant marine at the end of the sixteenth century had driven Venetian sailors to seek employment in other places, such as Leghorn. Venetian ship operators became so dependent on Greek sailors that the navigation laws of 1602 counted Greeks as Venetians in requiring that crews of ships of Venetian registry must be two-thirds Venetian. When the merchant marine enjoyed a revival in the eighteenth century, naval commanders complained that they lacked good crews because the pay was irregular, whereas merchantmen which paid regularly were well manned.

THE LOSS OF
ADRIATIC
LORDSHIP
While Venice defended her lordship of the Adriatic successfully against the Turk, she became too weak to defend it against the rising great powers of Europe.

The Turkish wars made more complete the withdrawal of the nobility from commerce. Although trade with the Ottoman Empire did not cease entirely, it had to be conducted through intermediaries. Restrictions on foreigners at Venice were removed so that they would keep wares moving and supply the customs revenue on which the government heavily depended. Some Venetian nobles made money out of the wars, to be sure; some captains brought home notable amounts of booty, as did Francesco Morosini. Timber merchants and other suppliers of war materials made fortunes. On the other hand, the French, Dutch, and English established themselves firmly in the Levant. They obtained from the Turks treaties limiting their tariff payments to 3 percent (whereas the Venetians paid 5 percent and more in some ports) and completed their conquest of what had been markets for Venetian manufactures.

Both direct and indirect taxes were increased to meet the costs of the wars. By 1710, the yearly revenue of the Serenissima was about 5 million ducats, and more was obtained by extraordinary measures. The legal tender was debased so that a ducat of state debt could be paid in 1718 with coins containing only 17 grams of pure silver, whereas in 1630 the coins required would have contained 22 percent more silver (20.8 grams). Offices and honors were more extensively sold than ever. Even the honor of Procurator of San Marco could be bought by nobles who contributed 20,000 ducats; forty were elected during the Cretan War. Young nobles could buy the right to enter the Great Council at 20 instead of 25. A general proposal admitting into the nobility men who offered 60,000 ducats was rejected, but individual offers of 100,000 ducats were acted on favorably to such an extent that new admissions yielded more than 10 million ducats.

In spite of all these devices, the long-term public debt skyrocketed. From about 8 million ducats in 1641 it soared over 50 million in 1714 partly through forced loans, partly through the sale of annuities by the Mint. In wartime, life annuities were sold paying 14 percent, inheritable annuities paid 7 percent. Intervals of peace were used to refund the latter at 2 to 5 percent. So low a rate as 2 percent had to be imposed, but the government felt justified in forcing conversion at the low rate on those who had bought bonds at heavy discounts during the war. To pay more than 5 percent on the purchase price would be to pay usury, it was felt. Short-term borrowing through the Banco del Giro was pushed to the danger point again in 1713 as it had been in 1630, and reached a total of 2,300,000 ducats. The relative importance of the bank in financing war was of course much less at the later date, since the long-term debt had in the meantime grown about sevenfold. Both bank credit and the bond market were put under severe pressure.

Thus burdened, Venice clung the more rigidly to the neutrality which was her traditional posture in wars between the Bourbons and the Hapsburgs. A vigorous anti-Hapsburg policy, as the Young had advocated, became quite impractical in view of the periodic need of a Hapsburg alliance against the Turks. In the War of the Spanish Succession, 1701–14, which was fought to decide which dynasty should rule Spain and how Spanish possessions would be divided, Venice spent heavily to maintain an armed neutrality. But Austrian troops came through the Brenner Pass and across Venetian territory to fight the French for Milan and win it. France then sent a fleet to cruise off the mouth of the Po, so as to prevent the Austrians from sending reinforcement into Lombardy from Trieste by sea. Similar violations of Venetian territory and Venetian waters occurred in later wars, and Austria tightened dangerously her control of northern Italy. In negotiating with Russia alliances against the weakening Turkish Empire, envisaging its partition, Austria specified that Venetian territories should be considered within her sphere.

Venetian lordship of the Adriatic was composed of two elements, one military, the other commercial. War fleets should not operate there without her permission. As late as 1630, Venice enforced this claim when the King of Spain wished to send his sister with an appropriate fleet to Trieste on the way to her marriage with the Emperor in Austria. The Serenissima insisted that it would provide the armed escort; otherwise, its ambassador declared, the princess would have a wedding shower of cannon balls. By contrast, in May, 1702, when news reached Venice of the French fleet operating off its coasts against the Austrians, alarm caused cancellation of the traditional Ascension Day ceremony of Wedding the Sea. That cancellation symbolized the end of Venetian pretension to control the operation of foreign warships in the Adriatic. Later in the eighteenth century, the Adriatic was casually entered frequently by English warships operating against the French and by the Russians whose fleets destroyed the declining Turkish navy by actions in the Aegean and Ionian Seas, waters which Venice had once ruled.

Commercially, lordship of the gulf had meant that merchant shipping should bring specified cargoes to Venice and obey various Venetian navigation laws, such as those regarding her salt monopoly, health quarantine, and tariffs. After the relaxation of medieval staple rights which would have compelled wares to come physically to Venice, Venetian patrols enforced the collection of customs duties on wares headed for other ports, and persistently harrassed enfringers of the salt monopoly. As Venice's general political position grew weaker and weaker, however, her navigation laws and customs regulations were increasingly violated with impunity.

Venice's weakness permitted the growth of rival ports within the Adriatic. The challenge of Trieste was trumpeted by the Austrian emperor in 1719, when he proclaimed it a free port where goods might enter and leave without paying any tolls. Of more immediate success was the pope's proclamation in 1732 of a similar free port at Ancona; but in the long run, Trieste proved the more dangerous rival both because it had the backing of a large powerful state and because it was well located to displace Venice as the center of exchange between two regions of different and complementary endowments. The emperors improved Trieste's connections northward through Austria into Germany and Bohemia and eastward through Hungary, facilitating its collection of their mineral and forest products. In return, Trieste supplied those regions with goods they could not produce, such as the oil, fruits, nuts, and wines of the Mediterranean and a variety of wares from further overseas. Trieste's trade grew rapidly only after 1763, however, when the trade of Venice also expanded.

REVIVALS IN MERCHANT SHIPPING Although no longer a main crossroads of world commerce, Venice was still the metropolitan market for a rich, densely populated area. Similarly, its merchant marine no longer competed for European leadership, but regional needs created dependable cargoes, and when the fleets of the main sea powers were absorbed in their own wars, Venice's merchant marine enjoyed bursts of prosperity.

During the Turkish wars, local demand for ships was strong. Many were consumed in battle or employed in supplying the fleets and overseas bases. As in previous wars, Ragusa boomed during hostilities, but its merchant marine had fallen to a third of what it had been in the second half of the sixteenth century and Ragusa was in 1667 destroyed by an earthquake from which it recovered slowly. Long-distance trade was carried largely in English and Dutch vessels, and Venetian expansion was in smaller types which plied the Adriatic, concentrating at Venice stocks of olive oil from Apulia, sulphur from the Marches, raisins from the Ionian Islands, and other local products, so that the ships from the Atlantic entering the Adriatic knew Venice was a port where they could quickly load a full cargo.

Foreigners came to Venice in large numbers while the restrictions on them were relaxed during war. Some of those who became Venetian citizens were prominent shipowners. The Jews expanded their commerce and also owned ships. Indeed, the kind of merchants who crowded the Rialto changed during the seventeenth century. Increasingly, the Venetian nobles and citizens of old families devoted themselves entirely to government or the navy. The ruling class no longer included merchants, not even the richest, many of whom were recently naturalized immigrants. They felt they needed and indeed acquired organizations of their own, not a formal guild, but less formally instituted *Capi di Piazza* or, for the shipowners, *Capi de Parcenevoli*, who were consulted by the Board of Trade when called on by the Senate for an advisory opinion. When that Board of Trade was created in 1516, it could get the businessman's point of view from its members' own experience or from talking to their brothers or brothers-in-law.

The gap between the ruling class and the traders may explain an unwise, half-hearted measure taken by the Senate in 1662. To compete with Leghorn's success as a "free port," customs on imports by sea were lowered. But since reexport was taxed as heavily as ever, the move reduced customs receipts without attracting more transit trade and was repealed twenty years later. Moreover, the prior loading right of Venetian ships was reestablished in each interval of peace. Venice persisted in using its advantages as a port to favor a Venetian merchant marine, even when foreign vessels could have provided cheaper and safer transport.

To protect the Venetian vessels in Levantine waters from Barbary pirates, the Senate ordered them to sail in convoys. Shipowners protested that convoys used eight to fourteen months for a voyage that could be made in three or four, required excessive escort fees, and made markets always unfavorable because of the competition of the many ships arriving at once. The Armenian colony told the Board of Trade that they would rather send their ships accompanied only by prayers to the Almighty and accept God's unknowable gifts of good and evil rather than submit to predictable losses from shipping in convoys.

Whether in or out of convoys, their reputation as superior navigators enabled the Dutch to pay lower insurance rates than Venetians paid, 5 percent instead of 8 to 10 percent, according to the report of an Undersecretary of the Marine who recommended in 1671 the establishment of a school in the Arsenal to teach navigation. Admitting that it had fallen woefully behind in an art in which it had once led, Venice in 1683 founded such a school for the training of masters and mates.

A vigorous expansion of both trade and shipbuilding followed sweeping reforms made in 1736. Tariffs on both imports and exports were much reduced for wares in transit, and Venetian ships were encouraged to provide safe transport in more flexible form. Those *navi* that carried at least 40 men and 24 cannon and were at least 70 feet long in the keel were declared "fit ships" (*navi atte*), that is, fit to defend themselves, and were allowed to sail unescorted. They were generally successful in fighting off pirates and, in the 1740's, 10 to 12 a year went to Cyprus or Syria and 6 or 7 to Alexandria. In trade to the West, more important in the eighteenth century than the Levant trade, Venetian merchantmen expanded as "neutral shipping" during the War of the Spanish Succession and again during the War of the Austrian Succession. At least vessels flying the Venetian flags multiplied in western waters; their ownership and previous registry may have been in many cases suspect. In 1746, five Venetian "fit ships" sailed to London, one to St. Petersburg (Leningrad), and one from Lisbon to America.

Many such Venetian ships took along a French or English flag to hoist in case they encountered corsairs from Barbary, for while the Venetian flag might discourage French or English privateers, North African Moslems still viewed it as an invitation or a challenge. The English and French had negotiated treaties with these Barbary states protecting their ships from seizure. Some Venetian merchants urged that Venice likewise make treaties with the Moors and pay them tribute, but others objected to the expense and doubted that a peace treaty would be respected. The Senate clung to its traditional policy of regarding Barbary as subject to the Ottoman sultan and trying to deal through him. Although unsuccessful, such a policy seemed more dignified than paying tribute. The profits to be made in western voyages became so alluring, however, during the Seven Years War (1756-63), that the Senate permitted merchants and a high-ranking interpreter, but not any high-ranking noble, to undertake negotiations. Treaties were arranged, in 1763-65, by which Venetians gained much more in profits than they paid in tribute.

The Barbary treaties were followed by a boom in Venetian shipbuilding which, after faltering, benefited during the wars of the American and French Revolutions from the fact that the banner of Saint Mark was one of the very few neutral flags. In Levantine waters also, Venice's policy of neutrality gave its shipping some advantages during the wars which the Turks and Russians fought at sea as well as on land in 1768-74 and 1787-92. From the 60 to 70 ships recorded in 1763, the Venetian merchant marine grew to 238 counted as "ships" in 1775, and 309 in 1794, in addition to smaller types. Unfortunately, there is no assurance of consistency in the determination of what was ranked as a "ship." There were fewer big ships in use in the eighteenth than in the sixteenth century, if we classify as "big" only those rated 240 tons or more. But the reversion to smaller vessels was not a sign of Venetian inferiority; it occurred in all ports. Although changes in types and units of measurement cloud statistical demonstrations, it seems likely that the total tonnage moving through the port of Venice was larger in 1783, the peak of this boom, than ever before in the thousand years of the city's history.

When this upswing was near its peak, Venice's maritime laws and regulations were systematically codified for the first time since Doge Ranieri Zeno's code of 1255. The *Codice per la Veneta Mercantile Marina*, approved by the Senate in 1786, was broader in scope and neater in arrangement than Zeno's code. And it was a model of clarity, in spite of the fact that commissions had been working at it for nearly forty years.

Compared to the medieval regulations, the code of 1786 reveals the high authority assumed by the naval administration over all seamen, although the code was naturally concerned with sailing ships only, not galleys. Earlier, merchant shippers had been arbiters in disputes between masters and mariners; now the Magistracy for Naval Personnel (*Magistrato all'Armar*) were the judges. On the crucial issue of punishing a sailor for desertion, the code specified that he be sentenced to the galleys or prison, but provided that any sailor accused of jumping ship could file an affidavit setting forth his side of the case and be absolved at the discretion of the Magistrato all'Armar.

The code also reflected the way social classes connected with shipping had changed since the days of Doge Ranieri Zeno. It assumed a sharper separation between employees and capitalists, who were even referred to as *capitalisti*. The rights of the shareholders, the parcenevoli, were carefully stipulated and separated clearly from those of the ship's master, who was now assumed to be a salaried employee, not one of the owners. Few provisions recall the days when the crew had been semi-partners in a sailing and trading venture. Each seaman's right to his own portage or "venture" was specified, to be sure. From a voyage outside the Gulf, a properly enrolled seaman in good standing could bring back free of freight and customs two barrels of wine, four 50-pound sides of salt meat, four cheeses not over 50 pounds, 10 ducats worth of merchandise, and, from some voyages, a limited quantity of olive oil. But the clause specified that these were to be considered assistance in providing for his family! Lest he sneak other merchandise past customs, the code forbade his bringing in other wares or engaging in commerce. But reports sent in by Venetian consuls indicate that Venetian sailors were the most notorious of smugglers and that they often turned the whole ship into a kind of bazaar as soon as it entered a harbor, just as the commander of the Venetian galleys had not been ashamed to do in Alexandria two centuries earlier (see Chapter 24).

Sailors, captains, and share owners were all required to enroll in the seaman's guild, the Scuola dei Marineri di San Nicolò, which had been founded in 1573. From the dues it collected in varying amounts from its diverse members, it maintained a hospital for sick seamen and the usual guild functions such as religious services. It provided the "surveyors" who passed on the seaworthiness of vessels before they left port. It lobbied for more jobs for its members and for their exemptions from customs, but all its activities were in the eighteenth century rigorously subject to the Magistrato all'Armar.

There was resurgence in Venice's navy also during the 1780's. To compel observance of the treaties by the Barbary states, Venetian war fleets staged demonstrations off Tripoli and Algiers in the 1760's and attacked Tunis in the 1780's. In these expeditions, Angelo Emo, the last famous Venetian admiral, displayed the kind of capacities which had formerly been common among the nobles but which had become so rare as to be sensational. Scion of a distinguished family, fascinated from boyhood with ships and the sea, after service as a gentleman cadet (*nobile*) Emo was given command of a ship-of-the-line almost as soon as he was twenty-four. While commanding a convoy to Lisbon in 1758, he made a reputation by his display of courage and resolution during an Atlantic storm and by his ingenuity in devising make-shift substitutes when his ship's rudder was carried away. In the bombardment of Tunis in 1785, he devised floating batteries, rafts or pontoons made out of spars and casks and able to carry heavy guns protected by parapets of sandbags. His achievements put new life into the Arsenal. After the peace with the Turks in 1718, work in the Arsenal had almost ceased; completion of ships begun was so delayed that one was 55 years on the ways. Under the impetus given by Emo, new keels were laid in the 1780's. When he died in 1792, the fleet with which he was cruising between Sicily and Tunis contained 4 first-rates, ships-of-the-line; 2 heavy frigates; 4 light frigates; 3 transport frigates; and 26 smaller sailing ships or rowed vessels.

Until Venice's war fleet, its merchant marine, and the Republic itself were destroyed in the Napoleonic wars, Venice continued to be the leading port and the busiest center of shipbuilding and shipping in the Adriatic.

A TENACIOUS DEFENSE · III

The Death of the Republic

CHAPTER TWENTY-NINE

For almost eighty years, from 1718 to 1797, while Europe's great powers were engaged in major wars, Venice enjoyed peace (except for actions against pirates). One might expect that Venetian statesmen would be praised for thus avoiding the horrors of war, especially in light of what Venice produced during those years in music, literature, and the fine arts; but historians have labeled Venice's eighteenth century its age of decadence. Venetians of the time called themselves decadent in that they were not doing what their forefathers had done. Modern historians call them decadent because they were so much concerned with doing what their ancestors had done, and because they did not build new institutions contributing to the making of the future Italian nation.

AN ECONOMY NOT IN DECLINE A member of the Venetian nobility who became an archivist after Napoleon destroyed the Republic in 1797, Carlo Antonio Marin, composed what he called a civil and political history of its commerce. While he wrote, Venice as a port was being killed by England's war with Napoleon, but Marin still had hopes that Bonapartist rule would sustain Venice's traditional economic role. He was convinced that Venice's decadence was moral and military but not economic, and in the eighth volume of his history Marin maintained that Venice's trade in 1797 was as great and as enriching as when depicted in 1423 in the famous speech of Doge Tommaso Mocenigo. The figures Marin used to demonstrate his point emphasized Venice's export of the products of her own domains, such as the textiles manufactured at the foothills of the Alps and the newly

important agricultural products, most notably silk and rice. Thanks to the cultivation of rice, beans, and corn in addition to wheat, the Venetian domains could
not only feed themselves but export foodstuffs—a striking change since 1423!
Also, a tacit confession that the city was a less important part of the state over
which it ruled! In official documents such as the budget, Venice was always
referred to as *La Dominante*. But economically it was no longer as dominant
as it had been.

Modern scholars have made comparisons of 1797 and 1423 more sophis-
ticated than Marin's and they point to much the same conclusions. Economic
growth rather than decline characterized the Venetian state in the eighteenth
century, but the growth was greatest in Venetian possessions in mainland Italy.
Total population reflected this, although it was relatively stable. After the
plague of 1630-31 had reduced the city's population from roughly 150,000 to
about 100,000, it recovered within a decade to 120,000 and fluctuated thereafter between that figure and about 150,000. In 1764-66, the census reported
141,056; in 1790, 137,603 inhabitants. The Mainland domain, which had a
population of only 1,500,000 in the mid-sixteenth century, grew to more than
2,000,000 by 1770. The chief explanation of the demographic growth is found in
improvements in agriculture, of which the most important was the cultivation of
corn (maize) which became the chief food of the peasants.

Industrial surveys show declines within the city of Venice, although
brocades, lace, glass, and books were still important. Levantine markets for
Venetian products were gradually recovered after the Venetians, in making
peace with the Turks in 1718, won the low 3 percent tariff which their western
competitors had gained earlier. France had replaced Venice as the leader in
luxury industries, however, and the manufacture of traditional types of woolen
cloth within the city almost disappeared. For manufacture of cloth of the new
"Dutch type," a certain Isaaco Gentile received privileges in 1763. He had
spinning machinery, thirty-two looms, and a thousand employees on a location
with fifteen rooms. That was an isolated case; the manufacture of textiles grew
more vigorously on the Mainland. One of the few noble industrialists was Nicolò
Tron, who established textile manufactories at Schio, in the foothills back of
Vicenza. Nicolò Tron had been ambassador to England and, being impressed by
the factories he had seen there, he introduced similar improvements under
English supervisors. Within six years of Kay's invention of the flying shuttle,
Tron's employees were using it. Linen manufactories expanded in Friuli and
metal works around Brescia. Water-driven silk mills multiplied around Padua
and Bergamo. Industrial as well as agricultural products from the Mainland
were important in giving Venetian trade as high a total value in 1797 as it had
had three hundred years earlier.

Of course the rest of Europe had not stood still in the meantime.
Venice did not have as large a share of Europe's trade or wealth in 1797 as in
1423.

The decline of textile industries within Venice was a drop not only by
comparison with growth elsewhere, but compared to cloth production within the
city itself one or two hundred years earlier. It changed the occupational distribution of its population. Together with the expansion of maritime activity in the
eighteenth century, it shifted the proportion of craftsmen to seamen in favor of
the latter. Venice did not again become as much a nation of seamen as it had

been in the thirteenth and earlier centuries; but, compared to the industrialized city of 1600, which depended on foreign shipping, the Venice of 1797 was in much of its economic structure a return towards the Venice of the mid-fifteenth century. Censuses recorded a growing number of sailors (*marinari*). Within the six city districts, 2,200 were counted (fishermen and boatmen not included) in 1766-70; 4,500 in 1770-75. There were many more whose homes were in the villages of the lagoons. The French consul reported during the War of the American Revolution that there were 7,250 Venetian sailors, not counting the 3,000 taken into the British fleet. The shipmasters were no longer Venetian nobles, to be sure, as many had been in the fifteenth century. They were mostly Dalmatians with Slavic names. And the ownership belonged to Jews or to relatively new immigrants, not to Venetian old families. But the revival of Venice's position in the Levant in the second part of the eighteenth century recalls earlier centuries. The first European firm to establish a branch within the Red Sea were the Venetians, Carlo and Balthazar Rossetti. They opened up in Jiddah, the port of Mecca, in 1770. Their first big shipment was not pepper or ginger, but a newer "colonial product," coffee. In the Levant trade generally, Venetians were in second place behind the French, but they moved into first place, particularly in the main Syrian center, Aleppo, when in the 1790's the trade of France was disrupted by its revolution.

Within the Adriatic, Trieste's growth was for a long time subordinate to that of Venice, Trieste being served by Venetian ships and Venetian capital. The kind of business which in both cities took on the most modern form of organization was marine insurance. In the 1780's and 1790's, several joint-stock companies were formed to combine the capital and prestige of old families and newcomers in the booming business of insurance. This is just one example of the way Venice was expanding its commercial and transport services as the port and capital of a rich hinterland.

In most of this commercial and maritime expansion and in developing mainland industries, the names of old Venetian families are conspicuous by their absence. Rich Venetian nobles preferred to invest in land for reasons already explained, or to loan funds directly or indirectly to the government.

The government's bonds seemed increasingly secure as neutrality permitted solid improvement in its financial situation. During the first third of the century, its yearly income was about 5 million ducats. As in earlier centuries, very little of it, less than one fourth, came from direct taxation on Venetians; three fourths came from mainland cities and levies on consumption or turnover.

The public debt was roughly stabilized after the extraordinary expenditures in the wars against the Turks and in vain efforts to protect Venice's neutrality during the wars of the Spanish and Austrian successions. It amounted to over 50 million ducats but it had been made less burdensome by forcing many bondholders to take a cut in interest to 2 percent. Then for a time, borrowing was done at 4 percent so that in 1750 the debt was as follows, in par values:

Old debt paying 2 percent .... 52,000,000 ducats
New debt paying 4 percent 22,000,000
Medium term debt 6,000,000

Total debt, nominal value .... 80,000,000 ducats

Near the end of the century, revenues increased so that they totaled about 6 million ducats. Meanwhile, the proportion expended on the army and navy declined, especially after 1736 when Venice no longer made much pretense of keeping armed in its neutrality. In 1736, military expenditures were one third of the total and were more than the sum being paid to bondholders. In 1755, military expenditures absorbed something less than one-third, while considerably more than a third was being used to service the public debt. With this use of resources, the government was able after 1752 to reduce the rate on the "new debt" from 4 to 3½ percent by a purely voluntary refunding. Later, the old debt was refunded or retired, not at its nominal par value but at its market value. By 1797, the total debt was thus down to 44 million ducats.

REVENUE AND DEBT 1313-1788

Payments on the long-term public debt, compared with total revenue in ducats of account

Year	Payments in Ducats	Total Revenue in Ducats	Ratio of Payments to Revenue
1313	54,000		
1343	79,000	250,000	.31
1344	19,000	260,000	.07
1378	150,000		
1413	500,000		
1422	300,000	1,500,000	.20
1464	150,000		.15
1469		1,000,000	
1490	211,000		.20
1500		1,145,000	
1508	230,000		
ca 1550	300,000		.18
1551		1,717,000	
1555	200,000		.10
1569		2,000,000	
1577	800,000		.40
1602	200,000	2,444,000	.08
1608-10	55,000	2,588,000	.02
1621	192,416	3,436,361	.06
1633-41	520,000	3,000,000	.17
1736	1,841,255	5,341,059	.34
1755	2,061,604	5,602,095	.37
1788	1,770,000	6,000,000	.295

NOTE: For content and comparability of figures, see Bibliographical Note for Chapter 29.

In contrast with the "old debt," which had been created partly by forced loans and partly by the sale of annuities, the "new debt" issued during the eighteenth century was largely held by guilds and fraternities, the scuole, in a form called *capitali instrumentati* which had no maturity but paid regular interest. The scuole had accumulated endowments partly from dues but mainly from bequests, some of which they invested in real estate and some in government bonds. As good real estate investments in the city became harder and harder to find, they turned increasingly to government bonds. Then they added to their funds available for investment by accepting interest-bearing deposits. The scuole made arrangements with investors individually as to the annuities and maturities they desired. Apparently, the investors trusted them more than the government, partly perhaps because of the real estate backing the obligations of the scuole, and partly because the scuole were managed by men they knew well. The financial commissioners who began refunding the government's 4 percent obligations in 1752 felt sure they could do so in a free market because the scuole were paying less than 4 percent to their depositors. In effect, the scuole were providing Venetians with services like those of savings banks, and channeling savings indirectly into government bonds. Their activities explain the ability of the Venetian government to borrow at a low rate.

The lightening of the burden of public debt depended very little on any depreciation of the money. The coinage was not debased. The zecchino continued to be minted as 3.5 grams of pure gold, as it had been ever since 1284. The *scudo*, the most used silver coin, had decreased about one-tenth in the early decades of the century, but was maintained after 1739 at 30.2 grams fine. The "ducat" used in keeping government accounts represented in 1739 only 6 percent less silver than in 1718 and from 1739 to the fall of the Republic was unchanged.

Bank money was equally stable. As in the fourteenth century, it existed only in the form of entries on the books of the bank; a proposal to print bank notes was rejected in 1721. The last overissue of credits by the Banco del Giro was that referred to in the previous chapter, which raised the bank's liabilities to 2,300,000 ducats. The depreciation of bank money which it caused was corrected in 1718 by offering depositors long-term government obligations or 6 percent four-year notes. By this conversion and other steps, the bank's liabilities were brought down in 1739 to 820,000 ducats, which was considered about the amount needed to settle commercial balances. The bank then resumed cash payments and continued them until some years after the fall of the Republic.

THE APEX OF OLIGARCHY   The transformations of Western civilization at the end of the eighteenth century are conventionally characterized as the Industrial Revolution and the Democratic Revolutions. While the economy of the Venetian Republic showed many signs of adjustment to the new tempo of economic life, its political institutions remained entirely hostile to the new democratic spirit. In theory, the essence of the Democratic Revolutions was equal rights for all men regardless of who their fathers were. In practice, it lay in the transformation of upper classes by intrusion into them of men who based their claims to be there on their wealth and ability, not their ancestry. In the Venetian Republic, in contrast, almost every man owed his position to what his father had been— from the stevedores at the customs house, through the privileged craftsmen of the Arsenal, and the secretaries in the government bureaus up to the nobles in the Senate and Council of Ten. The right to govern was regarded by the nobles as a God-given right which was theirs because of their birth.

Venice's ruling nobles were so steeped in their aristocratic conceptions of society that they were hostile to the men not of their own class who were re-animating Venice's commercial life. The most powerful spokesman of the ruling circle during the second half of the century was Andrea Tron, son of the Nicolò Tron who was one of the few Venetian nobles to finance an industrial development. In a celebrated speech to the Senate in 1784 surveying the state of the economy, Andrea called on rich fellow nobles who had their wealth in land or public funds, or who were wasting it in conspicuous consumption, to turn to commercial maritime enterprises as their ancestors had done. But he did not do that himself. And he disparaged the spurt of Venetian shipping and trade during the War of the American Revolution because the profits did not go to solid, established Venetian families but to foreigners or new men, agents of foreigners. Jews had become important shipowners and also manufacturers. Andrea Tron helped put through new restrictions on Jews. He thought that they, like other upstart groups, should be kept in their place, well regulated by those born to rule, like himself. He proudly reproached his fellow nobles for decadence, but in himself he epitomized the kind of decadence which infected the ablest of the ruling class.

Within the nobility, the inner circle had become smaller during the seventeenth and eighteenth centuries, and those ruling became less dependent on winning freely given support from the whole nobility (see Figure 40). The three State Inquisitors, one of whom was a Ducal Councillor and two of whom were members of the Council of Ten, increasingly exercised the power of the Ten (who, it will be recalled, were really seventeen, since the doge and his six Ducal Councillors were also voting members). The three Inquisitors commanded a much feared corps of informers and secret police, and they suppressed any organization suspected of seeking a radical change in the form of government. Their proceedings were so secret that they were suspected of abuses of power for personal vengeance and ambition (see Chapter 27). Foreign affairs and regular business were handled in the Collegio by the six Savii Grandi. More and more these Savii decided important questions on their own. They felt so confident of their capacity to manage the Senate that they often did not bother to report to it dispatches from ambassadors. There was enough laziness or indifference among the Senators to tolerate this usurpation. The doge and his Councillors were more than ever absorbed in ceremonial. The effective chiefs of state were the six Savii Grandi and the three Inquisitors. None of these nine men held office for more than a year or could be reelected to the same post immediately, but the same nobles moved from one of these posts to the other or to important embassies or commissions, so that power remained in their hands.

Next in importance for the operation of the government were the secretaries, who were not nobles but were from the class of citizens-by-birth. Since they served the same agencies for years on end, they generally knew the functions to be performed and the rules to follow better than the nobles over them, many of whom took their positions as pure sinecures. Even those able nobles who spent practically their whole lives in conscientious government service did not become bureaucrats, that is, they were not attached by either material or sentimental ties to any particular bureau through which they exercised power, in which they became experts, and for which they felt responsible. They gained their positions and moved from one post to another, some paying better salaries

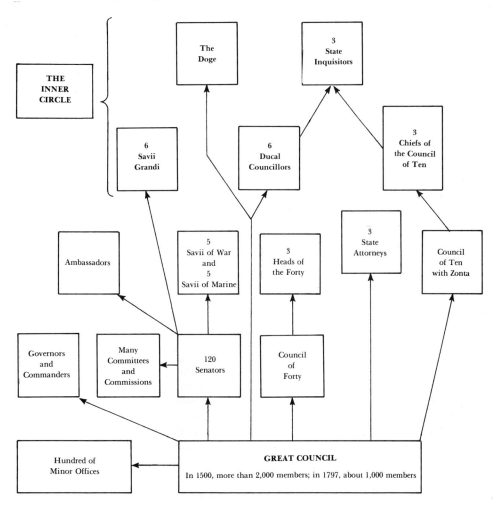

FIGURE 40 *The Structure of the Government.*

The arrows indicate by which councils officials were elected. The Signoria consisted of the doge, the Ducal Councillors, and the Heads of the Forty. More powerful in the eighteenth century were the Savii Grandi and the three State Inquisitors of whom one was a Ducal Councillor and two were members of the Ten.

and some less, according to the balloting in the Great Council which has already been described and which was at least as corrupt in the eighteenth century as in the sixteenth. One way in which such men as Andrea Tron were able to dominate the Senate and Great Council was by swinging elections for men who depended on such jobs for their livelihood.

The kind of positions to which nobles were elected gradually established as a matter of custom a threefold division within the nobility. At the top was a Senatorial order, in the middle a kind of judicial order of men with sufficient education in the law to be elected to the Forty and many other quasi-judicial posts, and at the bottom the Barnabotti whose poverty and lack of education kept them from holding any posts of importance although they were legally eligible for all. Debarred by the honor of their birth from lowly commercial or manual labor, the Barnabotti lived in misery, selling their votes and lobbying for jobs.

During the fifteenth and sixteenth centuries, the nobles seemed well satisfied with their membership and rejected all suggestions for reforms. During the seventeenth century, they became aware of deficiencies. An effort to improve the condition of impoverished nobles was the establishment in 1617 of a special school for the education of their children, the Accademia della Giudecca. It enabled a few to prove their capacity and rise to high office, but the number of poor nobles was increased when the loss of Crete drove refugees from that island to Venice. Few were any longer able to reestablish a family fortune by beginning as a noble bowman or gentleman cadet on a captain's staff.

The number of nobles began to shrink alarmingly after the plague of 1630–31. Most seriously felt was the lack of men with sufficient wealth and capacity to hold the highest offices. An insider commented late in the seventeenth century that there were then only fourteen or fifteen men capable of serving as Savio Grande. The post called for a man who had been ambassador to such courts as Rome and Paris and had upheld there the honor of the Republic by displays not only of manners, intelligence, and loyalty but also of wealth. For nearly three centuries, noble ranks had been closed against new blood and thus against men with newly made fortunes, except that nobles could and did marry the daughters of rich respectable citizens. Within the nobility, marriage alliances among the rich families caused wealth to become more and more concentrated in the hands of a few. In families with many children, all except one or two refrained from marriage so that the family fortune would not be scattered but would be passed on to finance political careers for the one or two offspring planned for the next generation.

The need of recruiting new men of wealth into the nobility was used, as was the extraordinary need for revenue during the later Turkish wars, to justify granting membership in the Great Council to rich worthies who contributed sufficiently. Between 1645 and 1718, nobility was conferred on 127 persons, each of whom put up 100,000 ducats and was personally recommended by the Collegio. These additions failed to stop the decline in numbers. From about 2,500 in the mid-sixteenth century, the total shrank after the plague of 1630–31 to 1,660 and then failed to recover. In 1775 it was down to 1,300, in 1797 down to 1,090. Among the adult Venetian males, about 6.4 percent were nobles in 1520, about 3.2 percent in 1797.

Of the 127 new families, one fifth were nobles from mainland cities, one fifth lawyers and chancery officials belonging to the class of citizens-by-birth, and three fifths merchants. Those who had been merchants promptly abandoned trade more or less completely, partly because the payment of 100,000 ducats (socially comparable to perhaps $10 million in 1970) seriously depleted their capital, partly because they felt that their new noble status required luxurious display, and mainly because they imitated the established old families who by this time regarded land as the one form of investment appropriate to their grandeur. The additions did not therefore undo the change in the character of the nobility. Having been for about three centuries strictly hereditary, it had become and remained a landowning, officeholding class.

The additions also failed to effect an amalgamation of the Venetian nobility with that of the Italian territories subject to Venice. Local nobles ruled as the upper class in their own cities but subject to the commands of the Venetian Senate and a few Venetian officials. The score or so elected to the Venetian Great Council during the Turkish wars either moved to Venice and were absorbed into its ruling class, losing all their local roots, or they stayed at home and never functioned as part of the Venetian nobility. The degree of alienation of the mainland nobles became evident in 1775, when the Venetian nobility made a new effort to overcome the shrinkage of its ranks. After heated debate, the Great Council approved offering membership to 40 families of mainland nobles who could prove their local status as nobles through four generations. Only 10 families applied.

It is generally said that the new nobles were never accepted as equals of the old. None were elected Savio Grande or a member of the Ten. But some certainly advanced to high office: at the fall of the Republic the commander of the main fleet stationed at Corfu, Carlo Aurelio Widman, and the last doge, Ludovico Manin, were of new families.

The policies of Venice towards the Italian cities raise many complex questions beyond the scope of this history. How far did Venice sacrifice their economic interests to her own? Should she or could she have overridden their liberties and leveled their social structures so as to have made a unified state? Could she have won the loyalty of mainland nobles by sharing from early date membership in the Great Council? Or by using in the eighteenth century, as she had tried in vain to do in the sixteenth, the slogan of Italian liberty in an adventuresome foreign policy like that which helped the kings of Savoy to become in the course of time kings of Italy? These questions naturally arise from concern with the genesis of the modern Italian nation. It suffices for our theme, however, to note only that the lion of St. Mark never came fully ashore. As befitted the symbol of a maritime republic, the lion was commonly depicted half on land, half on water. In retrospect, it is clear that Venice's future lay with Italy. But in spite of the growing economic importance of their mainland possessions, Venetians thought of themselves as a city apart and international. The Serenissima still drew much of its strength from a mixture of nationalities. It was comparable in this respect to its larger and growing neighbor, the empire of the Austrian Hapsburgs. The Greeks, Dalmatians, Friulians, and Lombards subject to the city in the lagoons were all vital elements in the Venetian state, so that the lion of St. Mark never planted all four feet firmly on Italian soil.

A STOP ON THE GRAND TOUR   In contrast to the declining political weight of Venice in the seventeenth and eighteenth centuries was its influence as a center of European culture. From the days of medieval pilgrims flocking to the Holy Land down to modern mass tours, Venice had catered to tourists. In the seventeenth and especially the eighteenth century, the tourism was aristocratic; many of Venice's visitors were members of Europe's upper classes, such as Montesquieu or Goethe, making "the Grand Tour" which was considered part of a gentleman's education.

Among the many features that drew them to Venice were its theater and its music. Venice was the opera center of the world in the seventeenth century. A union of music, staging, and acting produced the first opera at the courts of Florence and Mantua about 1600, but after 1613 Venice took the lead when

Claudio Monteverdi came to Venice to be Choirmaster of San Marco. Moreover, the first public opera house was opened in Venice in 1637. Operas were performed elsewhere at that date only as court functions. Because Venice was a republic, it erected opera houses open to a seat-purchasing public. For such an audience Monteverdi wrote in 1642, shortly before his death, his finest opera, *L'incoronazione di Poppea*. At the end of the seventeenth century, there were seventeen theaters in Venice with at least four giving performances simultaneously every season. Imagine all that opera in a modern city with a population of only 140,000!

In most of the 388 operas produced in Venice between 1637 and 1700, the staging was more important for acclaim than the words or the music. The Venetian public enjoyed a startling succession of contrasting scenes: pastoral idylls, spectral apparitions, incantations, battles, and shipwrecks. Painting scenery and devising machinery to move it rapidly became Venetian specialities, and artist-engineers who had proved their skill at Venice carried their art to such courts as Paris and Vienna.

Successors of Monteverdi such as Pierfrancesco Cavalli and Marcantonio Cesti kept Venice in the lead in opera during the seventeenth century, and in the eighteenth century Venice's most distinguished composer, Antonio Vivaldi, composed forty-four popular operas. But by that time, Naples and other capitals had developed competing styles in opera. Vivaldi, the red priest, so-called because of his red hair, is more celebrated for his orchestral concertos. As a music center, Venice was famous also for its organ makers and organ recitals, its violinists, its cantatas, and its girl choirs.

In the eighteenth century, Venice's theaters gave more time to spoken drama. Both tragedies and comedies attracted audiences which expressed their reactions vociferously. "Claques" organized to boo or cheer were recruited particularly from among the gondoliers who were rewarded with free admission. Among the hundreds of productions, it is the comedies that are of most interest, especially those of Carlo Goldoni. Venetian-born, son of a physician and with sufficient education in the law to derive from it part of his income, Carlo ran away from schooling several times to join troupes of players. He found them performing comedies in which the parts were improvised by the actors, who wore masks which signified to the audience what kind of character they portrayed: for example, Harlequin, a childish amorous buffoon, or Pantalone, a stuffy bourgeois. Being ex-temporized, this *commedia dell'arte* depended largely on pantomime that was almost acrobatic and on humor that was either slapstick or smut. Italy had at that time no tradition of written comedies comparable to those of England or those of France which Molière had perfected. Goldoni composed plots for the commedie dell'arte and persuaded the actors to use the lines he composed for them. At first, they acted the parts he created only because, living with the troupes, he conceived his characters to fit roles of the kind that the performers naturally acted. Once his compositions had been applauded by audiences, the troupes were eager to have them and he created his own kind of comedy, still containing some masked figures and stock characters, but purged of dirt and crudities while depicting with the utmost realism the characters to be met on the squares of Venice. His realism led him to write many in the Venetian dialect and he wrote also in French as well as in Italian. Notable was his transformation of the character Pantalone from a stupid cuckold, a butt for the jokes and tricks played by lying servants and young lovers, into a solid Venetian bourgeois, clinging instinctively to sensible standards of right and wrong.

Just as Goldoni was reaching the peak of his popularity in Venice, he was attacked by reactionaries who accused him of imitating the French and destroying the national Italian tradition of extemporaneous comedy. Leader of the attack was Carlo Gozzi, who produced some pieces directly satirizing Goldoni and many that were fantastic stagings of fairy tales, more like pageants than drama. Gozzi's shows were immensely popular, however. Rather than fight it out in Venice, Goldoni in 1762 accepted the position of director of the Comédie Italienne in Paris, where he died shortly after the French Revolution cancelled his position and pension.

Tourists in eighteenth-century Venice found her gambling halls even more popular than the theaters. The best-known were, like the theaters, owned by Venetian nobles. Many nobles became so addicted to gambling that they sat all day or night at the tables as bankers. The most famous gambling hall, the Ridotto at San Moisè, had besides its ten gaming rooms, salons devoted to conversation, to wine and cheeses, or to taking coffee; but in Venetian usage *ridotto* came to mean a gambling parlor.

Coffee houses multiplied also as places for diversion by mere sociability. There were a dozen around the Piazza, including Florian which opened in 1720 and Quadri in 1775. A few of the coffee houses attracted men who found each others' political views sympathetic. The Spadaria was the gathering place of those adhering to the new ideas coming from France.

From early date, tourists reporting on Venice included enthusiastic or disgusted comments on its prostitutes. In the eighteenth century, Venice was famous also for the charms of the singers and dancers who were the stars of the Venetian stage and who were highly rewarded for their favors. The most notorious picture of Venetian licentiousness is in the memoirs of Giacomo Casanova, who was the son of an actor and actress.

A new myth of Venice was woven from the comments of some travelers and from memoirs such as those of Casanova. Just as the early history of Venice is wrapped in the myth of pristine independence and its period of greatness is veiled by myths of the unfailing wisdom of the Venetian Senate, so the old age of the Republic is befogged by a myth of unsurpassed vice. The tourists do indeed generally testify to the loosening of morals among the women of the nobility. They found quite irreconcilable with even the pretense of marital fidelity the custom that a noble's wife be always accompanied by a *cicisbeo*, a man not her husband, who waited on her from morning to night even in the most intimate circumstances. They reported worldliness and worse in the convents. One French traveler, De Brosses, reported in 1739 that three convents were competing for the honor of supplying a mistress for the newly arrived papal nuncio — a report not worth repeating as evidence of such a state of affairs but as an indication of the kind of comment in common circulation.

On the other hand, the vices most commented on in Venice, gambling and the lack of marital fidelity, were common to all European capitals. Many a cicisbeo suffered all the tedium of chaperonage without the pleasures of a lover. Convents not praiseworthy for religious zeal yet fullfilled the social function of providing a way of life for widows and daughters who had no prospects of marriage. Better attested than their licentiousness is their holding of many musical recitals and elegant receptions. What distinguished the vice of eighteenth-century Venice was not the depths of its iniquity but the pervasiveness of its frivolity.

Eighteenth-century Venice had the reputation of being the gayest and most inconsequential of European capitals. The carnivals in which men and women went masked and indulged the liberties of make-believe created a spirit which lasted the year around, a pervading spirit of festivity.

LAST DAYS   *Men are we, and must grieve when even the Shade*
Of that which once was great, is passed away.
WORDSWORTH, SONNET III, LAST LINES

Underlying Venetian light-heartedness was the absence in all except a small minority of any serious purpose arising from political involvement. Even the handful of nobles who were thoroughly committed, who ruled the state and made that their lives, lacked stamina and courage.

When reports of revolutionary events in Paris and of revolutionary armies on the march poured into the Collegio, only a few voices advocated that Venice arm and prepare to fight for survival. They were not listened to. Her navy had been somewhat modernized by Angelo Emo, but her fortresses and her army were hopelessly out of date. Even if the money had been voted, men could not have been found among Venice's nobles to organize and lead the kind of army needed. Nor was Venice capable, under the new conditions created by the French Revolution, of managing a balancing of power between France and Austria. Passively it refused to ally with either and rejected proposals for a defensive league of Italian states. The traditional policy of unallied neutrality took less effort. The result was that, when Napoleon drove the Austrians from Milan and was pursuing them across Venetian territory into the Tyrolese Alps, Venice was at his mercy.

In the mainland cities occupied by the French, many members of the noble and middle classes mouthed the slogans of the French Revolution and used the occasion to set up governments hostile to Venice. The common people, on the other hand, unmoved by ideology and furious at the requisitions and abuses of French soldiers, showed firm loyalty to her, rioting under the rallying cry "Marco! Marco!"

Within the city of the lagoons, only a small number embraced democratic ideals and plotted an overthrow of the oligarchy. They were encouraged and organized by Bonapartist agents and in their support Napoleon advanced his troops to the water's edge. The Venetian commanders to whom the defense of the city had been entrusted all reported a lack of any adequate means of defense. There was evidence of a will to fight among lower ranks, especially among the Slavic militia brought from Dalmatia, but there was no fighting spirit among the nobles in charge. Fear dominated their last days: fear lest Napoleon confiscate their mainland estates which were already completely in his power, exaggerated fear of democratic plotting within the city, panicky fear of a sack by French soldiers. As reports of the French preparations to cross the lagoon came in, the

FIGURE 41   *Strolling Maskers (Photo Böhm).*

Pietro Longhi, who painted everyday scenes in the lives of eighteenth-century nobles, included many wearing the masks that were customary during the long carnival season.

unnerved Doge Manin exclaimed: "Tonight we shall not be safe even in our beds!"

Napoleon peremptorily demanded that the government dissolve itself and turn power over to a democratic municipal council to be protected by French soldiers. The doge urged acceptance of Napoleon's will, and the Great Council, in its last meeting, May 12, 1797, hurriedly voted itself out of existence. Four thousand French soldiers entered to keep order and paraded in the Piazza which had never before been occupied by foreign troops.

Napoleon plundered Venice systematically: its Mint, its Arsenal, its fleet, its archive, and its art treasures. Then, to buy time for his imperial schemes, he turned it over to Austria by the Treaty of Campo Formio, October 17, 1797. This bartering away of the once glorious republic plunged into despair the few enthusiasts who had sincerely hoped that Venice could have a glorious future also under democracy. One of them at least is worthy of note, Ugo Foscolo. As a youthful dramatist, he scored the last stage hit of the Venetian Republic with a play denouncing tyranny. Later, in his agonized strivings under Napoleon for a free Italy, he became for the emergent Italian nation "the first lyric voice of the new literature" (De Sanctis).

Eight years after transferring Venice to Austria at Campo Formio, Napoleon took Venice back, having meanwhile defeated Austria more thoroughly. In 1805 he added it to his Kingdom of Italy. A decade of French rule combined with the hardships of the British blockade then completed the ruin of Venice as a shipping center. The Congress of Vienna in 1815 reassigned it to Austria, from which it was freed by its union finally in 1866 with the Italian nation.

A TENACIOUS DEFENSE · IV

The Completion and Preservation of the City

CHAPTER THIRTY

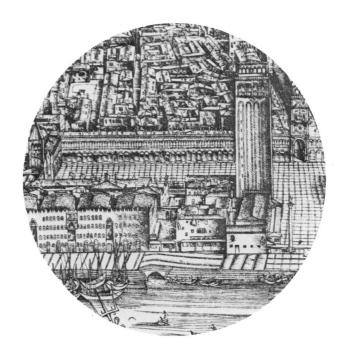

The gods returned to earth when Venice broke
Like Venus from the dawn-encircled sea.
Wide laughed the skies with light when Venice woke
Crowned of antiquity
WILLIAM ROSE BENET, *GASPARA STAMPA*

Visitors on the Grand Tour in the eighteenth century saw a Venice architecturally much changed from that depicted by Bellini and Carpaccio. Venice's distinctive beauty, rooted in the nature of the site and the Venetian way of life, shone through the Byzantine, Romanesque, Gothic, and Early Renaissance styles used before 1500, but there was much new construction in the sixteenth century when a fifth style dominated, that of the High Renaissance. In the completion of the city which survived as the tomb of the Republic, the High Renaissance was joined by the Baroque.

New building or rebuilding was frequently due to fires, which were the more devastating because the medieval city was so largely built of wood. Only gradually were wooden bridges and muddy lanes replaced by stone bridges and paved alleys and squares. No fire department was organized before the eighteenth century. The workers from the Arsenal were called in when government buildings were threatened, but a great fire which in 1514 consumed almost all the shops of the Rialto raged all night before the Arsenalotti were sent across town to prevent its spread. Meanwhile owners of shops, taverns, and palaces worked frantically to carry their possessions out of the path of the flames; no one, says the contemporary Marino Sanuto in his detailed description of the catastrophe, gave thought to extinguishing the conflagration.

Repeated fires occasioned gradual changes in the appearance of the city's oldest and most important building, San Marco. The brick domes of its vaulting, shining on the inside with Byzantine mosaics, were shielded on the outside by wooden cupolas covered with thin lead plates. Several times they burned and were rebuilt higher. The fire of 1419 was remembered as blazing so fiercely that the Piazza in front of the church was flooded with molten lead. In the restoration after 1419, the basically Byzantine edifice, with its façade already dominated by Romanesque portals, was crowned by Gothic pinnacles and flowery tracery.

Frequent also were fires in the Ducal Palace. In rebuilding its eastern wing after the fire there in 1483, Antonio Rizzo introduced a Renaissance style into that otherwise Gothic building. Even more than the buildings designed about the same time by Mauro Coducci, such as the Scuola di San Marco (Figure 20), it manifested the delight in profuse ornamentation characteristic of Venice's Early Renaissance architecture (see Chapter 15 and Figure 18).

THE HIGH RENAISSANCE   The more imposing style of the High Renaissance, closer to the spirit of imperial Rome, was being created almost contemporaneously at Rome by architects from Lombardy and Tuscany such as Bramante and Michelangelo. Artistic and literary circles in Rome and Venice were intimately entwined; Pietro Bembo, whose literary powers and popularity were then at their peak, was a leader in both. When armies sacked Rome in 1527, many artists fled to Venice for refuge and brought with them the prestige of their achievements in Rome. But the style of the High Renaissance could not easily be moved to Venice unmodified.

Renaissance architects dreamed of rationally, mathematically planned cities, dominated by buildings of harmonious proportions, even though they knew that the existing big cities, tangled masses housing 50,000 to 150,000 people, could not be made over to fit such schemes. In Rome, St. Peter's and the Vatican Palace were located according to a plan to create, apart from the medieval city, a new quarter in which structures would be designed with reference one to another so as to afford scenic vistas. The new papal capital aroused so much admiration that it incited many kings to create palace-cities in which order and stateliness were the dominant ideals. Could Venice survive the embrace of such a style?

No king or pope could plan a rebuilding of Venice. Decisions about what and where to build were made piecemeal by committees and councils of ever-shifting membership, so that in the end they reflected a kind of group judgment. The last word lay with members of the nobility. Many of them had a humanist education and, like Pietro Bembo, took a keen and intelligent interest in the arts. Of much humbler rank were the artists who formulated and executed proposals, but they were recognized as being of a different order than ordinary craftsmen. What we call "the fine arts" were coming to be regarded as superior to mere manual arts because they involved design according to mathematical principles, such as the laws of perspective, and because they showed an appreciation of the classical models which the humanists so much admired. The high intelligence of many leading artists and their versatility in "the art of design" were winning them a new place in society. Most architects were also sculptors. At Venice, separate guild membership and artistic tradition set apart the painters, to be sure, and the achievements of the Bellini, of Giorgione, and of Titian gave them positions of much influence. Their eminence strengthened the taste for pictorial effects in architecture which was rooted in Venice's eastern traditions. This taste and the conservatism resulting from action through committees shaped the expression of the High Renaissance at Venice.

Adjustment to Venetian conditions was made skillfully by Jacopo Tatti, called Sansovino, who after the sack of Rome came to Venice at the age of forty-one with a high reputation because of the works of architecture and sculpture he had executed in Rome. He was at once made Foreman (*Proto*) of San Marco and formed a close friendship of mutual admiration with Titian, with Pietro Bembo and other nobles, and with Pietro Aretino, the poet and humanist whose scandal-mongering earned him the sobriquet of "The Scourge of Princes." Together they dominated Venetian artistic circles at mid-century.

Sansovino's first responsibility was the church of San Marco. After surviving several earthquakes and fires, it was in danger of crumbling. He built buttresses to contain the vaults and bound the domes with heavy iron bands which prevented them from collapsing. The designs Sansovino contributed for the continuing decoration of the interior, especially for bronze bas-reliefs, were not his best works, but when his son, Francesco Sansovino, wrote a guidebook praising Venice's beauty, he could justly boast that his father had saved San Marco.

In August, 1532, fire destroyed the great palace of Giacomo Corner. Marino Sanuto tells how he and Gasparo Contarini went together in a boat up the Grand Canal to see the blaze and describes flames shooting high up from the attic floor where the fire had started amidst the great quantity of sugar being there stored and candied. The owner, the son of one of Venice's richest men and nephew of the retired Queen of Cyprus, promptly called on Sansovino to design a new palace. It became known as the Palazzo Corner della Cà Grande because it was so large (it is now the Prefecture; see Figure 42). In his design, Sansovino followed the tradition of Venetian palace architecture, focusing rich ornamentation on a façade towards the canal, with three stories and superimposed loggias. He combined Roman arches, architraves, and engaged columns to give an effect of magnificence gratifying to its owner. This Corner palace was under construction for more than twenty years, soaring in rivalry with the palace of equally imposing but heavier design by Michele Sanmicheli, another refugee from Rome, being built further up the Grand Canal during the same decades for the Grimani family. Several later structures reflect with less grace the new style of palace architecture introduced by Sansovino.

The most famous of Sansovino's buildings is the Library which faces the Ducal Palace across the Piazzetta. Pictorially it balanced the square, in spite of the contrast between the Gothic style of the palace and the entirely Renaissance style of the Library. The exuberance and refinements of its ornament suggest that Sansovino was essentially more a sculptor than an architect. That comment was made sneeringly when the vault over the main hall of his Library collapsed in 1545, almost as soon as it was built. Sansovino was immediately clapped into jail. The intervention of such friends as Bembo and Titian soon secured his release and he was even restored to his position as Foreman of San Marco, but only after some years and after he had rebuilt the fallen roof at his own expense, using heavy timbers to make a flat but more secure structure.

Sansovino showed a fine feeling for the beauty of the buildings around the Piazza and Piazzetta as a group. He contributed decisively to their present visual relation to each other by disengaging the towering Campanile from the structure which had hitherto adjoined its base. He began his Library at the end nearest the Campanile but so distant from it that there could be an unimpeded view from the Piazza across the Piazzetta. On the side of the Campanile facing San Marco and the Ducal Palace, he built the graceful little Loggetta where nobles could drop in for a rendezvous on the way to the palace. It contained some of his best statuary. At the west end of the Piazza facing San Marco he constructed the little church of San Geminiano (see Figure 43). Behind the Library and facing the water front he built the Mint with an appropriately robust design. His plan provided only two stories, but a third one was added soon after because the expanding business of the Mint required more space. Only after Sansovino's death was the Library completed down to the Molo to form a front facing the harbor parallel with the Mint. At last, the library begun by Bessarion and under Bembo's charge for a time had a worthy home. Today, Mint and Library together house the national library, the Marciana.

LATE RENAISSANCE AND AFTER   The subsequent history of the Piazza and surrounding buildings will carry us far beyond Sansovino's time, but can be summarized briefly. A successor of much learning and industry but little imagination, Vincenzo Scamozzi, finished his Library as just described. He used the same motifs, with the addition of a third story, in his building of the Procuratie Nuove on the south side of the Piazza. The design and the simpler arcades of Coducci's Procuratie Vecchie were extended until the two series of arcades met, on the western side, the façade of Sansovino's church of San Geminiano. Under Napoleonic rule, the church of San Geminiano was removed, and an arcade similar to that of the Procuratie Nuove extended around the west end. Behind them was built a ceremonial entrance and ballroom for the palace of the Bonapartist King of Italy (now the entrance to the Civico Museo Correr). The grain warehouses which had been on the south side of the Procuratie Nuove were removed to create there a royal garden with an outlook over the Bacino San Marco. It is still called the Giardinetto Reale.

The history of the Piazza di San Marco would not be complete without more detail about the Campanile. It had been many times shaken by earthquakes and damaged by fire. A celebration of the victory over Boucicault's Genoese fleet in 1403 burned the top off so that it had to be rebuilt, and it was then for the first time covered with gilded copper. In 1489, a stroke of lightning shattered that spire and broke the bells. Rebuilding in stone on the design we now see was ordered at once, but it was not completed until about 1513 when Antonio Grimani, the financier who had nearly ruined his career by his handling of the fleet in the Turkish war in 1499, spent of his own funds, as well as from the reserves of the Procurators of San Marco, and enhanced his reviving popularity by finishing it. The credit he received helped him crown his rehabilitation by election to the dogeship in 1521.

FIGURE 42   *Palazzo Corner della Cà Grande (Photo Böhm).*

Begun in 1532 by Sansovino who coated the traditional form of Venetian palace with the style of High Renaissance (compare Figure 15). The richly decorated façade on the Grand Canal does not extend along the sides, even when—as was unusual—the side wall also overlooked a canal.

Since the spire was topped by a copper-covered statue of the angel Gabriel three hundred feet above the pavement, it is not surprising that it attracted lightning at least five times in the sixteenth century and continued to do so until a lightning rod was inserted in 1776, a couple of decades after this way of diverting thunderbolts had been explained by Benjamin Franklin.

Signs of weakening cracks appeared early in July, 1902, but were not taken seriously enough, and at 10 a.m. on July 14, the whole tower collapsed.

The Venetians, who called the Campanile the father of all Venice's many parish bell towers, said that "papà fell like a gentleman," killing no one and doing almost no damage to either the church of San Marco or Sansovino's Library. It crumbled straight down, destroying only Sansovino's Loggetta. Meeting that same day, the Venetian city council resolved to rebuild it "where it was as it was," and with aid from many quarters finished it in 1912.

Church architecture of the High Renaissance at Venice took its inspiration less from Sansovino than from Andrea Palladio (1508–80), who got his start and did much of his finest work at Vicenza and on the country homes which Venetian nobles built in that neighborhood. He was a simple stonemason when one of his employers recognized his unusual capacities, talked with him about the Latin authors who had written on architecture, took him to Rome to study both its modern and antique monuments, and recommended him to other nobles who were erecting new villas. Palladio studied both archaeological remains and Latin texts, so that he was able in 1556 to collaborate with Daniele Barbaro, a Venetian humanist noble, in the publication of the ancient Roman authority on architecture, Vitruvius. In 1570, which by coincidence was the year when Sansovino's death left Palladio's preeminence unchallenged, he published his *Four Books of Architecture*. In it Palladio described with precise, practical drawings both the structures he had built and the solutions he considered appropriate for various kinds of buildings. Its translation and the reproduction of its plates made it for centuries the chief guide of English and American gentlemen who took a hand in designing their own country houses, as did Thomas Jefferson at Monticello.

The appeal of the country mansions designed by Palladio did not depend on a richly decorated façade like that of Sansovino's Library or Palazzo Corner, but on the harmonious proportions of the building as a whole and a few ornamental features strategically placed. For a porch or as a frame for the main entrance, Palladio designed columns and pediments combined as on the temple fronts he had measured among Roman ruins. Desiring to apply such temple fronts on a larger scale to the façades of churches, he and other Renaissance architects faced the problem of adapting the Roman type of temple front to a building which, unlike Roman temples, had a main aisle, the nave, which rose a full story higher than the side aisles. Called on to design a front for the church of San Francesco della Vigna in Venice, which Sansovino had begun but left unfinished, Palladio devised a solution which combined two temple fronts, both starting from the same base, one as high as the nave and intersecting another which was as wide as the whole church. He applied the same solution most harmoniously in a church entirely of his own design, Il Redentore, built in fulfillment of the vow made during the plague of 1575–77, and again in the church completed after his death for the monastery of San Giorgio Maggiore (see Figure 44).

Palladio's country houses were placed so as to be seen from a distance. Venice's network of alleys and canals offered few such vistas, and the government was not prone to override property rights in order to clear space so that a building could have a desired special setting. But Venice's harbor provided it with architectural space which most cities gained only by extensive demolition. Il Redentore rose above the wide canal that separates the Giudecca from the rest of the city. Little demolition was necessary to clear the view of San Giorgio

FIGURE 43   *The Piazza before Napoleon (courtesy of Museo Correr, Venice).*

Facing San Marco was a much smaller church, San Geminiano. On one side of it was the Procuratie Vecchia designed by Coducci, on the other side the Procuratie Nuova built by Scamozzi. On the left, in front of the Campanile, is Sansovino's Loggia. Booths, such as those shown in this eighteenth-century engraving, but simpler and much more numerous, normally included from early date those of guilds collecting dues and hearing complaints. During the Fair of the Ascension, the whole Piazza was filled with shops built for the occasion.

Maggiore across from the Ducal Palace. When Palladio designed the church and monastery, nondescript structures in front of the church interfered with such a view, but at the request of Doge Leonardo Donà and the Collegio they were removed so as to give an unimpeded view from the Ducal Palace of the façade of the church.

Without such buildings as Palladio designed for San Giorgio Maggiore, that side of the Bacino San Marco would merge into the low, unstructured horizon of the island-spotted lagoon. As it is, the great sheet of water is enclosed within the architecture of the city.

The skyline of the Bacino San Marco was completed with the building of Santa Maria della Salute and of Custom House Point (la Punta della Dogana). When the government vowed a new church to the Virgin in 1630 in gratitude for the passing of the plague of that year, they destroyed an old church and hospital to make a conspicuous place available and accepted the plans of Baldassare Longhena. He designed more in the pictorial style of Sansovino than in the relatively sedate style of Palladio. Classical motifs yielded to the new, more excited Baroque manner, while unity was obtained by planning a central octagonal church dominated by a towering dome (see Figure 45). Driving piles to support so lofty a monument took decades. Construction went on all through the Cretan War and was not finished until after fifty-six years of work, in 1687.

Meanwhile, the custom warehouses between the Salute and the Bacino San Marco were rebuilt in solid unpretentious style. To finish the Punta della Dogana in a manner worthy of its setting—with the Salute rising behind it, the Ducal Palace shining to the left and San Giorgio in front — was a severe challenge. There was the usual competition before an awards committee. The winners who completed the assignment and filled the gap were Giuseppe Benoni and Bernardo Falcone.

In contrast to the Renaissance and Baroque structures rising around it, the Ducal Palace preserved its Gothic exterior unchanged. In its interior courtyard, where Antonio Rizzo had displayed the delicate exuberance of the Early Renaissance, his ceremonial staircase was renamed the Scala dei Giganti when Sansovino punctuated its dominance of the courtyard by placing on it two giant statues, Mercury and Neptune, symbolizing the sources of Venetian wealth and power, trade and the sea (see Figure 18). Sansovino designed also the Scala d'Oro within the east wing leading gorgeously upward to the seats of power: the meeting places of the Collegio, the Senate, and the Ten. Palladio also designed some of the rooms which were magnificently rebuilt and redecorated after a fire there in 1574.

Another fire, on December 20, 1577, burned the upper floors of the wings overlooking the Bacino and the Piazzetta, ruined the big hall of the Great Council, and was so destructive as to raise the question whether the whole Ducal Palace should not be rebuilt in "up-to-date" Renaissance style. Fifteen leading architects were asked for opinions. Some of those consulted wished to pull down the old palace and construct according to a new design with Doric, Ionic, and Corinthian columns ordered in classical style one above the other. A contemporary chronicler wrote that Palladio was the leader of those proposing such a complete rebuilding, and that statement is still repeated because it was embedded in the eloquence of Ruskin, the Victorian art critic who hated the Renaissance. Full publication of Palladio's proposals has enabled his admirers to exonerate him from planning such a desecration as the destruction of the palace's Gothic arches, but he did describe the damage from the fire as sufficiently extensive as to require much new construction from the ground up, and he took the opportunity to disparage any building dependent on timber, iron clamps, and chains. He argued from ancient examples the superiority of masonry in which solid lower stories supported lighter stories above.

The Senate's decision was conservative. As its committee of inquiry recommended, it voted to rebuild the two ruined wings by strengthening the foundations and rearranging the interior — moving to a separate building the prisons which had been in the southeast corner — but to preserve the façades unchanged. Until September 30, 1578, the Great Council met in the huge shed in the Arsenal which had been used for the making and storage of oars. Meanwhile, foremen ship carpenters found in the Arsenal's lumberyard the massive timbers needed. With the wood and iron work that Palladio scorned, the palace's top floors were rebuilt and covered in much less time than the two to four years Palladio had tentatively judged necessary. Credit for this quick construction

FIGURE 44   *San Giorgio Maggiore, as painted by Francesco Guardi (Photo Böhm).*
The façade designed by Palladio shows here as seen across the Bacino San Marco.

went to a foreman from the Arsenal. The administrative supervisor was also a carpenter by training, Antonio da Ponte, the Foreman of the Salt Office (*Proto al Sal*). He held that position not because of expertise in saltmaking, but because the Salt Office dispensed much of the money appropriated by the Senate for contruction. Under Da Ponte's supervision also was built the adjoining prison, which included the police headquarters. Its rough style and lower elevation sets off the Ducal Palace. The famous Bridge of Sighs, providing a secure passage for bringing prisoners from their cells to the rooms of the Ten or the Inquisitors for questioning, was finished in 1614.

San Marco and the Rialto had been Venice's two main centers since its inception. While the Piazza and the Bacino San Marco were being wreathed with handsome structures in the sixteenth century, the Rialto was relatively neglected. The wide-ranging fire of 1514 was not used as an occasion for laying out a larger, more decorous gathering place for merchants and financiers; nothing was built comparable to the Bourse which Antwerp inaugurated in the 1530's. A proposal for such a replanning was doomed in advance by the government's preoccupation with reopening as soon as possible the stalls and shops from which it was accustomed to draw substantial revenue. The War of the League of Cambrai was raging; Venice's control of a mainland domain was still in doubt; it was a poor time for expensive long-range planning. Moreover, property values in the neighborhood were extremely high. When emphasizing the intensity of the trade around the Rialto, Marino Sanuto noted that his family possessed there a tiny tavern which yielded a higher rental than the finest of the city's palaces. Many nobles had that kind of interest in pieces of property adjoining the small open area at the foot of the Rialto bridge near the government offices and the portico of the church of San Giacomo which formed the heart of the Rialto. No replanning found substantial support. To be sure, the Fondaco dei Tedeschi on the other side of the Grand Canal had recently been rebuilt, and the Palace of the Treasurers, which also survived the fire, was refurbished in style by 1525. About 1554, Sansovino was called on to design an additional government office building and a profit-yielding shopping center near it along the Grand Canal, one of his more humdrum products.

A new bridge, however, was called for, since the old wooden one was in decay. A more enduring and elegant structure in stone was authorized in 1551 and designs invited, but the Council of Ten failed to appropriate funds. Only after the powers of the Ten were curbed did an award committee in 1587 seriously investigate possibilities. There was agreement that the bridge should be lined with two rows of revenue-yielding shops, and that it should rise twenty-four feet above water to permit passage under it of the bucentoro. Whether there should be three arches or one was a subject of long and harsh debate among the half-dozen architect-engineers consulted. Scamozzi insisted arrogantly that three were necessary. Antonio da Ponte said it could be done with one and that a single span would make a more impressive structure. The committee of nobles split two to one in favor of Da Ponte and the Senate approved their decision. The minority committee member, probably incited by Scamozzi, kept up his criticism, questioning the solidity of the foundations even after Da Ponte had been at work some years. The bridge was finished in 1592 and proved its soundness by surviving a severe earthquake in July of that year.

The contrast between the half-hearted urban renewal around the Rialto and the multiplication of splendid buildings around San Marco reflected the dominance of affairs of state over commercial business in the Venice of the sixteenth and seventeenth centuries.

LEADERSHIP IN PAINTING   The fires in the Ducal Palace have deprived us of many works of famous Venetian painters. None of the scenes painted there by Gentile and Giovanni Bellini, Giorgione, and Carpaccio survived, and of Titian's only his *Saint Christopher* on a back stairway to the doge's personal quarters. Happily, the government was not the only employer in Venice. Many paintings for churches and scuole were more fortunate in escaping fires so that Gentile Bellini and Carpaccio are known to us through their paintings for scuole, mentioned in Chapter 15. Titian painted so largely for an international market that relatively few of his many famous paintings are in Venice itself. Three at least are: *The Presentation of the Virgin at the Temple,* which he painted in 1534–38 for the religious fraternity Santa Maria della Carità, one of the Scuole Grandi. It shows to all the better advantage because it is still in the place for which he painted it, the Carità's building being now incorporated in the Venetian museum of fine arts, the Accademia. Two others are in the Frari church, the *Pesaro Altarpiece* and *The Assumption of the Virgin.* They showed new possibilities in the design and coloring of large canvases on religious themes. When the *Assumption* was

FIGURE 45   *A Festival at the Salute. Pen and ink by Canaletto (Photo Böhm).*

unveiled in 1518, it immediately established Titian as the leader of a Venetian school rivaling Rome.

For some years in the mid-sixteenth century, Venice was the foremost artistic center in Europe, partly because of the skill of its artisans in many traditional Venetian crafts bordering on the fine arts, such as engraving and jewelry work, but mainly because of the fame of its painters, led by Titian. In addition to his great religious canvases, he created many small imaginative compositions, mostly on pagan themes, which he called "poesie." He was also the most sought out of portraitists (see Figures 19 and 25). His large and busy bottega received innumerable commissions from foreign princes. He went to Rome to execute portraits of the pope with his nephews, and he went to Augsburg to paint Emperor Charles V victorious in full armor. Not only was he the leader in the technique of his art; Titian also ran his bottega as a very profitable business. It was a big workshop, filled with models and with canvases awaiting finishing touches and shipment after his sons and assistants had executed orders according to his ideas. He was certainly nearly ninety, perhaps nearly a hundred, when he and his sons died in 1576 during the plague. In the general confusion, his treasures were plundered or scattered.

When Sansovino had rebuilt the roof of his Library, he engaged painters in 1556-57 to execute his plans for interior decoration and promised the prize of a golden chain to the one whose work would be judged the best. The judges, Sansovino and Titian, gave the award to a younger artist who had been attracted, as had Titian, from the mainland to the capital city, Paolo, called Veronese because of the city he came from. When the upper rooms of the Ducal Palace were rebuilt and redecorated, Veronese was in his prime, and some of his most beautiful compositions are on the ceiling of the hall redecorated for the meeting of the Collegio, where the doge received ambassadors. Veronese is famous above all, however, for huge frescoes, designed and colored so as to fill the whole wall of a vast room with light and color, as does *The Feast of the House of Levi*, painted for the dining hall of the Dominicans of San Giovanni e Paolo and now in the Accademia, and *The Marriage Feast at Cana*, which was painted for the dining hall that Palladio designed for the monks of San Giorgio Maggiore but is now, thanks to Napoleon, in the Louvre.

In the repainting of the Ducal Palace after the fires, the most important artist was Jacopo Robusti, nicknamed Tintoretto because he was short and the son of a dyer. He hardly ever went outside Venice, painted almost entirely for fellow Venetians, and had none of the aristocratic and literary connections that distinguished the household of the princely Titian. It is reported that he was once apprenticed to Titian and was dismissed as soon as Titian noticed his style in drawing. Certainly Tintoretto's lines vibrate with an entirely different spirit. His first great success, *Saint Mark Freeing the Slave*, showed already in 1548 that Tintoretto could paint more dramatic pictures than did Titian, then at his peak. "Michelangelo's drawing and Titian's color" was said to have been the motto on the wall of Tintoretto's bottega. As a diligent craftsman, he sought to learn from every conceivable source and leapt at opportunities to buy models, sketches, and antiquities from which to take ideas. Other painters found him terrifying; he would try anything in attempting striking effects, generally successfully. He executed commissions with extraordinary rapidity and bid most aggressively in the competitions announced by the scuole and government agencies. His methods made enemies. One member of the Scuola di San Rocco responded to a drive for funds to complete the decoration of its meeting hall by making his contribution conditional on the work not being done by Tintoretto. But Tintoretto's partisans were equally vehement, and in 1564 he won that contract. He won by a trick and then executed it better than it could have been done by any other artist; it includes many of his masterpieces. He had painted much in the Ducal Palace before the fires, and he and his assistants led in the redecoration, leaving many examples of his versatility, from massive battle scenes in the hall of the Great Council to graceful pagan fantasies in the ante-chamber of the Collegio. Jacopo Tintoretto was above all a painter of large dramatic scenes, however, a man of the people who painted miracles with unquestioning conviction and startling energy.

After Tintoretto died in 1594, painters of comparatively mediocre talent turned out picture after picture to meet the demand which had been heightened by the creations of the three great masters: Titian, Veronese, and Tintoretto. During their lifetimes also they overshadowed many other capable Venetian painters such as Paris Bordone and Lorenzo Lotto. Compared to the present, the demand then for paintings seems insatiable. To be sure, the style of interior

FIGURE 46   *Tintoretto, Self-Portrait (Photo Böhm).*

decoration initiated for Venetian Renaissance churches by Coducci and perfected by Palladio excluded any painting, mosaic, or other such colored decoration on the brick-built walls and vaults. They were covered with stucco, as were even the half columns and entablatures, and were repainted white or cream every few years. "Palladio could control in this way the color and quality as well as the quantity of light" (Ackerman) and created a kind of pictorial effect within his churches simply by the lighting. In the side chapels, however, each altar called for one or several paintings on themes appropriate to that particular chapel. In addition, large paintings ornamented not only the walls of public buildings and the club houses of the scuole, but also the palaces of the nobles. The interior of the Barbaro villa which Palladio built at Maser, near Asolo, was resplendent with frescoes by Veronese.

In the eighteenth century, one of the painters employed in this sort of interior decoration, Giovanni Battista Tiepolo, 1696-1770, displayed a genius which again made Venice for some years the artistic capital of Italy, as it had been in the sixteenth century. Tiepolo's specialty was the painting of ceilings so that they seemed to open upward into ascending clouds peopled by angels, cherubs, and sacred or symbolic figures, with portraits of patrons among them, all in extraordinarily bright light colors. Among the many examples in Venice are the Scuola dei Carmeni, the church of the Gesuati, and the Palazzo Rezzonico. Equally famous are those he was summoned to execute outside Venice, at Milan, Würzburg, and Madrid.

One of his sons, Giandomenico Tiepolo, although completely overshadowed by his father as a decorative painter, had real talent for genre. Pietro Longhi, however, was the most effective painter of this new style — small scenes of Venetian social and domestic life (see Figure 41).

Venice became so famous in the eighteenth century for the art treasures in its palaces, churches, and meeting halls that the Council of Ten took measures to have them inventoried and to prevent their being bought and taken away by wealthy foreigners. To meet the demands of rich tourists, a special type of painting developed, namely, views of Venice. Giovanni Antonio Canal, generally known as Canaletto, whose father was a painter of sets for the theater, turned in the 1720's to producing views of Venice (see Figures 1 and 45). He received so many commissions from English nobles passing through Venice on the Grand Tour that he decided high prices could be obtained in London and went there to work for ten years. Most of his views were meticulously accurate and were less popular in Venice than the more romantic and sparkling views painted by Francesco Guardi (1712-93) (see Figures 18 and 44). Guardi used color with such a touch of fantasy as to make him "the last great master" in "the most fruitful tradition of Venetian art" (Haskell).

As the dying Venetian republic bequeathed to the nascent Italian nation its "first lyric voice," Ugo Foscolo, so also from Venice came the foremost sculptor of the new style, Antonio Canova (1757-1822). His *Daedalus and Icarus,* created in his stone-cutting shop in Venice in 1778, revealed the classicizing tendency which he later transformed into the neo-classical works executed in Rome for the popes and in Paris for Napoleon.

THE LAGOON   While painters were preserving Venice on canvas and the Council of Ten sporadically acted to secure its art treasures from foreign millionaires, the physical, biological basis of the city's life, the lagoon, was the constant concern of the Senate and the long-established Magistrato all' Acqua.

An old Venetian proverb recognized three enemies of the lagoon: the land, the sea, and man. From the land, rivers brought the silt and fresh water which threatened to clog the lagoon with canebreaks. After Venice's conquests on the mainland removed political obstacles, more canals were built to divert the rivers. Dikes were constructed on the landward side of the lagoon to keep out fresh water, and locks and portages were used to lift barges up from the lagoon to the inland waterways essential for Venice's commerce. But the execution of this program was incomplete, hampered, as programs for the preservation of the lagoon are today, by conflicting interests and theories. Some people argued that the water brought by the rivers helped enlarge the port. On that theory, a mouth of the Brenta that had been ordered closed in 1391 was opened in 1437, only to be closed again a few years later because of the extent of silting in the meantime near the Bacino San Marco.

The debate which rages now in the 1970's over filling-in a part of the lagoon so as to enlarge a nearby industrial zone was strikingly anticipated in the sixteenth century. At that time, narrowing the lagoon was advocated not for industrial purposes but for agriculture. In his campaign to make Venice independent of foreign grain, Alvise Corner defended damming off and draining the part of the lagoons which he called "the high marshes." He was making money that way himself and proud of it (see Chapter 21). He claimed it would help preserve the rest of the lagoon, because the stormy high tides which occasionally invaded these marshes carried back silt and vegetation to fill up other parts of the lagoon nearer the sea. Opposed to such reclamation were experts employed by the Magistrato all' Acqua, who argued for extending as widely as possible the flow of salt water, so as to make the lagoon healthier and the ports deeper.

Danger from the sea took two forms. The most dramatic appeared during fierce storms when a wind-driven Adriatic threatened to engulf the protective sand bars, the lidi. Early steps for keeping them intact included the prohibitions (mentioned in Chapter 2) against burning the pine groves on the lidi and against indiscriminate loading for ballast of the sand from their beaches. Some shores were strengthened by palisades or stone walls. On the lidi towards the south, at Pellestrina and Sottomarina (in front of Chioggia), what was left of such protection was carried away by high seas in 1686 and 1691. In their place, after many years of delay, massive sea walls called the Murazzi were built from huge blocks of Istrian stone. The Murazzi were finished in 1783, just a few years before the fall of the Republic, and withstood the sea until broken by the storm of November, 1966.

For many centuries, an equally dangerous and more subtle threat was the formation of underwater sandbars at the three ports or "mouths" of San Nicolò, Malamocco, and Chioggia. Ebb tides dropped their load of silt as they lost momentum in the Adriatic, and storms dredged sand from the beaches of the lidi and moved the submerged bars across the "mouths" of the port. Expert pilots and the buoys positioned by the Admiral of the Port provided only partial answers to this threat, although Venice's life as a port depended on keeping channels open both within the lagoon and between the lagoon and the Adriatic.

Until the sixteenth century, the mouth at San Nicolò of the Lido, being the nearest to the Bacino San Marco, was considered the port of Venice. But the Malamocco entrance was five times as large, or at least carried five to ten times as much water, according to a contemporary estimate. Some experts thought this the cause of the relatively sluggish movement of sea water in the northern and Venetian sections of the lagoon. The Grand Canal and the channel from it through the Bacino to San Nicolò was silting up alarmingly. The engineer or harbor master in charge reported in 1558 that the channel at San Nicolò was long, twisting, and dangerous, with a depth of only 11½ feet (Venetian) at mean tide. Since 1525 big ships had used the entrance of Malamocco.

During the rest of the life of the Republic and until almost the end of the nineteenth century, Malamocco was the port of Venice, the only one through which big ships could enter. Channels were dredged from the Malamocco entrance to the Bacino San Marco and to the Arsenal; otherwise those old centers of maritime life would have been inaccessible for large merchantmen. Ships-of-the-line were brought from and to the Arsenal by attaching to them the kind of pontoons called "camels" to reduce their draught (see Figure 39).

While Napoleon ruled Venice, the Malamocco entrance showed signs of silting up also. He ordered its protection by jetties, but they were not built until much later, between 1838 and 1857. These stone breakwaters projecting far out to sea, one on each side, made a relatively narrow channel to be scoured deep by the rush of tides.

Meanwhile, a railroad bridge connected Venice to the mainland, and after Venice was annexed to Italy in 1866 and the railroad network on the mainland was completed, dredging was begun to create facilities for freighters to unload next to railroad cars. By 1890, ships entering through Malamocco went to this new harbor called the Stazione Marittima (see Map 11). Only passenger ships went to the old harbor, the Bacino San Marco.

Between 1882 and 1892, the port of San Nicolò, now called commonly the Lido entrance, was reopened by dredging and by building two jetties to create a self-scouring channel like that of Malamocco. The Malamocco entrance sank into insignificance as big ships, even trans-Atlantic liners, moved past the Lido and through the Bacino San Marco and the Canale Grande della Giudecca to the Stazione Marittima. As modern industry developed in its hinterland, Venice became again a great port, second only to Genoa among the ports of modern Italy.

THE PERILS NOW   Industrialization intensified man-made threats to the life of the lagoons. An industrial "Venice" was begun in the 1920's at Porto Marghera, next to Mestre at the end of the bridge or causeway which had brought the railroad to Venice. In the 1930's this was broadened to bring also automobiles. They stopped at the nearby bus terminals and parking garage near the Stazione Marittima which marked the limit of the auto's penetration, at least until the 1970's, although motor-driven boats had by then changed the rhythm of life throughout the lagoons and the city's canals. In the 1960's, a Second Industrial Zone spread southward from Marghera over what until 1953 had been tideland. By 1970, the industries at Marghera — chemicals, petroleum, plastics, etc. — provided nearly 40,000 jobs. Overcrowding and urban sprawl changed much of Mestre from "garden suburb" to "workers' slums."

For political purposes, Marghera and Mestre as well as the Lido were combined with the Historical Center (the old six sestieri and the Giudecca) into one unit of urban government, a *Comune*. Most of the population of this newly defined "Venice" lived on the Mainland. Of a total population of 367,759 in 1969, there were in the Historical Center 115,685; on the Lido and lagoon islands 50,096; in Mestre and Marghera 201,978.

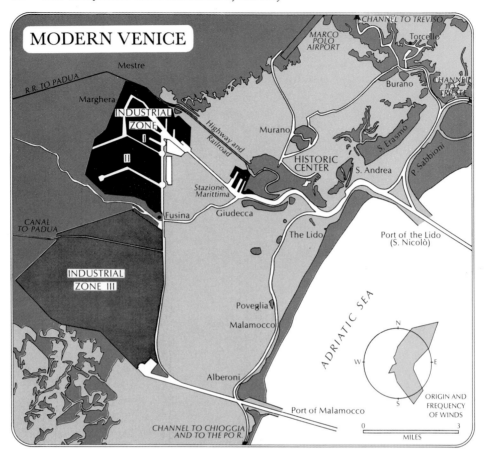

MAP 11

The dangers from this industrialism made world-wide headlines in November, 1966, when historic Venice was submerged six feet under water. Heavy rains created disaster at the same time in other Italian cities, from Belluno to Florence. In the lagoons, many days of southeast winds backed up flooding rivers to give Venice the highest "high tide" in its history. The Adriatic seemed to have swallowed up the lidi as its waves dashed directly against the Ducal Palace and San Marco. Headed by the world-wide organization of UNESCO, a movement to save Italy's artistic treasures broadened out to concern itself not simply with repairing as far as possible the damage done during the floods of 1966, especially at Florence, but also with preventing and correcting the slower, less dramatic crumbling of statues and blackening of paintings to which the floods served to call attention. Committees were formed, not only in Italy but in many nations, to collect voluntary gifts so as to supplement government expenditures and spur the salvation of selected art treasures. Helped generously by funds and experts from many nations, the directors of monuments, museums, and fine arts in Venice effectively trained and organized the skilled labor on which such restoration depended.

To strike at the causes, however, required decisions and adequate appropriations by the Italian government. Against a new flood, some steps were taken fairly quickly. The Murazzi at Pellestrina and Sottomarina were rebuilt. Observation posts at sea and a system of reporting enabled Venetians to have warning a few hours before their streets, their showrooms, shops, and homes were next inundated. Experts were consulted and plans drafted for gates that could be raised from the floor of the channels to close the three "mouths" at the Lido, Malamocco, and Chioggia. Controlling the tidal flow of the lagoons by such gates was an exciting possibility. But how would it affect the marine life? Or the flow of canals? These questions were urgently raised also by the proposal to dig a channel deep enough for 60,000-ton tankers from the Malamocco entrance directly to a new Third Industrial Zone. At first art lovers welcomed the thought that they need no longer tremble at the sight of half-empty tankers maneuvering past carriers of high-test gasoline between San Marco and San Giorgio Maggiore. But second thoughts about the effects on the tides of such a deep channel from Malamocco to Marghera and general opposition to more industry within the lagoons prevented completion of that "tanker canal" as far and as deep as originally planned, pending further research.

Opponents of the Third Industrial Zone emphasized how much the water and air were polluted by the already existing industries. The danger to such a city as Venice of destroying the life-giving qualities of surrounding waters was obvious, and the pollution of the air had even more immediately obvious effects on works of art. While motorized transport pounded their foundations, sulphuric oxides combined with the salt air to eat away the stones of Venice which Ruskin had so meticulously and lovingly traced. Their crumbling was not caused altogether or even chiefly by the industrialized zones; prevailing winds dumped most of Marghera's outpourings on the Mainland. The atmosphere of the Historic Center was poisoned mainly by the fuel used in the oil heating which became general in Venice after World War II. A law was passed requiring in principle conversion to gas. Its loopholes were deliberately made large because rapid conversions would be costly to the Comune and to house-owners, but in 1972 the largest and most modern establishments were heated by pollution-free gas.

National laws and subsidies were even more necessary to preserve Venice from sinking with accelerating speed below sea level. After electric pumps were introduced at Marghera in the 1930's to draw from the subsoil the water demanded by its industries, the sinking which had been going on slowly, about a half inch in ten years, became relatively rapid, about two inches in ten years, the exact amount differing from place to place. Although other geological changes contributed to raising the high water line, the pumping of water from the subsoil was the main cause of Venice's sinking beneath the waves, and was certainly the cause most clearly subject to human control. The pumping was only partly for industrial purposes; some was for irrigation, and some for Venice's municipal water supply. Instead of capping the wells, there was talk of pumping salt water back down under pressure. Where and how that could be done required research, long drawn out. But there was prospect that some wells would be capped after the completion of aqueducts from the headwaters of the Piave and from the river Sile above Treviso (see Map 1).

Changes in industrial technology may take a turn favorable to the survival of the city of the doges. The big industrial corporations, although dominated from Milan, not by Venetians, are discovering the economic disadvantages of congestion and talk of building their new plants not in Venice's Third Zone but north of its lagoon or much further south, nearer Ferrara. Tankers have grown to such a size that it may be more efficient to run a pipe line out to sea, beyond the port of Malamocco, than to dig for them a way into the port.

But in the Republic of Italy, as under the Serenissima, the government takes a hand in big entrepreneurial decisions. To be sure, there is now no government in Venice itself with the necessary jurisdiction, resolution, or financial resources. The political leaders of the present Comune function only as one among many pressure groups. They transmit to Rome the wishes of land speculators or art lovers or local residents demanding jobs and housing. Some 20,000 commuters enter the Historic Center every day and return at night to Mestre or beyond, because they cannot find adequate housing in Venice's "inner city." Italy's problems of industrial urbanism are not of course limited to Venice. Many other cities compete for funds to fight urban sprawl, local unemployment, pollution, and destruction of art treasures. In Rome, the national government formulated a law providing the funds needed to combat Venice's floods, pollution, and subsidence. Its passage was urged and its content fought over by local interests and nation-wide Italian committees devoted to preserving the many beauties of their national inheritance. The delay of its passage until after the parliamentary elections of 1972 left unanswered the question whether the Republic of Italy would prove capable of preserving the city created by the Republic of Venice.

Bibliographical Notes

These notes have the limited purposes of indicating: (1) the guides from which a more complete bibliography could be constructed; (2) recent publications, so far as I am aware of them, through 1971, particularly items in English; (3) specific references on some points of interest, for which the sources might not be found easily from the guides; (4) the secondary studies on which I have chiefly relied, especially when differing from the usual account. This latter purpose explains my many references to my own other writings, for they present evidence for my conclusions to an extent that would be inappropriate here.

An auxiliary bibliographical aid is the general index. When a publication is referred to, in these notes, with an abbreviated title or by the name of the author only, fuller bibliographical facts have been given at an earlier mention which can be located by the use of the general index. All authors are entered in that index. *Festschriften* and other collections of essays are indexed under the names of the men honored and of the editors, but not under their titles. Serials are indexed only if cited more than once and in abbreviated form.

Abbreviations frequently used are:

Arch. ven.	— *Archivo veneto*, edited and published by the Deputazione Veneta di Storia Patria, now Deputazione di Storia Patria per le Venezie
Atti Ist. Ven.	— *Atti* dell'Istituto Veneto di Scienze, Lettere ed Arti, Classe di Scienze Morali, Lettere, ed Arti
Colloque, Hist. Mar., 1962	— Méditerranée et Océan Indien: Travaux du Sixième Colloque International d'Historie Maritime, ed., M. Cortelazzo, No. 23 of Civiltà veneziana, Studi, of the Fondazione Giorgio Cini, Venice, and part of the Bibliothèque géné-

rale of Ecole Pratique des Hautes Etudes, 6e Section
(Paris: S.E.V.P.E.N., 1970)

EPHE-6 — Ecole Pratique des Hautes Etudes, 6e Section

Fonti stor. ven. — *Fonti per la storia di Venezia*, edited and published by the
Comitato per la Pubblicazione della Fonti relative alla
Storia di Venezia

Mon. stor. — *Monumenti storici*, edited and published by the Deputazione Veneta di Storia Patria, now Deputazione di Storia
Patria per le Venezie

N. arch. ven. — *Nuovo archivio veneto*

Riv. stor. ital. — *Rivista storica italiana*

Studi ven. — *Studi veneziani*

In these notes, as in captions under pictures, I have abbreviated references to
depositories in Venice. I wish again to express my appreciation for their courtesies:

Accademia — Gallerie dell'Accademia, Sopraintendenza ai Monumenti

ASV — Archivio di Stato, Campo dei Frari

Correr — Civico Museo Correr

Marciana — Biblioteca Nazionale Marciana

Querini-Stampalia — Biblioteca della Fondazione Querini-Stampalia

VENETIAN
HISTORY
AS A WHOLE
A still useful guide to the older literature and basic sources, although of course out of
date in many respects, is Heinrich Kretschmayr, *Geschichte von Venedig*, vol. I
(Gotha, 1905), vol. II (Gotha, 1920), vol. III (Stuttgart, 1934). An invaluable mine
of information is Pompeo Molmenti, *La storia di Venezia nella vita privata*, 3 vols.
(Bergamo, 1927, and later editions). The English translation, being from an earlier edition, contains much less. Still basic is S. Romanin, *Storia documentata di Venezia*, 10
vols. (Venice, 1853-61; reprint 1912), and the massing of material in chronological order
makes useful G. Cappelletti, *Storia della Repubblica di Venezia*, 13 vols. (Venice,
1850-55). Notable recent surveys are Roberto Cessi, *Storia della Repubblica di Venezia*,
2 vols. (Milan and Messena, 1944-46; 2nd ed., 1968), and his *La Repubblica di Venezia e
il problema Adriatico* (Naples, 1953) which contains a useful bibliography. On Venetian
chronicles, Kretschmayr's brief indications can be supplemented by Antonio Carile, *La
cronachistica veneziana* . . . (Olschki, 1968), as indicated in my review in *Speculum*,
XLVII (1972), 292-98.

My indebtedness to Gino Luzzatto, *Studi di storia economica veneziana* (Padua:
Cedam, 1954), and *Storia economica di Venezia dall xi al xvi secolo* (Venice: Centro
Internazionale delle Arti e del Costume, 1961) will be emphasized by many, more spe-
cific, references.

Interesting recent French surveys are Jacques Goimard *et al.*, *Venise au temps des
galères* (Paris: Hachette, 1968), imaginatively illustrated; and P. Braunstein and R. Delort,
Venise, portrait historique d'une cité (Paris: Editions du Seuil, 1971).

In English, the least unsatisfactory of the old surveys are F. Marion Crawford,
Venice, the Place and the People: Salve Venetia: Gleanings from Venetian History, 2 vols.
(New York, 1909), in which a professional novelist skillfully retells the old stories; and
William Roscoe Thayer, *A Short History of Venice* (Boston and New York, 1908), brief,
well organized. D. S. Chambers, *The Imperial Age of Venice, 1380-1580*, in History of
European Civilization Library, ed. Geoffrey Barraclough (New York and London, 1970),
very well illustrated, gives a useful up-to-date bibliography and a spritely survey of its
period.

Many current reinterpretations will be found in the nine attractive volumes in
which have been published the lectures of the series *Storia della Civiltà Veneziana* given at

the Centro di Cultura e Civiltà della Fondazione Giorgio Cini, Isola di San Giorgio Maggiore at Venice (Sansoni, 1955-65). Important periodical publications are (1) *Studi veneziani*, the continuation of the *Bollettino dell'Istituto di Storia della Società e della Stato Veneziano* of the same Fondazione Giorgio Cini; (2) the *Archivio veneto*; (3) the *Ateneo veneto*, for some periods and especially for the bibliographical articles of Giorgio E. Ferrari; and (4) the *Atti dell'Istituto Veneto*. These periodicals, especially the *Studi veneziani*, contain many more recent important articles than I cite below, since they are obvious series for anyone to consult in compiling a complete bibliography.

Recent Italian publications are surveyed in Congresso Nazionale di Scienze Storiche, *La storiografia italiana negli ultimi vent'anni*, 2 vols. (Milan: Marzorati, 1970), in which Giuseppe Martini devotes pp. 209-39 to Venetian history and in which other work on Venetian history is referred to in the contributions of Sestan, Berengo, Quazza, Pertusi, Brezzi, De Rosa, and Cozzi.

CHAPTER 1.
THE BEGINNING

For the early period in general: Volumes I and II, the only volumes published in the *Storia di Venezia* (planned in sixteen volumes) by the Centro Internazionale delle Arti e del Costume (Venice, 1957-58), especially the long chapters by Roberto Cessi, with extensive bibliographical notes; and the first chapter of Gino Luzzatto's *Storia*, planned as a part of the same series and similarly beautifully published by the Centro Internazionale delle Arti e del Costume.

For the early shoreline as shown on Map 1, see Map 23 in Van der Meer and Christine Mohrmann, *Atlas of the Early Christian World* (London: Nelson, 1958); and for detail, the maps in the above-cited *Storia di Venezia*, vol. II, chapters 11 and 15. On the lagoon from its beginning, the chapters by Bianca and Luigi Lanfranchi, G. G. Zille, and by others in that *Storia* and in Ministero dell'Interno, Direzione Generale degli Archivi di Stato, *Mostra storica della laguna veneta* (Venice: il Ministereo e Palazzo Grassi del Centro Internazionale delle Arte e del Costume, 1970).

On the early salt industry, see Jean Claude Hocquet's chapter in that *Mostra storica* and his "Histoire et Cartographie. Les Salines de Venise et Chioggia au Moyen Âge," *Atti Ist. Ven.* CXXVIII (1969-70), 525-74. An edition of Cassiodorus's letter with useful notes is in the edition by Ester Pastorello of *Andrea Dandolo, Chronica per extensum descripta* in *Rerum Italicarum Scriptores*, 2nd ed., vol. XII, pt. I (Bologna, 1938-40), pp. 69-70. It is translated at more length in Thayer, pp. 9-10.

On the river boats and their operators, see *Deliberazioni del Maggior Consiglio di Venezia*, Roberto Cessi, ed., *Atti delle Assemblee costituzionali italiane dal medio evo al 1831*, published by the R. Accademia dei Lincei, ser. III, sec. I, vol. II (Bologna, 1931), p. 263; vol. III (Bologna, 1934), pp. 15, 89. On the legal situation, see G. P. Bognetti, "La nave e la navigazione nel diritto pubblico mediterraneo dell'Alto Medioevo," in *Colloque hist. mar. 1962*, pp. 41-56.

On the slave trade, see Johannes Hoffmann, "Die östliche Adriaküste als Hauptnachschubbasis für den venezianischen Sklavenhandel bis zum Ausgang des elften Jahrhunderts," in *Vierteljahrschrift für Sozial- und Wirtschaftsgeschichte*, vol. 55 (1968), no. 2; and the second volume of Charles Verlinden, *L'Esclavage dans l'Europe médiévale*, expected shortly to round out his many specific studies, some of which are cited below.

CHAPTER 2.
THE PORT-CITY

The growth of the city from isolated islands is clearly illustrated in Eugenio Miozzi, *Venezia nei secoli: La Città*, vol. I (Venice, 1957), pp. 111-57. See also Cristoforo Tentori, *Della legislazione veneziana sulla preservazione della laguna* (Venice, 1792); contributions of R. Cessi and P. Leonardi to *Atti del Convegno per la Conservazione e Difesa della Laguna e della Città di Venezia* (Venice: Istituto Veneto, 1960); R. Cessi and A. Alberti, *Rialto: l'isola, il ponte, il mercato* (Bologna, 1934).

Lewis Mumford, *The City in History* (New York, 1961), chap. 11, sec. 2, and plate 21. He is magnificent in his general analysis of the model for city planning, although he mistakenly associates with the medieval period, in which the model took shape, a style of government that developed much later.

On the sale of overlarge ships about 1300, see *Cassiere della Bolla Ducale: Grazie — Novus Liber* (1299-1305), sez. I, Archivi Pubblici in *Fonti stor. ven.*, (1962), nos. 532, 544. On the Admiral of the Port, see ASV, Arsenale, buste 5 and 6; Senato Misti, reg. 47, ff. 152, 154; Paris, Bibl. Nat. Fonds Français, no. 5599, f. 136. The *capitolare* of the pilots is in ASV, Cattaver, busta 3, cap. 5. Reports on the depths and difficulties of the channels are in ASV, Savii alle Acque, busta 120.

General demographic background: R. Mols, *Introduction à la démographie historique des villes d'Europe du xiv au xviii siècle*, 3 vols. (Louvain, Gembloux, 1954-56); David Jacoby, "La population de Constantinople à l'époque byzantine: un problème de démographie urbaine," in *Byzantion* XXXI (1961), 81-109; L. Fabian Hirst, *The Conquest of Plague* (Oxford, 1953).

Venice's population: Karl Julius Beloch, *Bevölkerungsgeschichte Italiens*, vol. III (Berlin, 1961), and the earlier studies by Beloch and Contento there cited, which were published in the *Nuovo archivio veneto* in 1900 and 1902. On age distribution and migration from the villages to Venice, Daniele Beltrami, *Storia della popolazione di Venezia dalla fine del secolo xvi alla caduta della Repubblica* (Padua, 1954), although it contains errors. On specific epidemics, Mario Brunetti, "Venezia durante la peste del 1348," in *Ateneo veneto* XXXII (1909), and E. Rodenwaldt, "Pest in Venedig, 1575-1577," in *Sitzungsberichte der Heidelberger Akad., der Wissenschaften, Mathem.-Naturwissenschaftliche Klasse*, Jahrgang 1952 (Heidelberg, 1953), 2 Abhandlung, pp. 1-263. On the size of the nobility, James Cushman Davis, *The Decline of the Venetian Nobility as a Ruling Class*, Johns Hopkins Studies in Historical and Political Science, ser. lxxx, no. 2 (Baltimore, 1962).

My interpretation of the figures for 1338 is different from that of Beloch and Contento because they ignore the fact that the chronicle of Caroldo from which the figure of 160,000 is derived says explicitly that it is referring to the whole Dogado (Correr, Venice, Gradenigo MS 78, f. 519). It is therefore perfectly consistent with the smaller figure given for the sestieri on either side of the canal (i.e., the city only) by the manuscript which Beloch, *Bevölkerungsgeschichte* III, 3, calls the Giustiniani chronicle.

My figure of "nearly 190,000" for Venice's population before the plague of 1575 is reached by adding about 14,300 to the census figure of 1563, which is 168,627, in order to allow for categories not included (transients, etc.) and for undercounting, as does Beloch (*N. arch. ven.*, 1902, pp. 12-23 and 44), and adding about 7,000 for some continued growth 1563-74 at the rate indicated by comparing the censuses of 1540, 1552, and 1563.

CHAPTERS 3 AND 4. CONQUEST OF SEA POWER   Basic: Camillo Manfroni, *Storia della marina italiana dalle invasioni barbariche al trattato di Ninfeo* (Livorno, 1899). On the "sea harbor," *ibid.*, pp. 126-27. The quotation on the battle of Durazzo is from *The Alexiad of the Princess Anna Comnena*, translated by Elizabeth A. S. Dawes (London, 1928; and New York, 1967), book IV, sec. 2. On Greek fire, see in the same, XI, 10. Compare Agostino Pertusi, "Venezia e Bisanzio nel secolo xi," in *La Venezia del Mille* (Sansoni for the Fondazione Giorgio Cini, 1965). On the battle of Ascalon, see William, Archbishop of Tyre, *A History of Deeds Done Beyond the Sea*, vol. I, translated by E. A. Babcock and A. C. Krey, Records of Civilization, XXXV (Columbia University Press, 1943), book XII, 22-23; and Foucher de Charter (Fulcherius Carnotensis), *Historia Hierosolymitana, Recueil des historiens des croisades publié par les soins de L'Académie des Inscriptions et*

Belles-Lettres, 16 vols. (Paris, 1841-1906), *Hist. occid.* III, 452-53. In that collection, William's account is vol. I, pp. 546-49.

On the crusades, in general: *A History of the Crusades*, Kenneth M. Setton, ed.-in-chief, 2 vols. (University of Pennsylvania Press, 1958, 1962), wherein see, on Saladin's control of the sea, II, 52-53, and on the importance of the Palestinian sea ports, also I, 98, 375-76, 385-87.

On the Fourth Crusade and the position of Venetians in Constantinople: Charles M. Brand, *Byzantium Confronts the West, 1180-1204* (Harvard University Press, 1968), with full bibliography; Donald E. Queller and Susan J. Stratton, "A Century of Controversy on the Fourth Crusade" in *Studies in Medieval and Renaissance History*, ed. W. M. Bowsky (University of Nebraska Press, 1969), VI, 233-78; and Queller's little volume, *The Latin Conquest of Constantinople*, in Major Issues in History series (Wiley, 1971). On the size of some other armies, F. Lot, *L'art militaire* (Paris, 1946) I, 229; II, 442.

On piracy: P. Charanis, "Piracy in the Aegean during the reign of Michael VIII Paleologus," *Annuaire de l'Institut de Philologie et d'Histoire Orientales et Slaves* X (Brussels, Université Libre, 1950), 127-36; F. Sassi, "La guerra di corsa e il diritto di preda secondo il diritto veneziano," *Rivista di storia del diritto italiano* II (1929), 99-128; Fredric L. Cheyette, "The Sovereign and the Pirates, 1332," *Speculum* XLV, no. 1 (Jan., 1970), pp. 40-68; and Manfroni, pp. 262-64, 271, 278.

CHAPTER 5.
SHIPS AND
THE SHIP'S
COMPANY

On ships: Frederic C. Lane, *Navires et constructeurs à Venise pendant la Renaissance* (EPHE-6, Oeuvres Étrangères, V, Paris, S.E.V.P.E.N., 1965), a revised edition of my *Venetian Ships and Shipbuilders of the Renaissance* (Baltimore: Johns Hopkins University Press, 1934); and on the merchantmen of this period, my introductory note "Le navi raffigurate nello zibaldone" in *Zibaldone da Canal*, in *Fonti stor. ven.*, sez. V — Fondi Vari (Venice, 1967), and the more general works there cited. Also: Louise Buenger Robbert, "A Venetian Naval Expedition of 1224," in *Economy, Society, and Government in Medieval Italy: Essays in Memory of Robert L. Reynolds*, ed. David Herlihy *et al.* (Kent, Ohio: Kent State University Press, 1969), pp. 141-52. On the size of ships (tonnage and the botte), see below, supplementary note to Chapter 26.

Concerning the maritime law of the period: Riniero Zeno [Vallo] , *Storia del diritto marittimo italiano nel Mediterraneo*, 2nd ed., in Pubblicazione della Fondazione Vittorio Scialoia per gli Studi Giuridici, 3 (Milan: A. Giuffre, 1946); A. Lattes, *Diritto marittimo privato nelle carte liguri dei secoli xii e xiii* (Rome, 1939); and Guido Bonolis, *Diritto marittimo medievale dell'Adriatico* (Pisa, 1921) add significantly to the old, basic work of W. Ashburner, *Rhodian Sea Law* (Oxford, 1909).

The basic Venetian codes are edited by Riccardo Predelli and Adolfo Sacerdoti in the *N. arch. ven.*, n.s., IV-VI (1902-3); and separately, *Gli statuti marittimi veneziani fino al 1255* (Venice, 1903). See also my "Maritime Law and Administration, 1250-1350," in *Venice and History: The Collected Papers of Frederic C. Lane* (Baltimore: Johns Hopkins University Press, 1966), reprinted from *Studi in onore di Amintore Fanfani* (Milan: A. Giuffre, 1962), III, 21-50; and G. Cassandro, "La formazione del diritto marittimo veneziano," *Annali di storia del diritto* (Milan: A. Giuffre, 1968-69), XII-XIII, 131-59.

On the traveling merchants and their contracts: Luzzatto, *Storia*, pp. 20-29, 80-93; *Studi*, pp. 56-116; and Alfred E. Lieber, "Eastern Business Practices and Medieval European Commerce, *Economic History Review*, ser. 2, vol. XXI, no. 2 (August, 1968), pp. 230-43.

On the status of seamen: my contribution, "Venetian Seamen in the Nautical Revolution of the Middle Ages," presented to the Convegno Internazionale di Storia della Civiltà Veneziana, on *Venezia e il Levante fino al secolo xv*, June, 1968, at the Fondazione Giorgio Cini, and being published by Casa Editrice Leo S. Olschki, Florence.

CHAPTER 6.   The pertinent parts of the *Storia* and *Studi* of Gino Luzzatto already cited; W.
LORDSHIP OF   Lenel, *Entstehung der Vorherrschaft Venedigs an der Adria* (Strasbourg, 1897); A.
THE GULF   Battistella, "Il dominio del Golfo," in *N. arch. ven.*, n.s. XXXV (1918); Roberto
Cessi, *La Repubblica di Venezia e il problema adriatico* (Naples, 1953); E. Sestan,
Venezia Giulia: Lineamenti di una storia etnica e culturale (Bari, 1965); L. Bettini, *Le
saline dell' antico delta padano*, from *Atti e Mem. della Deputazione Provinciale Ferrarese
di Storia Patria*, n.s., XXIV (Ferrara, 1962); B. Krekić, *Dubrovnik (Raguse) et le levant au
Moyen Âge* (Paris: Mouton, 1961); and for a handy yet scholarly view of Ragusa's
general position, Bariša Krekić, *Dubrovnik in the 14th and 15th Centuries* (Norman:
University of Oklahoma Press, 1972).

On the legends concerning the wedding of the sea: Gina Fasoli, "Nascita di un
mito," *Studi storici in onore di Gioacchino Volpe* (Florence, 1958), pp. 463, 473–77;
Lina Padoan Urban, "La festa della Sensa nelle arti e nell' iconografia," in *Studi ven.* X
(1968), 291–98, 312. The ancient liturgy quoted is published in Pastorello's edition of
Dandolo's *Chronica per extensum* in *R.I.S.*, 2nd ed., t. XII, pt. 1, p. 265n.

On "staple policy" in general, see the chapter by A. B. Hibbert, in *The Cambridge
Economic History of Europe*, vol. III (Cambridge, 1963); and A. Schaube, *Handelsgeschichte der romanischen Völker des Mittelmeergebiets bis zum Ende der Kreuzzüge*
(Munich and Berlin, 1906). On the salt monopoly, Clemens Bauer, "Venezianische Salz-
handelspolitik bis zum Ende des 14. Jahrhunderts," in *VJS f. Soz.- und Wirtschaftsgeschichte* XXII (1930), 273–323. On the grain trade, Hans C. Peyer, *Zur Getreidepolitik
oberitalienischer Städte in 13 Jahrhundert* (Vienna, 1950).

CHAPTER 7.   Most basic, in addition to the works of Luzzatto and Schaube already cited, is
THE LEVANT   Wilhelm Heyd, *Histoire du commerce du levant au moyen age*, 2 vols. (Leipzig,
1886). On the sailing routes from Egypt, see F. C. Lane, "Economic Meaning of the
Invention of the Compass," *American Historical Review* LXVIII (1963), 605–17, and in
Venice and History, especially p. 336. On Romania, Freddy Thiriet, *La Romanie vénitienne au moyen âge*, Bibliothèque des Écoles Françaises d'Athènes et de Rome, vol.
193 (Paris, 1959), and Silvano Borsari, *Studi sulle colonie veneziane in Romanie nel
xiii secolo* (Naples, 1966); *idem., Il dominio veneziano a Creta nel xiii secolo* (Naples,
1963); *idem.*, "Il commercio veneziano nell'impero bizantino nel xii secolo," *Rivista
storica italiana* LXXVI, 4 (1964), 982–1011.

On the Genoese rivalry: R. Caddeo *et al.*, *Storia marittima dell'Italia dall'evo
antico ai nostri giorni* (Milan: Garzanti, 1942); the difficult-to-find second volume in
Camillo Manfroni's series, *Storia della marina italiana dal trattato di Ninfeo alla caduta di
Costantinopoli*, of which only Part I was published (Livorno, 1902); *idem.*, "Sulla battag-
lia dei Sette Pozzi e le sue conseguenze," *Rivista marittima*, XXXIII, pt. 1 (1900); G.
Caro, *Genua und die Mächte am Mittelmeer 1257–1311*, 2 vols. (Halle, 1895–99); Rober-
to Lopez, *Storia delle colonie genovesi* (Bologna, 1938); Deno J. Geanakoplos, *Emperor
Michael Paleologus and the West, 1258–1282: a Study in Byzantine-Latin Relations*
(Cambridge, Mass., 1959); Angeliki Laiou, *Constantinople and the Latins: The Foreign
Policy of Andronicus II, 1282–1328* (Harvard University Press, 1972); Hélène Glykatzi-
Ahrweiler, *Byzance et la mer* (Paris, 1966).

On the Black Sea, the Mongols, and Marco Polo: George I. Bratianu, *La Mer Noire,
des origines à la conquête ottomane*, Societas Academica Dacoromana, Acta Historica,
t. IX (Munich, 1969), and his earlier works there cited in the bibliography; Robert S.
Lopez, "European Merchants in the Medieval Indies: the Evidence of Commercial Docu-
ments," *Journal of Economic History* III (1943), 164–84; Bertold Spuler, *Die Goldene
Horde: Die Mongolen in Russland, 1223–1502* (Leipzig, 1943); R. Morozzo della Rocca,
"Sulle orme di Polo," *Italia che scrive*, 1954; and "Catay," in *Misc. in onore di Roberto
Cessi* (Rome, 1958), I, 299–303; R. Almagia, R. Gallo, *et al.*, *Nel centenario della*

nascita di Marco Polo (Venice, Istituto Veneto di Scienze, Lettere ed Arti, 1955); F. Borlandi, "Alle origini del libro di Marco Polo," *Studi in onore di Amintore Fanfani*, vol. I.

Henry H. Hart in his *Marco Polo, Venetian Adventurer*, rev. ed. (Norman: University of Oklahoma Press, 1967) uses Marco as a central figure in a general description of Venice of that time. Marco is vividly presented in Eileen Power, *Medieval People*, 5th ed. (Barnes and Noble, 1950). The illustrations, Figure 5, are from MS Français 2810, Bibliothèque Nationale, Paris. For the routes on Map 6, see John Frampton, *The Most Noble and Famous Travels of Marco Polo*, edited by N. M. Penzer (London, 1929), Penzer's introduction.

For the concepts "cut and dried" and "cut and run" command of the sea, I am indebted to J. M. Kenworthy [Strabolgi] and George Young, *Freedom of the Sea* (London, [1928]), chap. II.

CHAPTERS 8 AND 9. THE COMMUNE Important earlier works are mentioned in Roberto Cessi's long chapter in vol. II of the *Storia di Venezia*, published by the Centro Internazionale delle Arti e del Costume (Venice, 1958); in Giorgio Cracco, *Società e stato nel medioevo veneziano* (Florence, 1967); and in Frederic C. Lane, "The Enlargement of the Great Council of Venice," in *Florilegium Historiale: Essays presented to Wallace K. Ferguson*, eds. J. G. Rowe and W. H. Stockdale (University of Toronto Press, 1971), pp. 236–74. See also: Giovanni Cassandro, "Concetto caratteri e struttura dello stato veneziano," in *Bergomum* XXXVIII (1964), no. 2, pp. 33–55 and in *Rivista di storia del diritto italiano* (Milan) XXXVI (1963), 23–49; Gina Fasoli, "Governanti e governati nei comuni cittadini italiani fra l'xi ed il xiii secolo," *Etudes suisses d'histoire générale* XX (1962–63), pp. 141ff; and Agostino Pertusi, "Quedam Regalia Insignia," *Studi ven.* VII, (1965), pp. 3–124.

On the early church and relations with Constantinople, Otto Demus, *The Church of San Marco in Venice: History, Architecture, Sculpture* (Washington, D.C.: The Dumbarton Oaks Research Library and Collection, 1960), book I.

On the number of *custodes* employed by the Signori di Notte, see Melchiore Roberti, *Magistrature giudiziare veneziane*, 3 vols; vol. III in *Monumenti storici* XVIII (Venice: Deputazione Veneta di storia patria, 1911) pp. 25, 29. On the ideal of equal justice, *ibid.*, vol. II (XVII of the *Monumenti*), p. 26, in the 1227 oath of a Ducal Councillor: "Studium quoque et curam habebo quod dominus dux omnes homines Venecie maiores et minores equaliter portet in racione et iusticia et in offensionibus." On practice: Stanley Chojnacki, "Crime, Punishment, and the Trecento Venetian State," in Lauro Martines, ed., *Violence and Civil Disorder in Italian Cities, 1200–1500* (University of California Press, 1972).

On Venetian colonies: Guido Astuti, "L'organizzazione giuridica del sistema coloniale e della navigazione mercantile delle città italiane nel Medioevo," in *Colloque hist. mar., 1962*, pp. 57–89; Vsevolod Slessarev, "*Ecclesiae Mercatorum* and the Rise of Merchant Colonies," *Business History Review* XLI, no. 2 (Summer, 1967), 177–97; Wilhelm Heyd, *Le colonie commerciali degli Italiani in Oriente nel Medio evo*, 2 vols. (Venice, 1866–68); Robert Lee Wolff, *Politics in the Latin Patriarchate of Constantinople, 1204–1261* (Dumbarton Oaks Papers, no. 8, Harvard University Press, 1954), and Wolff's articles there cited; and the books of Thiriet and Borsari, cited for Chapter 7.

On Nicolò Querini's "gran pratica" to be bailo of Negroponte, see Marino Sanudo Torsello, *Istoria del Regno di Romania*, in Karl Hopf, *Chroniques Gréco-Romanes inédites ou peu connues* (Berlin, 1873; reprint, 1966), p. 112.

Enforcing on the Procurators the freezing of the rent as reward for help against Bajamonte Tiepolo is recorded in the chronicle in the Marciana, MS Ital. Cl. VII, Cod. 779, f. 160.

I am grateful to Stanley Chojnacki for enabling me to consult prior to its publication his paper, "In Search of the Venetian Patriciate: Families and Factions in the Fourteenth Century," forthcoming in the volume of *Renaissance Venice*, edited by John Hale.

CHAPTER 10.   On navigation in general, E. G. R. Taylor, *The Haven-Finding Art* (London, 1956),
NAUTICAL   and on dead reckoning in particular, her "Mathematics and the Navigator," *Journal*
REVOLUTION   *of the Institute of Navigation* (London, 1960). On the compass and its effects, my
"Economic Meaning of the Invention of the Compass" in the *American Historical Review* LXVIII (1963), 605–17 and in *Venice and History*. On new types of ships, my *Navires et constructeurs à Venise*. For comparison with Genoese developments, see Jacques Heers, *Gênes au xvᵉ siècle* (EPHE-6, Affaires et gens d'affaires, XXIV, 1961) and "Types de navires et spécialisation des trafics en Méditerranée à la fin du Moyen-Age," in *Le Navire et l'économie maritime du Moyen-Age au XVIIIᵉ siècle principalement en Méditerranée*, Travaux du Colloque International d'Histoire Maritime tenu 1957 (EPHE-6, Bibliothèque générale, 1958), pp. 107–18.

The "mappamundi" of Francesco and Marco Pizzigani are reproduced, as are other sea charts, in Prince Yusuf Kamal, *Monumenta cartographica Africae et Aegypti*, 16 vols. (Cairo, 1926–51), IV, 1285–86, 1289. There is mention of "Marcus Pizzigani patronus juratus navis vocate Cornaria que nuper venit de Tana" in Dec., 1330, in ASV, Avogaria di Commun, Delb. M. C., Brutus, f. 123t.

On protection costs in general, see my "Economic Consequences of Organized Violence," *Journal of Economic History* XVIII (1958), 401–17, reprinted with related essays in my *Venice and History*; on the early galley voyages, my "Venetian Merchant Galleys, 1300-1334," *Speculum* XXXVIII (1963), 179–205, also reprinted in *Venice and History*. On the loss of part of the Flanders fleet in 1336, see *I libri commemoriali della Repubblica di Venezia, Regesti*, ed. R. Predelli (in *Monumenti storici pubblicati dalla Deputazione Veneta di Storia Patria* [now di Storia Patria per le Venezie], ser. 1, Venice, 1976 ff.), lib. III, no. 465; *Venetiarum historia vulgo Petro Iustiniano Iustiniani filio adiudicata*, eds. Roberto Cessi e Fanny Bennato (in *Mon. stor.* above cited, n.s., XVIII, Venice, 1964), p. 217. In ASV, Maggior Consiglio, Deliberazioni, Spiritus copia, ff. 193–94, it is noted that so many of the Senators and relatives of Senators lost personally from the capture that, if the usual rules banning from voting those with a possible conflict of interest had been applied, the Senate would have lacked a quorum.

On the slave trade: Charles Verlinden, "Le Recrutement des esclaves à Venise aux XIVᵉ et XVᵉ siècles," *Bulletin de l'Institut Historique Belge de Rome* XXXIX (1968), 83–202, and his many earlier articles there cited; also his "La Législation vénitienne du bas moyen âge en matière d'esclavage (XIIIᵉ–XVᵉ siècles)," *Ricerche storiche ed economiche in memoria di Corrado Barbagallo* (Naples: E.S.I., 1969), 147–72. For Venetian penetration of the Black Sea: Heyd, *Commerce du levant;* G. I. Bratianu, *La Mer Noire* as cited and, specifically, G. I. Bratianu, *Les Vénitiens dans la Mer Noire au XIVᵉ siècle: La politique du Sénat 1332-33 et la notion de latinité*, Académie Roumanie, Etudes et Recherches XI (Bucarest, 1939).

On the shift of crusading activity to the Aegean, see Heyd and Thiriet as cited above; A. Laiou, "Marino Sanudo Torsello, Byzantium and the Turks: The Background of the Anti-Turkish League of 1332-1334," *Speculum* XLV, 3 (July, 1970), 375–92; and A. T. Luttrell, "Venice and the Knights Hospitallers of Rhodes in the Fourteenth Century," *Papers of the British School at Rome* XXVI (1958), 195–212.

On free navigation, see the article of Luzzatto on that subject in his *Studi*.

Recent studies of the trade through Germany which cite earlier basic literature are Philippe Braunstein, "Relations d'affaires entre Nurembergeois et Vénitiens à la fin du XIVᵉ siècle," *Mélanges d'archéologie et d'histoire de l'Ecole Française de Rome* LXXVI

(1964), pt. 1; *idem.*, "Wirtschaftliche Beziehung zwischen Nürnberg und Italien im Spätmittelalter," in *Beiträge zur Wirtschaftsgeschichte Nürnbergs* I (Nuremberg: Stadtarchiv, 1967); and Wolfgang von Stromer, "Nürnberg in the International Economics of the Middle Ages," *Business History Review* XLIV (1970), 210–25.

On the cotton industry in the West: Maureen Fennell Mazzaoui, "The Cotton Industry of Northern Italy in the Late Middle Ages; 1150–1450," *Journal of Economic History* XXXII (1972), 262–86.

CHAPTER 11.
COMMERCIAL
REVOLUTION

Basic are Luzzatto's *Storia*, his *Studi*, and his *Il Debito pubblico della Repubblica di Venezia* (Milan-Varese, 1963), a reedition of his volume, *I Prestiti*, which was vol. I of series III of *Documenti finanziari della Repubblica di Venezia*, published by the Accademia dei Lincei (Padova, 1929).

On finances: also in the *Documenti finanziari*, ser. I, vol. I, Robert Cessi's *La Regolazione delle entrata e delle spese* (Padua, 1925) and *idem.*, in ser. IV, vol. I, *Problemi monetari veneziani* (Padua, 1937). Series II of those *Documenti finanziari*, entitled *Bilanci Generali*, vol. I, pt. 1, and vols. II and III were published by R. Commissione per la Pubblicazione dei Documenti Finanziari della Repubblica di Venezia (Venice, 1912 and 1903). Minor printer's errors in the Table II of my calculations of the size of the Monte Vecchio as presented in an appendix to Luzzatto's *Il debito pubblico* are corrected in its presentation in English as item 6 in *Venice and History*.

The "commercial revolution" I have here referred to was so named and well characterized by Raymond de Roover, "The Commercial Revolution of the Thirteenth Century," *Bulletin of the Business Historical Society* XVI (1942), 34–39. He gave details and bibliography concerning it in his chapter in *The Cambridge Economic History of Europe*, vol. III (Cambridge, 1963).

On Loredan's trip to India, see Roberto S. Lopez, "Venezia e le grandi linee dell'espansione commerciale nel secolo xiii" in *La civiltà veneziana del secolo di Marco Polo* (Venice: Sansoni and Fondazione Cini, 1955), as well as his "European Merchants in the Medieval Indies," *Journal of Economic History* III (1943), 174–80. On Federico Corner: the studies of Luzzatto, which are summarized in my "Gino Luzzatto's Contributions to the History of Venice," *Nuova Rivista Storica* XLIX (1965), 72–74. On Marino Cappello, *capitanio* as well as *armator* of the galleys of Flanders of 1334, see Senato Misti, reg. 16 (copia) ff. 90–91, 96, 121–22. On the cement pool and the government's renting out of kilns: *Le deliberazioni del consiglio del XL della Repubblica di Venezia*, t. II, ed. A. Lombardo, *Mon. stor.* (Dep. ven., n.s., vol. XII (1958), nos. 452–63.

Also on business organization, fairs, and usury, see items 3, 4, 7, 8, and 9 in my *Venice and history*, especially no. 8 which is an English version of "Ritmo e rapidità di giro d'affari nel commercio veneziano del Quattrocento," *Studi in onore di Gino Luzzatto*, 4 vols. (Milan: Giuffre, 1949), I, 254–73; and no. 3, "Family Partnerships and Joint Ventures" from *Journal of Economic History* IV (1944), 178–96; Gino Luzzatto, "Tasso d'interesse e usura a Venezia nei secoli xiii–xv," in *Miscellanea in onore di Roberto Cessi* (Rome, 1958) I, 191–202; J. Kirshner, "The Moral Theology of Public Finance: A study and Edition of Nicholas de Anglia's *Quaestio disputata* on the Public Debt of Venice," *Archivum Fratrum Praedicatorum* XL (1970), 47–72; Giulio Mandich, "Forme associative e misure anticoncorrenziali nel commercio marittimo veneziano del secolo xv," in *Rivista delle società* (Milan: Giuffre), anno VI (1961), 471–508; and Antonio Scialoja, "Le galee grosse della Repubblica Veneta, I, Un precedente dei 'Pools' marittimi," in his *Saggi di storia del diritto marittimo* (Rome, 1946), reprinted from *Studi in Memoria di Bernardino Scorza*, a cura del Università di Bari (Rome, 1940); Reinhold C. Mueller, "Procurators of San Marco in the Thirteenth and Fourteenth Centuries" forthcoming in *Studi veneziani* XIII (1971).

Commission agency as fully developed in the fifteenth century is pictured in my *Andrea Barbarigo, Merchant of Venice* (Baltimore, 1944, reprinted in 1967 by Octagon Books, N.Y.); and in *Il libro dei conti di Giacomo Badoer*, eds. Umberto Dorini e Tommaso Bertelè, Il Nuovo Ramusio, Raccolta di Viaggi, Testi e Documenti relativi ai Rapporti fra l'Europa e l'Oriente a cura dell' Istituto Italiano per il Medio ed Estremo Oriente, III (Rome: Liberia dello Stato, 1956), which is analyzed thoroughly by Guido Astuti in "Le forme giuridiche della attività mercantile nel libro dei conti di Giacomo Badoer (1436–40)," *Annali di storia del diritto* XII–XIII (1968–69).

On changes in bimetallic ratios, A. M. Watson, "Back to Gold — and Silver," *Economic History Review*, ser. 2, XX (1967), 1–34. On the value of the ducat as legal tender, F. C. Lane, "Le vecchie monete di conto veneziane ed il ritorno all'ore," *Atti Ist. Ven.*, CXVII (1958–59), 49–78. On insurance, the elaborately illustrated volumes of Giuseppe Stefani, *Insurance at Venice, from the origins to the end of the Serenissima*, 2 vols. (Venice: Assicurazioni generali di Trieste e Venezia, 1958).

On cittadini in general: Molmenti, *Vita privata*, vol. I; and Beltrami, *Storia della popolazione*. On Scuole Grandi, Brian Pullan, *Rich and Poor in Renaissance Venice* (Oxford: Basil Blackwell, 1971). On the number of noble families in the fourteenth century, Chojnacki, "In Search of the Venetian Patriciate," above cited.

CHAPTER 12.
CRAFTSMEN
AND SEAMEN

On Venetian industries and guilds in general, Luzzatto's *Storia* and the works cited in its bibliography, especially *I capitolari*, ed. Monticolo, who gives much supplementary material, as in vol. I on hemp and ropemaking. On the Mint, regulations printed in Cessi, *Problemi monetari (Documenti finanziari*, ser. IV, vol. I). The contract for steel bolts is recorded in ASV, Libri Commemoriali, reg. 1, f. 57, no. 157. On the breaking up of the monopoly in building materials, see *Delib. del Consiglio del XL*, vol. II, nos. 452–63; on the furriers, R. Delort, "Un aspect du commerce vénitien au XVᵉ siècle: Andrea Barbarigo et le commerce des fourrures (1430–1440)," *Le Moyen Age* LXXI (1965), 29–70, 247–73. On citizenship for immigrant artesans, Molmenti, *Vita privata*, I, 72–78.

On technology, especially of the chemical industries: Charles Singer *et al.*, *A History of Technology*, 5 vols. (Oxford, 1955–60). The praise of the mix used by Venetian glassmakers is from vol. III, p. 233. The earliest description of glassmaking with specific reference to Venice is in book XII of Georgius Agricola, *De Re Metallica*. I quote from the translation by Herbert C. and Lou H. Hoover (London: The Mining Magazine Salisbury House, 1912), p. 584.

On seamen: my above-cited contribution to the Convegno in Venice in June, 1968, still in press, "Venetian Seamen in the Nautical Revolution of the Middle Ages"; and on the shipbuilding industry, my *Venetian Ships*. On Venetian crews of Aegean pirate ships: Marino Sanuto Torsello, *Istoria del regno di Romania*, in Karl Hopf, *Chroniques Gréco-Romanes*, pp. 146–47; on "le menue gent" at Trapani, Martino da Canale, *Cronaca veneta*, eds. Filippo Luigi Polidori and Giovanni Galvani, in *Archivio storico italiano* VIII (1845), pp. 518–21.

CHAPTERS
13 AND 14.
TRIUMPH BY
COHESION

Since Manfroni's general naval history does not include this period, it may prove useful to list, in the order of the events they describe, special articles that do much to fill the gap: Albano Sorbelli, "La lotta tra Genova e Venezia per il predominio del Mediterraneo, I, 1350–1355," *Mem. d. R. Accademia d. Sci. d. Bologna*, Cl. di sci. morali; Sez. di sci. storico-filologiche, ser. I, t. V (1910–11), pp. 87–157, reprinted, 1921; Mario Brunetti, "Contributo alla storia delle relazioni Veneto-Genovesi dal 1348–1350," in *Miscellanea di Storia veneta*, Deputazione veneta di storia patria ser. 3, t. IX (1916); *idem.*, "La battaglia di Castro (1350) ed il regolamento delle prede marittima della Repubblica di Venezia," *Rivista marittima*, Feb., 1910, prima trimestre, pp.

270-282; Camillo Manfroni, "Il piano della campagna navale venete-aragonese del 1351 contro Genova," *Rivista marittima*, Aug.-Sept., 1902, pp. 323 et seq.; Vittorio Lazzarini, "La battaglia di Porto Longo nell'isola di Sapienza," *N. arch. ven.*, VII (1894); *idem.*, "Aneddoti della vita di V. Pisani," *Arch. ven.*, ser. 5, XXXVI-XXXVII (1945); *idem.*, "La battaglia di Pola e il processo di Vettor Pisani," in *N. arch. ven.*, n.s., XXV (1913), 177 et seq.; *idem.*, "La morte, il monumento di Vettor Pisani," *N. arch. ven.*, XI (1896), 395 et seq.; *idem.*, "Due documenti della guerra di Chioggia," *N. arch. ven.*, XII (1896), 137-47; I. Tiozzo, "Una pagina sulla battaglia di Pola," *Arch. ven.*, ser. 5, XXI (1937); Vittorio Lazzarini, "Frammento di registro del tempo della guerra di Chioggia," *Arch. ven.*, ser. 5, XXI (1937); *idem.*, "La presa di Chioggia," *Arch. ven.*, ser. 5, XLVIII-IX (1951); *idem.*, ed., *I dispacci di Pietro Cornaro ambasciatore a Milano durante la guerra di Chioggia, Mon. stor.*, (Dep. Ven.) ser. 1, vol. XX (1939); and *idem.*, ed., *Daniele di Chinazzo, Cronica de la Guerra da veneciani a zenovesi*, in the same *Monumenti*, n.s., vol. XI (1958); Francesco Surdich, *Genova e Venezia fra Tre e Quattrocento*, in Collana storica di Fonti e Studi editi da G. Pistorino (Genoa: Fratelli Bozzi, 1970); and at least in part in *Atti della Società Ligure di Storia Patria*, n.s., VII (1967), and C. Manfroni, "Lo scontro di Modone," *Rivista marittima*, Oct., 1897, p. 75 et seq., and Nov., 1897, p. 319 et seq.

Michel Balard, "A propos de la bataille du Bosphore: l'expédition génoise de Paganino Doria à Constantinople, 1351-52," in Centre de Recherches d'Histoire et Civilisation Byzantines, *Travaux et Memoires* IV (Paris, 1970), 431-69, uses the logs of Genoese galleys.

Only some of the above are cited in the bibliography to R. Caddeo *et al.*, *Storia marittima dell'Italia* (Milan: Garzanti, 1942), in which M. Nani-Mocenigo wrote libri IV and V, which provide a coherent narrative of the whole period 1261-1453. On a number of points on which his account differs from the specialized studies, I have followed the latter.

Manfroni's articles on the lack of discipline on Venetian galleys are cited in my "Venetian Seamen" forthcoming in the Atti del Convegno of 1968 above cited.

The passages quoted from Daniele di Chinazzo concerning Pisani are on pp. 44, 57-58, 148. Daniele's account of Zeno's voyages are taken directly from day by day records kept by a scribe of the fleet, pp. 154-59, 179-85, 199-201, 212-22.

Vittorio Lazzarini, *Marino Faliero* (Florence, 1963), collects articles published earlier in the *Archivio veneto*.

The theory that Falier's act was not an effort at monarchy but the effort of a faction is presented by Giovanni Phillinini, "Marino Falier e la crisi economica e politica della metá dell' 300 a Venezia," *Arch. ven.*, ser. 5, vol. 84 (1968), with emphasis on the accompanying economic crisis. On the monarchical ideas in Venice, particularly on Andrea Dandolo's, see Cracco, *Società e stato*, 399-440. Also, Mario Brunetti, "Per la riabilitazione di un doge; Lorenzo Celsi," in *Studi di arte e storia a cura della direzione del Museo Civico-Correr* (Milan-Rome: Alfieri, 1920), vol. I, pp. 143-47. On Andrea Dandolo's legal and historical studies, Girolamo Arnaldi, "Andrea Dandolo, Doge-Cronista," in *La storiografia veneziano fino al secolo xvi: Aspetti e Problemi*, ed. A. Pertusi (Florence: Olschki, 1970).

On Cyprus, see Sir George Hill, *A History of Cyprus*, 4 vols. (Cambridge University Press, 1948), vol. II. On rivalries in Romania, Max Silberschmidt, *Das orientalische Problem zur Zeit der Entstehung des türkischen Reiches* (Leipzig and Berlin, 1923); N. Jorga, "La politique vénitienne dans les eaux de la Mer Noire," *Bulletin de la Section Historique de l'Academie Roumaine*, II, 2-4 (1913-14), 289-370; G. I. Bratianu, "Les Vénitiens dans la Mer Noire . . . après la Deuxième Guerre des Détroits," *Echos d'Orient* XXXIII (1934); and on Venetian expansion of its empire, Thiriet, *Romanie vénitienne*, Part III.

On the public debt and the financial recovery, Luzzatto, *Il debito pubblico*, cap. III and IV.

CHAPTER 15.
ARTS AND
LETTERS

General: Giulio Lorenzetti, *Venezia e il suo estuario: guida storico-artistica* (Venezia: Bestetti & Tumminelli, 1928; or later English translation, slightly revised, Rome: Istituto poligrafico dello Stato, Liberia dello Stato, 1961); Terisio Pignatti, *Venice* (New York, 1971). On the Byzantine in Venice: Sergio Bettini, *Mosaici antichi di San Marco* (Bergamo, 1944); *idem., Venezia* (Novara, 1953); and his chapters in *Le origini di Venezia* and other volumes of the series *Civiltà veneziana* of the Fondazione Giorgio Cini; M. Brunetti, S. Bettini, F. Forlati, and G. Fiocco, *Torcello* (Venice: Libreria Serenissima, 1940); Otto Demus, *The Church of San Marco in Venice: History, Architecture, Sculpture* (Washington, D.C.: Dumbarton Oaks Studies VI, 1960); *idem., Die Mosaiken von San Marco* (Baden, 1935); *idem., Byzantine Mosaic Decoration* (Boston Book and Art Shop, 1955); Pietro Toesca and Ferdinando Forlati, *Mosaics of St. Mark's* (Greenwich, Conn.: New York Graphic Society, 1958); and, for the Pala d'Oro especially, the chapter by Andrè Grabar in M. Muraro, *Treasures of Venice* (Skira for *Horizon Magazine*, distributed by The World Publishing Company, Cleveland, 1963), and Klaus Wessel, *Byzantine Enamels from the 5th to the 13th century*) Greenwich, Conn.: New York Graphic Society, 1968), with bibliography.

On later architecture, Luigi Angelini, *Le Opere in Venezia di Mauro Codussi* (Milan, 1945); Edoardo Arslan, *Venezia gotica* (Electa Editrice, 1970); Michelangelo Muraro, "Scala senza giganti," in *De artibus opuscula XL: Essays in Honor of Erwin Panofsky*, ed. Millard Meiss, 2 vols. (New York University Press, 1961); Teresio Pignatti, *Palazzo ducale Venezia* (Novara, 1964).

On the painters: Molmenti, *Vita privata*, vols. I and II; Vittorio Michini, ed., *Disegni di Jacopo Bellini* (Bergamo, 1943); Giles Robertson, *Giovanni Bellini* (Oxford, 1968); Millard Meiss, *Giovanni Bellini's St. Francis in the Frick Collection* (Princeton University Press, 1964); Michelangelo Muraro, *Carpaccio* (Firenze, 1966); Pietro Zampetti, *Vittore Carpaccio* (Venice: Alfieri, 1966); Terisio Pignatti, *Giorgione* (Milan: Alfieri, 1969).

On literature and learning, see the general essays and specialized studies in the two collections: *Umanesimo europeo e umanesimo veneziano*, ed. Vittore Branca, and *Venezia e l'Oriente*, ed. Agostino Pertusi. They are vols. 2 and 4 in the series *Civiltà europea e civiltà veneziana: aspetti e problemi*, published for the Centro di Cultura e Civiltà della Fondazione Giorgio Cini, San Giorgio Maggiore (Venice: Sansoni, 1963 and 1966). On James of Venice particularly, L. M. Paluello in *Venezia e l'Oriente*; on tne organization of Padua, Pearl Kibre, *Scholarly Privileges in the Middle Ages* (Mediaeval Academy of America, 1962); on Petrarch and Aristotelianism, Paul Oskar Kristeller, "Il Petrarca, l'Umanesimo, e la scolastica a Venezia," in *La Civiltà Veneziana del Trecento*, 147-78, and the introduction to and the translation of Petrarch's reply to the four friends in *The Renaissance Philosophy of Man*, eds. Ernst Cassirer, Paul Oskar Kristeller, and John Herman Randall, Jr. (Phoenix Books, University of Chicago Press, 1948, 1967). On the same themes and the school at San Marco especially, Bruno Nardi, "Letteratura e cultura veneziana del Quattrocento," in *La Civiltà veneziana del Quattrocento*, and "La scuola di Rialto e l'Umanesimo veneziano" in *Umanesimo europeo.* . . . The quotation from Valentini's will is taken from the latter article, p. 94.

On medicine in Venice and Master Gualtieri, B. Cechetti, "La medicina in Venezia nel 1300," *Arch. ven.*, XXV (1883), 361-81; XXVI (1883), 77-111, 251-70; Ugo Stefanutti, *Documentazioni cronologiche per la storia della medicina, chirugia e farmacia in Venezia dal 1258 al 1332* (Venice: Ongania; and Padua: Antenore, 1961).

On civic humanism, see the appreciative essays on its chief expositor, Hans Baron, and his complete bibliography in Anthony Molho and John A. Tedeschi, eds., *Renaissance: Studies in Honor of Hans Baron* (DeKalb, Ill.: North Illinois University Press, 1971); and Wallace K. Ferguson, "The Interpretation of Humanism: The Contribution of Hans Baron," *Journal of the History of Ideas* XIX (1958), 14-25. On Venetian examples: N. Carotti, "Un politico umanista del Quattrocento," *Riv. stor. ital.* 1937, fasc. II. pp. 18 ff.; Patricia Labalme, *Bernardo Giustiniani: A Venetian of the Quattrocento*, Uomini e dottrine, 13 (Rome, Edizioni di Storia e Letteratura, 1969); Gianni Zippel, "Ludovico Foscarini ambasciatore a Genova nella crisi dell'espansione veneziana sulla terraferma (1449-50)," *B. Ist. Stor. Ital. Medioevo*, no. 71 (1959), pp. 181-255.

On Greeks in Venice, Deno John Geanakoplos, *Greek Scholars in Venice* (Harvard University Press, 1962); and on Bessarion's library, Lotte Labowsky, "Il Cardinale Bessarione e gli inizi della Biblioteca Marciana," in *Venezia e l'Oriente*.

On Bembo's personality, G. Meneghetti, *La vita avventurosa di Pietro Bembo, umanista-poeta-cortigiano* (Venice: Tipografia commerciale, 1961). On his history, Gaetano Cozzi, "Cultura politica e religione nella 'pubblica storiografia' veneziana del '500," in *Bolletino . . . veneziano* V-VI (1963-64), 215-96; and more generally on humanist historiography, Agostino Pertusi, "Gli inizi della storiografia umanistica nel Quattrocento," in *La storiografia veneziana*, above cited.

CHAPTERS 16 AND 17. CONTESTS FOR POWER   General view and bibliography: Nino Valeri, *L'Italia nell' età di principati* (Milan: Mondadore, 1949); Luigi Simeoni, *Le Signorie*, 2 vols. (Milan, 1950); Romanin's *Storia Documentata*; and for the later period, Fernand Braudel, *La méditerranée et le monde méditerranéen à l'époque de Philippe II*, 2nd ed., 2 vols. (Paris, 1966). An English translation by Siân Reynolds is announced by Harper and Row. Special: Bortolo Belotti, *La vita di Bartolomeo Colleoni*, 2nd ed. (Bergamo, 1933); Garrett Mattingly, *Renaissance Diplomacy* (Boston, 1955); James C. Davis, ed., *Pursuit of Power: Venetian Ambassadors' Reports. . .* (Harper Torchbooks, 1970). On the Turkish wars, see note to Chapter 25.

More specialized: Alessio Bombaci, "Venezia c l'impresa turca di Otranto," *Riv. stor. ital.* LXVI (1954), 159-203; Federico Seneca, *Venezia e Papa Giulio II* (Padua, 1962); Giovanni Soranzo, "Il clima storico della politica veneziana in Romagna e nelle Marche nel 1503," *Studi romagnoli* V (1954), 513-45; *idem.*, "L'ultima campagna del Gattamelata al servizio della Repubblica Veneta," *Arch. ven.* (1957), pp. 79-114; F. Bennato, "La partecipazione militare di Venezia alla lega di Cognac," *Arch. ven.* (1956), pp. 70-87.

On the Italian league, Giovanni Soranzo, "Studi e discussioni su *La lega italica del 1454-1455*" in *Studi storici in onore di Gioacchino Volpe* (Florence: Sansoni, 1958), pp. 971-95. Recent discussions of issues and bibliography: Vincent Ilardi, " 'Quattrocento' Politics in the Treccani *Storia di Milano*," in *Bibliothèque d'humanisme et Renaissance, Travaux et Documents*, XXVI (Geneva, 1964), pp. 162-90; Giovanni Pillinini, "L'umanista veneziano Francesco Barbaro e l'origine della politica di equilibrio," *Arch. ven.* (1963); *idem, Il sistema degli stati italiani, 1454-1494* (Venice: Libreria universitaria, 1970).

Venetian policy in the crucial years 1502-3 is excellently analyzed in P. Pieri, *Intorno alla politica estera di Venezia al principio del Cinquecento* (Naples: Tipomeccanica, 1934).

The praise of civic humanism is quoted from Zippel, "Ludovico Foscarini ambasciatore. . .," as cited, p. 215.

The budget given for about 1500 is a reconciliation of various figures in *Bilanci Generali*, in *Doc. finan.*, ser. II, vol. I, t. I. The off-duty conversation of the condottieri is recounted in *The Commentaries of Pius II*, translated by Florence Alden Gragg, notes by Leona C. Gabel, *Smith College Studies in History* XLIII (1957), p. 788. The praise of "la plus triumphante cité" is from Philippe de Commynes, *Mémoires*, ed. B. de Mandrot, 2 vols. (Paris, 1901-3), II, 208-9. The quotation from Mocenigo's "Farewell Address" is my translation from the text given in Kretschmayr, *Geschichte*, II, 618. Extensive translation from other versions are given by W. Carew Hazlitt, *The Venetian Republic*, 2 vols. (London, 1915), I, 840-47.

The passages referred to in Priuli are in *Rerum Italicarum Scriptores*, 2nd ed., tomo XXIV, pt. III, Girolamo Priuli, *I Diarii*, ed. R. Cessi, vol. IV (Bologna, 1938), pp. 15–18, 29–55. See also *ibid*, vol. II (Bologna, 1933–34), 193, 196, and vol. IV, 112, for Priuli's ideas on the causal importance of sin.

On Venice's government of mainland cities: Angelo Venturi, *Nobilità e popolo mella società veneta del '400 e '500* (Bari, 1964) and Benjamin G. Kohl, "Government and Society in Renaissance Padua," *Journal of Medieval and Renaissance Studies* II, no. 2 (Fall, 1972), 205–21.

CHAPTER 18. Enrico Besta, *Il Senato veneziano (origini, costituzione, attribuzioni e riti)* in *Mis-*
THE *cellanea di storia veneta*, ser. 2, t. V (Venice: Deputazione, 1899), is still basic, as is
CONSTITUTION the manuscript of Giovanni Antonio Muazzo, "Del antico governo della repubblica di Venezia," on which see A. Lombardo, "Storia e ordinamenti delle magistrature veneziane in un manoscritto inedito del secolo xvii," in *Studi in onore di Riccardo Filangieri*, 3 vols. (Naples, 1959), II, 619 ff. Muazzo (Civico Museo Correr, Cod. Cicogna 2000, ff. 90–91) gives the numbers voting for Procuratori. Giuseppe Maranini, *La costituzione di Venezia dopo la serrata del Maggior Consiglio* (Rome, 1931) adds a prolix quilting of constitutional theory. Also, especially for the size and exclusiveness of the nobility, Davis, *The Decline*.

Special: M. Brunetti, "Due Dogi sotto inchiesta: Agostino Barbarigo e Leonardo Loredan," *Arch. veneto-tridentino* VII (1925), 278–329; Roland Mousnier, "Le trafic des offices à Venise," *Revue historique de droit français et étranger*, ser. iv, année 30 (1952), no. 4, pp. 552–66; Donald E. Queller, *Early Venetian Legislation on Ambassadors* (Geneva: Droz, 1966), and *The Office of Ambassador in the Middle Ages* (Princeton University Press, 1967); and "The Civic Irresponsibility of the Venetian Nobility," in *Economy, Society, and Government in Medieval Italy: Essays in Memory of Robert L. Reynolds* (Kent, Ohio: The Kent State University Press, 1969), pp. 223–36. On relations with the nobility of the mainland cities, see Ventura, *Nobilità e popolo*, and the long review of it, with bibliography, by Cecil H. Clough in *Studi veneziani* VIII (1966).

Philippe de Commynes's comment on the common people is in his *Mémoires*, ed. Mandrot, II, 213. The comment by Jean Bodin on the equality of Venetian justice is quoted from *The Six Bookes of a Commonweale*, the facsimile reprint of the English translation of 1606 by Richard Knolles, ed. K. D. McRae (Harvard University Press, 1962), p. 785.

On equality in dress: M. Magaret Newett, "The Sumptuary Laws of Venice," in *[Manchester] Historical Essays*, eds. T. F. Tout and James Tait, Publications of the University of Manchester, Historical Series, no. VI (Manchester University Press, 1907), pp. 245–77.

In Marino Sanuto, *I Diarii*, eds. Rinaldo Fulin, Federico Stefani, Nicolò Barozzi, Guglielmo Berchet, Marco Allegri, under the auspices of the R. Dep. Veneta di Storia Patria, 58 vols. (Venice, 1879–1903), significant passages are: on his nominating himself, VIII, 143–44; on his own speeches, XXV, 344–47, XXXIX, 24–29; on his bitterness in defeat, XII, 92; XXII, 7, 65–66; XXIV, 677; on the *censori* and electioneering, XXV, 170; XXIV, 656–59; on Gritti's anger at illegal electioneering, LI, 610–11; on votes for sale, LIV, 7–8; on Doge Loredan's effective eloquence, IX, 29–30.

On Gasparo Contarini: James Bruce Ross, "The Emergence of Gasparo Contarini: A Bibliographical Essay," reprinted from *Church History* XXXXI, 1 (March, 1972), and the articles she there cites by Felix Gilbert and herself. On his land survey: Sanuto, *Diarii* XXVI, 483; XXVII, 111, 154, 466, 625. On his purchase of 20,000 *campi*: Marcantonio Michiel, "Diarii," MS in Civico Museo Correr, Cod. Cicogna 2848, f. 300. The translation of Contarini's *De Magistratibus et Republica* by Lewes Lewkenor, *The Commonwealth and Gouvernment of Venice* (London, 1599), was reprinted in Amsterdam, 1969.

On Florentine views of the Venetian constitution: Felix Gilbert, "The Venetian Constitution in Florentine Political Thought," in *Florentine Studies: Politics and Society in Renaissance Florence*, ed. Nicolai Rubenstein (London: Faber and Faber, 1968), pp. 463–500.

In regard to nominations by Senatorial *scrutinio* and by the Signoria, and their restriction early in the sixteenth century, the statements in Besta and in Maranini are inadequate. The number of such nominations in the late fifteenth century is made clear by the opening folios of ASV, Segretario alle Voci, Proposte, reg. 15 (ex. 9 bis), reg. 16. On the changes, see Sanuto, *Diarii*, III, 661, 769–70; XVIII, 291, 305, 312. Also on the nominations, Sanuto, XVIII, 418, 422–23, 427, and the extensive, although not for all years complete, record of men nominated and votes received: Bibl. Marciana, MS, It. Cl. VII, Cod. 813–19. Nominations, elections, and other aspects of Venetian practical politics are being analyzed more thoroughly than ever before by the use of such sources by Robert Finlay in a doctoral dissertation, Chicago.

On control of church appointments, C. Piana and C. Cenci, eds., *Promozioni agli ordini sacri a Bologna e alle dignità ecclesiastiche nel Veneto nei secoli xiv-xv* (Quaracchi-Florentia: Coll. S. Bonaventura, 1968).

For personal, family, and funereal details on the doges and on ducal elections: Andrea da Mosto, *I Dogi di Venezia nella vita pubblica e privata* (Milano: Aldo Martello Editore, 1960).

CHAPTER 19.
OCEANIC
DISCOVERY   On Fra Paolino and Fra Mauro: Roberto Almagia, *Planisferi, carte nautiche e affini del secolo xiv al xvii esistenti nella Biblioteca Apostolica Vaticana, Monumenta cartographica Vaticana* I (Città del Vaticano, 1944); *Il mappamondo di Fra Mauro*, ed. Tullia Gasparrini Leporace (Libreria dello Stato, 1956); Heinrich Winter, "The Fra Mauro Portolan Chart in the Vatican," *Imago Mundi* XVI (1962). On Alvise da Mosto, *The Voyages of Cadamosto*, trans. and ed. G. R. Crone, Hakluyt Society, ser. 2, no. LXXX (London, 1937).

In general on Venice and oceanic discovery: Comune di Venezia, Celebrazioni in onore di Alvise da Mosto, *Catalogo*, *Mostra dei navigatori veneti del quattrocento e del cinquecento* (Venice: Biblioteca Nazionale Marciana, 1957); Boies Penrose, *Travel and Discovery in the Renaissance, 1420–1620* (Harvard, 1952, and Atheneum, 1962); Prince Yusuf Kamal, *Monumenta cartographica* above cited. Bibliographies on Zeno, Cabot, and Samuel E. Morison, *The European Discovery of America: The Northern Voyages, A.D. 500–1600* (New York: Oxford University Press, 1971). See also A. da Mosto, "I navigatori Nicolò e Antonio Zeno," in *Ad Alessandro Luzio, Miscellanea de studi storici* (Gli archivi di stato italiani, Florence, 1933); E. R. R. Taylor, "A Fourteenth-Century Riddle — and Its Solution," *Geographical Review*, LIV (1964), 573–76; David B. Quinn, *Sebastian Cabot and Bristol Exploration* (Bristol Branch of the Historical Association of the University, Bristol, 1968).

For Ramusio, his *Delle navigationi e viaggi* (Venice, 1550, 1554) and A. Del Piero, "Della vita e degli studi di Gio. Battistia Ramusio," *N. arch. ven.* IV (1902), pt. 2, pp. 5–109.

CHAPTER 20.
THE SPICE
TRADE   The account in Heyd's often-cited *Histoire du commerce du levant*, II, 427–552, is still basic and is relied on for essentials by many later studies. For example, Ahmah Darrag, *L'Egypte sous le règne de Barsbay, 825–841/1422–1438* (Damascus, 1961) and Subhi Y. Labib, *Handelsgeschichte Agyptens im Spätmittelalter*, Beihefte 46, *Vierteljahrschrift für Sozial- und Wirtschaftsgeschichte* (Wiesbaden, 1965) take from Heyd their account of Venetian pepper purchases from the Soldan. Darrag adds much about Barsbay's activities in the Red Sea. Heyd made some mistakes in spite of his general

excellence. For example, he misreports Piloti's statement that the exactions of the soldan raised prices "plus la moitié," as "doubled it" (p. 448). On Piloti, see the new edition by Pierre-Herman Dopp, *Traité d'Emmanuel Piloti sur le passage en Terre Sainte* (1420), Publications de L'Université Iovanium de Léopoldville, IV (Louvain-Paris: Nauwelaerts, 1958). On prices, see my note "Pepper Prices before Da Gama," in *The Journal of Economic History* XXVIII, 4 (December, 1968), 590–97; and on the volume of the trade, my earlier articles reprinted in *Venice and History*. The treaty obtained by Donato in 1442 is fully printed by John Wansbrough, "Venice and Florence in the Mamluk Commercial Privileges," *Bulletin of the School of Oriental and African Studies* (1965), 487–97. Piero Marcello's scandalous conduct is recorded in the Cronaca Zancaruol, Marciana, MS, Ital. Cl. VII, Cod. 1275, Coll. 9275, f. 674.

On immediate reactions to the Portuguese: Vitorino Magalhaes-Godinho, "Le repli vénitien et égyptien et la route du cap, 1496–1533," in *Eventail de l'histoire vivante: Hommage à Lucien Febvre* (Paris: Colin, 1953), II, 283–300, and Ruggiero Romano, Alberto Teneti, and Ugo Tucci, "Venise et la route du cap: 1499–1517," and its discussion in *Colloque Hist. Mar. 1962*, pp. 109–39.

On the painting representing Venetians at a Mamluk court: questions of identification and attribution have been thoroughly reviewed by C. Dana Rouillard in an article expected to appear in 1973 in the *Gazette des Beaux Arts*.

On the spice trade later in the sixteenth century: Braudel, *La Méditerranée* I, 493–517; Donald F. Lach, *Asia in the Making of Europe*, vol. I (Chicago, 1965), chap. III; Ugo Tucci, *Lettres d'un marchand vénitien, Andrea Berengo (1553–1556)* EPHE-6, Affaires et Gens d'affaires, X, (Paris, 1957); and on the later Portuguese trade: V. Magalhaes-Godinho, *L'économie de l'empire portugais aux XVe et XVIe siècles* (EPHE-6, Ports – Routes – Trafics, XXVI, 1969).

On a canal at Suez, F. Charles-Roux, "L'Isthme de Suez et les rivaltés européennes au XVIe siècle," *Revue de l'histoire des colonies français* (1924), 174–85. On the proposal of Philip II in 1584, see Braudel, above cited, and I. Cervelli, "Intorno alla decadenza di Venezia," *Nuova rivista storica*, L (Sept.-Dec., 1966), 596–642.

CHAPTER 21.
OTHER TRADES

The classic by Fernand Braudel, *La Méditerranée*, is basic for the situation generally. On competition within the Adriatic, see Peter Earle, "The Commercial Development of Ancona, 1479–1551," *Economic History Review*, ser. 2, XXII, 1 (April, 1969), pp. 28–44; R. Paci, "La scala di Spalato e la politica veneziana in Adriatico," *Quaderni storici* (continuation of *Quaderni storici delle Marche*), anno V, no. XIII (Ancona, 1970); F. W. Carter, "The Commerce of the Dubrovnik Republic," *Economic History Review*, ser. 2, XXIV, 3(1971), 370–94, with bibliography. The publication is announced for 1972 of F. W. Carter, *Dubrovnik (Ragusa): A Classic City-State* (London and New York: Seminar Press). The figures on Ragusan customs are from J. Tadic, "Le commerce en Dalmatie et à Raguse et la décadence économique de Venise au XVIIe siècle," in *Aspetti e cause della decadenza economica veneziana nel secolo xvii*, Atti del Convegno, 27 giugno–2 luglio, 1957, Venezia (Istituto per la Collaborazione Culturale, for the Fondazione Giorgio Cini, Venice and Rome, 1961), p. 251. See also, J. Tadic, "Le porte de Raguse et sa flotte au XVIe siècle," in *Le Navire et l'économie maritime du Moyen Age au XVIIIe siècle, principalement en Méditerranée*, Travaux du Colloque d'Histoire Maritime, 1957, ed. M. Mollat, EPHE-6, Bibl. gen. (1958), and T. Stoianovich, "The Conquering Balkan Orthodox Merchant," *Journal of Economic History* XX (1960), 234–317. The quotation is from p. 240.

On the shipment of *verzino* from Portugal to Syria, see Sanuto, *Diarii*, XVIII, 268; and on dyes in general, William F. Leggett, *Ancient and Medieval Dyes* (Brooklyn, 1944). On the sugar and cotton trades of Cyprus, M. L. de Mas Latrie, *Histoire de l'île de Cypre*, vol. III (Paris, 1855), and Sir George Hill, *A History of Cyprus*, vol. III (Cambridge, 1948); and on the fall in sugar prices, E. O. von Lippmann, *Geschichte des Zuckers*, 2nd ed. (Berlin, 1929), pp. 720-21, Sanuto, *Diarii*, I, 270-71, and Herman Van der Wee, *The Growth of the Antwerp Market and the European Economy* (The Hague, 1963), vol. I, pp. 318-24. On wine, Sanuto II, 477-78; and on raisins, *Calendar of State Papers, Venetian, passim*.

On trade with Germany, Kellenbenz's study in the volume, *Aspetti e cause* and bibliographies in Braustein's "Wirtschaftliche Beziehung," and Stromer's "Nürnberg," cited for Chapter 10.

On .the Jews, Part III of Brian Pullan, *Rich and Poor in Renaissance Venice* (Oxford: Basil Blackwell, 1971). To his bibliography might be added, for Jews in the Levant: J. Starr, "Jewish Life in Crete under the Rule of Venice," *Proceedings of the American Academy for Jewish Research* XII (1942), 59-114; and Ellis Rivkin, "Marrano-Jewish Entrepreneurship and the Ottoman Mercantilist Probe in the Sixteenth Century," in *Proceedings of the Third International Conference of Economic History, Munich, 1965* (volume still in press); and on Daniele Rodriga, the above cited article of R. Paci in *Quaderni storici* no. 13. I could read only the cryptic summary in English of David Jacoby, "On the Status of the Jews in the Venetian Colonies in the Middle Ages," *Zion* (in Hebrew) XXVIII, 1 (1962-63), 59-64. See also: David Kaufman, "Die Vertreibung der Marranen aus Venedig im Jahre 1550," *The Jewish Quarterly Review*, ser. I, XIII (1901), 520-25; and Constance H. Rose, "New Information on the Life of Joseph Nasi, Duke of Naxos: The Venetian Phase," *Jewish Quarterly Review* LX (April, 1970).

On the grain trade and agricultural development: Aldo Stella, "La crisi economica veneziana della seconda metà del secolo xvi," in *Arch. ven.*, LVIII-LIX (1956), 17-69; Maurice Aymard, *Venise, Raguse et le commerce du blé pendant la seconde moitié du XVIe siècle* (EPHE-6, Ports — Routes — Trafics, XX, 1966); and Marino Sanuto, *Cronachetta*, ed. R. Fulin, per Nozze Papadopoli-Hellenbach (Venice, 1880), pp. 124-25, 207-8. His comment on high rents at the Rialto, *ibid.*, p. 47. Also, Giuseppe Fiocco, *Alvise Cornaro, il suo tempo e le sue opere* (Vicenze: Neri Pozza, 1965); and with current bibliography, A. Ventura, "Considerazione sull' agricoltura veneta e sulla accumulazione originaria del capitale nei secoli xvi e xvii," *Studi Storici* IX (Istituto Gramsci, 1968), pp. 674-722; and for general background, Ruggiero Romano's article in that same issue of *Studi Storici*.

CHAPTER 22. On the growth of the woolen industry, Domenico Sella, "The Rise and Fall of the
MANU- Venetian Woolen Industry," in Brian Pullan, ed., *Crisis and Change in the Venetian
FACTURING Economy* (Methuen, 1968); on its organization, at the Correr, MS, ser. IV, Marie-gole no. 129, and on the strike, ff. 213-33.

On the silk industry, their statutes in the series of Mariegole, at the Correr, MS, IV, nos. 48 and 49 and, at ASV, their Capitolare Nuovo, Sala Margherita, Legature, LXXVII, no. 48 bis. Quite misleading is R. Broglio d'Ajano, "L'industria della seta a Venezia," republished in Carlo M. Cipolla, *Storia dell'economica italiana*, vol. I (Einaudi, 1959), for he tries to excuse himself for not dealing with the period after 1500 by saying on page 213 that the industry had then seen its best days.

On printers, Horatio F. Brown, *The Venetian Printing Press* (London, 1891); A. Tenenti, "Luc'antonio Giunti il Giovane, stampatore e mercante," in *Studi in onore di A. Sapori* II, 1022-1060. For Erasmus's remarks, see his "Colloquy, Opulentia Sordida," in Mangan, *Life, Character and Influence of Erasmus*, 2 vols. (New York, 1927), I, 245-59, and *Epistles*, ed. F. M. Nichols (New York, 1962), I, 446-47. On Aretino's role and bookseller' hacks, see Paul F. Grendler, *Critics of the Italian World, 1530-1560* (University of Wisconsin Press, 1969). Production figures are from L. Febvre and H. J. Martin, *L'Apparition du livre* (Paris, 1958).

On cost accounting at the Mint, Correr, MS, Arch. Donà della Rosa, busta 161, ff. 77, 79, and *passim*. On the candlemakers or wax workers, ASV, Cinque Savii all Mercanzia, Risposte, busta 138. On the kiln of Nicoletus Grimanus, see ASV, Grazie, reg. 3, f. 13, no. 162 (Nov. 19, 1329). On the gig mill, Correr, MS, IV, Mariegole, no. 129, f. 209 v. On a new invention for fulling, ASV, Cinque Savii, busta 137, f. 187.

On Venetian patents to encourage invention, G. Mandich, "Le privative industriali veneziane (1450-1550)," *Rivista di diritto commerciale* XXXIV (1936), pt. 1, 511-47.

On religious fraternities, Lia Sbriziolo, "Per la storia delle confraternite veneziane," in *Atti Ist. Ven.* CXXVI (1967-68), 405-42; and for that of San Girolamo, E. A. Cicogna, *Delle iscrizioni veneziane*, 6 vols. (1824-53), VI, 870-71, 945-55.

On the connection of the guilds with conscriptions for the Navy, see Pullan's *Rich and Poor* and the dissertation of Richard Tilden Rapp, "Industry and Economic Decline in Seventeenth Century Venice," University of Pennsylvania, 1970, which he kindly placed at my disposal. The interesting decrees permitting the organization of guilds by workers in the woolen industry so that they could be assigned oarsmen are in ASV, Consiglio di Dieci, Deliberazioni, Comune, reg. 13, ff. 37, 52. They are in Latin!

CHAPTER 23.
PROFITS OF
POWER

On government finances, much valuable information can be dug out of the *Bilanci generali*, and on the public debt see my "Public Debt and Private Wealth, particularly in Sixteenth-Century Venice," in the *Mélanges en l'honneur de Fernand Braudel* (Toulouse, Editions Edouard Privat, 1973). Various estimates of the total number of noble office holders are given in many chronicles. For example, MS Riant 12, f. 201 v, at Harvard University, gives a total of 780, naval commanders included, for about 1450. Valuable on the financial relations of Venice and the Terra Ferma is one of Gino Luzzatto's very last articles, "L'economia veneziana nei secoli '400 e '500," *Bergomum*, anno LVIII (vol. 38), no. 2 (1964), 57-71.

On banking, Luzzatto's article in his *Studi* and mine in *Venice and History*. On both banking and public finance I have drawn much directly from Sanuto's diary. For example, the insults scrawled against the bankers are in *Diarii*, XXXV, 140, 148. Still basic is the material in E. Lattes, *La libertà delle banche a Venezia dal secolo xiii al xvii* (Milan, 1869). The clearest explanation of how the Banco del Giro collected a commission of $1^{1}/_{3}$ percent on each exchange through the way the value of the bank ducat was set is in Renato Sandrini, "Considerazioni sull'opera 'Banche e problemi monetari a Venezia nei secoli xvi e xvii," in *Giornale economica della Camera di Commercio, Industria, Arte, et Agricultura di Venezia*, no. 3, May-June 1969, pp. 10-12, a comment on the study by Lucio Balestrieri there cited.

On money: Nicolò Papadopoli-Aldobrandini, *Le Montete di Venezia*, 4 vols. (Venice, 1893-1919) and the explanation of the later forms of moneys of account by Giulion Mandich, "Formule monetarie veneziane del periodo 1619-1650," in *Il Risparmio* V (April, 1957) and in *Studi in onore di Armando Sapori* (Milan: Cisalpino, 1957), pp. 1143-83. On the bill market and exchange fairs see Giulio Mandich, "Delle fiere genovesi di cambi particolarmente studiate come mercati periodici del credito," *Rivista di storia economica* IV (1939), 257-76; *idem, Le pacte de ricorsa et le marché italien des changes au XVIIe siècle* (EPHE-6, Affaires et Gens d'Affairs, VII, 1953); and, with full bibliography, José-Gentil Da Silva, *Banques et crédit en Italie au XVIIe siècle*, 2 vols. (Paris: Klincksieck, 1969).

On poverty and wages: Brian Pullan, "Wage-Earners and the Venetian Economy, 1550-1630," in *The Economic History Review*, ser. 2, XVI (1964), and in the volume edited by Pullan, *Crisis and Change in the Venetian Economy* (London: Methuen, 1968). Also Brian Pullan, "Poverty, Charity, and the Reason of State: some Venetian examples," in *Bolletino . . . Veneziano*, II (1960) and "The Famine in Venice and the New Poor Law,

1527-29," in *Bollettino . . . Veneziano*, V-VI (1963-64), from which (p. 153) I have taken his quotation from Luigi da Porto. On poverty also, but on prices particularly, see Fernand Braudel, "La vita economica di Venezia nel secolo xvi," in *La civiltà veneziana del Rinascimento* (Venice: Centro di Culture e Civiltà della Fondazione Giorgio Cini and Sansoni, 1958), and his general survey, with F. Spooner, in *The Cambridge Economic History of Europe*, vol. IV, to which should be added the study by Romano, Spooner, and Tucci on prices at Udine and Chioggia, in preparation.

The figures concerning Venetian mainland palaces are those of Philip Jones in *The Cambridge Economic History of Europe*, vol. I, 2nd ed. (Cambridge, 1966), p. 418.

CHAPTER 24.
MERCHANT
GALLEYS

General: Jules Sottas, *Les messageries maritimes de Venise au XIVe et XVe siècles* (Paris, 1938); Alberto Sacerdoti, "Note sulle galere da mercato veneziane nel xv secolo," in *Bollettino . . . veneziano*, IV (1962), pp. 80-105; Lane, *Navires*, chap. I, and "Venetian Shipping during the Commercial Revolution," in *American Historical Review* XXXVIII (1933), 219-39, and in *Venice and History*, pp. 3-24.

On the relevant commercial organization, see the studies of business organization cited for Chapter 11, and also F. Braudel and A. Tenenti, "Michiel da Lezze, marchand vénitien (1497-1514)," in *Wirtschaft, Geschichte, und Wirtschaftsgeschichte: Festschrift zum 65. Geburtstag von Friedrich Lütge*, ed. W. Abel et al. (Stuttgart, 1966). The contrast between law and practice is most clearly illustrated in a contract generously called to my attention by Stanley Chojnacki specifically negating the Senate's requirement for the pooling of freights — ASV, Archivio Notarile, Cancelleria inferiore, B 79, Gasparino Favacio, protocollo, Nov. 10, 1357. Rebates that Andrea Barbarigo received from the *patroni* on a cloth shipment are recorded in his Journal B under Feb. 7, 1442 (modo veneto) and in his Ledger B, k. 83 and referred to in Andrea's letter to Bertuzi Contarini, Aug. 9, 1440.

On the Council of Twelve: Ugo Tucci, "Le Conseil des Douze sur les navires vénitiens," in *Le Navire, Colloque, 1957*, ed. Mollat, pp. 119-26; Bibl. Nat., Paris, Fonds Français MS 5599, f. 148; Lane, *Venice and History*, p. 211; and ASV, Senato Misti, reg. 38, ff. 58, 71.

Manuscript notebooks of Venetian nautical lore are Egerton MS 73 and Cottonian MS Titus A 26, both in British Museum, London; Ital. MS, Cl. IV, Cod. 170 of Pietro Versi in the Marciana, Venice; and that of Michele di Rodi, advertized by Sotheby and Co. for the sale of July 11, 1966, appendix, pp. 116-19. On the captain's table, see ASV, Senato Misti, reg. 53 doppio, f. 488, Dec. 23, 1421 and Bibl. Nat., Paris, Fonds Français MS 5599, f. 156.

Benedetto Sanuto's memo to his brother was printed by Luigi Fincati, "La nobiltà veneziana e il commercio marittimo," in *Rivista marittima*, July-Aug., 1878, from Cod. Cicogna 3101/IV. Admiral Fincati accepted the suggestion in Cicogna's notes as to its date, but the copy of the *estratto* at the Museo Civico has notes by F. Stefani showing that its date is 1548 since the capitano it refers to, Alessandro Bon, commanded in that year, as I have confirmed from other sources. In Henry Barnaby, "A Voyage to Cyprus in 1563," *The Mariner's Mirror* LVI (1970), 309-14, a Jewish merchant describes interestingly the galley in which he made the voyage.

On Venetian galley crews at the siege of Constantinople, Nicolò Barbaro, *Giornale dell'assedio di Costantinopoli, 1453*, ed. E. Cornet (Vienna, 1856). The quotation is my translation from pp. 37-38, before I saw the translation by J. R. Jones on p. 47 of his edition of Nicolò Barbaro, *Diary of the Siege of Constantinople* (New York: Exposition Press, 1969).

On pilgrim voyages: the regulation is described in M. Newett's introduction to *Canon Pietro Casola's Pilgrimage to Jerusalem in the Year 1494* (University of Manchester

Historical Series V, 1907). Colorful accounts well documented are R. J. Mitchell, *The Spring Voyage* (London: Murray, or New York: Potter, 1964) and Hilda F. M. Prescott's two volumes on Felix Fabri.

On ventures and customs exemptions of seamen, see ASV, Compilazione leggi, busta 27 and Cinque Savii, n.s., busta 91.

Sanuto's *Diarii* gives much detail for 1496–1533, including summaries of several reports of capitani. Other of their *relazioni* are ASV, Senato Relazioni (indice 322), busta 61; Museo Correr, Venice, MS Wcovich-Lazzari, busta 24/4; and Bibl. Nat., Paris, Fonds ital., MS No. 328. There are a number of copies of *commissioni* of capitani at the Correr, and the formulas in use at the beginning of the fifteenth century are in ASV, Senato, Commissioni, Formulari, reg. 4.

Details on the African slave trade: in Egypt, Piloti (edition by Dopp, above cited), pp. 135, 143–44; on galleys, forbidding them to load any except blacks, ASV, Senato, Deliberazioni, Incanti galere, reg. II, f. 8. On the incident at Rhodes in 1464, Domenico Malipiero, *Annali veneti dell'anno 1457 al 1500* in *Archivio storico italiano*, ser. I, vol. VII (Florence, 1843), pp. 614–18; on the last voyages to Northwest Africa, Sanuto, *Diarii*, s.v. galee; and Marc Antonio Michiel, "Diarii, 1511–21," MS in the Correr, Cod. Cicogna 2848, ff. 291–98, 310, 350. On cargo for the African voyages see also E. W. Bovill, *The Golden Trade of the Moors*, 2nd ed. (Oxford, 1970).

CHAPTER 25.
THE WAR
FLEETS
Camillo Manfroni, *Storia della marina italiana dalla caduta di Costantinopoli alla battaglia di Lepanto (1453–1571)* (Rome, 1897); and for earlier wars, *idem.*, "La battaglia di Gallipolli e la politica Veneto-Turca (1381–1420)," in *Ateneo veneto*, anno XXV, vol. II (1902), pp. 3–34, 129–69; *idem.*, "La marina veneziana alla difesa di Salonicco, 1423–1430," in *N. arch. ven.*, n.s., XX (1910), pt. 1; Roberto Lopez, "Il principio della guerra veneto-turca nel 1463," *Arch. ven.*, ser. 5, vol. XV (1934); F. C. Lane, "Naval Actions and Fleet Organization, 1499–1502," in the forthcoming *Renaissance Venice*, ed. J. Hale; *idem.*, *Navires*; and a forthcoming article on "Wages and recruitment of crews on Venetian ships, 1382–1620," probably in *Studi veneziani*; C. Capasso, "Barbarossa e Carlo V," in *Riv. stor. ital.* XLIX (1932), 169–209, 304–48; Alberto Tenenti, *Cristoforo da Canal: La marine vénitienne avant Lépante* (Paris, 1962); *idem.*, *Venezia e i corsari* (Bari, 1961) or *Piracy and the Decline of Venice, 1580–1615*, Introduction and glossary by Janet and Brian Pullan (Berkeley, 1967); Braudel, *La Méditerranée* . . . ; R. C. Anderson, *Naval Wars in the Levant, 1559–1853* (Princeton University Press, 1952); Mario Nani-Mocenigo, *Storia della marina veneziana da Lepanto alla caduta della Repubblica* (Rome, 1935).

On Turkish cannon against Constantinople, Franz Babinger, *Maometto il Conquistatore* (Rome and Turin, 1957); and against Negroponte, "Due ritmi e una narrazione in prosa di autori contemporanei intorno alla presa di Negroponte fatta dai Turchi . . . 1470," ed. F. L. Polidori, in *Arch. stor. ital.*, app. vol. IX (1953), pp. 399–440.

On the composition of the Christian fleet in 1571, Giovanni Pietro Contarini, *Historia delle cose successe del principio della guerra mossa da Selim. . . .* (Venice, 1572); and on dispositions at Lepanto, E. von Normann-Friedenfels, *Don Juan de Austria als Admiral der Heiligen Liga und die Schlacht bei Lepanto* (Pola, 1902). The best description I have seen of the campaign of 1570 is in Sir George Hill, *History of Cyprus*, vol. III (Cambridge, 1948), chap. xiv.

The commission of Vincenzo Capello is in ASV, Arch. privati, Correr, no. 225.

Unfortunately its late date prevented my profiting from the papers presented at the Convegno organized by the Fondazione Giorgio Cini at Venice in October 1971 and reviewed by Felipe Ruiz-Martin, "The Battle of Lepanto and the Mediterranean," *Journal of European Economic History* I (Rome: Banco di Roma, 1972), 166–69.

CHAPTER 26. Basic are the works above cited of Braudel (especially additions in the 1966 edition,
ARGOSIES as I, 271–85), of Tadic, and of Tenenti, plus the latter's *Naufrages, corsaires et
assurances maritimes à Venise, 1592–1609* (EPHE-6, Ports — Routes — Trafics, VIII,
1959), and my *Navires*; Gino Luzzatto, "Per la storia della costruzione navali a Venezia
nei secoli xv-xvi," in his *Studi*. See also, Ruggiero Romano, "La marine marchande
vénitienne au xvi siècle," and my "La marine marchande et la trafic maritime de Venise à
travers les siècles," both in *Les Sources de l'histoire maritime en Europe, du moyen âge
au XVIIIe siècle*, Actes du Quatrième Colloque International d'Histoire Maritime tenu
1959 (EPHE-6, Bibl. gen. Paris: S.E.V.P.E.N., 1962); Ugo Tucci, "Sur la pratique vénitienne de la navigation au XVIe siècle," *Annales (Economies, sociétés, civilisations)*,
Jan.-March, 1958, pp. 72–86; Stefani, *Insurance*.

On the wine trade and channel voyages in general: Alwyn A. Ruddock, *Italian
Merchants and Shipping in Southampton, 1270–1600*, Southampton Records Series (Oxford, 1951), but for the 5-ducat tax on wine in 1473, which Ruddock missed because it is
ignored in the *Calendar of State Papers, Venetian*, see ASV, Senato Mar, reg. 9, ff. 162,
172, 186. For complaints from Crete and freight rates on wine, *ibid.*, reg. 12, ff. 156–57;
Senato Secreta, reg. 40, f. 133; Sanuto, *Diarii*, II, 477–78, 483.

My generalizations about freight rates on cotton and ashes are based on comparison
of the rates specified for several years in Senato Misti, 1417–33 with those in the law of
1502, Senato Mar., reg. 15, ff. 145–46. The insurance rates are taken from Priuli, *Diarii*,
IV, 77 and Tenenti, *Naufrages*, pp. 59–60.

On the importance of alum for the competing Genoese shipping, see Heers, *Gênes*,
chap. 3; and on sixteenth-century comparisons, Edoardo Grendi, "Traffico portuale,
naviglio mercantile, e consolati genovesi nel Cinquecento," *Riv. stor. ital.* LXXX (1968),
593–638. On the marciliane, Domenico Sella, *Commerci e industria di Venezia nel secolo
xvii* (Venezia, Fondazione Giorgio Cini, Civiltà veneziana, Studi, no. 11, 1961), p. 106
note; and other Resposte of the Cinque Savii such as that Sella quotes. On the Uskoks, in
addition to Tenenti's *Corsari*, see Gunther E. Rothenberg, "Venice and the Uskoks of
Senj, 1537–1618," *Journal of Modern History* XXXIII, no. 2, June 1961, pp. 148–56.

The travel diary of Alessandro Magno is in the Folger Shakespeare Library, Washington, D.C., MS V.a. 259 (former shelf number 1317.1).

SUPPLEMENT: My statements about the size of Venetian ships are all expressed in the number of
TONNAGE metric tons they could carry, which is practically the same as deadweight tonnage.
AND THE SIZE That seems among various meanings of tonnage the best to use in general compari-
OF SHIPS sons, as I explained in "Tonnages, Medieval and Modern," *The Economic History
Review*, ser. 2, vol. XVII, no. 2 (1964), pp. 213–33. The botte used by the Venetians to indicate the size of ships was about .6 of these tons by my estimate. See *ibid.*,
pp. 222–23; *Venetian Ships*, p. 249; and with additional evidence *Navires et leur constructeurs*, pp. 241–42. Recently Ugo Tucci, in "Un problema di metrologia navale: la
botte veneziane," *Studi ven.* IX (1967), 201–46, converting also to metric tons (*tonne-
lata metriche*) and utilizing much additional evidence, reached the conclusion that before
1771, the botte equalled .8 tons. A law of 1771 changed the botte and made it equal
thereafter to one English ton.

The real disagreement between Professor Tucci and myself is very little, however.
We agree on the size of the Cretan cask or barrel called a botte (bota in Venetian,
according to Boerio's *Dizionario*) from which the ship measure used in rating Venetian ships
was derived (compare "Un problema," pp. 215–17, and *Navires*, p. 241). Our findings
almost agree on the weight of a botte, namely, that of ten Venetian bushels (*stara*), of
which I gave the weight as 132 Venetian lbs. each, and he gives, with better evidence, 128
lbs. The difference in our conclusions arises from ambiguities concerning the way the

tonnage (or bottage) of a ship was determined. One way was to take such measures as the beam and the length of keel, and then to multiply and divide according to a conventional formula. He adds much to my exploration of such rules, especially much of later date. We thoroughly agree that the methods were such as to allow a large margin of error and also a large margin of favoritism to a shipowner or collector. Another way to estimate a ship's tonnage was to count how many units it loaded. By a "Tarrifa" of 1681, he demonstrates how wide a range of equivalents could be worked out on that basis, partly because of different densities of various kinds of cargo, partly because very rough equivalents were used for practical administrative purposes. On the other hand, the fifteenth-century evidence offered in my *Venetian Ships* and hundreds of references in Sanuto's diary indicate a rough equivalence then between official ratings and commonly accepted estimates of cargo-carrying capacity. Tucci believes that official ratings underestimated the real size and real weight-carrying capacity, or, to put it in terms such as I used in my "Tonnages" (p. 226), that Venice did develop "official ratings in registered tons different from the generally recognized carrying capacities." Indeed it must be admitted that it would be surprising if the Venetians had not done so, since so many such official ratings developed elsewhere during the centuries between 1500 and 1800. See, for example, the contrasts between "portata" and "carico" in Edoardo Grendi, "I Nordici e il traffico del porto di Genova, 1590-1666," *Riv. stor. ital.* LXXXIII, 1 (1971), 38-39, 51-53. I would be ready to agree accordingly that Venetian official ratings in botti were sufficiently below real capacity *in the seventeenth century* so that .8 should be used in converting to tons. But .6 seems to me still to be more appropriate for medieval centuries.

For the botte used in the western Mediterranean, the estimate of .5 ton (Lane, "Tonnages," p. 222) is substantially confirmed from the Datini archives by Federigo Melis, "Werner Sombart e i problemi della navigazione nel medio evo," in *L'opera di Werner Sombart nel centenario della nascita*, Biblioteca della rivista, *Economia e storia* VIII (Milan: Giuffre, 1964), 95n-98n.

I regard the sixteenth century as a borderland in which one probably needs to ask about each figure: Whose estimate was it? And for what purpose? For example, Ruggiero Romano found a document (reported p. 34 in his "La Marine," above cited) which says that the Venetian merchant marine contained in 1567, not counting any surviving merchant galleys, 42 ships of 400 botti or more with total bottage of 53,400 botti, of which 35 ships were of 1,000 botti or more. Using Tucci's figure for conversion would give a total of 35 ships, each of 800 tons or more. Conversion similarly with .8 gives a total of 42,720 tons in ships of 320 tons or more. These figures are strikingly large. Even conversion with .6 gives Venice many more big caracks than Genoa had at that time; see Edoardo Grendi, "Traffico portuale, naviglio mercantile e consolati genovesi del Cinquecento," *Riv. stor. ital.* LXXX, 3 (1968), 612-13. The figures for 1567 seem suspiciously large also in comparison with figures which Romano and I both give for Venice in 1560, namely only 12 ships of 1,000 botti and a total tonnage of vessels of 400 botti and over of 29,000 botti. Neither the figures for 1560 or for 1567 are taken directly from official records, however. The figures for 1567 come from a petition of shipowners in 1590 seeking higher freight rates so as to regain their past prosperity; see my *Navires*, p. 102n. I doubt that in picturing that prosperity they used figures which underestimated the size of the fleet in 1567. Compare Manlio Calegari, "Navi e barche a Genova tra il xv e il xvi secolo," in Consiglio Nazionale delle Ricerche, Centro per la Storia della Tecnica in Italia, *Guerra e commercio nell'evoluzione della marina genovese tra xv e xvii secolo*, in Miscellanea storica ligure, n.s., II (Genoa, 1970), pp. 28n-29n. Such doubts are reflected in my frequent use above of such vague expressions as "at least 40" or "mostly of 600-700 tons."

CHAPTER 27.
SOVEREIGNTY

On the controversy with the papacy and the intellectual-political atmosphere generally: William J. Bouwsma, *Venice and the Defense of Republican Liberty* (Berkeley: University of California Press, 1968), from whom I quote a phrase taken from p. 529; and Gaetano Cozzi, whose basic book *Il Doge Nicolò Contarini: richerche sul patriziato veneziano agli inizi del seicento*, Fondazione Giorgio Cini, Centro di Cultura e Civiltà, Civiltà veneziana, Studi 4 (Venezia, Rome, 1958) is supplemented by many articles. Far more than its title suggests, Cozzi's "Una vicenda della Venezia barocca: Marco Trevisan e la sua eroica amicizia," *Bollettino...veneziano*, II (1960) is an analysis of the degeneration of Venetian politics. Many other articles are cited in Bouwsma's bibliography and in notes to the edition by Gaetano e Luisa Cozzi of Paolo Sarpi, *Opere*, La Letteratura italiana, Storia e Testi, vol. 35, t. 1 (Milan, Napoli: Riccardo Riccardi, 1969). The papal point of view dominates Ludwig von Pastor's account in his *History of the Popes*, vol. 12 of *Geschichte der Papste* (Freiburg in Breisgau, 1928), and is reflected in Aldo Stella, *Chiesa e stato nelle relazioni dei nunzi pontifici a Venezia* (Citta del Vaticano, 1964). On Leonardo Donà, Federico Seneca, *Il Doge Leonardo Donà: la sua vita e la sua preparazione politica prima del dogado* (Padova: Antenore, 1959) and James C. Davis's forthcoming *Family and Fortune*, to be published by The American Philosophical Society, Philadelphia.

On the academies, Paul Lawrence Rose, "The Accademia Venetiana, science and culture in Renaissance Venice," in *Studi ven.* XI (1969), 191–242.

On international politics generally: R. Quazza, *Preponderanza spagnuola (1599–1700)*, in *Storia politica d'Italia*, VIII (Milan, 1938); Federico Seneca, *La politica veneziana dopo l'Interdetto* (Padova, 1957); and Kretschmayr, *Geschichte*, III. Also, and for the Spanish Conspiracy especially, Leopold von Ranke, *Zur venezianischen Geschichte*, in *Sämmtliche Werke*, 2nd ed., 48 vols. (Leipzig, 1873–81), Bd. 42; G. B. Rubin de Cervin, "Galleons and 'Q' Ships in the Spanish Conspiracy against Venice in 1618," *Mariner's Mirror* XXXVIII (1952), 163–83; Giorgio Spini, "La congiura degli Spagnoli contro Venezia del 1618," *Arch. stor. ital.* CVII (1949), 17–53 and CVIII (1950), 159–64. Ranke's comment on Italian mercenaries is in his *Sammtliche Werke*, Bd. 42, p. 189.

On the naval war with Ossuna: A. Battistella, "Una campagna navale veneto-spagnuola in Adriatico poco conosciuta," *Arch. veneto-tridentino*, 1922–23, and *idem.*, "Un diario navale veneziana sulla campagna navale veneto-spagnola del 1617–18," *Arch. ven.*, ser. 5, vol. IV (1928), and Anderson's *Naval Wars*.

On Venice's republican reputation in the seventeenth century: William Bouwsma, in *Renaissance Venice*, John Hale, ed.; Franco Gaeta, "Alcune considerazione sul mito di Venezia," *Bibliothèque d'Humanisme et Renaissance* XXIII (1961), 58–75; and on its influence in England, Christopher Hill, *Intellectual Origins of the English Revolution* (Oxford, 1965), pp. 276–78.

On the economic downturn about 1602 and the seventeenth-century decline: Domenico Sella's *Commerci e industrie* and his articles in English above cited. More detail on many aspects in *Aspetti e cause della decadenza*. On the English competition, Ralph Davis, "England and the Mediterranean, 1570–1670," in *Essays in the Economic and Social History of Tudor and Stuart England in Honour of R. H. Tawney*, ed. F. J. Fisher (Cambridge, 1961). On the nobility of the time, Brian Pullan, *Service to the Venetian State: Aspects of Myth and Reality in the Early Seventeenth Century*, estratto da *Studi Secenteschi, Rivista annuale* a cura di Carmine Jannaco e Uberto Limentani, V, 1964 (Florence: Olschki, 1965), pp. 95–148.

CHAPTER 28.
NEW AGE OF
SEA POWER

On naval actions and conditions: Nani-Mocenigo, *Storia della marina veneziana*; Anderson, *Naval Wars*; and on Angelo Emo, Anderson's "The Unfortunage Voyage of the *San Carlo*," *Mariner's Mirror* XXXII, 1 (Jan. 1946), 50–54; Vincenzo Marchesi, "La marina veneziana dal secolo xv all rivoluzione del 1848," *Atti e Memoria dell' Accademia di Agricoltura, Scienze e Lettere di Verona*, ser. 4, XX (1919), 145–75; F. Sassi, "La politica navale veneziana dopo Lepanto," *Arch. ven.*, ser. 5, XXXVIII–XLI (1946–47), 99–200. Also the 5 volume manuscript of Giacomo Nani, "Memorie sopra le imprese militari e marittimi di veneziani" at the Biblioteca Universitaria di Padova, MS, no. 161, which contains extracts from dispatches and other sources. For the Turkish side, J. de Hammer [-Purgstall], *Historie de l'empire ottoman depuis son origine jusqu' à nos jours*, 18 vols. (Paris, 1936–44); my quotations are from X, 392 and XI, 330. On Francesco Morosini: Gino Damerini, *Morosini* (Milan: Alpes, 1928); R. Bratti, "I nemici di Francesco Morosini," *Arch. Veneto-Tridentino*, VII (1925); and the sketch in Andrea da Mosto, *I Dogi*. Production of ships-of-the-line is itemized in C. A. Levi, *Navi da guerra costruite nell' Arsenale di Venezia* (Venice, 1896). Figures on ships and casualties in 1718 are from Anderson, *Naval Wars*, pp. 266–69, 358 (not counting carronades which would make the total French guns 1,084 and the British 1,138).

Richard Tilden Rapp's dissertation, "Industry and Economic Decline in Seventeenth Century Venice," gives detail on service in the fleet by guild masters.

On mercantile shipping, Ugo Tucci, "La marina mercantile veneziana nel Settecento," in *Bollettino . . . veneziano*, II (1960); R. Romano, *Le Commerce du Royaume de Naples avec la France et les pays de l'Adriatique au XVIIIᵉ siècle* (EPHE-6, Ports — Routes — et Trafics, III, 1951); Alberto Caracciolo, *Le port franc d'Ancône* (EPHE-6, Ports — Routes — et Trafics, XIX, 1965), and for Trieste, A. Tamaro, *Storia di Trieste*, 2 vols. (Rome, 1924), and recent works cited and summarized in Ph. Braunstein, "A Propos de l'Adriatique entre le XVIᵉ et le XVIIIᵉ siècle," *Annales* XXVI, 6 (1971), 1271–78. On the Barbary States, see A. Sacerdoti, "Venise et les Régences d'Alger, Tunis et Tripoli (1699–1760)," *Revue africaine* CI (1957); and on the Ottoman Empire in general, Robert Mantran, "La navigation vénitienne et ses concurrentes en Méditerranée orientale aux XVIIᵉ et XVIIIᵉ siècles," *Colloque hist. mar. 1962*, pp. 375–91.

See the previously cited works of Luzzatto on the Banco del Giro and of Stefani on insurance (also on the merchants' association and the preparation of the maritime code of 1786). On the size of the debt, the *Bilanci Generali*; the MS in the Correr, Cod. Morosini, 531/vi; and Ventura, as cited in *Studi storici* (1968), pp. 713–19.

The *Codice per la veneta mercantile marina* of 1786 was published that year by the sons of Antonio Pinelli, Stampadori ducali, Venice. The fate of Venice as a port is brilliantly summarized in Gino Luzzatto's "Le vicende del porto" in his *Studi*.

CHAPTER 29.
DEATH OF
THE REPUBLIC

On finances, see the *Bilanci Generali*, Luzzatto's "Les Banques," Papadopoli's *Le Monete*; Luigi Einaudi, "L'economia pubblica veneziana dal 1736 al 1755," *La Riforma sociale* XIV (1904), 177–96, 261–82, 429–50, 509–37; and [Lorenzo Antonio da Ponte], *Osservazione sopra li depositi nella Veneta Zecca* (Verona, 1801). On industrial development in general, Gino Luzzatto, *Storia economica dell' età moderna e contemporanea*, vol. II, (1960), especially pp. 180–87, and the dissertation above cited of R. T. Rapp. On Nicolò Tron: Bruno Caizzi, *Industria e commercio della Repubblica Veneta nel xviii secolo* (Milan: Banca Commerciale Italiana, 1965), pp. 62–65. On Andrea Tron: Giovanni Tabacco, *Andrea Tron (1712–1785) e la crisi dell' aristocrazia senatoria a Venezia* (Istituto di Storia Medievale e Moderna, no. 2, Università degli Studi di Trieste, 1957). The passages of Carlo Antonio Marin referred to are in his *Storia civile e politica del commercio de' Veneziani*, 8 vols. (Venice, 1798–1808), VIII, 313, 336–43. For comparison of the eighteenth century with "the blackest period of Venetian economy" under Napoleon: Gino Luzzatto, "L'economia veneziana dal 1797 al 1866," in *La civiltà veneziana nell'età romantica* (Sansoni, 1961).

On the relation of Venice to its mainland domain: S. J. Woolf, "Venice and Terra-ferma: Problems of the Change from Commercial to Landed Activities," in the *Bolletti-no . . . veneziano*, IV (1962). It is republished in *Crisis and Change in the Venetian Economy*, ed. Brian Pullan. Woolf presented a broader discussion of political problems in "The Problem of Representation in the Post-Renaissance Venetian State," in *Liber Memorialis Antonio Era, Studies presented to the International Commission for the History of Representative and Parliamentary Institutions* XXVI (UNESCO, Cagliari and Brussels, 1961 and 1963).

On the shrinkage of the nobility and the new families added, Davis, *The Decline*. On the decay of the nobility in a broader sense, see the general histories, and Pullan's review of Davis in the *Bollettino . . . veneziano*, V–VI, 406–25. Frances Haskell, *Patrons and Painters* (New York, 1963), part III, characterizes the society of eighteenth-century Venice as vividly as the painting. See also Maurice Rowdon, *The Silver Age of Venice* (New York, 1970).

On the last days, G. B. McClellan, *Venice and Bonaparte* (Princeton, [1931]) and Guy Dumas, *La fin de la République de Venise: aspects et reflets littéraires* (Thèse, Paris-Rennes, 1964–65). The quote from De Sanctis concerning Ugo Foscolo is from p. 906 of a Naples 1936 edition of his *Storia della Letteratura italiana*.

I have benefited greatly from the generosity of J. Georgelin, who placed at my disposal in typescript much of his forthcoming study of Venice in the Age of Enlightenment. I have drawn on it not only for specific facts from the reports of French consuls but also for his view of the Venetian economy in the eighteenth century, based on extensive use of the Venetian archives. On the firm of Carlo Rossetti, see also his "Compagnies de commerce vénitiennes au Levant au XVIIIᵉ siècle," in *Sociétés et compagnies de commerce en Orient et dans l'Océan Indien*, Actes du Huitième Colloque International d'Histoire Maritime, Beyrouth, 5–10 Septembre, 1966, ed. Michel Mollat (EPHE-6, Bibl. gén., 1970).

SUPPLEMENT: Tabulation of the par value of the total debt would be misleading, since in both the
THE LONG-TERM fifteenth and eighteenth centuries bonds paying only 1 or 2 percent were valued at
PUBLIC DEBT a fraction of par, both on the market place and in redemptions. Comparison of
total income over the centuries can be misleading also because of the changing value of the "ducat" (see index under "Moneys of Account"). Consequently, the table in Chapter 29 was constructed to show the changes in the proportion of total revenue absorbed by payments on the debt. There is much chance of error, however, in calculating the ratio of Payments to Revenue, even assuming the figures given in the *Bilanci generali* and other sources cited above are accurate.

One difficulty arises in distinguishing the long-term debt from short-term borrowings which took such varied forms as loans from banks, discounts for advance payment of taxes, and deferring the payments due to be made by various bureaus such as the Salt Office. When totals of short-term obligations are given, they are less than one-tenth of the par value of the long-term debt, but the interest paid was relatively high. I have considered long-term all borrowing on which regular interest payments were promised, for on such loans the date of repayment was either undetermined or more than five years.

Some of the totals of revenue are more net than others. It is impossible to determine in most cases to what extent local expenses or expenses involved in collecting revenue have been deducted from the returns reported. The consolidation of accounts in 1736 probably made the figures for that and ensuing years less net than earlier figures and explain some of the apparent increase in revenue. For example, receipts of 240,730 ducats from the sale of wheat or flour in 1736 are almost balanced by expenses of 220,416 for buying wheat (*Bilanci*, III, 284–85). There are no similar entries in the accounts for 1621–24.

To distinguish between payment of interest and repayment of principal is in many years impractical. After 1570 an important form of borrowing was the sale of life annuities. The yearly payments amortizing these and other annuities of limited duration were recorded under "interest (pro)." On the other hand, in some years redemptions are separately recorded but are less than new borrowing, and in such cases, for example, in 1736 I have included under "Payments" only the total given for "pro" and not the total of "affrancazione di capitali." For 1755, I assumed that "provvedimenti extraordinarii" referred to new borrowing and therefore deducted that amount, 293,513 ducats, from the "affrancazione," 419, 284, and added the difference to what appeared in the balance sheet as "pro," namely 1,867,834. Lack of data prevented making such corrections for all years.

CHAPTER 30. On architecture: Leonardo Benevolo, *Storia dell architettura del Rinascimento*, 2
COMPLETION vols. (Bari, 1968); *idem*., *La città italiana nel Rinascimento* (Milan, 1969); James S.
AND Ackerman, *Palladio* (Penguin Books, 1966); G. Mariacher, *Il Sansovino* (Milan,
PRESERVATION 1962). Also Lorenzetti's guide and other works cited for Chapters 1 and 2 and 15;
R. Wittkower, *Architectural Principles in the Age of Humanism* (London, 1949); and articles by Wittkower and others in *Barocco europeo e barocco veneziano*, ed. V. Branca (Venice: Sansoni for Fondazione Giorgio Cini, 1962).

On Palladio and the Ducal Palace, Giangiorgio Zorzi, *Le opere pubbliche e i palazzi privati di Andrea Palladio* (Venice: Nero Pozza Editore, 1965), p. 157; and, with the quotation from the chronicle Molin, *idem*, "Il contributo di Andrea Palladio e di Francesco Zamberlan al restauro del palazzo ducale di Venezia dopo l'incendio del 20 decembre 1577," in *Atti Ist. Ven.* CXV (1956-57), 11-68. Ruskin's comment is in *Stones of Venice*, par. xxviii of his chapter on the Ducal Palace.

On clearing the view of San Giorgio from the Ducal Palace, see Gino Damerini, *L'isola e il cenobio di San Giorgio Maggiore* (Venezia, 1956), p. 84. On the Campanile and its collapse: Comune di Venezia, *Il Campanile di San Marco riedificato*, 2nd ed. (Venice, 1912); Laura M. Ragg, *Crises in Venetian History* (London: Methuen, 1928), chap. xxi, with excellent photographs; Rosolino Gattinoni, *Storia del Campanile di San Marco* (Venezia, 1912). On Rialto: Roberto Cessi and Annibale Alberti, *Rialto: L'isola, il Ponte, il mercato* (Bologna, 1934). On high real-estate values there, Marino Sanuto, *Cronachetta*, ed. Fulin per Nozze Papadopoli-Hellenbach (Venice, 1880), p. 47.

On painting, Haskell's *Patrons and Painters*, already cited; Erwin Panofsky, *Problems in Titian* (New York University Press, 1969); Pietro Zampetti, *A Dictionary of Venetian Painters*, 4 vols. (Leigh-on-Sea: F. Lewes, 1969-71). Also Alice Binion, "The 'Collegio dei Pittori' in Venice," and David Rosand, "The Crisis of the Venetian Renaissance Tradition," both in *Arte* (December 1970).

Oliver Logan, *Culture and Society in Venice, 1470-1790: The Renaissance and its Heritage* (New York, 1972) became available too late for me to benefit from its discussions, which include literature and society as well as the fine arts.

The treatises on the lagoons of Alvise Cornaro are published in Fiocco's book already cited and with other treatises on the same subject in *Antichi scrittori d'idraulica veneta*, published by R. Magistrato alle Acque, Ufficio idrografico, Venice, vols. I–IV (Venice: Ferrari, 1919-52), with explanation of the editorial plan in vol. III.

On industrial development and present perils: UNESCO, *Rapporto su Venezia* (Milan: Mondadori, 1969); *Difesa di Venezia*, edited by Giorgio Bellavitis for Italia Nostra (Venice: Alfieri, 1970); Eugenio Miozzi, "La verità sugli sprofondamenti di Venezia," *Ateneo veneto*, n.s., VIII (1970), 109-20; *Mostra storica della laguna veneta*, cited for Chapter 1; Rudolfo Pallucchini, "Il problema della salvaguardia del patrimonio artistico veneziano. Prospettive e speranze," *Atti Ist. Ven.*, anno CXXXIII, t. CXXIX (1970-71), 153-82; Tullio Bagiotti, *Venezia da modello a problema* (Cassa di Risparmio di Venezia, 1972); Judith and Walter Munk, "Venice Hologram," *Proceedings of the American Philosophical Society*, vol. 116, no. 5 (Oct., 1972), pp. 432-42.

Index

THE JOHNS HOPKINS UNIVERSITY PRESS

This book was composed in Baskerville text
by Jones Composition Company, Inc. with
Bauer Text Initial and Poliphilus Italic display type
supplied by Monotype Composition Company from
a design by Victoria Dudley. It was printed
on S. D. Warren's 60-lb., Bookman Matte,
and bound in Joanna Arrestox cloth
by Universal Lithographers, Inc.

Library of Congress Cataloging in Publication Data

Lane, Frederic Chapin, 1900-
    Venice, a maritime republic.

    Bibliography: p.
    1. Venice—History. 2. Venice—Commerce—History.
I. Title.
DG676.L28   945'.31   72-12342
ISBN 0-8018-1445-6
ISBN 0-8018-1460-X (pbk.)